A Companion to Phenomenology and Existentialism

Blackwell Companions to Philosophy

This outstanding student reference series offers a comprehensive and authoritative survey of philosophy as a whole. Written by today's leading philosophers, each volume provides lucid and engaging coverage of the key figures, terms, topics, and problems of the field. Taken together, the volumes provide the ideal basis for course use, representing an unparalleled work of reference for students and specialists alike.

A Companion to Phenomenology and Existentialism

Edited by

Hubert L. Dreyfus

and

Mark A. Wrathall

A John Wiley & Sons, Ltd., Publication

This edition first published 2009

© 2009 Blackwell Publishing Ltd
except for chapter 32 © Andreas Brenner.
Editorial material and organization © 2009 Hubert L. Dreyfus and Mark A. Wrathall

Edition history: Blackwell Publishing Ltd (hardback, 2006)

Blackwell Publishing was acquired by John Wiley & Sons in February 2007. Blackwell's publishing
program has been merged with Wiley's global Scientific, Technical, and Medical business to form
Wiley-Blackwell.

Registered Office
John Wiley & Sons Ltd, The Atrium, Southern Gate, Chichester, West Sussex, PO19 8SQ, United Kingdom

Editorial Offices
350 Main Street, Malden, MA 02148-5020, USA
9600 Garsington Road, Oxford, OX4 2DQ, UK
The Atrium, Southern Gate, Chichester, West Sussex, PO19 8SQ, UK

For details of our global editorial offices, for customer services, and for information about how
to apply for permission to reuse the copyright material in this book please see our website at
www.wiley.com/wiley-blackwell.

The right of Hubert L. Dreyfus and Mark A. Wrathall to be identified as the authors of the editorial
material in this work has been asserted in accordance with the Copyright, Designs and Patents Act 1988.

Wiley also publishes its books in a variety of electronic formats. Some content that appears in print may
not be available in electronic books.

Designations used by companies to distinguish their products are often claimed as trademarks. All brand
names and product names used in this book are trade names, service marks, trademarks or registered
trademarks of their respective owners. The publisher is not associated with any product or vendor
mentioned in this book. This publication is designed to provide accurate and authoritative information
in regard to the subject matter covered. It is sold on the understanding that the publisher is not engaged
in rendering professional services. If professional advice or other expert assistance is required, the services
of a competent professional should be sought.

Library of Congress Cataloging-in-Publication Data

A companion to phenomenology and existentialism / edited by Hubert L. Dreyfus and
Mark A. Wrathall.
       p. cm. — (Blackwell companions to philosophy; 35)
    Includes bibliographical references and index.
    ISBN: 978-1-4051-9113-5 (paperback : alk. paper)
    1. Phenomenology. 2. Existentialism. I. Dreyfus, Hubert L. II. Wrathall, Mark A.
III. Series.

    B829.5.C557 2005
    142'.7—dc22

                                                                    2005017581

A catalogue record for this book is available from the British Library.

Set in 10/12.5pt Photina by Graphicraft Limited, Hong Kong
Printed in Singapore by Ho Printing Singapore Pte Ltd

3 2010

Contents

Illustrations

Notes on Contributors

Daniel Andler holds doctoral degrees in mathematics from the University of California, Berkeley and Paris. He is now Professor of Philosophy of Science and Epistemology at the Université Paris-Sorbonne (Paris IV). He was for many years co-director and then director of the Centre de Recherche en Épistémologie Appliquée (CREA), the École Polytechnique, and CNRS, Paris. He heads the new Department of Cognitive Studies at the École Normale Supérieure, Paris, and is founding President of the Société de Philosophie des Sciences. He has published extensively on the foundations of cognitive science, and is co-author of a two-volume work in the philosophy of science, *Philosophie des sciences* (2002). He is currently working on a couple of connected book projects, one focusing on knowledge, the other on mind.

William Blattner is Associate Professor of Philosophy at Georgetown University. He is the author of *Heidegger's Temporal Idealism* (1999) and is currently working on a *Reader's Guide to "Being and Time"* and *Pragmatist Confrontations: Heidegger, Dewey, and the Primacy of Practice*.

Manuel Bremer teaches philosophy at the University of Düsseldorf, Germany. His English publications include the books *Information and Information Flow* (2004) and *Introduction to Paraconsistent Logics* (2005), as well as papers on analytical philosophy of language and epistemology. Since 1998 he has been a member of the Centre for the Study of Logic, Language and Information at the University of Düsseldorf.

Andreas Brenner is Lecturer in Philosophy at the University of Basel, Switzerland. His publications include: *Ökologie-Ethik* (1996), *Lexikon der Lebenskunst* (2002), *Tiere beschreiben* (2003), and *Bioethik und Biophänomen* (forthcoming, 2006).

John B. Brough is Professor in the Department of Philosophy at Georgetown University. He has translated Edmund Husserl's *On the Phenomenology of the Consciousness Internal Time* (1991) and *Phantasy, Image Consciousness, and Memory* (2005), and is the co-editor of *The Many Faces of Time* (2000). He has written several essays on Husserl's phenomenology of time, as well as a number of papers on phenomenological aesthetics.

Taylor Carman is Associate Professor of Philosophy at Barnard College, Columbia University. He has written articles on topics in phenomenology and is author of *Heidegger's Analytic: Interpretation, Discourse, and Authenticity in "Being and Time"* (2003) and coeditor of *The Cambridge Companion to Merleau-Ponty* (2005). He is currently writing books on Merleau-Ponty and Heidegger.

Steven Crowell is Mullen Professor of Philosophy and Professor of German Studies at Rice University. He is the author of *Husserl, Heidegger, and the Space of Meaning: Paths Toward Transcendental Phenomenology* (2001), the editor of *The Prism of the Self: Philosophical Essays in Honor of Maurice Natanson* (1995), and co-editor of the *New Yearbook for Phenomenology and Phenomenological Philosophy*.

Craig DeLancey is Assistant Professor of Philosophy at the State University of New York, Oswego. His publications include *Passionate Engines: What Emotions Reveal about Mind and Artificial Intelligence* (2002).

Hubert L. Dreyfus is Professor of Philosophy in the Graduate School at the University of California, Berkeley. His publications include *What Computers (Still) Can't Do* (3rd edn, 1992), *Being-in-the-World: A Commentary on Division I of Heidegger's Being and Time* (1991), *Mind over Machine: The Power of Human Intuition and Expertise in the Era of the Computer* (with Stuart Dreyfus, 1987), and *On the Internet* (2001).

Dagfinn Føllesdal is C. I. Lewis Professor of Philosophy at Stanford University. His publications include *Husserl und Frege* (1958), *Referential Opacity and Modal Logic* (1961 and 2004), and *The Philosophy of W. V. Quine* (editor, 5 vols., 2001).

Shaun Gallagher is Professor and Chair of Philosophy and Cognitive Sciences at the University of Central Florida. He is co-editor of the interdisciplinary journal *Phenomenology and the Cognitive Sciences*. His most recent book, *How the Body Shapes the Mind*, was published in 2005. His previous books include *Hermeneutics and Education* (1992) and *The Inordinance of Time* (1998).

Michael Allen Gillespie is the Jerry G. and Patricia Crawford Hubbard Professor of Political Science and Professor of Philosophy at Duke University. He works on modern continental theory and the history of philosophy. He is the author of *Hegel, Heidegger and the Ground of History* (1984) and *Nihilism before Nietzsche* (1995). He also co-edited *Nietzsche's New Seas: Explorations in Philosophy, Aesthetics, and Politics* (1988) and has written articles on Montaigne, Descartes, Kant, Hegel, Nietzsche, and Heidegger. He is the Director of the Gerst Program in Political, Economic, and Humanistic Studies.

Peter Eli Gordon is Professor of History at Harvard University. He is the author of *Rosenzweig and Heidegger: Between Judaism and German Philosophy* (2003), as well as a variety of essays on topics in both modern European intellectual history and Jewish thought. He is currently writing a book on the Davos encounter between Heidegger and Cassirer.

Charles Guignon is Professor of Philosophy at the University of South Florida, Tampa. He is the author of *Heidegger and the Problem of Knowledge* (1983) and *On Being Authentic* (2004), co-author of *Re-envisioning Psychology* (1999), and has edited or co-edited a number of books, including *The Good Life* (1999), Dostoevsky's *The Grand Inquisitor* (1993), *Existentialism: Basic Writings* (2001), and *The Existentialists* (2004).

Béatrice Han-Pile is Reader in Philosophy at the University of Essex, England. Her publications include *Foucault's Critical Project: Between the Transcendental and the*

Historical (2002) and numerous articles on Nietzsche, Foucault, and Heidegger. She is currently working on a book entitled *Transcendence without Religion*.

Sara Heinämaa is Senior Lecturer of Theoretical Philosophy at the University of Helsinki, Finland. She also works as Professor of Humanist Women's Studies at the Centre for Women Studies and Gender Research, University of Oslo, Norway. She has published several articles in phenomenology, focusing on the problems of the method, embodiment, and sexuality. Her latest publications include *Toward a Phenomenology of Sexual Difference: Husserl, Merleau-Ponty, Beauvoir* (2004), and the collection *Metaphysics, Facticity, Interpretation* (2003), co-edited with Dan Zahavi and Hans Ruin.

Piotr Hoffman studied philosophy in Poland and France. He taught philosophy at the University of California, Berkeley, and is now Professor of Philosophy at the University of Nevada, Reno. His most recent book is *Freedom, Equality, Power: The Ontological Consequences of the Political Philosophies of Hobbes, Locke and Rousseau* (1999).

David Couzens Hoy is Professor of Philosophy and Distinguished Professor of Humanities at the University of California, Santa Cruz. His most recent book is *Critical Resistance: From Poststructuralism to Post-Critique* (2004). In addition to writing *The Critical Circle* (1978) and editing the Blackwell anthology, *Foucault: A Critical Reader* (1986), for Blackwell's *Great Debates in Philosophy* series, he also debated Thomas McCarthy in their book, *Critical Theory* (1994).

Martin Jay is Sidney Hellman Ehrman Professor of History at the University of California, Berkeley. Among his publications are *The Dialectical Imagination* (1973 and 1996), *Marxism and Totality* (1984), *Adorno* (1984), *Permanent Exiles* (1985), *Fin-de-siècle Socialism* (1989), *Force Fields* (1993), *Downcast Eyes* (1993), *Cultural Semantics* (1998), *Refractions of Violence* (2003), and *Songs of Experience* (2005).

Shunsuke Kadowaki is Professor of Philosophy at the University of Tokyo, Komaba, Japan. He is the author of three books (in Japanese): *Contemporary Philosophy* (1996), *Phenomenology of the "Space of Reasons": A Critique of Representational Intentionality* (2002), and *Husserl: How is the Mind Connected to the World?* (2004).

Dieter Lohmar is Professor of Philosophy at the University of Cologne, Germany. His publications include *Phänomenologie der Mathematik* (1989), *Erfahrung und kategoriales Denken* (1998), and a commentary on Edmund Husserl's "Formale und Transzendentale Logik" (2000).

Clancy Martin earned his PhD from the University of Texas, Austin in 2003 and is Assistant Professor of Philosophy at the University of Missouri, Kansas City. He has published many articles on ethics and nineteenth-century European philosophy and existentialism, and he has written or edited several books in ethics, including, most recently, *Honest Work* (2005).

Wayne M. Martin is Reader in Philosophy at the University of Essex, England. He is the author of *Idealism and Objectivity: Understanding Fichte's Jena Project* (1997) and *Theories of Judgment: Psychology, Logic, Phenomenology* (2005), and is the General Editor of *Inquiry: An Interdisciplinary Journal of Philosophy*.

J. N. Mohanty is Professor of Philosophy at Temple University. His publications in the field of phenomenology include *Husserl and Frege* (1983), *Phenomenology: Between Essentialism and Transcendental Philosophy* (1997), *Logic, Truth and the Modalities: From a Phenomenological Perspective* (1999), and *The Self and Its Other: Philosophical Essays* (2003).

Ann V. Murphy is currently NewSouth Global Postdoctoral Fellow in the School of Philosophy at the University of New South Wales, Sydney, Australia. Her background is in twentieth-century French philosophy, phenomenology, political philosophy, and feminist theory. Her current research focuses on violence, vulnerability, and embodiment. She has published on Beauvoir, Irigaray, Merleau-Ponty, Foucault, and Levinas.

Frederick A. Olafson is Professor Emeritus of Philosophy at University of California –San Diego.

Matthew Ratcliffe is Lecturer in Philosophy at the University of Durham, England. He has published numerous articles on phenomenology, philosophy of mind, and philosophy of science. Most of his recent work is concerned with intersubjectivity and the phenomenology of feeling.

François-David Sebbah is Maître de Conférences at the Université de Technologie de Compiègne (TSH-COSTECH). Formerly a program director at the Collège International de Philosophie, Sebbah is currently on the editorial boards of the academic journals *Alter, Intellectica,* and *Cahiers d'Études Lévinassiennes*. He is the author of the books *Lévinas: Ambiguïtés de l'altérité* (2000) and *L'épreuve de la limite: Derrida, Henry, Lévinas et la phénoménologie* (2001), as well as some twenty articles, mostly on contemporary French phenomenologists and/or the uses, effects, and extensions of phenomenology.

David Sherman is Associate Professor of Philosophy at the University of Montana, Missoula. Journals in which his articles have appeared include *Philosophy Today, Telos, Philosophy & Social Criticism, The Philosophical Forum,* and *Philosophy and Literature,* and he is the co-editor of the *Blackwell Guide to Continental Philosophy* (2003).

Charles Siewert is Professor of Philosophy at the University of California, Riverside. He is the author of *The Significance of Consciousness* (1998) and a number of articles on the philosophy of mind and its relationship to phenomenology.

Robert C. Solomon is Quincy Lee Centennial Professor of Philosophy and Distinguished Teaching Professor at the University of Texas, Austin, and past President of the International Society for Research on Emotions. He is the author of over forty books including *The Passions* (1993), *In the Spirit of Hegel* (1983), *About Love* (1988), *A Passion for Justice* (1995), *Up the University* (with Jon Solomon, 1993), *A Short History of Philosophy* (1996), *Ethics and Excellence* (1992), *A Passion for Wisdom* (1997), *A Better Way to Think About Business, The Joy of Philosophy* (both 1999), *What Nietzsche Really Said* (with Kathleen M. Higgins, 2000), *Spirituality for the Skeptic, Living with Nietzsche* (2003), and *Not Passion's Slave* (2003) and *In Defense of Sentimentality* (2004), vols. I and II of a three-volume series, *The Passionate Life*.

Fredrik Svenaeus is Associate Professor of Philosophy in the Department for Health and Society, University of Linköping, Sweden. He has published one book in English:

The Hermeneutics of Medicine and the Phenomenology of Health: Steps Towards a Philosophy of Medical Practice (2001). Currently he is working in a research project on phenomenology and new medical technologies.

Iain Thomson is Associate Professor of Philosophy at the University of New Mexico. He is the author of *Heidegger on Ontotheology: Technology and the Politics of Education* (2005) and has published more than a dozen articles on Heidegger and other leading figures in phenomenology and existential philosophy. He is currently writing a book on Heidegger's phenomenology of death and its impact on contemporary continental philosophy.

Udo Tietz is Professor of Philosophy in Marburg, Germany. His publications include *Sprache und Verstehen in analytischer und hermeneutischer Sicht* (1995), *Hans-Georg Gadamer zur Einführung* (1999, 2001, 2004), *Hinter den Spiegeln. Beiträge zur Philosophie von Richard Rorty* (Mithg. 2000), *Ontologie und Dialektik. Heidegger und Adorno über das Sein, das Nichtidentische, das Urteil und die Kopula* (2002), *Die Grenzen des Wir. Eine Theorie der Gemeinschaft* (2002), *Hegel für Eilige* (2004), *Vernunft und Verstehen. Perspektiven einer integrativen Hermeneutik* (2004), *Heidegger* (2005), and various essays on the theory of rationality, the philosophy of language, phenomenology, critical theory, and social philosophy.

Mark van Atten is Researcher for the Centre National de Recherche Scientifique (CNRS) at the Institut d'Histoire et de Philosophie des Sciences et des Techniques (IHPST), Paris, France.

Frederick J. Wertz is Professor and Chair of Psychology at Fordham University, editor of the *Journal of Phenomenological Psychology*, and a former President of the American Psychological Association's Society of Theoretical and Philosophical Psychology and Division of Humanistic Psychology. He has published works in phenomenological psychology, many on qualitative research methods, and edited the volumes *The Humanistic Movement: Recovering the Person in Psychology* (1994) and *Qualitative Research in Psychology* (1987).

Robert Wicks is Associate Professor of Philosophy at the University of Auckland, New Zealand. His publications include *Hegel's Theory of Aesthetic Judgment* (1994), *Nietzsche* (2002), and *Modern French Philosophy* (2003). His most recent work is on the philosophy of Arthur Schopenhauer.

Mark A. Wrathall is Associate Professor of Philosophy at the University of California at Riverside. He is the author of *Heidegger on Truth, Language, and History* (2009) and *How to Read Heidegger* (2005). He has edited a number of volumes, including *Religion after Metaphysics* (2003), and *Appropriating Heidegger* (with James Falconer, 2000).

Julian Young is Professor of Philosophy at the University of Auckland, New Zealand. His publications include *Nietzsche's Philosophy of Religion* (2006), *Schopenhauer* (2004), *The Death of God and the Meaning of Life* (2003), *Heidegger's Later Philosophy* (2003), *Heidegger's Philosophy of Art* (2002), and *Heidegger, Philosophy, Nazism* (1997). He is currently working on a philosophical biography of Nietzsche.

Acknowledgments

We owe thanks to many who have assisted with various aspects of the planning of this volume and the preparation of this manuscript, including James Faulconer, Catherine Curtis, Amy Wrathall, Jeffrey Johnson, Daniel Wood, Ariane Uhlin, and Enoch Lambert.

Chapter 30 is a shortened and revised version of Iain Thomson, "Ontology and ethics at the intersection of phenomenology and environmental philosophy," *Inquiry*, 47, 4 (2004), pp. 380–412. By permission of Taylor & Francis.

1

A Brief Introduction to Phenomenology and Existentialism

MARK A. WRATHALL AND HUBERT L. DREYFUS

Phenomenology and existentialism are two of the most influential movements in twentieth-century philosophy. During the heyday of existentialism in the middle decades of the twentieth century, there were heated disputes about whether the movements belonged together or were even compatible with one another. Herbert Spiegelberg, for example, argued that, while phenomenology and existentialism are independent movements, they are compatible in principle and, indeed, that they have "at least enough affinity for fruitful cooperation" (1960: 70). Asher Moore, by contrast, saw the relationship between existentialism and phenomenology as an "unholy alliance," and argued that phenomenology was "unfit . . . for existential inquiry" because it necessarily had to overlook individual existence in its search for universal structures (1967: 408, 409).

Martin Heidegger and Jean-Paul Sartre were the two figures crucial to this debate – crucial in the sense that each could, with right, be claimed by both phenomenology and existentialism. In fact, they disagreed on the subject of the relationship between existentialism and phenomenology. Heidegger always thought of his work as true to the genuine spirit of phenomenology (although he stopped referring to his work as "phenomenological" in order to distance himself from Husserlian phenomenology). He was dismissive, however, of existentialism, contending that it was a continuation of the errors of modernism (Heidegger 2000: 225). Heidegger concluded in 1966, perhaps unrealistically, that "it is hardly necessary anymore today to expressly observe that my thought deals neither with existentialism nor with existence-philosophy" (Heidegger 1986: 649–50). Despite his rejection of twentieth-century existentialism, Heidegger's work carried on the existential tradition of thought as it had been developed by the nineteenth-century progenitors of existentialism, Kierkegaard and Nietzsche, and also was tremendously influential on the later development of existentialism. Heidegger's standing in the existential tradition is secured by his exploration of the existential structure of Dasein or human being, his historicized account of essences, his critique of the banality of conformist everyday life, and his reflections on guilt, anxiety, death, and authenticity.

Sartre, on the other hand, embraced the label of existentialism, arguing that it was "the least scandalous, the most austere of doctrines" (1947: 15). Existentialism, he claimed, was "a doctrine which makes human life possible and, in addition, declares that every truth and every action implies a human setting and a human subjectivity" (1947: 12). At the same time, Sartre saw his existentialism as fundamentally grounded in a phenomenological approach. He gave *Being and Nothingness* the subtitle "A Phenomenological Essay on Ontology." And in *The Transcendence of the Ego*, he wrote of phenomenology that "for centuries we have not felt in philosophy so realistic a current. The phenomenologists have plunged man back into the world; they have given full measure to man's agonies and sufferings, and also to his rebellions" (1962: 105).

Before saying any more about existentialism's and phenomenology's compatibility with and relevance to one another, we should briefly introduce the two movements.

Phenomenology

The term "phenomenology" has been in common use in philosophy since Hegel's monumental work, *The Phenomenology of Mind* (1807). During the nineteenth century, the word denoted a descriptive as opposed to a hypothetical–theoretical or analytic approach to a problem.

Phenomenology began as a discernible movement with Edmund Husserl's (1859–1938) demand that philosophy take as its primary task the description of the structures of experience as they present themselves to consciousness. This description was meant to be carried out on the basis of what the "things themselves" demanded, without assuming or adopting the theoretical frameworks, assumptions, or vocabularies developed in the study of other domains (such as nature).

Husserl apparently began using the term in the 1890s in his lectures "Phänomenologie: ein Abschnitt in Brentanos Metaphysik (Klärung von Grundbegriffen)" (see Heidegger 1993: 13 n. 6). Franz Brentano (1838–1917) had a decisive influence on Husserl's development of phenomenology owing to Brentano's own descriptive approach to the study of psychic phenomena, and also through his arguments regarding the structure of consciousness. Also of influence was Wilhelm Dilthey's (1833–1911) argument against naturalistic accounts of the psychic domain, and his attempt to develop a more descriptive approach to the human sciences.

In Husserl's hands, "phenomenology" came to have a more precise, methodological sense (see Chapter 2). For Husserl, phenomenology is a study of the structures of consciousness (see Chapter 6), which proceeds by "bracketing" the objects outside of consciousness itself, so that one can proceed to reflect on and systematically describe the contents of the conscious mind in terms of their essential structures (see Chapters 8 and 9). This was a method, Husserl believed, which could ground our knowledge of the world in our lived experience, without in the process reducing the content of that knowledge to the contingent and subjective features of that experience (see Chapter 7).

On the basis of this method, Husserl believed, philosophy could be established as a rigorous science that could "clarify all species and forms of cognition" (Husserl 1964: 4), because it could discover the structures common to all mental acts. Following

Brentano, Husserl saw intentionality, object-directedness, as the mark of the mental (see Chapter 5). Intentional acts, Husserl argued, have a meaningful structure through which the mind can be directed toward objects under aspects. Another essential structural feature of the mental, Husserl argued to great influence, was temporality (see Chapter 10).

Early followers of Husserl extended his work into a variety of domains – Max Scheler (1874–1928), for instance, into an examination of the essence of emotions and intuition; Roman Ingarden (1893–1970) into art and aesthetics; Edith Stein (1891–1942) into the nature of empathy; Karl Jaspers (1883–1969) into psychology. Martin Heidegger (1889–1976), Husserl's most brilliant student and influential critic, along with Jaspers, moved phenomenology in a new direction.

Heidegger rejected Husserl's focus on consciousness and, consequently, much of his basic phenomenological method. For Heidegger, the purpose of phenomenological description was not to discover the structures of consciousness, but to make manifest the structure of our everyday being-in-the-world. Because Heidegger's interest was worldly relations rather than mental contents, he rejected both the usefulness of the phenomenological method as practiced by Husserl and the need for mental meanings to account for many if not most forms of intentional directedness. Indeed, Heidegger argued that the intentionality on which Husserl focused – the intentionality of discrete mental judgments and acts – is grounded in something more basic, the intentionality of a general background grasp of the world. Maurice Merleau-Ponty (1908–61) extended Heidegger's account of being-in-the-world to a study of our bodily experience of the world in perception (see Chapter 3). Sartre as a phenomenologist shared Heidegger's focus on existential, worldly relationships, but sought to account for those relationships in a Husserlian fashion by focusing on consciousness.

Heidegger and Husserl both had a formative influence on many of the most prominent philosophers of the latter half of the twentieth century. These include Heidegger's students Hans-Georg Gadamer (1900–2002), who developed Heidegger's philosophical hermeneutics, and Hannah Arendt (1906–75), whose work on politics and public ethics developed many of Heidegger's insights into our being with one another in a shared public world. Emmanuel Levinas (1906–95), Michel Foucault (1926–84), Jacques Derrida (1930–2004), and Jürgen Habermas (1929–) have all been influenced by and, to some degree, defined their work by opposition to, the phenomenologies of Heidegger and Husserl.

Existentialism

Existentialism was self-consciously adopted as a label for a movement only in the twentieth century. But existentialist writers see themselves as carrying on a tradition that was first anticipated by Blaise Pascal's (1623–62) rejection of Cartesian rationalism, which tried to define human being in terms of our rational capacities. Pascal saw human being as an essential paradox, a contradiction between mind and body. Søren Kierkegaard (1813–55), usually acknowledged as the founder of modern existentialism, shared Pascal's sense for the inherent contradiction built into the human condition. Kierkegaard reacted to Hegel's systematic and, purportedly, total account of human being and history in terms of rationality, arguing for the essential absurdity of human existence, and the need for a fundamentally irrational, but faithful and passionate commitment to a Christian form of life. Nietzsche (1844–1900) and Dostoevsky (1821–81) likewise criticized the philosophical tradition's emphasis on rationality as undermining the passionate attachment to the world necessary to support a worthwhile life. Together, Pascal, Kierkegaard, Dostoevsky, and Nietzsche form the historical background to twentieth-century existentialism (see Chapter 11).

In the twentieth century, the existential approach to religion pioneered by Pascal, Kierkegaard, and Dostoevsky was developed by a surprising range of theologians and religious thinkers (see Chapter 13). These include, among others, Gabriel Marcel (1889–1973), Nicholas Berdyaev (1874–1948), Paul Tillich (1886–1965), Rudolf Bultmann (1884–1976), Miguel de Unamuno (1865–1936), Lev Shestov (1865–1938), Karl Barth (1886–1968), and Martin Buber (1878–1965).

In the public imagination, however, twentieth-century existentialism was most well known in its atheist form as popularized by French thinkers like Sartre, Simone de Beauvoir (1908–86), and Albert Camus (1913–60) (see Chapter 14). This branch of existentialism was deeply influenced by Nietzsche's proclamation of the "death of God," his rejection of the Judeo-Christian tradition, and his consequent critique of traditional metaphysics and ethics.

Like the phenomenology of Heidegger, Merleau-Ponty, and Sartre, existentialism as a movement starts its analysis with the existing individual – the individual engaged in a particular world with a characteristic form of life. Thus, an emphasis on the body (see Chapter 17) and on the affective rather than rational side of human being (see Chapter 16) are characteristic of existentialism. For existentialist thinkers, the focus is on uncovering what is unique to that individual, rather than treating her as a manifestation of a general type. Existentialists thus tend to be anti-essentialists, to deny that there are essential features or properties that determine the being of a thing. Many go further and insist that the world is not just lacking in essence, but absurd, and thus incapable of being made sense of (see Chapter 19). Indeed, existentialists like Sartre and Camus argue, human being itself is rendered meaningless and absurd by the inevitability of death (see Chapter 20).

With their focus on the individual and a denial of any meaningful sense of what constitutes an essential or absolute goal for human existence, existentialists emphasize human freedom and responsibility (see Chapter 18), and hold that the only goal consistent with that freedom and responsibility is to live authentically (see Chapter 15). Finally, existentialists tend to share an opposition to rationalism and empiricism alike, and often define themselves by their opposition to the main currents of modern philosophy.

Because existentialist analysis takes as its starting point an involved stance within an individual's experience of the world, some of the most powerful works in existentialist thought have taken the form of novels, plays, or pseudonymous tracts. These forms are effective ways for an existentialist author to explore a way of being in the world from the inside, as it were. As a consequence, existentialism has been, in the nineteenth and twentieth centuries, at least as influential in the literary arts as it has been in philosophy. Dostoevsky was, of course, primarily a writer of fiction, but many of Sartre's, Beauvoir's, and Camus's most influential writings were also works of fiction. Camus received the Nobel Prize for literature in 1957; Sartre was awarded (and refused) the prize in 1964. Literary figures influenced by existentialism, or recognized as existentialists in their own right, include novelists,[1] playwrights,[2] and poets.[3]

* * *

Let us return, then, to the issue of the compatibility of existentialism and phenomenology. To a large extent, the arguments over the issue have been rendered moot. With the benefit of few more years of historical distance, it no longer seems pressing to decide to what extent existentialism can be phenomenological, or whether phenomenology leads one inevitably to existentialist views on the self and the world. What is clear is that there is no merely accidental relationship between the two traditions. Indeed, the ultimate compatibility of the movements is resolved in practice. Both movements are now routinely drawn upon in addressing current concerns in the philosophy of mind and action (Chapters 21–25), cognitive science (Chapter 26) and psychology (Chapter 27), the philosophy of science and technology (Chapters 29 and 31), ethics broadly construed (Chapters 30, 34, and 35), politics (Chapter 36), history (Chapter 37), art (Chapter 38), and mathematics (Chapter 39).

The phenomenological and existential traditions have now largely merged into a common canon of works and ways of doing philosophy. If we had to try to summarize what these two traditions have in common, we could perhaps do no better than identify the following four approaches that they both share:

1   A concern with providing a description of human existence and the human world that reveals it as it is, without the distortion of any scientific presuppositions. This leads to:

2   A heightened awareness of the non-rational dimensions of human existence, including habits, non-conscious practices, moods, and passions.

3   A focus on the degree to which the world is cut to the measure of our intellect, and a willingness to consider the possibility that our concepts and categories fail to capture the world as it presents itself to us in experience.

4   A belief that what it is to be human cannot be reduced to any set of features about us (whether biological, sociological, anthropological, or logical). To be human is to transcend facticity.

Existentialism develops these concerns in a particular direction, coming to hold the following:

5   Everyday life is at best banal and at worst absurd and meaningless.

6   Anxiety in the face of death can disclose to us the banality or absurdity of life; hence, there is a constant motivation to flee from anxiety back into conformism and a reaffirmation of everyday life.

7   The most pressing philosophical task is to help us cope with anxiety and despair in such a way that we can affirm *this* life in all its absurdity.

8 The ideal human life will be authentic, that is, accept responsibility for the exercise of freedom.

* * *

The Organization of the Book

This book is divided into three main parts: Part I is devoted to phenomenology and Part II is devoted to existentialism. Each of these parts contains longer chapters devoted to the main movements of the respective traditions, and a number of shorter chapters highlighting some of the central concepts of the movement. In Part III we abandon the attempt to treat phenomenology and existentialism as movements in isolation from one another. Indeed, we abandon the effort to treat them as *historical* movements at all. Instead, we present chapters devoted to taking up contemporary problems, issues, and fields of philosophy from an existential and/or phenomenological perspective. Some of these chapters are more influenced by one movement or the other. As a whole, however, we believe that they demonstrate the continued vitality of phenomenology and existentialism.

Notes

1 These include Ivan Turgenev (1818–83), Franz Kafka (1883–1924), Hermann Hesse (1877–1962), André Malraux (1901–76), Walker Percy (1916–90), John Updike (1932–), Norman Mailer (1923–), and John Barth (1930–).
2 These include Samuel Beckett (1906–89), Eugène Ionesco (1912–94), and Arthur Miller (1915–2005).
3 Such as Rainer Maria Rilke (1875–1926).

References and Further Reading

Heidegger, M. (1986) *Seminare. Gesamtausgabe* vol. 15. Frankfurt am Main: Klostermann.
—— (1993) *Grundprobleme der Phänomenologie [1919/20]. Gesamtausgabe* vol. 58. Frankfurt am Main: Klostermann.
—— (2000) *Vorträge und Aufsätze. Gesamtausgabe* vol. 7. Frankfurt am Main: Klostermann.
Husserl, E. (1964) *The Idea of Phenomenology* (trans. W. P. Alston and G. Nakhnikian). The Hague: Martinus Nijhoff (original work published 1907).
Moore, A. (1967) Existential Phenomenology. *Philosophy and Phenomenological Research*, 27, 408–14.
Sartre, J-P. (1947) *Existentialism* (trans. B. Frechtman). New York: Philosophical Library.
—— (1962) *The Transcendence of the Ego* (trans. F. Williams and R. Kirkpatrick). New York: Noonday Press.
Spiegelberg, H. (1960) Husserl's Phenomenology and Existentialism. *Journal of Philosophy*, 57, 62–74.

Part I

Phenomenology

Main Movements

2

Husserlian Phenomenology

STEVEN CROWELL

Phenomenology and Twentieth-Century Thought

Though the term "phenomenology" was in use prior to Edmund Husserl – it is found, for instance, in Kant and Lambert, and, with a very different signification, in Hegel – it is in its Husserlian form that phenomenology came to exert decisive influence on twentieth-century thought. To understand Husserlian phenomenology it is pointless going back to the previous uses of the term, since Husserl paid no attention to these (Spiegelberg 1982: 6–19); instead, his thinking developed in debates over the foundations of arithmetic and logic carried out in the school of the Austrian philosopher, Franz Brentano. Nor is Husserlian phenomenology a static entity. Initially a method for tackling certain epistemological problems, phenomenology became, over the four decades of Husserl's mature philosophical life, the basis for a complete "system" that "has within its purview all questions that can be put to man in the concrete, including all so-called metaphysical questions, to the extent that they have any possible meaning at all" (Husserl 1989: 408; translation modified). So understood, phenomenology was to be a platform for generations of researchers who would contribute, as in the natural sciences, to a growing stock of philosophical knowledge. In so doing they would shore up the threatened legacy of European civilization: a culture based not on tradition and opinion, but on rational insight into universally valid truths and values. The fate of Husserlian phenomenology in the twentieth century turned out quite differently, however. Husserl's project did provide the starting point for several generations of philosophers, beginning with contemporaries such as Alexander Pfänder, Adolf Reinach, and Moritz Geiger, and continuing through Martin Heidegger, Jean-Paul Sartre, Maurice Merleau-Ponty, Emmanuel Levinas, Hans-Georg Gadamer, and Jacques Derrida, among many others. Yet in each case adoption of the phenomenological approach was accompanied by rejection of much of Husserl's actual doctrine. As a result, though phenomenology remains a vital contemporary movement, *Husserlian* phenomenology is often treated as a mere historical antecedent.

And yet, it is no exaggeration to say that only now is it possible to see just what Husserl's phenomenology actually *is*. The historical reception – in which Husserl's philosophy is dismissed as an arch-essentialist version of Cartesian foundationalism, a radical idealism that flirts with solipsism, a philosophy of "reflection" that cannot do justice to the realities of the body, history, and sociality – is largely a function of Husserl's manner of working and the difficulties he had in bringing his thoughts to print. Husserl's output is divided into the relatively few books he published during his lifetime – which, after the *Logical Investigations* (1900; cited as Husserl 1970b and 1970c), mostly have the character of introductions to phenomenology's methods and programmatic aspirations – and a vast store of research manuscripts representing the fruit of Husserl's daily writing schedule: applications of phenomenology to specific topics such as perception, temporality, embodiment, social reality, history, culture, and value. Upon Husserl's death in 1937 this entire output was threatened with destruction at the hands of the Nazis, but a Belgian cleric, H. L. van Breda, smuggled it out of Germany and established the Husserl archive at Leuven. The editing and publishing of this material – including its translation into many languages – has now reached a point where a new picture of Husserl has begun to emerge. What on the basis of Husserl's publications might look to be a confusingly discontinuous series of positions – an early "realism," a middle-period Cartesian "idealism," a late rejection of Cartesianism – can be seen from the *Nachlass* to be the outgrowth of a sustained, and remarkably consistent, internal development. Further, these manuscripts suggest that phenomenology has far more to contribute to contemporary debates – in epistemology, philosophy of language, philosophy of mind, and social ontology, for instance – than the traditional picture might lead one to suspect. This is not to say that the "new" Husserl is free of paradox, nor that the standard criticisms get no grip on his thought. But it does mean that presenting Husserlian phenomenology now involves something other than assessing it as a mere precursor.

Since the present chapter cannot hope to take the full measure of Husserl's thought, its goal shall be to examine what is most distinctly *phenomenological* about it. What, then, *is* phenomenology? It is not impossible to give a reasonably concise characterization – if not definition – of Husserlian phenomenology through a series of contrasts. First, phenomenology is a *descriptive* enterprise, not one that proceeds by way of theory construction. Before one can develop a theory of something – say, an account of how perception is caused by the interaction of eye and brain, or how mental representations must be postulated to explain it – it is necessary, according to Husserl, to provide a careful description of what perception itself is, to get clear about the phenomenon that one is trying to explain. Thus, second, phenomenology aims at *clarification*, not explanation. Phenomenological descriptions neither employ nor provide causal laws that explain the existence of things; instead, they mark those distinctions – such as those between memory and perception, or between depictions and signs – that allow us to understand what it is to be a thing of this or that sort. This means, third, that phenomenology is an *eidetic* and not a factual inquiry; it is not concerned to describe all the properties of some particular thing but to uncover what belongs to it *essentially* as a thing of that kind. Phenomenology studies some concrete act of perception only as an example for uncovering what belongs necessarily to perception as such – for instance, that it gives its object "in person," or that it apprehends its object against a co-given background or "horizon." Finally, phenomenology is a *reflective* inquiry; it is not concerned directly with entities, as are the natural sciences, but with our *experience* of entities. It is committed to the view that descriptive clarification of the essential conditions for being X cannot be achieved by *abstracting* from our experience of X but

10

only by attending to how X is *given in* that experience. Of the four features just mentioned, this reflective character is most distinctive of phenomenology, and richest in implications. For it challenges entrenched philosophical theories about "mind" and "world" and demands that we attend to how "the things themselves," as Husserl put it, show themselves.

Why did phenomenology – this reflective, descriptive clarification of eidetic features – have such an extraordinary impact on twentieth-century thought? One could point here to its discoveries about consciousness and intentionality, its critique of the epistemological dilemmas of modern philosophy, the resources it provides for a new ontology or theory of categories; and so on. Yet such contributions themselves rest upon a more fundamental achievement, namely, phenomenology's recognition that meaning (*Sinn*) is the proper topic of philosophical inquiry, one that cannot be grasped with traditional categories of mind and world, subject and object. Here phenomenology shares a motive with the "language-analytic" philosophy that emerged simultaneously with it. Both movements sought to break free of traditional philosophy, and for the same reason: in order to do justice to meaning. In contrast to early analytic philosophy, however, phenomenology does not see meaning as *primarily* a linguistic phenomenon. Rather, it comes into its own when Husserl takes the "important cognitive step" of extending terms like meaning and signification "to all acts, be they now combined with expressive acts or not" (Husserl 1982: 294). This allows phenomenology to break decisively with mentalism and representationalism and explore meaning as encountered directly in the world of our practical and perceptual life. This chapter will examine how this focus on meaning leads to Husserl's most distinctive innovations, and to his most controversial claims.

Husserl's "Breakthrough" to Phenomenology: Intentionality and Reflection

Husserl was born on April 8, 1859, in Prossnitz, Moravia. His "breakthrough" to phenomenology came some forty years later, in the *Logical Investigations* (Husserl 1970b, 1970c). His initial studies had been in mathematics, in which he finished a doctoral dissertation in 1882 in Vienna. While in Vienna he attended lectures by Franz Brentano, whose call for an empirical scientific philosophy based on a kind of descriptive psychology had attracted much attention. At its core was the concept of a "mental phenomenon," which Brentano defined by appeal to "what the Scholastics of the Middle Ages called the intentional (or sometimes mental) inexistence of an object, and what we should like to call . . . the reference to a content, the directedness toward an object" (Spiegelberg 1982: 36). Drawn by questions in the foundation of number theory, Husserl switched his attention to philosophy and began to explore Brentano's notion of "intentionality" as a way to clarify our concept of number – a topic on which he wrote his second dissertation, in Halle, in 1887.

While teaching as a *Privatdozent* in Halle until his move to Göttingen in 1901, Husserl continued to study what he then thought of as the "psychological" foundations of arithmetic, though his first major book, *Philosophy of Arithmetic* (1891; cited as Husserl 2003), already breaks with many of the particulars of Brentano's approach.

Especially unclear in Brentano was the relation between the "content" that is bound up with mental acts and the "directedness toward an object" that such acts involve. While his contemporary, Gottlob Frege, held that the content through which such directedness is achieved is the content, or meaning (*Sinn*), of sentences – a concept or "thought" that has nothing to do with the mental – Husserl wondered how sentences could come to *have* meaning at all. For him, it would not be enough to develop a sentential logic. It would be necessary to show how the inten*s*ionality of terms depends on the inten*t*ionality of consciousness, since no content or meaning is intelligible without reference to the *subject* who thinks, judges, and perceives. Husserl's "breakthrough" to phenomenology began the slow process of disengaging this appeal to subjectivity from the psychological trappings of its Brentanian origins.

The problem of psychologism

The birth of phenomenology in the *Logical Investigations* has always had something paradoxical about it. For there Hussserl introduces phenomenology as "descriptive psychology," arguing that it is the only way to approach foundational problems in philosophy of logic; yet he does so only after devoting 200 pages to a critique of "psychologism," the view that logic must be founded upon psychology. To get a sense for the dilemma that would exercise Husserl throughout his career, let us take a closer look at this paradoxical breakthrough.

Logical psychologism is a cluster of positions, all of which claim that because the laws of logic are laws of thinking they must ultimately derive from psychological facts and the evolution of human thought-processes. Husserl objected to what he saw as the skeptical and relativistic consequences of such a view. Psychologism yields relativism, since logical validity is taken to depend on the contingent psychic make-up of the human being, such that a different make-up would produce different laws. And it yields skepticism since, by denying logic unconditional validity, it renders every truth-claim undecidable. Husserl seizes on this last point to demonstrate the self-refuting character of psychologism. As a theory – that is, a set of propositions whose explanatory power comes from the material and logical laws that organize it – psychologism asserts, as true, propositions concerning logic that, if they *were* true, would undermine the epistemic authority of the theory itself (Husserl 1970b: 135ff.). Husserl's rejection of psychologism appears uncompromising: logical laws have *ideal* validity; they are normative for human thinking because they are necessary conditions for *truth* as such. Husserl thus places two constraints on any account of logical validity: first, it must preserve the link between logic and the norm of truth; and second, it must be "presuppositionless" in the sense of refusing (on pain of circularity or outright skepticism) to derive logical validity from any contingent fact.

This latter requirement actually rules out any *explanation* of logical validity at all, if by "explanation" is meant a theory that accounts for such validity without presupposing it. Husserl acknowledges this point when he claims that "theory of knowledge, properly described, is no theory." That is, its "aim is not to *explain* knowledge in the psychological or psychophysical sense as a *factual* occurrence in objective nature, but to *shed light* on the *Idea* of knowledge in its constitutive elements and laws" (Husserl 1970b: 264, 265). As a descriptive method, phenomenology is appropriate for theory of knowledge in this sense. But, surprisingly, Husserl calls it descriptive *psychology* (Husserl 1970b: 262). How did he imagine that it could avoid his own anti-psychologistic arguments?

The answer here – to the extent that the *Logical Investigations* provides one – lies in the fact that Husserl examines cognitive acts (thinking, judging, perceiving, etc.) not as mental items but as *truth*-bearers, i.e., in light of the norm of truth. On this view, intentionality is not simply the static presence of a "presentation" in a mental experience (*Erlebnis*) but a normatively oriented *claim to validity*. This claim need not take the form of an explicit judgment, but in every case of a consciousness-of-something it is there.

To say that a mental experience is intentional is to say that it is "of" something, that it refers to something. But such reference cannot be a simple relation between two things – an act and its object – since there are "objectless presentations" such as hallucinations, which possess intentional directedness without an existing object. This led Husserl to recognize that the content of an intentional act is complex, involving both a putative intended object as well as an "intentional object" or manner in which the intended object is given. To avoid infinite regress, the intentional object cannot be another object toward which the act is directed; it must be an aspect of the act itself. Husserl's breakthrough is to see that this aspect is a normative or inferential structure, not a "psychic" one. The intentional object provides something like satisfaction conditions that must hold of the intended object *if* the claim inherent in the act is veridical. Thus, to say that I currently perceive "a coffee cup" is to say that what I currently experience (these white, gleaming surfaces, etc.) is taken as (partially) satisfying a rule inhabiting my act as its meaning, determining that it is "of" this rather than that. In the *Logical Investigations* Husserl had not yet freed himself from psychological assumptions. For instance, he initially held that this meaning arises when sensory input is formed by an interpretive mental act (*Auffassung*). Yet even here the essential point is attained: relations between acts cannot be understood in causal terms but are functions of *meaning*. The two most important of these are "foundation" (*Fundierung*) and "fulfillment" (*Erfüllung*). Together, they yield the distinctive phenomenological epistemology of *Evidenz*.

Founding, fulfillment, and Evidenz

In turning to these relations, one should recall that phenomenology is not concerned with particular intentional experiences except as examples of their *kind*. It aims at the essence of acts and the essential relations between them; it is an eidetic science, not a factual one. In the *Logical Investigations* Husserl defends a strongly anti-empiricist theory of universals, and throughout his career he practiced an "eidetic reduction" in which the factual is probed for its essential constitution by "freely varying" a particular example until the limits of its variability are grasped. There is nothing particularly phenomenological about this reduction, however. It is practiced in eidetic sciences such as geometry and is at work in the conceptual analyst's pursuit of necessary and sufficient conditions. What *is* distinctly phenomenological is the connection Husserl establishes between this method and what he calls "intuition" (*Anschauung*), to which we shall return.

In his analysis of the logic of wholes and parts, Husserl defines the relation of *Fundierung*: When "an *A* cannot as such exist except in a more comprehensive unity which associates it with an *M*" then *A* is "founded" in *M* (Husserl 1970c: 463). Intentional acts exhibit such relations among themselves. For instance, memory is founded upon perception, since the content of a memory (what Husserl calls the "matter" of that act) cannot exist without reference to a prior act of perception: When I remember the cup of coffee I had yesterday the content of this memory is not simply the cup, conceived as an item in the world, but the cup *that* I drank from, admired, in short, *perceived*. "Having perceived" belongs necessarily to the memory's "intentional content" even when I turn out to be wrong, for that is what distinguishes the memorial act from an act of imagination. The crucial point here is that *Fundierung* is not a real relation – causal, mechanical, psycho-associative – but a *meaningful* one: neither strictly logical nor inferential (since there is no logical connection between the acts of perception and memory), it is what Husserl calls an "*intentional* implication." Thus it is also not a genetic relation in the causal sense. Husserl will eventually come to recognize a genetic dimension to relations of foundation, but the laws of such genesis concern "compossibility" (Husserl 1969a: 74) and not causal sequence.

An important example of a founded act is judgment or assertion, an instance of what Husserl calls a "categorial" act. The sense (or act matter) of the assertion, "my coffee is cold and milky," points back to acts of perception in which cold, milky coffee is directly perceived. In an assertion categorial forms (such as part/whole) that "are not genuinely present in the unarticulated percept" but are there as "ideal possibilities" get "articulated" explicitly, thereby constituting a new, founded object, a "state of affairs" (Husserl 1970c: 792ff.; translation modified). In our example, the categorial forms "is" and "and" bring out ideal possibilities contained in the content of my perception (not the object of perception as a thing in the world but as the intentional content of *this* act of perception); they thus necessarily point back to *some* intuited founding content. But what can that content *be*? In the *Logical Investigations* Husserl seems to hold that categorial forms are not "genuinely present in the unarticulated percept," but he later expresses dissatisfaction with his doctrine of categorial intuition, in part because perception's meaningful content seems neither to be that of an unarticulated whole nor something founded upon conceptual or categorial acts. The issue of how to understand such content thus became a spur to the development of phenomenology.

The relation of founding between perception and judgment also illustrates a second, perhaps even more important, phenomenological relation among intentional acts – that of "fulfillment" (*Erfüllung*). For it is not just that the judgment refers back to some perceptual content; rather, it is *fulfilled* by it. Articulation of the perceptual content is the *telos* of the judgment, the measure of its success or failure. To express this relation Husserl introduces the distinction between "empty" or "merely signitive" acts and "fulfilling" or "intuitive" acts (see Husserl 1970c: 728). When, in the absence of the corresponding perception, I assert that my coffee is cold and milky, the content of my assertion is presented in an empty or merely signitive way. But if I make the same assertion after having raised the cup to my lips, the content is intuitively given and I can experience how this intuition fulfills the sense of the assertion: the very same cup that is the object of my judgment, and in *just the way* that it is judged by me, is presented "in person," intuitively, by the perception, and I experience this "coincidence" (*Deckungs-synthesis*) of the matter of the two acts. Again, this is not a causal relation between acts, or their objects, but one that pertains to the *meaning* through which the objects are given in the acts.

Though Husserl introduces the notion of empty intentions and their intuitive fulfillments on the example of judgments, the distinction cuts across the whole field of intentionality. Perception, for instance, is itself a combination of intuitively given and emptily intended moments: in perception, my coffee cup is given in person, but the intuitively given aspects are limited to the sides I can see of it. The rest is co-intended, but as "hidden from view," and thus with a certain emptiness. This emptiness is not, however, a sheer blank; rather, the content of the perceptual act prescribes certain possible "fulfillings" for the back of the cup (e.g., that it will be the back "of a cup") and rules out others (e.g., that it will be a human face). For Husserl, phenomenology has the task of tracing the essential interconnections of fulfillment among acts, reflecting on the interplay of presence and absence in intentional experience as a whole.

Husserl's initial reason for turning to such relations was epistemological, and perhaps the major achievement of his early phenomenology is his recasting of the old correspondence view of truth as a matter of "fulfillment." To speak of correspondence is not to adopt an impossible standpoint from which to judge that some mental content maps the thing-in-itself. Rather, it is to recognize the relations of fulfillment between certain categorial acts (judgments) and their founding perceptual contents. Consciousness of truth (the correctness of the judgment) is consciousness of the synthesis of identification between the judgment's meaning and the intuitive fulfillment provided by an act of perception with the same meaning. This yields a phenomenological reformulation of epistemology: not a theory constructed to answer the skeptic but an elucidation of the meaningful relations of foundation and fulfillment that obtain among cognitive acts.

First, the concept of fulfillment permits a *functional* characterization of intuition. Where traditional empiricism defined intuition in terms of sense perception, phenomenology defines it as "any fulfilling act whatever," i.e., any act in which "something appears as 'actual,' as 'self-given' " (Husserl 1970c: 785; translation modified). Husserl's general term for this intuitive epistemic component is *Evidenz*. This does not mean "evidence" in the sense of a trace from which something is inferred; rather it is the self-presence of the thing itself, its "self-givenness" according to its own type. Thus in mathematical calculations I can operate "emptily" with symbols. But I can also calculate on the basis of *Evidenz*, that is, on the basis of the intuitive self-presentation of the operations (e.g., addition) and their intentional contents (numbers, etc.). Though such things are not given through the senses, the distinction between merely empty calculating and "authentic" or intuitively fulfilled thinking remains.

Second, the phenomenological insistence on the epistemic authority of *Evidenz*, together with the structure of presence and absence that characterizes even intuitive acts such as perception, suggests an intentional, teleological *hierarchy* among levels of knowledge. For fulfillment itself is a relative notion. If my judgment that the coffee is cold and milky is fulfilled in a corresponding percept, this percept, in turn, is not fully intuitive; it includes emptily intended moments that are also subject to fulfillment. Should they fail to be fulfilled, then my judgment will also fail to be fulfilled. If it turns out that I am only hallucinating (when I try to taste the coffee there is nothing in the cup), my judgment will be undermined. For Husserl, this means that the fulfilling *Evidenz* for the judgment was neither adequate (i.e., complete) nor apodictic (i.e., yielding *necessary* truth). Obviously, no perceptual evidence could ever be adequate or apodictic, but Husserl believed that such evidence *was* obtainable in first-person reflection on the meaningful content of mental life. If philosophy is to be a genuinely "presuppositionless" and founding science, then it must be based on such first-person *Evidenz*.

But this demand led to a major aporia in Husserl's *Logical Investigations*. For even if reflection on intentional acts yields an apodictic ground for elucidating what knowledge and cognition mean, the relation between this intentional sphere and the "intended object" remains obscure. Husserl argues that "the intentional object of [an act] is the same as its actual object . . . and that it is absurd to distinguish between them" (Husserl 1970c: 595), and this has led some commentators (Drummond 1990; Sokolowski 1974) to attribute a kind of direct realism to the *Logical Investigations*. But the "sameness" here is merely that of intentional *sense*: Husserl is asserting that the intentional object is not a second, distinct object or mental representation but a certain *way* in which "the object (period) which *is* intended" is intended (Husserl 1970c: 578). The question of whether "the object (period) which *is* intended" is itself given *in* the act is not settled thereby. Indeed, Husserl writes that "*intentional* objects of acts, and *only* intentional objects, are the things to which we are at any time attentive" (Husserl 1970c: 585) – which suggests that the "object (period) which *is* intended" precisely does *not* belong to our attending experiences, but is only "meant" in them. In general, Husserl's anti-representationalist theory of mind does not add up to direct realism. Instead, he saw the question of "the existence and nature of 'the external world'" as "a *metaphysical* question" toward which phenomenology, as descriptive clarification of the terrain of intentionality, should remain neutral (Husserl 1970b: 264).

Yet Husserl's position was not in fact neutral; rather, as the claim that we attend *only* to intentional objects makes plain, he had not entirely freed himself from psychologistic assumptions. The sphere of intentional implications appears here as something like a circle of light surrounded by a sea of darkness (de Boer 1978), a sea of the "object (period) which is intended" that eludes the reach of reflective *Evidenz*. Soon after the *Logical Investigations* Husserl came to see that this stance wholly undermined the philosophical potential of phenomenology, and, identifying it with the fallacy of "naturalism," he abandoned it in favor of a kind of "transcendental," or non-metaphysical idealism.

Philosophical Implications of Phenomenology: Transcendental Idealism

After publishing the *Logical Investigations* in 1901 Husserl moved from Halle to Göttingen. There he fell into a long personal and philosophical crisis, as reflected in these lines from his diary: "I have been through enough torments from lack of clarity and from doubt that wavers back and forth . . . Only one need consumes me: I must win clarity, else I cannot live; I cannot bear life unless I can believe that I shall achieve it" (Spiegelberg 1982: 76). The impasse of the *Logical Investigations* was finally over-come with the theory of the phenomenological reduction, which had been developing since Husserl's lecture courses of 1905–07 but which attained systematic expression only in his 1913 *Ideas*. To understand this most controversial of Husserlian notions correctly – and to appreciate the "constitutive" phenomenology that arises from it – it will be useful to recall two related steps: the rejection of naturalism and the reconceived distinction between "transcendence" and "immanence."

Naturalism and the concept of immanence

By 1911 Husserl had come to see phenomenology as more than an epistemological clarification of logic and mathematics. It was to be a rigorous philosophical science in which the norms governing every sphere of human experience – the evaluative and practical no less than the cognitive – would be rationally grounded and clarified. The greatest danger to such a project, as he argued in "Philosophy as Rigorous Science," is "the naturalizing of consciousness, including all intentionally immanent data of consciousness," and with it "the naturalizing of ideas and consequently of all absolute ideals and norms" (Husserl 1965: 80). What Husserl means by "naturalism" is essen-tially what John McDowell calls "bald naturalism" – the claim that "whatever is belongs to psychophysical nature," understood as a domain of "rigid laws" (Husserl 1965: 79) – and his arguments against it are essentially those he earlier leveled against psychologism. Now, however, Husserl clearly sees that the *normativity* of intentional relations exceeds the naturalistic conception of nature, which excludes all but *causal* relations. Phenomenological reflection on experience concerns normative questions. For instance: "how can experiences be mutually *legitimated* or *corrected* by means of each other, and not merely replace each other or confirm each other subjectively" (Husserl 1965: 87; emphasis added)? If consciousness is understood naturalistically, such questions cannot be answered; but if one takes the normative structure of inten-tionality to *define* what "consciousness" is, the field of "phenomena" opens up, governed by non-causal, (quasi) *inferential* laws. Consciousness in this sense is a "monadic unity" of meaningful relations between acts and their contents; "in itself [it] has nothing to do with nature, with space and time or substantiality and causality, but has its thoroughly peculiar 'forms'" (Husserl 1965: 108). Phenomenology thus becomes the study of how the meaningful world of our experience is constituted on the basis of such "forms." And because natural science is itself a tissue of meaning, its own theses (and so those of philosophical naturalism) are *founded* upon the meaningful relations uncovered by phenomenology.

But why is this world of phenomena not a merely *subjective*, merely "phenomenal," world? In what sense has Husserl overcome the restriction, found in the *Logical Inves-tigations*, to a kind of mental immanence? Husserl's transcendental turn is designed specifically to overcome such mentalism by bringing the "object (period) which is intended" into the space of reasons. The key is found in his theory of *Evidenz* and the new concept of *intentional* immanence it entails.

In his lecture course of 1907, later published as *The Idea of Phenomenology*, Husserl distinguishes between two senses of the pair "immanence/transcendence." The first sense is defined in terms of the metaphysical and naturalistic assumptions common to modern philosophy and science, with its notion of the mind as a *forum internum*: "Genuine" immanence pertains to what is actually "contained" in a mental act, as an "idea" is supposed to be contained in the mind according to traditional empiricism (Husserl 1964: 27–9). The "transcendent," in contrast, is what is *not* a part of the act, i.e., what lies outside the mind. For Husserl, what is genuinely immanent is given to reflection with adequate evidence and so belongs to the proper field of phenomenology. The "intentional object" (the act-matter or meaning) is clearly immanent in this sense, but the "object (period) which is intended" is most often *not*. It is transcendent and so beyond the reach of phenomenological inquiry. In order to make the object phenomenologically accessible without denying its transcendence by making it a mental content, Husserl introduces a second sense of "immanence," governed not by a metaphysical assumption about mentality but by the concept of *Evidenz*. Evidential immanence is "absolute and clear givenness, self-givenness in the absolute sense," whereas the transcendent is what is in no way self-given. On this view mental processes remain immanent (because they are adequately given), and physical things remain transcendent in the first sense – not adequately given, not "part" of the mental. But they are *not transcendent in the second sense*, i.e., not "in no way self-given." They are indeed given, though inadequately.

Note that Husserl has not here figured out how consciousness can, after all, get outside the "mental" to grasp the "real" things that, according to the *Logical Investigations*, lie beyond its ken. He has shown why all such attempts at bridge building are superfluous. The "object (period) which is intended" is *given* to consciousness and can be studied in its modes of givenness. "Noematic" phenomenology thus emerges as the study of the modes of givenness precisely of those things that transcend consciousness.

The noema

The concept of the noema, which grows out of Husserl's new evidential conception of immanence, is one of the most disputed in phenomenology. Controversy begins with Husserl's description of the noema as the "sense" (*Sinn*) that belongs to "every intentive mental process" (Husserl 1982: 213). Having in this way extended the notion of sense beyond language to all acts, it is tempting to see the noema in the manner of a Fregean *Sinn*, an abstract entity *through* which the transcendent object, distinct from the noema, is intended. This reading – developed by Dagfinn Føllesdal (Føllesdal 1982) and adopted by Dreyfus (Dreyfus 1982), Smith and MacIntyre (Smith and MacIntyre 1982), and others – fits many of Husserl's texts. On the other hand, Husserl also describes the noema as the transcendent thing itself in its manner of being given. "Perception, for example, has its noema, most basically its perceptual sense, i.e., the perceived as perceived" (Husserl 1982: 214). Because the noema includes *perceptual* moments – not just "this cup" but "this-cup-as-perceived-from-here-in-this-light" – it is difficult to see it as an abstract entity, and on this basis Robert Sokolowski (Sokolowski 1974), followed by the definitive work of John Drummond (Drummond 1990), disputes the distinction between noema and transcendent object. To maintain it is to preserve the kind of representationalism that transcendental phenomenology had intended to avoid.

The dispute over the noema is integral to the dispute over Husserl's transcendental idealism. We will not be able to settle the matter here, but each side has its strengths.

The Fregean interpretation nicely captures the fact that noematic relations are normative rather than associative or causal, but it insinuates a version of representationalism – seized upon by Dreyfus to accuse Husserl of Cartesianism – clearly in conflict with Husserl's intentions (Husserl 1982: 219). The competing view – which holds the noema to be nothing but the transcendent thing viewed from the phenomenological attitude – does justice to Husserl's stated aims, but it struggles to explain how the perceptual elements of the noema can stand in normative, and not merely associative or phenomenalistic, relations. However, this was clearly a problem that Husserl himself faced, for he did not take relations within and among noemata to be simply logical. Instead, he sought the origin of logical relations precisely in the sphere of the perceptual (see Husserl 1973, and below). Perception itself is merely *proto*-logical, its content in some ways non-conceptual, relations between noemata only *quasi*-inferential. To say that the noema of my perceiving a coffee cup adumbrates the hidden back side is not, for Husserl, to say that my *concept* of a cup demands that there be a back side. Of course, it does demand it, but perception – its noematic meaning – has a "logic" of its own.

The idealism in which the noema plays such a significant role was publicly introduced in *Ideas I* (1913; cited as Husserl 1982), and this text governed the reception of phenomenology throughout the century. Here phenomenology expands from a limited epistemological enterprise to a full transcendental philosophy that explores the conditions for the possibility of all "being and validity." The key to this universal scope lies in the phenomenological reduction, which Husserl introduces as a version of the Cartesian strategy of first-person reflection and methodological doubt. This has led many to see Husserl's phenomenology as a kind of Cartesianism, subject to the same limitations as its historical model. The final section of this chapter will address some of these issues, but at present we shall concentrate on notions introduced in *Ideas I* that remain in play throughout Husserl's subsequent thought: the idea of the "natural attitude" and its suspension; the primacy of "transcendental subjectivity"; and the doctrine of the "constitution" (*Konstituierung*) of meaning.

The natural attitude and the epoché

By 1913 Husserl had come to see naturalism – the uncritical incorporation into philosophy of "truths" borrowed from other sciences – as an instance of a much more pervasive "naïveté" that would undermine the effort to establish a radically self-responsible, presuppositionless philosophy. Husserl calls this the "general thesis" of the "natural attitude" and introduces the reductions – the *epoché* and transcendental-phenomenological reduction – to expose the dimension that the natural attitude conceals: the intentional sphere in which the meaning that is taken for granted within the natural attitude is constituted. In describing the natural attitude Husserl makes an important advance beyond the *Logical Investigations*, for he discovers the phenomenon of "world" as *horizon* – that is, he uncovers a kind of intentionality that is not the correlate of a specific intentional object but of that context wherein any intentional object can show itself. The concept of "horizon" will play an increasingly important role in Husserl's phenomenology after *Ideas I* (see Welton 2000).

Husserl attempts to make the natural attitude descriptively evident by pointing out that our everyday way of going about our business – dealing with things of all sorts,

19

other people, engaged in scientific activities, recreation, and so on – involves various modalities of "belief." I simply take for granted that what I am dealing with exists and is, more or less, as it presents itself as being. Furthermore, "other actual objects are there for me as determinate, as more or less well known, without being themselves perceived or, indeed, present in any other mode of intuition" (Husserl 1982: 51) – that is, they belong within a co-intended *horizon* of "indeterminate actuality" (Husserl 1982: 52). The horizon does not merely accompany the entity upon which I am focused; it in some sense *belongs* to that entity. I would not be perceiving *this* coil of rope did it not carry with it the "internal" horizon of "indeterminate yet determinable" properties that are hidden from view, or rest within the "external" horizon that establishes the rope as a "man-made" thing, a "real" thing (and not a hallucination), and so on. These horizonal implications are not, strictly speaking, conceptual or logical, though they are normative; they are intentional implications that go to constitute the thing as it is experienced. But I, in my concern to find a piece of rope to hang a piñata for my children, am aware of none of this. I simply take the rope's being for granted.

Now this taken-for-granted belief can become challenged: I go to pick up the rope and it turns out to be a snake. Yet – and here is Husserl's point – all such doubt takes place against an horizon, the world, that remains firm. " 'The' world is always there as an actuality," even if "this or that is . . . to be struck *out of it*" as an illusion (Husserl 1982: 57). The natural attitude is defined in terms of this unshakeable world belief, which Husserl calls the "general thesis of the natural attitude" and which others have, perhaps more aptly, called "animal faith." Like the later Wittgenstein, Husserl holds that this world horizon is the background that necessarily stands firm whenever I come to doubt something within it; it itself, then, cannot be doubted. Nevertheless, Husserl holds that world-belief can be *suspended* or "bracketed." Such bracketing – a freely exercised "refraining from judgment" about the existence of the world (and so of all the beliefs that depend upon it, all natural "positing") – is the *epoché* of the natural attitude, the first step in the phenomenological reduction. My ordinary beliefs remain in force – I do not attempt to doubt them, as Descartes did – but I "make no use" of them. I no longer take them for granted. The question of the real being of what presents itself is explicitly *set aside*.

But what is the *point* of the *epoché?* Though Husserl's motivations are complicated, the phenomenologically decisive one is this: Husserl has his eye on the sphere of intentional correlation between act and object, *noesis* and *noema*, that he had uncovered in the *Logical Investigations*. Under the *epoché* my belief in the world-horizon is put out of play, and with it all the *explanatory theories* (including psychological theories) that depend on it. This has the effect of neutralizing the tendency, inherent in the natural attitude, to treat the sphere of intentional correlation as itself an entity in the world – perhaps falling under the categories of psychology or anthropology – and to take for granted that its laws will be the sort found in everyday and scientific inquiry. The *epoché*, then, has the essentially negative function of inhibiting the ontological assumptions that keep "the life of the plane" from recognizing its dependence on the sense-constituting "life of depth" (Husserl 1970a: 118).

It is worth noting that while Husserl held the *epoché* to be absolutely central to phenomenology, many subsequent phenomenologists found it either unnecessary or impossible. Heidegger, for instance, held it to be unnecessary: phenomenology was destined to be ontology, and as a "bracketing" of existence "the reduction is in principle inappropriate" for providing a positive account of being (Heidegger 1985: 109). Merleau-Ponty, on the other hand, saw that the *epoché* was to "break with our familiar acceptance" of the world in order to thematize it. But he held that a "complete reduction" was impossible: the attempt to bracket the world only reveals its "unmotivated upsurge" (Merleau-Ponty 1962: xiv). Both objections seem to question the idea that phenomenology can or should be ontologically neutral, about which we shall have more to say below. But such objections can be hard to assess. Not only do they often run aspects of "the" reduction together that Husserl kept apart; more importantly, the concepts of "being" and "ontology" at work in the objections are already explicitly phenomenological, as resistant to traditional metaphysics and contemporary naturalism as Husserl himself was. Suffice to say that the issue of ontological commitment is an open question in phenomenological philosophy.

Transcendental reduction and constitution

In order to disclose the "life of depth" the essentially negative *epoché* must be supplemented by a transcendental phenomenological reduction in which intentional correlation is made thematic. Husserl characterizes this as a reduction to "pure" consciousness, that is, to intentionality purified of all psychological, all "worldly" interpretations and described simply as it gives itself. What shows up in the natural attitude as simply there for me – the hammer I use, the rope I notice in the corner – now comes into view as a unity of *meaning* (a pure "phenomenon") that is what it is precisely because of its place in the nexus of intentional acts and experiences in which it comes to givenness. The transcendental reduction thus allows phenomenology to study the intentional constitution of things – that is, the conditions that make possible not the *existence* of entities in the world (the issue of existence has been bracketed), but their *sense as* existing, and indeed their being given *as* anything at all.

When Husserl speaks of objects being "constituted" (*konstituiert*) by consciousness, he means neither that the mind composes a mental representation from subjective data nor that it creates objects in a causal way. The basic idea is relatively simple. The same entity can be experienced in a variety of ways: this rock, which I kick out of the way as an impediment, is subsequently picked up by my friend in order to pound a stake into our tomato patch; it is then admired by my geologist neighbor as a fine specimen of Texas granite. The same rock is given each time with a different meaning. According to Husserl, we must attribute these differences not solely to the thing itself (though they do *belong* to it) but to the consciousness that experiences them in these ways, because only the conscious act explains why at this moment just *these* aspects of the object are experienced, why my experience has *this* content. And since, under the reduction, the object "is" nothing but the rule that governs the various noemata in which it can be given, the object is in this sense constituted by consciousness. Anything that presents itself *as* something can therefore be analyzed reflectively in terms of the intentionalities that constitute it, the experiences in which it is meaningfully given. Reflection on constitution uncovers normative satisfaction conditions embedded in experience itself; it does not impose such conditions on experience as logical desiderata. To take something as a hammer is not to be able to *define* it but to be able to do something *appropriate* with it, to use it. In Husserl's language, it is to be conscious of an internal and external horizon of co-implications (what is properly expected of things of this kind, what it will do under specific transformations, the social practices of building, and so on). Being a hammer is constituted in such horizons.

Transcendental idealism

The doctrine of constitution contains the essence of Husserl's transcendental phenomenological idealism. Constitution is *transcendental* because it is the condition of possibility of something being there *as* something; it correlates what is experienced with the "subjectivity" in which it is experienced. But Husserl argues that this correlation authorizes a kind of idealism because it seems to involve a certain asymmetry between constituting consciousness and the worldly being that is posited in the natural attitude: as a structure of meaning, the latter cannot be (be given) without being constituted, whereas consciousness (understood as "pure" consciousness) is not similarly dependent on the constitution of a world. Because questions of what lies beyond the phenomenologically given are ruled out by the *epoché*, some have argued that this sort of idealism is *neutral* with regard to traditional metaphysical questions (Carr 1999; Crowell 2001). In particular, it cannot have the sense of a subjective idealism in which the world is "my representation." Yet Husserl's text is ambiguous enough to admit of various interpretations. Some – for instance, A. D. Smith (Smith 2003) – have understood his references to the "absolute being" of consciousness and the "merely relative" being of worldly things as authorizing a full-blown metaphysical idealism. Others – Dan Zahavi (Zahavi 2003), for instance – argue that while Husserl's transcendental reduction is not itself a metaphysical position, it does have metaphysical *implications*. It rules out the kind of representationalism that invites skeptical thing-in-itself doctrines, for example. Husserl did believe that certain questions often deemed "metaphysical" are rendered meaningless by phenomenological analysis, and he also developed his own phenomenologically based personalistic metaphysics. Such personalism far transcends anything that can truly be based on phenomenological *Evidenz*, however, so I will pursue the issue no further here (see Brainard 2002: 1–32).

Husserl's phenomenological idealism is distinct from Kant's transcendental idealism in that, while the latter's concept of transcendental subjectivity is a formal principle arrived at by way of an argument, the former is a concrete field of *Evidenz*, of intentional correlation and syntheses of meaning. For this reason, Husserl comes to speak of "transcendental *life*" as an anonymously functioning depth-dimension within ordinary experience. In the years following the publication of *Ideas I* reflection on transcendental life led phenomenology into questions not merely of static correlation, but of the *genesis* of the intentional contents that show up as noemata. In some ways, genetic phenomenology presents a challenge to the idea of phenomenological method as reflective and intuitive – for how can one reflect on and intuit what is irrevocably past? – and some have argued that it must incorporate elements of conceptual "construction" (see Welton 2000). But it is certain that genetic questions – carried out not as empirical-psychological, but as transcendental investigations – dominated Husserl's later philosophy. This is already prefigured in three notions mentioned in *Ideas I*, though not developed until later.

Temporality, passive synthesis, transcendental ego

First, Husserl suggests that the most fundamental structure of pure consciousness is not intentionality itself but "temporality" as the "necessary form combining mental processes with mental processes" in one continuum, or "stream" (Husserl 1982: 194). The rules governing such combination are not those of objective "clock" time, since the latter, as a measurable quantity, requires a standard for measurement, whereas the former, as the ground upon which all such standards are constituted, cannot be standardized. In a series of manuscripts dating from 1905, Husserl analyzed the peculiar structure belonging to consciousness of "inner" time, in which all noematic unities arise within a temporal horizon of *protentions* (non-thematic anticipations of subsequent experiences) and *retentions* (aspects of the "just experienced" that are not thematically recollected but held in the present as "just passed"), thereby giving current experience its temporal depth. Since intentional acts are themselves constituted *as* perceptions, recollections, judgments, and so on, they, too, belong within this universal temporal framework. Here Husserl faced a dilemma: if the intentional acts ("noeses") that constitute noematic unities of meaning are themselves identifiable unities within the stream of consciousness, what constitutes *them* cannot have the character of an intentional act. Husserl's analysis of temporality thus purports to uncover an "absolute" self-constituting and pre-intentional "flow" of consciousness as the ultimate basis for genetic phenomenology (see Brough 1972). The descriptions leading to this absolute level are extremely subtle, however, and are disputed by specialists.

A second element of genetic phenomenology, connected with the theory of temporality, is the notion of "passive synthesis." This somewhat paradoxical term belongs to Husserl's "transcendental aesthetic," his account of those elements of intentional constitution that precede the explicit, or "active," synthesis carried out in conceptual thinking and judging. A unity of meaning is constituted every time I judge that "the cup is white," for instance. But Husserl argues that this rests upon a level of "pre-predicative" synthesis in which the white cup itself is constituted perceptually as an identity of manifold changing aspects. At bottom these aspects involve something that is "pre-given" to consciousness – what Husserl calls "hyletic data," the dimension of sensation. On Husserl's view, the sensuous does not inhabit consciousness as meaningless atoms awaiting conceptual fixation; rather, it is genuinely synthesized, though "passively" (i.e., without ego-involvement), according to what Husserl, following empiricist psychology, calls rules of "association" – for instance, prominence (in the field), contrast, homogeneity, and heterogeneity (Husserl 1973: 72–6). Through a phenomenology of passive synthesis Husserl hoped to trace the genesis of logic, to show how predicative logical forms are rooted in pre-predicative modes of perceptual synthesis. Such investigations have much to contribute to recent debates over non-conceptual content, but the difficulty of distinguishing genuine description from theoretical construction here is evident. Can the norms of conceptual thought be bootstrapped out of content that is not already governed by them? Are the rules of association actually phenomenologically evident? Does it make sense – as Merleau-Ponty, for one, denied – to speak of neutral hyletic "data" that get passively synthesized as "properties" of objects? The recent translation of Husserl's manuscripts on passive synthesis should foster discussion of these important issues (Husserl 2001).

Finally, the turn toward genetic phenomenology has implications for Husserl's treatment of the ego. In the *Logical Investigations* Husserl had denied the necessity of an ego for the stream of consciousness, but by 1913 he came to argue that "each mental process" – each instance of intentionality – "is characterized as an act of the ego" (Husserl 1982: 190). Even after the *epoché* – in which the empirical, psychological human subject as an entity in the world is bracketed, taken simply as a constituted phenomenon – the stream of consciousness is "owned," is centered upon the first person. But how does such a "transcendental" ego give itself in reflection? Husserl never quite brings his views into line on this matter, but he highlights three essential aspects of the ego.

First, the ego shows itself as "ego pole" – a point from which intentional acts "emanate" and to which they "belong" as "its" (Husserl 1982: 191). This conception is phenomenologically motivated both by the fact that active synthesis (such as judging) is a matter of an ego "taking a stand," and by the fact that upon reflection I find that even acts in which the ego does not directly take a stand (such as perception) nevertheless involve objects being there *for*, evident *to*, a first-person consciousness.

This latter point leads to the second guise of the ego, namely, as a principle of *self-awareness*. Phenomenological analysis shows that the stream of consciousness – the ongoing awareness of the world around us – entails an awareness of *itself in* being aware of the world. Husserl's commitment to a transcendental ego is in part motivated by this demand. But as Zahavi – following Sartre – has shown, this self-awareness cannot be conceived on the model of an intentional act directed upon the ego engaged in intentional acts. To block the fatal regress, self-awareness must be an *original* non-objectifying function of intentional consciousness itself. Whether this undermines Husserl's doctrine of a "pure" ego is a matter of some dispute (see Zahavi 1999).

Finally, in his genetic phenomenology Husserl introduces a third conception of the transcendental ego, namely, as the "substrate of habitualities" (Husserl 1969a: 66). Considered genetically, the temporal stream in which the ego (in the first sense) takes stands and makes judgments not only constitutes a "world" of noematic meaning, but achieves a kind of *self*-constitution: each judgment becomes an "abiding accomplishment" and forever marks the ego as the one who has judged thus; each practical attempt at something becomes the basis for subsequent habits, inclinations, abilities, and skills – "secondary passivities" – that come to characterize a distinct transcendental style. "The ego constitutes itself for itself in, so to speak, the unity of a 'history'" (Husserl 1969a: 75). At this level, phenomenological reflection on constitution is nothing more than the "self-explication of the transcendental ego" as *monad* (Husserl 1969a: 68).

Not surprisingly, this has given rise to the objection that phenomenology is not only a subjective idealism but a solipsism as well. Husserl vehemently denied that phenomenology is a metaphysical solipsism (the reduction ensured neutrality there), but he was acutely concerned about the charge of "transcendental solipsism." Isn't the meaningful world as constituted merely "my" world – or, more pointedly, aren't the others who are there in the world with me merely constituted products of my constituting consciousness? We cannot explore the details of Husserl's attempt to solve this problem in the *Cartesian Meditations*, but it points to a larger set of issues that, according to a widespread view, lie beyond the reach of Husserl's phenomenology: the phenomena of *embodiment, intersubjectivity,* and the *historicity* of the *lifeworld.* I shall conclude this chapter, then, by sketching something of these disputed horizons.

Horizons of Husserlian Phenomenology

Ideas I was to be followed up by two further volumes, one demonstrating the phenomenological method through constitutional analyses of two major regions of being, "nature" and "spirit" (*Ideas II*), and the other providing phenomenological foundations for the system of sciences (*Ideas III*). These works, however, were never published. In 1916 Husserl moved to Freiburg as the celebrated founder of the phenomenological movement, yet, thanks to his idealistic turn, he was estranged from many of his former colleagues. Though he worked feverishly on topics that would have found their way into the two further *Ideas* volumes – as well as on many other projects – his thought was constantly developing and he published nothing further until 1929, when *Formal and Transcendental Logic* appeared (Husserl 1969b). Husserl's Freiburg period, which lasted until his death in 1938, thus has an aspect of painful paradox: no period in Husserl's life was richer in philosophical ideas and none less fruitful in the kind of publication that would show the full scope of phenomenology's contribution to philosophy. As the material from this period becomes better known, however, we can begin to appreciate something of Husserl's achievement.

While producing phenomenological analyses in his research manuscripts, Husserl also devoted attention to phenomenological method. Some commentators argue that these reflections are generally a step behind the analyses, attempts to fit new insights into old methodological commitments (Welton 2000; Steinbock 1995). Be that as it may, Husserl did come to identify a "great shortcoming" in the approach to the reduction laid out in *Ideas I* (the so-called "Cartesian way") since, "while it leads to the transcendental ego in one leap, as it were, it brings this ego into view as apparently empty of content" (Husserl 1970a: 155). In contrast, Husserl began to emphasize how access to the evidential field of intentional syntheses could be motivated through problems arising in phenomenological psychology, and through ontological issues in the foundations of the empirical sciences (see Kern 1977). It was in Husserl's research manuscripts, however, and not in his reflections on method, that a different picture of transcendental subjectivity began to take shape, one that anticipated – and perhaps in part responded to – issues that were then current in so-called *Lebensphilosophie.* These would send the phenomenological movement off in an "existential" direction in subsequent years (see Natanson 1973). In particular, Husserl struggled to reconcile the idea that the constituting transcendental subject is *embodied, social,* and *historical,* with the claim that it cannot be *part* of the world that it constitutes. This "paradox of human subjectivity" (Husserl 1970a: 178) shows itself in each of the three horizons.

Embodiment

Phenomenological analysis shows that constitution of the perceptual world entails more than vision conceived as a mental act; it requires an *embodied* subject. The noema of my perception of this coffee cup on my desk, for instance, includes not merely the sides that are currently open to view but also the underside and back side that are there but not now visible. What does it mean that these out-of-view aspects are "there"? Husserl argues that a disembodied subject would be incapable of entertaining such a sense; rather, to say that they are "there" but not visible is to say that were I to *move* around the cup, or move the cup itself, I could bring new facets into view. These facets appear in a specific order keyed to the kind of movements I can make and the kind of manipulations of the cup I can exercise. The noematic rule of the perceptual object's identity, then, refers to an embodied subject, to an "I can" that stands in "conditional" – that is normative, not causal – symbiosis with its environment: reaching out to touch the cup, what it manifests to touch confirms what sight has disclosed, fulfills it evidentially thanks to the "synaesthesia" – or original combination of sensory modalities – that characterizes my bodily engagement with the world. The subject who sees a *real world*, then, cannot be a disembodied one (Husserl 1989: 70–80).

However, the body is itself something *seen*; it too is constituted as a thing in the world. Husserl responds to this paradox by distinguishing between *Körper* (the body as a constituted natural object) and *Leib* (the "lived body" as a dimension of constituting subjectivity itself). Even after bracketing the *Körper* through the reduction, the first-person experience of transcendental subjectivity retains a unique aspect of embodiment, of the "I can." I *am* my *Leib*. Husserl shows how this identity arises through the reflective arc established in the sense of touch. Embodiment becomes "subject" when, in sensing the world through touch, it at the same time senses itself sensing. Only subsequently does this original embodiment get constituted as a *Körper*, a natural object that "belongs" to me by means of a self-enworlding, or "mundanization," in which I come to understand myself as an animal, a human being, and so on.

Husserl's solution is, of course, not without its difficulties. At times he still speaks as though the reflexive self-constitution of the lived body proceeds from an "absolute" ego, and his analysis of the "I can" in terms of systems of kinaesthetic sensations (i.e., those belonging to my own embodied movements) retains elements of an intellectualistic construction. But Husserl went quite far toward demonstrating how embodiment is a normative condition of intentional content. Perhaps it is best to say that he was trying to do justice to two phenomenologically evident facts: first, that the meaning-structure of the world is intelligible only as something given to an embodied subject; and second, that the body at issue cannot be identified with the body-as-object but must be understood as "ego-logical," that is, the center of a reflexive, first-person "point of view."

Sociality

Similar issues arise when Husserl begins to consider the contribution that *sociality* or "intersubjectivity" makes to the constitution of the world. Returning to our example, what makes it the case that the currently unseen facets of the cup before me nevertheless have the sense of being *currently visible* facets? This cannot be derived from the idea that I could move around the cup to see them, for this would only establish that they were visible when facing me. According to Husserl, it is because I take them as visible for *an other* who could now stand where I *would* stand if I moved around the cup. Thus the subjectivity capable of having the intentional content, "visible real thing," is necessarily a *social* subject; such meaning would remain closed to the solipsist. And since, for Husserl, perception is the bedrock upon which all other constitutive achievements are built, to show that perception is possible only for a social subject is to show that transcendental subjectivity is transcendental *intersubjectivity* (Husserl 1970a: 172, 262). The full notion of transcendence – the idea of a real world "out there," other than me – depends on there being others for whom it is "there too."

Here again, however, an objection arises: Aren't others themselves parts of the world as I find it, subject-objects in the world? If so, are they not also noematic unities whose meaning depends on *my* constitutive accomplishments? It cannot be said that Husserl worked out a finally satisfactory answer to this problem; it operates as an horizon of his developing thought, and, as in the case of embodiment, he seeks to do justice to two compelling phenomenological demands. On the one hand, the world's meaning makes reference at every turn to a plurality of subjects in communication. The normativity that makes intentional content possible depends on a kind of publicity, and indeed my very sense of myself is as "one" among others "like me." Husserl develops these insights in manuscripts on the "personalistic attitude" (Husserl 1989) and in several volumes on the social world. On the other hand, no genuine subjectivity is conceivable that would not be the first-person singular, an "I." If transcendental intersubjectivity is genuinely *subjectivity*, then, it must be centered on an individual ego that, to the extent that it *is* individual, is "unique and indeclinable" (Husserl 1970a: 185). Husserl develops this thought above all in *Cartesian Meditations*, where he shows how transcendental intersubjectivity arises from a primordial "analogizing" encounter between the embodied ego in its "sphere of ownness" and the body of the other. The other's subjectivity is registered as an irrevocable "absence" thanks to which there arises in me the *sense* of something being radically "other" – a sense that subsequently attaches to the whole constituted world (Husserl 1969a: 107).

History

Finally, in reflecting on the cultural crisis of Europe Husserl came to recognize that intentional content of whatever sort, and the meaningful relations it exhibits, involves reference to an *historical* horizon, to a generational process whereby the constitutive achievements of *temporally distant* subjectivities come to be "sedimented" in current experience. The world constituted in the ongoing life of transcendental subjectivity – which Husserl now begins to call the "lifeworld" (*Lebenswelt*) – comes to be seen as a complex interplay of memory and forgetting, of faithful transmission and fateful emptying of original experiences and intentional accomplishments. For instance, Husserl explored the intentional implications sedimented in the history of mathematized physics in an attempt to show how such physics – then as now taken to be the model of rationality – had become an empty *techne* obscuring the genuine sources of rationality in transcendental subjectivity (Husserl 1970a; Hopkins 2003). But if one can only understand the meanings that circulate in the contemporary world by recourse to their (intentional, not empirical) history, then transcendental subjectivity itself must be "historical." If constitution takes place not merely along the axis of an individual life but also along the "generative" axis (Husserl 1970a; Steinbock 1995) of cultural worlds embodying specific historical narratives, then the reduction to transcendental subjectivity cannot stop at the sort of individual "consciousness" with which Husserl began. Nowhere is the tension between the path of phenomenological inquiry and Husserl's early framework for elucidating it – the framework of nineteenth-century psychology – more apparent than in his late forays into the historical lifeworld as the ultimate horizon of meaning.

And yet, it is understandable that Husserl would shrink back from what look to be the implications of his historical meditations, insisting that "reduction to the absolute ego as the ultimately unique center of function in all constitution" remains necessary (Husserl 1970a: 186). For the generative concept of transcendental subjectivity has strayed far from the epistemological considerations that turned phenomenology toward subjectivity in the first place: the demand for first-person *Evidenz*, the interest in reflective description, givenness, and intuition in the service of ultimate philosophical *self*-responsibility. The line between a truly phenomenological inquiry and a merely empirical one dressed up in philosophical garb – to say nothing of a metaphysics of objective spirit in the Hegelian manner – is easily transgressed in Husserl's late work, and it is to his credit as a phenomenologist that he was keenly aware of the danger. It may be that concrete phenomenological investigations point ineluctably toward a concept of transcendental subjectivity that is richer than the original psychologically forged concept of "consciousness" – one that would include embodiment, sociality, and historicality. Certainly, later existential and hermeneutic phenomenologists held this to be so. But in the case of history, as in the case of embodiment and sociality, Husserl retained a sharp sense (perhaps sharper than those who followed him) of the twin demands made by the things themselves: meaning comes to us as a trace of sedimented constitutive activity, as something bound up with a specific historical genesis; but at the same time it is always and only understood in current intentional experience. It is there and there alone that meaning – including the meaning of history itself – is concretely *given*. If philosophy is to recover historical sedimentations of meaning it can only do so by *making* them current, and if it is to remain *phenomenological* (beholden to the given as it is given) it cannot abandon reflective analysis of experience. Many things, of course, escape the "original" grasp of first-person reflection: historical generativity, my birth and death, my early development, dreamless sleep, the "unconscious," and so on. In every case, however, as Husserl insists, "this sort of thing has its manners of ontic verification, of 'self-giving,' which are quite particular but which originally create the ontic meaning for beings of such particularity" (Husserl 1970a: 188). In other words, if we speak meaningfully of the "unconscious," "death," and other such things, it is because these things *are* self-given to us in some way, are *not* mere abstract constructs. The challenge of phenomenology is to remain attuned precisely to those modes of givenness, and some of the most interesting phenomenological work – in Husserl as well as in his "followers" – is the result of taking up that challenge.

References and Further Reading

Bernet, R., Kern, I., and Marbach, E. (1993) *An Introduction to Husserlian Phenomenology*. Evanston, IL: Northwestern University Press.

Brainard, M. (2002) *Belief and its Neutralization: Husserl's System of Phenomenology in Ideas I*. Albany: State University of New York Press.

Brough, J. (1972) The emergence of an absolute consciousness in Husserl's early writings on time-consciousness. *Man and World*, 5, 298–326.

Carr, D. (1999) *The Paradox of Subjectivity*. Oxford: Oxford University Press.

Cobb-Stevens, R. (1990) *Husserl and Analytic Philosophy*. Dordrecht: Kluwer.

Crowell, S. (2001) *Husserl, Heidegger, and the Space of Meaning*. Evanston, IL: Northwestern University Press.

de Boer, T. (1978) *The Development of Husserl's Thought* (trans. D. Plantinga). The Hague: Martinus Nijhoff (original work published 1966).

Dreyfus, H. (1982) Husserl's perceptual noema. In H. Dreyfus & H. Hall (eds.), *Husserl, Intentionality, and Cognitive Science* (pp. 97–123). Cambridge MA: MIT Press.

Drummond, J. (1990) *Husserlian Intentionality and Non-Foundational Realism*. Dordrecht: Kluwer.

Føllesdal, D. (1982) Husserl's notion of *noema*. In H. Dreyfus & H. Hall (eds.), *Husserl, Intentionality, and Cognitive Science* (pp. 73–80). Cambridge MA: MIT Press (original work published 1969).

Heidegger, M. (1985) *History of the Concept of Time: Prolegomena* (trans. T. Kisiel). Bloomington: Indiana University Press (original work published 1925).

Hopkins. B. (2003) The phenomenological project of desedimenting the formalization of meaning: Jacob Klein's contribution. *Philosophy Today*, 46/5, 168–77.

Husserl, E. (1964) *The Idea of Phenomenology* (trans. W. P. Alston and G. Nakhnikian). The Hague: Martinus Nijhoff (original work published 1950).

—— (1965) Phenomenology as rigorous science. In *Phenomenology and the Crisis of Philosophy* (trans. Q. Lauer) (pp. 71–148). New York: Harper & Row (original work published 1911).

—— (1969a) *Cartesian Meditations* (trans. D. Cairns). The Hague: Martinus Nijhoff (original lectures delivered 1929).

—— (1969b) *Formal and Transcendental Logic: An Attempt at a Critique of Logical Reason* (trans. D. Cairns). The Hague: Martinus Nijhoff (original work published 1929).

—— (1970a) *The Crisis of European Sciences and Transcendental Phenomenology* (trans. D. Carr). Evanston, IL: Northwestern University Press (original work published 1954).

—— (1970b) *Logical Investigations, Volume One* (trans. J. N. Findlay). London: Routledge & Kegan Paul (original work published 1900–1; 2nd edn. 1913).

—— (1970c) *Logical Investigations, Volume Two* (trans. J. N. Findlay). London: Routledge & Kegan Paul (original work published 1900–1; 2nd edn. 1913).

—— (1973) *Experience and Judgment* (trans. J. S. Churchill and K. Ameriks). Evanston, IL: Northwestern University Press (original work published 1939).

—— (1982) *Ideas Pertaining to a Pure Phenomenology and to a Phenomenological Philosophy, First Book I* (trans. F. Kersten). The Hague: Martinus Nijhoff (original work published 1913).

—— (1989) *Ideas Pertaining to a Pure Phenomenology and to a Phenomenological Philosophy, Second Book* (trans. R. Rojcewicz and A. Schuwer). The Hague: Martinus Nijhoff (original work published 1952).

—— (2001) *Analyses Concerning Passive and Active Synthesis* (trans. A. Steinbock). Dordrecht: Kluwer (original lectures delivered 1918–26).

—— (2003) *Edmund Husserl: Collected Works: vol. 10, Philosophy of Arithmetic* (trans. anonymous). Dordrecht: Springer.

Kern, I. (1977) The three ways to the transcendental phenomenological reduction in the philosophy of Edmund Husserl. In F. Elliston and P. McCormick (eds.), *Husserl: Expositions and Appraisals*. Notre Dame: University of Notre Dame Press (original work published 1962).

McKenna, W. (1982) *Husserl's "Introductions to Phenomenology": Interpretation and Critique*. The Hague: Martinus Nijhoff.

Mensch, J. (1988) *Intersubjectivity and Transcendental Idealism*. Albany: State University of New York Press.

Merleau-Ponty, M. (1962) *The Phenomenology of Perception* (trans. C. Smith). London: Routledge & Kegan Paul (original work published 1945).

Mohanty, J. N. (1982) *Husserl and Frege*. Bloomington: Indiana University Press.

—— (1997) *Phenomenology Between Essentialism and Transcendental Philosophy*. Evanston, IL: Northwestern University Press.

Moran, D. (2001) *Introduction to Phenomenology*. London: Routledge.

Natanson, M. (1973) *Edmund Husserl: Philosopher of Infinite Tasks*. Evanston, IL: Northwestern University Press.

Ricoeur, P. (1967) *Husserl: An Analysis of his Phenomenology* (trans. E. G. Ballard and L. E. Embree). Evanston, IL: Northwestern University Press.

Smith, A. D. (2003) *Husserl and the* Cartesian Meditations. London: Routledge.

Smith, B., and Smith, D. W. (eds.) (1995) *The Cambridge Companion to Husserl*. Cambridge: Cambridge University Press.

Smith, D. W., and McIntyre, R. (1982) *Husserl and Intentionality*. Dordrecht: D. Reidel.

Soffer, G. (1991) *Husserl and the Question of Relativism*. Dordrecht: Kluwer.

Sokolowski, R. (1974) *Husserlian Meditations and How Words Present Things*. Evanston, IL: Northwestern University Press.

—— (2000) *Introduction to Phenomenology*. Cambridge: Cambridge University Press.

Spiegelberg. H. (1982) *The Phenomenological Movement*, 3rd edn. The Hague: Martinus Nijhoff.

Steinbock, A. (1995) *Home and Beyond: Generative Phenomenology After Husserl*. Evanston, IL: Northwestern University Press.

Welton, D. (2000) *The Other Husserl*. Bloomington: Indiana University Press.

Zahavi, D. (1999) *Self-Awareness and Alterity: A Phenomenological Investigation*. Evanston, IL: Northwestern University Press.

—— (2003) *Husserl's Phenomenology*. Stanford, CA: Stanford University Press.

3

Existential Phenomenology

MARK A. WRATHALL

The terms "existential phenomenology" and "existentialist phenomenology" came into widespread use in the late 1950s and early 1960s as a way of designating what was common to the thought of Heidegger, Sartre, Merleau-Ponty, and the philosophers influenced by them. So far as I can tell, none of these philosophers designated their own work "existential phenomenology," although they did describe their projects in related ways. Heidegger, following the emergence of existentialism as a movement in France, denied that his thought dealt with "existentialism or existence-philosophy" (Heidegger 1986: 650), but he described his approach to phenomenology in *Being and Time* as an "analytic of existence" (*Existenz*) (Heidegger 1962: 62). Sartre called his "special phenomenological method" "existential psychoanalysis" (Sartre 1984: 617). In the preface to *The Phenomenology of Perception*, Merleau-Ponty explained that "phenomenology is also a philosophy which puts essences back into existence, and does not expect to arrive at an understanding of man and the world from any starting point other than that of their 'facticity' [i.e., their actual, definite ways of being]" (vi).

A word of caution is in order, however. To pay inordinate attention to these verbal similarities is to invite confusion. For example, in the passages I just quoted, "existence" means different things for Heidegger and Merleau-Ponty. For Heidegger, "*Existenz*" names the human mode of being; Merleau-Ponty's "*l'existence*" refers to a much broader range of phenomena, and would include worldly things. And Sartre's focus on consciousness (a focus indicated by his description of his method as "psychology") sets him apart in important ways from what is distinctive about the existential phenomenologies of Heidegger and Merleau-Ponty.

All the same, there is a justification for grouping these philosophers together under the heading "existential phenomenology." This justification is grounded in commonalities in their understanding of the phenomena upon which they focus (section I), and in the phenomenological method they use to account for such phenomena (section II).

Existential phenomenologies have included descriptions of the meaning of being (Heidegger), the role of the lived-body in perception (Merleau-Ponty), and skillful coping (Hubert Dreyfus). One can also see Arendt's account of the public domain, Sartre's account of bad faith and our concrete relations with others, de Beauvoir's descriptions of sex and aging, Levinas's reflections on our encounter with the other, and Marion's work on the "saturated phenomenon" of divine transcendence, as works in existential phenomenology. Even Nietzsche's efforts to illuminate existence through the notion of the will to power, or Kierkegaard's and Pascal's efforts to redescribe religious faith in non-philosophical terms, belong with some justification to the canon of works in existential phenomenology. I will, however, explore the idea of existential phenomenology primarily through the works of Heidegger and Merleau-Ponty, as their works are undisputed paradigms of what existential phenomenology is.

I Existential Phenomena

Existential phenomenologists all share the view that philosophy should not be conducted from a detached, objective, disinterested, disengaged standpoint. This is because, they contend, certain phenomena only show themselves to one who is engaged with the world in the right kind of way. I propose calling such phenomena "existential phenomena." Insofar as they are *phenomena*, existential phenomena exist in revealing themselves to us: "the expression '*phenomenon*' signifies that which shows *itself in itself*, the manifest" (Heidegger 1962: 51). Insofar as they really *exist*, they don't depend for their being on our knowing them as such – they are what they are independently of whatever we happen to think of them. As Heidegger observes, "entities *are*, quite independently of the experience, acquaintance, and comprehension by which they are disclosed, discovered, and determined" (Heidegger 1953: 183).

If one thinks that something can show itself to us, make itself manifest, only to the extent that we have a determinate and explicit awareness of it as such, then the idea of an existential phenomenon might seem paradoxical. But one of the key elements of existential phenomenology is the view that there are a number of different ways in which entities can show themselves to us. Indeed, both Heidegger and Merleau-Ponty agreed that the most fundamental way in which we encounter entities, our "primary perception" of them, in the words of Merleau-Ponty, "is a non-thetic, pre-objective and pre-conscious experience" (Merleau-Ponty 1962: 242). For Merleau-Ponty, we have a "non-thetic" perception of something when it is not posed or placed squarely before us as an object for perception – that means "we have no *express* experience of it" (Merleau-Ponty 1962: 258). Something is "pre-objective" when it has a structure that resists articulation into a content that allows it to be grasped in thought – it is a "positive indeterminate which prevents the spatial, temporal and numerical wholes from becoming articulated into manageable, distinct and identifiable terms" (Merleau-Ponty 1962: 12). Other existential phenomenologists describe such phenomena using different terms, but their aim is the same – they want to direct our attention to things which bear on us not by being available to thought, nor because we are expressly aware of them as such, but rather because they shape or influence our comportment with things.

Thus, as Merleau-Ponty explains, the existential phenomenologist's aim is "to return to that world which precedes knowledge, of which knowledge always speaks, and in relation to which every scientific schematization is an abstract and derivative sign-language, as is geography in relation to the country-side in which we have learnt beforehand what a forest, a prairie or a river is" (Merleau-Ponty 1962: ix). Because existential phenomena may show themselves best when we are not focally aware of them, not reflecting on them, or not thinking about them, they may well present to our view something that can only be imperfectly and partially captured in theoretical statements. Thus, the method of existential phenomenology must be descriptive, and consists always only in leading us to an apprehension of the objects of research.

Before returning to the nature and problems inherent in phenomenological description, however, let's try to get a better grasp of what the "existential phenomena" are. We'll do this by examining some paradigmatic instances of things which exist in "showing themselves" to us, but which are perceived in "non-thetic, pre-objective and pre-conscious experience." We will look, in particular, at existential-phenomenological accounts of (1) the entities with which we cope in our everyday practices, (2) the world, and (3) human being-in-the-world.

1 Worldly entities

By "worldly entities," I refer to those things which would not exist without an organized context of human equipment, activities, purposes, and goals. For example, if there were no need to build things, and no such things as nails and boards, then there would be no hammers. This is not to deny the reality of the raw materials from which hammers are made – wood and iron, for example. Those sorts of physical objects presumably exist whether there is a human world that incorporates them or not. A physical object, as Merleau-Ponty notes, "exists *partes extra partes*, and . . . consequently it acknowledges between its parts, or between itself and other objects only external and mechanical relationships" (Merleau-Ponty 1962: 73). That means that its existence in no way depends on its being incorporated into a world of human uses and activities.

For much of the philosophy of the early twentieth century (including both Neo-Kantian and transcendental phenomenological approaches), an object could only be given to thought if it had already been "constituted" by thought. "Constitution," in its most general sense, means allowing something to be seen as what it is by giving it a place in an ordered context. Thus for Kant, for instance, an object could only be seen as an object if it was brought under certain categories of thought. The result of such a view of constitution is that an entity can only show itself when it is already structured conceptually. This view of constitution, in other words, commits one to a denial of the existence of existential phenomena.

Heidegger accepted the importance of constitution – he believed that something could only be given to us as an existing entity once it had been placed into an ordered context. But Heidegger argued that this constitution didn't need to be performed by thought or in the categories proper to the intellect. "Constituting," Heidegger explained in a traditional sense, "means *letting the entity be seen in its objectivity*." But, he argued, "this objectivity . . . is not a result of the activity of intellectual understanding upon the external world. It is not a result of an activity upon an already given mix of sensations or throng of affections, which are ordered to form a picture of the world" (Heidegger 1985: 71). Instead, Heidegger argues that entities are constituted – allowed to show themselves as they are in themselves – when they have a place in a whole context of relations to other worldly entities and human activities. A hammer is constituted as the thing it is by the way it relates to nails and boards, and activities like pounding and building. If the very same object physically described were found in a different context, it would be a different worldly entity. It would be, in the terminology of existential phenomenology, differently constituted, even though it would be physically identical.

Even though worldly entities are thus constituted through their relations to us, existential phenomenologists argue that these constitutive relationships do not necessarily have the logical or conceptual structure of thought. The aim of a phenomenological description of worldly entities is to help us recognize how things are constituted and available for us without needing to be constituted by us in thought.

It might seem paradoxical that we could learn to recognize the mind-independence of things by attending to the way they are given *to us*, or perceived and coped with *by us*. (It was for this reason that Husserl didn't believe phenomenology could immediately arrive at any conclusions about the being of entities. He thought that the description of experience required us to "bracket" the existence of entities, meaning that we would focus on the way they appear in consciousness without considering how they exist independently of that appearance.) The seeming paradox is a result of the fact that we inhabit a philosophical landscape shaped by Descartes and the empiricists, who all believed that the objects of perception are ideas given to consciousness (this same landscape also lends credence to the intellectualist views of constitution we've already touched on). Of course, there is a kernel of truth to the tradition; there is a sense in which the things we encounter in the world normally present themselves as unmysterious, as completely available to be thought about.

But this familiarity with things doesn't imply that they are completely constituted by and for thought. As Merleau-Ponty notes:

> the fact remains that the thing presents itself to the person who perceives it as a thing in itself, and thus poses the problem of a genuine *in-itself-for-us*. Ordinarily we do not notice this because our perception, in the context of our everyday concerns, alights on things sufficiently attentively to discover in them their familiar presence, but not sufficiently so to disclose the nonhuman element which lies hidden in them. But the thing holds itself aloof from us and remains self-sufficient. (Merleau-Ponty 1962: 322)

The traditional view that the objects of perception are ideas cannot do justice to our experience of beings as mind-independent. Ideas, as Berkeley showed, can't have any substantiality to them – that is, there can't be anything more to them than can be thought. But that, of course, is not how we experience things. Even the ones with which we are completely familiar "hold themselves aloof from us and remain self-sufficient."

The key to understanding how things can be both aloof and given to us depends on seeing how they can have a significance not of the order of thought. As Merleau-Ponty argues, we grasp the significance of ordinary objects primarily in our bodies, in knowing how to move ourselves and hold ourselves as we explore them perceptually and practically: "We understand the thing as we understand a new kind of behavior, not, that is, through any intellectual operation of subsumption, but by taking up on our own account the mode of existence which the observable signs adumbrate before us" (Merleau-Ponty 1962: 319). In other words, the thing shows its various aspects to us as invitations for specific ways of dealing with it. An ashtray, to focus on one of Merleau-Ponty's favorite examples, presents itself in terms of particular ways to hold it, to position ourselves by it, and so on:

> The significance of the ash-tray (at least its total and individual significance, as this is given in perception) is not a certain idea of the ash-tray which co-ordinates its sensory aspects and is accessible to the understanding alone, it animates the ash-tray, and is self-evidently embodied in it. That is why we say that in perception the thing is given to us "in person", or "in the flesh." Prior to and independently of other people, the thing achieves that miracle of expression: an inner reality which reveals itself externally, a significance which descends into the world and begins its existence there, and which can be fully understood only when the eyes seek it in its own location. Thus the thing is correlative to my body and, in more general terms, to my existence, of which my body is merely the stabilized structure. It constitutes itself in the hold of my body upon it; it is not first of all a meaning (*signification*) for the understanding, but a structure accessible to inspection by the body. (Merleau-Ponty 1962: 319–20; translation modified)

I understand the ashtray, in other words, not by having ideas of it, but by knowing how to hold it, how to move it or move my hands relative to it, which requires that I be able to anticipate and respond to the ways it will show itself as I move myself around it. The ashtray gives itself to me when it reveals the unified sensory-motor significance that it has for my body. Any intellectual discoveries we make about the object are subsequent to, and dependent on, this manifestation of it.

Heidegger makes the same point regarding the existentiality of objects of use, the available or the ready-to-hand. Things are given to us as they are in themselves only when we possess the skills for dealing with them in an appropriate manner: "equipment can genuinely show itself only in dealings cut to its own measure (hammering with a hammer, for example)." "But," Heidegger observes, "in such dealings an entity of this kind is not *grasped* thematically [i.e., explicitly] as an occurring thing, nor is the equipment-structure known as such even in the using. The hammering does not simply have knowledge about the hammer's character as equipment, but it has appropriated this equipment in a way which could not possibly be more suitable" (Heidegger 1962: 98).

Heidegger's description of tool use, like Merleau-Ponty's description of the ashtray, is not meant as a *proof* of the mind-independence of things, but rather aims to orient us in such a way that we can see for ourselves how they normally give themselves to us. When hammering, we understand and encounter a hammer without having to have any reflective thoughts about it at all. Indeed, we hammer best when we are not deliberately trying to do so (see Heidegger 1962: 99). This is because for Heidegger, as for Merleau-Ponty, the meaning of the hammer is meaning not for thought, but for our own existence, our own way of being in the world.

Another way to recognize the mind-independence of things is to acknowledge that things are not uniformly familiar to us. Let's look at Heidegger's description of "a trivial example," and the conclusions he draws from the example:

> If we observe a shoemaker's shop, we can indeed identify all sorts of extant things on hand. But which entities are there and how these entities are handy, in line with their

inherent character, is unveiled for us only in dealing appropriately with equipment such as tools, leather, and shoes. Only one who understands is able to uncover by himself this environing world of the shoemaker's. We can of course receive instruction about the use of the equipment and the procedures involved; and on the basis of the understanding thus gained we are put in a position, as we say, to reproduce in thought the factical commerce with these things. But it is only in the tiniest spheres of the beings with which we are acquainted that we are so well versed as to have at our command the specific way of dealing with equipment which uncovers this equipment as such. The entire range of intraworldly beings accessible to us at any time is not suitably accessible to us in an equally original way. There are many things we merely know something about but do not know how to manage with them. They confront us as beings, to be sure, but as unfamiliar beings. Many beings, including even those already uncovered, have the character of unfamiliarity. This character is positively distinctive of beings as they first confront us. (Heidegger 1982: 304)

The description directs our attention to the way that things show up in the world as, admittedly, understandable, sorted already into the types and classes that we pick out with names. If we walk into a shoemaker's shop, we don't see mere entities, we see tools and other familiar things. But if we pay attention, we notice that our ability to identify things is not matched by an ability to let them show themselves as they genuinely are in themselves, because we lack the skills for using them. Even if we "receive instruction about the use of the equipment," that is, even if we acquire a kind of propositional knowledge about how it is used, we would not be in a position to fully grasp the meaning of things. We wouldn't for example, know how to hold the tools or manipulate them on the basis of being able to "reproduce in thought the factical commerce with these things." Thus, the world shows up as given to us for action and thought and perception but, nonetheless, as distinguished into more and less familiar and transparently available regions and objects. But this difference is not a difference in their givenness to thought – we can be equally able to think about a familiar object and an unfamiliar object.[1] Thus, to be an object of thought is not the same thing as being given to the understanding. As Heidegger concludes, "we must keep in mind the point that the usual approach in theory of knowledge, according to which a manifold of arbitrarily occurring things or objects is supposed to be homogeneously given to us, does not do justice to the primary facts." Our ordinary perception of the world therefore attests to the mind-independence of things – they present themselves as available for us to use and think about, but as containing in themselves their own "inherent content" or "specific whatness" which exceeds and is independent of what we happen to think about them, or even what we are capable of thinking about them.

For existential phenomenologists, then, worldly things are structured by the ways that they relate to and condition other things, bodies, and activities. That they are constituted by such relations points to the fact that to be an object of perception or use is to belong to a world, that is, to that wherein these relational structures can exist. Existing entities are thus independent of any particular thoughts or conscious experiences we have of them only to the extent that the world is not itself an ideal entity, something that only exists for thought. Let's look now at existential-phenomenological accounts of the world.

2 The world

For the existential phenomenologists, the world is an existential phenomenon in its own right. We've seen already Merleau-Ponty's argument that things are given to us in virtue of a sensory-motor meaning they possess, and therefore can be available to us without being fully available to thought. In an analogous way, Merleau-Ponty sees the world as given to us as a unity behind all our particular experiences of particular things. This unity is something that we grasp without having a mental representation or theory of it: "The world has its unity, although the mind may not have succeeded in inter-relating its facets and in integrating them into the conception of a geometrized projection." The unity takes the form of a kind of style with which we can get in tune, but which we can't reduce to an object for reflection:

> This unity is comparable with that of an individual whom I recognize because he is recognizable in an unchallengeably self-evident way, before I ever succeed in stating the formula governing his character, because he retains the same style in everything he says and does, even though he may change his place or his opinions. A style is a certain manner of dealing with situations, which I identify or understand in an individual or in a writer, by taking over that manner myself in a sort of imitative way, even though I may be quite unable to define it: and in any case a definition, correct though it may be, never provides an exact equivalent, and is never of interest to any but those who have already had the actual experience. I experience the unity of the world as I recognize a style. (Merleau-Ponty 1962: 327)

That is, we understand the world by sensing the unity in the way that objects and activities are organized and presented. I grasp the style of an individual when I see, for instance, how her way of wearing her clothes is like her hairstyle and her interior decoration, but also how these suit the things she does and the places she goes, how they match the way she carries herself, talks, laughs, etc. A style is a recognizable way of being-in-the-world that, despite being recognizable, evades definition. Merleau-Ponty is suggesting that the world exists like a style – as something that organizes and unfolds the things we encounter. It is thus something we can get a sense or feel for without being able to conceptualize or even become fully aware of.

As an example in which one can see this kind of world-structure manifesting itself, Merleau-Ponty describes the way the natural world opens itself up to vision. Imagine approaching a distant city, which presents to us a certain skyline or outline against the horizon. One might try to treat the world as the synthesis of all the different perspectives (each of which presents a slightly different skyline). But, in fact, as we approach the city, we don't see a series of discrete outlines which need to be cobbled together into a whole unless we look away from the city as we approach. In that case, when we look back, we might have the experience of seeing a different outline or skyline. In the normal case, however, what we see is a single, unified, unfolding whole:

> The world does not hold for us a set of outlines which some consciousness within us binds together into a unity ... The town to which I am drawing nearer, changes its aspects, as I realize when I turn my eyes away for a moment and then look back at it. But the

outlines do not follow each other or stand side by side in front of me. My experience at these different stages is bound up with itself in such a way that I do not get different perspective views linked to each other through the conception of an invariant. The perceiving body does not successively occupy different points of view beneath the gaze of some unlocated consciousness which is thinking about them. For it is reflection which objectifies points of view or perspectives, whereas when I perceive, I belong, through my point of view, to the world as a whole, nor am I even aware of the limits of my visual field. (Merleau-Ponty 1962: 328–9)

The perceptual world, in other words, is not a constructed unity, composed out of a series of snapshots linked together in thought. A particular perspective on the world, to the contrary, is an abstraction. Rather than snapshot views, what we experience as we move through the world temporally and spatially is the unfolding of a unity, the changing aspects of a unified whole that precedes and underwrites my particular apprehension of it:

I do not have one perspective, then another, and between them a link brought about by the understanding, but each perspective *merges into* the other . . . The natural world is the horizon of all horizons, the style of all possible styles, which guarantees for my experiences a given, not a willed, unity underlying all the disruptions of my personal and historical life. (Merleau-Ponty 1962: 329–30)

While Merleau-Ponty focuses on the world of perception (i.e., the unified field that unfolds itself in our changing experiences of the world), Heidegger's concern is typically the work world – the unified setting of action. This, too, has an existential structure, a significance we grasp in order to act at all, but of which I ordinarily lack focal awareness, and which certainly cannot be reduced to an effect of my consciousness. In the last section, we saw that our ability to encounter particular worldly things depends on their standing already in contexts of significance. The world is revealed for us as we understand these contexts, as we understand the whole ordered way that objects and activities are referred to each other. The world is revealed, then, every time we successfully deal with worldly entities, because the world is simply that total context within which relations of objects and activities are organized and make sense. "If Dasein is to be able to have any dealings with a context of equipment . . . *a world must have been disclosed* to it. With Dasein's factical existence, this world has been disclosed" (Heidegger 1962: 415). The world – "that wherein Dasein already understands itself" – is thus "something with which it is primordially familiar." But, "this familiarity with the world does not necessarily require that the relations which are constitutive for the world as world should be theoretically transparent" (Heidegger 1962: 119), because the familiarity consists in having a practical grasp of how to navigate in the world.

But what of us, the entities who know the world and experience things? Are we existential phenomena for ourselves? According to the existential phenomenologists, we are not primarily thinking beings, but rather embodied active beings in the world. Once again, the description is meant to point us back to our experience of being ourselves – an experience that puts the lie to modern subjectivism.

3 Being-in-the-world

We are thinking beings, but we are not *just* thinking beings. For the existential phenomenologists, the traditional philosophical focus on our rational being – a tradition stretching from Plato to Descartes and beyond – may succeed in grasping one aspect of our nature. But it misses the whole of human existence, which includes our non-reasoning capacities for willing, desiring, and acting in the world. "One's own Dasein," Heidegger argues, "itself first becomes 'find-able' from itself in looking away from 'experiences' and the 'center of action,' or rather does not yet 'see' them at all. Dasein finds 'itself' first of all in what it pursues, needs, expects, prevents – in what is environmentally available, which first of all concerns it" (Heidegger 1962: 155, translation modified). Who we are, then, is not in the first instance revealed through an awareness of a self, an acting and experiencing center point, but rather in a way of being with the worldly things with which we are most familiar.

Even when we do become aware that we are having experiences or thinking thoughts (which is phenomenologically different than experiencing things and thinking about them), these "subjective" experiences are by and large experiences of the world we encounter through embodied action. When I become aware of myself as tasting chocolate, for example, I am still aware of myself *as* experiencing the world; I am not aware of myself as having a subjective experience. Thus, Heidegger is justified in concluding that we understand ourselves "proximally and for the most part in terms of its world" (Heidegger 1962: 156).

Merleau-Ponty agrees, and argues that the starting point for understanding ourselves is the lived body, which, as the "vehicle of being in the world" (Merleau-Ponty 1962: 82), is an existing being in its own right. Our ability to understand a world that can't be fully grasped in thought requires that we ourselves are not simply representing minds. Because the existing world is never presented to us as a whole, as completely determinate and available for thought, Merleau-Ponty argues, the world "does not require, and even rules out, a constituting subject" (Merleau-Ponty 1962: 406). We encounter the world, in other words, not as subjects thinking thoughts of the world, but as ourselves a kind of "open and indefinite unity of subjectivity." Merleau-Ponty explains that my unity as an experiencing being is like the unity of the world – it is not something I experience directly, but rather it is the background against which each particular experience can stand out.

> What remains, on the hither side of my particular thoughts, to constitute the tacit *cogito* and the original project towards the world, and what, ultimately, am I in so far as I can catch a glimpse of myself independently of any particular act? I am a field, an experience. One day, once and for all, something was set in motion which, even during sleep, can no longer cease to see or not to see, to feel or not to feel, to suffer or be happy, to think or rest from thinking, in a word to "have it out" with the world. There then arose, not a new set of sensations or states of consciousness, not even a new monad or a new perspective, since I am not tied to any one perspective but can change my point of view, being under compulsion only in that I must always have one, and can have only one at a time – let us say, therefore, that there arose a fresh possibility of situations. (Merleau-Ponty 1962: 406–7)

Merleau-Ponty thus conceives the unity of the self as something that is not itself fully given in experience. It is a "possibility of situations," a "field" which encounters the world in a unified way, but which is not itself fully explicit and understandable to itself. We understand ourselves as we understand the world, progressively manifesting ourselves as we unfold our existence in the temporal world:

> In one sense, there are no more acts of consciousness or distinct *Erlebnisse* [experiences] in a life than there are separate things in the world. Just as, as we have seen, when I walk round an object, I am not presented with a succession of perspective views which I subsequently coordinate thanks to the idea of one single flat projection, there being merely a certain amount of "shift" in the thing which, in itself, is journeying through time, so I am not myself a succession of "psychic" acts, nor for that matter a nuclear *I* who bring them together into a synthetic unity, but one single experience inseparable from itself, one single "living cohesion", one single temporality which is engaged, from birth, in making itself progressively explicit, and in confirming that cohesion in each successive present. (Merleau-Ponty 1962: 407)

The "subject" is itself, in other words, an existential phenomenon. It is so because it has its existence in being in a world, which means, in acting and experiencing and responding to the meaningful things and people and situations it encounters in the world.

> In so far as, when I reflect on the essence of subjectivity, I find it bound up with that of the body and that of the world, this is because my existence as subjectivity is merely one with my existence as a body and with the existence of the world, and because the subject that I am, when taken concretely, is inseparable from this body and this world. (Merleau-Ponty 1962: 408)

Heidegger likewise argues that, in understanding ourselves, the best we can do is to describe perspicuously our experience of being in the world so that we come to recognize what we already understand. "A bare subject without a world," he noted, "never 'is' in the first instance, nor is it ever given" (Heidegger 1962: 152; translation modified). This means that, methodologically, we can't come to understand ourselves through reflection or introspection – these methods only remove us from the world and bring us before our thoughts of the world. Thus, he observes, "the Dasein, as existing, is there for itself, even when the ego does not direct itself to itself . . . The self is there for the Dasein itself without reflection and without inner perception, *before* all reflection. Reflection, in the sense of a turning back, is only a mode of *self-apprehension*, but not the mode of primary self-disclosure" (Heidegger 1982: 159). But as beings in the world, we can only be seen through a method that "exhibits us phenomenally" (see Heidegger 1962: 152), that is, that points out how we actually are constituted as the entities we are through our engagement with things in the world. But how is such a description possible? This is the subject which we take up in the next section.

II The Existential-Phenomenological Practice of Description

In the last section, we reviewed several of Heidegger's and Merleau-Ponty's descriptions of worldly things, the world itself, and us as worldly beings. If these descriptions are correct, then they put us in a position to understand the central claim of existential phenomenology – that there are phenomena which can be seen but not grasped through an analysis of the way such things present themselves to thought.

Suppose there are existential phenomena. That means that there are significant entities and structures which reveal themselves by "speaking" to my lived body or to me as I am involved in particular practical projects. These things will move me to act, to see things, to think thoughts, but without giving me a *reason* for doing those things. When the shape of the ashtray leads me to move my hand in a particular fashion, for example, it does so without giving me any thoughts about how I should move my hand. Indeed, any effort to deliberately move my hand will be less smooth and skillful than simply allowing my hand to respond to the ashtray in its situation.

What method could we possibly use, then, to come to understand them? Traditional philosophical methodologies of argumentation, the use of formal logic, etc., will be virtually worthless, because the things we are interested in are not functioning argumentatively. That is, the apprehensions that we do have of them are not the rational consequence of their conceptual content. We thus can't deduce the essence of things from the way they show themselves to us when we reflect on them as objects and articulate properties that we can predicate of them. This is because what is essential about them as existential phenomena is precisely not what they give us to think about. As Heidegger puts it, "there is no proof in phenomenology because it constantly describes" (Heidegger 1993: 219). That is, no clear and determinate content ever gets fixed through which we can capture things as they present themselves to us in our "prepredicative" "having-to-do-with-things" (see Heidegger 1995: 145).

For the same reason, a phenomenological method that consisted in bracketing our involvement with things and focusing on the way they give themselves to our conscious reflection will equally miss the mark:

> These primary phenomena of encounter . . . are of course seen only if the original phenomenological direction of vision is assumed and above all seen to its conclusion, which means letting the world be encountered in concern. This phenomenon is really passed over when the world is from the start approached as given for observation or, as is by and large the case even in phenomenology, when the world is approached just as it shows itself in an isolated, so-called sense perception of a thing, and this isolated free-floating perception of a thing is now interrogated on the specific kind of givenness belonging to its object. There is here a basic deception for phenomenology which is peculiarly frequent and persistent. It consists in having the theme determined by the way it is phenomenologically investigated. For inasmuch as phenomenological investigation is itself theoretical, the investigator is easily motivated to make a specifically theoretical comportment to the world his theme. Thus a specifically theoretical apprehension of the thing is put forward as an exemplary mode of being-in-the-world, instead of phenomenologically placing oneself directly in the current and the continuity of access of the everyday preoccupation with things, which is inconspicuous enough, and phenomenally recording what is encountered in it. (Heidegger 1985: 187–8)

The problem with focusing on things as they are given in our reflective awareness of them, in other words, is not that we will end up falsely describing the objects of consciousness, but that we will miss the pre-reflective, pre-conscious mode of being in the world.

41

The existential-phenomenological method is meant to avoid this error by keeping the focus, not on the description of the phenomena, but on the phenomena themselves. The description is useless unless one has access to the phenomena being described, because what we gain through the description is not a definitive account of the phenomena, but an awareness of the conditions under which these phenomena can manifest themselves as they are in themselves. The description is checked by using it to orient ourselves to the world in the right kind of way, and it is "verified" when that orientation allows the phenomena to show themselves. Thus, the key to a good description, a description that helps us achieve apprehension of the phenomena, is that it avoids distorting how we direct ourselves to the world through false theories or presuppositions about the phenomena we seek.

At a certain level, it ought to be perfectly obvious that an unbiased description of the object of inquiry plays a central role in any inquiry whatsoever, if only as a preliminary step toward explaining the object. Thus, when phenomenologists claim that their method consists in describing the phenomena without presuppositions or without imposing any prior theoretical framework, this hardly seems to distinguish them from scientists, analytical philosophers, or any other serious researcher. Everybody ought to want to return "to the things themselves," to let the things that interest us dictate what we say about them and how we think about them. Indeed, most careful thinkers, whatever their discipline, believe that they are doing just that.

And yet phenomenologists routinely insist that their practice of description has a kind of priority over the descriptive practices of the sciences or of other philosophers. Before we can assess such claims, we obviously need to understand them. What is the descriptive practice of phenomenology? How does it differ from other modes of description?

Analytical philosophers sometimes think of description very broadly as any attribution of properties to an object. In existential phenomenology, by contrast, "description" is reserved as a term for a particular kind of activity – one that aims at assisting in the apprehension of a phenomenon. This means that many sentences which would qualify as descriptions in a broad analytical sense would not, in fact, be useful phenomenological descriptions. It might be correct to classify the sentence "water is two parts hydrogen and one part oxygen" as a description, insofar as it ascribes properties to an object, but this would not serve for most people as a phenomenological description, because they are not equipped to discover the property described (the ratio of hydrogen and oxygen atoms) and, thereby, apprehend the object.

Phenomenological description, then, is a particular practice, something we do with language, rather than a type of linguistic structure. In fact, the purpose of phenomenological description is in some ways quite similar to everyday, non-philosophical practices of description. In the ordinary course of affairs, a description is of use only when one is unacquainted with the thing being described, and the description is good only to the degree that it helps one recognize or better understand the thing. When one doesn't know what a person or a thing or an event looks like, then one seeks out a description of its visual properties. Likewise if one doesn't know what it tastes likes, smells like, feels like – in each case, one seeks out a description sufficient to at least give one a sense for how it is experienced, if not an ability to recognize it through the appropriate mode of sensory exploration. Objects can also be described for thought – if one lacks acquaintance with a concept, one can have it described in terms of its conceptual implications, thus deepening one's grasp of it, or allowing one to mentally apprehend the concept.

Phenomenological descriptions are offered for the same kinds of reasons. To illustrate more carefully the important features of this kind of description, let's look at some familiar, everyday examples. Suppose that I am looking for an acquaintance's house. She might describe it as "the house at 40.225 degrees north latitude, 111.646 degrees west longitude." This is a precise description, but useless to me without considerable knowledge of the theoretical framework used to divide the surface of the earth up into degrees of longitude and latitude. If this were her description, I might reasonably respond that she had succeeded in ascribing properties to an object, but that in order to find the house I need a description suited to my capacities for exploring the world. "It is a brick house with cream trim and a green roof, six blocks west of University Avenue" would be a less precise, but much more useful description. Note that the success of the description is tied to the purpose for which it is sought – if my acquaintance is listing her house for sale, rather than giving directions to a party, she would tailor the description accordingly. In that case, the aim is not to lead someone to the house, but to give them a feel for the way the house affords living. In that case, "the house has 1800 square feet of finished living space, four bedrooms, two baths, a fireplace, and hardwood and tile floors throughout" would be a much better description.

In phenomenology, as we have said, the purpose for the description is to bring us to an apprehension of the phenomenon as it is in itself. We are thus not primarily interested, in contrast to the sciences, in fitting the phenomenon into a preexisting framework. Scientific description, in general, aims less at describing things in accordance with the particular capacities and predilections of the reader, and more at a neutral description that will allow anyone to identify the object being described. And the point of scientific description is to identify objects using just those properties which will allow one to recognize how the objects instantiate a general statement that describes all similar objects in a uniform manner. For these reasons, scientific description is driven by a theory, and couched in terms of a theory (which is not the same as saying that it is theory-relative in any insidious sense). It is driven, in particular, by the desire to fit the phenomenon into a broader structure that explains and predicts the properties and interactions of the objects of inquiry.

Existential phenomenological description aims, by contrast, at staying with the phenomenon itself, in order to produce in the reader an understanding of the circumstances under which the thing shows itself as it is in itself, rather than an ability to recognize the thing from a certain view of or perspective on the thing. This is what phenomenologists mean when they say that phenomenology aims at a "presuppositionless" description. Behind this claim is the idea that it is possible to see something in radically different ways, and that one way of seeing it will actually obstruct our ability to see it in other ways. Take, for example, the effect that medical detachment has on a doctor's perception of the people she treats. Richard J. Baron, a medical doctor, has argued that the clinical and technological practices developed by contemporary medicine have made the patient's humanity virtually invisible. "Physicians look through their patients," he argues, "to discover the underlying pure disease." As he explains:

> The patient functions, more than anything else, as an obstruction, an impediment, a
> screen that is unfortunately translucent but which, in the hands of a skilled physician,
> can be made totally transparent. In a sense, the paradigm ideal would be a medicine
> without patients altogether. And indeed, this is very much the direction in which
> medicine is tending. (Baron 1981: 21)

In a similar way, our ability to see things the way they present themselves to us in the course of our everyday affairs can be impaired by certain descriptions – because these descriptions will attune us to some aspects and thus tend to inure us to others. The faulty descriptions can be quite correct insofar as they go, and they might even have their own kind of "freedom from presuppositions" of a certain sort. For example, the success of a doctor's clinical detachment in diagnosing and describing disease is, to some degree, attributable to the way it blinds her to the human experience of suffering and illness that presents itself to a less detached observer. The aim therefore is not freedom from all presupposition, but freedom from those presuppositions which prevent the appearance of the phenomena we seek. Each different kind of thing, Heidegger asserts, has a different mode of encounter (*Begegnisart*) proper to it. Only when we let it encounter us in the right way, only then can it show itself as it is in itself. The existential phenomenologist seeks a freedom from any presuppositions that will prevent her from encountering existential phenomena as such.

Compare, for instance, one common reading of Husserl, according to which he argues that we preserve a freedom from presuppositions by refusing to accept any proposition which could not be completely fulfilled in intuition or apprehension (put roughly, that means that we don't accept any proposition unless we are capable of apprehending everything we need to in order to verify the truth of the proposition). Since propositions regarding non-ideal, mind-transcendent things cannot ever be completely fulfilled (there are always some sides or views or features of them which exceed what any finite being can apprehend of them), it follows that a presuppositionless inquiry would be one which refuses to assume that such things exist. Without the assumption of the existence of, for example, physical entities, in turn, one would need to suspend all natural-scientific theories, which are grounded in the supposition of the real existence of the things they study.

From an existential-phenomenological perspective, however, freedom from presuppositions is purchased by a refusal to substitute a description or theoretical account of an entity for the apprehension of the entity itself. One of the "fundamental maxims of the phenomenological method" is the injunction that we "must not reinterpret what is phenomenologically given into expressions," because the expressions of the phenomenon "first originate in that one expresses them" (Heidegger 1993: 219). This means that, in existential phenomenology, the end goal of description is to guide the reader to the practical orientation for the world in which the phenomenon can show itself. In the end, the description is of no independent value. Its merit as a description is completely a function of its ability to lead us to apprehend the thing itself, not its suitability for serving as a foundation for theorizing.

By contrast, on the Husserlian view that we just reviewed, the end result of phenomenological description is a proposition that can stand on its own, verifiable without the need for apprehending anything outside of the domain of consciousness.

From an existential-phenomenological perspective, this amounts to turning one's back on the things themselves in favor of mere conscious states. And that itself amounts to a tacit acceptance of an unsupported presupposition – namely, that the description of our experience of an object can tell us all that we need to know about it. As Merleau-Ponty explains:

> philosophy is not a lexicon, it is not concerned with "word-meanings," it does not seek a verbal substitute for the world we see, it does not transform it into something said, it does not install itself in the order of the said or of the written as does the logician in the proposition . . . It is the things themselves, from the depths of their silence, that it wishes to bring to expression. (Merleau-Ponty 1968: 4)

It is for this reason that Merleau-Ponty distinguishes phenomenology from the methodology of both analytical philosophies and the natural sciences. "The demand for a pure description," Merleau-Ponty notes, "excludes equally the procedure of analytical reflection on the one hand, and that of scientific explanation on the other" (Merleau-Ponty 1962: ix). "Analytical reflection" on Merleau-Ponty's account would include both Husserl's phenomenology of consciousness, and much of analytical philosophy. This approach "starts from our experience of the world and goes back to the subject as to a condition of possibility distinct from that experience, revealing the all-embracing synthesis as that without which there would be no world" (1962: ix) – that is, it looks for those acts through which entities and the world itself are constituted for consciousness. Because it turns away from the things we experience to offer an account of the conceptual structure of experience, Merleau-Ponty argues, "it ceases to remain part of our experience and offers, in place of an account, a reconstruction" (1962: ix). The objection, in short, is that analysis begins in the right place – our experience of the world – but it immediately leaves that experience behind to conduct a conceptual analysis of the structure and make-up of that experience. By "going conceptual" – by treating the experience as if it is on a par with judgments, inferences, beliefs, and other cognitive states and acts – analysis ends up looking for a "subject" who possesses those states and performs those acts, and thus misses what it is really like to be in the world. And, in a parallel error, analysis ends up treating the world itself as the product of the subject's cognitive states and acts, and thus misses what it is really like to be a world.

Existential phenomenologists, in other words, believe that their way of using descriptions assures us that we never abandon the phenomena for a mere thought or representation of the phenomena. As a result, they believe that their approach to description is the best way to let certain phenomena show themselves – namely, those phenomena which we have called existential phenomena, the ones that give themselves to us pre-reflectively.

The phenomena will only "show themselves with the kind of access which genuinely belongs to them" (Heidegger 1962: 61). But if they are existential phenomena, the only access to them is in the way that we live in the experience of them, rather than in a conscious reflection on them. That introduces an unavoidable tension into the phenomenological project – we must try to describe something which threatens to conceal itself the moment that we slip into the kind of reflective mode that allows us to describe it. The first "fundamental maxim of the phenomenological method," according to Heidegger, is that we highlight and present and lift something into relief through the formulation of a phenomenological description. But, Heidegger is quick to remind us, what is thereby expressed "is not (always) known phenomenally in its context, is not a correlate of knowing" (Heidegger 1993: 219).

That means that the only way to check on the description we have offered is constantly to return from the description to an apprehension of the object, that is, for phenomenology to "constantly renew itself in bringing itself before the givenness" (one of the "fundamental maxim(s) of phenomenology"; Heidegger 1993: 219). This means there is no final, all-encompassing statement of the nature of existential phenomena, nor of the lessons to be learned from them. Indeed, we would only expect such a statement if they were not existential phenomena, if they could be reduced to the order of either the mental or the physical. But that we can never lay down definitive propositions doesn't deprive phenomenology of rigor or its descriptions of correctness. If the existential phenomenologists are right, we all have potential access to the phenomena, and are thus able to check on the accuracy of the descriptions ourselves. "The visible," Merleau-Ponty writes,

> and the philosophical explicitation of the visible are not side by side as two sets of signs, as a text and its version in another tongue. If it were a text, it would be a strange text, which is directly given to us all, so that we are not restricted to the philosopher's translation and can compare the two. And philosophy for its part is more and less than a translation: more, since it alone tells us what the text means; less, since it is useless if one does not have the text at one's disposal. (Merleau-Ponty 1968: 36)

Acknowledgments

I am indebted to David Cerbone, Steven Crowell, Hubert Dreyfus, Sean Kelly, and Daniel Wood. They have helped me immensely in my thinking about the matters discussed here through their comments and, in some cases, their objections. Research for this chapter was funded in part by the David M. Kennedy Center for International and Area Studies.

Note

1 Of course, *what* we can think about objects depends to some degree on our familiarity with them. But our ability to think about them as such does not.

References and Further Reading

Baron, R. J. (1981) Bridging the clinical distance: An empathic rediscovery of the known. *Journal of Medicine and Philosophy*, 6, 5–23.

Heidegger, M. (1953) *Sein und Zeit*, 7th edn. Tübingen: Max Niemeyer.

—— (1962) *Being and Time* (trans. John Macquarrie and Edward Robinson). New York: Harper & Row.

—— (1982) *Basic Problems of Phenomenology* (trans. Albert Hofstadter). Bloomington: Indiana University Press.

—— (1985) *History of the Concept of Time* (trans. Theodore Kisiel). Bloomington: Indiana University Press.

—— (1986) *Seminare. Gesamtausgabe* vol. 15. Frankfurt am Main: Vittorio Klostermann.

—— (1993) *Grundprobleme der Phänomenologie. Gesamtausgabe* vol. 58. Frankfurt am Main: Vittorio Klostermann.

—— (1995) *Logik: Die Frage nach der Wahrheit. Gesamtausgabe* vol. 21. Frankfurt am Main: Vittorio Klostermann.

Merleau-Ponty, M. (1962) *The Phenomenology of Perception* (trans. C. Smith). London: Routledge.

—— (1968) *The Visible and the Invisible* (trans. Alphonso Lingis). Evanston, IL: Northwestern University Press.

Sartre, J.-P. (1984) *Being and Nothingness* (trans. Hazel E. Barnes). New York: Washington Square Press.

4

French Phenomenology

FRANÇOIS-DAVID SEBBAH
TRANSLATED BY ROBERT J. HUDSON

Phenomenology is alive. It is one way in which philosophy incessantly reinvents itself today, one way that it brazenly takes upon itself the task not to completely fold upon itself within its own history, not to timidly abandon the territories of truth, especially that of perception, to the sciences – whether they deal with humanity or nature. Phenomenology is particularly alive in France, in the French language, and in French writing.[1]

If one takes a closer look at "French Phenomenology," one could perhaps distinguish two "families." There is one family of those who, following Merleau-Ponty, maintain tangible perception as the initial opening for all things to appear. To trace how things appear, they turn their attention in the direction of that which, in perception, is prior to the complete and static thing in its face-to-face relation with a subject that is, itself, complete and static. The works of Henri Maldiney, Jacques Garelli, Marc Richir, and Renaud Barbaras,[2] for example – without trying in the least to "compress" them all together – may be classified, up to a certain point, in this family. It is thus a question of getting back to a pre-originary stage of experience, paralyzed by instability and ambiguity because it comes before the clean division of determined identities – and that because the latter is the place where we find ourselves, the place of logical and ontological determination. In other words, we must put to work a reduction that is already inchoate or incomplete. To paraphrase Merleau-Ponty: a reduction that tends toward that which, by definition, escapes stabilization at a glance; a reduction that, in every instance, requires by the same token its never-ending renewal. Thus this gesture leads toward the anonymity of the World: anonymity if it goes toward that which precedes the subject that is fixed in its identity; the World, if the "World" is fixed as the name of the prior horizon on which all that appears can be shown.

We can distinguish another family of thought that branches off from the same phenomenological requirement that we return to the event of appearance. This family, concerned as it is with a reduction that seeks to be even more radical, attempts to turn its view to that which would be more originary than the World itself. One immediately sees the paradox to which this phenomenology exposes itself – whether it asserts the paradox, or, on the contrary, claims to disqualify it. The very necessity of radicality, in its concern for exposing the manner of appearing, leads phenomenology to (or beyond) what generally presents itself as the norm of appearance: the visible, in its essential structure. This phenomenology tends toward that which comes to rupture the visible, that which comes to disrupt it and does not allow itself to be captured by it. From whence comes, without doubt, the violence of its style, which cannot be reduced to the violence in the act of writing, as exemplified not only by Levinas in *Otherwise Than Being, Or, Beyond Essence* (Levinas 1974), but also by Michel Henry when it pertains to describing the structure of Immanence – Immanence that conceals itself from the light of the World and whose movement flirts with tautology without ever collapsing into it. A traumatic – and traumatizing – way of testifying to the ordeal that consists in exposing oneself to that which, older than the visible, overcomes and escapes it, but at the same time forgives it – or at least gives it meaning. This phenomenological family shares with the first family mentioned, the "Merleau-Pontian" family, the concern for dismissing the subject as the pole of initiative and sovereignty. However, because it seeks to be even more radical, this critique of the subject will not lead to an originary anonymity, but rather toward "the passivity older than all passivity" of a named Self, evoked, precisely, as an example of endurance of the test at hand; a Self that, in one sense, consists entirely of the one proven by this very ordeal.

One cannot fail to wonder, in light of this briefly sketched "table of families," "Where is French phenomenology going?" One may very well look like a "bad pupil" if one does not ask the question: How did Husserlian rationalism and the responsibility of rigor that it constantly affirmed, give birth to a philosophy that concerns itself with that which precedes the determination of stable identities, with that inchoateness which, by so doing, unceasingly escapes into the ambiguously winding "neither . . . nor" in which the visible is interwoven and to which painters bear witness so well (as in the first-evoked "Merleau-Pontian family")? Must not poetic suggestion come to replace the rigorous discourse that seeks to fittingly describe the order of essences? Irrationality raises its head; but, one could well say, it could have been "worse." The worst would be the second family evoked – which this chapter prefers to examine.

Before delving deeper into this study, let us quickly attempt to introduce the most significant representatives – while understanding that such a perilous exercise runs the risk of caricaturing each of the movements somewhat and blurring that which individuates them and makes them resist easy classification into a "family" (such classification into "families" only sheds light by temporarily obscuring the thing that is classified).

Emmanuel Levinas

Levinas deserves credit for having introduced phenomenology to France (see Levinas 1988, 1989). Above all else, he would not desist in asserting himself to be a phenomenologist – in the meantime, however, evoking "the ethical language, which phenomenology resorts in order to mark its own interruption" (Levinas 1974: 120n.35). It is necessary to insist that Levinas, often suspected of veering from phenomenological description in the name of a speculative construction of the Other (with a capital "O") or of its praise, has, for his own part, always claimed to practice phenomenological description – especially at the beginning of his career, without ever contradicting this claim, even if it did complicate the meaning of his work. "Description," in a sense, is truly renewed: it is not relevant to identify and establish essences, but, on the contrary, to "de-formalize," to surrender, through the act of writing, the phenomenon to a dynamic indetermination of the horizons of sense. The question will always remain, by the same token, of how to understand the phenomenological imperative as the impossibility of separating the "concepts" from the empirical examples by which they are solidified. However, we would now like to underline another aspect of the relationship that Levinas has with phenomenology. Describing the way in which the face of another appears simultaneously in frankness and in ambiguity, he insists on the following: the face obscures all power of constitution; it disrupts any predetermined horizon. The face of another is always "out of context." Thus, it opens a dimension of significance (in that it is pure address and pure injunction; it summons, issues a call): more and more clearly over Levinas's career, it is this ethical dimension that would come to endow phenomenality with signification, with "significance," as he put it. This said, the "transcendence to the point of absence" that Levinas names the "Infinite" or even "*Illéité*" (that is, the absolute "it") *appears* however in its own paradoxical manner: in – or like – the very disruption of phenomenality, as "a trace of that which will have never been present." Nevertheless, the trace always holds to the horizon that it *divides* (*Illéité* is, precisely, only offered like the face), and the disruption of phenomenology is only allowed to inhabit the same horizon that it disrupts and opens to signification: a *radical* disruption of phenomenology which is, nevertheless, only given as a trace or an echo of the very thread that is always already bound to phenomenology.

Michel Henry

Since *The Essence of Manifestation* (Henry 1990a), his first master work, Michel Henry has incessantly practiced the following gesture which can only be qualified as transcendental: if that which is shown is taken in a movement of transcendence, of "exit outside itself," then such a reality would not be able to provide a foundation. Only radical immanence is substantial reality. Radicalizing this description in his most recent works (see especially Henry 1996, 2000, 2002), Henry describes what he calls the duplicity of appearance: the *ek-static* appearance of the World that is then opposed to the auto-appearance of self-immanence, of that which he calls "Life." The appearance of the World brings to light – and this light is purely an exteriority endowed with a power to exteriorize – to draw out any being that shows itself within itself: the appearance of the World is de-realizing. If phenomenology, subordinated to its Greek origin, is based on the principle according to which "whatever appears, is," and if it comprehends only the appearance of the World, then it describes nothing of that which, at the same time, is and actually appears; and, it even fundamentally participates in this enterprise of the de-realization of all existence. It is thus necessary not to abandon phenomenology but to *reverse* it into an authentic phenomenology (this reversal is explicitly evoked in Henry 2000: 238). That is, the denunciation of the World, of the visible, would not be the denunciation of all appearance: in truth, if the World is that which "expels from itself" all beings by its *ek-static* movement, if it is that which defeats interiority, then only that which comes from the self, is brought to the self, and likewise, brings each being into itself, endows it with an interiority and an ipseity, and will in actuality be an effectivity. What it all amounts to is this motion of bringing into itself that which truly exists, a purely immanent motion that "*ipséizes*" or "subjectifies": a grasping of Life itself in which each Living Thing is grasped. We must insist, according to Henry, that this immanent movement of Life into itself makes its appearance the most authentic auto-revelation by which it appears to itself without any detour through the World where beings are shown. Henry qualifies this radical phenomenology as "material phenomenology" (see Henry 1990b) to express the fact that it owes *nothing* to form or to essence. This phenomenology is more than "possible": even obscured by the phenomenology of the World, it cannot, in any sense, be always already at work beneath the surface, in the same way that Life, in its absoluteness, supports the World.

It will be noted that the material phenomenology of Henry does not choose to privilege phenomena (as does that of Jean-Luc Marion – as we will soon see – or of Levinas, in a certain sense, when he grants privilege to this "contra-phenomenon" – in both meanings of the word "contra" ("opposed to" or "butted against") – that is, the face).[3] A constant of the Henrian gesture consists, not in dismissing phenomena that seem irreducibly marked by their ek-static structures, but, on the contrary, in attempting to renew them: a *tour de force*, aimed at the specific auto-revelation with which each is endowed, from the point of view of the immanence of Life (Flesh, for example, will provide the opportunity of a description that singularizes it as such, in such a way that it would owe its appearance to absolutely nothing else in the World).

Jacques Derrida

The Derridean gesture is, undoubtedly, of all those presented, the most reticent to allow itself to be included in a family in general, and in this one in particular. Nevertheless, we will attempt to show in what ways it is not without legitimacy that we invite him to this "family reunion." Derrida's relationship with phenomenology, from his earliest texts – meticulous commentaries on Husserl (see Derrida 1962, 1967) – was constant, even if he never accepted phenomenology as such. Without a doubt, he radically deconstructed the metaphysics of presence that would have animated the movements of phenomenological reduction (eidetic and transcendental reduction) – insofar as these would ultimately lead back to the present-living of the consciousness. However, deconstruction is never a negation or a simple critique. Thus, from a certain point of view, Derrida could have asserted the reduction "as a resource of deconstruction," because "reduction" always signifies, in the work of Husserl, the reception, without reservation or prejudice, of phenomena – what Derrida would radicalize through "exposure," in "saying yes" (*dire oui*) to the limitlessness of what would come: deconstruction itself (see especially Derrida 1987). Of all the threads through which Derrida would never cease weaving the problems of phenomenology, here we will only mention two: the motif of the trace and the problem of the gift (*don*) (see especially Derrida 1991, 1993). Referring explicitly to Levinas (but also drawing from other sources, such as Nietzsche), the notion of the trace in Derrida finds itself at the crossroads of a reflection on the sign and a description of phenomenality: the trace declares at the same time, the originary contamination of the transcendental with the empirical (in virtue of which there is no pure origin), and, in as much as it always presupposes the motif of the *archi*-trace, that there is never full presence of phenomena, that there are no such phenomena and, in closing, no "phenomenology as such." This last point lends itself to the paradox of the same movement: that the phenomenon will have always already been taken into the paradigm of the spectral. This is because the spectral affirms itself, explicitly in Derridean texts beginning in the 1990s, as the paradigm of all phenomenology: the specter is neither the least presence nor a mixture of presence and absence that could be grasped as two autonomous terms, pure from the origin. In the same motion, the specter is neither purely life nor purely death, nor a mixture of the two (which would assume the prior purity of the two terms), but originary "survival," all life being survival "from the origin" (when set in the crisis of all plenitude and purity of origin). Even if one should not imprudently force the problem of the gift onto that of donation in phenomenology, one will notice that Derrida's description of the gift – as a gift, by definition, is never given without lacking in generosity – goes in this same direction, creating a crisis of phenomenology as a reception free of prejudice, of a phenomenality that is offered without remnants (traces): according to Derrida, phenomena are only given from an "originary" absence, which would never allow itself to be apprehended as pure absence. Always already spectralized and deceptive, it creates a crisis in the clean division between presence and absence, in a *contamination* that does not allow it to be derived from a supposed purity, since this purity is what would have been the distinction and the prior opposition of the two terms (presence and absence). Phenomenology is, consequently, impossible as such. However, this impossibility of espousing the phenomenological necessity and method renders it equally impossible to be absolutely and definitively detached. One cannot adopt both the principles of phenomenology according to Derrida and naïveté at the same time – however, neither can one abandon them.

Jean-Luc Marion

The phenomenology of Jean-Luc Marion shares an affinity, often explicit or asserted, between the movements we have just rapidly covered. It could be said only with some reservations – because thought, of course, can never be reduced to the sum of affiliations and associations – that Marionian phenomenology, with that of Henry, affirms the liberation of phenomena from the limitations of intentionality – of Seeing – and explores the radicality of an auto-affection preceding any variation (Flesh); it could further be said that, along with Levinas, his phenomenology designates an inverse intentionality and "destroys" the subject only to discover an "instance," integrally organized by what is shown by itself (an instant that he names, for his part, the "devoted"[4]). Again, with affinity to Levinas, this phenomenology designates that which exceeds all horizons of visibility. Neither is it without relation to the Derridean gesture, from which it recognizes having experienced, for example, in the name of *différance*, a rupture with the horizon of the object or of the being. It would first acknowledge Derrida for having prepared the terrain through his deconstruction of the primacy of presence, to a donation that would no longer be reduced to the different models of presence we have at our disposal (this consequence being, as such, definitely not Derridean).

The phenomenology of Marion explicitly contemplates the phenomenological method and means to radically implement it. From this point of view, it is closer to the Henrian gesture than to those of Levinas or Derrida. In fact, it is explicitly opposed to the Derridean movement, in that the latter, as we have stated, contemplates "the imposs-ibility of phenomenology as such." Nor does it align with Levinas, taking into account his type of phenomena, that tear away from or exceed the horizon of the visible, imply-ing a phenomenology that tested by its own limitations, if not interrupted. On the contrary, phenomenology according to Marion must be measured with a certain fidelity to Heidegger, in as much as this is possible. Marion proposes to liberate the reduction of any presupposed limitation and thus to give access to the donation (which will itself, in a certain circularity that should be questioned, allow this reduction and free it of its prejudices). To evoke the giving (*Gegebenheit*) is to call upon a Husserlian concept that would make it possible to be freed from the limitation to the object (constituted by intentionality) and even to being (a radical liberation that Husserl and Heidegger would have questioned, each in his own manner, and just as soon stepped back from). To state it all too rapidly, in the "donation," according to Marion, the phenomenon is presented as unconditioned, as never limited by any way of measuring that would precede it. Consequently, the phenomenon shows *itself* only as it gives *itself*. Marion proposes to describe phenomenality, not by describing regions, but rather degrees of phenomenality: there are phenomena that are poor in intuition – in particular, those that are understood in the form of the object seen in light of intentionality – and this because their weakness in intuition guarantees them a certain assurance, that is, permits the subject to keep them under the control of its view, which has always traditionally been the model for all phenomenality. Opposing these, Marion designates that which exceeds the limits of the object, of what can be constituted by intention-ality: "the saturated phenomenon." A phenomenon saturated by the donation is never limited to what a subject can submit to the control of its view. But, we must insist that the saturated phenomenon, according to Marion, far from being exceptional or eccen-tric, will serve the function of the norm or the paradigm of phenomenality, since in it, the donation is, in a way, liberated (and we must necessarily describe how, in even the poorest phenomenon, something of the saturated phenomenon remains – because it is well given). Let us note that Marion produces a typology of saturated phenomena. He constructs this typology beginning with the categories of understanding according to Kant, each type of phenomenon implying an additional donation compared to each of these categories: they include the event (saturated according to quantity), the idol or the table (saturated according to quality), the flesh (saturated according to relation), and the icon or the face of the other (saturated according to modality). Finally, there is the phenomenon, saturated par excellence, which groups the four types of saturation and thus elevates saturation as such. Qualified as "phenomenon saturated with power" or as "paradox of paradoxes," Marion speaks of the phenomenon of revelation (which we will later consider).

As we see at the end of this brief presentation, the four authors presented here can all be considered as assuming a phenomenology of excess (understood according to both the objective and subjective genitive); but only Derrida and Levinas can be explicitly regarded as assuming or asserting something like a test of the limits of phe-nomenology, or proving its impossibility – an impossibility that remains fruitful. Henry and Marion, each in his own way, claims, on the contrary, to have released the phenomenon from its limitation to the Seen and/or to the form and/or to the object, and to be able to practice a reduction whose radical possibility, precisely, makes it possible to skip over these various obstacles. Significantly, Marion writes: "Therefore, in the driving figure of the saturated phenomenon, phenomenology finds its last possibility: not only the possibility that surpasses effectivity, but also the possibility that surpasses the same conditions of the possible, the possibility of the unconditioned possibility – otherwise stated, the possibility of the impossible, the saturated phenomenon" (Marion 1997: 304).

It is, therefore, only at the price of an interpretive gesture, which could not be completely implemented here, that one could show in what, and how, authors such as Henry and Marion, in their practices of excess, productively (or not) test the limits of phenomenology. We will, however, at the end of this chapter, venture to outline this gesture.

* * *

Regardless of these distinctions and oppositions that we present as being "parts of a family," and in order to widen our perspective, let us emphasize the fact that our approach broaches the problem proposed by Dominique Janicaud in configuring this field: the opposition between the "theological turn" that characterizes these works on one side, and, on the other, a "minimalist"[5] phenomenology that is disabused of a fascination with the originary and of the pretension to pose as first philosophy. And, it is, of course, in this second phenomenology, which holds to different types of phenomena given in their singularity, that we find Janicaud's convictions.

But in a difference – decisive in our eyes – from Janicaud, we are not inclined to diagnose a simple escape from phenomenology in authors such as Henry or Levinas. We attempt once again to comprehend the reproach addressed in this "theological" French phenomenology from an appropriately phenomenological motif, that is, *while trying to grasp that which, from the most intimate phenomenological obligation, was able to present the latter as being, so to speak, its complete auto-transgression.* It would be a question of refusing to allow oneself to be confined by the way in which Janicaud poses the problem – by refusing in the same motion to erase the real problem that he indicates – and by attempting to understand this problem as an integral part of phenomenology itself in what it contains that is, at once, irreducibly paradoxical and fertile – fertile in and by the aporia.

It is useful to pause on the problems of *phenomenological reduction* (which we set aside at the beginning of the chapter and which we must now address), because it appears as though it is the phenomenological operator par excellence, in the sense that, at the very least, all phenomenologists stop at the gesture that consists in tearing oneself from that which appears to the appearance itself. In saying this, we here propose a (doubtless poor) definition of phenomenological reduction, one that is simply negative, not indicating which "domain" is attained by the reduction – whether it should even be described as consciousness, for instance. And this so as to find the lowest common denominator that makes phenomenologists of phenomenologists.[6] One could designate as a "phenomenologist" the one who holds himself or herself to the necessity of reduction. Did Merleau-Ponty not write that "the greatest teaching of reduction is the impossibility of a complete reduction"? (Merleau-Ponty 1981: Introduction, p. VIII). Still, all *concern* themselves with phenomenological reduction, and – in this sense – all practice it, even if testing the impossibility of its accomplishments without abandoning the test remains a method of its practice.

Undoubtedly, the motif of phenomenological reduction is not single-faceted within Husserl's own writing. We will not enter into a discussion of the different modes of reduction – which consists, at heart, in asking ourselves the different ways to carry out a reduction – but, as a prerequisite, we will speak of the ambiguities that affect the very necessity indicated by the word "reduction," as taken from Husserl. The ambiguities, we hasten to stress, according to our own judgment – and this working hypothesis will necessarily have to be supported hereafter – do not signify anything incoherent or inconsistent from the reduction, only its proper place and fruitfulness.[7]

The distinction between the two families of contemporary French phenomenology (the Merleau-Pontian family and the other to which we more particularly attach ourselves here) allows us to develop our own outlook on the problem of reduction.

Thus, the Merleau-Pontian family understands and applies reduction more like a placing between parentheses that brings us back to the horizon of the World than as a renewed drive to an ultimate ground.[8] (Things are never quite the caricatures that we present here, and it must be said that, in a sense, this family also shares the need to return upstream toward the originary, in themes of presupposition or perceptive faith, for instance, but it is never a question, in any case, of returning to an ultimate, absolute founder.)

Across from the "Merleau-Pontian" family, the spectrum of contemporary French phenomenologists that interests us here opens up: starting with the specific desire not to yield to the requirement of renewal toward the originary – from beyond which one is unable to return – we hold to the end of auto-appearance (at the very least, an end to the ability to make appear, or provide meaning, which can no longer be understood as auto-appearance – the Infinite operates thus in Levinas's work), to which we can relate all appearance; beginning from such a desire, subjectivity assumes a central place.

However, a distancing occurs in connection with the Husserlian movement that results precisely and paradoxically from a will to radicalize it even more, if that is possible – or, more exactly, not to yield to the radical requirement of the Husserlian movement to return toward something originary. This "radicalization of (Husserlian) radicalism" straightforwardly reverses the point of arrival. Also, suspecting – as Patočka does – the "Husserlian transcendental subjectivity" of being merely a speculative construction, a naïveté created and left outside of the reach of *épokhè*, these phenomenologists seek something more originary. Still, that which they arrive upon is not an *épokhè* of transcendental subjectivity that would convey the horizon of the World. On the contrary, true will to rejoin an absolutely original originary (by giving themselves ground, so to speak, to rest on the theme of transcendental subjectivity) does not consist, especially not for them, in suspending the movement of renewal. Not trying to mislead with the requirement of renewal will clearly signify radically assessing subjectivity as the finality of a point of view that in fact examines an irreducible delay of what it provides itself. That which gives subjectivity to itself only does so in a paradoxical mode of proving it by means of an irreducible overflow, and, consequently, driving it back against itself into the most radical passivity. The concern for respecting the character of the originary, its position prior to anything, requires that these authors do not identify this originary, or more exactly, that they identify it as the unidentifiable, as that which irreducibly surpasses the act by which *I* give it to myself. (Thus, it comes from the Infinite, according to Levinas, and even, in a sense, from Life, according to M. Henry, because if Life is given to itself and embraces itself, in each Self, then no Self, in any situation, can give itself Life.) Such is the paradox that, at heart, forces these authors to inscribe the *épokhè* as the requirement to neutralize all positions of being (*l'être*) to the very core of reduction, as a renewal toward the originary that produces a sort of "drive" for the originary – a higher bid for the originary.

Consequently, one could reproach them for the whole lot: for exceeding the given limit – in the sense of the limit of appearance – in an effort to seize the root of appearance as such,[9] in an endless, vertiginous movement, since all identification of the originary, suspected of being a hypostasis, will necessarily have been ineluctably deconstructed to enable the very movement of appearance that, by definition, can only be solidified in a being. Or, one could reproach them for the contrary – but this second risk is engendered by the first – for deferring to hypostasis at the worst moment, that is, when the constraints of appearance have been transgressed in an attempt to offer, despite the break, a place for hyperbolic reduction and incomplete definition,[10] and without an end result of their own, finally and inconsequently finding, in a manner of speaking, a term.[11] (One will recall on this matter the capitalizations of the Other and Life that were denounced by Janicaud.) At base, the desire for reduction that characterizes this family of French phenomenology is contradictory. This renders the following question impossible: Is it true to itself when it incessantly restarts itself, expecting all beings to recover an event that is always older and, as such, unidentifiable; or, on the contrary, when it pretends precisely to succeed in rejoining the absolutely originary?

This phenomenology would thus fall victim to excess *and* the "excess of excess." This excess leads beyond the field of appearance and then *fails* to provide the grounds of originary auto-appearance (but is therefore also true to the radicality of the return upstream, which makes no disillusion in giving itself an identifiable, non-phenomenological origin). The "excess of excess" is that which consists of wanting to make it so that the effort of reduction is labeled a success and points to itself as indisputable evidence of the source of all giving – without the ability to avoid the suspicion that this phenomenological evidence is nothing but phenomenological pseudo-evidence, a speculative construction, a naïve thesis, the naïve position on existence of an absolute being that is beyond appearance.[12] With so much suspicion that the motivating dilemma is impossible to circumvent, one is obliged to leave it alone. (What is given as the result of *épokhè* is necessarily *already* external and escapes methodological control.)

Therefore, in all these cases, is this phenomenology untrue, in part, to the phenomenological requirement in order to be true to another part of this requirement – as though the phenomenological requirement was contradictory at its origins? These contradictions being the following: first, to respect *épokhè and* to deprive oneself of the renewal (toward the originary) and second, to completely carry out the renewal *and*, to accomplish this, yield to *épokhè*.[13] The family of contemporary French phenomenology

56

that interests us here assumes this very position of exemplary confrontation with this double-constraint that seems to be inscribed as the heart of the requirement, as the phenomenological imperative. Unceasingly passing from excess to "excess of excess," and inversely, since none of these moments is completely satisfactory from the point of view of phenomenological injunction (which is actually a contradictory injunction), this phenomenology cannot be stabilized in a final, definitive and inapprehensive figure of itself, but becomes, properly stated, a "sporadic phenomenology" (*phénoménologie clignotante*) (Sebbah 2001a).

There is a significant conclusion to be drawn: this phenomenology that we just recognized calls for a complete reflection as to what *use* we can make of it. The real question it poses to its reader is: How will you make good use of me? Indeed, its unceasingly excessive character – regardless of what side we take – prohibits (or protects) us – from being able to completely adhere to and state it definitively: we cannot, it seems, find comfort and peace of mind; neither in a reading of Levinas nor in one of Henry can we adhere to these authors to the very end. Yet, is it not this that makes good masters of them, masters who caution their readers – if they know how to read them – from all epigonal conduct? Conversely, these are the main truths of phenomenology, if their transgressive practice of phenomenological method testifies, in fact, to a fidelity, to a contradictory injunction of phenomenology itself. We can neither completely adhere to these phenomenologies, nor completely detach ourselves, without yielding to the phenomenological requirement.

* * *

This matter has undoubtedly suffered from its great generality (since it proposed to find the means of reconfiguring the entire field of contemporary French phenomenology by evaluating its paradoxical fruitlessness). Allow us to attempt to outline, obviously too schematically, using examples from each author that we have discussed, the manner it endures (or, at times, circumvents?) the test of excess that forges their common bond.

Jacques Derrida

It is, of course, significant that Jacques Derrida is not included as part of the group of authors identified by Janicaud as attempting to negotiate a theological bend within phenomenology. This is due to the fact that – if "theology" here means (what is, after all, a rather derived meaning!) passage beyond the borders of that which is given as evidence of the essence and reception of something given beyond this evidence – it should indeed be affirmed that Derrida *never* carries out such a transgression without return. To meditate upon and test this crisis of evidence – its impossibility as such being found in its purity – certainly never returns, as we have suggested, offering a presence in excess to the sovereignty of evidence. The test of the limit of the phenomenological, according to Derrida, does not open one to that beyond the phenomenon, as Husserl defines it: this is why he is not a target of Janicaud's criticism. If he is sometimes the object of bitter criticism, it is owing to the positions by which his movement – such as we have described it – would be found to be *irrational* (i.e., weakness of the argument, effects of seduction, identification of the paradoxes halting the eidetic description forced by obviousness, etc.). The test of the phenomenological, the setting into crisis, and even the continuation of the crisis, are not reducible by us according to what is envisioned by these types of objections (which are sometimes reduced to a great deal of brutality and poverty; but this is another debate). The Derridean test of the phenomenological always maintains an intimate rapport with that which is being put to the test (and the accusation that it is non-phenomenological could not be held except from a position that would identify phenomenology with Husserlianism and Husserlianism with a transcendental type of rationalism supporting no setting into crisis). This rapport will never be noticed often enough in the description and reduction proposed by Derrida, as they resist such exposure. Moreover, to really reflect upon it, the Derridean movement – in that which implies as much the impossibility of forsaking the "as such" of phenomenology as the impossibility of this "as such" – is one of the rare movements that reflects the same movement that it practices.

The Saturated Phenomenon According to Jean-Luc Marion

We had, when considering an earlier work (Marion 1997: 304), designated Marionian phenomenology as precisely that which justified Janicaud's objections; like that which, precisely, validates the economy of the test of the phenomenological limit, of its domain in law (evidence) and, in the same gesture, of its methodical constraints. Exempt, always already and even in advance, from the limitations of the domain of the given (which, in Husserlian terms, is usually only allowed for that which concerns objectifying acts), will it not have difficulty playing out the giving of that which exceeds intuition without one being able to rationally discuss it on the standard norm of that which is given (or not)? Among these French phenomenologists, it would be no less than the appearance of a paradox that Marion would be the one who asserts most of all phenomenology as a method, its practical application and the success of reduction. If the sequence of reductions functions so well with Marion (after the Husserlian reduction to the object, then the Heideggerian reduction to being, the third and final – since it succeeds in leading to the most radical – reduction is the Marionian reduction to the saturated phenomenon), is this not because this exercise, and its implicit risk-taking – the opening of the un-anticipatable – is in some way feigned? Precisely, since one pretends to provide himself the means of succeeding in reducing the un-anticipatable, does he not provide himself the means to anticipate, and thus miss as such – to miss as such for having excessively pretended to have provided himself with such?

Such was, in substance, the argument that we presented to oppose Marion's *Réduction et donation* (*Reduction and Givenness*; Marion 1989). Without attempting here to distinguish between what is to be ascribed to the insufficiency of our earlier reading, and what is to be ascribed to the increasingly profound investigations and displacements of Marionian thought itself since this seminal work, we should be precise in stating that it is impossible to take back this criticism and announce its lack of accuracy and justice toward the phenomenology of the saturated phenomenon. That leads us, not to discount our objection, ourselves, but to attempt to nuance it, to moderate, renew, and deepen it. Henceforth, concerning the saturated phenomenon of Marion, the objection for which Janicaud would have furnished the seminal form seems to have, so to speak, been "exceeded."

If the question really is: "From whence comes the right to consider as an attested phenomenological example an element of *revealed* theology, for example, Christ?" then one cannot merely hold to pointing out, while being scandalized, that Marion gives himself allowances for that which exceeds the norm of evidence (and camouflages the violence of this simple *fait accompli* with a façade of methodological rigor). This is because Marion's work deepened: if we grant that it is, at the very least, possible to deliver the giving from its limitation to the object (which is, undoubtedly, debatable, but, in any state, constitutes a philosophically admissible statement and is thus *philosophically* debatable), then Christ *can offer himself*. The most important step produced by Marion is the following: "can offer" is changed to "offers."

The Marionian movement consists, in fact, of saying that if one takes the Heideggerian definition seriously, then the phenomenon that "shows itself" would not, by definition, be preceded and determined by its condition of formal possibility: the phenomenon does not surprise me except when it is preceded by *nothing*, which conditions the possibility in advance – and especially not by categories such as those on the side of a subject that one could qualify as a constituent. This description applies to any phenomenon inasmuch as it is phenomenalized; even the poorest of phenomena, if one remains, must maintain its bond with this additional category. From this (Marionian) point of view, it could be said that the advantage of phenomenology consists in canceling out the Kantian question, that of the right or legitimacy of appearance. The questions of "What right?" or "What is the condition of possibility?" make no sense phenomenologically and can only, in their very formulation, miss the phenomenon. This excess on the condition of possibility will be, in the same movement, an excess on the phenomenon to any empirical or objective effectivity: no longer measuring itself alongside the right, the phenomenon is thus no longer measured with the fact, at least with the fact of the object. This is what the Marionian theme means when speaking of the "possibility that surpasses not only affectivity, but also the very conditions of possibility."[14] From this point, it becomes insufficient to declare that saturated phenomena – especially the saturated phenomenon par excellence, revelation – absolutely transgress any norm or right of appearance. It becomes insufficient in comparison with the gesture that we have just indicated. Of course, no one is held to do it, but, it should at least be noted that this gesture was produced, that it rests all the same on a description of the phenomena (would this description force the opening of what we held until now as indescribable?) and on a series of arguments: for this reason, it is justifiable as a subject of phenomenological discussion. We must add something: Marion, in order to be prudent, insists that, in this way, he simply establishes phenomenologically the *possibility* of revelation. In the same movement, he insists that the effectiveness of this revelation, the ontic status of this revelation, concerns a revealed theology that he carefully avoids producing himself in his works on phenomenology (this is especially the case in Levinas 1961).

The radical phenomenologist, Marion exempts himself from all rational theology (where the question is of beings and of the relation of causality between beings and the "super-being" we call "God"). Acceptance of the phenomenology that he proposes implies the possibility of the "giving" of the "saturated phenomenon par excellence," revelation, this possibility, consequently, culminating in putting into play the very idea of phenomenology: the release of the framework of the object being like the release of a giving beyond the very question of intuition (fulfilling the concept), of its excess or of its deficiency.

It is out of the question to simply dismiss this objection according to which Marion never attempts to test the limits of phenomenality – because he does well to assert a transgression, so that he, himself, is liberated from the very idea of a limit (a limitation to the form of the object and just the same for whatever limit); however, it is necessary to produce this objection due to the rigorous reception of argumentation and description produced by Marion in his most recent texts.

Such a task exceeds the limits of this presentation. Nonetheless, we will suggest a direction of research: Marion allows for the possibility of a phenomenon that is without *any further rapport* with the "phenomena of common right." For example, concerning the traits proper to the face, is it not that case that these are not given except at the very core of the upheaval of the visible, to which they are ineluctably attached? To justify this excess of the visible (in the sense of what is given in the paradigm of form, evidence, or object), perhaps it is this point that characterizes all these French phenomenologists; but, can this reception *cut off* all the accumulation of common visibility? Whereas, according to Marion, the historical event or the face of another are saturated phenomena, their excess to the visibility of common right never entirely extracts them from the ordinary world. They contaminate it as much as they are contaminated by it – the saturated phenomenon par excellence, revelation, is absolved of any rapport with ordinary phenomenology, for it is not shown "there" except in the event of an absolutely *other* giving, showing no bond of common visibility.

The Face According to Levinas

There is a way of determining the precise location of the objection we are outlining, which is at the place of the saturated phenomenon par excellence, that boils down to determining the difference between the Levinasian description of the face and the one put forward by Marion. From the beginning of this presentation, let us recall that the face according to Levinas – as well as according to others whose arguments we will not develop here – presents two decisive characteristics: "frankness" and "expression"; it "speaks," and thus, it is true, it is "given" fully and as – in addition to the visible – an ethical language (Schonfeld 2005). However, the face – more so in *Otherwise than Being* than in *Totality and Infinity* – is characterized as much by its ambiguity as by its frankness: ambiguity in that it is not given, so to speak, save as a void, that like the upheaval of the appearance of the World, that is: still and ineluctably the same – visible; it is a *trace* of that which will never be present, and the trace gives only insofar as it implies the absently irreducible. Without going into all the details here, it could be said that already in his interpretation of Levinas, and especially in his description of the face that he proposes under his own name, Marion favors the first of these two characteristics and tends to rescind the second, or at least, envelop it within the first:

if there is a certain "deficiency" of the face, something like the absence that haunts it, this deficiency will be interpreted by Marion as a deficiency of intuition signaling, in fact, an addition, an additional giving. Such is, according to us, the difference between a movement that legitimizes the giving of revelation within phenomenology, liberates giving beyond any limit to the point that the absently irreducible trace cannot find at its heart any status of radicality (Marion), and the movement (that of Levinas) that never ceases to test the limit of phenomenality, the absently irreducible marked by the trace of the face to the World itself, is thus apprehensive with regard to revelation. For Levinas, revelation, although beyond theoretical or objectifying knowledge, is still not the otherwise than knowing appropriate for the otherwise of being, but still a form of knowing, if we take this last term to mean a sort of giving (which, circumstantially, would give as any other form of giving constrained by the rule of the object or by evidence would give).

The Levinasian movement would never cease to test the limits of phenomenology, whereas the Marionian movement, dismissing all limits, could propose itself as allowing the possibility of revelation and thus being the most radical form of phenomenology. However, one could, "from the exterior," so to speak, designate this second gesture as providing an excess through a simple transgression that, consequently, is cut off from any rapport with the extremities of phenomenology, and maybe even from phenomenology altogether. Would such a transgression, an absolute transgression, be one from which one could never again transgress (if all transgressions are tested in relation to limits)?

We should emphasize here that the Derridean rapport with phenomenology recognizes a deep affinity with the relationship of the Levinasian movement with phenomenology. Like the latter, Derrida favors the problematic of the *trace* and never ceases to test the limits of the phenomenal while simply demanding that it not be transgressed. One could even say that Derrida accentuates this tendency. One would, in turn, find a sort of confirmation *a contrario* of this hypothetical reading in that if Marion minimizes the ambiguity of the face in order to favor his additional giving, Derrida, for his part, tends, on the contrary, to accentuate the dimension of the absence of the trace as forming a crisis surrounding any presence and leaving aside the frankness of the face that is given (his rapport with ethics plays itself out differently). It is significant from this point of view that Eli Schonfeld, in a text sensitive to Jewish lineage in the work of Levinas (Schonfeld 2005: 446), accentuates the difference between Levinas and Derrida at the exact point where we have the tendency, for our own part, to accentuate the proximity. It is true that the Levinasian description of the face carries within itself a tension between these two directions (contradictory up to what point?): the positivity of the ethical frankness of the face on one side, and, on the other, the ambiguity of the trace working the phenomenal horizon in absence. Schonfeld emphasizes, for his part, that if the trace fails to return to any positivity for Derrida (we are incessantly returned from trace to trace, and the archi-trace is "first"), for Levinas, it returns to the positivity of ethical language and even, he says, beyond the ethical, "the trace returns us to a Jewish God, with the God of the book of Exodus" (ibid.). In all consistency, this Levinas would be more suitable for Marion.

Thus, we clearly see two manners of practicing excess in phenomenology distinctly taking form. There is the one that tests the limits: the Derridean movement; but there is also the Levinasian movement. (We should, of course, concede that there is, in the work of the latter, a certain ethical "positivity," but it seems to us – though arguing would take us too far from the scope of this chapter – that one can, in no case, concede that the frankness of the face leads one directly and ineluctably back to the God revealed at Sinai. Levinasian phenomenology remains fixed to this pole of phenomenality, the face overwhelming the visibility of the visible itself as a trace of that which will have never been present.)

In light of this gesture, there is one that liberates the giving from the limit of the visible (constrained by the norm of evidence), that being Marion; and, as we demonstrated above, the movement of Henry, which is, from this point of view, closest to that of Marion.

The Auto-Revelation of the Figure of Christ in Michel Henry

Henry, nevertheless, if he dismisses the authentic phenomenality of his attachment to any ek-static structure still does not allow for any giving that would not be limited by some unit of measure, but once again takes up the discussion of the immanence of the proof of Life, that, at base, holds the place of a criterion of authentic phenomenology: this is, no doubt, debatable – in true sense of debate, discussion – but it institutes a norm that returns to the certification that the living self creates from the source of this auto-affection (for example, but not exclusively, through suffering). The auto-revelation in question, in order to radically free itself from the World, is all the more strongly attached to that which always *also* constituted a norm in phenomenology, the lived experience, the "auto-effective" certification, if you will. Henry's "revelation" looks to nothing other than to this: that in the description he proposes, the pressure of Life alone, which is always pressure exerted from the self of a Living Thing, constitutes immediately the very expression and the source of all signification.

It seems that the relationship of excesses (concerning the visible) is offered in a manner strikingly and perceptibly different between the work of Henry and that of Marion. We would, therefore, like to conclude with a simple outline of a precise example, a precise textual sequence of the method of reading that we have just proposed, to locate within his work a moment of phenomenological transgression that attests at the same time to the proof that this limit has been endured.

Let us focus on the question that is absolutely central to the status of Christianity, and more precisely, to the status of the figure of Christ, in the economy of the latest work published to date by Henry, *I am the Truth* (Henry 1996). To what point should we follow Henry in his use of Christianity in phenomenology? Is there a point where we can no longer follow him on this path? Can we identify this point? In what ways does this final point still testify to the center of the matter of transgression of the phenomenological – a transgression that, we must emphasize, is not completely proven and reflected upon as such by Henry – of infidelity to the phenomenological requirement?

We must first point out that Henry does not seem to endorse Christianity in exactly the same way that he did, for instance, Cartesian or Marxist thought (see, for Descartes,

Henry 1985; and for Marx, Henry 1976). Addressing the manner that he is comparable to Descartes and Marx, let it be said that he was sometimes reproached for carrying out a sort of "forcing" (*forçage*) by which he succeeds in finding in them an annunciation of his own basic intuition. Of course, in Henry's eyes, it is Life that is omnipresent in his auto-revelation – up to the very symptoms of its negation: barbarism – which is revealed most particularly in these works (although less completely so, of course, than in his own!). In any event, at the very most, we can expect a Henrian description to take excessive liberties with the texts that it employs. Whereas, in *I am the Truth* – although no one can judge it as a being anything but a very specific "account" of Christianity – it is the opposite question that arises. That is, to know the following: was the Henrian phenomenology of Life not surreptitiously subordinated to a motif and an intuition that were, at first, foreign to him, and, that threaten to control it from this exteriority? From Henry's point of view such is, of course, not the case: he would claim to have simply known to recognize in Christianity an exemplary revelation from the very movement of Life. There would be no place for him to be scandalized by subordination to philosophy in general, and by phenomenology in particular, to a particularized faith in the whole of specific dogmas in their positivity. There would also be, except in the case of misapprehension, a poor way of articulating the question: indeed, for Henry, it is Life that reveals itself in different ways in the philosophies – as in other types of work. In the same way, Life reveals itself in different ways in the different religions. Consequently, there is nothing anti-phenomenological to be found in the particular way that Christianity reveals Life: there would be nothing reprehensible; on the contrary, in continuing the revelation of Life that takes place in Christianity in and by philosophical discourse that would take into consideration Christian faith without distorting it with its own constraints (those, in particular, of a requirement of rigorous, rational explanation of the sequence of its expressions).

If, in examining Christianity, we suspect that something else is coming into play and asserting itself in Henrian philosophy outside the – absolutely legitimate – Henrian conception of philosophical practice, it is for the following reason: the question that arises here is of knowing if it is, indeed, the Henrian phenomenological description that *ends* in the figure of Christ, or if, on the contrary, it is not *rooted* as a prerequisite. Is this not the irruption of a non-phenomenological theme, not produced by phenomenological constraint, in Henry's phenomenology that brings to him, from without, the possibility of resolving a problem that arose in this phenomenology and has not managed to resolve itself by its own means?

We will content ourselves here with outlining the problem at hand: in *I am the Truth*, the issue is to know how each Living Thing (*Vivant*) *ipseizes* itself in the movement of Life. How does a Living Thing acquire its *ipseity* from the sovereignty of Life? This question arises if we must hold that Life absolutely gives life to every being and that, even so, from the point of view of a Living Thing, to be oneself always supposes a meaning – even if it is only one meaning – to be tested absolutely separately, absolutely autonomously, in its singularity, to be held absolutely to oneself. How do we make this event of the singularity of the Self thinkable and describable in the sovereignty of Life without always already compromising the latter, this first event toward which the whole is, however, entirely predisposed?

Very precisely, the answer is in Christ, as he will be designated as the "First Living Thing," as the "Archi-Son" who will allow the paradoxical double-constraint that we have just explained to be rendered intelligible.[15] As the Archi-Son, Christ is, rightfully, the unheard-of first occurrence of *ipseic* singularity in Life that, in a sense, owes nothing to Life, but, on the contrary, offers it something in the possibility to *ipseize* Living Things by inaugurating this possibility. Consequently, Christ offers to each Being to be itself. As such, the event of the coming of Christ is a transcendental event. It also escapes the linear and cumulative temporality of objective time, and it is not absurd to say that the event of the "Archi-Son" has always already taken place in Life, making possible in itself the *ipseization* of Living Things; and that, still, in the same motion, must be characterized by the unrepeatable singularity of the event, that which is supposed to identify it (being about Christ and not another, and this because Christ has no trace of general abstraction), even if this identification has nothing to do with the World or the object (it is certainly not initially about spatio-temporal individualization) and is strictly transcendental?

From this point, it is legitimate to wonder, as we do, if Christ is not a motif imported from outside the phenomenology of Life, allowing Him to face a double constraint that we were unable to manage to produce or govern using our own resources. Therefore, everything is held up: by pointing toward Christ, does Henry not provide a precise identification of the transcendental? Does he not *identify* the most originary source of all giving (would this identification indicate a transcendental event)?

It is now time to tie up the loose ends of this rapid analysis of the status of Christ as the Archi-Son in the Henrian phenomenology of Life,[16] as well as those of the hypothesis that we presented above, in order to help configure the field of contemporary French phenomenology and orient ourselves within it.

One will have understood that the figure of Christ would occupy, according to us and within Henrian phenomenology, the function and the place of the motif, undiminished by *épokhè*, through which reduction as hyperbolic renewal would be able to stabilize itself on an ultimate ground, thus inverting the excessive movement by which it is prone to an "excess of excess" that identifies the unidentifiable, despite everything and in contradiction with the inclinations of its own requirements, to give a term to the anxiety it accommodates.

It is useless to specify that the movement we are attempting to characterize here is, in fact, neither linear nor sequential, and that the production of the figure of Christ in phenomenology does not simply negate the phenomenological character of the Henrian system. This philosophy is sufficiently complex so as not to be subject, in any event, to a case of easy exit without returning to phenomenology, while at the same time, retaining the necessity of knowing how to indicate the present transgression of the imminent constraints of phenomenology.

To conclude, let us reiterate that if, for our part, we cannot accompany Henry when he allows himself to use Christ, which we have diagnosed as an "excess of excess," we hold that the "excess of excess" itself, which disallows complete agreement with the phenomenological course of an author, is still, and perhaps more so than ever, the testimony of the radicality of the phenomenological movement in question, of the risk that it knows to take.

Notes

This chapter takes up, builds upon, and significantly modifies portions of Sebbah 2001b and 2000.

1 So that we are not mistaken here, the affirmative position of this statement in no way implies an "apology" for any school: likewise, there is no way of judging except for the gestures of thought that will be evoked in the following lines that testify to an exit from, or a treason against, phenomenology; others, or even the same, speak of a "post-phenomenology." It would be useless to mention that the stakes that we claim here are not those that concern the guardians of vaults – or of temples.

2 See, for example, Maldiney 1973; Garelli 1991, 2000; Richir 1987, 1992; and Barbaras 1993, 1999.

3 Except when considering that Life is this privileged "phenomenon," because nothing is revealed except in Life or as Life.

4 From Marion 1997, the book that we favor most particularly here, written in the wake of Marion 1989; we also make reference, in this presentation, to Marion 2001, which takes up the contributions of Marion 1997 in a concern for systemization, depth, and clarification.

5 See Janicaud 1998. Let it be noted that Janicaud had criticized the authors that we are treating here – we must stress with the exception of Derrida – for the motif of the others of trying to negotiate a "theological turn" of phenomenology. See Janicaud 1991.

6 At least pertaining to that which no one would qualify as a "continental" use of phenomenology: the analytical use and the use of phenomenology in the cognitive sciences being precisely characterized by that. These uses seem to us, for the most part, to ignore and even explicitly divert the requirement of reduction. It is, at least, necessary to point out, however, a notable exception concerning the rapport between cognitive sciences and phenomenology: the recent work of Natalie Depraz and Francisco Varela (see Depraz, Varela, and Vermersch 2003).

7 One could speak of "fruitfulness" if such an ambiguity of reduction, prohibiting all pretension of a definitive description as to the way of appearance, does not, however, result in abandoning the requirement, but on the contrary, indefatigably starting it over again.

8 To make the distinction operative, in our own way, let us particularly draw on the method worked out by Patočka that differentiates between "*épokhè*," in the sense of a simple movement of suspicion or placing between parentheses of the thesis of the world, and "reduction," in the sense of a "renewal toward the source of any appearance" (Patočka 1988).

9 This would then produce, at the very heart of phenomenology, a sort of dialectic of appearance, in the Kantian sense of the term.

10 And all the while entirely aiming at this accomplishment.

11 These hypostases would still be even more detached from the field of appearance than was Husserlian transcendental subjectivity: these authors would do "worse" than Husserl to want to rightly radicalize the Husserlian gesture of reduction.

12 "Beyond appearance": that is to say, beyond perceptive actions and all the actions that modify or are founded upon them.

13 One could, furthermore, wonder – we will simply suggest it here – that if this way of presenting oneself entirely is proof of this double-constraint with the impossibility of constituting oneself in the definitive figure of the self, then, it does not constitute an overall greater fidelity to phenomenology than the practices of phenomenology that, to be entirely and definitively faithful to the branch of double-constraint, completely dodge the imperative charge of the other. This is evident, but one still needs to more deeply support this

hypothesis. In formulating this suggestion, we keep in sight the alternative between the phenomenology that is considered "theological" and that considered "minimalist" as proposed by Janicaud – and we would readily propose to short-circuit this alternative in the name of anything else. In addition, we will have understood that happy medium in an affected, quantitative, and inconsistent sense. The strictly Aristotelian idea of the "happy medium" would be more appropriate for what we have in mind, if, for Aristotle, "happy medium" maintains within itself the opposing excesses.

14 The prudent call to this distinction between simple possibility and effectivity can, in addition, be surprising, from the point of view of an author who seems to have, so to speak, short-circuited it in liberating the giving as the "possibility of the impossible."

15 See Henry 1996, in particular ch. 5, "Phénoménologie du Christ" [Phenomenology of Christ], and especially chs. 6 and 7, "L'homme en tant que 'Fils de Dieu'" [Man as "Son of God"], and "L'homme en tant que 'Fils dans le Fils'" [Man as "Son in the Son"].

16 We looked longest at part II, ch. III of Sebbah 2001a.

References and Further Reading

Barbaras, R. (1993) *De l'être du phénomène; sur l'ontologie de Merleau-Ponty*. Grenoble: Éditions Jérome Millon (*The Being of the Phenomenon: Merleau-Ponty's Ontology*, trans. T. Toadvine. Bloomington: Indiana University Press, 2004).

—— (1999) *Le désir et la distance. Introduction á une phénoménologie de la perception*. Paris: Vrin.

Depraz, N., Varela, F. J., and Vermersch, P. (2003) *On Becoming Aware. An Experiential Pragmatics*. Amsterdam: John Benjamins.

Derrida, J. (1967) *La voix et le phénomène* [Voice and phenomenon; only available in English as part of anthologies; the French subtitle is "introduction to the problem of the sign in the Phenomenology of Husserl"]. Paris: Presses Universitaires de France.

—— (1962) *Edmund Husserl: L'origine de la géométrie*. Paris: Presses Universitaires de France (*Edmund Husserl's Origin of Geometry: An Introduction*, trans. and intro. J. Derrida, Lincoln: University of Nebraska Press, 1989).

—— (1987) *Psyché. inventions de l'autre*. Paris: Galilée (expanded 1988) (*Psyche: Invention of the Other*, Chicago: University of Chicago Press, 1993).

—— (1991) *Donner le temps*. Paris: Galilée (*Given Time*, Chicago: University of Chicago Press, 1992).

—— (1993) *Spectres de Marx*. Paris: Galilée (*Specters of Marx: The State of the Debt, the Work of Mourning, and the New International*, New York: Routledge, 1994).

Garelli, J. (1991) *Rythmes et mondes – au revers de l'identité et de l'altérité*. Grenoble: Éditions Jérôme Millon.

—— (2000) *Introduction au Logos du monde esthétique – de la Chôra platocienne au schématisme transcendental et à l'expérience phénoménologique du monde*. Paris: Beauchesne.

Henry, M. (1976) *Marx: une philosophie de la réalité, une philosophie de l'économie*. Paris: Gallimard (*Marx: A Philosophy of Human Reality*, Bloomington: Indiana University Press, 1983).

—— (1985) *Généalogie de la psychanalyse: le commencement perdu*. Paris: Presses Universitaires de France (*The Genealogy of Psychoanalysis*, Stanford, CA: Stanford University Press, 1993).

—— (1990a) *L'essence de la manifestation*. Paris: Presses Universitaires de France (original work published 1963) (*The Essence of Manifestation*, The Hague: Martinus Nijhoff, 1973).

—— (1990b) *Phénoménologie matérielle*. Paris: Presses Universitaires de France.

—— (1996) *C'est moi la vérité. Pour une philosophie du christianisme*. Paris: Seuil (*I Am the Truth: Toward a Philosophy of Christianity*, Stanford, CA: Stanford University Press, 2003).

—— (2000) *Incarnation. Une philosophie de la Chair* [Incarnation: a philosophy of flesh]. Paris: Seuil.

—— (2002) *Paroles du Christ* [Words of Christ]. Paris: Seuil.

Janicaud, D. (1991) *Le tournant théologique de la phénoménologie française*. Combas: Editions de l'Éclat (*Phenomenology and the "Theological Turn": The French Debate*, New York: Fordham University Press, 2000).

—— (1998) *La phénoménologie éclatée*. Paris: Éditions de l'Éclat (*Phenomenology "Wide Open": After The French Debate*. New York: Fordham University Press, 2005).

Levinas, E. (1961) *Totalité et infini*. The Hague: Martinus Nijhoff (*Totality and Infinity: An Essay on Exteriority*, Pittsburgh, PA: Duquesne University Press, 1969).

—— (1974) *Autrement qu'être, ou, Au-delà de l'essence*. The Hague: Martinus Nijhoff (*Otherwise Than Being, Or, Beyond Essence*, Pittsburgh, PA: Duquesne University Press, 1998).

—— (1988) *En découvrant l'existence avec Husserl et Heidegger* [Discovering existence with Husserl and Heidegger]. Paris: Vrin (original work published 1949).

—— (1989) *Théorie de l'intuition dans la phénoménologie de Husserl*. Paris: Vrin (original work published 1930) (*The Theory of Intuition in Husserlian Phenomenology*, Evanston, IL: Northwestern University Press, 1995).

Maldiney, H. (1973) *Regard, Parole, Espace*. Lausanne: Éditions L'Âge d'Homme.

Marion, J-L. (1989) *Réduction et donation. Recherches sur Husserl, Heidegger et la phénoménologie*. Paris: Presses Universitaires de France (*Reduction and Givenness: Investigations of Husserl, Heidegger, and Phenomenology*, Evanston, IL: Northwestern University Press, 1998).

—— (1997) *Étant donné. Essai d'une phénoménologie de la donation*. Paris: Presses Universitaires de France (*Being Given: Toward a Phenomenology of Givenness*, Stanford, CA: Stanford University Press, 2002).

—— (2001) *De surcroît: études sur les phénomènes saturés*. Paris: Presses Universitaires de France (*In Excess: Studies of Saturated Phenomena*, New York: Fordham University Press, 2002).

Merleau-Ponty, M. (1981) *La Phénoménologie de la perception*. Paris: Gallimard (original work published 1945) (*Phenomenology of Perception*, London, Routledge, 2002).

Patočka, J. (1988) Epokhè et réduction. In *Qu'est-ce que la phénoménologie?* (pp. 249–61). Grenoble: Éditions Jérôme Millon.

Richir, M. (1987) *Phénomènes temps et êtres – ontologie et phénoménologie*. Grenoble: Éditions Jérôme Millon.

—— (1992) *Méditations phénoménologiques – phénoménologie du langage*. Grenoble: Éditions Jérôme Millon.

Schonfeld, E. (2005) Hommage à Jacques Derrida. "*Jewgreek is greekjew*": les extrêmes se rejoignent-ils vraiment? ["Jewgreek is greekjew": do the extremes every really meet?]. *Cahiers d'Études Levinassiennes*, 4, 441–51.

Sebbah, F-D. (2000) Une réduction excessive: où en est la phénoménologie française contemporaine? [An excessive reduction: where is contemporary French phenomenology?]. In in E. Escoubas and B. Waldenfels (eds.), *Phénoménologie française et phénoménologie allemande* (pp. 129–55). Paris: L'Harmattan.

—— (2001a) *L'épreuve de la limite. Derrida, Henry, Levinas et la phénoménologie* [The test of the limit: Derrida, Henry, Levinas, and Phenomenology]. Paris: Presses Universitaires de France.

—— (2001b) L'exception française [The French exception], *Le Magazine littéraire*, 403, November.

Central Concepts

5

Intentionality

J. N. MOHANTY

Beginnings

Intentionality has occupied a central role in modern phenomenology beginning with Edmund Husserl. But, at the same time, its precise nature and status have been a matter of controversy within the larger philosophical movement. Even within Husserl's own philosophy, its analysis, function, and interpretation have had a long, winding, and extremely complex history. In this chapter, I will try to follow some of these controversies and lines of development, looking specifically at work by Husserl, Heidegger, and Merleau-Ponty.

We now know that the concept of intentionality antedates Brentano's lectures on psychology, that we find it in the scholastics, and far back in Aristotle, such that even Brentano's famed statement about it has Aristotelian overtones. However, without stopping to trace that fascinating history of the concept, let us be satisfied with citing the passage in which Brentano's formulation first surfaces:

> Every mental phenomenon is characterized by what the Scholastics of the Middle Ages called the intentional (or mental) in-existence of an object, and what we might call, though not wholly unambiguously, reference to a content, direction upon an object (which is not to be understood here as meaning a thing), or immanent objectivity. Every mental phenomenon includes something as an object within itself; although they do not all do so in the same way. In presentation something is presented, in judgment something is affirmed or denied, in love loved, in hate hated, in desire desired, and so on.
>
> This intentional in-existence is characteristic exclusively of mental phenomena. No physical phenomenon exhibits anything like it. We can, therefore, define mental phenomena by saying that they are those phenomena that contain an object intentionally within themselves. (Brentano 1973: 88–9)

Interpreting this justly famous paragraph has led to various problems. We must, first of all, be clear about what he means by "mental phenomena" (correspondingly, by "physical phenomena"); we should also be clear about what he means by "object" and by that phrase "intentional (or mental) in-existence of an object." We are also left wondering how and in what sense mental phenomena can "contain an object intentionally within themselves." Mental phenomena for Brentano are mental *acts*, designated by such verbs, or rather gerundial nouns, as "believing," "perceiving," "desiring," and "hoping" – not, to be sure, mental contents such as images or sensory data. The former alone are intentional in his sense.

It is generally thought that Husserl took over the thesis of intentionality from Brentano, and then considerably modified it. As Brentano's pupil, Husserl attended Brentano's lectures on psychology and certainly would have learned about the concept of intentionality. However, as recent researchers have shown, Husserl did not introduce the concept of intentionality in his own work until years later. At last, in 1894, we find him, finally overcoming, after a long struggle beginning with his *Philosophie der Arithmetik*, Brentano's "immanentism." He does this by discovering for himself that presentations (*Vorstellungen*) were of two kinds: *intuitive* (where a content is given in the act although even here he recognizes that when an external object is given, the whole system of contents corresponding to such an object goes far beyond the contents which are actually immanent to the act) and *representative* (in which the represented object is not at all immanent). The latter sort of *Vorstellung* is rather directed toward the intuition of what is *not* given.

With this, he had discovered a concept of intentionality which is directed toward a transcendent object, and which is "fulfilled" when that object is given. He also discovered the same intentionality in the heart of intuitive presentations as pointing to what is not yet, but can be, given. With the overcoming of "immanentism," the basis was laid for the *Logische Untersuchungen* (the *Logical Investigations*).

Husserl's Theory of Intentionality

Overview

In the *Logical Investigations*, Husserl introduced the thesis of intentionality in three stages. In the First Investigation, he begins with a semantic thesis, a theory of meaning, in connection with "expressions." In the Fifth Investigation, he takes up the theme of consciousness, and directly relates to the Brentanian thesis. He defines the notion of "act," rejects Brentano's immanentism, and sharply distinguishes between the content and the object of an intentional act. In the Sixth Investigation, all this is taken up into the concepts of knowledge as fulfillment of intention, and of truth as evidence. We will briefly expound the theory in these three stages.

First, the semantic theory, on the face of it, bears a close resemblance to Frege's, but we shall avoid the hasty conclusion that he may have derived it from the latter. He formulates the theory thus: "Each expression not merely says something, but says it *of* something: it not only has a meaning, but refers to certain *objects* . . . the object never coincides with the meaning. Both, of course, only pertain to an expression in virtue of the mental acts which give it sense" (Husserl 1970a: vol. I, 287). An expression refers to its *object* via its meaning. The meaning, here called *Bedeutung*, is later said to be an *ideal* entity, a species whose instances are the acts intending it – *ideal* in the sense that it is not spatio-temporally individuated and is closer to what some philosophers call "abstract" entities.

In the Fifth Investigation, the Brentano thesis is addressed. Between the widest concept of "consciousness" as the totality of one's mental life, and the narrowest concept of it as one's inner perception of one's mental experiences, Husserl cuts out a middle region consisting only of intentional experiences which he designates by the technically defined term "act." By insisting on the *terminus* "act," he wants to free the notion of intentional experience from the idea of a specific sort of activity, especially an act of the will.

Husserl, however, disagrees with Brentano's thesis that all experiences are intentional. There are, he insists, experiences or, in Brentano's words, mental phenomena which are not intentional, for example, "sensations and sensation complexes" (Husserl 1970a: vol. II, 556; translation modified). He prefers to drop Brentano's use of the term "mental phenomena," in view of the ambiguities that surround his doctrine of "inner perception." The location "intentional experience referring to an object" should not be construed as meaning that two things are present in experiences, an object and an intentional act directed toward it. Only one thing is present, an intentional experience, and "(I)f this experience is present, then *eo ipso* and through its own essence (we must insist), the intentional 'relation' to an object is achieved, and an object is 'intentionally present'" (Husserl 1970a: vol. II, 558). He thus rejects a relational understanding of intentionality. He is *not* trying to understand *how* consciousness (which is allegedly within me) relates to an object out there. There is no intentional experience without already having an intentional object. Likewise, the alleged consciousness that is to achieve its relation to an object is already, to begin with, consciousness of this object and of no other.

An important aspect of the concept of intentionality, as it is elaborated in the Fifth and the Sixth Logical Investigations, is that it is presented in the context of a theory of perception. As it now stands, the theory, in very simple outlines, amounts to this: the intentional object of perception transcends the act of perceiving. The act, however, has its immanent contents, which are also called "primary contents," which are sensory complexes, later to be called hyletic data. The intentional act has then two functions, one built, as it were, upon the other: it first confers sense or meaning upon the primary contents, and thereby objectivates, or makes possible an object, to which *then* it intentionally refers (in this account, "first" and "then" are to be understood not in a chronological sense but in a logical order). This is how one should understand this crucial text: "Apperception is our surplus, which is found in experience itself, in its descriptive content as opposed to the raw existence of sense: it is the act-character which as it were ensouls sense, and is in essence such as to make us perceive this or that object" (Husserl 1970a: vol. II, 567). This perceptual model is extended by Husserl to understanding an utterance: here, too, a meaning-giving act supervenes upon the presented acoustic "primary content"; the latter is interpreted, resulting in the auditor's grasping of a meaning. We now understand why Husserl would say later that although Brentano was the discoverer of intentionality, he did not see the objectifying role of intentionality.

In the last phase of the theory of intentionality, as it is developed in the *Logical Investigations*, the discussion of intentionality is undertaken in the context of *knowing*. The distinction between meaning intention and meaning fulfillment, already introduced in the First Investigation, is extended beyond logical thinking to all objectifying acts. Intentionality may now be said to be *striving* after truth and as a temporal process.

The meaning as noema

Husserl's manuscripts written between 1906 and 1910 abound in various ways of articulating this new theory of meaning, which was made possible by Husserl's momentous discovery of the "epoche" in 1905. With the subjecting of the object in the natural attitude to the reduction, the component of doxic positing or belief which belongs to every act which confers on the object its being-character (e.g., "real," "possible," "imaginary") now becomes available for study; Husserl calls it *noesis*. Its correlate becomes the object *in the how of its givenness* together with its thetic characters, now called the *noema*. The noema is also said to be the *Sinn* of the act. We thus arrive at the famed thesis of noesis–noema correlation, which is often said to be the essential feature of intentionality. Husserl speaks of the noema as the phenomenologically reduced object, as the intended as such, especially as the perceived as perceived, as the ideal-identical *Sinn* or meaning of the act, as the appearing object, etc.

Let me now give a rather simple analysis of the structure of what Husserl calls *the full noema*. Although Husserl sometimes calls the full noema *Sinn*, *Sinn*, "in the most pregnant sense," is the noematic nucleus to which belong all the objective predicates constituting the "how" of the object's givenness. The full noema includes the nucleus with its central point, the X, and the thetic character which is then the *posited meaning*. This thetic character is, in general, predicates corresponding to the doxic quality of the act whose noema we are considering. This X is to be construed neither as the substance underlying the objective predicates, nor as a phenomenon apart from the latter predicates, but as a component of the *meaning* of the act, by virtue of which the predicates are unified as "belonging to one and the same thing." It indicates *a function* whose concretizations are different in different cases.

Now, I will distinguish between (i) the psychological noema, (ii) the logical noema, (iii) noema as a semantic function, and (iv) the transcendental noema. The psychological noema may be identified as the total content of the appearing object prior to "epoche." It is distinctly different from the object that is presented. The logical noema is the noematic *Sinn* consisting of the nucleus and the objective predicates ascribed to the object. It is logical inasmuch as its ideality makes logical discourse possible. Propositions, syllogisms, and theories are noemata in this sense. From the semantic point of view, the noema is a function whose arguments are possible worlds and values are individuals in the actual world. The transcendental noema *is* the object as it appears within the epoche. There is, then, no distinction between the transcendental noema and the object. The sense of constitution of the object varies from one interpretation of the "noema" to the other.

Subsequent developments of Husserl's theory

Further developments of Husserl's theory of intentionality were stimulated by his discovery of and growing concern with the horizonal characteristic of every act as well as of its noema, by his continuing, and developing, researches into inner time-consciousness, and both leading to the realization that the act-intentionalities, having noetic-noematic structure, are surrounded and penetrated by intentionalities which are not acts.

Let us recall that intentionality, for Husserl, constitutes the object by conferring meaning upon the non-intentional stuff or *hyle*. Using now the idea of *noema*, we can say that one and the same object is constituted by the noematic nuclei of those acts carving out, as it were, a common and shared area. This notion of constitution and the theory of intentionality associated with it surely underwent some revision, though not radical change, in later years of Husserl's thinking. It does appear that many aspects of intentionality came to be revised without, however, radically affecting the central core of the theory.

Heidegger on Intentionality

For about fifteen years, Heidegger was captivated by the *Logical Investigations*. The key concepts in the *Investigations* which he isolated for special attention are "intentionality," "categorial intuition," and "a priori." While Brentano set him on his philosophical path as much as he also influenced Husserl, it was Brentano's essay on the concept of Being in Aristotle – "On the Manifold Sense of Being in Aristotle" – and not his lectures on psychology, which determined his thinking. This explains why early on he sought to give an ontological interpretation to those three key concepts.

In the *Basic Problems of Phenomenology*, Heidegger points out several misinterpretations of intentionality (Heidegger 1982). The most pervasive misinterpretation is to construe it "as an extant relation between two things extant, a psychological subject and a physical object" (Heidegger 1982: 60; translation modified). To the contrary, intentionality belongs to the structure of the subject. But then, a second misinterpretation arises when we construe the intentional experiences of the subject as being immanent to the subject, and there, in order to explain how immanent experiences can be of a transcendental object, end up by regarding the objects of intentionality also as immanent to the subject – in which case, intentionality becomes something that occurs within the subject. However, intentionality is neither objective, nor subjective. It is indeed prior to, and "more original" than both, the subject and the object.

It seems that while defending the thesis of intentionality, Heidegger's goal, toward which he moves slowly over the years, is to overcome the Husserlian version of it. When he rejects "erroneous objectivism" and "erroneous subjectivism" and sets aside any construal of it as a relation between two "extant" entities, clearly he is reformulating, in his own language, Husserl's rejection of objectivism as well as of psychologism. He still has to find a way to articulate his own distinctive position. He does this by asking what is the *ontological status of intentionality*, which on his view Husserl left indeterminate. Heidegger asks us to think of intentionality more radically. How is it possible for the subject to escape the confines of its immanence and relate to the other? Or, even, why does a subject "require" an object, and conversely? This relating must belong to the ontological constitution of the subject itself. Intentionality must belong to the existence of Dasein. It is of the nature of Dasein that it exists in such a way that it is "always already with other beings" (Heidegger 1982: 157).

Dasein's "transposition" of itself to the things is possible because its very nature is *transcendence*. This leads Heidegger to a discussion of *temporality*, especially to what he calls the "ecstatic-horizonal constitution of temporality" (Heidegger 1982: 314). What we have in the end is the following order of foundational dependence:

Temporality → transcendence → being-in-the-world → Intentionality

In this chain, the preceding member founds the succeeding. Intentionality is only a surface phenomenon of deeper ontological structure.

Let me turn now to the concepts of *meaning*, *Sinn*, and noema, which, for Husserl, have their origin in intentionality. For this purpose, I will go back to Heidegger's still earlier writings. In his lectures of 1920, he tells us that factual life-experience has the character of meaningfulness (*Bedeutsamkeit*), which consists in three kinds of meaning: *Gehaltssinn* (contentual meaning), *Bezug-sinn* (relational meaning), and *Vollzugsinn* (performance-meaning). The first is the content of what is experienced, the second is relational meaning which lies in the "how" of that content's being presented or experienced. The third is, for Heidegger, the most important; it consists in the temporal reenactment of the event of meaning. This last is the primary task of phenomenology, the Husserlian "clarification" of sense by returning to the original experiencing moment when the meaning emerges. For Heidegger, it is to return to the historical origin.

Merleau-Ponty

Merleau-Ponty's original contributions to the theme of intentionality may be brought under four headings, "operative intentionality," "bodily intentionality," "intentionality and transparence," and, finally, the relation between consciousness and the world.

Operative intentionality

The intentional act which posits the world or an object in the world is not the primary intentionality. What precedes it is the lived experience of the world "as already there." Kant held that the categorial constitution of the objective world already presupposes that "the hidden art of imagination" has already constituted the world. The task of understanding is to conceptualize, objectify, and render "conscious" what has already been achieved (Kant 1965). This fundamental, most primary experience (not "act") of world-constitution is called by Merleau-Ponty "operative intentionality," following a suggestion by the late Husserl (Husserl 1970b). In Merleau-Ponty's world, it is "the natural and antepredicative unity of the world and of our life, being apparent in our desires, our evaluations and in the landscape we see, more clearly than in objective knowledge, and furnishing the text which our knowledge tries to translate into precise language" (Merleau-Ponty 1962: xvii). Husserl had treated desires, evaluations, and the like as non-objectifying but still as acts, and as presupposing objectifying acts. Merleau-Ponty, rightly I think, treats feelings, emotions, desires, and evaluations as experiences which are *not acts*, nevertheless intentional in a rather extended sense, and he reverses the Brentano–Husserl relation of priority between objectifying and non-objectifying intentionalities. Merleau-Ponty writes that Husserl's originality does not consist in the discovery of intentionality but rather in: "The elaboration of this notion and in the discovery, beneath the intentionality of representation, of a deeper intentionality, which others have called existence" (Merleau-Ponty 1962: 121fn.). Note that whereas Heidegger does not want to call this existence or Dasein's being-in-the-world intentional on the ground that being is not an object, Merleau-Ponty, closer to Husserl, still regards it as the deeper level of intentionality, or as "operative intentionality."

Bodily intentionality

Although, as is well known, Merleau-Ponty rejects the absolute dualism advocated by Sartre, between consciousness and the world, and situates body in the ambiguous middle, the body is still on the side of the subject (Merleau-Ponty 1964: 5). It is "our point of view on the world." The subject of perception is not "an absolute thinker," but the body. The body-subject is not a *thing*, but an intentional movement directed toward the object, or at least is a potential movement. "The body itself is a motor power, a "motor project" (*Bewegungsentwurf*), a "motor intentionality." As one's hand moves to grasp a tumbler of water, it is *not* that there is first a thought about raising and stretching one's arm and then this thought causes a mechanical bodily motion. It is the bodily movement that directs itself toward the object, and this movement has its own *sui generis* intentionality. "Motility," writes Merleau-Ponty, "is not, as it were, a handmaid of consciousness, transporting the body to the point in space of which we have formed a representation beforehand" (Merleau-Ponty 1962: 139). The intentionality of bodily movement confers the primary meaning on things in the world, which thought subsequently conceptualizes by a process of idealization.

Bodily intentionality has the feature of being "anonymous," it is not fully transparent to itself, nor is it totally opaque; it is not incurably particular, as characterized by Heidegger's *Jemeinigkeit*, but has a certain generality about it such that the meanings it confers are empirically general, not strict idealities; it is also characterized by a certain circularity, it both is a project towards the world and also is an openness towards the world (Merleau-Ponty 1962: 254).

Intentionality and transparence

Sartre famously regards consciousness, which is, in his jargon, so fully intentional that its entire being consists in being directed toward the world, such that in itself it is sheer nothingness, it has no contents, no Husserlian *hyle* nor Husserlian noema. Being fully intentional, it is also fully transparent to itself. Intentionality implies complete transparency, and excludes all opacity. Being-in-itself is both non-intentional and opaque. Rejecting such oppositional thinking, Merleau-Ponty regards intentionality as always *a matter of degrees*, and so also is the transparency of intentional subject (Merleau-Ponty 1962: 124–5). Intentionality never grasps its object in its totality, nor it is completely aware of all its background and presuppositions. An absolute positing of the object, we are told, would mean "death of consciousness" (Merleau-Ponty 1962: 71).

Consciousness and the world

The idea of intentionality seems to suggest an initial separation of consciousness and the world, and then an attempt to reconnect them. On Merleau-Ponty's view, this is a mistake. We are "through and through compounded of relationships with the world" (Merleau-Ponty 1962: xiii). We are intimately bound to the world by "intentional threads." This tie can be loosened, as by the epoché, but cannot be cut off – which explains Merleau-Ponty's recognition that we need the epoché, but a complete reduction is not possible. I think he saw clearly that the pure subject of classical transcendental philosophy and the pure object of classical science are both products of *thinking*, and it is by rejecting both that we begin to see that embodied and situated consciousness and the pre-objective perceived world are two aspects of the same intentionality.

An attempt to reconcile the various perspectives on intentionality

I may now bring this account of intentionality to a conclusion by way of ordering the different approaches to this topic in a sort of hierarchical order. We may begin with a psychological thesis along Brentano's lines, characterizing all mental *acts* as containing within themselves a directedness toward an object, a directedness which cannot be explained otherwise than by recognizing this as an irreducible and intrinsic feature. The next stage in our thinking would consist in trying to accommodate this feature within a naturalistic–causal framework à la Sellars and Dretske. If both the "immanentism" of the Brentano thesis and the physicalism of the causal account fail, then we have to find a place for what is important in each. The intentional content must be grounded in the natural and the cultural orders, and intentionality in Dasein's being-in-the-world, especially in its temporality. The representative content of the Brentano thesis has to be grounded in the non-representational, but actional projects of the Dasein. Finally, the opposition between a mentalistic representational theory of intentionality – both theoretical as well as practical and affective – as a transcendental –constitutive function, according to which the intentional content is not an internal representation but a publicly sharable meaning, and the world in which Dasein finds itself is the product of prior constitutive accomplishments of an intentionally implicated community of egos. With this progressive deepening of our understanding of the nature and function of intentionality, the relevant philosophical *problem* continues to be transformed.

References and Further Reading

Brentano, F. C. (1973) *Psychology from an Empirical Standpoint* (trans. A. C. Rancurello, D. B. Terrell, and L. L. McAlister). New York: Humanities Press (original work published 1874).

Chisholm, R. (1972) Intentionality. In P. Edwards (ed.), *Encyclopedia of Philosophy* (pp. 201–4). New York: Macmillan and Free Press.

Chisholm–Sellars correspondence (1972) In Ausonio Marras (ed.), *Intentionality, Mind, and Language*. Urbana: University of Illinois Press.

Dreyfus, H. (ed.) (1982) *Husserl, Intentionality, and Cognitive Science*. Cambridge, MA: MIT Press/ Bradford Books.

Føllesdal, D. (1969) Husserl's notion of noema. *Journal of Philosophy*, 66 (20), 680–7.

Gurwitsch, A. (1966) *Studies in Phenomenology and Psychology*. Evanston, IL: Northwestern University Press.

Heidegger, M. (1962) *Being and Time* (trans. J. Macquarrie and E. Robinson). New York: Harper & Row (original work published 1927).

—— (1982) *The Basic Problems of Phenomenology* (trans. A. Hofstadter). Bloomington: Indiana University Press (original lectures delivered 1927; original work published 1975).

Husserl, E. (1962) *Ideas: General Introduction to Pure Phenomenology* (trans. B. Gibson). New York: Collier/Macmillan (original work published 1913).

—— (1970a) *Logical Investigations* (trans. J. N. Findlay). New York: Humanities Press (original work published 1900–1).

—— (1970b) *The Crisis of European Sciences and Transcendental Phenomenology: An Introduction to Phenomenological Philosophy* (trans. D. Carr). Evanston, IL: Northwestern University Press (original work published 1954).

—— (1993) *Cartesian Meditations: An Introduction to Phenomenology* (trans. D. Cairns). Boston: Kluwer (original work published 1931).

Kant, I. (1965) *Critique of Pure Reason* (trans. N. K. Smith). New York: St. Martin's Press (original work published 1781).

Merleau-Ponty, M. (1962) *Phenomenology of Perception* (trans. C. Smith). New York: Routledge (original work published 1945).

—— (1964) *The Primacy of Perception* (trans. J. M. Edie). Evanston, IL: Northwestern University Press (original work published 1947).

Mohanty, J. N. (1964) *Edmund Husserl's Theory of Meaning*. The Hague: Martinus Nijhoff.

—— (1982) *Husserl and Frege*. Bloomington: Indiana University Press.

—— (1985) *The Possibility of Transcendental Philosophy*. Dordrecht: Kluwer.

Searle, J. (1983) *Intentionality: An Essay in the Philosophy of Mind*. New York: Cambridge University Press.

Welton, D. (1983) *The Origins of Meaning: A Critical Study of the Thresholds of Husserlian Phenomenology*. The Hague: Martinus Nijhoff.

6

Consciousness

CHARLES SIEWERT

Introduction

Consciousness figures as a central – sometimes dominant – theme in the phenomeno-logical tradition initiated by Franz Brentano and Edmund Husserl. This chapter describes key elements of Brentano's and Husserl's seminal discussions of consciousness. It then briefly notes some ways in which these views were received by some of the best-known ("existential") phenomenologists who followed: Martin Heidegger, Jean-Paul Sartre, and Maurice Merleau-Ponty.

Writings in phenomenology reasonably seen as about consciousness (in some widely recognizable, if initially loose sense) tend to take as basic some notion of *appearance* or *experience* – or a notion of *consciousness of objects* – for which perceptual appearances and imaginings, but also episodes of conceptual thought, furnish paradigms. Working then from some initial, broad understanding of consciousness, experience, or appear-ance, philosophers in the phenomenological tradition try to characterize the forms it takes, and how they are related – especially in terms of their *intentionality* – in terms, that is, of how they are "directed at" or "refer" to things. This characterization comes from a critical reflection on these forms, one that relies on the sort of understanding of them available through occupying (or adopting in imagination) the point of view of someone who is conscious of things (or has experiences, or to whom things appear) in the manner characterized. Phenomenological accounts are not aimed at providing either a causal or reductive explanation of consciousness. The aim is rather to give a highly general descriptive account that employs distinctions one can understand by being someone to whom the account applies. The value of such an enterprise may be taken to lie in the understanding it provides of the subject matter of psychology and related fields, and of the sources of knowledge and symbolic meaning. It may be taken as bearing on the character of aesthetic evaluation and ethical choice. And it can form the basis for reflection on the human condition.

Such statements may help situate the treatment of consciousness in phenomeno-logy roughly within a wider sphere. But given the difficulty of generalizing about phenomenologists as a group, it would be best at this point to discuss their views individually.

Brentano

Brentano sought to establish the framework for a scientific study of the mind. He saw his project as distinct from but required for a successful casual explanatory (in his terms, "genetic") psychology, and as providing foundations to logic, ethics, and aesthetics. Its immediate aims are: to delimit the subject matter of psychology; to lay out the principal distinctions applicable to it; and (partly by means of this) to clarify the manner in which it can be studied. Brentano variously calls this endeavor "descriptive psychology," "psychognosy," and "phenomenology." His account of consciousness needs to be understood in the light of this project and the primary notions he develops in connection with it.

Central to the execution of Brentano's program is his famous claim that intentionality is the mark of the mental. Mental phenomena are distinguished by (as he variously puts this) "the intentional inexistence of an object . . . reference to a content, direction to an object." Thus: "[e]very mental phenomenon includes something as object within itself" (1972: 88). Brentano proposes that these phenomena are to be analyzed in terms of three fundamental classifications: "presentations"; "judgments"; and emotional/volitional phenomena (such as loving and hating). And he holds not only that all these are marked by intentionality; they are also universally possessed of a specially *self-reflexive* form of intentionality – a kind of perception – whereby mental acts are directed at or refer to themselves. For a mental phenomenon to be *conscious* is for it to contain such a perception of itself: consciousness is "*inner perception.*" Thus, according to Brentano, all mental phenomena are conscious. Inner perception (unlike "outer perception") is infallible, and provides the basis for psychological knowledge generally, including the taxonomical variety sought in phenomenology.

One might classify Brentano's view among "inner-sense" theories of consciousness. However, this can be misleading, since these can vary widely with different conceptions of "sensing" (or perception). In Brentano, perception of any kind essentially includes *presentation* – and presentation is fundamental to the mind. Presentations (or presentings) cover whatever might be described as an *appearing* – including not only sensory appearances (of, e.g., colors, shapes, sounds, odors, flavors), but also "conceptual" appearances such are found in non-sensory thought (intellectual or "noetic" consciousness, in Brentano's terms) (1972: 81, 198). Presentings are necessary but insufficient for judgings – and a perception consists in a judgment that *accepts* something presented. It is important to recognize that a theoretically primitive notion of presentation or appearance is built into Brentano's account of consciousness as inner perception in two ways: an inner perception is a presentation of a mental phenomenon – and also, the mental phenomenon perceived/presented is itself a presentation (or based on a presentation).

Brentano's is a bold view about consciousness, its scope, and its role in self-knowledge. But its content can be properly understood only by seeing how he develops and defends it through addressing a number of interesting problems.

(1)   There is a concern (derived from Comte's criticism of introspection) that perception requires some sort of split between perceiver and perceived. *Inner* perception,

then, since it would require these to *coincide*, not only is not (as Brentano claims) *ubiquitous*; it is not even *possible* (1972: 32–3).

(2) One may object that Brentano's theory leads to an infinite regress: if all mental phenomena are conscious, this includes all inner perceptions. And if each inner perception is conscious then each needs to be the object of a further inner perception. But this is unacceptable (1972: 105, 121–2).

(3) One might argue, against Brentano, that there is, in any case, more to the mind than consciousness, for the postulation of unconscious mental phenomena is justified in virtue of its explanatory power (1972: 105–12).

(4) One may worry that, since knowledge of mental phenomena from inner perception would be based on data from a single subject, it would not be sufficiently general to provide the basis for a scientific study (1972: 37).

Brentano answers these challenges as follows.

In response to (1): though he does not consider the criticism, as it stands, to be particularly cogent, Brentano thinks Comte is on to something – for there is a sense in which inner *observation* is not possible. However, inner *perception is* possible. For Brentano, the difference between the two lies in the fact that observation (but not perception) essentially involves the discovery of what is already there through increased *attention* to an object observed. While we can learn about visible objects by observing them – looking at them *more closely* – we cannot learn about our own mental phenomena by similarly directing our attention to them. An attempt to attend in this way to one's current mental state alters its very character, instead of just revealing how it already was. However, in granting this we do not preclude *perceiving* our own mental phenomena in Brentano's (presentation plus judgment) sense, and using this, together with memory, to characterize them knowledgeably (1972: 29–30, 34–5, 43, 124–8).

Brentano proposes a way of dealing with (2), the regress problem, without retreating on his claim that all mental phenomena are conscious. Rather than blocking such a regress by postulating unconscious inner perceptions, he maintains that the inner perception of a given presentation (such as hearing a tone) is conscious, not because there is a yet further perception trained on it, but because it is part of the very mental act of which it is the perception. For the inner perception to be conscious, it is enough that it is part of the hearing of which it is the perception. Brentano also tries to forestall objections here by emphasizing that, when we perceive a color or tone, we only "incidentally," "implicitly," and "secondarily" perceive our own perceiving as well. For Brentano *implicit* perception and *unconscious* perception are not the same (1972: 122–7, 129, 275ff.).

In answer to (3) Brentano argues, on a case-by-case basis, and with reference to views of his contemporaries (pre-Freudian proponents of the unconscious), that equally or better warranted forms of explanation are available that do not appeal to unconscious mental processes (1972: 113–17).

In response to (4), Brentano says we can avoid the danger that reliance on inner perception will yield only idiosyncratic features of the perceiver's own mind, if we focus on basic types of mental phenomena that we can confirm are widely or universally shared (such as perception, attention, judgment, memory, and so on), and if descriptive psychology is carried on in critical dialogue with others (1972: 37–8).

80

These and other aspects of Brentano's account of consciousness, interesting in their own right, form a background essential to appreciating the discussions of later phenomenologists, because of Brentano's considerable influence on Husserl's philosophy.

Husserl

Much of Husserl's early philosophy arises from his attempt to apply what he took from the descriptive psychology of his teacher Brentano to epistemological issues. Husserl's abiding conviction is that philosophy should attempt to account for various types of *evidence* by tracing them to their characteristic *sources in experience* – and to do so in a rigorous, critical, and systematic manner. This interest in constructing a systematic framework for understanding experience adequate to clarify its evidentiary role appears to have been a major motive for Husserl's preoccupation with questions of consciousness and perception. In any case, what grows out of Husserl's encounter with Brentano is a complex, challenging and original view of the nature of consciousness and its place in knowledge.

In *Logical Investigation* V Husserl explicitly addresses himself to the project of disambiguating "consciousness" to the extent needed for his foundational philosophical concerns. This leads him to distinguish three senses or concepts of consciousness (2001: vol. 2, V, §1):

(a)   What is conscious is whatever is a part of someone's occurrent experience – what belongs to someone's "stream of consciousness."
(b)   What is conscious is whatever is the object of "inner awareness" (i.e., inner perception).
(c)   What is conscious is any mental act or intentional experience.

Senses (b) and (c) are to be found in Brentano; ultimately it is sense (a) that Husserl favors. His initial account of consciousness (a) relies heavily on examples. He says, in effect, that consciousness in this sense is what is shared by experiential occurrences such as "percepts, imaginative and pictorial presentations, acts of conceptual thinking, surmises and doubts, joys and griefs, hopes and fears, wishes and acts of will" that are *unified* in the way these are when they belong to a particular person – an "*ego*" (2001b: vol. 2, V, §2, p. 82). Husserl argues that we can (and should) make sense of (a), independently of adopting either Brentanian usage (b) or (c), on the following grounds.

(1)   If we suppose all that is conscious in sense (a) is conscious in "inner awareness" sense (b), we are beset by "grave difficulties" – in particular, the threat of infinite regress (2001: vol. 2, V, §5, p. 85).
(2)   Brentano's attempted resolution of that difficulty assumes the "unbroken activity of inner perception" – but this cannot be demonstrated phenomenologically (*ibid.*).
(3)   Talk of "inner perception" is plagued by a certain ambiguity that makes it unsuitable for epistemological purposes. We might take it narrowly, so that something conscious in sense (a) is "perceived" only if it is an object of "adequate perception" – where an *adequate* perception attributes to its object no more than what is strictly "given" or

"apprehended" in that very perception of it. While the narrow sense is philosophically preferable to a broader one, it is also to be distinguished from consciousness (a): not everything conscious in that sense is the object of adequate perception (2001b: vol. 2, 87, pp. 335ff.).

(4)   What is conscious in sense (a) includes but is not limited to intentional (directed, referential) acts. We can recognize that certain sensory contents (e.g., color sensations) form a part of conscious perceptual experience that is distinct from the "interpretation" these "data" are given in the experience. Thus senses (a) and (c) need to be distinguished (2001b: vol. 2, V, §2, pp. 83–4, §15b).

Early on Husserl also tries to distinguish the class of what is conscious in his preferred sense (a) by reference to Descartes's method of doubt: what is conscious is understood in terms of what it is about oneself that would be untouched by Cartesian doubt (2001b: vol. 2, V, §6). This way of interpreting "consciousness" is revised and elaborated through Husserl's theory of perception, and his closely associated notion of a "phenomenological reduction," both of which are central to his philosophy as a whole. To understand his views on consciousness, it is essential to have some understanding of these.

Important aspects of Husserl's theory of perception appear in the *Logical Investigations* (2001b: vol. 2, V, §14; VI, §§4–6, 10, 14, 40). But it is in full bloom by the time of the first book of his *Ideas*, published in 1913. Centrally, his account concerns what it is to experience a natural thing – or more particularly, what it is for something to appear in space. Husserl notes that when we experience some object in space (say, a cube lying on a surface) we experience the object only partially, "one-sidedly," perspectivally, via an "adumbration" or "profile" of it. We can distinguish changes in these adumbrational appearances from apparent changes in the object itself, which we recognize as appearing *constant* in, e.g., color or shape, through a "flux of experience." Now we experience in this manner not only an object, but also – less attentively and "*determinately*" – its close surroundings. And the way we experience what we do cannot be properly understood apart from a sense – a kind of "*anticipation*" or "*predilineation*" – of how things could *potentially* be *more* determinately given to us than currently, were we to direct attention appropriately. This anticipation, Husserl thinks, extends to what is not "authentically or genuinely given" (what does not *appear* to us) at all, even indeterminately – for example, the side of a cube facing away from the viewer. The cube looks to one – as it does – *cubical* from a given angle, only insofar as one "anticipates" other appearances: how it would look from other angles, were one to do what is needed to see its hidden aspects (1982: §§35, 41, 42, 44; 1960: §§19, 20; 2001bv: §§1–3).

This account, in which actual appearances are linked to potential further appearances "anticipated," is an account of the intentionality of perception. For only in virtue of a relation between current actual spatial experience and potential experience that would *fulfill* (in some sense confirm or corroborate) it, can one identify an object to which the experience refers or is directed. Without that relation between the experience, and what is anticipated – its "horizon" – a sensory experience would be without directedness to an object altogether, without intentionality.

Husserl's novel, holistic view about the intentionality of spatial experience raises many questions it is impossible to explore here. But it is only against its background that we can understand his way of interpreting consciousness (a). A few more steps will make this clear.

Because spatial perception is essentially perspectival in the way described, Husserl says we can never (in the sense earlier indicated) fully *adequately perceive* anything spatially (and so we cannot have "adequate *evidence*" regarding any such object of experience) (1982: §§42, 138). For current experience is of an object at all only insofar as it "points" beyond what is authentically given in it to merely potential experience that would fulfill it. But the possibility can never be ruled out that the future course of experience will be such as to frustrate a fulfillment that would allow one to conclude one had identified stable persisting objects in space. Ultimately, Husserl holds, appreciation of this truth about experience shows that it is possible to have experience that never reveals *any* actual spatial objects that transcend the experience. As Husserl puts it, "the possibility of the non-being of the world is never excluded" (1982: §46).

Now, in recognizing that spatial experience in this way fails to guarantee the existence of things outside itself, in space, we are able also to recognize the possibility that one may form judgments about one's experience that do not commit one to the actual existence of spatial objects. To restrict one's judgments to ones of this sort is to do what is required for the suspense of judgment involved in Husserl's famous "phenomenological reduction," crucial to his official philosophical method. This cognitive feat of reduction, Husserl thinks, was foreshadowed by the method of doubt in Descartes's philosophy. But here it is finally made possible, not by contemplation of some deviant causal hypothesis involving an evil demon (or, we might add, a mad scientist and a brain in a vat), nor by inducing any *doubt* (hyperbolic or otherwise). Rather this reduction of judgment is made possible through insight into the essence of spatial experience.

This has important consequences for Husserl's conception of consciousness. For he concludes that consciousness (a) is none other than the "phenomenological residuum" – the "residue" of the phenomenological reduction – which residue nonetheless retains its intentionality as an object of study (1982: §§33, 34, 49, 50; see also the paragraph interpolated into the Second Edition of the *Logical Investigations* [2001b: V, §2, p. 82]). So, in Husserl, what is conscious becomes not whatever is the object of Brentanian inner perception, but whatever belongs to a "stream" of consciousness. And *that* is ultimately interpreted to mean: whatever concrete events are left to consider, once one has suspended judgment about the natural world – the world of objects in space and time, partly – as one can – by means of the just-rehearsed Husserlian reflections about the essence of spatial experience. Husserl's conception of consciousness is thus made dependent on his methodological reduction – easily among the most controversial aspects of his philosophy, even for those who consider themselves phenomenologists.

If this conveys something of how Husserl understood his "stream" sense of consciousness ((a) above) without appeal to Brentanian consciousness-as-inner-perception, it still leaves unclear the extent of his disagreement with Brentano about self-consciousness. To get clearer about this, we must go again to Husserl's theory of perception. For he wishes to emphasize that we are *not* given our own experience as we are given spatial objects to judge about, through partial appearances and anticipation of further, different, confirming ones that allow us to identify constant objects of reference (1982: §44). Nonetheless, Husserl thought one's own experience is – in some *other* way – "intuitively given" to one to form (reflective) judgments about. This mode of being given, whatever it is, Husserl sometimes speaks of as "perception," though it is crucially unlike the way things are given to us spatially, in this respect: *this* manner of givenness will not admit the possibility that there is in fact nothing there given in that manner for one to judge about. "It would be a countersense to believe it possible that a mental process *given in that manner* does *not* in truth exist" (1982: §46, p. 100). Since this way of being given something to form judgments about *guarantees* that there is something about which to judge, our judgments about experience can possess especially strong evidentiary status; we can have (in Husserl's sense) "adequate evidence" for such judgments, as we can never have regarding what appears to us in space (1982: §§46, 137, 138, 144).

But just what *is* this special way in which one's own experience is "given"? We have here, in his view, a sort of intentionality – a species of consciousness *of* something – but one which can be had without yet "*positing*" what one is conscious of "*as an object.*" The *general* difference between *positing* and *non-positing* consciousness is, at least initially, to be understood against the background of Brentano's distinction between judgment and "mere" presentation. One may be merely presented with something, it may appear to one – in imagination, say – in such a way that this presenting is directed at or refers to what is presented, though one neither *affirms* nor *rejects* the existence of what is presented; one does not (in Husserl's terms) "posit" its existence or non-existence (as in judgment) (2001b: vol. 2, V, §§23, 38). Husserl would also offer, as examples of such non-positing consciousness, our indeterminate experience of what lies in the unattended (but still apparent) surroundings of what we are looking at (1982: §113). And here he draws an important analogy. What appears to us inattentively in spatial perception is not an object of perceptual judgment. But by appearing to us in such inattentive fashion, it is such that we *can*, though attending to it, *form* such judgments about it. Somewhat similarly, by having a non-positing (but intentional) consciousness of one's own experience, the experience is always *available* for one to form a reflective judgment about, through a direction of attention (1982: §45).

Husserl's view of "the consciousness of internal time" also plays an important part in his attempt to flesh out his notion of the "self-givenness" of experience. On his view, when we experience something current – such as the note of a melody we hear – we also are "retentively" conscious of the past experience, in a way that makes it possible for us to hear the melody as a whole. This *retention*, however, is to be distinguished from a *recollection* that certain notes have been experienced. To focus on the simple case of hearing a single tone: hearing the tone for a time, one "retains" one's *just having heard* the tone as one *continues* to hear it, even when one does not "posit" that the tone was just heard (as in recollection). And this retention "points back" to the tone's having been heard, though the preceding experience is not an *object* of the retention. Thus it seems the retention is not only *non-positing* (like imagination), it is also (evidently *unlike* imagination) "*non-objectivating.*" It is, in Husserl's view, an inescapable part of this view of the consciousness of internal time that there will be such a non-objectivating consciousness, not simply of experience just past (retention), but of experience *as it is occurring* (1982: 113; 1991: §§12–14, 39; Appendices VII–IX).

We might gloss Husserl's view by saying that while we do not have a *reflective self-consciousness* wherever we have conscious experience (there is no unbroken activity of Brentanian inner perceptual judgment), we do always have a *non-positing self-consciousness*: for one's every conscious experience is *itself* something *of which* one is thus conscious. But this leaves unclear just how Husserl thinks self-consciousness, in the sense of consciousness of a *self* or *ego*, figures in all this. Among the relevant materials to consider are these. In the *Logical Investigations* Husserl evidently holds that experience conscious in sense (a) is necessarily *someone's*. For the unity of a given "stream" is none other than the unity belonging to experiences that are all (e.g.) *mine*. Experience conscious in sense (a) is, after all, described as the "phenomenological being of the ego" (2001b: vol. 2, V, §§1, 2). Further, he thinks one can, in conceiving of a Cartesian style doubt, retain a reflective self-consciousness even while excluding any conception of one's bodily self (the "body-ego"). But he does not (any more than does Brentano) think this affords one the right to think of oneself as an immaterial substance or Cartesian ego. Rather, the conception of one's self then at play – the "mind-ego" – is just that of a certain unity of experience. And finally, Husserl recognizes that this sort of self-concept is specially expressible using the first-person singular pronoun or other essentially "occasional" (i.e., demonstrative or indexical) words, which are resistant to any rephrasal in other, general terms (2001b: vol. 1, I, §26; 2001: vol. 2, VI, §5).

But an additional wrinkle in Husserl's (post-*Investigations*) view of self-consciousness must be mentioned. In the second edition of the *Investigations*, Husserl claims to have discovered, since the time of the first, what he did not previously recognize: a "pure" or "transcendental" ego (2001b: vol. 2, V, §8). Husserl thinks that the *full* reduction excludes more than we explicitly noted above: it comprises a "transcendental" reduction that not only excludes judgment that particular objects exist in space and time. It also "puts out of action" the affirmation that any particular occurrences (including one's own experiences) are happening or have happened at certain times, even though it somehow still allows one to consider these experiences – albeit purely with respect to their essence. So one comes to consider "pure consciousness," the proper concern of phenomenology as Husserl ultimately understands it. Indeed the "phenomenological residuum" earlier alluded to is for Husserl *pure* consciousness. But in this reduction to pure consciousness one also attains, as distinct from the forms of more ordinary empirical self-consciousness, a consciousness of the *transcendental ego*. Even where one has taken the reduction so far as to exclude affirmation of the existence of a particular "empirical" self with a certain history, existing at a particular time, the essence of experience one is then still free to consider is seen to require it to have the form of being *someone's* – someone, moreover, regarded as the *source* of mental activity. In phenomenological reflection, one is aware not just of the unity of consciousness, but of a *unifier*. Thus the idea of the pure ego involves that of *agency* (1982: §122).

Heidegger

Two general conceptions of consciousness have emerged from our discussion. One, associated most with Brentano, joins consciousness closely to presentation – *appearance* in a broad sense – and to a form of self-consciousness supposedly bound up with it. To be conscious is to be a presentation that contains a perception of itself. The other, associated with Husserl, has us consider consciousness as that concrete "region of being" left for judgment even when we are not judging that particular spatio-temporal objects exist – the *phenomenological residuum*.

While the originality of Brentano's and Husserl's views should not to be minimized, we can say that both broad conceptions of consciousness just highlighted have recognizable roots in the Cartesian philosophical tradition. Heidegger, though strongly marked by his study of both Brentano and Husserl, strove to make a radical break with this tradition. Prior to the publication of his central work, *Being and Time*, Heidegger explicitly criticizes Husserl's reduction-derived conception of consciousness on the grounds that it neglects the "question of the being of consciousness" (and neglects the question of the "sense of being" altogether) (1985: §§10–13). Whatever the force of these criticisms, one might have expected them to lead Heidegger to suggest an improved way of thinking about consciousness that does *not* neglect these questions. However, what we find is that talk of consciousness (and intentionality) drops away, and Heideggerean phenomenology in *Being and Time* is oriented towards a general account of our "way of being" – that is, the way of being specific to "Dasein."

This abandonment of consciousness-talk seems to have been an attempt to make a fresh start, by refusing to use terms heavily laden with assumptions Heidegger wants to question or reject. Specifically, Heidegger hears in talk of consciousness a tendency, derived from Descartes, to oppose the "inner" realm of consciousness or mind to the "external world," and to accept an associated "problem of knowledge," which demands we explain how we can know anything "outside of" what is "in" consciousness. Heidegger regards this "problem" as illusory. The illusion arises from a failure to appreciate that our way of being is not primarily a "knowing," but involves a practical encounter with entities in our environment, in which they show themselves as "equipment" for our use. This way of being is properly understood by our *engaging* in it, and is deeply *mis*understood, if we interpret ourselves in terms of Descartes's model of consciousness, or its contemporary descendants (1985: §§20–4; 1962: Division One, II, §13).

Could Heidegger be said to discuss consciousness in *any* sense that would allow us to see him as sharing a common topic of discourse with Brentano and Husserl? One might consider a possible affirmative answer. Heidegger does want to account broadly for the ways in which things *show* themselves to us (that is, to beings such as ourselves with Dasein's way of being). And this account of "ways of showing" is such as is available from the perspective of one to whom things are thus "shown," just in virtue of being shown that way (1962: Intro., II, §7). We might then propose that these *showings* would include what Brentano would have described as a "presenting" or a phenomenon based on a presenting, as well as those occurrences Husserl would point to as paradigm cases of consciousness (a). On this view, Heidegger would not be ignoring consciousness, or denying its importance; he would just be rejecting the "inner perception" and "phenomenological residue" conceptions of it, and proposing a rather different framework for describing its forms – one in which beings showing themselves (or being "disclosed") as "ready-to-hand" equipment, or "present-at-hand" occurrent entities in the world – would constitute fundamental classifications (1962: Division

One, III, §§14–16). Perhaps we could even see, in Heidegger's talk of Dasein's pre-ontological understanding of its own being, some thematic continuity with Brentanian "implicit self-perception" and Husserlian "non-positional self-consciousness" (1962: Intro., I, §4). Assessing the feasibility of this way of looking at Heidegger would take us much farther into his philosophy than we can go here. However, it should be acknowledged he would likely see it as liable to taint his philosophy with the traditional ontology he is struggling to escape.

Sartre

Sartre – although certainly not shy in embracing radical positions, and heavily influenced by his reading of Heidegger – is considerably happier than Heidegger to adopt traditional terminology and philosophical apparatus – particularly that involving "consciousness." Indeed, in many respects he adopts as his own Husserl's view of reflection, and a ("non-reflective") non-positing consciousness. For Sartre every (positing) consciousness of an object includes a (non-positing) consciousness of itself. To suppose otherwise would, he maintains, commit one to the absurdity of an "unconscious consciousness" – a "consciousness ignorant of itself." This non-positional consciousness of consciousness is evident, Sartre argues, in our inarticulate awareness of what we are doing as consciousness is directed this way or that – e.g., as one is counting cigarettes (1956: Intro., III; 1957: 40–1).

However, this just-offered gloss, though perhaps useful as a first approximation, obscures a crucial aspect of Sartre's view. As part of a deliberate break with Husserl, Sartre denies (in *Transcendence of the Ego*) that one is non-positionally conscious of *oneself* being conscious of something. No conscious self, no "ego" is included within this primitive *non-positional* consciousness of consciousness. To be sure, Sartre thinks, when one *reflects* on consciousness, one attributes the consciousness reflected-on to an ego (to oneself). But, he holds, one does so falsely. For what consciousness is, is a direction to an object that transcends it, and consciousness is thus essentially negative: it is what it is not, in Sartre's teasingly paradoxical formulation. From this Sartre argues that consciousness brings with it a radical freedom, the recognition of which is incompatible with attributing consciousness to an enduring self possessed of stable psychological character (1956: 56–112; 1957: 93–106). By interpreting its intentionality so as to allow consciousness only such negative character as comes from the way it contrasts, in its spontaneous activity, with its objects (and filtering all this through Heideggerean themes of anxiety and authenticity), Sartre arrives at a dramatic conception of consciousness as the source of an intolerably vertiginous freedom.

Merleau-Ponty

Merleau-Ponty responds to Husserl's legacy in a notably different way than his classmate Sartre. His response also differs from that of Heidegger, partly in that, while Merleau-Ponty no more than Heidegger accepts the notion of consciousness as a region of being, in essence detachable from the world, he is (at least in *Phenomenology of Perception*) content to use the term "consciousness," and sees himself as appropriating and developing Husserlian insights regarding perception. Thus with Merleau-Ponty we are on somewhat safer ground, if we say he offers up a philosophy of consciousness.

It does seem, however, that Merleau-Ponty (unlike Brentano, Husserl, and Sartre) was not much exercised by the question of what all that is conscious in sense (a) has in common. He seems rather more interested in trying to draw attention to certain (elusive, if pervasive) *forms* of consciousness. He is particularly taken with the idea – for which he partially credits Husserl – that in ordinary spatial perception we have a kind of "pre-predicative," "pre-objective," and "non-positing" consciousness of our surroundings and our own bodies (2003: 116–29). One way this idea shows up is in Merleau-Ponty's interpretation of the Husserlian notion that to perceive space is in part to "anticipate" how it will appear to us if we direct attention appropriately. In Merleau-Ponty, it seems, this anticipation of further, different, or more determinate spatial experience consists in the exploratory *motor activity* we engage in, or are prepared to engage in, as we perceive – for example, what we know how to *do*, to get a better *look* at something. We perceive by moving in the right ways, and how we move anticipates further experience of a kind that would confirm the experience we have had. Such anticipatory movement is not the product of a separate internal representation of space; it *is* a way of being conscious – "non-positionally" (hence non-representationally) conscious – of space (2003: 77–88; 158–70; 348–54). The subject of this "motor-intentional" consciousness is conceived of in neither Cartesian nor Husserlian terms, but as a *body*-subject. *Contra* Sartre, to attribute consciousness to such a self is not to flee from freedom in bad faith, but to recognize the background of sensorimotor dispositions and skills that make intelligible the situations in which personal choice – human freedom – can arise (2003: 510–15; 523–7).

Although Merleau-Ponty does not try to say what consciousness in general is, he does have some notable things to say that indicate an unwillingness to accept either Brentanian or Husserlian ways of doing this. To take the latter first: Merleau-Ponty agrees with Husserl that nothing about spatial experience of a particular thing guarantees that one's further experience will link up harmoniously with it, and not disconfirm it or cast it into doubt. But he denies it follows that one might be in continual sensory error, or that one can render it truly intelligible to oneself that one is subject to global hallucination (2003: 344–7; 394–402). Thus while Merleau-Ponty retains the language of consciousness, he evidently rejects Husserl's conception of consciousness as "phenomenological residuum."

Merleau-Ponty's discussion of doubt and certainty reveals that he would also reject a Brentanian conception of consciousness as the realm of what is infallibly perceived. He goes at this issue piecemeal, discussing: (1) sensory consciousness (2003: 435–8); (2) emotive and volitional consciousness (2003: 439–42); and (3) intellectual consciousness (2003: 444–59). He argues that in judgments about each of these we are vulnerable to error and capable of entertaining doubts. Regarding (1): he says that, in normal circumstances, a faithful description of how one experiences would (in the case of vision) commit one to the existence of an object seen. Visual consciousness (of an ashtray or a hand, say) is either to be described as *seeing* an ashtray or hand, in a sense of "seeing" that requires there be a thing seen, or else it is to be described in such a way that implies it *resembles* cases of genuine seeing in this sense. Thus one cannot rationally suppose one is in error about whether there really are any things one sees or has seen, while making no error about one's sensory consciousness. In connection with (2), Merleau-Ponty points out that we recognize in such cases a distinction between what is authentic and what is not, and he argues that to be mistaken (as one may be) about whether one authentically feels something (whether one is, for example, genuinely in love) is to be mistaken about what one's feelings are, the very character of one's consciousness. Finally, in case (3), Merleau-Ponty says that such judgment renders itself intelligible in words, and our grasp of what we mean by our words, even in our most abstract thought, relies on a perceptual and cultural background we can never make fully explicit. This makes our understanding of our words susceptible to indefinitely further reconsideration and revision, with the result that, even here – in our apprehension of what we are thinking or judging – rational doubt is possible. So once again consciousness is not a sphere in which we are invulnerable to error and incapable of doubt, and Husserl was mistaken in supposing we ever have truly "adequate perception."

Still, Merleau-Ponty thinks, this does not leave one engulfed in endless doubt. In doing what we do – including what we do perceptually and cognitively – we have a kind of tacit understanding of what we are doing that warrants what we are inclined to say about this, absent any special reasons to doubt it. Any rational doubt about one's manner of being conscious in a particular case can arise only against the background of understanding in another case what one is conscious of, or how one is conscious, where one's engagement in conscious activity precludes one's being able to entertain a doubt about it (2003: 461–75).

In these remarks about the reception of the Brentano/Husserl legacy by Heidegger, Sartre and Merleau-Ponty we have, inevitably, only scratched the surface, and we have neglected the views of many interesting philosophers reasonably labeled phenomenologists, as well as many topics associated with phenomenological discussions of consciousness. But it is hoped that this summary conveys something of the richness and originality of discussion relating to consciousness in phenomenology, and will encourage its use as a resource for further investigation.

References and Further Reading

Brentano, F. (1972) *Psychology from an Empirical Standpoint* (trans. T. Rancurello, D. Terrell, and L. McAlister). London: Routledge (original work published 1874).

Carman, T., and Hansen, M. (eds.) (2004) *The Cambridge Companion to Merleau-Ponty*. Cambridge: Cambridge University Press.

Dreyfus, H. (1991) *Being-in-the-World: A Commentary on Heidegger's* Being and Time, *Division I*. Cambridge, MA: MIT Press.

Heidegger, M. (1962) *Being and Time* (trans. J. MacQuarrie and E. Robinson). New York: Harper & Row (original work published 1927).

—— (1985) *History of the Concept of Time* (trans. T. Kisiel). Bloomington: Indiana University Press (original work published 1979).

Husserl, E. (1960) *Cartesian Meditations: An Introduction to Phenomenology* (trans. D. Cairns). The Hague: Martinus Nijhoff (original work published 1931).

—— (1982) *Ideas Pertaining to a Pure Phenomenology and to a Phenomenological Philosophy, First Book: General Introduction to Pure Phenomenology* (trans. F. Kersten). The Hague: Martinus Nijhoff (original work published 1913).

—— (1991) *On the Phenomenology of the Consciousness of Internal Time (1893–1917)* (trans. J. Brough). Dordrecht: Kluwer (original work published 1928).

—— (2001a) *Analyses Concerning Passive and Active Synthesis: Lectures on Transcendental Logic* (trans. A. J. Steinbock). Boston: Kluwer (original work published 1966).

—— (2001b) *Logical Investigations* (trans. J. Findlay). London: Routledge (original work published 1900–1).

Merleau-Ponty, M. (2003) *Phenomenology of Perception* (trans. C. Smith). London: Routledge (original work published 1945).

Mulligan, K. (1995) Perception. In B. Smith and D. W. Smith (eds.), *The Cambridge Companion to Husserl* (pp. 168–238). Cambridge: Cambridge University Press.

—— (2004) Brentano on the mind. In D. Jacquette (ed.), *The Cambridge Companion to Brentano* (pp. 66–97). Cambridge: Cambridge University Press.

Rollinger, R. D. (2004) Brentano and Husserl. In D. Jacquette (ed.), *The Cambridge Companion to Brentano* (pp. 255–76). Cambridge: Cambridge University Press.

Sartre, J-P. (1956) *Being and Nothingness* (trans. H. Barnes). New York: Philosophical Library (original work published 1943).

—— (1957) *Transcendence of the Ego* (trans. F. Williams and R. Kirkpatrick). New York: Noonday Press (original work published 1937).

Thomasson, A. (2000) After Brentano: A one-level theory of consciousness. *European Journal of Philosophy*, 8, 190–209.

Wider, K. (1997) *The Bodily Nature of Self-Consciousness*. Ithaca, NY: Cornell University Press.

Zahavi, D. (1999) *Self-Awareness and Alterity: A Phenomenological Investigation*. Evanston, IL: Northwestern University Press.

—— (2003) *Husserl's Phenomenology*. Stanford, CA: Stanford University Press.

7

The Lifeworld and Lived Experience

MARTIN JAY

In the struggle to define itself in opposition to its predecessor, the generation in France that fashioned itself as post-phenomenological took special pleasure in deriding the concept of "lived experience." Jacques Derrida, to take a salient example, charged in *Of Grammatology* that experience is an "unwieldy" concept that "belongs to the history of metaphysics and we can only use it under erasure (*sous rature*). 'Experience' has always designated the relationship with a presence, whether that relationship had the form of consciousness or not" (Derrida 1976: 60). The phenomenological attempt to raise it to a transcendental level, above the vagaries of historical and cultural change, was deeply problematic, he continued, because it "is governed by the theme of presence, it participates in the movement of the reduction of the trace" (Derrida 1976: 61–2).[1] It therefore fails to understand the temporal disunity of "*différance*." Moreover, phenomenology naively believes that "all experience is the experience of meaning" (Derrida 1981: 30).

Likewise, Michel Foucault complained in *The Order of Things* that phenomenology was a philosophy that resolved itself into "a description – empirical despite itself – of actual experience, and into an ontology of the unthought that automatically short-circuits the primacy of the 'I think'" (Foucault 1973: 326). And in the interviews he gave in l978 to the Italian journalist Duccio Trombadori, he argued that

> the phenomenologist's experience is basically a way of organizing a reflective examination (*regard réflexif*) of any aspect of daily, lived experience in its transitory form, in order to grasp its meaning. Nietzsche, Bataille, and Blanchot, on the contrary, try through experience to reach that point of life which lies as close as possible to the impossibility of living, which lies at the limit or the extreme. They attempt to gather the maximum amount of intensity and impossibility at the same time. (Foucault 1991: 31; translation modified)

Whereas phenomenology sought to find within daily experience an ultimately integrated subject, the more transgressive thinkers he preferred gave experience

> the task of "tearing" the subject from itself in such a way that it is no longer the subject as such, or that it is completely "other" than itself so that it may arrive at its annihilation, its dissociation. It is this de-subjectifying undertaking, the idea of a "limit-experience" that

tears the subject from itself, which is the fundamental lesson that I have learned from these authors. (Foucault 1991: 31–2)

Accordingly, Gilles Deleuze could claim Foucault's major achievement was "the conversion of phenomenology to epistemology . . . Everything is knowledge, and this is the first reason why there is no 'savage experience': there is nothing beneath or prior to knowledge" (Deleuze 1988: 109).

Jean-François Lyotard, himself an early adherent of Maurice Merleau-Ponty's version of phenomenology, ultimately came to similar conclusions. In *The Differend* (1983), he acknowledged that "an experience can be described only by means of a phenomenological dialectic," but then added that

the idea of an experience presupposes that of an I which forms itself (*Bildung*) by gathering in the properties of things that come up (events) and which constitutes reality by effectuating their temporal synthesis. It is in relation to this I that events are phenomena. Phenomenology derives its name from this. But the idea of the I and that of experience which is associated with it are not necessary for the description of reality. They come from the subordination of the question of truth to the doctrine of evidence (Lyotard 1988: 45–6).[2]

Auschwitz, or more precisely the way it has become a proper name for the ineffability of history and the impossibility of its capture by speculative discourse, had given the lie to the phenomenological concept of experience, which could be traced all the way back to Hegel's *Phenomenology of Spirit*. "Can one still speak of experience in the case of the 'Auschwitz' model?," Lyotard asked, and then, following Theodor Adorno, responded firmly that one could not (Lyotard 1989: 364).

How valid, we need to ask, was this denunciation of "lived experience" so insistently leveled by post-phenomenological critics? Did they do justice to the multiple ways in which experience was evoked in the phenomenological tradition? Were perhaps some of their own alternative usages anticipated in the work of certain of their targets? To answer these questions, it will be necessary to step back and provide a less tendentious recapitulation of the role of experience in the thought of the major phenomenological theorists. To make this dauntingly ambitious task a bit more manageable, we will restrict ourselves to the work of Edmund Husserl and Martin Heidegger with only an occasional nod to others who also explored its implications.

Any historian of the phenomenological movement will be immediately struck by the ironic fact that it was launched precisely in opposition to one powerful current of thought that had itself privileged experience in epistemological terms. What became stigmatized in Husserl's 1900 *Logical Investigations* as "psychologism" meant the genetic reduction of ideas to their contingent, experiential context, in either the individual psychologies of those who held them or the social groups out of which they came.[3] Even the grounding of ideas in a philosophical anthropology, species-wide in scope, was suspect. That is, Husserl was intent on rescuing secure knowledge from the relativist and naturalist implications of its situatedness in the lives of those who were the knowers. Insisting on disentangling Mind from the minds of fallible mortals, he disdained Protagorean anthropocentrism, in which man was the measure of all things. Included in the denunciation was the empiricism of a John Stuart Mill based on inductive method. "Truths" may seem persuasive for those who hold them as such, but it is wrong to confuse that conviction with an a priori criterion of veracity. The precise content of the ideal Mind might vary – mathematical truths, as Frege had stressed, or logical ones, as both he and Husserl argued, or even values, as other critics of psychologism like the neo-Kantian Heinrich Rickert had claimed – but in all cases, the point was to resist its reduction to judgments, assertions, or worldviews, in short, the subjective or intersubjective experiences of those who held them. "Logical absolutism" meant the rigorous separation of genesis from validity, the rejection of probability for certainty, and the denial that logic needed to be validated by any criteria of reasonableness outside its own intrinsic value.

But Husserl went beyond formal logic narrowly construed. It was possible, Husserl insisted, to get more direct and unmediated access to "the things themselves" and, indeed, to do so in such a way that they would yield up their essential truth, understood as their inherent sense or meaning, to the "scientific" eye of the phenomenologist. The ordinary world of everyday opinions, mere "doxa" with all of its fallibilities, could be transcended in the search for universally true knowledge, "episteme" that earns the right to be honored as pure intelligibility. All genetic questions about the contingent origins of those truths in the flux of becoming could be successfully suspended. "True beginnings, or origins, or rizōmata pantōn" (Husserl 1965: 146),[4] he argued, stood outside the ephemerality of the moment and overcame the prejudices of the day.

What distinguished Husserl's method of phenomenological description from that of more traditional rationalist or scientific approaches, however, was his provocative contention that experience, understood in a fresh and unexpected way, could itself be the immanent location for the appearance of those essential truths. In A. D. Smith's gloss of his position, "we should not, as self-responsible philosophers, accept as absolutely binding mere second-hand opinions or things of which we have some vague intelligence, but only those things which we have *directly experienced for ourselves*" (Smith 2003: 17). This meant overcoming both naïve naturalism and relativist historicism. A naturalist understanding of the world as comprised entirely of physical objects existing independently of conscious minds, which then experienced them through sense data, was as problematic as a historicist one that saw them in entirely genetic and culturalist terms. Opposed to the epistemological method derived from Cartesian dualism, with its strict separation of subject from object, and to more traditional methods of introspective self-reflection, Husserl sought to explore consciousness itself for "evidence" – and that was a critical word in his vocabulary, implying the unmediated and unqualified force of what is given to us[5] – of the ideal world. Describing the contents of that consciousness in a "rigorous" way, looking for the logos in the phenomena rather than proving it deductively, could yield up essential knowledge that was superior to the objectivist belief in a correspondence between what was "out there" in the world and "in here" in our minds. Against all odds, a passage was possible between the level of impure psychological events, temporal and relative to the knowing subject, to atemporal, ideal truths and meanings purified of any contingent, contextual dross.

The bridging concept was, of course, intentionality, derived in part from Franz Brentano,[6] which meant that consciousness was not self-contained and solipsistic, but always led out into – or was directed toward – the world of objects that appeared to it.

Every *cogito* contained an equally immediate and compelling *cogitatum*. Intentionality meant the tendency of subjective consciousness to strive toward an object as its teleological goal, the object providing the terminal focus for the subject. In Husserl's special lexicon, the intentional content or "noema" manifests itself in the "noetic" multiplicity of perceptions of its apparently objective existence.

Using Kant's vocabulary, but subtly altering its meaning by underplaying its active implication, Husserl argued that the subjectivity for whom the manifestation of noetic perceptions takes place can justly be called "transcendental." It suspends the empiricists' natural attitude, which takes for granted the givenness of external reality, and seeks understanding not in a naïve reflection in the mind *of* that external world, but in reflection *on* consciousness and its contents. Getting back to "the things themselves" can be accomplished only by returning to the apodictic self-evidence and presence of the data of our consciousness, the evidence of our lived experience. Going beyond Kant's purely formal understanding of knowledge, which eschewed any contact with noumenal things-in-themselves, Husserl believed his method would provide access to the essences of material reality as well. Through what he called an *épochè* (abstention from or bracketing of), all contingent aspects of a phenomenon and the subsequent "reduction" of its residue to an essential core, a noema (which he sought to distinguish from the inductive abstraction underlying objectivist natural science), absolute, not relative, knowledge of being could be achieved. Or more precisely, what was achieved through an act of immediate intellectual intuition – the kind of inspired, primordial seeing he called "eidetic" – was knowledge of ideal essences, the "ideas" of his first major work (Husserl 1980). What is revealed are meanings, which are themselves ultimately understood as rational.

What is not discovered, however, is whether or not these essential "ideas" actually exist in a world exterior to the mind that grasps them. For Husserl, in fact, the question of existence is itself bracketed as irrelevant to the scientific search for essential meanings. No logical law, he went so far as to insist in *Logical Investigations*, "implies a 'matter of fact,' not even the existence of presentations or judgments or other phenomena of knowledge. No logical law, properly understood, is a law for the facticities of mental life" (Husserl 1970: 104).

An enormous amount of ink has already been spilled in explicating, defending, and criticizing these ambitious claims, and this is not the place to attempt yet another serious analysis. For the issue of experience, however, the following points need to be emphasized. First, as Husserl put it in his *Crisis of European Sciences* of 1936, the crucial question was not "what do I experience?" but "what is my experience?" (Husserl 1954: 236–7). This meant that experience is not something a subject has of something outside, which then can be represented by internal imitation or reflection, but is itself the englobing site of consciousness and its intended object, whose ideal essence can be found only there. Phenomenology thus shared with other modern schools of thought, such as pragmatism and hermeneutics, a desire to expand experience beyond the narrow confines of its traditional epistemological understanding, whether Cartesian, Humean, or Kantian in inspiration. Experience was more than perception, sensation, or even synthetic a priori judgments about a world of phenomenal objects.

At times, the most fundamental version of experience seemed to earn Deleuze's dismissive label of "savage" (a term that had earlier been given a positive connotation in the work of Merleau-Ponty; see Lefort 1978). As Husserl put it in his *Cartesian Mediations*, "this beginning is the pure – and, so to speak, still dumb – experience which is now to be brought to the pure expression of its own meaning" (Husserl 1973a: 38fn.). Dumb experience involves what he called "indication" (*Anzeige*), in which one sign can point to another, but without any meaningfulness (e.g., a smiling face indicates happiness, but doesn't tell us its intrinsic significance). Only when it becomes "expression" (*Ausdruck*) will a sign bring out the meaning of originary experience, allowing access to the essential truths a rigorous science sought. In fact, because existence is irrelevant to essential meaning, an expression need not indicate any actual object in the world or the subjective state of a subject. Later commentators like Merleau-Ponty and Derrida would challenge the plausibility of this distinction (Merleau-Ponty 1962; Derrida 1973),[7] but it allowed Husserl to think he could find ideal essences amidst the flux of contingent subjective states and objective existences.

In fact, where Husserl's phenomenology differed from other anti-empiricist alternatives such as hermeneutics and pragmatism was in its far more ambitious goal of finding eternal, essential, ideal truths amid the flux of passing encounters between self and world or self and other, a goal that seemed to many ultimately comparable to Platonic idealism in its search for a priori truths. As Quentin Lauer has noted, Husserl optimistically sought a "logic of experience" by virtue of which "the 'reconciliation' of reason and experience will ultimately be complete, since reason itself will be a kind of experience, and experience itself will be rationalizable" (Lauer 1965: 77).

In *Experience and Judgment*, the work compiled posthumously in 1948 from several of Husserl's manuscripts, he emphasized that all predicative judgments in logic have to be grounded ultimately in prepredicative experience, defining the latter as the "self-evidence of objects." In fact, the very distinction between experience and subsequent judgments about experience Husserl sought to efface. Grounding judgments of all kinds, he argued, involves

> the task of the *retrogression to the world* as the universal ground of all particular experiences, as the *world of experience* immediately pregiven and prior to all logical functions. The retrogression to the world of experience is a *retrogression to the "life-world,"* i.e., to the world in which we are already living and which furnishes the ground for all cognitive performance and all scientific determination. (Husserl 1973b: 41)

If in Husserl's earlier work, the impulse was to leave behind experience in order to find essential truths that would transcend their contingent, contextual origins, in his later work, he stressed more and more retrogression into the lifeworld of prepredicative experience. What he called "founded experiences," which included more active reflections, were always grounded in "simple experiences," which were more passive in nature.

The audacity and ambition of Husserl's influential project have to be acknowledged, but its plausibility is another thing entirely.[8] For those of his followers who could not accept his scientific ideals or believe in the possibility of knowing pure, rational essences or pursue his search for transcendental subjectivity purged of all presuppositions and prejudices, it was his focus on the pre-reflective, environing world (*Umwelt*) of doxa and sensations, habits and beliefs that constituted Husserl's true legacy. As Merleau-Ponty was to put it, he kept getting a clearer and clearer picture of the residue left behind by all reflexive philosophy and of the fundamental fact that we exist before we reflect; so that, precisely to attain complete clarity about our situation, he ended by assigning, as the primary task of phenomenology, the description of the lived world (*Lebenswelt*), where Cartesian distinctions have not yet been made. (Merleau-Ponty 1964: 135)

This insight made it possible to mobilize the insights of phenomenology for progressive political projects, including the Marxism that Merleau-Ponty himself embraced for a while. For, "having started with a 'static phenomenology,' he ended with a 'genetic phenomenology' and a theory of 'intentional history' – in other words, a logic of history" (ibid.).

Whether or not the Marxist appropriation of phenomenology was fully persuasive – Merleau-Ponty himself came to doubt it at the end of his career – other aspects of the de-transcendentalization of Husserl's original project continued to attract positive attention. For example, his crucial distinction between the body as an object of observation from without, a body for natural scientific control (what he called *Körper*), and the body as lived from within and intertwined with subjective interiority (*Leib*), inspired a slew of phenomenological investigations of how the body had been alienated by modern science into an object of manipulation. It also led via the work of Sartre and Merleau-Ponty to a richer understanding of race relations explored by Third-World theorists like Frantz Fanon. Husserl's stress on the prepredicative *Lebenswelt* (lifeworld) as the a priori ground of all scientific thought likewise redirected attention to the concrete practices, institutions, and unreflected beliefs that subtended even the most seemingly disinterested, objective, and value-neutral procedures. It would, however, only be a short jump to seek the historically and culturally specific features of distinct lifeworlds, which Husserl's stubbornly transcendental essentialism had tried to deny.

For in addition to the uncertainty about his goal of grounding rigorous scientific knowledge and eternal ideal essences in the *Lebenswelt*, doubts were also often expressed about the ability of "experience" to lose its associations with psychologistic subjectivity. This latter doubt helps explain the initial hesitancy of Husserl's most distinguished follower, Martin Heidegger, in endorsing the concept of experience at all in his earliest work. For not only did he reject the goal of disinterested inquiry into ideal essences and jettison any transcendental notion of subjectivity, Heidegger also worried that "experience" – even in the form of the subjective *Erlebnisse* that Dilthey and other exponents of *Lebensphilosophie* had elevated over scientific *Erfahrungen* – suggested an inner, psychological event, which was separate from body and world.[9] Dasein's moods could not be reduced to mere private experiences, Heidegger warned, because they were able to disclose the world rather than merely express interiority. Openness to the world, not psychological richness, was the road to the presencing of Being. Self-evidence was not sufficient to ground knowledge of essential reality, because the punctual "self" to whom the world was made "evident" could not be the point of entry for the unveiling of ontological truth. As he put it in *Being and Time*,

Our everyday environmental experiencing [*Erfahren*], which remains directed both ontically and ontologically towards intraworldly entities, is not the sort of thing which can present Dasein in an ontically primordial manner for ontological analysis. Similarly our immanent perception of experiences (*Erlebnissen*) fails to provide a clue which is ontologically adequate. (Heidegger 1962: 226)[10]

Did Heidegger ever lose his initial suspicion of experience in any of its various acceptations? Was it always a synonym for the psychological subjectivism he was so much at pains to discredit? According to one commentator, Calvin O. Schrag,

> Heidegger never succeeds in formulating a consistent position on the role of experience in his *Existenz-ontologie*. For the most part, particularly in his earlier writings, he is discernibly critical of any "philosophy of experience." In *Being and Time*, he relegates – probably without due consideration – all philosophies of experience to the limbo of subjectivism. In his book on Kant [*Kant and the Problem of Metaphysics*, 1929] he takes pains to distinguish the design of the *Critique of Pure Reason* from the program of a possible philosophy of experience. Admittedly, in his later work, *Unterwegs zur Sprache*, he speaks more approvingly of experience, and suggests a close connection between experience and language. But the fact remains that the question about the structure and dynamics of experience is never squarely faced by Heidegger. (Schrag 1969: 265 n.4)

If Heidegger ever developed a more positive notion of experience, it was not by returning to traditional meanings of *Erfahrung*, which he associated with the experimental methods of modern science.[11] Indeed, he left behind Husserl's own methodological pretensions for a mode of thought that owed as much to poetic insight as rigorous *Wissenschaft*. Instead, a bit like Walter Benjamin, who famously defended *Erfahrung* against *Erlebnis* by giving it an entirely fresh reading,[12] he cautiously moved away from his disdain and embraced what might be called a notion of experience without the psychological subject. As Schrag indicates in the remarks cited above, this change involved a more positive attitude toward the relationship between language and experience, which are sometimes seen as opposed (especially when experience is tied to sense impressions and language is seen as merely a communicative medium). But it also involved a subtle revision of experience as a concept closer to what in his mature vocabulary would be called *Ereignis*.

The shift is hinted at in the gloss he made in 1950 of Hegel's *Phenomenology of Spirit* in *Holzwege*. This work has been translated into English as *Hegel's Concept of Experience* (Heidegger 1970).[13] In many respects, Heidegger distances himself from Hegel in his commentary: he criticizes the priority of the knowing subject in the notion of the Absolute Spirit, resists the triumphal recuperation of alienation in the narrative journey (the *Fahrt* implied by *Erfahrung*) of that subject's development, and challenges the ideal of full presence or *parousia* (the Christian idea of the "second coming") he sees underlying Hegel's dialectic. But significantly he reinterprets Hegel's notion of experience as a synonym for Being itself: "The parousia of the absolute takes place as phenomenology. Experience is Being, in accordance with which the Absolute wills itself to be" (Heidegger 1970: 149).[14] Hegel's still metaphysical understanding of ontology may have been faulty, according to Heidegger, but his linkage of Being and experience merits appreciation. "Because phenomenology is experience, the beingness of beings, therefore it is the gathering of self-appearance in concentration upon the appearance out of the light of the Absolute" (Heidegger 1970: 148).[15]

The role of *Ereignis* (normally translated as "event," but closer to "appropriation" in Heidegger's usage, and sometimes translated by the neologism "en-owning") gained in importance in his later work,[16] but even in his earlier work Heidegger had imbued it with the passive implication of experience, the waiting expectantly for something to happen rather than deliberately making it happen. As he put it in his later essay "On the Way to Language,"

> To undergo an experience with *something*, be it a thing, a person, or a god, means that this something befalls us, strikes us, comes over us, overwhelms us, and transforms us. When we talk of "undergoing" an experience we mean specifically that the experience is not of our making. To undergo here means that we endure it, suffer it, receive it as it strikes us, and submit to it. (Heidegger 1959: 59)

Heidegger also contrasted *Ereignisse* with experiences of objects that are set apart from a subject, the subject–object dualism he was so much at pains to overcome:

> Experience doesn't pass before me as thing that I set there as an object; rather I myself appropriate it (*er-eignes es*) to me, and it properly happens or "properizes" (*es er-eignet*) according to its essence. (Heidegger 1987: 75)

An *Ereignis* might well be a threatening one – expressing the link in German between *Erfahrung* and *Gefahr* (danger; see Heidegger 1994: 54)[17] – as in the case of modern technology, but it also might be an opportunity for the revelation of a deeper truth. The belonging that is suggested by the *eigen* in *Ereignis* (thus the plausibility of the neologism "en-owning") is not that of an object by a subject, but rather of *Dasein* by *Sein*. Because it is not the same as a natural process (*Vorgang*), an *Ereignis* can take the form of a radical rupture in the course of things, a sudden appearance of Being in the midst of quotidian existence.

Thus, the journey of experience – the *Fahrt* in *Erfahrung* – does not lead back to the point of departure, even at a higher level, as in the case of Hegelian dialectics, but is rather an interruption in the narrative flow. Charles Scott is thus able to say of *Beiträge zur Philosophie (Vom Ereignis)*, written in the late 1930s and published in 1989,

> Heidegger is in the midst of an *Erfahrung* – an experience of traveling along, a "progress" in older usage – as he writes; but instead of being centered in his own private world of feeling and observation, as many travelers are, he finds that he is drawn out by a troubling, persistent, indeterminate thought that is not his to own. "It" has no clear way leading to it. This thinking is thus more like exploring than a trip defined by a destination, and it does not present itself as naming any specific thing. (Scott 2001: 1)

Wandering with an openness to the world rather than purposefully thrusting oneself forward to ever-higher planes of truth and reason allows experience in this sense to happen.

Robert Bernasconi aptly summarizes the differences between Hegel and Heidegger in the following terms:

the former is tied to the rule of presencing and the latter commemorates it. Phenomenology for Hegel is a *parousia*, whereas for Heidegger it is letting the non-apparent appear as nonapparent. So Heidegger's word *Erfahrung* is not set up in opposition to Hegel's, but, in his remembrance of Hegel's concept of experience as a presencing, he lets the oblivion of Being appear as the unsaid of what is said. (Bernasconi 1985: 85)

Whereas Hegel is confident of overcoming the lack or alienation that occurs during the perilous journey that is experience, and understands the recollection at the end of the process as an anamnestic ingathering of what had been lost, Heidegger remains suspended at the level of the search. Experience thus confirms lack rather than overcomes it, and whatever commemoration occurs is not of the perpetual presence of Being, but rather of its oblivion.

This version of experience as *Ereignis* was, in fact, very different from the notion of "lived experience" that was so scornfully disdained by post-phenomenological critics. Perhaps because of their identification of it with the version they attributed to French disciples of Husserl and Heidegger, in particular the generation that called itself existentialist, they stressed its connection with traceless presence and self-contained interiority, even if the latter was not to be understood in psychological terms. Because of the traditionally subjective connotations of the term, they understood "lived experience" to be irrevocably tied to the notion of a strong self or agent able to learn from that experience. As such, this was a subject whose personal *Bildung* could be understood as a microcosmic variant of the learning process that Hegelian Idealism in particular had imposed on history. It was a subject whose life history was a coherent narrative, at least from a retrospective point of view. And if this version of experience as an emplotted story, whose meaning was established retrospectively, were problematic, so too was the prelinguistic alternative that Deleuze would dismiss as "savage experience." For it suggested a kind of innocence that was the very opposite of experience in most of its traditional acceptations.

There were, however, aspects of the phenomenological invocation of experience, as we have briefly outlined it above, that do not easily conform to either of these images. Ever since Husserl stressed the importance of intentionality, however much he may have wanted it to provide a smooth transition from the interior world of consciousness to essential things in themselves outside, there was an impulse in phenomenology to get beyond self-sufficient consciousness to something more. Experience (*Erfahrung*, if not *Erlebnis*) was, after all, always of an "other," either a thing or another consciousness, never entirely subjective in any solipsistic sense of that term. Experience inevitably involves an encounter with an alterity that cannot be reduced to a mere emanation of the constitutive subject. It transcended the model of possessive individualism that some critics argued tacitly informed the stress on "authenticity" or *Eigentlichkeit* in early Heidegger (Adorno 1973).

Moreover, although Husserl had struggled to find in experience rational essences, ideal truths, and eternal meanings that would transcend the contingent flux of existential becoming, his injunction to retrogress to the lifeworld of prepredicative experience meant that the latter in one guise or another inevitably crept back in. Heidegger and the existentialists thus put the question of existence back on the agenda, refusing to bracket it as irrelevant as had Husserl. The "dumb" experience of "indication" refused to disappear once the passage had been made to the more meaningful experience of "expression." However much it tried to purify its method, transcendental phenomenology could not keep its existential potential at bay forever.

A material eidetics could not, in other words, avoid going out into the world of historical and natural reality, however resolute its resistance to psychologism. Merleau-Ponty in particular would insist on its opening to biological and psychological discourses, even if he accepted the distinction between the body as lived (*Leib*) and the body as scientific object (*Körper*). In fact, among the most profound legacies of Husserl's phenomenology were the social and cultural investigations he inspired, which extended from cinema studies and art history to psychology and sociology, anywhere where the traditional dualism of subject and object might be challenged.

It was, however, in Heidegger's radical rethinking of experience under the rubric of *Ereignis* that the most explicit counter-example to the critique of "lived experience" can be found. As we have seen, it turned against any residue of Hegelian post-facto narrativization and meta-subjective constitution, as well as the idea of fulfilled temporal presence. Instead, it suggested a notion of experience as rupture and dislocation, which reintroduced the moment of passivity, even heteronomy, that always sets experience apart from more active concepts like action or agency or praxis.

Not surprisingly, there has been a recent reconsideration of the alleged conflict between the legacy of phenomenology and the theories of those who set themselves against it in the 1970s and after. A number of studies have found surprising anticipations of poststructuralist positions in the phenomenological tradition, broadly speaking. David Wood, for example, contends that "if phenomenology has an ethical dimension, it is not its alleged foundationalism or its search for essential intuition, it is this patience with *experience* . . . If negotiation with alterity is the locus of the ethical, 'experience' is the essentially contested marker of that site" (Wood 2000: 24–5). He goes on to claim that Derrida might thus be considered a "radical phenomenologist," despite his early critique of experience.[17] Tilottima Rajan also argues that Derrida plays off the transcendental and existentialist impulses in phenomenology, adding that the influence of Jewish thinkers like Edmund Jabès and Emmanuel Levinas alerted him to an idea of "experience no longer linked positivistically to presence but rather to 'that which is most irreducible within experience: the passage and departure toward the other'" (Rajan 2002: 127).

If there is any major implication of these reassessments of the relationship between phenomenological and post-phenomenological theories for the question of experience, it would be that no single formula can adequately do justice to the experience of "experience" in the tradition we have been discussing. That is, the journey that experience itself so often connotes, the encounter with otherness that produces something beyond what was present at its beginning, the opening to newness that takes whomever makes the journey beyond their point of departure, has itself been undergone by phenomenologists' disparate efforts to make sense of this vexed term. Along the way several alternatives were explored: experience purged of its psychologistic dross, understood transcendentally, and providing access to rational, eternal essences; experience as existentially meaningful and located in the body prior to the objectifying gaze of science; experience as the passive waiting for a disruption in routine existence producing an "event" opening up a deeper connection with Being. What all shared was an attenuation of the traditional link between experience and the strong, centered subject of consciousness subtending it, a subject, either individual or collective, capable of a process of self-improvement or *Bildung*. Whether in its Cartesian or Hegelian form, this was a subject that was rejected by the twentieth-century phenomenological tradition. Instead, its adherents contributed to the paradoxical idea of experience without a subject, which was also defended in their own vocabularies by pragmatists, Critical Theorists, and, indeed, post-structuralist thinkers as well.[18]

Notes

1   Derrida's critique of phenomenological notions of experience was likely reinforced by the connection between Husserl's notion of evidence and the privileging of sight, for example, in *Cartesian Meditations*, where he writes "Evidence is, in an extremely broad sense, an '*experiencing*' of something that is, and is thus; it is precisely a mental seeing of something itself" (Husserl 1960: 52). For a discussion of Derrida's complicated response to ocularcentrism, see Jay 1993, ch. 9. For an analysis of his claims about presence in Husserl, see Bernet 1983.

2   Later he would link the idea of experience in twentieth-century phenomenology to its predecessor in Hegel's *Phenomenology of Spirit* (see Lyotard 1988: 88).

3   Husserl's earlier work, *Philosophie der Arithmetik* (Husserl 1970), was itself castigated as psychologistic by Gottlob Frege, but he soon absorbed this lesson and resolutely attacked it wherever it appeared. For a general account of psychologism and Husserl's role in criticizing it, see Kusch 1995.

4   The Greek phrase means "the roots of all."

5   For a discussion of the implications of *Evidenz* (sometimes translated as "self-evidence") for Husserl, see Smith 2003: 50.

6   For a useful introduction to Brentano's notion of intentionality and Husserl's partial appropriation of it, see Chisholm 1967. The concept of intentionality can be traced back to the Scholastics, for example in St. Anselm's ontological proof of God.

7   For considerations of their critiques, see, respectively, Taminiaux 1990: 131–4; and D'Amico 1999: 230–42.

8   For a still valuable critique from a dialectical perspective, see Adorno 1983.

9   For a comparison of Heidegger and Dilthey, see Bambach 1995.

10 For a discussion of this passage, see Dreyfus 1991: 177.

11 For a summary of his various discussions of *Erfahrung*, see the helpful entry on "experience" in Inwood 1999: 63.

12 The literature on Benjamin's analysis of the two types of experience is voluminous. For my own attempt to sort it out, which cites the most important interpretations, see Jay 2004: ch. 8. For comparisons of Heidegger and Benjamin, see Caygill 1994 and Benjamin 1994; and van Reijin 1998; Long 2001; and Ziarek 2001: ch. 1.

13 The translations of Hegel are by Kenley Royce Dove, those of Heidegger are not credited. For a helpful gloss on this book, see Bernasconi 1985: ch. 6.

14 The German reads, "Die Parusie des Absoluten geschieht als die Phänomenologie. Die Erfahrung ist das Sein, demgemäß das Absolute bei uns sein will" (Heidegger 1977: 204).

15 The German reads, "Weil die Phänomenologie die Erfahrung ist, die Seiendheit des Seienden, deshalb ist sie die Versammlung des Sicherscheinens auf das Erscheinen aus dem Scheinen des Absoluten" (Heidegger 1977: 203).

16 See the entry under "Event" in Inwood 1999.

17   See also Terada 2001.
18   These variations on the theme of experience without a strong notion of the subject are explored in Jay 2004.

References and Further Reading

Adorno, T. (1973) *The Jargon of Authenticity* (trans. K. Tarnowski and F. Will). London: Routledge (original work published 1964).

—— (1983) *Against Epistemology: A Metacritique* (trans. W. Domingo). Cambridge, MA: Harvard University Press (original work published 1956).

Bambach, C. (1995) *Heidegger, Dilthey, and the Crisis of Historicism*. Ithaca, NY: Cornell University Press.

Benjamin, A. (1994) Time and task: Benjamin and Heidegger showing the present. In A. Benjamin and P. Osborne (eds.), *Walter Benjamin's Philosophy: Destruction and Experience* (pp. 212–45). London: Routledge.

Benjamin, A., and Osborne, P. (eds.) (1994) *Walter Benjamin's Philosophy: Destruction and Experience*. London: Routledge.

Bernasconi, R. (1985) *The Question Of Language In Heidegger's History of Being*. Atlantic Highlands, NJ: Humanities Press.

Bernet, R. (1983) Is the present ever present? Phenomenology and the metaphysics of presence. In J. Sallis (ed.), *Husserl and Contemporary Thought*. Atlantic Highlands, NJ: Humanities Press, 1, pp. 85–112.

Caygill, H. (1994) Benjamin, Heidegger and the destruction of tradition. In A. Benjamin and P. Osborne (eds.), *Walter Benjamin's Philosophy: Destruction and Experience* (pp. 1–30). London: Routledge.

Chisholm, R. M. (1967) Brentano on descriptive psychology and the intentional. In E. N. Lee and M. Mandelbaum (eds.), *Phenomenology and Existentialism*. Baltimore, MD: Johns Hopkins University Press.

D'Amico, R. (1999) *Contemporary Continental Philosophy*. Boulder, CO: Westview Press.

Deleuze, G. (1988) *Foucault* (trans. S. Hand). Minneapolis: University of Minnesota Press (original work published 1986).

Derrida, J. (1973) *Speech and Phenomena and Other Essays on Husserl's Theory of Signs* (trans. D. B. Allison). Evanston, IL: Northwestern University Press (original work published 1967).

—— (1976) *Of Grammatology* (trans. G. C. Spivak). Baltimore, MD: Johns Hopkins University Press (original work published 1967).

—— (1981) *Positions* (trans. A. Bass). Chicago: University of Chicago Press (original work published 1972).

Dreyfus, H. L. (1991) *Being-In-The-World, A Commentary On Heidegger's* Being and Time, *Division 1*. Cambridge, MA: MIT Press.

Foucault, M. (1973) *The Order of Things: An Archaeology of the Human Sciences* (trans. A. Sheridan). New York: Pantheon Books (original work published 1966).

—— (1991) How an "experience-book" is born. In R. J. Goldstein and J. Cascaito (ed. and trans.), *Remarks on Marx: Conversations with Duccio Trombadori*. New York: Semiotext(e).

Heidegger, M. (1959) The nature of language. In P. Hertz (ed. and trans.), *On the Way to Language*. New York: Harper & Row (original work published 1957).

—— (1962) *Being and Time* (trans. J. Macquarrie and E. Robinson). New York: Pantheon Books (original work published 1927).

—— (1970) *Hegel's Concept of Experience* (trans. A. Hofstadter). New York: Harper & Row (original work published 1942–3).

—— (1977) *Gesamtausgabe*, vol. 5, *Holzwege*. Frankfurt: Vittorio Klostermann.

—— (1987) *Gesamtausgabe*, vol. 56/57, *Zur Bestimmung der Philosophie*. Frankfurt: Vittorio Klostermann.

—— (1994) Die Gefahr. In *Gesamtausgabe*, vol. 79, *Bremer und Freiburger Vorträge*. Frankfurt: Vittorio Klostermann.

Husserl, E. (1954) *Krisis Der Europäischen Wissenschaft Und Die Transzendentale Phänomenologie* [Crisis of the European sciences and transcendental phenomenology]. The Hague: Martinus Nijhoff.

—— (1960) *Cartesian Meditations: An Introduction to Phenomenology* (trans. D. Cairns). The Hague: Martinus Nijhoff (original lectures delivered 1929).

—— (1965) Philosophy as rigorous science (trans. Q. Lauer). In *Phenomenology and the Crisis of Philosophy* (pp. 71–148). New York: Harper & Row (original work published 1910).

—— (1970) *Philosophie der Arithmetik*. Mit ergänzenden Texten (1898–1901). *Husserliana*, vol. 12 (ed. L. Eley). The Hague: Martinus Nijhoff.

—— (1973a) *Cartesian Meditations* (trans. D. Cairns). The Hague: Martinus Nijhoff (original lectures delivered 1929).

—— (1973b) *Experience and Judgment: Investigations in a Genealogy of Logic* (ed. L. Landgrebe, trans. J. S. Churchill and K. Ameriks). Evanston, IL: Northwestern University Press (original work published 1939).

—— (1973c) *Logical Investigations* (trans. J. N. Findlay). London: Routledge (original work published 1913).

—— (1980) *Ideas Pertaining to a Pure Phenomenology and to a Phenomenological Philosophy, Third Book* (trans. T. Klein and W. Pohl). Boston: Kluwer (original work published 1913).

Inwood, M. (1999) *A Heidegger Dictionary*. Oxford: Oxford University Press.

Jay, M. (1993) *Downcast Eyes: The Denigration of Vision in Twentieth-Century French Thought*. Berkeley: University of California Press.

—— (2004) *Songs of Experience: European and American Variations on a Universal Theme*. Berkeley: University of California Press.

Kusch, M. (1995) *Psychologism: A Case Study of the Sociology of Philosophical Knowledge*. London: Routledge.

Lauer, Q. (1965) *Phenomenology: Its Genesis And Prospect*. New York: Harper & Row.

Lefort, C. (1978) L'idée de être brut et d'esprit sauvage. In *Sur une colonne absente: Écrits autour de Merleau-Ponty* (pp. 8–44). Paris: Gallimard.

Long, C. P. (2001) Art's fateful hour: Benjamin, Heidegger, art and politics. *New German Critique*, 83, 89–115.

Lyotard, J.-F. (1988) *The Differend: Phrases in Dispute* (trans G. V. D. Abbeele). Minneapolis: University of Minnesota Press (original work published 1983).

—— (1989) Discussions, or phrasing "after Auschwitz." In A. Benjamin (ed.), *The Lyotard Reader* (pp. 360–92). Oxford: Oxford University Press.

Merleau-Ponty, M. (1962) *Phenomenology of Perception* (trans. C. Smith). New York: Routledge (original work published 1945).

—— (1964) *Sense and Nonsense* (trans. H. L. Dreyfus and P. A. Dreyfus). Evanston, IL: Northwestern University Press (original work published 1948).

Rajan, T. (2002) *Deconstruction and the Remainders of Phenomenology*. Stanford, CA: Stanford University Press.

Schrag, C. O. (1969) *Experience and Being*. Minneapolis: University of Minnesota Press.

Scott, C. E. (2001) Introduction: Approaching Heidegger's *Contributions to Philosophy* and its companion. In C. E. Scott, S. M. Schoenbohm, D. Vallega-Neu, and A. Vallega (eds.), *Companion to Heidegger's* Contributions to Philosophy (pp. 1–14). Bloomington: Indiana University Press.

103

Smith, A. D. (2003) *Husserl and the* Cartesian Meditations. London: Routledge.

Taminiaux, J. (1990) *Dialectic and Difference: Modern Thought and the Sense of Human Limits* (ed. and trans. R. Crease and J. T. Decker). Atlantic Highlands, NJ: Humanities Press.

Terada, R. (2001) *Feeling in Theory: Emotion after the "Death of the Subject."* Cambridge, MA: Harvard University Press.

van Reijin, W. (1998) *Der Schwarzwald und Paris: Heidegger und Benjamin* [The Black Forest and Paris: Heidegger and Benjamin]. Munich: W. Fink.

Wood, D. (2000) *Thinking after Heidegger*. Cambridge: Polity.

Ziarek, K. (2001) *The Historicity of Experience: Modernity, the Avant-Garde, and the Event*. Evanston, IL: Northwestern University Press.

8

Husserl's Reductions and the Role They Play in His Phenomenology

DAGFINN FØLLESDAL

The reductions were introduced by Husserl as part of his transcendental turn, which took place around 1905. He had used the word "reduction" before, in 1891, at the very end of his first work, *Philosophy of Arithmetic* (Husserl 1970b: 261ff.). However, the term is there used in the sense of reducing one kind of mathematical representation to some standard systematical form. For example, if we ask: "Which is greater, $18 + 49$ or 7×9?" we can answer this by "reducing" "$18 + 49$" to the standard form "67," and "7×9" to "63" and we then have an immediate answer to our question.

In his next major work, *Logical Investigations*, from 1900/1 (Husserl 1975, 1984), there is no talk of reductions. Then in the *Ideas* (1913; cited as Husserl 1950), *First Philosophy* (lectures delivered 1923/4; cited as Husserl 1956, 1959), *Cartesian Meditations* (lectures delivered 1929; cited as Husserl 1988a, 1988b), and his last work, the *Crisis* (1954; cited as Husserl 1970a), reduction, in a quite new sense, becomes a central topic. Husserl discusses several kinds of reduction, the main ones being the eidetic, the transcendental, and the phenomenological reduction. Husserl interpreters disagree on what the reductions are and how they relate to one another. Some scholars find them so enigmatic that they write them off, together with all the rest of Husserl's transcendental philosophy. This reaction testifies to the central role the reductions play in Husserl's later philosophy: the reductions are the basic methodological tools of his transcendental philosophy; the reductions and Husserl's transcendental philosophy require one another in order to make sense.

In this chapter we will give an interpretation of the reductions that fits in well with Husserl's texts and, I hope, makes sense.

Some Basic Ideas of Husserl's Phenomenology

In order to understand the reductions and the role they play, we must first know the basic structure of Husserl's phenomenology, and in particular notions and distinctions that he introduced in connection with his transcendental turn. A basic idea from the beginning of phenomenology, in the *Logical Investigations* and hence before the transcendental turn, is *intentionality*, the directedness of consciousness. Let us explain it with the help of one of Husserl's favorite examples, the seeing of a dice. When we see a dice, we see an object which has six sides, some of which can be seen from where we are, others can be seen if we twist it or move around it. The sides are square, but they appear as four-sided polygons unless we look at them from directly above. We have grown so accustomed to all of this we that we do not notice our complicated set of anticipations. Only when something goes wrong do we become aware that something disturbs. For example, if we move around and find no rear side, we may start reflecting and may discover that a lot of anticipatory structuring has been going on unnoticed. However, once we find a way of restructuring our experience, for example, by taking what we have in front of us as three square pieces put together to form a corner, which from some perspectives looks like a dice, we have an explanation of what happened and we can go on with our activities as before – until some other breakdown happens; according to Husserl there is no stage in perception where our anticipations are guaranteed to be successful.

The reflective attitude that we for a moment fell into when we tried to find out what disturbed, is a simple example of the *transcendental* reduction. We are reflecting on the structuring activity of our consciousness and the corresponding structure we expected to find in the experienced world. This reduction is not as mysterious as it might sound, and in a moment we shall expound and discuss it more systematically. Before we turn to this, however, let us notice that our dice example also may serve to illustrate the other main reduction in Husserl: the eidetic reduction. Let us now see how this happens. Looking at the dice, I may focus on this material object, which weighs approximately one-eighth of an ounce, which I inherited from my grandfather and which I would therefore not exchange with any other dice. I am seeing this particular physical object. When in this way I perceive a physical object, I am, Husserl says, in the natural attitude. However, looking at the dice I may also focus on its shape, I may disregard all the individual oddities of my dice and concentrate on the cubic form which is exhibited by my dice and also by many other objects. Further, my dice is not only a cube; it also exemplifies many other geometrical shapes, some of them more general, such as a polyhedron or a parallelepiped, or regularity, convexity, and so on. Each of these shapes can be the object I am focusing on when my eyes are directed toward the dice. What reaches my eyes may all the time be the same, but the object I am studying need not be this particular physical object, but may be any of the many features that are instantiated by it. The features need not be geometrical, they may be arithmetical, such as the five dots on the side turned toward me, or topological. They need not be mathematical at all; they can also be the color of the dice, its weight, etc. There is no limit to the number of features that a thing can instantiate.

All these features Husserl calls *eidos* (plural: *eide*), or *essences*. When Husserl writes about essences, he is hence not using the word as a label for something that is unique for each object, what is sometimes called individual essence. On the contrary, an essence is for him something that can be shared by many objects.

When we turn from observing a concrete physical object to studying one of these general features, we perform what he called the *eidetic* reduction. Again, this does not seem mysterious or difficult. It is something we do every day. Mathematicians do it more often than others, but we all do it, when we are turning from the concrete individuals to general features of the objects around us.

There remains the phenomenological reduction. But as we shall see, once we have the other two reductions, we also have the phenomenological one. Let us now, however, go through all of this somewhat more systematically.

Intentionality. Noema, Noesis, Hyle

First, intentionality: Husserl's teacher Brentano, from whom Husserl learned about intentionality, in two oft-quoted paragraphs defines intentionality as the *directedness* of our consciousness upon an object:

> Every mental phenomenon is characterized by what the Scholastics of the Middle Ages called the intentional (or mental) inexistence of an object, and what we might call, though not wholly unambiguously, reference to a content, direction toward an object (which is not to be understood here as meaning a thing), or immanent objectivity. Every mental phenomenon includes something as object within itself, although they do not do so in the same way. In presentation, something is presented, in judgment something is affirmed or denied, in love loved, in hate hated, in desire desired and so on.
>
> This intentional inexistence is characteristic exclusively of mental phenomena. No physical phenomenon exhibits anything like it. We can, therefore, define mental phenomena by saying that they are those phenomena which contain an object intentionally within themselves.[1]

Husserl was very much in sympathy with Brentano's idea, but he saw two problems: First, some acts have no object. For example, when we hallucinate or when we think about the largest prime number or Pegasus, there is no object, although we might think so. What then about the act's directedness? Second, even when the act has an object, how does the act come to relate to it? Brentano gives no account of how this happens, he just states that the act is directed toward an object. Husserl endeavors to overcome both of these problems by introducing the notion of a meaning associated with the act. This gets its fully developed form in the *Ideas*, where he develops a theory of a *noema*.

The noema is a structure that is associated with each act, corresponding to all the "anticipations" we have about the acts' object. I put the word "anticipations" in quotation marks, because normally an anticipation is something we are aware of, but for Husserl, the noema has constituents that we are not aware of, "anticipations" that we have tacitly taken over from our culture and never thought about, even bodily settings, which we would have great difficulty describing in words even if we should be made aware of them.[2] Also, among our "anticipations" when we perceive an object is the anticipation that the object has features that go far beyond what we anticipate, features that we have never thought about and that are not even tacitly anticipated, features that have nothing corresponding to them in the noema, except our recognition that the object goes far beyond our anticipations. It is *transcendent*, Husserl said; it is not exhausted by our anticipations, and it never will be. As we go on examining the object, walk around it, turn it around, explore it with our various senses or with scientific instruments, our anticipations always go beyond what "meets the eye" or our other senses. The object, in turn, goes beyond anything that we ever anticipate.

Husserl conceives of the noema as an answer to the second question above: How does the act relate to its object? It also provides an answer to the first question: Acts may have this kind of directedness without their having any object. We often have anticipations that fail to be fulfilled. Husserl's way of dealing with acts without objects is strikingly parallel to Frege's way of dealing with expressions without a reference: the expression may have a meaning, a *Sinn*, without there being an object that matches this meaning. Husserl himself points to this parallel between noema and linguistic meaning in several places. In the third volume of the *Ideas*, which he never completed, he writes: "the noema is nothing but a generalization of the notion of meaning (*Bedeutung*) to the field of all acts."[3] However, while Frege was rather taciturn concerning the notion of meaning and struggled with it mostly in his unpublished manuscripts, Husserl discusses the noema extensively. We need not go into his theory of the noema here. We shall however, take note of another, correlative notion, which is pertinent to our understanding the reductions: the *noesis*. Each act has a noesis, which is the experiential counterpart to the noema. The noeses are the structuring experiences, those that give structure, or meaning, to the act. While the noema is the meaning *given* in an act, the noesis is the meaning-*giving* element in the act.

The noeses are experiences, unlike the noemata, which are timeless structures. There is also a second kind of experience in our acts, that Husserl calls the *hyle* (using the Greek word for matter). The hyle are experiences we typically have when our senses are affected, but also can have when we have fever or are affected by drugs and the like. The hyle and the noesis have to fit in with one another; the hyle should be *filling* components of the noesis and correspondingly of the noema. This is what we meant by the metaphor "meet the eye" above: when we perceive, some of the "anticipations" in our noema are filled by hyle, others are not; they just point to further features of the object and may become filled when we go on exploring the object. These unfilled anticipations may conflict with the hyletic experiences we get when we explore the object, in that case, an "explosion" of the noema takes place, we have to revise our conception of what we perceive, we have to come up with another noema that fits in with our hyletic experiences. The hyle therefore *constrain* the noesis we can have in a given situation and thereby what noema we can have.

However, the hyle do not constrain us down to uniqueness; whatever hyle we have, there are always many different noeses that are compatible with them, noeses that differ in the anticipations that go beyond those that are presently filled. The object of an act, even an act of perception, is not uniquely fixed by the sensory experiences we have; there is always some slack, although we normally are not aware of this, except in special situations of the kind that Gestalt psychologists discussed under the heading "ambiguous" pictures. The hyle's constraining effect is crucial to bringing about our notion of *reality* and thereby the distinction between reality and fantasy. In fantasy there are no constraints, and as a consequence of this, fantasy lacks the reality character characteristic of perception. The reality character of the object is also reflected in the noema and noesis, in their so-called *thetic* component. This and the other components of the noema and noesis are, however, not needed in order to understand Husserl's reductions, and we shall therefore not discuss them here.[4]

As noted, in the natural attitude and also in the eidetic attitude we are not aware of these three elements of our acts, the noema, the noesis, and the hyle. They only come to our awareness when we reflect on our acts and their structure. These three elements, noema, noesis, and hyle, remain hidden, although they are crucial to the way we experience the world. Husserl called them *transcendental*. This should not be confused with transcendent, which was mentioned earlier. "Transcendent" means "inexhaustible," while "transcendental" means hidden, but crucial for our experience. It is this latter notion that is important in connection with the reductions.

Eidos. The Eidetic Reduction

We are now ready to go into the first of Husserl's three reductions, the *eidetic reduction*. This is so called because it brings us to the eidos, or essences, of things. We touched briefly on the eidos in our discussion of the dice. Let us now consider it more closely. When I am facing the dice, my consciousness can be directed toward a number of different objects: toward a dice or some other object that looks like a dice from where I am, for example, as we noted, three square pieces put together to form a corner, or any number of other physical objects, the only requirement being that the noema of the act directed toward that object be compatible with the hyletic experiences I have. However, as we noted when we discussed the dice, my consciousness can also be directed toward one of the features of the dice, for example, its cubic form. In that case, I have anticipations of what kind of experiences I will get when the circumstances change or I perform certain actions. For example, I expect that if I count the corners I will get eight, and if I count the edges, I will get twelve. Some of these anticipations are similar to those I have when the object of my act is this concrete particular dice. However, I have no anticipations concerning this particular dice. I may take it away and replace it with another dice, and none of my anticipations will be violated. My anticipations when the object of my act is the cubic form include therefore only a subset of the anticipations I have when the object of my act is the concrete particular dice. Hence the label "reduction" for the passage from the experience of a particular concrete object to the experience of an eidos.

The object of my act in a given situation need therefore not be a concrete physical object, it can be an eidos. Given an act and the constraints imposed upon us by the hyle, the object of the act can in fact be any one of a large number of different physical objects, and it can also be any one of a number of general features, or eide. What object I experience, is underdetermined by the hyle. Husserl calls any act that is constrained in this way an *intuition*. These acts make reality claims; their noema has a thetic component that corresponds to our regarding the object of the act as real. According to Husserl, intuitions and no other acts yield evidence for what the world is like. The three notions intuition, constraint, and reality are in this way intimately connected with one another.

Intuition that is directed toward physical objects Husserl calls perception. Intuition directed toward eidos or essences he calls eidetic intuition or essential insight (*Wesensschau*). Husserl regards himself an empiricist: all evidence reaches us through our senses. However, he argues that philosophers have jumped too quickly from empiricism to physicalism, the view that the only objects there are physical objects. Many of our acts are directed toward essences. And to the extent that they are constrained in the way we have described, they give us evidence concerning essences and their various properties.

The examples of essences that we have given so far have been cubes and other geometrical forms and the number of dots on the side of a dice. These all belong to mathematics. However, as noted earlier, Husserl conceived of the study of many other kinds of essences; any kind of similarity between objects points to an essence, for example, colors, and also "humanity," the feature all humans have in common. He conceived of a variety of eidetic disciplines in addition to geometry, arithmetic, and other mathematical disciplines. Each of them would study an essence or an inter-related group of essences. One of the methods they would use would be *eidetic variation*: one will focus on an essence and go through a number of examples that instantiate this essence. The examples need not be physical objects, it is easier and quicker to *imagine* new cases and variations and thereby explore what features this essence has and how it relates to other essences. Since we focus on essences when we study eidos, and not on the objects that exemplify these essences, it does not matter for us whether these objects exist or not. By varying the examples of objects that instantiate the essence, we may prove existence results: we may find an instance that instantiates a particular combination of features. However, negative results, that there is no object satisfying a certain combination of features, require other types of considerations.

Husserl knew the method of variation from the philosopher/mathematician Bernard Bolzano (1781–1848) who developed this method in his *Theory of Science*.[5] Husserl could also point to his mathematics teacher Karl Weierstrass, who used the method to discover a number of results in the foundations of mathematics, among them that there are continuous functions that are nowhere differentiable. (This result was proved 30 years earlier by Bolzano, but it was unknown to Weierstrass and Husserl, since Bolzano was not permitted to publish his results.)

The *eidetic reduction* is the transition from the *natural* attitude, where we are directed toward particular material objects, to the *eidetic* attitude, where we are directed toward essences (see Figure 8.1).

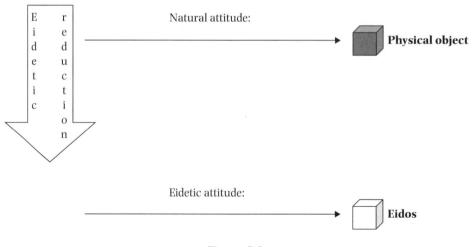

Figure 8.1

The Transcendental Reduction

Now on to the transcendental reduction. As already hinted at in our discussion of the dice in the beginning of the chapter, the transcendental reduction consists in our reflecting on the act itself rather than on its object. We then discover that our being directed upon the object consists of a complicated interplay of three elements: the structuring experiences in the act, *noeses*, the correlated structure given in the act, the *noema*, and the filling and constraining experiences, *hyle*.

Husserl argues that with some training one may be able to systematically study these three elements. One will then disregard the normal object of the act. One will not doubt that it is there, or wonder whether it is there, or check out one's anticipations by exploring the object further. Husserl calls this change of attitude an *epoché*, using the old Greek word for abstaining from judgment. He also calls this a *bracketing* of the object. One will simply not be concerned with the object, but solely with the structure of the act in which we experience the object. We will study the act's noesis, noema, and hyle. The *transcendental reduction* is this change of focus, from our object-directed attitude to an act-directed attitude. It leads us from the objects that we are concerned with in the natural or in the eidetic attitude to the transcendental objects, noema, noesis, and hyle, and also to the *transcendental ego*, the aspect of our ego that we are not aware of when we are considering ourselves as physical things in the material world, but that we become aware of when we discover the structuring activity of our own consciousness.

This reflective turn is called a reduction because it leaves out something that we were concerned with before the reduction started; the objects in the world and the eide. They are "bracketed", Husserl says (see Figure 8.2).

Transcendental reduction

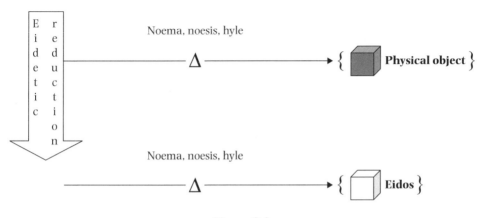

Figure 8.2

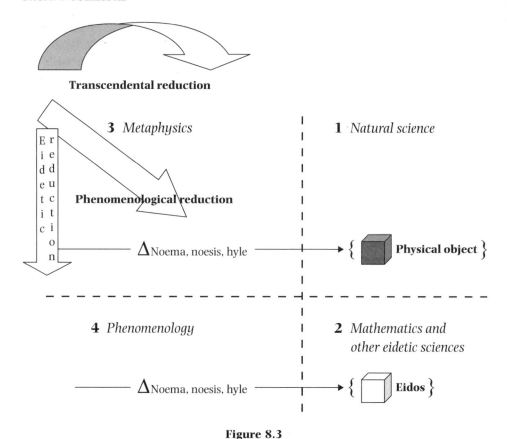

Figure 8.3

The *phenomenological reduction*, finally, is a combination of the eidetic and the transcendental reduction. It leads us from the natural attitude, where we are directed toward individual, physical objects, to an eidetic transcendental attitude, where we are studying the noemata, noeses, and hyle of acts directed toward essential traits of acts directed toward essences. Using a diagram with four quadrants we can illustrate the phenomenological reduction (see Figure 8.3).

The reductions separate the objects of acts into four realms, indicated as four quadrants in Figure 8.3, and four main disciplines. In quadrant 1 we have the concrete physical objects that we are studying in the natural sciences. The eidetic reduction leads us to the eidos, the general features of objects, which are studied in mathematics and other eidetic sciences. If we perform the transcendental reduction on acts directed toward physical objects, we study the noemata, noeses, and hyle of such acts (quadrant 3). Husserl does not say much about this realm, but he proposes to call it metaphysics, and he indicates that it includes the study of the transcendental structuring of what is typically individual, such as death in its uniqueness for an individual, as distinguished from death as a general feature of people and animals. Quadrant 4, finally, contains the noemata, noeses, and hyle of acts directed toward essences. The study of these entities is what Husserl calls phenomenology. Hence the name of the reduction that leads us from the natural attitude to the objects studied in phenomenology: the *phenomenological* reduction.

One final note concerning the reductions. In this presentation of Husserl's thought I have treated the phenomenological reduction as composed of the eidetic reduction followed by the transcendental reduction, in that order. It is clear that the order matters: if we were to start out with the transcendental reduction and then afterwards perform the eidetic reduction, we would arrive at the essential features of noemata, noeses, and hyle of acts directed toward individual concrete objects. This is not the same as the noemata, noeses, and hyle of acts directed toward essences. Husserl normally starts, as we have done, with the eidetic reduction and then follows it by a transcendental reduction. However, there are some few texts where he seems to permit the reductions to come in either order. In that case, phenomenology would presumably comprise the study of both realms.

Notes

1 Brentano 1924 (and later editions, pp. 124–5), vol. 1, book 2, ch. 1. Here quoted from D. B. Terrell's English translation of this chapter in Chisholm 1960: 50.
2 More on this in Føllesdal 1990. For more on the noema, see Føllesdal 1969.
3 Husserl 1950.
4 For more on this, see Føllesdal 2003.
5 Bolzano 1914–31.

References and Further Reading

Bolzano, B. (1914–31) *Wissenschaftslehre* (4 vols.). Leipzig (original publication Sulzbach, 1837, reprinted Vienna 1882).

Brentano, F. (1924) *Psychology From an Empirical Standpoint*. Hamburg: Felix Meiner (original work published 1874).

Chisholm, R. B. (ed.) (1960) *Realism and the Background of Phenomenology*. Glencoe, IL: The Free Press.

Føllesdal, D. (1969) Husserl's notion of noema. *Journal of Philosophy*, 6, 680–7.

—— (1990) The Lebenswelt in Husserl. In L. Haaparanta, M. Kusch, and I. Niiniluoto (eds.), *Language, Knowledge, and Intentionality: Perspectives on the Philosophy of Jaakko Hintikka* (Acta Philosophica Fennica, vol. 49). Helsinki, pp. 123–43.

—— (2003) The thetic role of consciousness. In D. Fisette (ed.), *Husserl's Logical Investigations Reconsidered* (Contributions to Phenomenology, vol. 48) (pp. 11–20). Dordrecht: Kluwer.

Husserl, E. (1950) *Ideen zu einer reinen Phänomenologie und phänomenologischen Philosophie. Erstes Buch: Allgemeine Einführung in die reine Phänomenologie* [Ideas: general introduction to pure phenomenology and to a phenomenological philosophy. First book]. *Husserliana* vol. 3 (ed. W. Biemel). The Hague: Martinus Nijhoff (original work published 1913).

—— (1956) *Erste Philosophie (1923/4). Erste Teil: Kritische Ideengeschichte* [First philosophy (1923/24). First part: the critical history of ideas]. *Husserliana* vol. 7 (ed. R. Boehm). The Hague: Martinus Nijhoff.

—— (1959) *Erste Philosophie (1923/4). Zweiter Teil: Theorie der phänomenologischen Reduktion* [First philosophy (1923/24). Second part: theory of phenomenological reduction]. *Husserliana* vol. 8 (ed. R. Boehm). The Hague: Martinus Nijhoff.

—— (1970a) *The Crisis of European Sciences and Transcendental Phenomenology* (trans. D. Carr). Evanston, IL: Northwestern University Press (original work published 1954).

—— (1970b) *Philosophie der Arithmetik. Mit ergänzenden Texten* (1890–1901) [Philosophy of arithmetic. With supplementary texts (1890–1901)]. *Husserliana* vol. 12 (ed. L. Eley). The Hague: Martinus Nijhoff.

—— (1975) *Logische Untersuchungen. Erster Teil. Prolegomena zur reinen Logik. Text der 1. und der 2. Auflage* [Logical investigations: first part. Prolegomena to pure logic. Text of the first and second edition]. *Husserliana* vol. 18 (ed. E. Holenstein). The Hague: Martinus Nijhoff (original work published 1900).

—— (1984) *Logische Untersuchungen. Zweiter Teil. Untersuchungen zur Phänomenologie und Theorie der Erkenntnis. In zwei Bänden* [Logical investigations. Second part. Investigations concerning phenomenology and the theory of knowledge. In two volumes]. *Husserliana* vol. 19 (ed. U. Panzer). The Hague: Martinus Nijhoff (original work published 1901).

—— (1988a) *Cartesianische Meditation. Teil I: Die Idee einer transzendentalen Methodelehre* [Cartesian meditations. First part: the idea of transcendental doctrine of method]. *Husserliana: Edmund Husserl Dokumente 2/1* (ed. E. Fink). The Hague: Kluwer (original lectures delivered 1929).

—— (1988b) *Cartesianische Meditation. Teil II: Ergänzungsband* [Cartesian meditations. Second part: Supplementary Volume]. *Husserliana: Edmund Husserl Dokumente 2/2* (ed. E. Fink). The Hague: Kluwer (original lectures delivered 1929).

9

Categorial Intuition

DIETER LOHMAR

Husserl's distinction between simple and categorial intuition in chapter 6 of the Sixth Logical Investigation (LI) is the basis for the phenomenological theory of knowledge. But the theory of categorial intuition is regarded as difficult. Some critics also think it is opaque or even completely wrong.[1] Sometimes it is even suspected that Husserl later completely rejected his theory of categorial intuition.[2] With the help of this last theory, Husserl tries to answer the question how intentions directed to "states of affairs" (*Sachverhalte*), such as "The book is green," are fulfilled. In these expressions elements occur which can be easily fulfilled in sense perception, for example, the book and the color green. But what gives fulfillment to the "being green" of the book? We might extend this question to all all elements of categorial form in propositions, like "one," "and," "all," "if," "then," "or," "no," "not," and so on. Intentions of real things are fulfillable by sense perception, whether inner or outer perception. Thus we might call ideal objects those objects which are only fulfilled in categorial intuition, as Husserl suggests (Husserl 1984: 674).

The contrast of simple and categorial acts is explained by means of act analysis. A simple intuition in the form of sense perception presents its object "directly," "immediately," in a "single step" (Husserl 1984: 674), "in one blow" (Husserl 1984: 676), and its presenting function does not rest on founding acts.

Categorial intuition is founded. In this case we do not use the concept of mutual founding but the concept of one-sided foundation.[3] In the less complex cases, categorial intuition is founded on simple perceptions. The condition for the intuitivity of the categorial act is its having passed through each of the founding particular intentions in a fulfilled way. As in the case of simple objects, in categorial acts there are also degrees of intuitivity, and thus of evidence. Categorial intuition does not refer to its object in simple, one-rayed acts but always in jointed, higher-order acts which rest on founding acts. The objects of founding acts are synthetically placed into a categorial relation within the founded categorial act. Thus in categorial acts new objects are intended, i.e., categorial objects which can only be intended (and given) in such founded acts. The intuitivity of categorial intuition is only thanks to acts which consist of stages of founding and founded.

If we consider the realm of language, we might pose the problem of categorial intuition in the following way: What fulfills the categorial elements of propositions which cannot be fulfilled by simple perception alone like "one," "some," "many," "is," "is not," "and," "or," etc. (Husserl 1984: 658)? These elements must also be somehow fulfilled, otherwise the intention as a whole cannot be fulfilled.

In the most simple cases the fulfillment of the categorical elements of propositions is somehow connected with simple perception, but for categorical intuition it asks more than perception. Perception is not founded in other acts. Categorial intuition is founded in acts in which we intend the objects (or the aspects of objects) which we relate to one another in categorial intuition. Thus in categorial intuition we intend objects which cannot be intended in the simple founding acts, like "being red," "being a book" (Husserl 1984: 674 ff.).

There are different forms of categorial intuition, and each has its particular type of synthetic fulfillment.[4] In the Sixth Logical Investigation Husserl analyzes only some basic forms of categorial intuition (identification, relations, collections, eidetic abstraction) to show that the concept of categorial intuition is justified, and that these forms can serve as a pattern for analyzing the other forms of categorial intuition (see Husserl 1984: 678 f., 681 f., 683 f., 688 f., 690 ff.).

In §48 of the Sixth Logical Investigation Husserl analyzes the stages of acts found in synthetic categorial intuition. Three clearly distinct steps or phases are to be distinguished. We will take the proposition "The door is blue" as an example.[5] The simple, founding perceptions must be those of the door and of the dependent moment of the color "blue." In the first step (1) we intend the object in one, unstructured glance. This is a simple act which is directed to the object as a whole; Husserl calls it a simple "*Gesamtwahrnehmung*" (Husserl 1984: 682). The parts of the object are, however, also intended, but in this first unstructured intention of the whole of the object, not yet explicitly so (Husserl 1984: 681 ff.). Nevertheless these partial intentions are elements of the unstructured intention of the whole object, and they are thus already conscious as potential objects of an explicit intention.[6]

In the second step (2) the object is intended in an explicit manner by highlighting our interest with respect to the parts which, up to now, had only been implicitly intended. Husserl calls this kind of objectification a "subdividing act" ("*gliedernde Akte*"; Husserl 1984: 681). Parts of the object which had been implicitly intended now become the intentions of explicit acts. But this does not mean that in this new kind of objectification of the object there is an intention of a new object: It is still the door we are perceiving. The subdividing acts are special intentions within the simple act which is directed at the door. We might say that in the "subdividing act" the door is intended through (or by way of) the medium of the blue color. There is no new object intended; rather we intend the same object in a subdividing manner.

In the first unstructured perception of the object the parts of it were also intended, but only implicitly. In a subdividing, specifying intention (*Sonderwahrnehmung*) they are intended explicitly – they (so to speak) stand in the foreground. Our interest is directed to the sense contents in which the object is presented: I am attentive to the color and the smell of the rose, the rustle of the leaves. In each continuous perception my attention wanders through the elements which present the object one after the other.

The shift from the unstructured perception of an object to the subdivided perception of an object might be interpreted as a "double apperception," i.e., as two different perceptions based on the same sense contents. But in this case it is not a change of apperception which results in another object, but in a different mode of the same object. Both are simple acts, but in the particular partial intentions we intend the door by way of an intention of its color, while in the initial unstructured perception of the same object we are only implicitly directed at the color. In the first case the sense contents serve as representatives of an implicit partial intention, in the second the same sense contents are representatives of an explicit partial intention.

As we have already pointed out in the example of continuous synthesis, there is a so-called "synthesis of coincidence" in the transition from the unstructured intention of the whole to the explicit partial intentions. In this "synthesis of coincidence" we are aware both that we are intending the same object, and that this object, the door, not only has a color in general but that this color is blue. One important remark: Both of these founding intentions are intuitively fulfilled and thus justify the thesis that the perceived object is a "real" object. This is one of the decisive functions of sensuality in the framework of categorical intuition.[7] Thus the synthetic transition from the one to the other is also suitable for justifying the claim of "reality" with respect to categorical intuition. This constitutes the difference between knowledge and mere hearsay.

This transition of founding acts and the "synthesis of coincidence" which happens in this transition somehow offer everything we need for knowledge. But for actual knowledge there must also be a synthetic act which performs a categorial appercep-tion of the "synthesis of coincidence" itself. In everyday life we often experience such "syntheses of coincidence" and thus "have everything needed for the performance of knowledge," but we nevertheless only actually carry out such a performance if it is relevant for our practice.[8]

In the third (3) decisive step of the process of categorial intuition we intend the objects of the particular subdividing perceptions synthetically in the new categorial intention. We can establish a relation between the objects of the founding acts, or between the object of the unstructured act as a whole and one of its dependent mo-ments ("The door is blue"). In this founded act the elements which are synthetically connected in a categorial relation take on a new character: they are syntactically formed by the categorial act. In all synthetic categorial intuitions we will find these three steps: (1) the initial, simple perception of the whole; (2) the particular, explicit subdividing perceptions; and (3) the actual categorially synthetic intention.

In the example of the door and its color, it is the "door" which takes on the categorial form of a "substrate" which bears qualities, while the "blue" becomes a "quality" of the substrate (substrate/accident). This categorial formation is not merely the per-formance of another type of simple apperception of the perceived object. The categorial act intends "that the door is blue" and is perhaps even the fulfillment of this matter of fact. Within categorial intention the "substrate capable to bearing qualities" and the "quality of the substrate" are dependent moments. Thus the fulfillment of a categorial intention is always dependent on founding perceptions and their intuitive fulfillment. But the dependence goes further: the fulfillment of perceptual intentions is in turn dependent on hyletic (reelle) contents.

But the fulfillment of categorial intentions is not only dependent on the intuitive character (evidence) of the founding acts.[9] Such a generalization, i.e., the thesis that the intuitive character of categorial intention is completely dependent on that of the founding perceptions, would lead to paradoxical results. For example, one of the consequences would be that axiomatic mathematics is not evident knowledge because its results are established completely within signitive intentions (i.e., only intentions with the means of a system of signs but without sensual fulfillment).

Thus, sense perception can contribute to the fulfillment of categorial intentions at least in the most simple cases. But there are many objects of categorial intuition which have only a very loose connection with sense perception, for example, the propositions of pure mathematics and algebra, where there is hardly any contribution of sensibility. But on the other hand, there are surely elements in categorial intuition which can be fulfilled with the help of sensible intuition – something like the "blue" of the door – and in each case there are elements which cannot be fulfilled in sensibility alone, like "being blue."

One of the decisive issues for this conception of knowledge concerns the function of the former stages of the categorial process in the intuitivity of the categorial act: to what extent is their performance in the third stage still "alive" or, respectively, "present"? On the one hand, this question concerns the intuitivity and the quality (i.e., its thetic character, "*Setzungsqualität*") of the founding acts. But it also concerns the "synthesis of coincidence": we need to make clear what the founding acts are, and whether we can somehow keep their performance in play in the complex process of knowledge.

Let us turn once again to the details of our example of the "blue door." After the simple perception of the whole is performed, the moment of the blue color of the door becomes the object of an explicit subdividing perception (Husserl 1984: 682). But in the explicit perception of the "blue" we do not intend and perceive the "blue" for the first time. For an implicit intention the "blue" already occurs in the initial, simple perception of the whole. This implicit, partial intention corresponds to a possibility of an explicit intention. In the transition from the first simple perception of the whole to the explicit subdividing intention there occurs a "synthesis of coincidence" between these two intentions (see Husserl 1984: 650 ff., 569 ff.). The coincidence occurs between the explicit intention of the moment "blue color" on the one hand, and the partial intention implicit in the intention of the whole on the other.

It is decisive for the understanding of the concept of "synthesis of coincidence" that what is brought into coincidence are the intentional moments of the respective acts. The fulfilling coincidence is not based on equal or similar hyletic data ("*reelle Bestände*"). Such a coincidence may occur, but it does not support the intuitivity of categorial intuition. The basis of intuitivity in the case of categorial intuition are the coincidences of the intentional moments of acts, i.e., synthesis of coincidence between partial intentions.[10]

These syntheses of coincidence which occur between partial intentions now have a new function: they are apperceived as representing or fulfilling contents of the new synthetic categorial intention "The door is blue." The synthesis of coincidence which arises in the active process of running through the subdividing acts – making, so to speak, all the partial intentions of the object explicit – are now representing the "being blue" of the door.

At this decisive point in the phenomenological theory of knowledge we find the schema: apprehension/apprehended content ("*Auffassung – aufgefaßter Inhalt*") which

118

is meant to understand the intuitivity of perceptions as based on sensually given contents. Thus we need to recognize that Husserl accepts this model of how to understand intuitivity for the categorial intuition as well as for sense perception. In the LI, as well as in many later writings, we find this model introduced many times at decisive points of the argument (see Husserl 1964: 94–103, 109 ff., 132 f., 138 ff.). For our limited purposes we do not need to take up Husserl's self-criticism with respect to the model of apprehension/contents of apprehension, which in the first place only points out the limits of the schema but does not reject it (see Husserl 1969: 7, Anm.1). Husserl criticizes the use of this model for the deepest level of constitution in inner time-consciousness and for acts of fantasy (Husserl 1980: 265 f., Husserl 1984: 884). For acts constituting intentional objects and categorial objects it is not defective, but unavoidable.

But the model of apprehension and apprehended contents leaves some questions unanswered. For it is obvious that the very special character of the way "given" contents fulfill categorial intuition, i.e., the syntheses of coincidence, requires a critical analysis. Therefore we have to analyze more closely what kind of contents syntheses of coincidence are. In relation to the special character of the synthesis of coincidence as a given content I will first present three negative insights. The discussion of these three negative insights will in turn reveal some positive insights into the character of the syntheses of coincidence which give intuitivity to categorial objects: we cannot identify that which is the representing content of categoriality (i.e., the synthesis of coincidence) with the representing content of sense perception (neither with respect to the simple perception of the whole nor the explicit perception of the subdividing acts). And syntheses of coincidence cannot be sense contents of outer perception at all.

One might think that a representing content of a perceived object could serve as a fulfilling content of a categorial intuition if it were apprehended in a new manner, i.e., in a "categorial apprehension," where formerly it had only been used in an "perceptual apprehension." But I do not think that this is the case in categorial intuition. Consider the representing contents of the objects of explicit and subdividing acts in sense perception. If it were the case (that they could also serve as contents of categorial acts), then we would not be able to argue for three essential and necessary stages in the active performance of a categorial intuition. In principle we would already have (or would be able to have) categorial intuition on the basis of sense perception alone. The same argument shows that categorial intuition cannot be fulfilled with a perceptual content of outer perception.[11]

We can now point to some positive aspects of the synthesis of coincidence. As we have seen in the example of the blue door, the representing contents of the door function in a double way: first in the simple perception of the whole object, then also in the explicit perception in which the color of the door is specifically intended. In the transition between these two acts there arises the synthesis of coincidence between the implicit intention and the explicit intention of the blue within the subdividing act that is aimed thematically at the color. This synthesis of coincidence now turns out to be able to function as a representing content for the categorial intuition of the "being blue" of the door (Husserl 1984: 682).

In this case the content which is apprehended is not a sense content at all – even if it rests on the coincidence of partial intentions fulfilled by sense contents, it is a synthesis between intentional moments of two or more acts which is imposed on us in the transition between the acts.[12] Experiencing the coincidence of the intentional moments of "blue" in the two acts at first only means that we "experience" the equality of these intentions; it does not mean that we have the fact of equality or equivalence as a theme, nor that we have the matter of fact "being blue" as a theme. The synthesis of coincidence is somehow imposed on us in a passive manner, even if it occurs in the framework of an actively performed activity. The content (the datum) is given to us – we must accept this seemingly paradoxical formulation – in a "sense" which has nothing to do with sensibility, but which is an irreducible relation between the intentional moments of acts. It is the apprehension of such contents which fulfills the intention "The door is blue." Syntheses of coincidence are non-sensible representing contents.

Obviously the concept of non-sensible contents is problematic within the framework of a phenomenology which begins its theory of knowledge with the analysis of sense perceptions. Yet we should not only dwell on the difficulties with this way of understanding categorial intuition, but also point to its advantages: the fact that non-sensible contents somehow fulfill categorial intuitions clearly justifies Husserl's extension of the concept of intuition beyond the realm of sensibility. Simple (founding) acts and founded, complex categorial acts do not only differ essentially in their structure, but also in the characteristics of the contents which make them intuitive. Beside this we have a clear hint how to understand knowledge in mathematics with the same model (i.e., synthesis of coincidence) as we use in all other forms of knowledge. Moreover, we have a clear argument for the necessity of running through the complete three-staged process of categorial activity in order to reach intuitive fulfillment. Without the performance of the first two stages of categorial activity (i.e., the simple perception of the whole and the subdividing explication of the partial intentions), the necessary fulfilling syntheses of coincidence cannot occur. We may even suppose that in every case of categorial intuition there is a necessary contribution of non-sensible contents. I will now examine more closely this last thesis.

Another important form of categorial intuition is the eidetic intuition ("*ideierende Abstraktion*" or "*Wesensschau*").[13] Husserl's theory of eidetic intuition begins with the fact that the human mind has the ability to become aware of common features in different objects. In §52 of the Sixth Logical Investigation Husserl analyzes this form of knowledge as a particular form of categorial intuition. The phenomenological method of eidetic intuition is the attempt first to understand and then to enforce this original ability of the human mind so that it becomes a method for a priori knowledge that is based upon common features of acts of consciousness as well as objects of thinking and perceiving.

The eidetic method is of crucial importance for the claim of phenomenology to be a philosophical science. In the *Investigations* Husserl still interprets his phenomenology as a version of "descriptive Psychology" – at least he uses this denotation – but on the other hand phenomenology is not meant to be an empirical discipline that only collects together arbitrary facts. Thus phenomenology has to find and establish methods which make it possible to arrive at a priori insights independent of the given particular factual case, i.e., to arrive at universal knowledge concerning the general features of consciousness.

120

Thus the claim of phenomenology to be a science depends on whether eidetic intuition can be established as a justified form of categorial intuition. We may also look at this from the point of view of the idea of self-justification that Husserl pursues for phenomenology: to establish eidetic intuition as a justified form of categorial intuition is a decisive aim of the LI.

Eidetic intuition is founded in simple intuition in a way similar to other forms of categorial intuition we have seen. We are only able to have an intuition of general features like "blueness" or "human" by running through a whole series of blue objects in perception or fantasy (see Husserl 1984: 111–15, 176 ff., 225 f., 690–3). The aim of the theory of eidetic intuition is not only (but also) to make clear how it is that we can gain general concepts of objects, but also how the intuition of general features works, i.e., how it is that we can have an intuition of the characteristics held in common by different objects. We may also speak in this respect of "common objects," and insofar as we usually identify such common objects with "concepts," it is also an investigation into the legitimating source of our intuition of concepts. Thus in performing the eidetic intuition of "blueness," we must run through a series of perceived or imagined blue objects in order to have the intuition of the common "blueness." This process is not circular, because in the founding acts the theme is single blue objects while in the founded eidetic intuition we apprehend the common feature of blue on the basis of the synthesis of coincidence which, as we already know, is a non-sensible content.

A detailed analysis of eidetic intuition as a form of categorial intuition in §52 of the Sixth Logical Investigation runs along the lines of the three stages found in every form of categorial intuition: first the simple perception of the object as a whole; then the explicit, subdividing acts; then finally the categorial synthesis. In the second stage, that is, in running through the subdividing acts explicitly pointing to the moment of color with respect to different perceptive or imaginative objects, there occurs a synthesis of coincidence with a particular style.

In order to arrive at an intuition of general objects it is of decisive importance that we have intuitive or imaginative acts for the subdividing acts during the second phase. Eidetic intuition cannot be founded on signitive acts alone (Husserl 1984: 607 ff.). But on the other hand, eidetic intuition is also possible if only one intuitively present object is given, for we can vary this example in imagination. In the *Investigations* Husserl states that it is indifferent for the intuitivity of eidetic intuition whether the subdividing acts of the second phase are intuitive acts or imaginative acts, that is, imaginative acts are admissible (Husserl 1984: 691 ff., 670). In the further development of his theory Husserl arrives at the insight that the imaginative acts are not only to be tolerated but that they are to be preferred – even that imaginative or "free" variation is necessary for eidetic intuition.[14] It is free eidetic variation that assures us that in eidetic variation we do not adhere to a limited realm of cases which may carry only contingently common features (see Husserl 1964: 419–25 and Husserl 1968: §9). The factual reality of the single cases in the eidetic variation is irrelevant in this concern (see Husserl 1968: 74).

In the third stage of the process of eidetic intuition we apprehend the synthesis of coincidence which occurs in running through the different acts of the second stage. We apprehend this synthesis as a representation of the common feature, i.e., the general object that we intend. As in the act in which a real thing is thematically identified, the synthesis of coincidence which occurs on the second stage between the subdividing acts is the apprehension of the coincidence as the identity of the general feature. The general feature, the (same) color, is intuitively given through the series of blue objects and the synthesis of coincidence between the acts directed at the moment of color.

We can understand higher order eidetic intuitions in the same way. We can perform eidetic intuitions founded in categorial acts. For example, we can have an intuition of the general aspect "color" based on the intuition of different colors, and we can have an intuition of the concept "act of consciousness" by running through eidetic intuitions of different forms of consciousness.

There are also problematic aspects of eidetic intuition, which is above all an experimental form of reflection. With the help of eidetic intuition we can supposedly have a clear idea about the limits of our concepts: by imaginative variation of particular cases of a general concept we might discover the point where the variation exceeds the limits of the concept, and at which we are imagining something else.[15] We can thus learn to recognize the limits of our concepts and experience them as non-arbitrary. But even in recognizing them as something fixable, it is not clear how their limits are determined.

The full extent of this problem is only realized in the attempt to intuit the essence of objects which carry some cultural meaning. Whereas in one culture we may intuit the essence of the divine as plural, in another we might intuit the essence of the divine as singular. The same turns out to be the case with the essence of woman, honor, justice, etc. There is no way of finding a common answer.

As a partial solution to this problem, we might try to draw a distinction between "simple" objects which carry no cultural meaning and those which do. Acts of consciousness – the preferred theme of Husserl's phenomenology – may turn out to be objects of the first class. On the other hand: complex objects which can only have their full sense in the intersubjective constitution of the community, objects such as cultural world, myth, religion, etc., all exceed this limit. Most everyday concepts are learned by each of us in a long process of formation within the intersubjective consensus of our community. In this way our everyday concepts have a genesis and a "history" closely connected to the convictions of our respective community.

The next important form of categorial intuition is collection. The fullfillment of "a and b" is dependent on the performance of founding acts directed at a and b making the members of a collection an explicit theme. But this is not enough as long as the synthetic intention on both together, the "and" is not performed. In this case the fulfilling factor is not to be found in synthesis of coincidence, because we can combine objects in a collection which have no partial intentions in common.

Thus we cannot understand how fulfillment works in collections without taking into account the contribution of the synthetic categorial intention "and" itself. Collections owe their intuitivity only to the fact that we synthetically combine objects, that we collect them. Only while synthetically combining the a and the b do we have the collection intuitively. But this leads to the strange result that the categorial act itself contributes to its own intuitivity. At least this makes us understand why we are completely free in collections to combine objects even of different realms of being, for we are not dependent on common partial intentions: "7 and justice and Napoleon."

An intention contributing to its own fulfillment might induce the impression of circularity. But it is the synthetic activity of combining the objects of the founding acts into a new object, the collection, which gives the fulfillment. This strange case raises questions about the kind of fulfilling, "representing" contents in collection. We might suppose that what serves as representant ("*Repräsentant*") is the experience of the performance of the act of collection (in inner perception). But it seems more reasonable to accept the fact that the categorical intention "and" itself can be viewed as a non-sensible content (in this respect it is similar to the synthesis of coincidence) and that it can serve as a fulfilling content of the intention of the collection.

It is obviously a special case, in fact an important exception, in the realm of intentions and categorical intentions that the will to perform a synthetic intention is enough to fulfill this intention. But it remains an exception for the fulfillment of intentions which count for knowledge in the narrow sense is dependent on synthesis of coincidence which occurs passively in the passing over from one founding act to the other. A collection itself therefore, is not already a contribution to knowledge but it can become an important element of further knowledge if we make further judgments about this collection (or set). Husserl writes in respect to the lack of independence of collectiva that they are no "states of affairs" (Husserl 1984: 688, 1964: 254), because there are no syntheses of coincidence fulfilling the categorical intention (see Husserl 1964: 135, 254, 297, 223).

Notes

1   The most important sources on the theme of categorical intuition in Husserl are: Tugendhat 1970: 111–36; Sokolowski 1970: 65–71; Sokolowski 1974: §§10–17; Ströker 1978: 3–30; Sokolowski 1981: 127–41; Willard 1984: 232–41; Lohmar 1989: 44–69; Lohmar 1990: 179–97; Seebohm 1990: 9–47, Cobb-Stevens 1990: 43–66; Bort 1990: 303–19; Lohmar 1998: 178–273 and Lohmar 2002: 125–45.

2   Husserl wrote that he no longer accepts the theory of the categorical representation (1984: 534 f.). An appropriate interpretation of Husserl's intentions, therefore, must free itself from the misleading elements of his initial interpretation of categorical representation in Ch. 7 of the 6th LI; see Lohmar 1990: 179–97.

3   In the 3rd LI the concept of mutual foundation is predominant but the 6th LI prefers the concept of one-sided foundation. See Husserl 1984: 270 f., 283–6, 369 and, for the 6th LI, Husserl 1984: 678. On Husserl's different concepts of foundation, see Nenon 1997: 97–114.

4   But there are differences in the kind of intention. Husserl makes a distinction between synthetic and abstractive forms of categorical intuition. Synthetic categorical intentions are co-directed to the objects of their founding acts, such as "A is bigger than B." The intention of abstracting intentions is not directed in the same way on the objects of the founding acts. In abstractive intentions the objects of the founding acts can only be a medium through which the intention is directed to something common, the eidos. The objects of the founding acts are only examples of this eidos (see Husserl 1984: 690, 676, 688).

5 In the 6th LI Husserl makes a difference between the relation of whole and independent parts (*Stücke*) and the relation of whole and dependent parts (*Momente*); see Husserl 1984: 680 f., 231; Husserl 1964: §§50–2. In Husserl 1964 he interprets the two forms "S has the part P" and "S has the quality m" as equivalent in relation to the structure of their constitution; see Husserl 1964: 262.

6 In *Ideas I* (1950) Husserl will regard this possibility of making an intention explicit as characteristic of horizon-intentionality. See Husserl 1950: 1, 57, 71 ff., 212 f.

7 See Husserl 1950: 239. For detailed discussion of the function of sensuality in categorial intuition see Lohmar 2002: 125–45.

8 Nevertheless, these opportunities for gaining knowledge do not disappear without trace. In the genetic phenomenology one of the prominent themes is the way in which this "trace" (of knowledge which is experienced but not conceptualized) is kept or stored in the human subject in different forms of prepredicative experience. See the first section of Husserl 1964 and Lohmar 1998: Ch. III, 6–8.

9 Husserl himself wrote once – in the problematic Ch. 7 of the 6th LI – about the possibility of a functional dependence of the evidence of the categorial act from the evidence of the founding acts (see Husserl 1984: 704). See Lohmar 1990: 179–97.

10 Husserl writes: "Zugleich 'deckt' sich aber das fortwirkende Gesamtwahrnehmen gemäß jener implizierten Partialintention mit dem Sonderwahrnehmen" (Husserl 1984: 682). It is important that this "synthesis of coincidence" can occur also between symbolic (and thus "empty") intentions, which is of crucial importance for the foundation of mathematical knowledge; see also Husserl 1985: 282.

11 We might think that syntheses of coincidence are a content of inner perception. At a time Husserl himself thought that such a solution may be promising. In Ch. 7 of the 6th LI (1st edn.), the "Studie über kategoriale Repräsentation," Husserl proposes the thesis that categorial intuitions can be fulfilled by the apprehension of so-called "contents of reflection." In this case, the content apprehended is the same content which represents the actual performance of the categorial act in inner perception. See Husserl 1984: 708, Lohmar 1990. E. Tugendhat takes up this misleading view of Husserl; see Tugendhat 1979: 118–27. Later on Husserl criticizes this attempt of the first edition of LI as defective; see Husserl 1984: 535.

12 The concept of coincidence has a problematic double sense in Husserl. In the LI Husserl uses the concept of coincidence often to name the coincidence of fulfilled intentions with empty intentions which fulfills the latter. But this is a trivial concept of fulfillment for it does not answer the question how fulfilled intentions become fulfilled at all. The other context of using the concept of coincidence is in analyzing categorial intuition as fulfilled by synthesis of coincidence between the partial intentions of the founding acts; this non-trivial use of the concept makes clear how the categorical intentions become fulfilled.

13 See Bernet, R., Kern, I., Marbach, E. 1989: 74–84; Mohanty 1959: 222–30; Tugendhat 1979: 137–68; Hopkins 1997: 151–78. The designation "Wesensschau" for the eidetic intuition seems to be a wrong choice in terminology because it suggests a nearness to platonic thinking which is not intended by Husserl.

14 See Husserl 1950: 146 ff., where he speaks of a priority of imagination; see also Husserl 1974: 206, 254 f. and 1964: 410 ff., 422 f. Th. Seebohm points out that imaginative variation is already to be found in the LI (Seebohm 1990: 14 f.).

15 Husserl has analyzed the accquisition and the determinations of the limits of concepts in his theory of types in his genetic phenomenology. See Lohmar 1998: Kap. III, 6, d. To this problematic see also Held 1985: S. 29 and Claesges 1964: 29 ff.

References and Further Reading

Bernet, R., Kern, I., & Marbach, E. (1989) *Edmund Husserl. Darstellung seines Denkens* [Edmund Husserl: portrayal of his thought]. Hamburg: Meiner.

Bort, K. (1990) *Kategoriale Anschauung*. In D. Koch and K. Bort (eds.), *Kategorie und Kategorialität* (pp. 303–19). Würzburg: Königshausen & Neumann.

Claesges, U. (1964) *Edmund Husserls Theorie der Raumkonstitution* [Edmund Husserl's theory of the constitution of space]. The Hague: Martinus Nijhoff.

Cobb-Stevens, R. (1990) Being and categorical intuition. *Review of Metaphysics*, 44, 43–66.

Held, K. (1985) *Einleitung*. In: E. Husserl, *Die phänomenologische Methode. Ausgewählte Texte I.* Stuttgart: Reclam.

Hopkins, B. (1997) Phenomenological cognition of the a priori. Husserl's method of "seeing essences." In B. Hopkins (ed.), *Husserl in Contemporary Context* (pp. 151–78). Dordrecht: Kluwer.

Husserl, E. (1950) *Husserliana III–1: Ideen zu einer reinen Phänomenologie und phänomenologischen Philosophie, erstes Buch* [Ideas pertaining to a pure phenomenology and to a phenomenological philosophy] (ed. K. Schuhmann). The Hague: Martinus Nijhoff (original work published in 1913).

—— (1964) *Erfahrung und Urteil: Untersuchungen zur Genealogie der Logik* [Experience and judgment: Investigations in the genealogy of logic] (ed. L. Ludwig). Hamburg: Claassen.

—— (1968) *Husserliana IX: Phänomenologische Psychologie* [Phenomenological psychology] (ed. W. Biemel). The Hague, Martinus Nijhoff.

—— (1969) *Husserliana X: Zur Phänomenologie des inneren Zeitbewussteseins (1893–1917)* [The phenomenology of internal time-consciousness (1893–1917)] (ed. R. Boehm). The Hague: Martinus Nijhoff (original works published 1893–1917).

—— (1974) *Husserliana XVII: Formale und transzendentale Logik* [Formal and transcendental logic] (ed. P. Janssen). The Hague: Martinus Nijhoff (original work published 1929).

—— (1980) *Husserliana XXIII: Phantasie, Bildbewusstsein, Erinnerung* [Imagination, image consciousness, and memory] (ed. E. Marbach). The Hague: Martinus Nijhoff (original works from the Husserl estate).

—— (1984) *Husserliana XIX: Logische Untersuchungen, Zweiter Teil* [Logical investigations, second part] (ed. U. Panzer). The Hague: Martinus Nijhoff (original work published in 1901, rev. edn. 1922).

—— (1985) *Husserliana XXIV: Einleitung in die Logik und Erkenntnistheorie* [Introduction to logic and theory of knowledge] (ed. U. Melle). The Hague: Martinus Nijhoff (original work presented 1906/7).

Lohmar, D. (1989) *Phänomenologie der Mathematik*. Dordrecht: Kluwer.

—— (1990) Wo lag der Fehler der kategorialen Repräsentanten?, *Husserl-Studies*, 7, 179–97.

—— (1998) *Erfahrung und kategoriales Denken*. Dordrecht: Kluwer.

—— (2002) Husserl's concept of categorial intuition. In D. Zahavi and F. Stjernfelt (eds.), *One Hundred Years of Phenomenology* (pp. 125–45). Dordrecht: Kluwer.

Mohanty, J. N. (1959) Individual fact and essence in Edmund Husserl's philosophy. *Philosophy and Phenomenological Research*, 29, 222–30.

Nenon, T. (1997) Two models of foundation in the "Logical Investigations". In B.C. Hopkins (ed.), *Husserl in Contemporary Context* (pp. 97–114). Dordrecht: Kluwer.

Seebohm, Th. M. (1990) Kategoriale Anschauung. *Phänomenologische Forschungen*, 23, 9–47.

Sokolowski, R. (1970) *The Formation of Husserl's Concept of Constitution*. The Hague: Martinus Nijhoff.

—— (1974) *Husserlian Meditations*. Evanston, IL: Northwestern University Press.

—— (1981) Husserl's concept of categorial intuition. *Phenomenology and the Human Sciences*, supplement to *Philosophical Topics*, 12, 127–41.

Ströker, E. (1978) Husserls Evidenzprinzip [Husserl's principle of *Evidenz*]. *Zeitschrift für philosophische Forschung*, 32, 3–30.

Tugendhat, E. (1970) *Der Wahrheitsbegriff bei Husserl und Heidegger* [The concept of truth in Husserl and Heidegger]. Berlin: De Gruyter.

—— (1979) *Selbstbewusstsein und Selbstbestimmung: Sprachanalytische Interpretationen* [Self-consciousness and self-determination]. Frankfurt am Main: Suhrkamp.

Willard, D. (1984) *Logic and the Objectivity of Knowledge*. Athens: Ohio University Press.

10

Temporality

JOHN B. BROUGH AND WILLIAM BLATTNER

Temporality as a fundamental concern of twentieth-century continental thought had its roots in the phenomenology of Edmund Husserl. Although time occupied Husserl throughout most of his philosophical career, it was his lectures and sketches from early in the century, eventually published in 1928 under Martin Heidegger's editorship, that influenced later figures in the phenomenological tradition, such as Heidegger himself, Sartre, and Merleau-Ponty. Husserl described time as the most important of all phenomenological problems, and also as the most difficult. The time Husserl investigates is not time understood as an empirical phenomenon tied to the movement of celestial bodies and measured by clocks. His interest is in the *consciousness* of time. Husserlian phenomenology is marked by a focus on consciousness as "intentional," by which Husserl meant not (simply) purposeful conscious activity but the directedness of every conscious experience toward something. Thus a perception is the perception of a bird in flight or of a melody playing on the radio, a memory is the memory of a dinner I had last week. The consciousness of time, Husserl thought, is an exceptionally important and complex form of intentionality, involved in virtually every aspect of conscious life. It not only exemplifies intentionality, but makes it possible in its many forms.

The facets of Husserl's phenomenology of temporal awareness match those of the phenomenon he investigates. Since acts of consciousness intend objects and since temporal objects play such a prominent role in our experience, Husserl has much to say about temporal objectivity. The most obvious sorts of temporal objects are those we encounter in perception. Perceived objects, whether relatively stable or caught up in change, are temporal because they endure, succeed one another or exist simultaneously, and display themselves in temporal modes of appearance. The restaurant in which I am enjoying a dinner appears to me as now existing, as having existed in the past, and as having an indefinite future ahead of it. I also experience the dinner itself in ever-shifting modes of now, past, and future, although, compared to the room in which it occurs, the dinner is a short-lived and temporally unique event. It is important to note that now, past, and future are not static containers, nor are they parts of temporal objects, or even points of time; they are, rather, the ways in which temporal objects and the points of time they occupy appear to us.

Among these modes of appearance, Husserl singles out the now for special attention. He is particularly concerned to avoid the presumption that we can be conscious only of what is now, that since past and future are, respectively, no longer and not yet, they are simply not available to consciousness. This prejudice of the now would leave us imprisoned in the present, forever locked away from past and future. Husserl argues to the contrary that temporal objects as they actually endure or run off appear as now, past, and future. Indeed, if they appeared only as now, they would never appear as *temporal* objects. The now is not sealed up within itself; it is in dynamic relation to the past and to what is to come. As such, now, past, and future are relative to one another. The now "is a relative concept and refers to a 'past,' just as 'past' refers to the 'now'" (Husserl 1991: 70). The now always has its fringe or horizon of past and future.

Although now, past, and future are mutually dependent for their sense, the now enjoys a "privileged" status (Husserl 1991: 26). It serves as the point of orientation for our conscious lives. What is past appears as past in relation to the now, and it is in relation to the now that what is future appears as future. The now is also privileged in the sense that it is open to the new. It is the "generative point" (Husserl 1991: 26), consciousness's moment of hospitality in which new moments of an object, or perhaps an altogether fresh object, present themselves. If we experienced nothing as now, we would be severed from this cornucopia of life. We could not even be said to be aware of the no longer or of the not yet, since we would never experience anything new that could become old. The spring of our experience would dry up.

The now is equally "the source-point of all temporal positions" (Husserl 1991: 74). To play host to a new object-point is to welcome a new time-point. "Each actually present now creates a new time-point because it creates . . . a new object point" (Husserl 1991: 68). Whatever appears at the new time-point will remain forever fixed to that point as it slips into the past. Hence the now is also the source of our experience of the temporal relation of before and after. Once a being or event has actually presented itself in the now, it will forever after be something that came before, and followed, something else. Furthermore, if the now is the source of new temporal positions and of the objects occupying them, and if individuation depends on appearing at a definite point in time, then the now "is a continuous moment of individuation" (Husserl 1991: 68). Finally, while the individual object has its abiding place in the sequence of temporal points, it has an ever-changing location in relation to the actual now. "Time is fixed, and yet time flows" (Husserl 1991: 67).

Not every object of consciousness is a temporal object. There are timeless objects such as the Pythagorean theorem that are no more bound to a particular moment in time than they are attached to a particular place in space. Even in these cases, however, time plays a role: it is only against the background of the temporality pervading the rest of our experience that we intend such objects as escaping time.

Husserl is not only concerned with the way in which temporal objects appear. He also investigates the constitution or structure of acts that enables them to bring temporally extended objects to appearance. If a melody I am hearing appears to me as in part now, in part past, and in part to come, then each phase of my act of hearing it must not only be conscious of the now-phase of the object but also reach out beyond the now to elapsed and future phases. If I did not preserve a consciousness of the elapsed tones as they slip ever more deeply into the past, I would hear only a single note and never the whole melody or even an extended part of it. Similarly, I must be open to further experience of the melody, or at least to the experience of something that will follow it. But preservation of what has elapsed and anticipation of what is to come will not by themselves account for the perception of the temporal object. For that to occur, presentation and anticipation must be tempered by modification. If I were simply to preserve the elapsed notes of the melody without modification, I would not hear a coherent melodic succession but "a disharmonious tangle of sound, as if [I] had struck simultaneously all the notes that had previously sounded" (Husserl 1991: 11).

Husserl claims that what makes possible this reaching out beyond the now, anticipating, preserving, and modifying, is that each momentary phase of the perceiving act possesses a threefold intentionality: primal impression, retention, and protention. Primal impression is the originary consciousness whose correlate is the phase of the object appearing as now. Primal impression is the moment of consciousness that presents a new object-phase in a new time-point as now, as there itself and in person. By contrast, retention, as Husserl sometimes says, is "perceptual" or impressional consciousness of the past. By this he means that it is the actual holding on to what has elapsed as it moves away from the now. Retention differs essentially from ordinary memory, as when I recall last week's dinner in the restaurant. Memory is an independent act, like the perception on which it is founded and that it recalls. Retention, on the other hand, is not an act but a dependent moment of a phase of an act. And unlike ordinary memory, it is presentation of the past rather than re-presentation. Ordinary memory assumes that retention (and primal impression and protention) have already done their work, leaving behind a constituted act and object to which it can return. Memory can then re-present a past event or object by running through the already constituted perception of it again. Memory thus re-collects the past, while retention "collects" it for the first time, and in immediate relation to the now. This collecting is intentional, a matter of consciousness and not like the retention of fluids in the body. Retention "transcends itself and *posits* something as being – namely, as being past – that does not really inhere in it" (Husserl 1991: 356). It is consciousness reaching out directly and originally to what has just elapsed. This means, too, that what is retained should not be thought of as an echo or afterimage: an echo is a present sound heard as now. The echo of a violin tone, for example, would not be the past violin tone but a weak present violin tone. To insist that what is retained is like an echo or image is an indication that the prejudice of the now – that one can experience only what is present – is still intact, while the whole thrust of Husserl's notion of retention is that consciousness can be directly and immediately aware of what is no longer now.

Protention is the impressional openness of consciousness to the future. It is essential to the perception of a temporal object "that there be an intention directed toward what is to come, even if not toward continuations involving the same temporal object" (Husserl 1991: 240). Just as retention is not ordinary recollection, protention is not an act of expectation. Expectation is a kind of memory in reverse: a full-blown act that rehearses some experience one expects to have in the future. Protention, on the other hand, is a moment of the actual phase of the ongoing perception that immediately opens me up to further experience, usually of what I am presently experiencing, without running through it in advance as if it were present. Perhaps because the future is indeterminate, Husserl has less to say about protention than about primal impression and retention.

129

Husserl presses his investigation of time-consciousness still further. The inventory of temporal objects is not exhausted by things such as houses and melodies: the acts of consciousness intending them are equally temporal objects. This is true of every act, not just of perceptions. The act of thinking of the Pythagorean theorem is a temporal object, even if the theorem itself is not. Acts are immanent to consciousness rather than transcendent, of course, but, like melodies and other transcendent things, they begin, endure for a time, and come to an end. Acts are the immanent temporal unities through which we intend objects, temporal and otherwise, transcendent to them. They have a place in the internal time of consciousness rather than the "external" time of the world. Unless we freely undertake an explicit act of reflection, we do not perceive or thetically posit our acts, but Husserl insists that we are nevertheless aware of them implicitly, and in the temporal modes of now, past, and future. I perceive a house and at the same time nonthetically "experience" or consciously live through my perception as an act extended in immanent time.

The final question Husserl asks is how these immanent temporal unities become constituted, and how, in the process, we become aware of the unity of consciousness itself. His answer is that the constitution is the achievement of "the absolute time-constituting flow of consciousness" (Husserl 1991: 77). The absolute flow is not a metaphysical absolute; it is absolute in the sense that it is the ultimate stratum of conscious life, responsible for its own constitution, for the constitution of acts as immanent temporal unities, and, through them, of transcendent temporal objects. Husserl is reluctant to apply the temporal predicates of now, past, and future to the flow (he reserves them for the constituted acts and their objects), but he does understand the flow to have successive phases, one of which will be actual while others will be post-actual and pre-actual. Each of these phases has the intentional moments of primal impression, retention, and protention, which together account for the flow's remarkable constitutional prowess. Thanks to them, the flow may be said to have a "double intentionality" (Husserl 1991: 84, 390): it constitutes the acts as temporal unities in internal time and it is conscious of itself as a single, ongoing flow. The two intentionalities require "one another like two sides of one and the same thing" (Husserl 1991: 87). Retention plays a particularly important role in the flow's double intentionality. Through its retentional moments, the flow experiences the elapsing phases of itself as they slip away; but since these phases in their primal impressional moment originally intended phases of the act as now, it holds on to the elapsed phases of the act as well, and through them the past phases of what the act intended. Hence Husserl can claim that "there is one unique flow of consciousness" in which both the unity of the act in immanent time "and the unity of the flow of consciousness become constituted at once" (Husserl 1991: 84).

The absolute flow may be seen as Husserl's way of explaining how the unity of my conscious life remains intact despite the myriad experiences I undergo. I live through innumerable acts, each with a finite duration, but their incessant beginnings and endings do not splinter my abiding sense of unity and identity. Husserl suggests that at the deepest level of my conscious being I *am* a flow, and in that sense my being is temporal being, but thanks to that very flow I remain one and the same being across the diaspora of time. Finally, Husserl's notion of the flow reveals how the awareness of both temporal presence and absence are fundamental to my conscious life. The flow flows away yet recaptures itself, becomes absent but overcomes its absence by intending its absent phases in their absence, not by making them present again in some surrogate. We are neither locked in presence nor condemned to wander in absence. Thanks to time-consciousness, our lives are complex tapestries of presence and absence, unity and diversity, and identity and difference.

Heidegger

Martin Heidegger worked and studied under Edmund Husserl as his "assistant" and protégé. Husserl's admiration for Heidegger was great enough that when Husserl decided to bring the core of his lectures on the phenomenology of internal time-consciousness into print, he asked Heidegger, then an associate professor at Marburg University, to edit them. Heidegger was, thus, steeped in Husserl's phenomenology of internal time-consciousness. What is more, Heidegger places the phenomenology of time and temporality at the center of the project of *Being and Time*: "*time* needs to be *explicated primordially as the horizon for the understanding of Being, and in terms of temporality as the Being of Dasein*" (Heidegger 1962: 39). Heidegger embraces Husserl's aspiration to work out an account of the temporality of the being of Dasein (us), that is, an account of how our experience is constituted temporally. His further project of developing an ontology of being in general on the basis of the temporality of Dasein's being is quite alien to Husserl's way of thinking. It is also, perhaps, less phenomenologically oriented. For both these reasons, we will focus on the first theme in Heidegger, his exploration of existential temporality.

As we saw above, according to Husserl time-consciousness is "absolute," and in three senses: (1) it is the ultimate foundation for intentionality; (2) it is characterized by "double-intentionality" and is thereby self-constituting; and (3) it is a condition of the possibility of any awareness of any object at all. Heidegger adopts these three theses as well, albeit in slightly modified form. He embraces (1) implicitly in *Being and Time*, and explicitly in *The Basic Problems of Phenomenology*, when he there characterizes the "ecstatic unity of temporality" as the final horizon of intelligibility and ontological understanding (Heidegger 1982: 308). He also shares Husserl's commitment to the notion of "double-intentionality" (2). This theme is central to *Being and Time*, but Heidegger again puts the point somewhat more clearly in *Basic Problems*, where he describes our own being as co-awaited (or co-protended) and co-retained in every protention and retention of objects (Heidegger 1982: §19b). Finally, Heidegger accepts (3) as well and gives it a new name: it is the ecstatic-horizonal unity of temporality. Temporality "carries Dasein away" or "enraptures" it to the horizons on the background of which the entities we encounter can show up at all. It thereby constitutes Dasein's "transcendence," its stepping over to a world, its "being outside itself" in a world (Heidegger 1962: §69c). Hence, he concludes, "The world is neither present-at-hand nor ready-to-hand, but rather temporalizes itself in temporality" (Heidegger 1962: 417). Therefore, Heidegger shares the fundamental contours of Husserl's account of internal time-consciousness.

Heidegger diverges from Husserl in important respects as well, however, and it is Heidegger's disagreements with Husserl that give life to the debate among

131

phenomenologists about temporality and time-consciousness. As we saw above, Husserl regards the primal now as the point of orientation for our conscious lives. Heidegger argues, however, that, the future is primary in human temporality (see, e.g., Heidegger 1962: 378). He places the future at the center of our temporal orientation, rather than the present, the now. Why? Because for Heidegger the life of Dasein is not primarily the life of *consciousness*, but rather, the life of a concrete social *agent*. It is on this basis that Heidegger rejects the language of *subject and object* and replaces it with *Dasein and world*. We (Dasein) are primarily and usually at work in the world being who we are, and in this regard, the future is primary. We are who we are in so far as we understand ourselves thus, but to "understand ourselves" is not to grasp, imagine, or know ourselves cognitively or reflectively. Rather, to understand ourselves is to be *capable* of being who we are. Understanding is having the knack of something, "being equal to it" or being "able to manage" it (Heidegger 1962: 183). Being *able* to manage something (even being ourselves), being equal to it, is a matter of "pressing ahead" into being it, forging forth into our way of life and self-understanding. In this experience, the "for-the-sake-of" predominates; the structure of this experience is one of "coming-towards-oneself." This is all to say that who I am is not primarily a matter of what I have done, nor primarily consists in what I am like just now, but rather resides in who I am trying to be. This who is futural, not present. The future is primary in primordial temporality.

The experience of the now and now-time is derivative of primordial futural temporality. In setting about being a teacher, I grab hold of the implements of my trade, chalk and erasers, textbooks and handouts, etc. I "make them present" by availing myself of them. This making-present is made possible, however, by my futural pressing ahead into being a teacher. I could not grab hold of the chalk and use it as chalk, unless I understood myself as a teacher or in some other way to which chalk is relevant. The now-dominated experience of perceiving and using things is grounded in the future-dominated experience of self-understanding. Heidegger thus grounds the *now*, the reference point of *consciousness*, in the *future*, the reference point of *self-understanding*.

Further, for Husserl it is distinctive of time-consciousness that it tails off into an indefinite and presumably infinite horizon of future and past. Time as the horizon of object-consciousness is focused on the now and diffuses into the indefiniteness of past and future. For Heidegger, time as the horizon of self-understanding is aimed toward a future into which I press, a future *for the sake of which* I act as I do. My self-understanding for the sake of which I act is not for the sake of anything further, however. My self-understanding is an ultimate or final horizon, beyond which I cannot see, beyond which it makes no sense to inquire. Unlike the infinite temporal sequence in which objects present themselves, the future of my self-understanding is finite. By *finite* here Heidegger does not mean that the time in which I understand myself stops. Rather, he means that it is limited, that it has an uttermost horizon. There is no reference point beyond my self-understanding. Indeed, the mathematical question whether time is infinite or finite gets no grip on primordial temporality, for primordial temporality is not a sequence of nows, but rather our self-constituting openness to our own existence.

Thus, although Heidegger shares Husserl's conception of time-consciousness, or better, temporality, as the framework and structure in terms of which experience is possible, and although he also shares Husserl's commitment to the absoluteness of temporality (though not Husserl's *word* "absolute"), he relocates temporality from time-*consciousness* to the structure of *agency*. The finite and futural temporality of active self-understanding supplants the infinite and now-oriented time of self-consciousness.

Sartre

Sartre's phenomenology of time does not offer any radically new departure. Rather, Sartre shares Husserl's orientation to *consciousness* and the *I*, but seeks to restate some of Heidegger's innovations in a language that is more consciousness-friendly. Sartre uses the terminology of ecstasis and horizon, and like Heidegger before him, views primordial temporality as the foundation for our "transcendence" or "openness" to a world. Sartre thought of himself as working out a critique of Husserl's account of time-consciousness. He viewed Husserl's theory as being too "egological" and trapped in the now, but in this regard, as we saw above, he was wrong. Husserl's view is not *trapped* in the now; protention and retention constitute our awareness of the flow of time, including past and present. Husserl's account is, however, *centered* on the now. Sartre was no doubt influenced by Heidegger's criticisms of this orientation to the now, but in order to fund Heidegger's objections to Husserl, one must make the move from the logic of subject and object to that of Dasein and world, agent and social context. Only by focusing one's phenomenology on engaged and absorbed action, and viewing consciousness as a secondary derivative of such action, does one win the ground necessary to opt out of Husserl's orientation to the now.

Merleau-Ponty

Like Heidegger, Merleau-Ponty focuses his phenomenology on action. Merleau-Ponty's advance over Heidegger lies in his insistence on not only conceding, as Heidegger sometimes does, that the social agent is embodied, but placing this embodiment at the center of his account. Merleau-Ponty's specific contribution to the phenomenology of temporality lies in his development of a theme that is suggested by Heidegger, but not worked out in the sort of detail for which one would hope. Heidegger insists upon the *unity* of the three "ecstasies" of existential temporality, that is, the unity of our being *ahead* of ourselves in pressing forth into a self-understanding (our *futurity*), our being *already* situated in a world that matters to us in determinate ways (our *beenness*), and the *presence* to us of objects of use and observation. He also argues that we "never have power over our ownmost being from the ground up," that is, that we are *subject to* who we already are, that we have "been released from our ground . . . so as to be *as this ground*" (Heidegger 1962: 330). Heidegger also links all this with freedom. He does not, however, connect the dots.

It is left to Merleau-Ponty to clarify the connection of these points in terms of temporality (Merleau-Ponty 1962: Part 3, chs. 2 & 3). He argues that we could possess no freedom, if the present and future were not linked to and bound by the past. If the present and future swung free of the past, then every decision we make would have to be made over again in every instant. No decision or resolution could count as an achievement on which we could rely as we press forward into being who we are. This means, in turn, we would never make decisions or form resolutions. To decide or resolve is to commit oneself in one's future. If the decision had to be remade in every instant, however, then one could never commit oneself. The decision I make now could not limit and commit my future, because in the next moment, I would be "free" to take it back. Such illusory "freedom" – sometimes called "radical choice" and sometimes attributed to Sartre – is no freedom at all. It is chaos and discontinuity. Freedom, the possession of the future by an act of resolution, requires that I be able to commit, bind, and limit my future, and this requires in turn that the now be grounded in the past. Decisions I have already made must remain controlling in the present.

References and Further Reading

Blattner, W. (1999) *Heidegger's Temporal Idealism*. Cambridge: Cambridge University Press.

Brough, J. B. (1977) The emergence of an absolute consciousness in Husserl's early writings on time-consciousness. In F. Elliston and P. McCormick (eds.), *Husserl: Expositions and Appraisals*. South Bend, IN: Notre Dame University Press.

Heidegger, M. (1962) *Being and Time* (trans. J. Macquarrie and E. Robinson). New York: Harper & Row (original work published 1927).

—— (1979) *Sein und Zeit*, 15th edn. Tübingen: Max Niemeyer Verlag.

—— (1982) *The Basic Problems of Phenomenology*. (trans. A. Hofstadter). Bloomington: Indiana University Press (original lectures delivered 1927).

—— (1997) *Die Grundprobleme der Phänomenologie*, 3rd edn. *Martin Heidegger: Gesamtausgabe* (ed. F-W. von Herrmann), vol. 24. Frankfurt am Main: Vittorio Klostermann.

Husserl, E. (1966a) *The Phenomenology of Internal Time-Consciousness* (trans. J. S. Churchill). Bloomington: Indiana University Press (original work published in 1928).

—— (1966b) *Zur Phänomenologie des inneren Zeitbewusstseins (1893–1917)*. *Husserliana*, vol. X. The Hague: Martinus Nijhoff.

—— (1980) *Vorlesungen zur Phänomenologie des inneren Zietbewußtseins*, 2nd edn. (ed. M. Heidegger). Tübingen: Max Niemayer Verlag.

—— (1991) *On the Phenomenology of the Consciousness of Internal Time (1893–1917)* (trans. J. B. Brough). *Collected Works*, vol. 4. Dordrecht: Kluwer.

Kortooms, T. (2002) *Phenomenology of Time: Edmund Husserl's Analysis of Time-Consciousness*. Dordrecht: Kluwer.

McInerney, P. K. (1991) *Time and Experience*. Philadelphia: Temple University Press.

Merleau-Ponty, M. (1962) *Phenomenology of Perception* (trans. C. Smith). London: Routledge & Kegan Paul (original work published 1945).

Sartre, J-P. (1953) *Being and Nothingness* (trans. H. E. Barnes). New York: Washington Square Press (original work published 1943).

Part I

Phenomenology

Main Movements

11

The Roots of Existentialism

HUBERT L. DREYFUS

Introduction

Existential thinking defines itself in opposition to the philosophical tradition, so the best way to find out what existentialism is is to lay out the essence of traditional philosophy from the point of view of the existentialists.

We can divide up Greek philosophy as formed by Socrates and Plato into three areas: theory of knowledge, ethics, and metaphysics.

Theory of knowledge: What can we know?

Plato was amazed by theory. He saw that, by becoming disinterested and objective, one could discover timeless truths about geometry and physics that held for all rational beings.

Plato also realized, and happily accepted, the fact that such theoretical knowledge had no place for perception, skill, intuition, emotion, the body, folk wisdom, and the tradition. In becoming a theoretical thinker, one leaves all that behind.

Ethics: How should we act?

The aim of Greek ethics was to get beyond personal preferences, prejudices, and desires in order to discover the highest good for all. For Socrates this took the form of seeking *universal* rules for right action. For Plato, it was based on finding out what all human beings really needed and how to act in order to get it. According to both philosophers, people are individuated only by the situation they happen to be in, and by their imperfections. All morally perfect people, in the same situation, would act in the same way.

Metaphysics: What is real?

If theory describes what is real, then the objects of theory – timeless, abstract, conceptual structures – are the most real. The truths of science and math have always been true and always will be. The cosmos is eternal and simply repeats itself in cycles. History, too, runs in cycles and so repeats the same general pattern. Even in a person's life there is nothing radically new. The true self was implicit from the start, like the tree in the seed. Thus we get the idea of human development as self-realization.

If you die to the body, which only gets in the way of being rational, you get out of time, change, conflict, and death. Ultimate reality is not temporal and historical, but eternal. As your rational soul merges with the rational structure of reality, you become eternal too.

To sum up: the Greek philosophers saw that, if one pursued perfection by doing theory, great things could be obtained. Disinterested theory revealed objective truth – a set of abstract principles that held for all men, at all places, and all times. This is still the goal of every discipline that claims to be scientific. Rational morality promised fulfillment of one's universal human needs, lucidity in one's actions, and the assurance that one's actions would be intelligible to any other rational being anywhere at any time. Merging with abstract reality, i.e. identifying oneself with one's rational capacities to produce and understand theories, promised freedom from time, change, conflict, and death.

From the Greek philosophers we have inherited our ability to think – to be detached, self-critical, reflective, and objective. But there is another aspect of our lives that existential thinkers claim is as important as Greek thought in shaping our concerns and our sense of human perfection. This is our Judeo-Christian inheritance. Although the Hebrews had no philosophical categories – they were too busy making history to reflect and do philosophy – it is illuminating to look at the Hebrew tradition under the same categories we used for understanding the Greeks.

Theory of knowledge

The Hebrews felt they grasped the truth not by detached contemplation but by total commitment – being true to God by keeping His covenant. He was their God, and this was their truth, unique to them, that gave them their identity. The difference from the Greeks is dramatic. For the Greeks, truth is open to all people since they all have universal, rational souls; for the Hebrews, truth is not universal. It is local and historical, revealed at a specific time and place to a particular people and preserved in a particular tradition.

Ethics

The ultimate authority is God, not reason. The difference this makes can be seen by looking at Plato's *Euthyphro*. Socrates asks Euthyphro whether an action is pious because the gods love it, or if the gods love it because it is pious. Euthyphro's Greek answer is: the gods approve what is pious. For the Greeks, what is pious or good is determined by rational criteria that are binding on all men, and even on the gods. The Hebrews answer is just the opposite: an action is good because God approves it or commands it, and what is good is different for each individual. God's command that Abraham should kill Isaac does not mean that all good fathers should kill their sons, but it was the right thing for Abraham as an individual to do.

Metaphysics

For the Hebrews, everything significant happens in history. The world was created from nothing roughly 6000 years ago. This was followed by crucial historical moments: The Covenant, the Ten Commandments, and (for the Christians) the Incarnation. Radical transformation is possible. After the Incarnation people lived in a different world. Likewise, self-realization is not our goal. The self is sinful but each individual can and must be reborn.

The above contrast shows that ours is a uniquely conflicted culture, the product of two powerful and opposed traditions. As heirs to the Greeks we have learned to *think* that the only access to truth is by means of detached and disinterested contemplation, so *truth is objectivity. The universal is higher than the individual*, so each person must subordinate his or her selfish interests to universal moral principles. Ultimate reality is being not becoming, and *to reach eternity you have to get out of time*. But we also *believe* that truth is involved, personal commitment to something or someone specific, and so is essentially *subjective*; that each person must do what God requires of him or her so the *individual is higher than the universal*; and that time is the locus of all that is meaningful so that *eternity must somehow be achievable in time*.

Other cultures have multiple traditions – China has Taoism and Confucianism, for example – but these traditions normally complement each other. No culture but ours has two traditions so totally opposed. The Greek discovery of detached, disembodied, timeless, universal, reflective rationality contradicts the Hebrew revelation of involved, embodied, historical, local commitment. One side gives us our ability to think; the other, our deepest experiences.

To make sense of our culture Christian thinkers were forced to conceptualize the Hebrew revelation in Greek philosophical terms. They have tried valiantly to put the Judeo-Christian *experience* into Greek *concepts*. The first to try were the early Christian philosophers, especially St. Augustine (354–430), who interpreted Christianity in Platonic terms. But, from the existentialist's point of view, the results were disastrous. Augustine couldn't make sense of the creation, the Incarnation, or of God's command to Abraham to kill Isaac. A thousand or so years later, St. Thomas Aquinas (1227–74) interpreted Christianity using Aristotle and did a bit better. But in the end, in his account too, life in time and history was subordinated to the contemplation of an eternal God.

By the middle of the seventeenth century, philosophers like Descartes (1596–1650) could simply assume that the philosopher's God, who was eternal, infinite, fully intelligible, universal, and good, must be the same as the Judeo-Christian God.

Blaise Pascal

But a generation after Descartes, Blaise Pascal (1623–62) one day had an overwhelming religious experience of Jesus the incarnate Christian God. It convinced him that the Hebrew/Christian God had nothing in common with the eternal, intelligible presence, described by the philosophers. He was a living God to whom individuals could pray, and who paradoxically both reveals and conceals Himself in history.

139

On that day Pascal wrote: "God of Abraham, God of Isaac, God of Jacob, not of philosophers" (Pascal 1966: 309). This insight and the experience that accompanied it was so important to him that he kept his note with him at all times, and he later noted that

> If [the Christian] religion boasted of having a clear view of God, and of possessing it open and unveiled, it would be attacking it to say that we see nothing in the world which shows it with this clearness. But, on the contrary, it says that men are in darkness and estranged from God, that He has hidden Himself from their knowledge, that this is in fact the name which He gives Himself in the Scriptures, *Deus absconditus*. (Pascal 1958: 53, #94)

This insight led to many other insights, which made Pascal a proto-existential thinker. Looking at various cultures and religions that were becoming known at the time, Pascal saw that human beings had no essence to self-realize, but rather defined themselves through their cultural practices. "Custom is our nature," he wrote (Pascal 1958: 28, #89). Since Pascal's time, people in the West have understood themselves as subjects over against objects, computers, and, most recently, resources that should get the most out of their possibilities. They then tend to become what they interpret themselves to be, but this just shows that human beings are none of these particular cultural interpretations of their essence. Precisely because they can be shaped by any of these understandings of human being, it becomes clear that they have no essence, but that they are open possibilities of self-definition.

Although the self has no nature, according to Pascal, it does have a structure. Plato already understood the self as combining two contradictory sets of factors: body and soul. On this Greek account, if both sets of factors were equally essential, the self would be in hopeless self-contradiction. It could not fulfill all its bodily, temporal needs while at the same time fulfilling its intellectual, eternal needs, and so would be pulled apart by its earthly and heavenly desires. Indeed, the more one tried to fulfill one set of factors, the less one would be able to fulfill the other set. Plato concluded that, happily, the factors were merely *combined*, and if one realized that only one set of factors was essential – for example, that one is an eternal soul, stuck with a temporal body and so one "died to the body" – the conflict and instability could be overcome. Thus, for the Greeks, life was a voyage from confusion to clarity and from conflict to harmony. Since the self was potentially whole and harmonious, all one had to do was to realize which factors were essential, and then live so as to satisfy one's true needs rather than one's superficial desires, and one would experience peace and fulfillment.

Pascal, however, realized, that, according to Christianity, *both* sets of factors are essential and the self is, thus, not just an unstable *combination*, but something much more upsetting, an unstable *synthesis* of two incompatible sets of factors. As Pascal put it: "What a chimera then is man! What a novelty! What a monster, what a chaos, what a contradiction, what a prodigy! Judge of all things, imbecile worm of the earth; depositary of truth, a sink of uncertainty and error; the pride and refuse of the universe!" (Pascal 1958: 121, #434). According to Pascal, a person's highest achievement was not to deny or overcome this contradiction – by getting rid of half the self – but to relate to one's self in such a way as to be fully alive to the tension. He noted that "we do not display greatness by going to one extreme, but in touching both extremes at once, and filling all the intervening space" (Pascal 1958: 98, #353). So he held that we must take a stand on ourselves in our way of life that expressed both our "greatness and our misery," avoiding both pride and despair, as Jesus did in humbly accepting that he was both God and Man. But Pascal had little to say about how we normal human beings should do this.

Søren Kierkegaard

Two hundred years later, Søren Kierkegaard, the first person to call himself an existential thinker, took up the insights of Pascal to combat the influence of Hegel, the last philosopher to attempt to synthesize our Greek and Judeo-Christian heritage. Kierkegaard argued that Hegel did not succeed. As usual, the detached reflection and the truth, universality, and eternity it allegedly revealed covered up the Christian message. So, instead of trying to understand the Judeo-Christian revelation in Greek terms, Kierkegaard highlighted the opposition. He showed that any attempt to rationalize the Christian experience resulted in claims that, to the Greeks, would have sounded absurd. According to Kierkegaard, truth is subjectivity, the individual is higher than the universal, and eternity is only possible in time. To see why he says such outrageous things, we have to begin with Kierkegaard's elaboration of Pascal's anti-Greek definition of the self as a contradiction that has to take a stand on itself in its way of life.

Kierkegaard affirms that the self is a *synthesis* between two sets of opposed factors, not just a combination. That is, that each set is essential and requires the other. Here is Kierkegaard's dense definition of the self:[1]

> *Despair is a sickness of the spirit, of the self, and so can have three forms: being unconscious of the despair of having a self (inauthentic despair), desperately not wanting to be oneself, and despairingly wanting to be oneself.*
>
> The human being is spirit. But what is spirit? Spirit is the self. But what is the self? The self is a relation that relates to itself . . . A human being is a synthesis of the infinite and the finite, of the temporal and the eternal, of freedom and necessity . . .
>
> Such a relation which relates to itself . . . must either have established itself or been established by something else . . .
>
> The self is such a derived, constituted relation, a relation that relates to itself, and in relating to itself relates to another . . . The self cannot by itself arrive at or remain in equilibrium and rest by itself, but only in relating to itself by relating to that which has established the whole relation. (Kierkegaard 1989: 43–4)

Ways of futilely attempting to be a self

Like all existential thinkers, Kierkegaard holds that the only test of what is the right way to live is to throw yourself into many ways of life until one discovers which way gets one out of despair. In his earlier works such as *Either/Or* Kierkegaard describes various ways of life and how they break down. In *Sickness unto Death* he lays out his conclusions, which we summarize in schematic form in Figure 11.1.

R₁ – This is what Kierkegaard calls "Spiritlessness." One has a sense that the self is a contradiction that has to be faced, but one lives in what Pascal called distraction – his examples were playing tennis and sitting alone in one's room doing geometry – so that one never takes a stand in action as to how to get the factors together.

Kierkegaard thought that the most dangerous distraction in his time was the Public Sphere, where one could discuss events and people anonymously without ever having to take responsibility for one's views. One could debate, on the basis of principles, how the world should be run, without running the risk of testing these principles in action. This form of distraction is now consummated in talk shows, and especially chat rooms and news groups on the internet (Dreyfus 2002).

R₂ – If a human being refuses to face the incompatible essential aspects of the self, he or she is not yet a self. To be a self, one must relate oneself to oneself in one's actions by taking a stand on both sets of factors. One must manifest that something about the self is essential by making something in one's life absolute. This existential stance can take a negative and a positive form [for an example of each, see Figure 11.2].

Negative R₂ – Kierkegaard says:

> In a relation between two things the relation is the third term in the form of a negative unity, and the two relate to the relation, and in the relation to that relation; this is what it is from the point of view of soul for soul and body to be in relation. (Kierkegaard 1989: 43)

When the relation is a negative unity, the relation relates to itself in the Greek way; denying one of the sets of factors and acting as if only the other aspect of the self is the essential one. One can, for example, take the soul to be eternal at the expense of the body as Plato did, or do the opposite, as did Lucretius.

This would work if the self were a combination, but it is a synthesis. Thus, if one lives just for the temporal one loses the eternal and doesn't have any continuity in his life at all, while, if one tries to make the infinite and the eternal absolute, one loses the finite and the temporal. As Kierkegaard puts it, such mystical types can't bring their God-relationship to bear on a decision as to whether or not to take a walk in the park.

Positive R₂ – Such selves try, by themselves, to express fully both sets of factors in their lives, but this turns out to be impossible. For example, if one makes possibility absolute and lives constantly open to new possibilities, one is in the aesthetic sphere of existence – Kierkegaard's anticipation of Nietzsche and the postmoderns – but one has no way to express the self's facticity. If one tries to make facticity absolute, one loses possibility and one is paralyzed by fatalism. (Kierkegaard 1992)

Once he has worked through all the stands the self can take on itself and shown how each leads to despair, Kierkegaard claims to have shown that "the self cannot by itself arrive at or remain in equilibrium and rest" (Kierkegaard 1989: 44). His Christian view is that the self does not have the truth in it. As a contradiction it does not have in itself the resources to live a stable and meaningful life. And, according to Kierkegaard, everyone who has not managed to perform the impossible task of getting his or her self together in a stable, meaningful life is in despair.

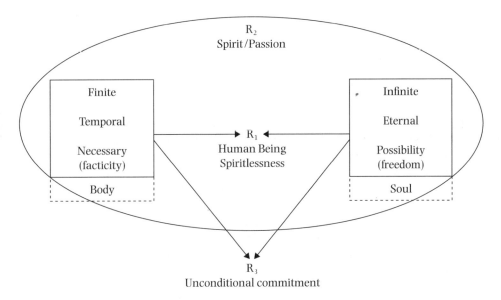

Figure 11.1   Illustration of Kierkegaard's Definition of the Self
[T]he common view overlooks the fact that, when compared with illness, despair differs dialectically from what one usually calls sickness, because it is a sickness of the spirit. And this dialectical aspect, properly understood, brings further thousands under the category of despair. If
at any time a physician is convinced that so and so is in good health, and then later that person
becomes ill, then the physician may well be right about his *having been* well at the time but now
being sick. Not so with despair. Once despair appears, what is apparent is that the person was in
despair. In fact, it's never possible at any time to decide anything about a person who is not
saved through having been in despair. For when whatever causes a person to despair occurs, it
is immediately evident that he has been in despair his whole life. When someone gets a fever on
the other hand, it cannot possibly be said that now it is evident that he has had a fever all his
life. But despair is a characteristic of the spirit, is related to the eternal, and therefore has something of the eternal in its dialectic. (Kierkegaard 1989: 54)

A person might well think that this is a preposterous claim, since I, at least, am not
in despair. One may feel that one is having a great time enjoying all one's possibilities,
or living a fulfilling life taking care of one's family, or that one's life is worth living
because one is working to eliminate suffering, and so forth. In general, one can feel
sure that one is fulfilling one's capacities and one's life is working out fine.

Kierkegaard would say that even when you think you are living a life worth living,
in fact you are in despair. What right does he have to say this? His answer is in *Sickness
unto Death*:

Despair differs dialectically from what one usually calls sickness, because it is a sickness
of the spirit. And this dialectical aspect, properly understood, brings further thousands
under the category of despair. If at any time a physician is convinced that so and so is in
good health, and then later that person becomes ill, then the physician may well be right

about his having been well at the time but now being sick. Not so with despair. Once despair appears, what is apparent is that the person was in despair. In fact, it's never possible at any time to decide anything about a person who is not saved through having been in despair. For when whatever causes a person to despair occurs, it is immediately evident that he has been in despair his whole life. (Kierkegaard 1989: 54)

Kierkegaard is pointing out that despair is not like sadness, regret, disappointment, depression, etc. Rather, unlike these downers, despair exhibits what Kierkegaard calls "the dialectic of eternity." If you are sad, you know that it is temporary. Even if something so terrible happens to you that you feel that you were happy once but that whatever has happened makes it impossible for you ever to be happy again, that is certainly misery, but it is not despair. Despair is the feeling that your life isn't working and, given the kind of person you are, it is impossible for things to work for you; that a life worth living is, in your case, literally impossible.

That means that once a person experiences despair – "it will be evidence that his 'previous' success was an illusion" – i.e., all that person's past joys *must have been* self-deceptions (Kierkegaard 1989: 51). So Kierkegaard concludes that, even though you now feel that things are going well for you, given the contradictory nature of the self, each of us, with the exception of those who have faced despair and been healed, must right now be in despair.[2]

The self in equilibrium and out of despair

Only when the self "in relating to itself relates to something else," Kierkegaard contends, can it get the two sets of factors into a positive relation (Kierkegaard 1989: 51). Only then is each set of factors defined in such a way as to support rather than be in conflict with the other. But how is this possible?

Whether you can get the factors together or whether they form a contradiction depends on how you define them. Or, to put it another way, the Greeks found that, if you define the factors from the point of view of detachment, you can't get them together. Kierkegaard tries to show that only if you define the factors in terms of a total involvement that gives you your identity as an individual can you arrive at a positive synthesis.

To illustrate what is at stake in having an identity, Kierkegaard draws on the chivalric romances. The example, on which he says "everything turns," is the case of "A young lad [who] falls in love with a princess, [so that] the whole content of his life lies in this love" (Kierkegaard 1985: 70). But Kierkegaard adds in a footnote, that "any other interest whatever in which an individual concentrates the whole of life's reality" would do as well (Kierkegaard 1985: 71).

Kierkegaard had been looking for just this sort of unconditional commitment. When he was 22 years old he wrote in his journal: "What I really lack is to be clear in my mind *what I am to do*, not what I am to know . . . The thing is to understand myself, to see what God really wishes *me* to do; the thing is to find a *truth* which is true *for me*, . . . *for which I can live and die*" (Kierkegaard 1951: 15). As he put it in his *Concluding Unscientific Postscript*, "Truth is subjectivity" (Kierkegaard 1968: 181).

The lad who loves the princess relates himself to himself by way of this relation to the princess. Thanks to it, he knows who he is and what is relevant and important in his world. Any such unconditional commitment to some specific individual, cause, or vocation, whereby a person gets an identity and a sense of reality, would do to make the point Kierkegaard is trying to make. In such a case, a person becomes an individual defined by his or her relation to the object of his or her unconditional commitment. The lad is the lover of the princess, MLK Jr. is the one who will bring justice to the American blacks, Steve Jobs identifies himself with Apple Computer, etc.

According to Kierkegaard, if and only if you let yourself be drawn into a defining commitment, can you achieve that which, while you were in despair, looked impossible, viz., that the two sets of factors reinforce each other, so that the more you manifest one the more you manifest the other. By responding to the call of such an unconditional commitment and thereby getting an identity, a person becomes what Kierkegaard, following the Bible, calls "a new creation" (Kierkegaard 1985: 70).

The necessary and the possible

We have seen that, when you have a defining commitment, your identity becomes as necessary as a definition. But, although your identity is fixed, it does not dictate an inflexible way of acting as if it were a rigid compulsion, infatuation, or obsession. That would not be an expression of freedom. Kierkegaard calls anyone who can sustain the risk of an unconditional commitment and let themselves be more and more involved a "Knight of Faith." Kierkegaard says the Knight is free to "forget the whole thing" but in so doing the Knight would "contradict himself," since it is "a contradiction to forget the whole of one's life content and still be the same" (Kierkegaard 1985: 72).

Still, in anything less than total loss and subsequent world collapse, one has to be able to adapt to even the most radical changes in the defining object. All such adaptive changes will, of course, be changes *in* the world but not changes *of* the world. Kierkegaard calls this "freedom" since, even though the central concern in one's life is fixed, one is free to adapt to all sorts of possible situations in all sorts of ways.

There is, however, an even more radical kind of freedom: The freedom to change one's world, i.e., to change one's identity. To be born again *and again*. Although Kierkegaard does not say so in so many words, once we see that eternity can begin in time, we can see that, not only can eternity *begin* at a moment of time, it can *change* in time. In Kierkegaard's terms, Abraham has faith that if he sacrifices Isaac, "God could give him a new Isaac" (Kierkegaard 1985: 65). This can happen because God is "that everything is possible" and that means even the inconceivable is possible (Kierkegaard 1989: 71). On Kierkegaard's view, one can only change worlds by being totally involved in one, deepening one's commitment, taking all the risks involved, until it breaks down and becomes impossible. As in Thomas Kuhn's *Structure of Scientific Revolutions*, revolutions depend on prior unconditional commitment to a paradigm (Kierkegaard 1967: 109).

The temporal and the eternal

For one to live fully in time, some moment must be absolutely important and make other moments significant relative to it. The moment when one is transformed by getting an identity is obviously such a moment. Kierkegaard, drawing on the biblical saying that we shall be changed in the twinkling of an eye, calls this moment the *Augenblick*. After the transformation, other moments also become significant since one's

145

unconditional commitment must be expressed in one's day-to-day activity. But the eternal is also expressed in one's life. Not the disinterested, abstract eternity of Plato, but the passionately involved eternity that Kierkegaard calls "eternity in time." Normally, the significance of events in one's life is subject to retroactive reinterpretation,[3] but, in an unconditional commitment that defines the self, one's identity is as eternal as a definition. The lad, who is a Knight of Faith, will henceforth always be the lover of the princess. Further events will be interpreted in the light of the content given the self in the *Augenblick*, not vice versa.

The way a commitment can produce a privileged moment is not something that can be understood by disinterested thought. Kierkegaard says: "A concrete eternity within the existing individual is the maximum degree of passion . . . The proposition inaccessible to thought is that one can become eternal although one was not such" (Kierkegaard 1968: 181). That is, if you are unconditionally committed to a particular person or cause, that will be your identity forever (for every moment of your life). The paradoxical fact is that, "only in existing do I become eternal" (Kierkegaard 1968: 506). But this does not make me any less temporal. "The existing individual *in time* . . . comes into relation with the eternal *in time*" (ibid.).

The finite and the infinite

Kierkegaard calls an unconditional commitment an infinite passion for something finite. But just what makes an infinite passion count as infinite? It can't be just a very strong feeling; rather, it must in some sense transcend the finite. For Kierkegaard, an infinite passion can legitimately be called *infinite* because it opens up a *world*. Not only *what actually exists* gets its meaning from its connection with my defining passion; anything that could *possibly* come into my experience would get its meaning for me from my defining commitment. As we saw earlier, according to Kierkegaard, one's commitment defines one's reality.

Of course, the object of my infinite passion is something *finite*. We are interested in the smallest particularities of our beloved. But any such finite being is vulnerable, and yet the meaning of one's life depends on it. This makes a defining commitment very risky. It would certainly be safer to define one's life in terms of some sort of theoretical quest or in terms of some abstract idea – say, the eventual triumph of the proletariat – but that is not concrete enough to satisfy the need to make the finite absolutely significant. So it follows, as Kierkegaard says, "without risk there is no faith" (Kierkegaard 1968: 188).

Kierkegaard holds that, given the risk, to let yourself be more and more involved with something finite, you need to live in a kind of absurdity. As he puts it: "Every moment to see the sword hanging over the loved one's head and yet find, not repose in the pain of resignation, but joy on the strength of the absurd – that is wonderful. The one who does that, he is great, the only great one" (Kierkegaard 1985: 79).

Such an individual, a Knight of Faith, can do this because he lives in the assurance that "God is the fact that everything is possible, and that everything is possible is God" (Kierkegaard 1989: 71).

In sum, when you have a defining commitment, the finite object of your commitment is infinitely important, i.e., the object of your passion is both something particular

146

and also world defining. Indeed, it is the condition for anything showing up as meaningful. But since such a finite commitment is always risky, and so security is impossible, one can only sustain one's infinite passion if one has faith that even the impossible is possible.

The teleological suspension of the ethical

Now we can see why Kierkegaard claims that, unless the self relates itself to "something else" with a total commitment, it is in despair, but that, if it has an absolute commitment, it will be able to get the two sets of factors together in such a way that they reinforce each other, and so be in bliss. But the idea that making an unconditional commitment is the highest thing a human being can do raises a serious problem.

Abraham had an unconditional commitment to some absolute we can call God, and his absolute commitment to that absolute required that he kill his son, Isaac. His anguish is not simply that he loves his son; it's that, if he kills Isaac, he would be putting himself as an individual with his own relation to the absolute above the ethical. But ethical principles are universal, that is, they are binding on everyone everywhere and they require that no one make an expectation of him or her self. Still, according to Kierkegaard, the fact that Jews and Christians consider Abraham the father of the faith shows that the Judeo-Christian tradition has, from the start, implicitly held that the individual is higher than the universal.

The ethical is absolutely important because it allows us to make sense of what we are doing. Only if we all share a public moral vocabulary that tells us what is right and what is wrong, worthy and unworthy, can we justify our actions to ourselves and to others. Nowadays, however, we no longer believe with Socrates, Plato, and Kant that there is just one rational shared moral vocabulary. Kierkegaard understands and accepts this. "Universal" need not mean for everyone for all times, but it can mean whatever standards are accepted by whatever group we respect. In any case, a shared morality is essential for us to recognize and resist our selfish impulses while taking on our social responsibilities, and explaining our actions to others and ourselves.

Kierkegaard contends that one has to get over what he calls "so-called subjectivity" – one's superstitions, obsessions, compulsions, prejudices, and the like – and he agrees with Socrates that critical thinking and a respect for the ethical enable one to do this. Kierkegaard is, thus, the first and last existential philosopher to see something worth saving in the philosophical tradition of critical rationality. Dostoyevsky, as we shall see, thinks philosophers are detached and so are dangerous, and Nietzsche thinks that Socrates, in wanting to die to his body, shows he is decadent, while recent existential thinkers such as Heidegger and Sartre hold that the ethical is just the voice of conformism. Kierkegaard, on the contrary, holds that being ethical, while not our highest end or *telos*, nonetheless enables people to get over being blinded and driven by their accidental particularity, thus enabling them to make a commitment that makes them an individual and so giving coherence and meaning to their lives. Kierkegaard thus is able to appreciate one of the principal achievements of Greek philosophy and, in this case, have the best of both worlds.

But in the end the Greek and Judeo-Christian worlds collide. Philosophers have always held that to leave the universal and act as a particular is selfish and immoral.

Kierkegaard agrees that people have always been tempted to make an exception of themselves, but he points out that philosophers can't distinguish such unethical acts from the unconditional commitments of the faithful like Abraham. "[But] then faith's paradox is this, that the single individual is higher than the universal, that the single individual . . . determines his relation to the universal through this relation to the absolute, not his relation to the absolute through his relation to the universal" (Kierkegaard 1985: 97). In short, our philosophical categories have no way to distinguish unconditional commitment from selfishness. And, indeed from the ethical point of view, in the shared public language in which we understand ourselves and others, Abraham is a criminal. If he tries to *understand* what he is doing as he gets ready to kill Isaac, he can only say to himself that he is a murderer. Yet, paradoxically, he feels he is doing his highest duty.

Criteria for judging the worth of ways of acting

Philosophers would say so much the worse for faith since it seems that someone going against the ethical like Abraham might well be driven by a compulsion like the child molester in Fritz Lang's *M*, or tempted to kill their son through insanity brought on by too much cortisone and reading too much Kierkegaard, as is the character played by James Mason in *Bigger than Life* (Nicholas Ray, 1956), or just plain crazy, like Jack Nicholson in Stanley Kubrick's *The Shining* (1980). Or, in real life, a dangerous psychopath like Charles Manson, or a fanatic like Hitler. How can one tell such dangerous criminals from Knights of Faith suspending the ethical? Granted there can't be any public criteria for recognizing a Knight of Faith, Kierkegaard suggests that there *are* criteria for "distinguishing the paradox from a temptation" (Kierkegaard 1985: 85).

There are at least three negative "criteria" and one positive one (Kierkegaard 1985: 106).

(1) Knights of Faith can't be driven to their action like Peter Lorre in *M*, who claims convincingly that he abhors killing children but that he can't help himself; they must be free. Kierkegaard says, "Abraham can refrain at any moment, he can repent the whole thing as a temptation" (Kierkegaard 1985: 139).

(2) Knights of Faith must respect the ethical. They must have subjected their impulses to critical reflection. In Kierkegaard's colorful terms, the Knight of Faith is not a "vagrant genius" (Kierkegaard 1985: 103). He can't just say "I'm a superior person and so I don't have to respect the ethical," as does Raskolnikov in Dostoyevsky's *Crime and Punishment*, or Charles Manson, as described in Vincent Bugliosi's *Helter Skelter*. The same would apply to Hitler if he took himself to be a charismatic leader above the ethical.

(3) But Knights of Faith can't justify themselves on the basis of some new universal principle, either. This rules out people who invent their own ethical. Kierkegaard says: "The true Knight of Faith is always [in] isolation; the false knight is sectarian" (Kierkegaard 1985: 106). Hitler would again be disqualified if he justified genocide by arguing that science showed that Jews were subhuman.

One positive criterion follows from all the above. Individuals who respect the ethical and yet feel that their unconditional commitment requires them freely to go against it feel, paradoxically, that what they are doing is the most despicable thing they could possibly do yet also the best thing they have ever done. From an everyday ethical point of view all suspenders of the ethical are crazy. As Kierkegaard says: "[Abraham] knows that higher up there winds a lonely path, narrow and steep; he knows it is terrible to be born in solitude outside the universal, to walk without meeting a single traveler . . . Humanly speaking he is insane and cannot make himself understood to anyone" (Kierkegaard 1985: 103). The result, Kierkegaard says, is a "constant tension" (Kierkegaard 1985: 106). Indeed, where Knights of Faith are concerned, "distress and anguish are the only justification conceivable" (Kierkegaard 1985: 137).

To see that this dramatic talk of the anguish of suspending the ethical is not just psychological science fiction, we need an example. Consider a homosexual "lad" in Denmark in 1850 who loved a "prince" rather than a "princess." The ethical at that time would consider this defining commitment terribly immoral. And so would the lover himself. Given the ethics of the time, he could only think of his love as perverted, unnatural, depraved, and disgusting. For him the ethical would be a temptation for, if he does not go straight, he would have to live with the anguished and paradoxical sense that his love is the best thing he ever did, while being at the same time the worst.

Kierkegaard was the first to see that we in the West live in a conflicted culture permeated by two contradictory understandings of the world and of who we are. The Greeks disclosed the universal ethical and we respect it as our highest goal because it enables us to make sense of our lives. But the Judeo-Christians' experience opened up the possibility of a calling that required that an individual go against the ethical. We can't give up the ethical and still *make sense* of what we are doing, but we can't give up our unconditional commitment and still have a *fully meaningful life*. These two demands are absolutely opposed. This situation is not to be deplored, however. Only a conflicted culture like ours, that respects the ethical and yet believes that people can be transformed into individuals, can be truly historical, that is, can radically change its understanding of what it means to be a human being.

Conclusion

Now we can see why Kierkegaard claims that, unless the self relates itself to something else with an unconditional commitment, it is in despair. Only if it has an unconditional commitment will the self be able to get the two sets of factors together in such a way that they will reinforce each other, and so be in bliss. Kierkegaard says rather obscurely: "This is the formula that describes the state of the self when despair is completely eradicated: in relating to itself and in wanting to be itself, the self is grounded transparently in the power that established it" (Kierkegaard 1989: 44). Grounded transparently means acting in such a way that what gives you your identity comes through in everything you do. But what is the power (lower case) that established the self? I used to think it was whatever finite and temporal object of infinite passion created you as a new being by giving you your identity. But that would only be the power that established your identity, not the power that established the three sets of contradictory factors to which your identity is the solution. What, then, is the power that established the whole relation?

The "power" doesn't seem to be the traditional Judeo-Christian God since the word is in lower case and Kierkegaard doesn't say that the power *created* the relation. But Kierkegaard does say that one could not despair "unless the synthesis were originally in the right relationship from the hand of God" (Kierkegaard 1989: 46). How are we to cash out this metaphor, especially if we remember that, for Kierkegaard, "God is the fact that everything is possible" – not an entity at all.

I think we have to say that "the fact that everything is possible" makes possible, indeed is incarnate in, the contradictory God-man. He is the paradoxical Paradigm who saves from despair all sinners – those who have tried to take a stand on themselves by themselves, either by relating only to themselves or by relating to an infinite, absolute, and eternal God (what Kierkegaard calls Religiousness A and sees as a kind of despair). The God-man saves them by calling them to make an unconditional commitment to Him: "The paradoxical edification [of Christianity] corresponds . . . to the determination of God in time as the individual man. If such be the case, the individual is related to something outside himself" (Kierkegaard 1968: 498).

But, given the logic of Kierkegaard's position, it follows that the object of such a defining relation does not have to be the God-man. Indeed, in the *Postscript* Kierkegaard says: "Subjectively reflection is directed to the question whether the individual is related to something *in such a manner* that his relationship is in truth a God relationship" (Kierkegaard 1968: 178). And even more clearly that "it is the passion of the infinite that is the decisive factor and not its content, for its content is precisely itself" (Kierkegaard 1968: 181).

The claim that God *established* the factors has to mean, then, that by making it possible for people to have a defining commitment – in the first instance to Him – and so be reborn, Jesus revealed that both sets of factors are equally essential and can (and must) be brought into equilibrium. This is the truth about the essential nature of the self that went undiscovered until Jesus revealed it. In this way he established the Christian understanding of the self, in which we now live. His is the call that demands "the decision in existence" which we cannot reject without despair (Kierkegaard 2001: 63).

So, on this reading, "to be grounded transparently in the power that established it" would mean that the saved Christian: (1) relates himself to himself by manifesting in all aspects of his life that both sets of factors are essential; by, that is, relating to someone or something finite with an infinite passion and so becoming eternal in time.

Whatever constituted the self as the individual self by giving it its identity, thereby making it "a new being" and healing it of despair – that "something" would be its Savior. And (2), all such lives are grounded in Jesus, the God-man, the Paradigm who first makes possible the radical transformation of people and of the world.

Fyodor Dostoyevsky

Like Kierkegaard, Dostoyevsky shares Pascal's insight that, to be a self, in the West at least, is to be composed of contradictory components and to have to take a stand on those factors in the way one lives. For Dostoyevsky, as for Kierkegaard, there is no moral or religious way to argue which stand is right; the right stand is the one that works. If your stand on the self leads you to despair and suicide, then that is not the right way to live. If it gives you joy, then you have found the right way to relate yourself to yourself. Dostoyevsky's affinities with existentialism are present in their clearest form in *The Brothers Karamazov*, so I will focus on that work.

In *The Brothers Karamazov* Dostoyevsky speaks not of the self but of the heart, and he has many different names for the factors as they are understood and lived by the father, Fyodor Karamazov, and his three sons, Ivan, Dmitri, and Alyosha. Still, his account maps perfectly on Kierkegaard's (see Figure 11.2).

Fyodor

Fyodor Karamazov is in the despair of not being conscious of having a self. He diverts himself by drinking and running after women so as not to be aware of his contradictory needs and the need to take a stand on them. But, unknown to him, his behavior expresses his double nature.

Ivan

Ivan's way of life is to be an objective, detached spectator. He is an intellectual, interested in philosophy and natural science. Like Plato, Ivan is seeking a kind of eternal perfection by dying to the world. Early on, Dmitri says, "Ivan's a tomb," and later, he adds, "Ivan has no God he has an idea" (Dostoyevsky 1996: 120, 677). Ivan is passionately trying to be dispassionate. He wants to be pure by throwing out all his imperfections – to get rid of what he calls the lackey, the Karamazov, the earthy side of himself. In Kierkegaard's terms, Ivan is in the despair of not wanting to be himself.

Dmitri

Dostoyevsky gives a revealing description of Dmitri when we first meet him. He is young, but he looks old; he is muscular, and yet his face looks thin and unhealthy; he seems to have firm determination and yet he has a vague look in his eyes; he has a melancholy gaze but then bursts into laughter. He is, in short, a walking contradiction (Dostoyevsky 1996: 70–1). When he speaks of the heart, he clearly is speaking of what Kierkegaard called the self. He says: "Here all contradictions exist side by side . . . Yes, man is broad, too broad, indeed. I'd have him narrower . . . God and the devil are fighting there and the battlefield is the heart of man" (Dostoyevsky 1996: 117–18).

Alyosha

Alyosha has a defining commitment to Father Zossima. His whole life thus far has been determined by that relationship. Like Kierkegaard's Knight of Faith, Alyosha is able to accept the risk of an unconditional commitment because he has faith that everything will always go well for him. "Alyosha was certain that no one in the whole world ever would want to hurt him, and, what is more, he knew that no one could hurt him. This was for him an axiom, assumed once and for all without question, and he went his way without hesitation, relying on it" (Dostoyevsky 1996: 110). Alyosha

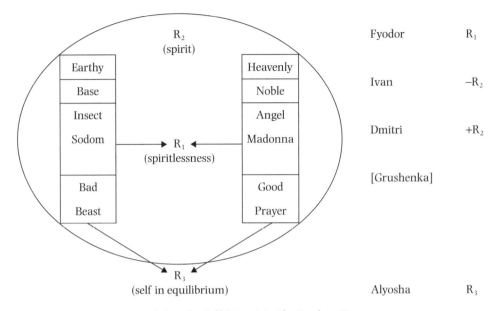

Figure 11.2 The Self (Heart) in *The Brothers Karamazov*

thus fits Kierkegaard's description of someone acting in a field of faith, "by virtue of the absurd," or "as though all things were possible."

To sum up, there are four Karamazovs and four ways the self can relate to itself:

1 Fyodor flees from facing up to the contradictory impulses in himself.
2 Ivan wants, in despair, to repress what he calls his base or lackey side.
3 Dmitri is trying desperately to accept both his sensuality and his spirituality and is flipping back and forth – unable to define the factors in a way that would allow them to support each other.
4 Alyosha has provisionally got himself together by sublimating all his impulses into his love for Father Zossima.

If we had space we could follow the lives of the four Karamazovs, each of whom lives out one of the ways the self relates itself to itself, but we will have to narrow our focus to Ivan, who represents Dostoyevsky's understanding of the traditional philosopher, and to Alyosha, whose life comes close to Dostoyevsky's ideal.

Dostoyevsky's critique of philosophy

In the revealing chapter called "Rebellion," Ivan sets out to tell Alyosha his basic stance toward life. Like Pascal, he insists that you can't prove or disprove the existence of God, but that religion is not about proving whether God exists, but about one's stance toward life. So, Ivan says he is going to give an argument about how one should live.

Ivan tells Alyosha that as soon as his involvement in the world lessens enough for him to be able to escape from it, he will commit suicide. This sounds like Socrates recommending that philosophers die to the world, and Ivan does want to resist the world's attraction, but he has different reasons for renouncing the world than did Socrates. He intends to prove that any decent person is obliged to leave the world as soon as possible because the world is such a corrupt and evil place that it is impossible for a moral person to accept living in it.

He makes his case by collecting a dossier of child abuse, cases of the torture of innocent children. No suffering of the child abusers in hell and no higher harmony can make up for the damage already done, so Ivan tells Alyosha: "I hasten to give back my entrance ticket, and if I am an honest man I am bound to give it back as soon as possible" (Dostoyevsky 1996: 272). Dostoyevsky wants us to be convinced by the argument, since when Alyosha is asked by Ivan, "would you consent to be the architect on those conditions?," Alyosha reluctantly answers, "no." Should each of us, then, give back our ticket? There seems to be something wrong with Ivan's argument. But what?

The way Dostoyevsky sets it up, what's wrong with Ivan's philosophical argument is that it is a *philosophical* argument. It presumes that Ivan is related to the world like a spectator at a play or someone being wooed by a club. If the play is pornographic or sadistic one can and should leave and give back the ticket; if the club is immoral one shouldn't join. But is that how we are related to the world? That may be how it looks to a detached, reflective philosopher like Ivan, but Dostoyevsky claims that each of us is already involved in the suffering in the world, and so we are not in a position to reject it. We are not pure innocent bystanders. Ivan turns out to be a sadist aroused by his "nice" collection of reports of the torture of children. More importantly, the plot shows that Ivan and almost everyone else is responsible for the crime at the heart of the book. So, what is wrong with Ivan's "rebellion" from Dostoyevsky's existentialist point of view is not Ivan's argument but the philosophical position from which it is made.

Alyosha doesn't see the mistake at the basis of Ivan's argument but instead makes the mistake of suggesting the traditional Christian doctrine that Jesus' innocent suffering balances the books. That leads Ivan to respond with the Grand Inquisitor Legend. Ivan's "poem" has been taken by many readers, who should know better, as a defense of an existentialist version of Jesus' teachings, and thus as the core of the book. For example, Nicholas Berdyaev, who takes himself to be an existentialist interpreter of Dostoyevsky, focuses on Jesus' demand that the believer come to Him with total freedom, and says: "The legend of the Grand Inquisitor contains the best of the constructive part of Dostoyevsky's religious ideas . . . It is noteworthy that the extremely powerful vindication of Christ (which is what the legend is) should be put into the mouth of the atheist Ivan Karamazov" (Berdyaev 1957: 204, 88). Nothing could be more wrongheaded! As becomes clear in the context of the book, both the Grand Inquisitor, Dostoyevsky's defender of Roman Catholic slavery, and his projection of a Jesus with a Protestant belief in total freedom, are equally wrong. The book defends a third position. It is the Russian Orthodox Church, interpreted by Dostoyevsky as a vision of how to live that is opposed to both, Catholic universalism and Protestant individualism. But Dostoyevsky had good reason to worry he would not be understood. He wrote to a friend after the publication of the Grand Inquisitor: "As my answer to all this negative side, I had planned this sixth book 'A Russian Monk' . . . And I'm trembling for it in this way: Will it be an adequate answer – especially since it's not a direct answer to the stand expressed before (in the Grand Inquisitor and before that) point by point, but only obliquely?" (Belknap 1967: 14).

Showing the way the Grand Inquisitor sets up a series of antinomies, each of which is answered somewhere in the course of *The Brothers Karamazov*, is too big a task to enter into here.[4] The answer culminates in Alyosha's experience of the connectedness of all human beings. To avoid man's relation to God drawing him away from his fellow human beings, Dostoyevsky claims not just that God is hidden as Pascal saw, but, like Kierkegaard, he holds that God is not an object at all, but rather the field of involvements – an "ocean of love" (Dostoyevsky 1996: 358).

Childhood memories

One of the least noted but most important aspects of *The Brothers Karamazov* is the stress Dostoyevsky puts on childhood memories. At the beginning of the book Dostoyevsky describes one of these: "He remembered one still summer evening, . . . the holy image . . . and on her knees before the image, his mother . . . snatching him up in both arms . . . and praying for him to the Mother of God, holding him out in both arms to the image as though to put him under the Mother's protection" (Dostoyevsky 1996: 17). And Dostoyevsky shows Alyosha producing such memories for the boys at the end of the book.

A key to the importance of such memories is in the account of the creation of Dmitri's childhood memory introduced as part of the testimony of a German doctor. The doctor tells of his first encounter with Dmitri – a neglected child. "I bought him a pound of nuts, for no one had ever bought the boy a pound of nuts before. And I lifted my finger and said to him, 'Boy, *Gott der Vater*' '*Gott der Sohn.*' '*Gott der heilige Geist*'" (Dostoyevsky 1996: 769). Now, God the Father, God the Son, and God the Holy Spirit are rather strange things to repeat when giving a child a bag of nuts. To understand what Dostoyevsky is up to here, it is important to realize that these words are pronounced at a baptism. The German doctor has, in effect, baptized Dmitri. He has put him in a dimension where salvation and damnation are possible. It was not done magically by sprinkling holy water on him, but it gives him a lasting sense of connectedness and love. We can now see, in retrospect, that Alyosha's experience with his mother, too, was like a baptism and that it inclined him toward a religious life. These special moments of love are important for Dostoyevsky because they are the condition for the possibility of one's later ability to love. Ivan never experienced such a moment.

This demagicalizing of baptism is an instance of one of Dostoyevsky's most important goals in *The Brothers Karamazov*. He is systematically existentializing the Christian revelation. He wants, thereby, to save the *existential truth* of Christianity from a literal reading that could put it in conflict with what he calls the laws of physics and chemistry. In the course of the book, Dostoyevsky clears away the magic from miracles, Confession, the Incarnation, Ordination, the Apostolic Succession, the Crucifixion, and the Resurrection, as well as angels and the devils, while showing *their existential meaning*. Kierkegaard can be read as doing the same job when he follows the trouba-dours in making romantic love an example of faith, and defining God, not as a Super-Being, but as a field in which all things are possible.

In a final *tour de force* in the last few pages of the book Dostoyevsky existentializes the founding of a church and eternity, as well as answering a remaining question left open by Ivan's Grand Inquisitor Legend. The Grand Inquisitor claims that, to have faith, human beings need a universal truth that all can believe in together – the universal church as a universal ant heap. Christ, according to the Inquisitor, insisted that human beings must relate to God in isolation.

Dostoyevsky's middle ground, enunciated by Father Zossima, is that, if two or more are gathered in love, a Christian community, "a world of living love," is formed (Dostoyevsky 1996: 871). The last pages of *The Brothers Karamazov* show us the existentialized founding of such a religious community.

Dostoyevsky always signals what he is existentializing, and those who are watching and know their New Testament will notice there are twelve boys present at a "big stone" (Dostoyevsky 1996: 871). With Alyosha's guidance the boys are given a childhood memory founded on their being together at the funeral of their friend, Ilusha. Even though they are tempted by the world, he tells them, they will never lose the memory of Ilusha and this moment at the rock. It will be a *shared* childhood memory for them. "You must know that there is nothing higher and stronger and more wholesome and good life in the future than . . . some good, sacred memory, preserved from childhood . . . If a man carries many such memories with him into life, he is safe to the end of his days" (Dostoyevsky 1996: 878). Such memories are "sacred" because, unlike ordinary memories, they cannot be changed by later events. So Alyosha can add: "All together at this stone, the cruelest and most mock-ing of us – if we do become so – will not dare to laugh inwardly at having been kind and good at this moment!" (Dostoyevsky 1996: 878–9). It is no accident that the meeting sounds like a church service. Alyosha sings out: "Ilusha, the good boy, the dear boy, precious to us for ever! . . . May his memory live for ever in our hearts from this time forth!" and the boys respond: "Yes, yes, forever, forever" (Dostoyevsky 1996: 879).

Alyosha has changed the boys *forever*. He has established an existentialized moment of eternity – produced what Kierkegaard calls eternity in time.

The saved self

All through the book, it has been an insult to be called a "Karamazov" for that name represented the base side of human nature. As Alyosha puts it: "My brothers are destroying themselves, . . . my father, too. And they are destroying others with them. It's 'the primitive force of the Karamazovs'" (Dostoyevsky 1996: 245). Being a Karamazov means being a self that is base, or, at best, having a heart that is base *and* noble but too broad to be in equilibrium. As the prosecutor remarks concerning Dmitri: "He was of the broad Karamazov character . . . capable of combining the most incon-gruous contradictions, and capable of the greatest heights and of the greatest depths" (Dostoyevsky 1996: 796). But at the very end of the book we see that the Karamazov self can be transformed by a loving relation to others outside itself. The earthly has been integrated with the heavenly and despair has been turned into joy. So the book fittingly ends with the newly created, eternal, sacred community of boys shouting in unison: "Hurrah for Karamazov!"

Nietzsche

Dostoyevsky and Nietzsche

Dostoyevsky and Nietzsche both wrote at the beginning of the last stage of our culture's living out the Socratic/Platonic promise that, by becoming critical and pursuing detached theoretical understanding, one could arrive at certainty in knowledge, universality in ethics, and eternal life. Both reacted against the Enlightenment promise that reason, disinterested objectivity, and scientific truth would save our culture from dogmatism, superstition, and fanaticism and, as Dmitri says, repeating what he has learned from Rakitin, the existentialized devil, a new man would arise, who would be free, in control of nature and society, master of himself, and – as Kant put it – at last, "mature."

All the existential thinkers share the view that what Nietzsche called "the Socratic will to truth" has not fulfilled its promise but, rather, has undermined the possibility of a good life. What they differ on is what the good life we are missing is and how to resist the result of the Enlightenment's making detached rationality the highest good. As we have just seen, Kierkegaard and Dostoyevsky think that existentialized Christianity (purified of Plato) is the source of resistance.

But Nietzsche is more radical. He sees Christianity as part of the problem. He held that it was no accident that, thanks to Augustine, Christianity merged with Platonism. He would see existentialized Christianity as a last desperate attempt to find ultimate meaning and purpose where there is none. So Nietzsche argued that, to save the West, he had to destroy Platonism's belief in the supersensuous and, in destroying it, free us from the debilitating effects of both Philosophy *and* Judeo-Christianity. In fact, our culture was already beginning to recover from its centuries of addiction to meaning. Nietzsche's account of this "greatest of all events" and whether we should despair over it or be joyful, is focused in his famous pronouncement at the center of *The Gay Science* that God is Dead.

> Have you not heard of that madman who lit a lantern in the bright morning hours, ran to the market place, and cried incessantly: "I seek God! I seek God!" . . . Do we smell nothing as yet of the divine decomposition? Gods, too, decompose. God is dead. God remains dead. And we have killed him. (Nietzsche 1974: 181)

Nietzsche adds:

> Here the madman fell silent and looked again at his listeners; and they, too, were silent and stared at him in astonishment . . . "I have come too early," he said then; "my time is not yet. This tremendous event is still on its way, still wandering; it has not yet reached the ears of men." (Nietzsche 1974: 283)

If many of the bystanders are atheists already, one might well wonder why they are astonished at the news, but Nietzsche holds that philosophers and scientists who believe in objective truth have not really given up God.

> [I]t is still a *metaphysical faith* upon which our faith in science rests – that even we seekers after knowledge today, we godless anti-metaphysicians still take our fire, too, from the flame lit by a faith that is thousands of years old, that Christian faith which was also the faith of Plato, that God is the truth, that truth is divine. – But what if . . . God himself should prove to be our most enduring lie? (Nietzsche 1974: 283)

But why does the Madman say that *we* have killed God? Nietzsche thinks that philosophers and scientists have killed God by finding out the truth about Him. God and the God's-eye point of view do not make sense:

> [Philosophers] demand that we should think of an eye that is completely unthinkable, an eye turned in no particular direction, in which the active and interpreting forces, through which alone seeing becomes seeing *something*, are supposed to be lacking; . . . There is *only* a perspective seeing, *only* a perspective "knowing." (Nietzsche 1967: 119)

Since there are only perspectives, all our so-called knowledge must be interpretation. Nietzsche consistently and happily affirms that: "this also is only interpretation . . . well, so much the better" (Nietzsche 1989: 30–1).

There is, thus, no objective truth, yet science is devoted to exposing self-deception. Nietzsche, like current constructivists, sees scientists, in their devotion to the truth, as bound to realize that all their discoveries are interpretations, thereby undermining scientists' claim to describe reality as it is in itself. Then, we can still admire science for its honesty and use its results for prediction and control. But science, done as if from God's point of view, will have undermined itself.

Nietzsche contends that Christianity too has undermined itself:

> You see what it was that really triumphed over the Christian god: Christian morality itself, the concept of truthfulness that was understood ever more rigorously, the father confessor's refinement of the Christian conscience, into intellectual cleanliness at any price . . . [I]nterpreting one's own experiences as pious people have long enough interpreted theirs, as if everything were providential, a hint, designed and ordained for the sake of the salvation of the soul – that is *all over* now, that has man's conscience *against* it. (Nietzsche 1974: 307)

Since our whole Enlightenment is built on the Platonic/Christian God, Nietzsche sees that this growing honesty and suspicion has not only killed God but will eventually bring down the West. Yet, he realizes that:

> The event itself is far too great, too distant, too remote from the multitude's capacity for comprehension even for the tidings of it to be thought of as having *arrived* as yet. Much less may one suppose that many people know as yet *what* this event really means – and how much must collapse now that this faith has been undermined because it was built upon this faith, propped up by it, grown into it; for example, the whole of our European morality. (Nietzsche 1974: 279)

Nietzsche calls the impending total cultural collapse of the foundation of our culture, a "cataclysm": "This long plenitude and sequence of breakdown, destruction, ruin, and cataclysm that is now impending – who could guess enough of it today to be compelled to play the teacher and advance proclaimer of this monstrous logic of terror?" (Nietzsche 1974: 279). And he adds: "Is not the greatness of this deed too great for us? Must we ourselves not become gods simply to appear worthy of it?" (Nietzsche 1974: 181).

It is worth noting that, in many ways, Dostoyevsky invented Nietzsche in order to refute him. Ivan in the *The Brothers Karamazov* already foresees the destruction of the bedrock on which our whole world is built. He proclaims the death of God, and sees the result as a "geological cataclysm" (Dostoyevsky 1996: 738). As he puts it: "I believe that a period, analogous with geological periods, will come to pass – the old conception of the universe will fall of itself without cannibalism and what's more the old morality, and everything will begin anew" (ibid.) Ivan, like Nietzsche, claims that, in response to the death of God, we must become gods ourselves (Nietzsche 1974: 181). But since Dostoyevsky holds that no one can live with such conclusions, by the end of the book, Ivan has gone crazy and seems about to die.

The free spirit

Nietzsche, on the contrary, thinks we Western human beings can recover from our meaning addiction. So for him, unlike for Dostoyevsky, the death of God is good news. Aphorism 343, which announces the impending cataclysm, is entitled "The Meaning of our Cheerfulness." For Nietzsche, just because *everything* was built into the Platonic/Judeo-Christian God, His death gives us a *total* freedom never before experienced by any culture.

> [T]he consequences for *ourselves*, are quite the opposite of what one might perhaps expect; they are not at all sad and gloomy but rather like a new and scarcely describable kind of light, happiness, relief, exhilaration, encouragement, dawn.
>
> Indeed, we . . . "free spirits" feel, when we hear the news that "the old god is dead," as if a new dawn shone on us. (ibid.)

We can now open new horizons: create new (polytheistic) gods, new suns, new values, and even create new selves (Nietzsche 1974: 143, 231, 266).

Such expansion is literally only natural. Life is constant overcoming. "The great and small struggle always revolves around superiority, around growth and expansion, around power – in accordance with the will to power which is the will of life" (Nietzsche 1974: 292). Getting over one's convictions is strong and healthy; holding onto them is weak and sick. Thus for Nietzsche: "The wish to preserve oneself is the symptom of a condition of distress, of a limitation of the really fundamental instinct of life which aims at *the expansion of power*" (Nietzsche 1974: 291).

But, according to Nietzsche, philosophers have always been too weak to accept this. "I recognized Socrates and Plato as symptoms of decay, as agents of the dissolution of Greece," he boasts (Nietzsche 1990: 39, 40). And Christians are also weak, so they have to deny death and meaninglessness and must believe in some version of eternal meaning. Nietzsche, on the contrary, holds that convictions are necessary, but one should not hang onto them but outgrow them. He concludes: "Convictions are prisons . . . Freedom from convictions of any kind, the *capacity* for an unconstrained view, *pertains* to strength" (Nietzsche 1990: 184). So Nietzsche would say to Dostoyevsky, since to live is to grow, if you don't outgrow and reinterpret your child-hood memories with more experience, it shows you are weak: "How much one needs a *faith* in order to flourish, how much that is 'firm' and that one does not wish to be shaken because one *clings* to it, that is a measure of the degree of one's strength (or, to put the point more clearly, of one's weakness)" (Nietzsche 1974: 287). The need for "something as unshakable as the vault of heaven" leads those who give in to it to miss "the marvelous uncertainty and rich ambiguity of existence" (Dostoyevsky 1996: 409; Nietzsche 1974: 76). So, happily, it turns out that the death of God, if we are able to accept it, is our opportunity to be most alive by taking part in our culture's "longest and most courageous self-overcoming" (Nietzsche 1974: 307). Indeed, free spirits can say: "we have . . . outgrown Christianity and are averse to it – precisely because we have grown out of it" (Nietzsche 1974: 340).

In exulting the free spirits who thrive on overcoming, Nietzsche is, in an important way, an anti-existentialist. All the existential thinkers we have been considering, as well as more recent existentialists like Sartre, inherit from the confluence of the Greek and Judeo-Christian traditions a need for something absolute and unchanging in human life. For Pascal, it was the hidden God of the Hebrews, for Kierkegaard, an unconditional commitment, for Dostoyevsky, the connectedness of all human beings. Kafka's K in *The Castle* is still longing for the authority of the castle, and Jaspers speaks of our need for getting in touch with "the encompassing" (Jaspers 1947). Even Sartre contends that the absence of an absolute makes human life a futile passion.

Yet while Nietzsche refuses to accept the account of God in either of our traditions, or to take seriously the pathos of His absence, he, nonetheless, shares many important insights with the founding existential thinkers. They all agree that:

1 There is no human nature. Pascal said: "Custom is our nature." Nietzsche adds: "Man alone among all the animals has no eternal horizons and perspectives" (Nietzsche 1974: 192).

2 Therefore human nature and the world can radically change – be transformed. History is more important than a fixed eternity outside of time.

3 Commitment is more important than ethical principles. The individual is higher than the universal.

4 The involved point of view reveals a reality more basic than that revealed by detached reason and theory. Truth is subjectivity.

5 Belief in God as a super-being is no longer possible or necessary for us, but that opens up the possibility of other ways of understanding and relating to the divine.

The founding existential thinkers, Pascal, Kierkegaard, Dostoyevsky, and Nietzsche, each begin with a description of the self and the culture in despair. Yet each of these thinkers make Christian bliss, or at least some sort of secular cheerfulness, the sign of a good life. It seems that only in the twentieth century did existential thinking take a turn to the darker side characteristic of the thought of Jaspers and Heidegger, or the outright despair of writers such as Kafka, and of Sartre, the only self-proclaimed existentialist.

Notes

1 I want to thank Jane Rubin who, over the many years we have taught Kierkegaard together, has helped me develop and refine the interpretation presented here.

2 The ultimate despair, Kierkegaard contends, is denying that one is in despair by denying the demand that we express the two sets of factors in our lives in a way that enables them to reinforce each other. This is not the distraction of the present age where one represses the call to be a self. Rather, someone, say Richard Rorty, in this ultimate form of despair sees that in our religious tradition the self has, indeed, been constituted as having two sets of essential but incompatible factors, but claims that this is merely a mistaken, essentialist view that we can and should opt out of. Since the traditional Judeo-Christian understanding of the self leads people to despair, we should simply give it up and adopt a vocabulary and practices that are more useful to us now.

How can we decide who is right here, Kierkegaard or the pragmatist? I think this is a question we can only approach experientially. In *Sickness Unto Death*, Kierkegaard tries to show that the Christian claim that the self is a contradiction is confirmed by a purportedly exhaustive categorization of all the ways of being a self available to us and how each fails. The only test is the test of existence.

3 Sartre gives the example of a person who has an emotional crisis as an adolescent, which he interprets as a religious calling and acts on by becoming a monk. Then, later, he comes to interpret the experience as just an adolescent psychotic episode, and leaves the monastery to become a businessman. But on his deathbed, he feels that his was a religious calling after all, and repents. Sartre's comments that our past is constantly up for reinterpretation, and the final interpretation is an accidental result of what we happen to think as we die.

4 My reading of *The Grand Inquisitor* is presented in Guignon 1993.

References and Further Reading

Belknap, R. (1967) *The Structure of* The Brothers Karamazov. The Hague: Mouton.

Berdyaev, N. (1957) *Dostoyevsky*. New York: Meridian Books.

Dostoyevsky, F. (1996) *The Brothers Karamazov* (trans. C. Garnett). New York: Modern Library (original work published 1880).

Dreyfus, H. (2002) *On the Internet: Thinking in Action* (ed. R. Kearney and S. Critchley). London: Routledge.

Guignon, C. (1993) *Dostoevsky: The Grand Inquisitor*. Indianapolis and Cambridge: Hackett.

Jaspers, K. (1947) *Von der Wahrheit* [On Truth]. Munich: Piper.

Kierkegaard, S. (1951) *Journals* (ed. and trans. A. Dru). London: Oxford University Press (original work published 1923).

—— (1967) *Training in Christianity and the Edifying Discourse which "Accompanied" It* (trans. W. Lowrie). Princeton, NJ: Princeton University Press (original work published 1855).

—— (1968) *Concluding Unscientific Postscript* (trans. D. F. Swenson and W. Lowrie). Princeton, NJ: Princeton University Press (original work published 1846).

—— (1985) *Fear and Trembling* (trans. A. Hannay). London: Penguin (original work published 1843).

—— (1989) *The Sickness unto Death* (trans. A. Hannay). London: Penguin (original work published 1849).

—— (1992) *Either/Or* (trans. A. Hannay; ed. V. Eremita). London: Penguin (original work published 1843).

—— (2001) *A Literary Review* (trans. A. Hannay). London: Penguin (original work published 1846).

Nietzsche, F. (1967) *On the Genealogy of Morals* (trans. W. Kaufman and R. J. Hollingdale). New York: Vintage Books (original work published 1887).

—— (1974) *The Gay Science* (trans. W. Kaufman). New York: Vintage (original work published 1887).

—— (1989) *Beyond Good and Evil* (trans. W. Kaufman). New York: Vintage (original work published 1989).

—— (1990) *Twilight of the Idols/The Anti-Christ* (trans. R. J. Hollingdale). London: Penguin (original work published 1889).

Pascal, B. (1958) *Pensées* (trans. W. F. Trotter). New York: Dutton (original work published 1660).

—— (1966) *Pensées* (trans. A. J. Krailsheimer). London: Penguin (original work published 1660).

12

German Existence-Philosophy

UDO TIETZ

When Jean-Paul Sartre sought to determine the relationship between existentialism and humanism shortly after the Second World War, he classified Karl Jaspers as a Christian existentialist and Martin Heidegger as an atheistic existentialist (Sartre 1947: 15). Jaspers and Heidegger maintained that the position taken by each of them is not to be equated with French existence-philosophy. However one might think today of Heidegger's and Jasper's dissociation from Sartre, it is certain that it is not merely a matter of establishing fine theoretical distinctions. Rather, both Jaspers and Heidegger thought that the existentialism advocated by Sartre could not suitably rely on the positions advocated by them. And if Heidegger is counted as an existence-philosopher at all, then surely this would be only the Heidegger of *Being and Time*.

Nevertheless, the French variety of existentialism in the version advocated by Jean-Paul Sartre is not the only one that falls under the term "existentialism." It may be that existentialism owes its international breakthrough "to the consequences of the Second World War, consequences that mesh still more deeply with the whole structure of our thought, and moreover to the total historical breakdown of our entire intellectual world" (Bollnow 1947: 126 f.). But existentialism is older than that, even though the term "existence-philosophy" is comparatively new – in *Neue Wege der Philosophie* ("New Paths of Philosophy"), Fritz Heinemann claims to have coined this term himself (Heinemann 1954: 11).

Søren Kierkegaard, who opposed Hegelian panlogicism with his "philosophy of existence," is existentialism's ancestor.[1] In this sense, existentialism follows in the line of anti-idealistic systems that want to put a rationally adulated reason on trial and want to situate it in its own domain of operation. Therefore, existence-philosophy continues the subject matter of the philosophy of life "in a deeper and more radicalized way," and outstrips it in the process. Life, called upon since Nietzsche as an opposition to rationality, reason, and truth, now, understood as the principle which is set against the principles of idealism, is further concretized by existence-philosophy through the concept of "existence." Thus, the concept of existence occupies the place which reason once had for Hegel: for Jaspers existence-philosophy is concerned directly with a fundamental new interpretation of "life," and Heidegger thinks that humans can only recognize themselves from their existence, "from the possibility: to become what they are, or not."

Both Jaspers and Heidegger in this context share with the philosophy of life not only a conviction of the limitations of reason and rationality, a criticism of subject–object dualism, and a criticism of the cognitivist reduction of the modern concept of the subject, but also a methodic irrationalism, insofar as "existential elucidation" is not supposed to be managed by the discursive understanding. According to Jaspers the existential elucidation takes place through an "existentiell" experience; according to Heidegger through the figure of a "radical questioning" within the framework of a "hermeneutic of Dasein."

* * *

Picking up from Kierkegaard, Jaspers argues that existence cannot be grasped rationally: "existence is . . . inaccessible to one who asks about it in terms of the purely objective intellect." It is to be grasped, then, "beyond the bounds of objective knowability in a *leap* that exceeds the capacity of rational insight. Philosophizing begins and ends at a point to which that leap takes me" (Jaspers 1970: 6). Jaspers wrote his habilitation thesis in 1913 with Wilhelm Windelband on *General Psychopathology* (Jaspers 1913), and in 1919 published the *Psychology of Worldviews* (Jaspers 1919). In the latter work he developed the basic positions of existence-philosophy, in which existence is already determined through the fact that it is that which is "never objectified." It is the "source of my thoughts and actions" (Jaspers 1969: 56) – which is why one can see this work as the birth certificate of systematic existence-philosophy. Jaspers, who, with this work, was appointed full professor of philosophy in Heidelberg in 1921 against the express opposition of Heinrich Rickert, fell back on the concept of "existence" as the basis for determining anew the essence of human being, namely as an essence that comports itself toward itself and thereby toward transcendence (Jaspers 1969: 56).

In the first place, the view that Jaspers maintains here – the view that existence cannot be rationally grasped – has nothing to do, as is frequently maintained, with a defensiveness against the sciences. To the contrary; Jaspers expressly stresses that there cannot be an "objective cognition as world-orientation" without science (Jaspers 1969: 69). Indeed, that without the sciences, which move in the medium of "conceptual thinking," "which is indirect and systematic," "philosophizing becomes immaterial and empty" (Jaspers 1969: 69). Jaspers merely believes that the knowledge that is supplied by the respective sciences must be joined together into a unified world picture by philosophy, proceeding from human existence. Precisely at existence, according to Jaspers, lie the boundaries of the sciences, boundaries which are not to be exceeded by means of a work of the understanding that is free of value judgments. Human existence has, for Jaspers, approximately the function which belongs to the "I think" within transcendental philosophy, inasmuch as Kant thought the whole of logic, indeed, transcendental philosophy itself, hangs from it. Human existence can itself not become an object of research for the sciences, because it is essentially non-objective, that is to say, it is freedom.

According to Jaspers, the methodic irrationalism of existential elucidation is thus not supposed to lead to the rejection of understanding and science. Existence-philosophy is, according to Jaspers, "the way of thought by means of which man seeks to become himself; it makes use of expert knowledge while at the same time going beyond it" (Jaspers 1957: 175). The path of philosophical existential elucidation is not supposed to lead to annihilation, but rather to the transcending of reason and rationality in their breakdown when confronted with the experience of "limit situations" – situations in which human beings see themselves set before the "nothing." When human beings become aware of their existence in "limit situations," and of their conditionedness in the grasp of their surroundings and through "transcendence," thinking raises itself above the empirically factical and begins to "float."

> The floating of thinking sets the authentically unconditioned free. The goal of elucidation is not a projection of being as such, not a possession of knowledge, not a result, but rather the methodic becoming aware of being. But this awareness is, as it were, a floating. In it occurs the dissolution of the ground in order to win a truer ground, until at last one achieves a free-floating groundlessness in the world with respect to the foundation of the one absolute ground of transcendence . . . In this way there is in the end no ground, no principle, but rather a floating of thought in groundless space. Contrary to a firm establishment and safeguarding that one finds in a system of thought, in which I hold myself and to which I submit myself, I remain master of my thoughts in order to be open for transcendence and to experience from transcendence the authentic unconditionedness of the world. (Jaspers 1947: 185)

Existence-philosophy, conceived of as *the critique of the culture of understanding*, here comes to itself as the philosophy of reason with, as it were, a "perceptual" reason. "Reason means the perception into the all-connecting being encountered of every essence and every possibility, of being and of nothing." This is a form of the "rational" critique of the understanding, which Jaspers shares with Heidegger, although he always rejected the latter's ontological mode of proceeding. For Jaspers, existence is not to be grasped in the form of an existential apriori that can be clarified through an analytic of Dasein within the framework of a "fundamental ontology." Existence always remains a "projection" and a call and an appeal to the "authentic." Heidegger surely noted this difference sooner than Jaspers, although he recorded already in 1928 some points of difference with Heidegger. Nevertheless it seemed initially to Jaspers that "for a short time" he and Heidegger "were on the same road," something which he thought "was, in retrospect, perhaps a mistake" (Jaspers 1981: 75/2).[2]

As we have already noted, existence lies beyond the boundaries of the knowledge that is scientifically knowable. It is not to be grasped rationally. "It gets beyond the bounds of objective knowability in a *leap* that exceeds the capacity of a rational insight" (Jaspers 1970: 6). At this point Jaspers calls attention to the fact that he has taken over this concept of existence from Kierkegaard: "To Kierkegaard I owe the concept of *Existenz*, which, since 1916, has become standard for me in order to understand that for which I had, until then, exerted myself uneasily" (Jaspers 1981: 86). "Through him . . . I came to see . . . what philosophy might be today" (Jaspers 1969: 9). But Jaspers also mentions a difference with Kierkegaard: "But of equal power [for me] was the concept and claim of reason, which, through Kant, now became constantly clearer" (Jaspers 1981: 86). World orientation and existential elucidation form for Jaspers a complementary relationship, whereby existence-philosophy becomes the alternative program to the scientific-technological rationality of our culture of understanding, without of course penetrating it and being able to place it thoroughly in question. This brought on the reproach of Jaspers' existence philosophy that its job is to provide edifying fancy speeches in the field of philosophy.

But be that as it may; for Jaspers existence philosophy represents a new "mode of thought" that indeed continues the discoveries of the particular sciences, in that it takes up their open questions. It is itself, however, not a science, since it has nothing to do with objects, but rather with human existence, which is essentially freedom. According to Jaspers, scientific thought is limited according to its content and its method because it always only focuses on beings, whereas for philosophy it is a matter of the totality of being. This is why he also thinks that there are two stems of knowledge that are not reducible to one another, between which there is no continuous passage, so that finally and ultimately only the Kierkegaardian leap, which is not rationally graspable, remains. The path to being is found through existence, which is defined in the first place as a non-epistemic self-relation, and also through its reference to the transcendent, which Jaspers also calls "the Encompassing of all encompassing" (Jaspers 1967: 70). "Existence is what relates to itself, and thus to its transcendence" (Jaspers 1969: 56).

Kierkegaard already saw things in a similar way, when he defined the "self" as a relation "which relates itself to itself, and in relating to itself relates to something else" (Kierkegaard 1989: 43). In fact, Jaspers rejects this thesis: "the more conception of God, the more self" (Kierkegaard 1989: 112), since with it the concept of existence receives a quasi-religious signature, which did not seem acceptable to Jaspers, at least not in this form. Thus, with Jaspers, even Kierkegaard's "terrible solitude" of human beings before God becomes the solitude of human being before the "nothing." Still, the formulation of existence as a non-epistemic self-relation, that always also has a reference to the transcendent, is something which he takes over from Kierkegaard.

It is significant in this context that Jaspers explains this antinomic character of existence more precisely through the concept of the "limit situation," inasmuch as the irreplaceableness of the individual who is conscious of his or her own finitude only shows itself in limit situations. Jaspers calls in existence against nihilism. But he does not want to understand existence solipsistically – this distinguishes Jaspers from Heidegger and later from Sartre, according to whom "hell is others." It is otherwise for Jaspers. For him, communication and, along with it, the reference to the other belong essentially to the authentic choice of the authentic self, with which an intersubjective space for a shared common lifeworld is opened up within existence philosophy, although Jaspers hardly thought seriously about the hermeneutic dimension of a intersubjective understanding of meaning within a common shared lifeworld. Existence is for Jaspers thus determined in three ways: first through its non-epistemic self-reference; second through its reference to the transcendent; and third through its communicative reference to the other.

Thus for Jaspers, then, the authentic self is indeed the last point of refuge in a world that is meaningless from the ground up. As he will say immediately after the the catastrophic experiences of the Second World War, however, the individual is only then him- or herself "when the other is also himself. Freedom is only in the degree to which all are free . . . But the individual is powerless. This spirit is the responsibility of us all . . . One of the possible ways into it is history" (Jaspers 1965:

29) – by which the shell of the existentiell innerliness is broken open more and more in the direction of an existence-philosophical "world philosophy."

* * *

"Existence" has replaced "life" in Heidegger's fundamental ontology also. *Being and Time* brings the philosophical end of the philosophy of life to our attention in that Heidegger replaces Wilhelm Dilthey's "Hermeneutic of Life" with an "existential analytic of Dasein," which is carried out within the framework of a "hermeneutic of Dasein." Existential ontology presents itself as the result of a fundamental questioning into the direction of inquiry of the philosophy of life itself, but in such a way that now " 'life' itself," which in the philosophy of life never became "a problem in its mode of being," is problematized – namely, as a question concerning the "being of Dasein" (Heidegger 1962: 73, translation modified). The "analytic of Dasein," which is supposed to achieve this, stands under the guiding principle: "*the 'essence' of Dasein lies in its existence*" (Heidegger 1962: 67). With this Heidegger himself also cites Kierkegaard, attesting that he "explicitly seized upon the problem of existence as an existentiell problem, and thought it through in a penetrating fashion," even though the "existential problematic" remained "alien to him, in that as regards his ontology, he remained completely dominated by *Hegel* and by ancient philosophy as Hegel saw it" (Heidegger 1962: 494, n.vi).

> That kind of Being towards which Dasein can comport itself in one way or another, and always does comport itself somehow, we call "*existence*". And because we cannot define Dasein's essence by citing a "what" of the kind that pertains to a subject-matter, and because its essence lies rather in the fact that in each case it has its Being to be, and has it as its own, we have chosen to designate this entity as "Dasein", a term which is purely an expression of its being. (Heidegger 1962: 32–33)

Thus Heidegger also, analogously with Jaspers, does not want to grasp existence objectively. A further common characteristic consists in the fact that Heidegger also wants to conceive of essence from out of existence. "Its being-what-it-is (essentia) must, so far as we can speak of it at all, be conceived in terms of its being (existentia)" (Heidegger 1962: 67) – a thesis which is characteristic of Kierkegaard and the entire existence-philosophy. "Accordingly those characteristics which can be exhibited in this entity are not 'properties' present-at-hand of some entity which 'looks' so and so and is itself present-at-hand; they are in each case possible ways for it to be, and no more than that" (Heidegger 1962: 67).

The "analytic of Dasein" and the question concerning the meaning of being that is clarified through this analytic, runs, according to Heidegger, "ahead of the positive sciences," because the "question of being," which Heidegger also calls "*the* fundamental question" of philosophy, must be answered before the question "what is there?" Being, according to Heidegger " 'is' only in the understanding of those entities to whose Being something like an understanding of Being belongs" (Heidegger 1962: 228).

Fundamental ontology would thus be an ontology which, with the "question of Being," wants to inquire into a domain that does not at all become especially thematic in traditional ontology. Or, put another way, fundamental ontology wants to enquire about the domain which lies behind the question: "what is there?" ("was '*es gibt*'?"). It does not simply ask about "what is there," but rather about the conditions of the possibility of ontology, and it would be in this respect a transcendental analysis in the Kantian sense. This is not to devalue traditional ontology. Heidegger claims that this ontology needs to be supported, which assumes of course that this ontology lacks support and is capable of being supported. If one should assume this with Heidegger, then the strategy that is connected with the question of being no longer seems absurd. The question of being aims, then, "at ascertaining the a priori conditions not only for the possibility of the sciences which examine entities as entities of such and such a type, and, in so doing, already operate with an understanding of Being, but also for the possibility of those ontologies themselves which are prior to the ontical sciences and which provide their foundations" (Heidegger 1962: 31). For if "the sciences are ways of being of Dasein," and if the "there is" (*es gibt*) is dependent on this Dasein, then the regions of being of the respective sciences first disclose themselves in the return to the understanding of being of those who comport themselves in their everyday existence toward entities in the world and who then methodically build up these naive dealings and cultivate the individual sciences to a precise form.

It is thus necessary to inquire back into the transcendental attitude behind the categorial constitution of entities, which is laid bare by transcendental philosophy, taking its lead from the sciences. The analysis of these prior understandings of being first becomes thematic with those structures of being-in-the-world which Heidegger calls "existentials"; this is why the existential analytic of being-in-the-world also deserves the name of a fundamental ontology.

Dasein also has for Heidegger a priority over the other entities that is based first in that fact that "this entity is determined in its being by existence" (Heidegger 1962: 34, translation modified) – this would be its ontic priority. It is based secondly in the fact that "Dasein is in itself 'ontological', because existence is . . . determinative for it" (Heidegger 1962: 34) – this would be the ontological priority. Finally, it is based in the fact that to Dasein an "understanding of existence" also always belongs, "an understanding of the being of all entities of a character other than its own" (Heidegger 1962: 34) – this would be its ontic-ontological priority.

To Dasein, which "is ontically distinguished by the fact that, in its very being, that being is an issue for it" (Heidegger 1962: 32), a privileged position is befitting because Dasein has an exceptional relation to the question of being and the question concerning the possibility of the understanding of being that is connected to it. "Of course only as long as Dasein is (that is, only as long as an understanding of Being is ontically possible), 'is there' Being'" (Heidegger 1962: 255). For "it is peculiar to this entity that with and through its being, this being is disclosed to it" (Heidegger 1962: 32), peculiar that Dasein "always already" has an understanding of being. "And this means further that there is some way in which Dasein understands itself in its Being, and that to some degree it does so explicitly" (Heidegger 1962: 32).

This "*understanding of being is itself a definite characteristic of Dasein's being*" (Heidegger 1962: 32; see Tietz 2003: 57 ff.). Heidegger wants to return with this concept to the totality of a non-objective context of meaning, which lies before each predication and makes it possible. And if it is true that "Dasein always understands itself in terms of its existence – in terms of a possibility of itself: to be itself or not itself" (Heidegger 1962: 33),[3] then the following thesis is not implausible: "fundamental ontology, from which alone all other ontologies can take their rise, must be sought in the existential analytic of Dasein" (Heidegger 1962: 34).

Dasein means being open in and for being. It is that place which Heidegger calls the site of the opening up of being (Heidegger 2000a: 220). The doctrine of the categories is also thereby tied into the ontology of Dasein – a doctrine which traditionally falls together with ontology and thus with the question concerning the being of entities. If Heidegger, in his book on Scotus (see Heidegger 1978), a book dedicated to Heinrich Rickert, wanted to renew the philosophy of language on the basis of the doctrine of meanings, the last ontological foundations of the understanding should now be specified. The doctrine of meaning, which traditionally ties the conditions of the possibility of a philosophical enterprise to language, falls under the conditions of existential ontology.

In accordance with the task which is contemplated by Heidegger, this ontology must, if it really wants to be a fundamental ontology and not a positive science, take on the form of an existential analytic, because the explanation of the meaning of being only proceeds from Dasein. For if Dasein interprets itself, then the transcendental reflection becomes an existential explication, which is unfolded by Heidegger within the framework of an existential analytic. With that the interpretation of a pre-ontological understanding of being and the explication of a context of meaning, in which everyday existence always already finds itself, steps into the place of self-consciousness Heidegger contrasts the self-relationship of the knowing subject to a Dasein who is existentially concerned about his being – a Dasein who, admitted into concrete world relations, comports himself to himself and others in his actions.

"It is not the case that man 'is' and then has, by way of an extra, a relationship-of-Being towards the 'world' – a world with which he provides himself occasionally. Dasein is never 'proximally' an entity which is, so to speak, free from Being-in, but which sometimes has the inclination to take up a 'relationship' towards the world. Taking up relationships towards the world is possible only because Dasein, as Being-in-the-world, is as it is" (Heidegger 1962: 84). Against the assumption of an idealistically stylized knowing subject, which relates itself to the world as if to a totality of knowable objects in order therein to objectify itself, by starting from being-in-the-world the characteristic of in-being as such is emphasized. This in turn stresses the attuned self-finding of Dasein in the midst of entities and therewith the impossibility of "think[ing] of the entirety of what is as an object" (see Gadamer 1994: 29). "World as a wholeness 'is not a being, but that from out of which Dasein *gives itself the signification* of whatever beings it *is able* to comport itself toward in whatever way'" (Heidegger 1998a: 121).

Heidegger thus, on the one hand, dissolves the transcendental subject, in whose veins no real blood flows, but rather merely the "diluted juice of reason as a mere activity of thought" (Dilthey 1989: 50, translation modified), and replaces it with a Dasein, which he, with the deeply flowing conceptuality of an existential ontology that proceeds transcendentally, intends to describe in such a way that all the domains of experience, which systematically overstretch the constitutive achievements of the transcendental "I," can become thematic in the conceptuality of the existential ontology. Heidegger adheres in a certain way to the transcendental attitude of an explanation that reflects on the conditions of the possibility of Dasein as being-in-the-world, in such a way however that he confers upon the transcendental problem an ontological sense.

Two things are interesting in this context; first the thesis that Dasein always understands itself from out of its existence, and second the thesis that this existence is represented as its possibility "to be itself or not to be itself," something that is supposed to depend on a choice that grounds authenticity and inauthenticity. Thus, before Heidegger clarified the meaning-theoretical and practical dimension of the hermeneutic understanding and of the understanding of action, he maintained that Dasein understands itself from out of its existence. This is a thesis which is made concrete in the course of the investigation in such a way that the practical self-understanding is supposed to provide the foundations of the understanding of meaning and action (see Tietz 2005: 59 ff.).

"Understanding is the existential being of Dasein's own potentiality-for-being; and it is so in such a way that this being discloses in itself what its being is capable of" (Heidegger 1962: 184). And this "understanding is either authentic, arising out of one's own self as such, or inauthentic" (Heidegger 1962: 186). The concept of understanding that Heidegger introduces in this way thus refers initially to the "understanding of existence." The concept of understanding is introduced without recourse to a linguistically parsed meaning, but rather with recourse to the practical self-understanding, from which we understand ourselves as such and such. First the concept of the ethical self-understanding is introduced and then the concept of the understanding is expanded onto the practical understanding in the sense of "know-how" and the hermeneutical understanding. "Meaning is that wherein the intelligibility of something maintains itself" (Heidegger 1962: 193). And only Dasein has this meaning: "only Dasein can be meaningful or meaningless" (Heidegger 1962: 193). This understanding of existence, the existence that is in each case one's own, has a circular structure, which "is rooted in the existential constitution of Dasein – that is, in the understanding which interprets" (Heidegger 1962: 195). This circular structure is not something to be avoided, but rather one is to enter into it in the "right way," since within it "is hidden a positive possibility of the most primordial kind of knowing" (Heidegger 1962: 195).

Now Heidegger pointed out already during the clarification of everyday being-in-the-world "that a bare subject without a world never 'is' proximally, nor is it ever given. And so in the end an isolated 'I' without others is just as far from being proximally given" (Heidegger 1962: 116). The others, which according to Heidegger "proximally" and "for the most part" encounter each other from out of the ready-to-hand, environmental context are precisely already "there with" us. Our encounter with them is different from the inner-worldly encounter of equipment or things, thus different from ready-to-hand and present-at-hand things. For the others are "*like* the very Dasein which frees them, *in that they are there too, and there with it*" (Heidegger 1962: 154). The "with" is of a kind with Dasein, that with-like everyday being-in-the-world is a shared world with others. For the "world of Dasein is a *with-world* [*Mitwelt*]. Being-in is *being-with* Others. Their being-in-themselves within-the-world

169

is *Dasein-with* [*Mitdasein*]" (Heidegger 1962: 155). Because Dasein is essentially in itself being-with, there always already lies in the being with others "a relationship of being from Dasein to Dasein" (Heidegger 1962: 162).

With this determination of Dasein as being-with and of the world as a with-world, Heidegger hits upon the important distinction between an objective world, in which natural objects and states of affairs are encountered as inner-worldly entities in manipulative dealings, and a social world of intersubjectively socialized subjects, who meet on the level of a common constitution of a world that is for them identical and for that reason objective. This has an obvious advantage over the monadological approach of the philosophy of consciousness, which explains our relations as symbolically mediated interaction – an approach that remained constitutive even for Husserl. It is true that Husserl, with his explanation of this phenomenon, returns to the foundational layer of the lived-world. Indeed he also understands all human achievements as objectivations of an everyday practice that is organized in accordance with the lived-world (see Husserl 1950: §49). However, through the fact that he thinks the "constitution of the lived-world" according to the basic principles of a constitution of knowledge, the attempt at a phenomenological grounding of intersubjectivity is clearly paradoxical. For how am I supposed as a monad, as a transcendentally achieving I, to constitute another I and at the same time experience the one that is constituted in me as another? But through a "change of perspective" of the ego and alter ego, one merely gains the grounding of a solipsistic-transcendental "community of monads," in which again every transcendental ego in turn merely has "his world," but does not arrive at an intersubjectively shared "we-world" (see Schütz 1957: 100). Husserl's change of perspective indeed guarantees a certain symmetry between ego and alter ego. The change of perspective is not capable, however, of breaking the immanence of the monad.

Heidegger is himself conscious of this paradox. For that reason he formulates the task to be "to make visible phenomenally the species to which this Dasein-with in closest everydayness belongs, and to interpret it in a way which is ontologically appropriate" (Heidegger 1962: 152). With this posing of the task, the social-ontological point of view of fundamental ontology comes into view, which is extremely significant for the analysis of being-with. Without mentioning Husserl's name, the analysis developed in the fourth chapter of *Being and Time* presents a single polemic directed at Husserl's theory of intersubjectivity, and seeks to clarify that problem on which Husserl toiled in vain. Heidegger succeeds with this through reconstructing being-with as an intersubjective relationship of Dasein to Dasein. Heidegger explicitly stresses that "an isolated 'I' without Others is [never] proximally given" (Heidegger 1962: 152), thus that when all is said and done, "being-with and the facticity of being with one another" is grounded in a simple "occurrence together of several 'subjects'" (Heidegger 1962: 157). And insofar as the mode of being of Dasein has the "kind of being of being-with-one-another," there is no requirement whatsoever "to provide the first ontological bridge from one's own subject, which is given proximally as alone, to the other subject, which is proximally quite closed off" (Heidegger 1962: 162).

In contrast to Dilthey, who must make being-with plausible by means of a psychologistically understood concept of empathy, and also different than Husserl, who in the *Logical Investigations* constructs the communication that is mediated by signs and mutual understanding from the one-sided "perception of the announcement" (see Husserl 1984: 39 f.) – even later, for instance in the *Cartesian Meditations* or in the *Crisis*, Husserl could not free himself from a model of understanding which conceptualizes the process of understanding from out of an "indeclinable primal-I"[4] – Heigger does not merely want to keep the concept of the understanding clear of all psychological additions, but rather he also wants to show being-with to be "a relationship of being from Dasein to Dasein" (Heidegger 1962: 162).

The analysis of the world is therefore reconstructed first of all from the point of view of an intersubjective relationship of Dasein to Dasein in being-with, with which being-with is shown to be a constitutive feature of being-in-the-world. Through this, Heidegger brings those processes of the understanding into view which hold present the intersubjectively shared, lived-worldly background – the background which supports hermeneutic understanding. Heidegger enters with a stroke the level of intersubjectivity, without having to construct it from the transcendental performances of individual subjects, using a theory of constitution. He thereby deepens the phenomenological theory of intersubjectivity in which he explains the analysis of the world from the point of view of an intersubjective relationship which I enter into with others. For the lifeworld, which is somehow suspended in the structures of linguistically mediated intersubjectivity, reproduces and maintains itself through the same medium in which subjects who are capable of speech and action come to an agreement with one another about something in the world. And yet Heidegger remains a prisoner of the Husserlian strategy.

Indeed, the special standing, maintained by Husserl, of a supposed pre-intersubjective self-consciousness is exposed as a fiction; the epistemically reduced subject of epistemology is dismissed by appeal to the contexts of involvements and references of the lifeworld that cannot be gotten behind, and it is submitted to the conditions of an innerworldly existence and historical facticity. The entire modern epistemology since Descartes has to accept the blame for proceeding from a subject in the figure of the "I think," a subject which has neither a world nor yet a with-world. This is something that affects even Husserl too, for while he indeed situates the transcendental ego in the world, he simultaneously, in order to not miss the possibility of a "universal critique," wants to make the lifeworld and therewith the intersubjective relationship between the ego and alter-ego understandable from out of a "primal-I" by using a theory of constitution. Heidegger is no more able to free himself from the stipulations of the phenomenological theory of intersubjectivity. "That the analysis of being-with nevertheless only reproduces and does not overcome the theory of intersubjectivity has its basis in its transcendental-philosophical conception, in the point of departure from projection as the transcendental constitution of the world" (Theunissen 1984: 171–2, translation modified).

Heidegger's problem is connected with his way of framing the other, which, more closely defined, appears as the "one." The "publicness" is a publicness that has been made average. It is supposed to be characterized not through belonging together, but rather through "distantiality," and in "averageness" it only meets the averaged expectations of everyone. In this way the "one," characterized as "neuter," levels out all positive possibilities of the being of Dasein. This interpretation of the "one" characterized as "neuter" has disastrous social-ontological consequences for Heidegger. For the "one-self," the "self of everyday Dasein," is the self who is completely fascinated by the world and the Dasein-with of others in the "one." It is consequently inauthentic. Authentic Dasein in a negative moment annuls the validity of the "objective we-world," and in a positive moment is supposed to lay open the transcendental horizon of the world and therewith also the "meaning of being." This authentic Dasein should be a Dasein that is freed from the domination of others. And this, as Heidegger tells us, exists only in "individualization."

With this formulation of being-with, Heidegger's advantage over the phenomenological theory of intersubjectivity immediately disappears again. Heidegger describes the structures of the lifeworldly background, which reaches out around the Dasein that is "in each instance mine," as structures of an everyday practice that has been made average, and which serve merely as a model of what authentic existence should not be. Because of this characterization, the analysis of being-with cannot be made fruitful for the question of how an intersubjectively shared world constitutes itself and maintains itself. Heidegger thus indeed succeeds in a first step at reconstructing the analysis of the world from the perspective of an intersubjective relationship between Dasein and Dasein in being-with, which is connected in the first instance with a change in perspective from isolated purposiveness to social interaction. In a second step, however, he lets the solipsistically positioned Dasein "as the entity which in each case I myself am" take the lead as opposed to Dasein-with. In fact this Dasein-with, including the structures of the lifeworldly background, are devalued as average and thoroughly deficient everyday practices. Because of this second step, Heidegger is thrown back onto the Husserlian starting point.

Because of that, Heidegger must make it plausible how now, once again, a being-with-one-another is made possible on the basis of individualization, but now a being-with-one-another that in comparison to the everyday kind turns out to be authentic. Heidegger seems to have supposed that, after the rise to power of the National Socialists, the people, built up to authenticity, will take over this task. Heidegger himself cannot enable this, for only death breaks through the environmental encounter of the other, an essential characteristic of inauthentic being-with-one-another. Authenticity as an abstract core of the self finds in death its measure and its ideal. In death alone are all relations to other Dasein undone. The solitude that arises from the non-relationality of the authentic self – Heidegger speaks in this context of an "existential solipsism" – thus becomes within social ontology the primordial fact of the authentic being one's self (see Theunissen 1984: 189 ff.).

This non-relationality of death, which gives Dasein to understand that ultimately it is alone, casts its shadow on all intersubjective relationships. For in what is most proper to it, the authentic Dasein is no less isolated than the transcendental ego is for Husserl. Insofar as, for Heidegger, authenticity "becomes a relationship to itself under which heading nothing further can be conceived" (Adorno 1973: 75), it is precisely not what an intersubjective relationship always already presupposes: a social relationship to others. No authentic self constitutes itself in being-with-one-another. Dasein gains its authenticity without a positive possibility of being-with. That means that an authentic understanding cannot find a place any longer in being-with others.

So in his discussion of being-with, Heidegger indeed included the others under the title the "one." But through this discussion the hermeneutical problem of the understanding also gets a paradoxical formulation, insofar as in the definition of the authentic relationship of the self to the self, the others are either completely missing or merely serve as a model of what it should not be. It is paradoxical because Heidegger couples two theses to each other. First the thesis that "being toward death" is a condition of the possibility of authenticity, and secondly the thesis that in the mode of authenticity a distinctive mode of the understanding lies before us.

The first thesis, with which Heidegger intends to place a "gap" between authenticity and inauthenticity, says that the confrontation with the possibility of death, a possibility that is "not to be outstripped," liberates Dasein "from one's lostness in those possibilities which may accidentally thrust themselves upon one" (Heidegger 1962: 308). Insofar as here the "the issue is nothing less than Dasein's Being-in-the-world" (Heidegger 1962: 294), "being toward death" is the condition of the possibility of a "choosing" which Heidegger calls authenticity. These theses, taken by themselves, do not seem problematic. The practical question can be posed in a radical and really fundamental manner, for instance as the question "How am I supposed to live?," where this is understood in such a way that it does not refer to this or that particular action, but rather to our way of acting and therewith places our life as a whole in question. Insofar as it is posed in this way, then it is a question which always addresses itself to a first person singular, which, Heidegger thinks, means that "what expresses itself in the 'I' is that Self which, proximally and for the most part, I am not authentically" (Heidegger 1962: 368).

This reference to a first person singular clearly has a normative sense. For the identity of an "I" is grounded in its self-understanding, however diffuse it might remain. In the "I," self-consciousness expresses itself, not as the self-relationship of a knowing subject, but rather as the ethical self-assurance of a person capable of being responsible. And this person who is capable of being responsible indeed always stands in an intersubjectively shared lifeworld, but "the individual projects himself as someone who *vouches* for the more or less clearly established continuity of a more or less consciously appropriated life history; in light of the individuality he has attained, he would like to be identified, even in the future, as the one into whom he has made himself" (Habermas 1992: 168).

From this first determination four further ones follow. The question concerning the "meaning of being" refers to a more or less immediate future; it refers to a self which is concerned with itself, it refers to a leeway of possibilities which should be questioned as a leeway, and it refers to those boundaries that limit these possibilities – for if these limitations were not available in the form of boundaries, they could not be considered here in any case (see Tugendhat 1979: 194 f.). It is indeed not necessary to pose this question. Instead of this, we could also go sailing or fishing. Heidegger designates with the expressions "authenticity" or "inauthenticity" this posing or this evasiveness before the question concerning the "meaning of being." Insofar now as the "one" always already relieves Dasein of the question concerning the "meaning of being," it also relieves him of the "projection" which gives an identity. Dasein lives as one lives, but not in such a way that it determines for itself what it wants to be. The "one" always already relieves Dasein of the freedom and authenticity of the choosing, which belongs to an autonomous self-determination and which authenticity first guarantees to a person who is capable of being responsible.

> With Dasein's lostness in the "one", that factical potentiality-for-being which is closest to it (the tasks, rules, and standards, the urgency and extent, of concernful and solicitous Being-in-the-world) has already been decided upon. The "one" has always relieved Dasein from taking hold of these possibilities of being. The "one" even hides the manner in which it has tacitly relieved Dasein of the burden of explicitly choosing these possibilities. It remains indefinite who has "really" done the choosing. So Dasein make no choices, gets carried along by the nobody, and thus ensnares itself in inauthenticity. This process can be reversed only if Dasein specifically brings itself back to itself from its lostness in the "one". (Heidegger 1962: 312, translation modified)

This is something that happens in the "limit situations" analyzed by Jaspers.[5] In these situations, Dasein is brought "back to its ownmost potentiality-for-being-its-Self" (Heidegger 1962: 354).

Heidegger here associates the analytic of Dasein which proceeds transcendentally and hermeneutically with the existence-philosophical theme that human Dasein understands itself from its own possibilities of being itself or not being itself, in such a way that it always stands before the alternatives of authenticity and inauthenticity. Heidegger in this way translates the theme of the responsibility for one's own salvation, a theme that came to a head with Kierkegaard, into the formula of care for one's own existence: "Dasein is an entity . . . [for whom] in its very being, that being is an issue for it" (Heidegger 1962: 32). And insofar as man is from the outset an ontological being, upon whom the question of being is existentially forced, Heidegger speaks here also of an ontical rootedness of the existential analytic. "The question of being is nothing other than the radicalization of an essential tendency-of-being which belongs to Dasein itself – the pre-ontological understanding of being" (Heidegger 1962: 35).

Heidegger's thesis, that the theoretical relation to the world is dependent upon our practical relation with the world, is thereby yet once again made more precise to the effect that theoretical and practical relations to the world are dependent on our practical self-understanding. This is true, Heidegger maintains, insofar as the "understanding of existence" is always also an "understanding of the world" (Heidegger 1962: 186). The practical self-understanding of one's own personal I-identity would then found, not only theoretical, but also practical world relations.

Now the first part of the thesis about dependence, according to which our theoretical world relation is grounded in our practical dealings, is well established. The second part appears problematic, insofar as the "understanding of existence" cannot provide a foundation to the hermeneutic understanding, since it is already tied to an intersubjectively shared language and therewith to the hermeneutic understanding. All the same, here Heidegger addresses an important aspect in connection with the problematic of self-consciousness. With recourse to practical comportment, Heidegger expands the concept of self-relations to me as a thinking and acting subject, beyond the concept of the theoretical self-consciousness, to which, from Descartes onward, the concept was restricted!

174

The care about one's own being which has been intensified into anxiety, which Heidegger joins to the introduction of temporal constitution, makes it understandable to the self that it cannot be understood in terms of the "one," but rather it must apprehend itself from its possibilities and must itself take its existence into hand. And who seeks to evade this decision – who believes the question concerning the life that is good or successful can be answered from the third-person perspective, so that one merely does oneself what "one" does – that person has already decided for a life in the mode of inauthenticity.

Even if one now does not want to go along in substantivizing the self and the others who are introduced as the "one," one must concede to Heidegger that the question concerning the "meaning of being," if it in fact is radically posed, must include in itself the possibility of being-no-longer! Just this ability-to-be-no-more is the possibility of death. And this is, as the negation of life, the last boundary, before which the question concerning a good or successful life is really meaningfully posed. The thesis, for its part – one can call it the *thesis of finitude* – thus appears well grounded, because the unsurpassable possibility of death is constitutive for every individual giving of meaning.

This is different from the case of Hegel, for whom self-consciousness first attains independence through the negation of all things external to it that condition it – these become null and void through the dialectically progressing process of the liberation of one's own finitude, through which the self-consciousness dissolves itself in its singularity and recognizes itself as the universal and therewith even as the individualized self-consciousness. Heidegger correctly insists on the irreducible finitude of "a Dasein which is in each case its own," which is to be debated neither through a dialectical procedure of sublation, nor through a theological promise of salvation from the world. For Hegel, self-consciousness itself does not need to be afraid of its own death, since it carries out in death only the mediated transition into the concrete eternity of the species of reason, in such a way that this appears as his home with which he "is reconciled," (Hegel 1979: 139). Heidegger, by contrast, recognizes that such a procedure of sublation makes unimportant the enabling conditions which place the finite Dasein – the Dasein who finds itself in determinate situations – before a choice in which it chooses itself.

We learn from Heidegger that an immortal being would not merely be an unbeing, but rather at the same time a being which could not get meaning from its perpetual Dasein. For a human being who would lose his mortality would also lose all interest in the lifeworldly concerns of mortal humans. In this respect, the question "Is death a condition of the possibility of the *significance of life* or: of the *meaning of life?*" must be answered positively (Apel 1978: 408). It is controversial whether this existentiell discovery also has a point for the theory of meaning, so that an immortal being, with the loss of its mortality, would not only lose every meaning-giving interest of and in the lifeworld, but rather together with this he or she would lose also the ability to genuinely communicate with others, that is, mortal humans. If it were like this, then "being toward death" at any rate would have to be understood not only as a "condition of the possibility of the *meaningfulness of life*," but also as a "*subjective-existential condition*" of the possibility of the "*understandability* of meaning" and therewith as a "necessary prerequisite for the constitution of all meaning content which is understandable for us" (Apel 1978: 413).

However one might stand with respect to this thesis now, if the existential result in fact has this consequence for the theory of meaning, then it must be spelled out in such a way that its meaning is a publicly accessible meaning, since a meaning that is not publicly accessible is an un-meaning. This is particularly true since, with the acceptance of the thesis of finitude, the question concerning the conditions of the possibility of an intersubjectively valid understanding of the meaning of something as something, and the question concerning the intersubjectivity of linguistically shared meanings, have not yet been answered. And it is precisely the answering of such questions that Heidegger attempts. He believes that the consequence of the thesis of finitude lies not only in the proof that the question concerning the good or successful life must be answered with an appeal to the "Dasein which is in each case our own." But he also believes that, with an appeal to this Dasein, the intersubjectivity of a common shared lifeworld and the intersubjectivity of a linguistically shared meaning can be made understandable. Nevertheless, precisely this proves to be impossible, since the priority of the intersubjectivity of the lifeworld over the mineness of Dasein, which is suspended in the structure of the linguistic intersubjectivity of meaning, goes beyond the way of conceiving things that remains trapped in the solipsism of Husserlian phenomenology.

In our context, the relevant problem results from the fact that Heidegger radicalizes the thesis of finitude into the thesis of authenticity and applies it to the problem of discourse and understanding. Heidegger thinks that the "understanding of existence" is "either authentic, arising out of one's own self as such, or inauthentic" (Heidegger 1962: 186). In this way Heidegger, in a first step, with an appeal to practical comportment, expands the concept of self-relations beyond the concept of the theoretical self-consciousness to the me as a thinking and acting subject. Then, in a second step, he switches the practical self-relation for the hermeneutic understanding, in such a way that the former is grounded in the latter. And since the human Dasein must apprehend itself in the horizon of its possibilities, if it does not want to lead a life in the mode of the inauthentic, "authenticity" grounds "authentic understanding."

But Dasein holds itself "proximally and for the most part" in the inauthentic kind of being. For "Dasein, as everyday Being-with-one-another, stands in subjection to Others" (Heidegger 1962: 164). This Dasein that stands in subjection to strangers, and hence is a non-autonomous Dasein, is characterized through the "distantiality, averageness, and levelling down" of its positive possibilities for being. The place at which this Dasein – the Dasein that is made non-autonomous by the "one" – keeps itself is the public. Heidegger attributes to the public not only a leveling, but also an authoritarian character. This authoritarian character becomes essentially fortified through "gossiping and passing the word along." And indeed, so far as it goes, in the public which is referred to by Heidegger as "authoritarian," "things are so because one says so. Idle talk is constituted by just such gossiping and passing the word along – a process by which its initial lack of grounds to stand on becomes aggravated to complete groundlessness" (Heidegger 1962: 212).

Later, in the "Letter on Humanism," Heidegger will say with respect to §§ 27 and 35 of *Being and Time* that this public, including the dictatorship of the public, is "the metaphysically conditioned establishment and authorization of the openness of beings in the unconditional objectification of everything" because "it stems from the dominance of subjectivity" (Heidegger 1998b: 242). This objectification is also the reason why "language thereby falls into the service of expediting communication along routes where objectification – the uniform accessibility of everything to everyone – branches out and disregards all limits. In this way language comes under the dictatorship of the public realm, which decides in advance what is intelligible and what must be rejected as unintelligible" (Heidegger 1998b: 242). In the "Letter on Humanism" the "decay of language" and the "devastation of language" are indeed diagnosed from the perspective of a philosophy of being. Nevertheless here, as in the account in *Being and Time* of the "one," an instance is identified which brings language under the subjection of the public, so that it becomes idle talk. Since the Dasein that has decayed to the "one" is able to express itself only in the leveled-down form of averageness – unlike Kant, Heidegger is not able to get anything more out of the public than its down-down, averaged, and authoritarian side – the "public" produced in this way must inevitably be understood as a pseudo-public, as a public which, instead of illuminating everything, obscures everything and in such a way that "what has thus been covered up gets passed off as something familiar and accessible to everyone" (Heidegger 1962: 165). This is achieved by idle talk.

Now one would misunderstand Heidegger's explanations of the fallenness of Dasein if one were to interpret this "as a 'fall' from a purer and higher 'primal status'" (Heidegger 1962: 220). Heidegger does not want to practice cultural criticism in the tradition of Nietzsche, Simmel, Klages, or Spengler. He also knows, it is true, that "unease with the culture" that marks the openly admitted or else hidden source of all the worries that are inspired by the philosophy of life and oriented to cultural criticism. And even the promise of the philosophy of life of a total renewal of the body-soul can be shown, using Heidegger's work, in a fundamental-ontological reformulation – and indeed in a solidly practical-political sense. Heidegger's assurance, however, that his account of the "one" does not represent a variety of cultural concern is to be taken seriously. "*The 'they' is an existentiale; and as a primordial phenomenon, it belongs to Dasein's positive constitution*" (Heidegger 1962: 167). The same can also be said of idle talk. The general fact that the mass culture is an average culture, which is essentially strengthened by "curiosity" and "ambiguity," becomes comprehensible precisely with the account of idle talk. Idle talk thus does not arise for example as a sediment and waste product of that average culture. Instead it belongs to that mode of being of being-with-one-another itself, and consequently one cannot join in it "from outside."

Heidegger explains this thought as follows:

> In the language which is spoken when one expresses oneself, there lies an average intelligibility; and in accordance with this intelligibility the discourse which is communicated can be understood to a considerable extent, even if the hearer does not bring himself into such a kind of Being towards what the discourse is about as to have a primordial understanding of it. We do not so much understand the entities which are talked about; we already are listening only to what is said-in-the-talk as such. What is said-in-the-talk gets understood; but what the talk is about is understood only approximately and superficially. We have the *same thing* in view, because it is in *the same* averageness that we have a common understanding of what is said. (Heidegger 1962: 212)

In the average culture, where everyone orients him- or herself to idle talk, communication is thus, strictly speaking, not shared at all anymore, at least not in an "authentic" sense. In the average common sense there is nothing which is left to be shared in discourse. This is because the average common sense is a common sense which *is* already shared, so that here nothing is left to *be* shared. Thus, insofar as being-with-one-another stands in "subjection to the others," it also "takes place in talking with one another and in concern with what is said-in-the-talk." And precisely because of that, "the genuineness of the discourse and of the understanding which belongs to it" can be guaranteed no longer (Heidegger 1962: 212).

The reason for this is not to be sought in the fact that a discourse, which holds itself in the discoursing-with-one-another of what is said in the discourse, has "lost" the "primary relationship-of-being" (212). For such a discourse has "never achieved" this "primary relationship-of-being," and as a consequence cannot lose it either. And just as little is the reason found in the fact that here there is present an "aim to deceive." For whoever wants to deceive would already need to have established this "primary relationship-of-being," if he wants to deceive. No, the idle talk, the "groundless saying and passing further along" (213, translation modified) is the reason that this genuine relationship-of-being is not established. Idle talk is itself the authority, which is thought to be responsible for the fact that the "act of disclosing" is perverted "into an act of closing off" (213). Thus it is not a function of the speaker being a more or less competent speaker of a language! In idle talk Heidegger sees a built-in mechanism which ensures an *effect of perversion*, which cuts Dasein off "from its primary and primordially genuine relationships-of-being towards the world, towards Dasein-with, and towards its very being-in" (214).

Now the thesis of the fallenness of idle talk can be understood in either a weak sense or a strong sense. If we understand this thesis in its weak variation, then it seems acceptable, but it cannot, however, be used by Heidegger to support his conclusions. At the same time the thesis in its strong variation appears for Heidegger indeed usable but becomes meaningless. In its weak variation we would use the concept of the understanding to designate the grasping of a linguistic meaning, whereby this thesis of the fallenness of idle talk is then conceived as expressing a truth-semantic theory of meaning. If we use the concept of understanding in this way, then it is clear that we have not authentically understood a statement if we do not know what a conversation is about. The problem is only that this way of taking the thesis doesn't allow us to distinguish between an authentic and an inauthentic understanding.

This cannot satisfy Heidegger. He must in addition show that idle talk per se can establish no "primary relationship-of-Being towards the entity talked about" and so to the "things themselves" – the reason for which is to be sought in the public as public. In addition, only if Heidegger can make this plausible can he cash out ontologically the distinction between authenticity and inauthenticity in relation to the problem of language and understanding. Heidegger must advocate the strong variation of the thesis of fallenness if he wants to direct it critically against idle talk. For this purpose two theses are coupled together: first is the thesis of "being toward death" as a condition of the possibility of choosing, which in a negative respect annuls "the objective we-world," and in a positive respect lays open the transcendental horizon of meaning that guarantees authenticity. Secondly is the thesis that in the mode of authenticity there is a corresponding discourse – an authentic discourse, to be exact. But precisely in this way the thesis of fallenness becomes meaningless. For the authentic discourse envisaged by Heidegger is not just simply the contrast picture to inauthentic idle talk, for example a discourse which establishes again the "relationship-of-Being towards the entity talked about" that has been cut off. It is rather a discourse which cuts off both all relations to being-with and all relations to the matters talked about. At this point, Heidegger's assurance that there really is this "primary relationship-of-being" is anything but plausible.

What Heidegger observes with regard to inauthentic idle talk can be stated in a much more precise form concerning authentic discourse: this discourse would not only be "groundless," "null," "not genuine," and "contrary to the facts," but rather a discourse that merely preserves silence. In the mode of authenticity, neither an authentic discourse nor an authentic understanding is possible, since in authenticity there can only be a reverent being quiet. It is thus also anything but a coincidence when Heidegger claims already in *Being and Time* that discourse has "another essential possibility": "*keeping silent*" (Heidegger 1962: 208).

Thus it is correct that the finitude of Dasein is a condition of the possibility for something appearing in the world as important for us. But it does not follow from this that the conditions of the possibility of the understandability of linguistically shared meanings are simply dependent on the conditions of the finitude of "that Dasein which is in each case one's own," a Dasein which authentically projects itself on its possibilities in the mode of authenticity. This is contradicted not only by the fact that the orientation to "that Dasein which is in each case one's own" cannot be constitutive for linguistic intelligibility in an intersubjectively shared language, but also by the fact that even this language transcends "that Dasein which is in each case one's own." An intersubjectively shared language is the condition of the possibility of and understanding of "death," for this is actually what first makes possible both an intersubjectively valid understanding and an existentially viewed understanding of what "death" really means (see Apel 1978: 416). In this respect, things are related in precisely the opposite way that Heidegger claims: the "understanding of existence" does not provide a foundation for the hermeneutic understanding, but rather the other way around.

Although Heidegger thus identified being-with as a constitutive feature of everyday being-in-the-world, he thinks that he can be guided by "that Dasein which is in each case one's own" in order to make plausible what he calls an authentic discourse. The orientation toward "that Dasein which is in each case one's own" is not only supposed to be constitutive for authentic choosing, but also for a discourse which Heidegger designates as "authentic." This has awkward consequences. In the first place, Heidegger is unable to show how this authentic understanding and discourse are to be understood. On top of that, Heidegger runs into the danger of rehabilitating a problem in the hermeneutical perspective that, in the epistemological perspective fell to his critique of meaning, which he directed at the presuppositions of the philosophy of consciousness: the problem of how the "knowing subject comes out of its inner 'sphere' into one which is 'other and external'" (Heidegger 1962: 87).

While Heidegger could, with regard to the subject–object relation of modern epistemology, expose this problem, and along with it the problem of the solipsism of epistemology, as an apparent problem, it returns however in a modified form, and in fact in the subject–subject relation of linguistically mediated interaction. Heidegger consistently refuses to conceive of knowing as "returning with one's booty to the 'cabinet' of consciousness after one has gone out and grasped it" (89), precisely because the "clarification of being-in-the-world" showed "that a bare subject without a world never 'is' proximally, nor is it ever given. And so in the end an isolated 'I' without Others is just as far from being proximally given," since they are always already "there with us in being-in-the-world" (152). On the hermeneutic level, however, Dasein is precisely locked in this "cabinet" if it authentically discourses. Precisely with that the problem of solipsism again arises for Heidegger in the framework of a private language. If being-with is originally supposed to keep Dasein from the path into the solipsism of epistemology, then authentic discourse also now opens the path into "existential 'solipsism'."

Indeed, Heidegger protests that "existential 'solipsism'" does not put Dasein as "an isolated subject-thing into the innocuous emptiness of a worldless occurring," but rather first "brings it" in the authentic sense "before its world" and "before itself as Being-in-the-world" (233, translation modified). "Everyday familiarity" is simply supposed to collapse. But it is very obvious that the language game in which and from which we understand ourselves also belongs to this everyday familiarity. If it in fact collapses, then the problem of solipsism arises in the form of a private language. In his critique of the theory of intersubjectivity of the philosophy of consciousness, Heidegger is, as it seems, still trapped in those premises which he opposes. For his theory of intersubjectivity also proceeds methodically from out of "that Dasein which is in each case one's own" – at least as concerning the mode of authenticity. And this Dasein bears all the consequences of a phenomenologically reduced being. Husserl demanded a phenomenologically altered comportment in opposition to "projecting oneself in thought and action." The phenomenological comportment is not merely supposed to permit the epoché-practicing phenomenologist to suspend the "general thesis of the natural attitude," but rather which allows the phenomenologist at the same time, by virtue of phenomenological self-reflection, to distinguish an absolutely indubitable basis from which the regress of grounding can be stopped and further questions concerning justification can be dismissed as meaningless. In the same way, Heidegger also demands, as against the thinking, acting, and speaking of everyday being-in-the-world, an existentially altered comportment in order to save Dasein in the mode of authenticity from the relativity and situatedness of everyday being-in-the-world. Heidegger indeed released the phenomenological reduction from the compulsion of the methodical. Individualization is conceived by him as an existentiell performance, while the phenomenological reduction presents a method that is handled by the disinterested spectator. Insofar as Heidegger demands, however, that authentic discourse and understanding have oriented themselves to the mode of authenticity, he reproduces the problem of intersubjectivity on an existential-ontological level.

With that, the explanatory advantage which Heidegger, with his analysis of being-with, had won on the level of the critique of the presuppositions of modern philosophy of consciousness is lost again on the level of the grounding of an authentic discourse. Having arrived at the gate of authenticity, no path leads back from here to an intersubjectively shared lifeworld. Indeed, Heidegger's fundamental ontology can "answer the question overlooked by platonist logicism concerning the subjective-existential constitution of understandable 'significance' . . . but it cannot answer the question concerning the grounds of the possibility of intersubjectively valid significations" (Apel 1978: 413). Heidegger recognizes a linguistically disclosed and inter-subjectively shared lifeworld as a fact. But he cannot make it understandable through fundamental ontology: Heidegger can merely universalize the unique existentiell solitude to a solipsistic-transcendental community of solitude, but he cannot raise it into an intersubjectively shared we-world. For the we is the "one." And the " 'public' we-world" (Heidegger 1962: 93) is the public "one-world," from which it is precisely necessary to get away. This is also why Heidegger in the end no longer has any place for an symmetrical I–Thou encounter of Dasein with Dasein in being-with.

Heidegger expressly opposes considering the I–Thou relationship as "the fundamental social structure" (Brandom 1994: 39), starting out from which one can explain not only the problem of intersubjectivity, but also the problem of the achievement of the disclosure of Dasein. Heidegger opposes the dialogic of Martin Buber, Franz Rosenzweig, and Heidegger's first habilitation student Karl Löwith, who emphasized in his habilitation thesis the dialogical I–Thou relationship as constitutive for discourse and understanding (Löwith 1981). Heidegger defends his position against such views with the argument that it would be an error "to assume that the I–thou relation as such primarily constitutes the possible discovery of the world" (Heidegger 1997: 214). What is constitutive for it is rather the "Dasein which is in each case our own" and its transcendence, through which it can first actually "be with another self as a thou in the world" (Heidegger 1997: 214). And precisely this is the reason why Heidegger cannot solve the problem of the dialogical constitution of meanings. Indeed, Heidegger, with the concept of the referential context of the lifeworld, which lies constitutively behind the participants in interaction, is able to make thematic the unquestionable context of processes of understanding. With the appeal to an authentic discourse, however, he changes straightaway his magnificent knowledge into an absurdity. For an authentic discourse would be a discourse which no one could understand any more – in the end not even he who believes that he can speak it.

Following Wittgenstein, we can designate such a discourse a "private language." As Wittgenstein showed, the speaker of such a private language would not be in a position to define the signification of linguistic expressions in such a way that one could meaningfully say he had used the linguistic expressions in correspondence with their respective significations. This is because to say this would require making reference to the public practice of everyday being-in-the-world, more precisely, to the ability to follow a rule. And one cannot, according to Wittgenstein's point, follow a rule privately. But now if the public practice of everyday being-in-the-world is a necessary condition for holding the "assignment of signs and significations" in a way that they can be controlled, and if the meaningful application of rules itself can be understood only in the context of the "custom" of a concrete "form of life," then the speaker of a private language places himself outside of this practice, insofar as he dismisses himself from this public practice of everyday being-in-the-world. But this is not all; he dismisses himself at the same time from an intersubjectively understandable language.

Now such a private-language argument could possibly be thought in the context of *Being and Time*. Analogously to Wittgenstein, Heidegger also shows that the skeptic presupposes something that he skeptically places into question: the reality of the external world. Therefore, there are, according to Heidegger no "'actual' sceptics" (Heidegger 1962: 271), because such a skeptic, if he were actually consistent, would not at all need to be refuted. Indeed not, because, differently "than one would innocently like to have true when one tries to bowl over 'scepticism' by formal dialectics" (272), the skeptic "has obliterated Dasein in the desperation of suicide, and in doing so, he has also obliterated truth" (271). Heidegger thus also begins from the premise that the skeptic, if he wants to present his skepticism meaningfully, must "always already" presuppose something that itself can no longer be doubted. From this perspective it is also meaningless and scandalous to demand a proof of the external world on the grounds that everything could possibly be merely my dream. And if Heidegger had now generalized this refutation of epistemological skepticism – a refutation based in the critique of meaning – he would have come to a comparably similar result with respect to the possibility of a private language, as we know it from Wittgenstein. For from the point of view of the theory of language and meaning, a private language is merely the counterpart to epistemological skepticism. One seeks in Heidegger in vain, however, for such a generalization to the philosophy of language of the meaning-critical refutation of epistemological skepticism (see Tietz 2004: 33 ff.).

This is because, in order to generalize the argument in this way, Heidegger would have had to be guided by the public use of an intersubjectively shared language. Such an orientation would not only offer the possibility of explaining the signification of a linguistic expression through its use within specific "language games." At the same time this orientation would open up the possibility of subjecting the use and misuse of linguistic expressions in the empty games of philosophy, in the sciences, and even also in everyday language to a critique that starts from immanence. Instead of this, Heidegger believes that the language of the everyday life-world can be surpassed in fundamental ontology through the laying open of an authentic discourse. It is the unsayable demand for authenticity which in the perspective of the philosophy of language rehabilitates that problem which Heidegger dismissed with respect to modern epistemology. For the immanence of the monad cannot be broken simply with this orientation to the "Dasein which is in each case our own." For Husserl, each *Cartesian Meditation* "leads back to the transcendental ego naturally," and is confronted "with its concrete monadic contents as this de facto ego, as the one and only absolute ego," by means of "the method of phenomenological reduction." In the same way, a solipsism is restored for Heidegger, albeit without the phenomenological reduction in the sense of a methodical procedure, which brings the problem of a private language in tow.

So the solitude, arising from the non-relationality of one's own self, overshadows every communicative understanding and in its ultimate consequence makes communication as communication impossible. The Dasein of the other mutates into a plurality of closed-off monads, which in their interiors contain mineness inaccessibly (see Sternberg 1981: 133). As we noted already, insofar as for Heidegger, like for Kierkegaard, "authenticity becomes a relationship to itself under which heading nothing further can be conceived, " it is precisely not that which linguistic understanding always already presupposes: a social relation to others. No authentic self constitutes itself in being-with, since being-with after all merely appears as a codetermining factor in relation to authenticity, and yet as a negative factor for it. Dasein gains its authenticity without a positive possibility of being-with; this thus means that something like an authentic discourse and understanding cannot occur here. The "gap" which the Heideggerian social ontology tears open between authenticity and inauthenticity is for Heidegger no longer bridgeable hermeneutically. In this respect, the analysis of being-with does not merely repeat the Husserlian theory of inter-subjectivity on the level of existential ontology, but rather radicalizes and intensifies it at the same time.

The dialogical structure of linguistic understanding disappears in favor of the monadological construction of the authentic self, which actually does not allow any further answer to its offer of language. This self is tied to an imagination which functions as a primary self-understanding and in contrast to which all offers of language of everyday being-in-the-world appear as ideological foreign infiltrations. The conceptualizing of death as a condition of authenticity thus does not merely have the consequence that Heidegger's project dismisses the principle of self-preservation in its traditional form, but rather also puts into question, on the basis of the monologue, the functioning of conventional language and its social content of signification. With this, the course is already set in *Being and Time* for explaining the "essence of language" from the "essence of poetry" (see Heidegger 2000b: 60 ff.).

But it is now clear that the monologue cannot be constitutive for linguistic under-standing by means of indentical significations. For the participation in linguistic interaction does not merely require the use of linguistic symbols, a use which is bound up with the competence to follow a rule, but rather also the attitude in which the ego and alter ego address each other. But precisely this addressing attitude is systematically misguided by the orientation to the "Dasein which is in each case our own." The consequence of this is that the monologue eats up the dialogue. This loss of dialogue is in its consequence the reverse side of the *negativism of the theory of intersubjectivity*, which the premises of the analysis of being-with force. The monadological involvement with "the Dasein which is in each case *our own*" com-pels Heidegger to reconstruct the intersubjective relationship between Dasein and Dasein in being-with from the perspective of an individual consciousness, through which the process of understanding falls into two disparate parts: in the declaration of a speaker on the one side, and in the taking notice of a hearer on the other side. Indeed, Heidegger assures us that speaking just as much as hearing is constitutive for discourse and understanding. Since however the "second person" appears "only in the levelled out form of the 'other' person, but not as my partner or as the thou belonging to an I" (Löwith 1942: 61, translation modified), a linguistically generated intersubjectivity of the understanding cannot be made plausible.

But with that the entire concept of language, as Heidegger takes it in *Being and Time*, is caught in a crisis. For that which is predicated cannot be "authentically" communicated in any case, because in the mode of authenticity there is no inter-subjectively understandable language whatever. And because every predication would compromise the priority of being, then language can ultimately communicate nothing more than something totally empty. Heidegger wanted originally to speak of

183

that of which Wittgenstein preferred to remain silent. In this way this emptiness, the absolutely inexpressible, that which is exempted from all predication under the name "being," finally becomes for him that *ens realissimum* that is capable of telling silence.

So then Heidegger indeed, following Dilthey and Husserl, adopted understanding and language as the basic characteristic of human Dasein and called attention to the constitutive role of the pre-understanding, which arises from the having-to-do with the same thing. But insofar as Heidegger with the orientation to "the Dasein which is in each case our own" gives the model for interpreting the understanding as a one-sided, say, monological, expression, it becomes impossible for him to solve the problem of the linguistic understanding of meaning. In contrast to the observations which everyone makes for themselves alone, the understanding of meaning is not feasible solipsistically. Linguistic signification can be derived from the performative attitude of participants in communication, which assumes a common orientation to an intersubjective practice – something Heidegger cannot guarantee through his orientation to "the Dasein which is in each case our own."

This is also the reason why the problem of intersubjectivity cannot be solved on the basis of Heidegger's premise of a Dasein which can project itself authentically on its possibilities only in solitude, something that then holds also analogously for an intersubjectivity of linguistically shared significations. For the signification of linguistic expressions cannot be made plausible, as Heidegger attempts to do, with a "Humpty-Dumpty-view" of language,[6] but rather only in relation to the rule-structure of language. Heidegger recognizes this in the consequences. He recognizes that Dasein is forced ultimately to watch helplessly the withdrawal of being from the deficient practice of the everyday understanding. And he recognizes, without of course freeing himself from the "Humpty-Dumpty-view," that the problem of intersubjectivity cannot be solved on the premises of fundamental ontology. That is why he attempts to spring back onto an ontologically even deeper foundation. But this foundation within Dasein, as it was conceived in *Being and Time*, cannot be exhibited.

The creative subject was indeed brought out from the realm of the intelligible and placed into the dimension of the lifeworld. And the philosophy of the subject, in which the transcendental formulation recovered an ontological sense, was indeed overcome through the more deeply conceived conceptuality of an existential ontology that proceeds transcendentally, which wants to make the conditions of the possibility of predication thematic with the concept of "disclosedness." "Precisely the concrete analysis of disclosedness in *Being and Time*, however, in which this is presented in its 'finitude,' had to lead to the realization that Dasein cannot bear any longer the grounding function which here was still transcendentally-philosophically expected. The later 'turning' is contained in advance in the content of the new problematic" (Tugendhat 1967: 273).

In his later philosophy Heidegger therefore searches for an alternative in order to get rid of the "founding communicationlessness" of Dasein (see Ebeling 1982: 30). Heidegger no longer wants to philosophize from Dasein, but rather from being. It is no longer Dasein, but rather being, to which Heidegger awards the power to disclose worlds. Therewith the problem of intersubjectivity now indeed becomes invalid. Now instead, being is at work in the grammatical change of the linguistic world picture, which in such a way takes over the place of a subjectless creator of meaning – with which then the chapter on existential ontology is ended and the chapter on the philosophy of being begins.

Notes

1   The early Georg Lukács dedicated an essay to him in 1909, in which he anticipated the basic theses of the later existence-philosophy. Lukács 1911: 61 ff. For more on this, see Tietz 1989: 561–80.

2   In the "Notizen zu Heidegger" Jaspers says: "among the German philosophy professors of our time only one interested me: Heidegger. All the others seemed to me intellectual bustle. Only here was another serious philosopher. In the years from 1920 to 1930 it united us" (Jaspers 1978: 75).

3   "In determining itself as an entity, Dasein always does so in the light of a possibility which it is itself and which, in its very Being, it somehow understands. This is the formal meaning of Dasein's existential constitution. But this tells us that if we are to Interpret this entity ontologically, the problematic of its Being must be developed from the existentiality of its existence" (Heidegger 1962: 69).

4   See Husserl 1976: 188. The exchange of roles between the ego and alter ego which Husserl contemplates can indeed guarantee a certain symmetry. Ultimately, however, every appresentation refers to its own primal presence. With that, Husserl's attempt to construct intersubjectivity from a pre-intersubjective "primal I," which lies before all exchange-understanding, remains stuck to a one-sided perspective. See Waldenfels 1980: 166 ff.

5   Heidegger refers in this context to Jaspers and his *Psychology of Worldviews*, insofar as "here the question of 'what man is' is raised and answered in terms of what he essentially can be," from which, according to Heidegger, "the basic existential-ontological signification of 'limit-situations'" is supposed to result (Heidegger 1962: 496 n. xv).

6   According to Humpty Dumpty: "When *I* use a word . . . it means just what I choose it to mean – neither more nor less" (Carroll 1872). Husserl also advocated such a Humpty-Dumpty view insofar as "a word or expression is invested with meaning by a mental act on the speaker's part conferring meaning upon it" (Dummett 1994: 104; see also Dummett 1994: 44 ff.).

References and Further Reading

Adorno, T. W. (1973) *The Jargon of Authenticity* (trans. K. Tarnowski and F. Will). Evanston, IL: Northwestern University Press.

Apel, K.-O. (1978) Ist der Tod eine Bedingung der Möglichkeit von Bedeutung? In J. Mittelstraß and M. Riedel (eds.), *Vernünftiges Denken. Studien zur praktischen Philosophie und Wissenschaftstheorie* (pp. 407–19). Berlin: Walter de Gruyter.

Bollnow, O. F. (1947) *Existenzphilosophie*. Stuttgart: Kohlhammer.

Brandom, R. B. (1994) *Making it Explicit: Reasoning, Representing, and Discursive Commitment.* Cambridge, MA: Harvard University Press.

Carroll, L. (1872) *Through the Looking-Glass.* London: Macmillan.

Dilthey, W. (1989) *Introduction to the Human Sciences* (ed. R. A. Makkreel and F. Rodi). Princeton, NJ: Princeton University Press.

Dummett, M. (1994) *Origins of Analytical Philosophy.* Cambridge, MA: Harvard University Press.

Ebeling, H. (1982) *Freiheit, Gleichheit, Sterblichkeit. Philosophie nach Heidegger*. Stuttgart: Reclam.

Gadamer, H.-G. (1994) Martin Heidegger's one path. In T. Kisiel and J. Van Buren (eds.), *Reading Heidegger from the Start* (pp. 19–34). Albany, NY: SUNY Press.

Habermas, J. (1992) *Postmetaphysical Thinking: Philosophical Essays* (trans. W. M. Hohengarten). Cambridge, MA: MIT Press.

Hegel, G. W. F. (1979) *Phenomenology of Spirit* (trans. A. V. Miller). Oxford: Oxford University Press.

Heidegger, M. (1962) *Being and Time* (trans. J. Macquarrie and E. Robinson). New York: Harper & Row.

—— (1978) *Die Kategorien- und Bedeutungslehre des Duns Scotus*. In *Frühe Schriften. Gesamtausgabe* vol. 1. Frankfurt: Klostermann.

—— (1997) *Phenomenological Interpretation of Kant's* Critique of Pure Reason (trans. P. Emad and K. Maly). Bloomington: Indiana University Press.

—— (1998a) On the essence of ground. In W. McNeill (ed.), *Pathmarks* (pp. 97–135). Cambridge: Cambridge University Press.

—— (1998b) Letter on "Humanism." In W. McNeill (ed.), *Pathmarks* (pp. 239–76). Cambridge: Cambridge University Press.

—— (2000a) *Introduction to Metaphysics* (trans. G. Fried and R. Polt). New Haven, CT: Yale University Press.

—— (2000b) *Elucidations of Hölderlin's Poetry* (trans. K. Hoeller). Amherst, NY: Humanity Books.

Heinemann, F. (1954) *Existenzphilosophie Lebendig oder Tot?* Stuttgart: Kohlhammer.

Husserl, E. (1976) *Die Krisis der europäischen Wissenschaften und die transzendentale Phänomenologie. Husserliana* vol. VI (ed. W. Biemel). The Hague: Martinus Nijhoff.

—— (1984) *Logische Untersuchungen*, vol. II/1. *Husserliana*, vol. XIX/1 (ed. U. Panzer). The Hague: Martinus Nijhoff.

Jaspers, K. (1913) *Allgemeine Psychopathologie*. Berlin: Springer.

—— (1919) *Psychologie der Weltanschauungen*. Berlin: Springer.

—— (1947) *Von der Wahrheit*. Munich: Piper.

—— (1957) *Man in the Modern Age* (trans. E. and C. Paul). Garden City, NY: Doubleday Anchor.

—— (1965) Geleitwort für die Zeitschrift "Die Wandlung." In *Hoffnung und Sorge*. Munich: Piper (original work published 1945).

—— (1967) *Philosophical Faith and Revelation* (trans. E. B. Ashton). New York: Harper & Row (original work published 1962 as *Der philosophische Glaube angesichts der Offenbarung*).

—— (1969) *Philosophy*, vol. 1: *Philosophical World Orientation* (trans. E. B. Ashton). Chicago: University of Chicago Press (original work published 1932 as *Philosophie*, vol. 1: *Philosophische Weltorientierung*).

—— (1970) *Philosophy*, vol. 2: *Existential Elucidation* (trans. E. B. Ashton). Chicago: University of Chicago Press (original work published 1932 as *Philosophie*, vol. 2: *Existenzerhellung*).

—— (1978) *Notizen zu Heidegger* (ed. H. Saner). Munich: Piper.

—— (1981) Philosophical autobiography. In P. A. Schilpp (ed.), *The Philosophy of Karl Jaspers*. La Salle, IL: Open Court.

Kierkegaard, S. (1989) *The Sickness Unto Death* (trans. A. Hannay). New York: Penguin.

Löwith, K. (1942) M. Heidegger and F. Rosenzweig, or, temporality and eternity. *Philosophy and Phenomenological Research*, 3: 53–77.

—— (1981) Das Individuum in der Rolle des Mitmenschen. In *Mensch und Menschenwelt. Beiträge zur Anthropologie. Sämtliche Schriften*. Stuttgart: Metzler.

Lukács, G. (1911) Das Zerschellen der Formen am Leben: Sören Kierkegaard und Regine Olsen. In *Die Seele und die Formen. Essays*. Berlin: Fleischel.

Sartre, J.-P. (1947) *Existentialism* (trans. B. Frechtman). New York: Philosophical Library (original lecture delivered 1945 as *L'Existentialisme est un humanisme*).

Schütz, A. (1957) Das Problem der transzendentalen Intersubjektivität bei Husserl. *Philosophische Rundschau*, 5, 81–107.

Sternberg, D. (1981) Der verstandene Tod. Eine Untersuchung zu M. Heideggers Existenzial-Ontologie. In *Über den Tod*. Frankfurt: Suhrkamp.

Theunissen, M. (1984) *The Other: Studies in the Social Ontology of Husserl, Heidegger, Sartre, and Buber* (trans. C. Macann). Cambridge, MA: MIT Press.

Tietz, U. (1989) Ästhetik und Geschichte. Eine philosophisch-ästhetische Analyse des Frühwerks von Georg Lukács. *Weimarer Beiträge. Zeitschrift für Literaturwissenschaft, Ästhetik und Kulturtheorie*, 4, 561–80.

—— (2003) *Ontologie und Dialektik. Heidegger und Adorno über das Sein, das Nichtidentische, die Synthesis und die Kopula*. Vienna: Passagen Verlag.

—— (2004) Heidegger und Wittgenstein über Sinn, Wahrheit und Sprache. *Allgemeine Zeitschrift für Philosophie*, 29/1, 19–38.

—— (2005) *Heidegger*. Leipzig: Reclam.

Tugendhat, E. (1967) *Der Wahrheitsbegriff bei Husserl und Heidegger*. Berlin: Walter de Gruyter.

—— (1979) *Selbstbewußtsein und Selbstbestimmung. Sprachanalytische Interpretationen*. Frankfurt: Suhrkamp.

Waldenfels, B. (1980) Der Sinn zwischen den Zeilen. In *Der Spielraum des Verhaltens*. Frankfurt: Suhrkamp.

13

Religious Existentialism

CLANCY MARTIN

It is from the viewpoint of night that I am considering the light.
                                        −Georges Bataille, *Inner Experience*

The philosophical literature collectively described as "religious existentialism" is vast. There are at least fifteen major thinkers, all of them prolific, who are properly understood as developing twentieth-century existentialism from a theistic, rather than an atheistic point of view. In fact, even among the atheists, who today are better remembered, the questions addressed by existentialism look suspiciously akin to religious (or perhaps better, spiritual) questions. This should not surprise us. Of the three great forerunners of the existentialists, Kierkegaard, Dostoevsky, and Nietzsche, the first two were profoundly religious thinkers, and the third understood his thinking as a response to our culture's loss of God. Gabriel Marcel, one of the great religious existentialists, who coined the term "existentialist," refused the label "Christian existentialist" as nonsensical because he thought the questions of existentialism and the questions of religion were ultimately inseparable.

But because of the size of the literature, the task of the commentator on this impressive tradition is daunting to say the least. He is confronted with an embarrassment of riches. So, rather than to try to survey in a superficial way many or most of the thinkers in the tradition, I have chosen to look a bit more carefully at only four: Miguel de Unamuno, Lev Shestov, Karl Barth, and Martin Buber. And I have chosen these four with an eye to their differences, rather than their similarities, in a hope at least to gesture toward the variety and complexity of the tradition. These four, while they are all of them Kierkegaardians – the work of the religious existentialists has been helpfully described as "apples from the tree of Kierkegaard" – have startling different views of God, the individual, and the possibility and nature of redemption. But they are all post-World War II thinkers, and they share the suspicion of the rationalist Enlightenment project that the devastating wars of the twentieth century aroused in so many minds, religious or no. They also share the suspicion that philosophy as it had been traditionally practiced had not been practiced well. Whether they share other classic "existentialist" concerns, we shall see as we proceed.

Miguel de Unamuno (1865–1936, Spanish–Basque)

Miguel de Unamuno was a poet, a novelist, and an essayist, but his masterpiece was a work of philosophy, *The Tragic Sense of Life* (1911–12; cited as de Unamuno 1921). In the famous introductory passage to the book, Unamuno declares that his concern is: "The man who is born, suffers, and dies – above all, who dies; the man who eats and drinks and plays and sleeps and thinks and wills; the man who is seen and heard; the brother, the real brother" (de Unamuno 1921: 1). He contrasts this man, who is both his subject and his audience, with man as (Unamuno thinks) he has been traditionally considered by philosophers, man who is "merely an idea . . . a no-man"(de Unamuno 1921: 1). He here announces the theme that will dominate the work: the opposition between life as it is actually lived and so must be understood, and life as it has been traditionally approached through rational categories that are inadequate to the task of comprehending existence. The significance of this opposition is demonstrated by the physical fact of death, which, he thinks, is meaningless when considered rationally, but takes on tremendous earnestness when considered from the perspective of an ordinary, actual human life.

Unamuno argues that our most basic impulse is the impulse to life itself. We want nothing more than to live and to go on living. But we are confronted with the frustrating and inescapable fact of the inevitability of death. Rationally speaking, he thinks, this should not cause any dismay: the impersonal fact of an end to life is not an affront to reason. Reason recognizes that we can never know that we continue to live beyond the fact of our physical dissolution, and moves on to other questions. Death is, however, a deeply personal affront to each and every one of us, who desire nothing more than immortality. (At this point Unamuno thinks that Catholicism does a better job of addressing religious experience than does Protestantism, because the former continues to insist on the centrality of the question of immortality, while the latter avoids the question by focusing on rational ethics). He argues that the personal question of immortality – that we desire it, despite the fact that we have absolutely no reason to expect it or even to hope for it – creates a *conflict* for us. We demand that existence provide to us something that we cannot see that it has to offer. For Unamuno, this experience of irreconcilable conflict is precisely the religious experience. Reason is at best unequipped to deal with, at worse dismissive of, this human and personal experience of inner conflict. But our experience of conflict, which provokes us to *struggle*, is what makes us genuinely alive.

A rational approach to life makes the further and related mistake of supposing that there is "a solution for every problem" (de Unamuno 1921: 93). It is not merely that reason is mistaken in supposing that every problem must have a solution (although Unamuno thinks this is a piece of "pious" naïveté). We also err when we rationally suppose that the *value* of every question is in its answer. Like Nietzsche before him, Unamuno insists that life is a questionable and even a terrifying thing; but to look for an "answer" to the question of life is again to find oneself confronting the meaningless solution of death. That death is part of life is not in itself meaningless – for Unamuno, the lived confrontation with the inevitability of death is part of how we come to create

189

meaning in our lives – but to understand and value death as some sort of "answer" to life's questions is of course utterly unsatisfying. You do not resolve the conflict presented by death by reasonably agreeing that it is the end of life. The point is that the end of life is irrationally unacceptable.

To make better sense of what Unamuno is after it will help to introduce a distinction he sometimes appeals to between truth and meaning. For Unamuno, reason is perfectly adequate to the task of discovering all sorts of truths about the world, and even truths about human psychology and how we relate to one another. However, those truths remain indifferent for us as persons, because meaning is not generated through our acknowledgment of facts. Meaning, he thinks, refers to the domain of human value, and is created in the human soul because of the traction of conflict. Reason discovers resolutions of problems in the world and calls these "truths," but irresolvable conflict creates passion in the soul and creates "meaning." We create meaning through our refusal to be reconciled to the differences we experience in the world between what it offers and what we desire. This is a crucial part of the "tragic sense" of human life: we find meaningful that which frustrates us, in the strongest sense of the word frustration.

Unamuno's account is fascinating here, in that he poses the question of how we actually come to value what we value. He has an easy account of a kind of immediate value: that is, the value of life, and presumably those good things that we need in order to live. (He simply asserts, albeit plausibly, that life is a kind of primary value or ground of value for us.) But what else becomes valuable to us? He argues that it is those things that are denied us: complete communication with others; happiness; love that wholly overcomes loneliness; a sense of personal completeness; self-knowledge. We struggle to achieve these things that we suspect are unachievable. The portrait he paints of the human condition is indeed a tragic one, because we find that we only want (or value, or find meaning in) what we cannot have. In a characterization of human existence that recalls Schopenhauer, life becomes a story of insatiable desire.

Unsurprisingly, then, life is experienced as suffering. He writes that "suffering . . . is the most immediate revelation of consciousness, and it may be that our body was given us simply in order that suffering might be able to manifest itself" (de Unamuno 1921: 211). This is not to say that the suffering of the body is the awakening of consciousness, but rather to show that consciousness emerges as precisely this conflict between what we want (or need) and what we get, which is repeated in the many frustrations of being embodied. Unamuno thinks that personality itself emerges out of the long series of frustrating conflicts that constitute human life. Each new experience of irreconcilable conflict is a new experience of suffering, which over time make us who we are. Without conflict, without suffering, we do not exist as persons.

Suffering raised to its highest pitch becomes anguish (we could also call it "dread" or "anxiety" – Unamuno takes the category directly from Kierkegaard's concept of *Angst*). While his characterizations of anguish are vague at best, he seems to think of anguish as a kind of generalized experience of the frustration of conflict. Rather than this or that experience producing conflict and suffering (even the experience of contemplating death), the individual in anguish experiences all of existence as this conflict. Existence itself is seen as endless, irreconcilable conflict and (thus) suffering, and so the individual despairs. But this experience of anguish is the highest experience to which a human can aspire. It is in fact the experience of God: "God, the Consciousness of the

Universe, is limited by the brute matter in which He lives, by the unconscious, from which He seeks to liberate Himself and to liberate us. God suffers in each and all of us . . . and we all suffer in Him. Religious anguish is but the Divine suffering, the feeling that God suffers in me and that I suffer in him"(de Unamuno 1921: 207). We come to love God, Unamuno claims, because in anguish we see that He is essentially the same sort of thing we are: a being torn between what it is and what it would be. We have sympathy for God. We even pity Him. And so faith, for Unamuno, does not become (as we might have expected) an expression of the most profound frustration, a reaching out for a God who does not offer His hand in return; on the contrary, faith is the moment at which we realize that even God cannot reconcile us to existence, because He suffers just as we do. Nor did the Son of God, Jesus Christ, come to bring us reconciliation and peace. He came rather to bring us conflict, struggle, and agony.

This is not, of course, a traditional characterization of God, and is hardly the perfect, all-powerful, all-knowing, all-good being of most descriptions of (or rational proofs of the existence of) God. Unamuno takes literally the scriptural assertion that we are made in the image of God but, rather than using the text to argue that we are ourselves perfect like God, turns the ordinary interpretation on its head by showing that God must therefore be limited and suffering as we are. That such an understanding of God is not a "rational" one is hardly an objection for Unamuno. We may want a perfect God, but what we get is this imperfect one, and so we find meaning again in the conflict.

So far Unamuno's portrait sounds a bit like a particularly depressing reformulation or inversion of Buddhism: life is suffering, suffering comes from frustrated attachment, and the acme of human existence (here's where he turns Buddhism on its head) is embracing that frustration. But Unamuno believes in a kind of redemption for us, and that redemption comes from the *comic*. Again following Kierkegaard, he argues that the religious experience is fundamentally a comic one.

He finds his illustration of the comic character of the religious experience – which in the end, for Unamuno, is all fully aware human experience – in Cervantes' fictional hero Don Quixote. He refers to Quixote, in the honorific normally reserved for Christ, as "Our Lord Don Quixote," and goes on to describe him as "a living and eternal man . . . worth all theories and all philosophies" (de Unamuno 1921: 323). For us, thinking about Quixote *after* Unamuno (his critical work on Cervantes is largely responsible for the enormous popularity of "the knight of the doleful countenance" in the twentieth century), it may be difficult to appreciate the philosophical weight Unamuno attached to the originality of the attitude displayed by Quixote. But let's try to think in the way that Unamuno did.

For Unamuno, the threat of ordinary experience, and the threat of our attempts to interpret ordinary experience rationally, is that we will fail to recognize those deep conflicts that actually constitute our experience. Through habit, superficiality, and the objective sorting of experience that reason excels at, we will lose our awareness of the things that really matter to us, and the conflicts that those things involve us in. So, he thinks, we can remove ourselves further and further from the hope of actually living life, by effectively ignoring the difficulty of love, of loneliness, of self-knowledge, of faith, etc. Quixote recognizes this danger, so he willfully creates conflict where superficially speaking none exists. He tilts at windmills not because he imagines they

191

are giants (although it does not matter, really, whether he so imagines or not), but because the point is to *tilt*. He fights for his love not because he knows that his beloved is worthy of his adoration (she is notoriously not so), but because he recognizes that without this effort his life becomes meaningless.

Love is not something given to him, it is something he must create, and must fight for. For Quixote, believing is creating. In creating what he believes he quite naturally becomes ridiculous; Unamuno argues that he becomes ridiculous even to himself. But ridiculousness is an expression of what is essentially human. Ridiculousness is the category of conflict: a conflict between what ought to be the case and what is presented as the case. And this, again, is our Quixotic human situation: the irreconcilable conflict between what we are and what we would be, between what we have and what we want. And the response to the ridiculous is not to despair, but to laugh. By making himself absurd Quixote redeems not only himself, but us as well, because the absurdity of his position and, if we are thoughtful, of our own position (as it is revealed by him) becomes an occasion for our good humor.

The key to Quixote's attitude is not just that he despises the opinion of the world, and insists on his own ability to create value for himself. (Quixote, like Unamuno, is a strong voluntarist: he insists we can choose to believe whatever we please.) It is also that he accurately understands the human condition, and responds to it in the most appropriate way. He does not merely observe the ridiculousness of our situation, he demands it, again, he creates it. Naturally this does not *make sense*: making sense would be a threat to the project of creating meaning. Quixote's virtue is precisely his absurdity. For Unamuno Quixote's recognition of the ridiculousness of being human also results in ordinary human virtues like forgiveness and pity: he cannot condemn the folly of anyone else, when he himself insists on the legitimacy of his particular brand of folly. Here Unamuno compares Quixote to Socrates, whose irony and denial of knowledge, he thinks, similarly create a kind of exemplary human goodness through the absence of a standard for condemning others.

Quixote's greatest strength, Unamuno argues, is his self-knowledge. He refuses to know the world, because he sees that meaning is not about *what is out there*. Consequently (and perhaps curiously), Unamuno claims, Quixote is incapable of fearing anyone or anything: all that matters to him is entirely in his own control. Quixote himself becomes, in a sense, God: his world (the world of meaning) is the world he has himself created. And Unamuno thinks that we too can become God-like, if we can come to know ourselves in this way. But self-knowledge here is also the awareness of our own limitations. We are limited because all we can do is insist on conflict, and recognize that the meaning of our lives is provided by that insistence. Like Quixote, then, we are tragic because we know only conflict and frustration, and so we struggle and suffer, but we can redeem ourselves by becoming comic, by making ourselves ridiculous, by laughing at ourselves, by quixotically insisting on the meaning of our suffering.

Lev Shestov (1866–1938, Russian)

While Kierkegaard was a crucial influence for the mature Shestov (interestingly, Edmund Husserl, a long-time friend and philosophical opponent of Shestov's, introduced him to Kierkegaard's work), Dostoevsky and Nietzsche were at least as important to the development of his thought, and Nietzsche's influence in particular is hard to underestimate. After an early work on Shakespeare, he wrote two books on Nietzsche, *Good in the Teaching of Tolstoy and Nietzsche* (1900; cited as Shestov 1969a) and *Dostoevsky and Nietzsche: The Philosophy of Tragedy* (1903; cited as Shestov 1969b). A third work, *The Apotheosis of Groundlessness* (1905; cited as Shestov 1920), attempts to further develop familiarly Nietzschean attacks on traditional accounts of reason and ethics. At one point he claims that Nietzsche is the only philosopher who took the question of the existence of God seriously. His style of writing also bears the mark of Nietzsche: he delights in aphorisms and polemic, he has a disdain for traditional philosophical argument, and he is often so extreme in his positions that one wonders if he meant them seriously or as rhetorical or skeptical foils. Shestov considered his two late works, *In Job's Balances* (1929; cited as Shestov 1975) and the magnum opus *Athens and Jerusalem* (1938; cited as Shestov 1966), to express his mature philosophical position. But his most intellectually exciting book is the collection of essays *Potestas Clavium* (1923; cited as Shestov 1968).

The religious existentialists were part of a memorably awful time in history. Born towards the end of the comparatively peaceful nineteenth century, with much of the optimism of the eighteenth century still in the air, all of them lived through World War I, and most of them lived through World War II as well. All four of the thinkers we are here considering were profoundly impacted by the events of World War I. But for Shestov the war was not just a terrifying indication of the limitations of human reason, rational ethics and science (as many of the others here tend to view it). For him it was God's bloody response to the Enlightenment. God laid His vengeful hands upon Western civilization and showed us where reason and merely conventional Christianity had taken us. The war, Shestov thought, was God's warning to us: continue down this path which chooses science over faith, reason over life, rational ethics over radical redemption, the nation over the individual, and you will be destroyed. (It may have been lucky for Shestov that he died in 1938. One can only imagine what he would have made of World War II.) The central and very old problem, Shestov thinks, is our obsession with knowledge:

> God forbade plucking the fruits of this tree not out of fear that man would obtain more than what had been granted to him and not out of jealousy. The accursed Serpent deceived Eve, deceived Adam, deceived Anaximander, and blinds all of us to this day. The tree of knowledge does not increase our powers but, on the contrary, diminishes them. We must choose between the tree of the knowledge of good and evil and the tree of life. (Shestov 1968: 157)

Shestov opens *Potestas Clavium* with the question: "Has there ever been a single philosopher who recognized God?"(Shestov 1968: 3). (His startling answer to the question is that there was only one: Nietzsche.) What Shestov attempts to show is that the entire history of Western philosophy has been built on what he takes to be a fundamentally godless claim: that reason will lead us to the truth. He thinks that, since the pre-Socratics, there have been almost no philosophers who have taken the possibility of a truly transcendent God seriously.

193

Shestov argues both that reason is insufficient to grasp God, and that experience is importantly irrational. The first attack is easier to make, so I will begin with it.

Reason, he thinks, can at best prove the existence of a rational God, but our idea of God is that He is greater than reason. "Every time reason set about proving the existence of God, it required as a first condition that God be ready to submit Himself to the fundamental principles that reason prescribed to Him" (Shestov 1968: 10). Rather than using reason to discover or indicate the existence of God, we have attempted to constrain God within the limited categories of our rational thought.

Shestov thinks the most egregious example of this tendency, though certainly not the only one, is that of Socrates. In his attempt to know the Good, Socrates wanted to use his own reason to be the arbiter of truth and falsehood (Shestov is not particularly worried about distinguishing Socrates from Plato, and surely many of his attacks might be better applied to the student than the teacher). In pursuing the Good with reason, Shestov argues, Socrates tried to place himself in the position of God. But all he succeeded in doing was reducing God to the Good. In this way, Shestov argues, following Nietzsche (who famously wondered if, on account of his rationalism, Socrates deserved his hemlock), Socrates initiated the Western crisis that resulted in the death of God. When Socrates insisted that the True and the Good were identical and discernible through reason, Shestov says, he in fact accomplished three things. First, he made God irrelevant, because the nature of the universe was penetrable by the merely human. The divine became nothing more than a kind of example of the rational categories of goodness and truth. Second, he devalued the universe as we actually experience it. By rationally insisting that truth and goodness are eternal and unchanging, he cast suspicion on our experienced and transitory reality. Third and finally, he extinguished all the mystery of life, the universe, and the Divine. Unless it is rational, Socrates taught us, it should be a source of distrust. For Shestov, Descartes, Spinoza, Kant, and even Husserl make this same Socratic mistake, of supposing that the universe is a rational place, and that our valuing (and the sources of our valuing) will be similarly rational. Begin with God, Shestov argues, rather than with reason, and you will develop a very different and more human understanding of the universe.

Moreover, the Socratic vision of the universe has failed to satisfy the human spirit. "Scratch any European," he writes, "even if he is a positivist or a materialist, and you will quickly discover a medieval Catholic who holds frantically to his exclusive and inalienable right to open for himself and his neighbor the gates of the kingdom of heaven" (Shestov 1968: 47). And why? Because reason, though it is capable of increasingly estranging us from our lived experience, cannot succeed in making us inhuman. We have fallen into knowledge, Shestov thinks, but we are also aware of our fallen condition, and in our every day lives we are constantly reminded of the presence of the Divine in our experience of *freedom*.

The experience of freedom, the daily need to choose and the ordinary lived confrontation of the fact that our choices change the future, demonstrates the irrationality (or the greater-than-rationality) of our experience and of the universe itself. Shestov argues that a rational investigation of the world shows us only causal necessity. Considered from the perspective of reason, the universe is wholly determined. And yet none of us will honestly deny the acute sensation of the difference between choosing and avoiding choice, between being active and being passive. In this context Shestov invokes the helpful example of laziness. How much easier is it, he asks, simply not to do what one knows one should? How much easier is it to relax into the comfort of laziness? The difficult thing is to will oneself out of the causal stream, to choose, to act. But with this difficulty comes the anxiety of confronting possibility. Once we recognize that we can choose, that we are not merely determined by causes or reasons, the future opens up in all its terrifying plenitude. And, in a classic move from Kierkegaard, the intense awareness of possibility creates anxiety. We can make almost anything happen. We could spontaneously hang ourselves, or murder another, or abandon our families, or set out to become a philosopher. Once we set our wills into motion, the order of necessity is destroyed. We ourselves can tear apart the fabric of what we liked to suppose was a rationally woven universe. And although we may tend to act according to reason, we are not compelled to do so. This inherent spontaneity of the individual, which, Shestov thinks, is essential to the creation of individual personality, reveals the divine component in our experience, which reason always misses.

In fact, Shestov argues, reason is directly opposed to that spontaneity, because reason would like to make us mere creatures of necessity. To acquiesce to reason is deeply comforting to us, because we need not confront possibility and assume responsibility for our choices. We can say, as it were, "it was the only logical thing to do." We are afraid of freedom; we would rather be told what to do. Continuing this line of attack, Shestov argues that reason seeks ultimately to eliminate human personality altogether, because it characterizes us as nothing more than a play of forces. For reason we do not choose our beliefs, we merely respond to the best evidence in forming them. And if we are always simply following the best evidence, why do we need the individual at all? Just as I involuntarily believe that the sun is shining because that is the evidence provided to my discerning eyes, and I believe the house is warm because of the evidence of my skin, so will I believe in the love of my wife, the beauty of a song, and the desirability of being a philosophy professor, all in involuntary response to the best evidence of my discerning reason. What am I in this complicated network of beliefs? Shestov thinks that Hume drew this (involuntarist) line of argument out to its logical (if completely unacceptable) conclusion: I am nothing, I am completely irrelevant. Rationally speaking, there is no "I." I am merely the point at which the controlling powers meet to play.

"God never uses coercion, but then, truth is not God: it coerces"(Shestov 1969c: 236). But again, it coerces us because it lends itself to our natural laziness. Our insistence on the kind of truth that reason can provide is "a desire dependent not on metaphysical considerations but on the profoundly inculcated habit of living and thinking in certain conditions of existence already well-known and comfortable" (Shestov 1968: 71). Shestov is not here suggesting a pragmatic criterion for truth: we do not accept rational truth because it works. Rather, in a line of argument that recalls many of Nietzsche's attacks on the notion of truth, he thinks that we accept rational truth because it is easier for us to do so.

In what looks like an interpretation of Hume's argument against induction (or it may be Hume by way of Nietzsche), Shestov argues that the "strange and monstrous" (Shestov 1968: 174) universe is fundamentally unpredictable: reason can accommodate itself to what experience actually presents to it, but it is incapable of deducing laws from experience. All reason can do is endorse those principles which seem to have described the universe so far – but that description is just the summary of the many surprises we have already encountered and, Shestov believes (injecting a curious empirical premise), the universe will always continue to surprise us. So our reliance on reason to tell us about the universe is not a reliance on truth, it is simply an expression of our need to *rely upon*.

For Shestov this is in fact the best we can hope for from philosophy: to show us the many failings of reason, so that we can free ourselves from its dulling characterization of experience. Even "the demands of logic finally have for their source a deep-seated human prejudice" (Shestov 1968: 167), namely, the prejudice in favor of rational order and our lazy acceptance of it. And the one consistent virtue of philosophers, he thinks, is that they have been dishonest about how they have developed their philosophical systems. They have pretended to reason their way into their conclusions, while in fact they began with some basic prejudice that they were determined to prove (here again he echoes Nietzsche, who made the same claim). The basic prejudice with which they began, Shestov argues, is the example of a good human choice; all the reasoning that comes afterward is a piece of distracting disingenuousness.

Shestov is particularly irritated with philosophers who advocate a rational ethics (like Plato and Spinoza, as he reads them). Such philosophers, Shestov claims, act as though reason itself has chosen between passion and rationality for the pursuit of the moral life. But reason is not in a position to make that choice, because the choice is prior to the operation of reason. Once reason is in play, the choice has already been made. (Some scholars have assigned this argument to Kierkegaard). Shestov here makes a claim that is being repeated in some recent work in contemporary meta-ethics: that the rational project of developing an ethics must accept certain ground assumptions that cannot be defended in the terms of that ethics, because those ground assumptions themselves provide for the possibility of normative claims in the ethics. But then, Shestov argues, the choice of those ground assumptions is an irrational one (it cannot be rationally defended), and the supposedly grand construction of reason collapses on its irrational foundation. It is not reason that dictates how we live, but a previous choice to live one way or another. The better way to live is to follow passion, because passion accepts and affirms that choice is fundamental.

The chief problem with reason is that it draws us away from freedom. But it also turns us away from life, by substituting concepts for experience. Like Gabriel Marcel, Shestov thinks that "real" experience is lived rather than known, and the individual who would truly experience her life should attend to the details of her actual living. It is the living that counts, not the thinking about living. What a non-conceptual description of experience might look like is of course notoriously difficult to say: once we start describing life, we begin to use concepts. But the description, Shestov insists, is different than that which is described, and our reliance on reason encourages us to substitute the former for the latter. For reason, he says, the ideal is to render life into abstract categories like those of mathematics. But abstraction is only a distraction from what experience actually is.

One is tempted here to ask Shestov to weaken his account slightly, and to include rational experience as a legitimate element of the larger set of all possible experience.

And Shestov recognizes the difficulty of living a life that is not at least informed by, if not dominated by, reason. But he insists that every application of reason results in a reduction of human freedom (the consistent application of reason, as we said above, eliminates freedom altogether). So, for Shestov, we can either rationally affirm our own irrelevance and despair, or we can irrationally champion absurdity and faith and find hope. Operating with the medieval idea that one believes in Christ precisely because it is absurd to do so, because no possible reason could or should be given for believing, he defines faith as "perfect freedom": the radical rejection of any reason for believing, the pure affirmation of belief as such. The believer believes just because she *can* believe. It is, he thinks, a "mad struggle" to maintain oneself in this state of faith – reason is always insidiously trying to find its way back in – but the mad struggle will open up a new dimension of thought that is otherwise inaccessible to us. If we reject the choice of reason and knowledge originally made by Adam and Eve, we can redis-cover an unknowable but experiential (and confessedly mystical) paradise.

Some of us, myself included, will find an argument that concludes with a mystery to be unsatisfying at best. But for Shestov the task of the true philosopher is just to take us to the mystery. If he had persuaded us of his position with good reasons he would only have contributed to our perdition. For better or worse, in the end our hope of salvation is to abandon reason and argument entirely.

Karl Barth (1886–1968, Swiss)

Like Unamuno and Shestov, Barth rejected Enlightenment rationalism, especially as it was applied to the questions of theology. In particular, the nineteenth-century attempt by many theologians to "humanize" Christ and religion was unbearable to Barth. The epitaph he once attached to his thinking was: "Man is made to serve God and not God man," by which he meant to indicate not only the radically subordinate role of man to God, but also the ahistoricity of God's relationship with man. Not only is there no need to historicize or in any other way temporalize what is eternal, it is in fact apostasy to do so. Accordingly, we should never attempt (as Rudolph Bultmann later will) to "make sense" of God for us today. The nature of God's relationship with us never changes, and we can never make sense of God.

Although contemporary theology owes its largest debt to his nearly 10,000-page magnum opus *Church Dogmatics* (1932–70), Barth's best philosophical work is his early *The Epistle to the Romans* (1919; cited as Barth 1933), a long and explosively controversial commentary on Paul's letter. The guiding principle of the work is the spiritual importance of humiliation. For Barth, God is the Absolute Other who created us, who provides the ground of all of our experience, and who we can know only through His grace. Barth is sometimes described as an "extreme realist" on the ques-tion of our knowledge of God's existence: the only thing that we can know that exists with absolute certainty is God. All the rest of our knowledge, including our knowledge of the outside world and, indeed, our knowledge of our own existence, is shadowy at best when compared with the fundamental truth that God exists. He thus turns our ordinary way (and traditional philosophical ways) of thinking about the existence of God on the head. For this reason he is among the philosophers we consider in this chapter perhaps the most difficult to appreciate for readers who do not themselves believe in the existence of God. In Barth's work one never escapes the feeling that all our efforts, our thinking, and even our lives are utterly insignificant when compared with the greatness that is God.

But that feeling of utter insignificance is precisely what Barth believes we have lost, and hopes to provoke. While Shestov believed that the Fall should be interpreted as a divine warning about the evils of reason, Barth interprets it (more traditionally) as a warning against the dangers of pride. (Our reliance on reason may be an example of our pride, but it is not the real problem.) For Barth our best hope of redemption is to completely abandon the idea that we can do anything to approach God. We are finite, and it is preposterous for the finite to seek to comprehend the infinite. So long as we believe that we are the sort of thing that might know God we will remain estranged from Him. Happily, our acknowledgment of our justified and radical estrangement from God contains the possibility that God may graciously embrace us.

"When we are blind and dumb," he writes, "then we see and speak; when we are bereft of question and answer, then we ask and find; when they suffer, then the children of God know and love their Father – triumphantly"(Barth 1933: 306). This deliberate invocation of paradoxical formulations may strike the reader as offensive. But it is supposed to do so. Paradox and offense are essential to Barth's understanding of the relationship between the human and the Divine. Following Kierkegaard, he insists that the lesson of Christ's appearance is a series of rationally offensive paradoxes: that the eternal should appear in time, that God should appear as man, that the wholly Other should appear and look just like us, that the immortal and all-powerful should die on the cross. God speaks to us in paradox in the effort to show us that reason cannot be the means to approach Him. Stronger, God speaks to us in paradox in order to offend and to *humiliate* reason. In paradox, Barth thinks, reason confronts its limitations; Christ as paradox emphasizes that reason is utterly inadequate to explain what God's sacrifice of his Son represents. And it is important that we are offended because God wants to rebuke us and challenge us. It is not sufficient for us to recognize that reason is not up to the task, and so to shrug our shoulders and give up. We should rather recognize that reason is precisely the wrong approach, and yet insist that we must find the way. Barth's idea of the religious seeker thus resembles Camus's later idea of Sisyphus: the striving believer who cannot explain why he believes, yet continues to struggle to do so.

"We confound time with eternity. This is the *ungodliness* of our relation to God. And our relation to God is *unrighteous*. Secretly we are to ourselves the masters of this relationship . . . In believing in Him, we justify, enjoy, and adore ourselves" (Barth 1933: 44). Barth once remarked that his thinking was an elaboration of Kierkegaard's idea that there is an "infinite qualitative distinction" between time and eternity. When we confound time with eternity, Barth thinks, we fail to recognize that our existence in time cannot provide us with the things we most need: truth, value, and immortality. In a familiar Platonic–Pauline move, Barth insists that all truth and value exist in the eternal realm: we have access only to the ephemeral things of the temporal world. But unlike Plato, Barth places the eternal realm entirely out of our grasp. In being estranged from God we are also estranged from the very possibility of knowledge and morality. That we would know and value, but cannot do so, is another form of our necessary humiliation.

The *ungodliness* of our relationship with God is the attempt to make eternal things temporal, to make the divine human. When we fail or refuse to acknowledge the paradoxical nature of our position as things that demand what exists out of time and yet are doomed to live in time, when we try with reason to pretend that we ourselves can discover truth or create value, we act as though we are ourselves God. And we can see the expression of this tendency in our *unrighteous* relation to God. Rather than admitting that we are nothing without God, and that our only hope for understanding is the complete and utter submission to God (which He may or may not reward with the grace of faith), we suppose that we can discover God through the application of our rational human categories.

Here again we see Barth's stringent opposition to Enlightenment rationalism. He not only opposes a rationalist account of God, he attacks the Enlightenment ideal of an autonomous conscience that may be the source of value. Because God is the transcendental source of all value, any value that does not derive directly from God must be rejected. To talk about ethics is not only silly, it is gravely misleading.

So what can we know? Barth says: nothing. We can experience humiliation, and through humiliation we may hope for the revelation of faith, which is always a miracle. This is the story of Christ, for Barth. The divine presence of God broke in "vertically from above": without expectation or explanation, the eternal entered time, and in so doing gave us hope that this can happen in our own lives, and showed the example of how it may happen, in Christ's humiliation and suffering on the Cross. Faith is irrational and even frightening. "There has been exposed to view a new rough river-bed, a very unfamiliar and strange impress of revelation, a disturbing form of faith" (Barth 1933: 67). He sees this exemplified in "the religion and the experiences in the characters in the novels of Dostoevsky" (Barth 1933: 68).

For Barth, God's self-relationship is expressed in the theological notion of the Trinity as a relationship of revelation: God is the revealer, the act of revelation, and the revealed. The hidden-ness of God can only be overcome by God's own complementary nature of revealing. Truth cannot be sought, it can only be granted. And if we are given faith, we are given it only through the grace of God. But Dostoevsky's characters show us one way in which this actually does happen. So Raskolnikov, for example, through suffering, desperation, and in the end complete abandonment of the notion that he himself can help himself (a complete abandonment of autonomy), at last is given the possibility of understanding. His coming to faith is a story that Dostoevsky does not write, and Barth thinks no one can write it, because it is irrational and wholly internal. But revelation does occur. And we can see the way it may occur, even though we can never have any reason to believe that it will occur for us.

Accordingly, for Barth, philosophy is pointless and should be rejected. His extreme realism on the question of God's existence leads him to argue that we cannot reason our way up to God, but should begin with God and allow the process of thinking to come from above. This is not the task of philosophy but theology, which attempts to trace the process of God's gracious condescension. We will not understand God, but we can see, as Paul and Dostoevsky saw, how He may choose to appear.

Martin Buber (1878–1965, Austrian and Israeli)

Buber's best known work is also his best work, the short, difficult essay *Ich und Du* (1923; cited as Buber 1958). Traditionally, the title of the work has been translated as *I and Thou*, but it is better translated as *I and You*, which also better conveys Buber's emphasis on the intimacy of the relationship between God and man.

Like Barth, Buber rejects a scientific, materialistic, or historical understanding of man's relationship with God. But it is hard to imagine a more unqualified rejection of Barth's view of the alienated relationship between God and man than what we find in Buber. For Buber, God is always present and available to us, if we attend closely to the way in which our experience reveals God. Buber thinks God is "the obvious that is closer to me than my own I" (Barth 1958: 127). While Barth gives us an almost Kafkaesque God, radically inaccessible and yet terrifyingly judgmental, Buber conceives of God in terms that remind one of a lover. Indeed, Buber repeatedly insists that love is the best intimation we have of the divine in our ordinary experience.

The key to Buber's work is a distinction he draws early in *Ich und Du* between two kinds of relationship (he also calls them "attitudes") that capture two different kinds of experience: I–It and I–You. These are, Buber thinks, the most basic "word-pairs" that we speak. The I–It relationship is characterized by the kind of ontological distance that it establishes between the subject and its object. When we relate to others or things in the manner of I–It, we suppose that those others or things are importantly separate from ourselves, that they are somehow distinct from us or removed from us. Our usual way of "knowing" depends upon an I–It relationship: some thing is other than us and so unknown, and to know it we approach it and investigate it, but all the while (or as part of the process of investigation) we keep it distinct from ourselves. In controlling or using a thing we separate it from ourselves. Thus Buber sometimes speaks of this kind of relation as a misrelation or a failure truly to relate. Similarly, the control or use of a person is an expression of an I–It relationship that fails to establish the kind of relation we desire between persons. When I use another person, I understand that person as a separate thing that serves my particular ends. In a move that recalls Kant's analysis of the immorality of treating other humans merely instrumentally, for Buber the disporting ourselves toward a person in the manner of "using" a person is to understand that person as an It, and to fail to understand that that person is another I. But for Buber it is a mistake to talk about either the I or the It as separate components of an interaction between them: the philosophically interesting space, he thinks, is where they come together, the manner of their interaction.

The "subject–object" relation, as we usually understand it, is just one example of the more fundamental I–It relationship. The subject is the I, the object the It, and the defining quality of the relation between the two is again their difference, their distance. The It is not the I but a place where the I may venture, inquire, or control. So, for example, to see the world as something distinct from oneself, as a place to pursue projects and to investigate truths and to have sensory experiences, is for Buber to comport oneself in the manner of I–It. Ultimately this way of relating to the world, if we engage in it alone, results in a complete alienation from the world, because all of one's attempts at relating at the same time establish and reaffirm the distance one has from the world. Solipsism is the natural consequence of the I–It relationship, as other human beings become simulacra: they are mere gatherings of sensory Its, no different, ontologically speaking, than desks, chairs, or computers. In reaction to this alienation, the I of the I–It relation may abandon selfhood altogether, and the person experiencing life in this way may come to see himself as an It: "As he accommodates himself to a world of objects that no longer achieve any presence for him, he succumbs to it" (Buber 1958: 103).

Of course, to think about the relationship of the I–It is to engage in one more I–It relation. We may even relate to inner experiences as Its. (Buber thinks that one way our attempts at self-knowledge go wrong is when we treat the "self" as an It. Here he anticipates recent work on the problems of the differences between first-person and third-person stances in the approach to self-knowledge.) But Buber does not want to indict the I–It relationship as such. He rather wants to show us that it is only one way – albeit a common, seductive, and potentially dangerous way – of experiencing the world.

The other way of experiencing the world, and the way that leads to love and to God, is through the "I–You" relationship. Again, I want to stress that for Buber this relationship should not be understood as an epistemological or psychological one; it is ontological. The being of the experience, when we experience the world in the mode of I–You, is in the way that particular mode establishes a relationship. The relationship exists in the "meeting" ("meeting" is one of Buber's central concepts) between the "I" and the "You."

A first approach to understanding the I–You relationship, which is difficult to speak about but after all is familiar (Buber thinks) to almost every human being, is to contrast it with the I–It. Buber suggests that we consider the difference between seeing a cat as a cat, the object, and then seeing the eyes of the cat, and seeing the cat looking back at you, the cat as another I like You. The experience is even more acute when we consider the eyes of another human being. If someone is not looking at you and you watch her eyes, you may comfortably observe her eyes as an example of an It: they are a certain color of lilac, they are moist, the lashes are dark, they look fatigued (although with this last we are already approaching the You). But now in mid-glance she turns and catches your eye. Suddenly you no longer see the It. You experience the You, there is a place "between" the two of you where you meet, there is a "recognition," an "encounter." She is seeing you as a You and you are experiencing her in the same way, and both of you are recognizing the I-ness and the You-ness of one another.

Buber argues that this experience, which is a "direct" experience of "presence," is both comforting and threatening. It is comforting because we transcend our aloneness. Suddenly we see that we are not in fact trapped in the prison of our own particular heads and lives; there are others out there just like us. But is it threatening because it stretches the bounds of who we are? With the I–It relationship we maintain a narrow sense of our own identity by keeping ourselves at a distance from others, by pretending that our experience of everything other than ourselves is in fact an experience of the otherness of everything. We feel a kind of security in our refusal to step beyond the closed bounds of the ordinary limits of selfhood. But when we meet someone as a You rather than as an It, we each encounter the other with mutual openness. We do not merely see one another, we meet one another, and so we are exposed to one another.

Without this exposure we cannot make sense of personality. For Buber, personality is not merely the collections of actions or dispositions to act that we come to know about a person. It is rather an intimate expression of each individual's subjectivity. It is an (unfortunately rather mysterious) "who we are" that can be understood only in the exposed, self-revelatory moment of the I–You relation.

There is also a problem created by the I–You relation. All human beings at some level understand and acknowledge the importance of this "being between" in order to relate to others. But because of its importance, and because of the threatening quality of being exposed, we have a desire to seem a particular way to others. We try to control the appearance of our personality to others, with the goal of expressing a personality that will be recognized and confirmed by others. But this effort itself destroys the crucial revelatory quality of the I–You experience – we are merely seeming rather than being – and the individual who tried to gain recognition through self-presentation finds himself further alienated from others. For Buber this is what we mean when we speak of "inauthenticity": the failed attempt to gain recognition by others through a false presentation of one's personality, which destroys the possibility of a genuine I–You experience. In an authentic I–You relation, each person will freely give of his or her personality without attempting to control the impression being created.

If we think about love we can see both the appeal of Buber's characterization of the I–You and a problem with it. Certainly the ideal of love is a kind of free giving forth of oneself that genuinely encounters another who is also freely giving forth. And we might agree that in that reciprocal exchange the love emerges. There is a kind of poignancy of experience in gazing into the eyes of a beloved, or sharing a moment of experience with a beloved (consider the look between a wife and a husband when a child is born), which seems both to confirm and to transcend personality. But is it that simple? There is an awful lot of lying in (at least some kinds of) love, of role-playing, manipulation, acting and maneuvering, all of which may also turn out to be in some complicated way constitutive of the love-relation. For Buber these ways of loving would be inauthentic modes of relation between the I and the You, and they should be avoided. He may well be right: perhaps ideal love does not need these kinds of games. But the fact that so much of our loving and so many other different ways we have of relating to one another look as though they depend upon what he would call inauthenticity may be a threat to his account.

To be fair to Buber, he does not think that maintaining an authentic I–You relationship is easy. To "make present" another person we must be constantly engaged in the difficult project of actively imagining what it is like to be that person (he calls this "imagining the real"). Buber insists that any time we meet another and see that other as a You rather than as an It we do this in some measure. Even the ability to have a successful conversation with another requires a kind of active imagining of that other person's position. But for us fully to imagine what it is like to be another is enormously difficult, and may be the project of a lifetime, most likely possible in the case of persons we know for a lifetime, such as friends, lovers, and family members.

When Christ asks us to "Love thy neighbor as thyself" this is what he is asking for: the complete recognition of another as a You, which also requires that the recognition is mutual (thus "the neighbor," the You who stands next to the I and understands the

I as a neighboring You). For Buber, our ethical efforts ultimately do not require more than this complete and mutual recognition. All of our moral dilemmas stem from the treating of others as Its, and can be overcome by our recognizing others as Yous. (Buber of course sees the Holocaust as a particularly striking and terrifying case of the ethical consequences of treating others as Its rather than recognizing them as Yous.)

But Buber's characterization of the I–You relationship does not end with other human beings, or even with other conscious entities. In an unabashedly mystical turn (Buber is rightly credited with the revival of the mystical Jewish movement Hasidism), he asserts that all of experience can be characterized as I–You. Consider a tree, he says. Again, we initially experience it in the mode of I–It. There is the object the tree and it is something other than what you are. It is an It and you are the I distinct from it.

> But it can also happen, if will and grace are joined, that as I contemplate the tree I am drawn into a relation, and the tree ceases to be an It . . . when I confront a human being as my You . . . then he is no thing among things nor does he consist of things. He is no longer He or She, limited by other hes and shes, a dot in the world grid of space and time . . . he is You and fills the firmament. (Buber 1958: 98–9)

Here the notion of "will" does not surprise us: just as it takes an active effort on the part of an I to recognize another human as a You, so it takes effort for appreciating the You-ness of other kinds of experience. But Buber's idea of "grace" is new to our account. For Buber, the human will and imagination can only accomplish so much. We have a natural and regrettable tendency to constantly slip back into an I–It relationship with our experience. But if we constantly strive to see that even the world itself is a thing like we are, God through his grace will help us overcome our mistaken idea that it is a different kind of thing. "Grace" may here sound to some ears like nothing more than "chance" or "good luck." But even if we are not theists we may sympathize with Buber's idea of grace. He is committed to the idea that will alone is not always sufficient to understanding all of experience as a You. But he need not argue any stronger notion of grace than this weak and so-to-speak negative notion: if the I does indeed strive, though its striving is not always sufficient to achieve the I–You relationship, it may yet happen that the I–You relationship emerges. For us this is the fortunate if inexplicable outcome of the sustained striving; for Buber it is grace. But in either case the change in experience is not a consequence of mere chance. The I–You experience of the world is there waiting for us, even if our efforts do not always guarantee its appearance to us.

Buber does not tell us what kind of thing the world is such that it is like us when we experience it as a You. He does not endorse a Leibnizian world of thinking monads, or a Spinozistic pantheism, or even some form of Idealism that infuses the world with God or mind. He is skeptical of the value of metaphysics of that kind, which he thinks moves us back into an I–It relation with the world. He insists that the only way to appreciate the You-ness of the world is to experience it. But he believes he can remind us of the You-ness of the world by showing us how prevalent it truly is in our lives. He argues that there are three distinct forms of the I–You relationship: the I–You with other conscious beings (he is most concerned, of course, with other people), the I–You with nature, and the I–You with "spiritual entities."

By spiritual entities Buber does not mean supernatural beings but those kinds of things we encounter in other than strictly material ways, such as aesthetic things (think of the kind of encounter one has with listening to Mozart) or contemplative things (think of the kind of encounter one may have while very carefully reading Wittgenstein). In each of these three kinds of I–You experience we are struck by the same phenomenon of meeting another that is like ourselves. Crucially, the meeting is not something that we can achieve alone. When we meet with the tree described above, it is like meeting with the mind of the painter when we contemplate her work: to see the painting as something more than pigment on canvas is to see the way in which it is infused with the mind and the vision of its creator. So too with the tree, Buber thinks: the tree makes the world present to us in revealing the mind and the vision of God. And so, in a Nietzschean twist that would have alarmed Nietzsche, Buber argues that artists – as the accessible revealers of truth – are directly in the service of God. Successful artistic creation is a demonstration of how meetings occur. In creating spiritual entities the artist is engaged in revelation, and our experience of beauty is really a kind of intimation of the I–You that exists between ourselves, the world and the divine.

For Buber, our experience of a beautiful piece of art, our experience of love, and our experience of the tree are all – from the perspective of I–You – experiences of *dialogue*. The I–It and the I–You do not refer only to relationships or ways of experiencing; they also refer to the possibility of communication. Buber calls them the "basic" word-pairs because the I–It expresses the negation of the very possibility of communication, and the I–You is the affirmation of dialogue (which is not mere communication, but successful communication at its best). As so often in Buber the language is metaphorical, but the idea is that the I–You is not just our awareness of another and being together with that other, but also learning from and growing with that other. Our communication is not just a conversation, it is a reciprocal exchange that benefits us both, and makes us each more aware of one another and ourselves. Ultimately this is a dialogue we are having with God. "Every single You is a glimpse of [God]. Through every single You the basic word addresses the eternal You" (Buber 1958: 123). But this is true also when each You addresses any other You, and consequently all experience is a kind of dialogue God is having with Himself. In experiencing the I–You, we experience ourselves as God.

References and Further Reading

Barth, K. (1933) *The Epistle to the Romans* (trans. E. Hoskyns). Oxford: Oxford University Press (original work published 1918; rev. edns. 1921 and 1933).

Buber, M. (1958) *I and Thou* (trans. R. G. Smith). New York: Charles Scribner's Sons (original work published 1923).

de Unamuno, M. (1921) *The Tragic Sense of Life* (trans. J. E. Crawford Flitch). New York: Dover Publications (original work published 1913).

Shestov, L. (1920) *The Apotheosis of Groundlessness* (renamed *All Things are Possible* in the English translation) (trans. S. S. Koteliansky). London: Martin Secker (original work published 1905).

——— (1966) *Athens and Jerusalem* (ed. and trans. B. Martin). Athens: Ohio University Press (original work published 1938).

—— (1968) *Potestas Clavium* (ed. and trans. B. Martin). Athens: Ohio University Press (original work published 1923).

—— (1969a) Good in the teaching of Nietzsche and Dostoevsky (trans. B. Martin). In B. Martin (ed.), *Dostoevsky, Tolstoy, Nietzsche*. Athens: Ohio University Press (original work published 1900).

—— (1969b) Dostoevsky and Nietzsche: The philosophy of tragedy (trans. S. Roberts). In B. Martin (ed.), *Dostoevsky, Tolstoy, Nietzsche*. Athens: Ohio University Press (original work published 1903).

—— (1969c) *Kierkegaard and the Existentialist Philosophy* (trans. E. Hewitt). Athens: Ohio University Press (original work published 1938).

—— (1975) *In Job's Balances* (ed. B. Martin, trans. C. Coventry and C. A. Macartney). Athens: Ohio University Press (original work published 1929).

14

French Existentialism

ROBERT WICKS

Eighteenth- and Nineteenth-Century Anticipations of French Existentialism[1]

Since all philosophies have an informing prehistory, it is no surprise that twentieth-century French existentialism rests upon historical and thematic sources that originate several centuries earlier. Central among these is the problem of human freedom that arose from the mechanistic view of the universe: from the times of René Descartes (1596–1650) to those of Immanuel Kant (1724–1804), it was fashionable among European intellectuals to regard the natural cosmos as an enormous mechanism. To them, the starry skies revealed a gigantic clockwork whose deterministic workings were believed to be knowable in the form of mathematically formulable laws.[2] It was also a time when mathematicians were often regarded as atheists.[3]

A disturbing side effect of this perspective was the reflection that human beings, had they not fortunately within them a counteracting divine quality and thereby a measure of freedom, could be understood predictably, scientifically, and exclusively as natural objects. The mechanistic worldview thus brought physical nature into conflict with human freedom, and insofar as the investigative methods of natural science slowly spread to all quarters of social activity, a foundation for human meaning and purpose became increasingly difficult to establish. With the arrival of the nineteenth century, mechanism was soon leading to nihilism.

In the late eighteenth century, Kant attempted to resolve this spiritual tension by rendering human freedom compatible with natural machinations: acknowledging that we cannot but assume that every event has a natural cause, he maintained that spatio-temporal experience must present itself as being deterministically governed. On top of this, however, he argued that nature appears to be a mechanism only conditionally, for it assumes this mechanistic guise only in the presence of our own inescapable mode of logically grounded comprehension. Kant concluded that what reality might be in itself is an independent issue, adding that we can speculate legitimately about the unconditional being of things in themselves and can locate reasonably the ground of human freedom and meaning therein.

In this philosophical style, Kant aligned the distinction between nature and freedom with the distinction between scientifically knowable appearance and essentially unknowable reality. He conceived of unpredictable human freedom in a manner independent of predictable natural processes, while he also attempted to establish in principle a compatibility between these two ways of interpreting our experience. To make room for religious faith, he drew limits famously upon what we can prove within the field of metaphysics.

Kant's recognition that we can conceive of human freedom independently of natural objectivity retained its attractiveness during the nineteenth century in its adoption by Søren Kierkegaard (1813–55), and it continued impressively into twentieth-century French existentialism as a centerpiece in the philosophy of Jean-Paul Sartre (1905–80). Both Kierkegaard and Sartre identified the source of human meaning concretely in the immediate experience of making ungrounded choices, and although their respective methods were less sympathetic to pure rational speculation than was Kant's, they also conceived of freedom in sharp opposition to nature.

During the nineteenth and twentieth centuries, as the awareness of the historical dimensions of experience became more salient in philosophical theorizing, Kantian solutions to the problem of rendering nature and freedom compatible became psychologically frustrating. This was the result of a more intense disposition to understand human freedom, not in reference to dimensions independent of the physical world, but in reference to spatio-temporal experience itself, and even more directly, in reference to one's own physical body and activity.

Moreover, as noted, understanding the spatio-temporal world scientifically as a mechanically driven entity had alienating effects: the cause-and-effect relationships that had proven to be so effective in scientific reasoning divided the world into a set of tiny parts, each of which has an effect on some other, and where each part is different from, and essentially alienated from, every other. This dispersive, atomizing, and linear style of interpreting our surroundings impeded an appreciation of the world's organic unity, along with an appreciation of the world as having a single inner principle of a more humanly recognizable sort.

Owing significantly to such perceptions, the nineteenth-century philosophical center of gravity drifted away from the physically objectifying, articulating and mechanistic focus of the seventeenth and eighteenth centuries. In reference to the natural world, the concept of "life" became salient and it soon took precedence over interpretations of nature that conceived of it as an automatic device. This new emphasis upon the concept of life yielded a variety of fertile implications, among which included a closer attention to growth, development, expansion, systematic arrangements and, most importantly and centrally to the history of French existentialism, a pronounced attention to both the passing of time and the importance of interpreting human experience in a down-to-earth manner.

Although Marxism (c.1840s–1870s) retained some mechanistic and automatic aspects, it is among the most representative and well-known optimistic views of the nineteenth-century European period, for it emphasized a practical economic style of analysis coupled with a historically centered vision of inevitable social progress. The equally optimistic, antecedent Hegelian philosophy of the 1820s that inspired Marxism relied even more explicitly and consistently upon the concept of life in the form of the "living concept." Later in the century, Friedrich Nietzsche (1844–1900) also grounded his philosophy of vitality (c.1870s–1880s) upon the healthy imperative of saying "yes" to life, even in its most vicious forms. This realistic emphasis upon "concrete thinking," as Hegel described it, is among the roots of existentialism in general and it is foundational to twentieth-century French existentialism.

Another major component of twentieth-century French existentialism – "the absurd" – overrides and outstrips the early-to mid-nineteenth-century idea of historical growth, for the idea of growth toward a definitive ideal temperately and restrictively adheres to an underlying rationality that governs natural and social phenomena. Hegel's and Marx's dialectical logics had a nontraditional and innovative structure, but they were nonetheless conceived of non-radically as alternative modes of rationality. In contrast, it is common knowledge among anyone who has had only a brief exposure to French existentialists such as Jean-Paul Sartre and Albert Camus (1913–60) that a hallmark of their thought is the recognition of the world's and the individual's utterly absurd and unfettered condition.[4]

By the time that Sartre and Camus were writing, the nineteenth-century confidence in rational historical development had been damaged by the destructive experiences of two world wars. In fact, Sartre's *Being and Nothingness* (1943; cited as Sartre 1956), along with Camus's *The Stranger* (1942) and *The Myth of Sisyphus* (1942; cited as Camus 1955) – three classics of French existentialism – were published in the midst of World War II's threat to human freedom and meaning. The social-psychological effects of World War I were shattering, but perhaps worse yet, in the midst of World War II it appeared that the Allied forces were engaged in a life-and-death struggle against Nazi Germany to preserve the very moral fate of Western civilization.

Existentialist Implications of the Nineteenth-Century Emphasis upon Life: Instinct, Individuality, and Absurdity

The nineteenth-century enthusiasm for interpreting the world in reference to the concepts of life, development, and progress – often in an effort to revivify the spiritually debilitating outlook that the mechanistic views of the Enlightenment had been generating – led in an unanticipated direction, namely, toward a more pronounced awareness of human qualities that had remained submerged in earlier theorizing. To articulate these qualities, we can identify at least three ways in which the nineteenth-century emphasis upon the concept of life precipitated the existentialist accentuation of the world's absurdity or non-rationality.

First, focusing upon life itself led to an explicit awareness of instinctual energies and biological qualities, which in turn stimulated the recognition of non-moral, destructive, and creative energies that are not clearly amenable to rationalistic understanding. An example is how the concept of the unconscious developed an importance at the beginning of the nineteenth century.[5] In later years, and more widely known, Sigmund Freud (1856–1939) – echoing views that appeared previously in the thought of Arthur Schopenhauer (1788–1860) and Eduard von Hartmann (1842–1906) – described the unconscious and instinctual aspect of the psyche (the "id") as an irrational psychic realm where contradictory drives and meanings stand side by side:

[The id] is the dark, inaccessible part of our personality . . . We call it a chaos, a cauldron full of seething excitations . . . it has no organization, produces no collective will, but only a striving to bring about the satisfaction of the instinctual needs . . . The logical laws of thought do not apply in the id, and this is true above all the law of contradiction. Contrary impulses exist side by side, without cancelling each other out or diminishing each other . . . There is nothing in the id that corresponds to the idea of time.

The id of course knows no judgments of value: no good and evil, no morality. (Freud 1965: 65–6)

Second, with a more concentrated attunement to life processes and to the attendant passing of time, nineteenth- and twentieth-century European thought highlighted the importance of individuality and personal uniqueness, as the historical and existential presence of the assorted things in the world, among which one's body is included, acquired a more pronounced intrinsic value. This valuation had the effect of intensifying feelings of human finitude and mortality – feelings that found their expression in a greater appreciation that one is a unique and contingent individual, and in the consequently more difficult task of comprehending what one is, since individuality and contingency in themselves resist easy explanation. For Sartre, the sheer existence of contingent individuals, not to mention the physical world itself, was an absurd and psychologically disturbing matter:

I knew it was the World, the naked World suddenly revealing itself, and I choked with rage at this gross, absurd being. You couldn't even wonder where all that sprang from, or how it was that a world came into existence, rather than nothingness. It didn't make sense, the World was everywhere, in front, behind. There had been nothing *before* it. Nothing . . . this nothingness had not come *before* existence, it was an existence like any other and appeared after many others. I shouted "filth! What rotten filth!" and shook myself to get rid of this sticky filth, but it held fast and there was so much, tons and tons of existence, endless: I stifled at the depths of this immense weariness. (Sartre 1964: 134)

Third, absurdity – since feelings of absurdity can arise from experiences of frustration and futility – emerged from the growing apprehension that one's given historical place is inescapable, and that "right now" is the only time when experience will ever take place. When one's present historical location is strongly emphasized, looking nostalgically toward the past for inspiration becomes futile, as it is realized that the celebrated times past whose spirit one once wished to revivify in oneself (e.g., for many nineteenth-century German thinkers, it was the healthy spirit of the ancient Greeks), no longer exist. Looking hopefully toward the future also becomes futile upon recognizing that from the standpoint of the present moment, tomorrow never arrives: when "tomorrow" arrives, it will have become another today, and the reference point of "tomorrow" will have shifted forward in a continuous process of deferral.[6] Looking transcendently toward a timeless and spaceless dimension is also regarded as hopeless, for within a more historically sensitive style of down-to-earth awareness, otherworldly dimensions strain against appearing to be fantastic and unbelievable.

Among many nineteenth- and twentieth-century thinkers, facing these assorted dead-ends generated a sense of disillusionment and of the world not making any sense, since the bulk of traditional sources of inspiration became unrealistic.

Nineteenth-century discussions concerning the death of God and nihilism have their place within this context of having perceived that there is no escape and no salvation from the frustrating present. Nietzsche is among the well-known nineteenth-century theorists who influenced French existentialism and who, writing from within this penned-in standpoint, addressed issues surrounding nihilism and the death of God. In later sympathy with such problems involving nihilism and the meaning of life, we find Camus at the outset of *The Myth of Sisyphus* stating that "There is but one truly serious philosophical problem, and that is suicide. Judging whether life is or is not worth living amounts to answering the fundamental question of philosophy" (Camus 1955: 3).

Camus wondered seriously whether suicide is the most appropriate reaction to the frustrating human condition, and he thereby defined French existentialism's major focus upon issues surrounding the meaning of life. His own Nietzschean answer was that life is indeed worth living, if only we are perceptive enough to appreciate the intrinsic value of each passing moment.

Since existentialist philosophy has been represented typically by atheistic thinkers, it is understandable that religious dimensions of French existentialism have remained underthematized within paradigmatic thinkers such as Sartre and Camus. We can nonetheless illuminate these dimensions in light of the above themes if we regard the existentialist movement in general as a reaction to the psychological effects of nihilism. As implied above, intense historical awareness impedes the acknowledgment of an otherworldly God that defines and maintains the universe, for the intensification of historical awareness tends to generate a stronger sense of individuality, a decreased recognition of universalist and transcendent aspects of oneself, a gradual emergence of relativism, and at the extreme point, meaninglessness and absurdity. In religious terms, this distancing from absolute grounds amounts to the familiar "dark night of the soul"[7] – a sense of emptiness and despair that stems from a perceived abandonment by what had been believed to be a permanent, caring, and divine upholder of the universe, whether it is conceived of as God, absolute truth, reason, or any other indication of unconditional being.[8]

Nineteenth-century theorizing produced an array of remedies for such feelings of meaninglessness, and these solutions expressed – even among atheists such as Nietzsche – a search for an unconditional or divine aspect of human being that is consistent with a this-worldly and individuality-centered outlook. From a theological standpoint, one could say that the traditional primacy of an otherworldly God-the-father gave way to a desire to render more comprehensible and experientially salient within the human individual, the spatio-temporal presence of the incarnated God-the-Son.

From this interpretive angle, we can discern both a distinctively Christian (i.e., Jesus-centered) and vaguely Oedipal aspect to the history of the atheistic and absurdist forms of French existentialism. Nineteenth-century attempts to revitalize Christianity through a more historically focused context required that more attention fall upon understanding the nature of Jesus as a combined historical and divine personage. Given the variations in understanding what it means to be a living, historical person, alternative conceptions of the unconditional aspect of human beings emerged. The most popular of these became the keynote of French existentialism.

Owing to the emphasis upon contingent individuality and the attendant frustration involved in the effort to comprehend the nature of accidentally occurring individuals, nihilism remained a threatening force within existentialist thought as a whole. All of the nineteenth- and twentieth-century existentialist theorists attempted to combat it in one way or another, as must every existentialist, and this was done mainly, as noted, through a drive to secure a sense of meaning by discerning an unconditional quality within daily human experience.

Among the candidates for this unconditional quality – traditionally and classically among which are self-consciousness, rationality, and sociality – the *freedom* of the contingent individual became the leading expression of the absolute quality of human beings within existentialist thought as a whole. No matter what else we happen to be, it was recognized generally that the individual person is fundamentally free. Moreover, that this freedom is immediately able to be experienced was seen to bear positively on resolving the nihilistic worries that threatened the perceived value of human existence. Kierkegaard, Nietzsche, Sartre, and Camus all emphasized the unconditional quality of human freedom. Even Hegel's earlier philosophy centered upon the historical development of freedom. Marxism also aspired to realize freedom more effectively within social organizations.

Within religious contexts, it has been common to appeal to freedom as a way to generate human meaning: linkages between an infinitely meaningful God and freedom reside foundationally in the speculation that God created the world by an ungrounded act of freedom. Appealing to the logic of the cosmological argument for God's existence that postulates an unconditional and "uncaused" cause of the physical universe, Kant formulated a speculative conception of God's freedom as a model for human freedom. In this he was hardly unique, and fifty years later Kierkegaard continued in this tradition by maintaining in a more experience-grounded manner that God's existence can be proven only in a practical way, namely, by instantiating an absolutely free consciousness within oneself.

For Kierkegaard, personally incarnating the divine involved the experience of freedom or "truth as subjectivity" – an experience of self-legislation that he believed is available to anyone who, within a life-and-death context, makes ungrounded decisions or leaps of faith. Such decisive leaps entail that one assumes full responsibility for the outcome, with all of its psychological implications: in finite beings, absolute responsibility generates anxiety as one carries the widespread and unforeseeable implications of one's decision upon one's shoulders. Sartre's own advocacy of absolute responsibility reiterates the same position, except that he recognized more explicitly how concrete circumstances tend to stand significantly in the way of exercising our absolute freedom and how they lead us into the temptations of self-deception.

Kierkegaard interpreted the unconditional nature of decisive action as the embodiment of a divine essence, for free acts characteristically embody pure self-determination.[9] In a related philosophical mode, Descartes also expressed the idea of an unrestricted freedom located within human beings: he stated in his *Meditations* that one's capacity to affirm or deny any proposition is an unlimited and divine capacity, for one can always say "no" to any given proposition.[10] In *Being and Nothingness*, Sartre maintained that we are condemned to be absolutely free, and he echoed both the Kierkegaardian sense of being absolutely self-determining and the Cartesian sense of always being able to say "no."

"Existence Comes Before *Essence"*

One of the most often-repeated slogans associated with French existentialism is "existence comes before essence" (Sartre 1948: 26). This expresses a philosophical attitude directly opposed to one of the most profound, natural, and influential intellectual dispositions and styles of interpretation in the history of Western philosophy, namely, the disposition to interpret the world upon analogy to how people make deliberate plans and then put them into action. Platonism is the classical example of this philosophical style.

Plato (427–327 BCE) regarded the imagined intellectual plans, forms, structures, definitions, idealizations, and perfections of physical things as timeless essences, ideas, or forms. These include numbers and geometrical conceptions as well as morally related ideas such as goodness, beauty, courage, and piety. Plato furthermore ascribed an unconditional being to these ideas – one that prevails metaphysically over their perishable instantiations in the world's many physical items and actions. Within this Platonistic vision, the plan definitively characterizes the essence of the anticipated instantiation or outcome, and the ideal instance or outcome would be the perfect realization of the prior plan. In the theological sphere, this idealizing style of reflection underpins the belief that God created the world as the expression of a good intention and that the world is unfolding accordingly.[11] Contrary to these approaches, existentialists of the paradigmatic, absurdist sort claim that the world simply "is" and was not "made." They deny that the world is an artifact and deny that its natural kinds, if there are any, have an overall systematic sense that informs their interrelationships.

Orthodox Platonism has also been renowned for maintaining that the physical realizations of the perfect, timeless, and unchanging plans never satisfactorily reflect the positive quality of the plans themselves, and for maintaining consequently that the plans have a higher truth value. Since the dominating spirit of the Western philosophical tradition has proceeded on the classical assumption that "essence" precedes "existence," it has often displayed an ahistorical tendency by directing our philosophical attention to purely intelligible or conceptual dimensions that are independent of space and time, and by diverting our attention from the "imperfect" world in which we find ourselves. In radical disagreement with the otherworldliness inherent in this perspective, Sartre wrote the following:

> What do we mean by saying that existence precedes essence? We mean that man first of all exists, encounters himself, surges up in the world – and defines himself afterwards. If man as the existentialist sees him is not definable, it is because to begin with he is nothing. He will not be anything until later, and then he will be what he makes of himself. Thus, there is no human nature, because there is no God to have a conception of it. Man simply is . . . Man is nothing else but that which he makes of himself. That is the first principle of existentialism. (Sartre 1948: 28)

Sartre's assertion that "existence precedes essence" more precisely expresses a pair of conflicting propositions: (1) human beings have an indefinable, indeterminable aspect – a free aspect – and lack a determinate essence that restricts this freedom, and (2) human beings appear on the scene within a physical world that existed prior to their presence, and this physical world strongly influences each individual's character. We are always free to say "no," but we nonetheless lack decisive control over when or where we will be born. This tension between our freedom and the implications of being a concrete and contingent individual located in space and time defines the philosophical atmosphere of French existentialism – an outlook that struggles to preserve triumphantly a measure of self-determination within an overwhelming historical world that determines the language we will speak, the social values we will initially absorb, and the sorts of daily problems we will need to manage, long before any one of us happens to appear.[12]

Given the existentialist attention to contingently given historical situations and things in their full detail, existentialist writings refer frequently to the human body, bodily functions, physical health and sickness, bodily conditions and orientations that necessarily influence philosophical reflection, all within a context of accepting the daily features of human experience as given facts, and upon which further reflection proceeds. When upon one's deathbed, the sky presumably will still appear to be blue, people will continue to speak the same language as the day before, the coughs and pains will be as they were, and life will be then as it fundamentally is now. Existentialist thought conveys a powerful and pervading sense of the daily world's corporeal reality that is augmented by a feeling of inescapability. For any transcendence of which is it reasonable to speak, the accompanying change in consciousness will not entail that one's pains will go away; changes in consciousness reside more stoically only in how one *interprets* daily events, just as one can interpret an ambiguous geometrical figure in several ways.[13]

From the standpoint of philosophical method, the above common-sense orientation entails that all philosophizing must first and foremost extend from the perspective of a flesh-and-blood person who is actively situated within a historical context, who is in effect a conscious body, and who has a limited set of senses and knowledge. Maurice Merleau-Ponty (1908–61) effectively expressed this outlook in his emphasis upon the primacy of perception: "The perceived world is the always presupposed foundation of all rationality, all value and all existence. This thesis does not destroy either rationality or the absolute. It only tries to bring them down to earth" (Merleau-Ponty 1964a: 12–42).[14] To be as down to earth and as realistic as possible is a motivating aim of existentialist thought, and varieties of French existentialism vary within this real-world sphere in reference to the degrees of emphasis they adopt respectively within the cluster of existential themes mentioned above. These include absurdity, individuality, alienation, sensuality, contingency, authenticity, freedom, and responsibility. With this background in hand, we can consider these themes in greater detail, using "concreteness" and "freedom" as focal points from which the other themes radiate.

Concreteness and Absurdity

As one's style of philosophizing shifts its attention from the contemplation of timeless universalities toward the details of concrete spatio-temporal contexts, an array of alternatives remains within this field upon which philosophical focus can be directed. These range from attending to the wider socio-historical contexts (e.g., the language that is being used, the particular society in question, the prevailing value systems, etc.) to attending to the details of individual people and personalities. Within the latter realm of attending to individuals, options range from considering individuals in a generalized way, as when one reflects upon a human existential condition that could be true for individuals in all times and places, to considering people as they are within some specific social context, to considering individuals in the most specific way, as when a person considers his or her own specific case, either more generally across the lifespan or as it is instantiated exactly here and now.

Given the difficulties in referring realistically to a determinate individual in abstraction from any social context whatsoever, existential thought oscillates between emphasizing the specific social context that determines the individual's historical orientation and emphasizing the supposedly irreducible and unique individual within that context. French existentialist thought of the 1930s and 1940s – especially in Sartre and Camus – attends closely to the situation of the irreducible and unique individual, in contrast to some of the corresponding German styles of existentialism that give greater weight to the specific social context within which the individual is situated.

We have seen that the theme of personal individuality appears in nineteenth- and twentieth-century existentialism in general, and we can reiterate that the desire to philosophize in a realistic fashion eventually leads to a contemplation of the individual person's experience, neither as a disembodied spirit nor as an abstract individual, but as a person who cannot be extracted from or theoretically held up for contemplation independently of the historical environment. Within this context of historically situated individuality there can easily emerge not only the baffling reaction to the fact that one exists at all, but an overwhelming sense of dissimilarity between oneself and other people. Heightening one's sense of individuality intensifies the difference between oneself and others, and this can lead to feelings of alienation and separation from the world at large. Thus arises the existentialist condition of not feeling well connected and at home in the world. Camus expresses this as the feeling of "the absurd," which he illustrates dramatically through an everyday episode within which one's mode of interpretation changes drastically:

> At certain moments of lucidity, the mechanical aspect of their gestures, their meaningless pantomime makes silly everything that surrounds them. A man is talking on the telephone behind a glass partition; you cannot hear him, but you see his incomprehensible dumb show: you wonder why he is alive. This discomfort in the face of man's own inhumanity, this incalculable tumble before the image of what we are, this "nausea," as a writer of today calls it, is also the absurd.[15] Likewise the stranger who at certain seconds comes to meet us in a mirror, the familiar and yet alarming brother we encounter in our own photographs is also the absurd. (Camus 1955: 11)[16]

In contrast, and bearing upon the question of how one ought to philosophize, Merleau-Ponty's existentialist and phenomenological emphasis upon the body and its natural immersion in the surrounding environment does not invoke profound feelings of alienation. In Camus's experience of absurdity, on the other hand, the same sort of bodily emphasis does produce distressing feelings of alienation. This occurs because Camus accentuates the awareness of one's own body to a self-centered point where it appears to be hopelessly cut off from the rest of one's environment. Unlike Merleau-Ponty, and also unlike the prior and inspirational views of Martin Heidegger (1889–1976) in the German existentialist tradition, the sense of personal individuality is so intense within Camus's and Sartre's varieties of existentialism, that disturbing feelings of solitude permeate their respective outlooks. Sartre's summary of the human condition human in *Being and Nothingness* is exemplary:

> The being of human reality is suffering because it rises in being as perpetually haunted by a totality which it is without being able to be it, precisely because it could not attain the in-itself [object] without losing itself as for-itself [subject]. Human reality therefore is by nature an unhappy consciousness with no possibility of surpassing its unhappy state. (Sartre 1956: 140)

Despite phenomenological analyses that suggest alternatively that the alienating distinction between "subject" and "object" itself rests upon our primordial connectedness to and continuity with the world,[17] Sartre's analysis of human relationships relies on the assumption that subjectivity and objectivity are fundamentally opposed and irreconcilable dimensions of the human social situation: in daily experience, one is either being objectified by being looked at by someone else, or one is being objectifying by looking at someone. Attempts to commune fully with other people are futile, since there remains always a unique sense of oneself that cannot be eliminated, dissolved, or rendered ineffective by any form of positive social community or oppressive social control. In light of his belief that humans aspire toward achieving full social community, Sartre concludes that we are condemned not only to be free, but are condemned to be alone with ourselves and alienated from other people, thus giving voice to a resounding existentialist theme.

Accompanying the theme of absurdity in French existentialism is an emphasis upon matters concerning aesthetics and art. Sartre's philosophical and literary works, for example, frequently contain references to bodily fluids, secretions, textures, sensory experiences of an associated viscous and gelatinous sort (e.g., shaking hands with someone and imagining that one is holding a large worm), and generally aesthetic qualities that are either stomach-turning, repulsive, or are at least non-beautiful. Camus is less explicitly focused upon off-putting aesthetic categories, but his key notion of the absurd is sometimes expressed in reference to feelings of sickness and nausea (as opposed to laughter, for instance).

We can account for this disconcerting aesthetic phraseology in reference to an intersection of themes, namely, the intensified focus upon bodily existence as combined with a recognition of non-rational aspects of human experience, the theme of attitudinal detachment as it appears in both the history of modern aesthetics[18] and twentieth-century phenomenology,[19] an underlying antagonism toward scientific thinking, along with an antagonism toward the traditional association of rationality with beauty. Once one attends to the physical body in detail and considers it in both an aesthetically distanced and concretist manner, the consequent weakening of the rationalistic mode of interpretation can lead to an awareness of the corporeal details as disorganized, non-beautiful and, potentially, as repulsive. In *Nausea*, Sartre describes the aesthetic feeling of the absurd in this disturbing light:

And I – soft, weak, obscene, digesting, juggling with dismal thoughts – I, too, was *In the way*. Fortunately, I didn't feel it, although I realized it, but I was uncomfortable because I was afraid of feeling it (even now I am afraid – afraid that it might catch me behind the head and lift me up like a wave). I dreamed vaguely of killing myself to wipe out at least one of these superfluous lives. But even my death would have been *In the way. In the way*, my corpse, my blood, on these stones, between these plants, at the back of this smiling garden. And the decomposed flesh would have been *In the way* in the earth which would receive my bones, at last, cleaned, stripped, peeled, proper and clean as teeth, it would have been *In the way*. I was *In the way* for eternity. (Sartre 1964: 128–9)

Sartre's aesthetics of the unattractive and imperfect aspects of daily life marks only one among several interpretive avenues that stem from adopting a down-to-earth outlook. Despite his attention to the upsetting experiences of the absurd, Camus often focuses alternatively upon the joyful appreciation of experience's sensory features, such as the sparkling of sunlight upon the ocean, the pleasure of breathing fresh air, and the generally fascinating play of variety within life. Merleau-Ponty, again in a less morbid and arguably healthier light, uses the example of painting to illustrate the phenomenological primacy of artistic awareness in contrast to scientific awareness.[20]

Freedom, Anxiety, and Authenticity

Although there is a dissonance between the earthbound quality of existentialist theorizing and Platonism's transcendently idealizing disposition, a positive association obtains between the existentialist analysis of the human condition and Aristotle's classically influential Greek conception of a good person. According to Aristotle, human beings are rational beings and good humans are humans who act rationally well (Aristotle 1998: Book I, Ch. 7). Being a good person entails realizing human potential. In the existentialist tradition, this human potential is defined as the capacity to experience one's freedom, so the ultimate existentialist would be someone who lives a life of freedom, or who maximizes his or her experiences of freedom. Those who remain confined by contingent and breakable constraints while believing falsely that these are absolute constraints, would be neither appreciating nor realizing their human potential well.

As traditional as the above framework happens to be, a distinguishing feature of existentialist thought resides in its conception of human freedom that defies rationalistic measures and constraints; here, human beings are not defined as "rational animals." If one can indeed choose between being rational and being irrational, then rationality need not govern or determine one's freedom, for one can say "no" to rationality itself as much as one can say "no" to anything else.

As it applies to concrete circumstances, this unconstrained individual-centered conception of freedom generates extended reflection upon which features of one's psyche and environment are contingent and changeable and which are not. Constant vigilance is advised against believing falsely that the contingent features of one's experience are unconditional features, for such beliefs land one in the position of living inauthentically and of not realizing one's freedom well. As the word "authentic" suggests, living authentically entails being the author of one's own life, being in command of one's destiny, and being a genuine human being and good example of what it means to be free. Doing otherwise involves living in a condition of self-deception or bad faith (*mauvais foi*), as Sartre would say. Simone de Beauvoir (1908–86) echoes Sartre's position: "Freedom is the source from which all signification and all values spring. It is the original condition of all justification of existence. The man who seeks to justify his life must want freedom itself absolutely and above everything else" (de Beauvoir 1991: 24).

Focusing upon the experience of freedom reveals a characteristic path for adopting an existentialist outlook, as one tries to live authentically within an experiential field riddled with contingencies. Given the acute sense of one's contingent place in the world, accompanied by a sense of the contingency of things in general, a keynote of French existentialism is that everyone's place in the world is fundamentally insecure and *non-securable*. Rationality provides an imperfect style of control and a sense of false security: we do not have and probably will never have a complete scientific and controlling knowledge of the world, and we do not know exactly what the future will bring. Things change, accidents happen, and holding on to supposedly timeless truths is futile and unnatural. Within this unsteady and capricious field of events, however, we can nonetheless exercise our freedom.

These considerations reveal an existentialist sense of insecurity and anxiety in the face of one's contingency in general, or in the face of the uncertain decisions one must make, or in the face of one's inevitable death. Hence arises the thought that an authentic person lives in a manner that directly incorporates the insecure condition of the world in which we live. We can thereby note two strands of theorizing within this sphere of French existentialism, each of which expresses an attempt to identify a dimension within the human being upon which one can depend, given that the world as a whole is undependable.

The first is the Sartrean view that we are condemned to be free and that focusing upon one's absolute freedom is the most authentic way to live. The second strand of theorizing, alluded to above in connection with nihilism, is Camus's observation that only the present moment is absolutely steadfast, and that we ought not to center our attention upon past, future, or otherworldly dimensions. The two strategies intend to disclose reliable and attractive aspects of human experience that counterbalance the loss of meaning that a continually fluctuating and contingent world tends to precipitate, without at the same time denying the elemental and inescapable presence of that fluctuating world in which we happen to be situated.

Sartre expresses his conception of authenticity by advocating a constant effort to avoid self-deception and bad faith. It can be comforting to accept social definitions and self-conceptions as if they were unconditional characterizations, but he emphasizes that all such artificial definitions are revisable or rejectable. When a person gravitates into a mode of interpretation that assumes that he or she has an unchangeable essence, opportunities are sealed off, potentialities remain unrealized, imagination becomes constricted and unauthentic lifestyles crystallize. Taking seriously Martin Heidegger's characterization[21] of the human being as a being whose existence is an issue for it, and also recalling Descartes's attempt to discover an absolutely reliable proposition by setting aside all doubtable propositions as if they were false, Sartre claims that the most authentic mode of being is to be a constantly questioning being, and to be especially questioning of oneself. This is the optimal expression of human freedom. Just as Descartes rested his philosophy upon the singly reliable awareness of his being able to doubt in general, Sartre finds a comparable security in the recognition of his ability to say "no" to any given proposition, and his associated ability to question all ossifying and constricting self-definitions, just as Descartes aimed to set aside all dubitable propositions.

Camus's conception of authenticity is similarly motivated, for he also sought stability amid a world of change and uncertainty. Recognizing that future, past, and timeless dimensions are unreliable, inaccessible or probably fictional, he maintained that the person who embodies the absurdity of the world lives fully in the present and enjoys the infinite value and constant variation of her or his aesthetic surroundings. He contracts and condenses the locus of value into a point defined by one's present moment – a moment that persists as long as one is alive.

For Camus, the most lucid person appreciates in every moment the exhilaration that can be imagined upon being released from prison, as one feels the fresh air upon one's face in one's new-found freedom, and as one imagines the wealth of new possibilities that each passing moment carries. Most interestingly, Camus intended his view to apply to the condition of being imprisoned – an imprisonment that is the existential one of being inescapably trapped in time and space. His characteristic figure was the mythic Sisyphus – a timeless laborer and prisoner – who, despite his bondage and eternal solitude, was able to extract an infinite value in the passing perceptual details as they stood in conjunction with his experience of perpetual struggle.[22]

Morality

Existentialist thought focuses in an earthly manner upon the nature of human being and the meaning of human life; its interests do not necessarily or immediately concern what is right or good. If "God is dead" and if everything is thereby permitted, then the human condition would rest upon a non-moral state of affairs. French existentialist thought recognizes this possibility. At the same time, insofar as the theme of freedom as self-determination is central to French existentialism, this factor introduces themes that are recognizable within moral philosophy.

The idea of self-determination quickly introduces traditional moral discourse, if we note the association between self-determination and self-legislation. From the abstracted perspective of the human being in general, we can speak of a person's setting a rule for themselves, not as an individual, but in reference to broader conditions that all humans would be obliged to recognize. This is the impartial and neutrally intersubjective self-legislating standpoint upon which Kant grounded his moral philosophy. He relied upon the concept of law in general, as he aimed to articulate the conditions for rule-governed behaviors that apply to everyone necessarily.

With the increasing sense of individuality that emerged in the nineteenth century, Kant's universalistic conception of self-legislation transformed into a more specified expression in, for instance, Nietzsche's celebration of a person-specific type of self-legislative morality. This is the morality of assertive individuals who declare for themselves that thus and thus will be so, merely as a matter of personal willpower. Nietzsche referred to this self-commanding style of thinking as a master morality and as a morality of leadership and self-glorification (Nietzsche 1996: 199–237). It is revealing that Nietzsche's conception of the strong-willed leading character – one that implicitly embodies Kierkegaard's and Sartre's notions of freedom – also reflects a particular conception of divine freedom. Unlike Kant's more rationally constituted conception of God, the implicit conception of God that informs Nietzsche's conception of master morality, not to mention Kierkegaard's experience of truth as subjectivity, closely approaches the idea of God as a pure authoritative will who is not subject to reason or any constraint. Here, God is an absolutely decisive, creative, and unlimited force. Kierkegaard's experience of truth as subjectivity aims to instantiate the consciousness of such a God within the human experience, as does Sartre's experience of personal authenticity in one's effort to avoid the ossifications and determinations of bad faith. These views regard the individual as being originally a self-legislator, self-determiner, and self-controller.

Within Sartre's view in particular, absolute self-determination is expressed in terms of Descartes's claim that one can always say "no," but it also appears in the positive idea of a "fundamental choice" that creatively determines one's personality and overall plan of life activity. One's fundamental choice and project can always be changed, and for this reason the kind of person one is is always subject to personal control and is always that for which one is responsible:

> If I am mobilized in a war, this war is *my* war; it is in my image and I deserve it. I deserve it first because I could always get out of it by suicide or by desertion; these ultimate possibles are those which must always be present for us when there is a question of envisaging a situation. For lack of getting out of it, I have *chosen* it. This can be due to inertia, to cowardice in the face of public opinion, or because I prefer certain other values to the value of the refusal to join in the war (the good opinion of my relatives, the honor of my family, etc.) Any way you look at it, it is a matter of choice. (Sartre 1956: 708)

The moral dimensions of Sartre's existentialist views of the 1940s focus upon responsibility, authenticity, and self-determination, rather than upon either goodness or rightness, pleasure versus pains, or behavioral consistency versus behavioral inconsistency. Sartre condemns people for adopting artificial and arbitrary labels in an essentialistic manner and for not fulfilling human potential. He does not (in 1943) envision a harmonious social condition toward which we aim in virtue of our common nature, and in reference to which one could derive the right to criticize others insofar as their actions do not contribute to producing this highly valued and communal end-state.

Sartre's position remains questionable on at least two points, however, the first of which assumes his claim in *Being and Nothingness* that human freedom is absolute. If our freedom is unconditional, then one can choose not to be rational, and if one can choose not to be rational, then one need not be setting a general example for anyone else when one chooses exclusively for oneself. Sartre's later (1946) and often quoted claim that when one chooses, one chooses for all humanity (Sartre 1948: 29) dramatically intensifies the social significance of one's choice, but it contradicts his crucial existentialist idea that each person is fundamentally unique and chooses only for himself or herself.

Second, upon assuming the irreconcilability of the subject–object distinction, Sartre maintains that human beings all aspire fruitlessly to be subjects and objects simultaneously and in effect are trying to be God. This effort to be God, he claims, is the impossible aim of all human relationships. For the purposes of articulating Sartre's position in a manner more consistent with his existentialist focus, however, we can distinguish between having within oneself an unconditional quality versus expressing this unconditional quality satisfactorily within the spatio-temporal world. In theological terms, it is the difference between saying "God is" as opposed to "Christ exists."

Sartre claims, as a matter of definition, that God embodies the fusion of subjectivity and objectivity and that it is impossible to be God. However, this obscures the sense in which within Sartre's own view, people are godlike insofar as they are absolutely free. Within the Sartrean outlook, the human problem does not reside in our not being "God" or in our not being like God, but rather in an inability to actualize perfectly our absolute freedom in the concrete world, since to some degree we are always in bad faith, and since our relationships with other people always remain unfulfilled owing to our own sense of personal individuality.

When expressed in theological terms, Sartre's outlook suggests that the human condition is essentially frustrating, not because people lack a divine quality, but because they cannot embody their absolute freedom perfectly in order to become instantiations of God in an earthly form.[23] This is to say that people are precluded from becoming Christlike figures and that the incarnation of the divine as a social phenomenon is an unrealizable ideal within this outlook.[24] Sartre is thereby more revealingly characterized as an anti-Christian than as an anti-theist, for his conception of human freedom closely reflects that of an absolutely free and authoritarian God.

Along different lines, if one believes that God is independent of rational constraint, then God could ask a person to act in defiance of traditional moral precepts, as one finds in the story of Abraham and Isaac – a story that inspired Kierkegaard's conception of absolute freedom. This introduces the question of whether any existentialist view that is grounded upon the idea of absolute freedom of the individual would imply a traditional moral content. It is difficult to see how it could, and this independence from traditional moral dictates is common theme within existentialist thought.

In *The Myth of Sisyphus*, Camus emphasized the importance of living authentically as an absurd, though not necessarily great, character who is synchronized with the irrational nature of the world. Specifically, he identified various personality types that embody this idea most effectively, namely, the conqueror, the traveler, the actor, the seducer, and the imprisoned worker. He gave prominence to these absurd types in reference either to living with a high degree of variation within one's experience (e.g., the actor, the conqueror, the traveler, the seducer), or living with an intense awareness of the present moment or "flame of life" (e.g., the imprisoned worker), even in a condition of what would otherwise be painfully monotonous.

Each of Camus's absurd personality types aims fully to appreciate the quality of the present moment in a struggle against inevitable death, but in doing so, traditional moral considerations are subordinated. The conqueror is responsible for many deaths, with only the number of conquests at stake; the seducer is responsible for many heartbreaks, with again, only the number of conquests at stake. The traveler and the actor intend to experience as many different places or to play as many roles as possible, and are morally neutral characters. In Sartre and Camus, the existentialist emphasis upon freedom and in having an intense awareness of the present tends to render traditional moral values secondary, although it does not exclude them. Living authentically and living morally are not contradictory, for one can choose continually to be moral.

French Existentialism's Influence

In later years, French existentialist thought of the 1930s and 1940s became influential in the fields of literary theory and social criticism. Inspired by Martin Heidegger's characterization of human beings as beings for whom their existence is an issue, Sartre developed an analysis of the nature of questioning itself. Specifically, Sartre maintained that any situation within which a question occurs involves posing alternative answers in light of the questioner's uncertainty. The difference between the possible answers, the possibility of receiving a negative answer, and the questioner's very uncertainty combine to establish a "triple non-being" within the situation (Sartre 1956: 36). This set of contrasts does not draw our attention to the positive elements of the questioning situation as one might naturally imagine, but rather to the gaps, the points of opposition, and the structures of differentiation that render the apprehension of the positive elements possible.

The deconstructive approach to linguistic meaning developed in the 1960s by Jacques Derrida (1930–2004) is an offspring of Sartre's analysis of questioning, for Derrida adopted the view – one inspired equally by the Swiss linguist Ferdinand de Saussure (1857–1913) – that the *differences* between words within a linguistic system are more decisive in determining meaning than are the positive significations of the words themselves. This approach expands methodologically upon the model of how the points of opposition between the questioner, a possible negative answer, and the contrast between the possible answers are more fundamental in understanding questioning than the positive contents of any particular questions and answers.

This gap-focused or fissure-focused style of analysis is held by its advocates to be more illuminating than traditional approaches: instead of examining, for instance, the positive structures of the bones to understand the human skeleton, one examines the locations of the joints between the bones; instead of examining the contents of the foreground presences, one examines the overlooked background; instead of considering what is said, one considers what remains unsaid or understated; instead of focusing upon the key figures in social institutions, one focuses upon the marginalized and dispossessed. In sum, one attends generally to what has been identified as "other," subordinate, implicit, or silenced within some subject matter, and then highlights this underprivileged element in a table-turning effort to reveal non-thematized or hidden features of the subject under consideration.

Sartre's emphasis upon experiential details also influenced Roland Barthes's (1915–80), Jean-François Lyotard's (1925–98), and Jacques Derrida's more concretist understandings of language. In the 1960s–1970s, Barthes, Derrida, and Lyotard observed that when language is used, one cannot abstractly separate the literalistic aspect from either the literary or narrative aspects of language; the several semantic dimensions always congeal together with the implication that purely literalistic

221

expressions are none other than false abstractions. In this manner, Sartre's views helped motivate the poststructuralist position that artistic modes of expression are more expressive of truth than literalistic modes, which are considered to be too narrowly one-dimensional.

Also in tune with the existentialist idea that "existence precedes essence," Michel Foucault (1926–84) advanced a non-Platonistic style of sociological and historical analysis in the 1970s, opposing the view that historical understanding should proceed typically by searching for a definition or essence to a given situation. Rather, Foucault maintained that the great majority of historical phenomena arise from an intersection of accidental happenings in the absence of any prior plan or essential meaning:

> The world we know is not this ultimately simple configuration where events are reduced to accentuate their essential traits, their final meaning, or their initial and final value. On the contrary, it is a profusion of entangled events. If it appears as a "marvelous motley, profound and totally meaningful," this is because it began and continues its secret existence through a "host of errors and phantasms." We want historians to confirm our belief that the present rests upon profound intentions and immutable necessities. But the true historical sense confirms our existence among countless lost events, without a landmark or point of reference. (Foucault 1977: 155)

Foucault broadens the French existentialist focus on individuality with a more Heideggerian attention to the wider social context and social-linguistic constitution of the contents of consciousness, while he respects the Sartrean idea that freedom and contingency are paramount. We are deeply influenced by our social environment, but since we live in a world of fluctuating contingencies, there are more opportunities available for social reform than are usually realized.

The same appreciation of Sartre's notion of bad faith is reflected in Roland Barthes's antipathy toward the ossification of meaning (the experience of which he calls "nausea") and his advocacy of constantly shifting one's position whenever one begins to sense that one's habits are tending to rigidify the situation. Just as Sartre advised us to resist the temptations of living in bad faith, Barthes advised us to resist the blind acceptance of myth that has assumed the guise of natural fact. Similarly, despite some of his Cartesian inheritances, Sartre's opposition to the idea of a permanent thinking substance that defines human subjectivity was shared by writers such Jacques Lacan (1901–81), and most of the French thinkers of the later twentieth century, who, in their emphasis upon the social construction of meaning and self, denied that consciousness has any permanent and definitive qualities.

The philosophical themes distinctive of French existentialism – freedom, the quest for personal human meaning, alienation, absurdity, individuality, resistance to oppression from without – are perennial, and the attractiveness of French existentialism is ensured for years to come. It embodies one of the main alternatives to the Platonistic philosophical mentality, and insofar as an earthly and historical presence is an ineradicable aspect of our experience, as long as finitude is an aspect of the human psyche, as long as detachment and the questioning of the *status quo* remain alive, as long as a strong sense of one's bodily presence and unique individuality remains pronounced and is sometimes maximized, as long as a feeling for the world's incomprehensibility persists, and as long as absolute freedom remains an inspiring ideal, French existentialist writers will continue to have a wide readership and influence in connection with their efforts to articulate our concrete human situation and search for meaning.

Notes

1   Some important nineteenth-century philosophers are referred to as "existentialists," but the terms "existentialist" and "existentialism" issued mainly from mid-1940s France. They were introduced significantly by Gabriel Marcel in 1945 in reference to Sartre, and became catchwords soon after owing largely to Sartre's public address in 1946 entitled "Existentialism is a Humanism" (Sartre 1948).

2   This attitude is consistent with Deism – a cluster of religious outlooks that were popular during the late seventeenth and eighteenth centuries in Britain, France, and North America. Deists respected God as the creator of the natural world, but they regarded God as a being who, after establishing natural laws, left nature to run at its own mechanical accord.

3   This is revealed in the full title of George Berkeley's (1685–1753) text, *The Analyst* (1734): *The Analyst, or A Discourse Addressed to an Infidel Mathematician, Wherein it is examined whether the object, principles, and inferences of the modern Analysis are more distinctly conceived, or more evidently deduced, then religious Mysteries and points of Faith.* The "infidel mathematician" referred to is believed to be Edmund Halley (1656–1742).

4   Owing to his emphasis upon concrete thinking, Hegel's philosophy inspires and illuminates French existentialist outlooks. Hegel maintained more specifically, however, that the highest realization of reason arises only within an actual social community, and he celebrated such an actualized rational community of human beings, in effect, as the incarnation of the divine. This form of humanism is consistent with the (non-orthodox) Christian view that a society of Jesus-like people (i.e., of mutually respecting, compassionate, moral people) is the most realistic instantiation of what has been more traditionally conceived of as an other-worldly heaven.

Hegel's image of an earthly moral society as the incarnation of the divine endured especially within twentieth-century French philosophers who express "Christian existentialism." This refers mainly to Gabriel Marcel (1889–1973) but also arguably to Teilhard de Chardin (1881–1955), although de Chardin is not typically referred to as an existentialist. Jacques Maritain (1882–1973) also advocated an optimistic, concretist, and humanistic view toward the possibility of a society of moral individuals, claiming that Thomism is the original existentialism.

The works of Marcel, Maritain, and de Chardin have existence-centered aspects, but it is more historically useful to associate the term "existentialism" with more extremist theorists whose apprehensions of the individuality of things leads us to wonder seriously whether the world is essentially rational, or whether rationality could ever prevail in the world.

This excludes Hegel from the set of nineteenth-century existentialists, since his faith in the incarnation of rationality was unsurpassed. Both absurdist existentialists in the sense here described, along with Christian existentialists, attend to the more realistic aspects of things – they both embody concrete styles of philosophy – but Christian existentialists deny that a down-to-earth orientation precludes the recognition of transcendent and universalistic essences. The present overview of French existentialism emphasizes the absurdist styles, owing to their more exclusive attention to individuality and existence, and their more radical departure from the nineteenth-century faith in social progress and ideal community.

5   The concept of the unconscious, for example, was salient in F. W. J. Schelling's *System of Transcendental Idealism* (1800).

223

6   Sartre's characterization of human consciousness as a forward-looking directedness (or "intentionality") – a view inspired by Edmund Husserl (1859–1938) – develops this thought. Sartre states that consciousness is always projecting itself forward in time and that it is therefore perpetually trying impossibly to live in the future. Consciousness, he says, is "what it is not" and it is not "what it is": we identify with a future point that we never attain, as we continue imaginatively to project our attention away from the moment in which we are situated.

7   The phrase "dark night of the soul" gained currency through the writings of St. John of the Cross (1542–91). See St. John of the Cross 1991.

8   In the *Phenomenology of Spirit* (Hegel 1977: §225), Hegel observed that nihilism arises when one's sense of individuality is intensified maximally in conjunction with a proportional minimization of one's sense of universality. When accompanied by the feeling that one is a contingent being through-and-through, utter self-centeredness conflicts with the recognition of universal foundations.

9   For a number of theorists, among whom is Benedict Spinoza (1632–77), freedom as self-determination is a defining feature of God.

10 Descartes influentially wrote the following: "The sole exception is the will or free choice; I observe it to be so great in me that I grasp an idea of nothing greater, to the extent that the will is principally the basis for my understanding that I bear an image and likeness of God" (Descartes 1979: 37).

11 In Plato's *Timaeus*, the physical world is similarly explained in reference to the craftsman-like activity of a godlike "demiurge" – a personage who fashions the material world in accord with his intellectual apprehension of the eternal essences that serve as his plans.

12 As noted, the views of Sartre and Camus are being taken to be the most representative of French existentialism. It is worth reiterating, however, that this emphasis is not universally accepted by those who can legitimately be called "French existentialists." Jacques Maritain, for instance, wrote the following in 1947: "Let it be said right off that there are two fundamentally different ways of interpreting the word existentialism. One way is to affirm the primacy of existence, but as implying and preserving essences or natures as manifesting the supreme victory of the intellect and of intelligibility. This is what I consider to be authentic existentialism. The other way is to affirm the primacy of existence, but as destroying or abolishing essences or natures and as manifesting the supreme defeat of the intellect and intelligibility" (Maritain 1956: 13).

Views such as those of Maritain, Marcel, and de Chardin accord more closely with Hegel's emphasis upon the concrete instantiation of rationality, and do not express a maximally intensified awareness of individuality to the detriment of the awareness of universality. The latter dissipation of the sense of universality, however, is what has made French existentialism's influential and controversial mark in the history of twentieth-century philosophy.

13 Husserl's phenomenology – a theory influential in the history of French existentialism – emphasized that perceptual presentations are typically subject to a multiplicity of interpretations. For instance, just as the sentence "the shooting of the hunters was frightening" can suggest either the frightening sound of the hunters' guns, or the frightening violence suffered by the hunters, the perception of a physical thing is ambiguous with respect to whether we are perceiving a solid thing, or a realistically painted image, etc. When we perceive an object, we do not ordinarily apprehend the reverse side of the object; interpreting the perceptual presentation just as it stands leaves it open that the reverse side of the object may or may not actually be there. Any semantically rich feature of experience has this ambiguous quality. Emmanuel Levinas's (1906–95) *The Theory of Intuition in Husserl's Phenomenology* (1930) helped introduce Husserl's phenomenology to Sartre and Merleau-Ponty.

14 The text is from Merleau-Ponty's address to the *Société Française de Philosophie* soon after the publication of his central work, *The Phenomenology of Perception* (1945).

15 Camus, writing in 1942, is referring to the views of Jean-Paul Sartre as expressed in his novel *Nausea* (Sartre 1964).

16 Fyodor Dostoevsky's (1821–81) *Notes from Underground* (1864) is an antecedent existentialist text – one that foreshadows the work of Franz Kafka (1883–1924) – that periodically expresses a comparable sense of alienation and objectification: "I should like to tell you now whether you want to hear it or not, why I couldn't even make an insect out of myself. I tell you solemnly that I have wanted to make an insect out of myself many times" (Dostoevsky 1972: 17).

17 Both Merleau-Ponty and Heidegger challenge the fundamentality of the subject–object distinction.

18 The notion of aesthetic disinterestedness – a mode of attention wherein one attends to an object with a conscious disengagement and psychical distance from the attraction of practical concerns (as in Camus's telephone booth example) – extends back to the eighteenth century into the writings of the Earl of Shaftesbury (1671–1713). See Stolnitz 1961.

19 Husserl's phenomenological attitude has an aesthetic dimension insofar as it prescribes that we attend to a perceptual presentation independently of considering whether the presentation refers to a physical or imaginary object. In his characterization of aesthetic contemplation, Kant also stated in his *Critique of Judgment* (Kant 1951) that as a matter of making aesthetic judgments, we should contemplate the object independently of the consideration of whether or not the object exists.

20 See Merleau-Ponty's 1948 essay on Cézanne, "*Le Doute de Cézanne*" [Cézanne's doubt], which appeared in *Sens et Non-Sens* [Sense and non-sense] (Merleau-Ponty 1964b).

21 See the beginning of Heidegger 1962.

22 Camus's enthusiasm for nurturing the "flame of life" within us reflects a passage from the highly influential conclusion of Walter Pater's *Studies in the History of the Renaissance* (1873):

> Well! we are all *condamnés*, as Victor Hugo says: *les hommes sont tous condamnés á mort avec des sursis indéfinis*: we have an interval, and then our place knows us no more. Some spend this interval in listlessness, some in high passions, the wisest in art and song. For our one chance is in expanding that interval, in getting as many pulsations as possible into the given time. High passions give one this quickened sense of life, ecstasy and sorrow of love, political or religious enthusiasm, or the "enthusiasm of humanity." Only, be sure it is passion, that it does yield you this fruit of a quickened, multiplied consciousness. Of this wisdom, the poetic passion, the desire of beauty, the love of art for art's sake has most; for art comes to you professing frankly to give nothing but the highest quality to your moments as they pass, and simply for those moments' sake. (Pater 1912: 238–9)

23 This peculiarly reiterates the Platonistic situation where spatio-temporal instantiations are unable to match the perfection of the timeless ideal.

24 Sartre's nausea conveys the frustration of not having the ideal situation match the existential situation. For instance, in *Nausea*, his main character becomes nauseated when he cannot comprehend a tree's root, because the root's details are always in excess of the root's conceptual definition and specification. In being unable to exist as God (i.e., in being unable to be a Jesus-figure, as here interpreted), the ideal condition similarly does not match the actual condition. Absolute freedom (our assumedly divine aspect) cannot be perfectly instantiated within a determinate social and historical context, just as conceptual definitions cannot be perfectly instantiated in material things.

References and Further Reading

Aristotle (1998) *The Nicomachean Ethics* (trans. D. Ross). Oxford: Oxford University Press (original publication date unknown).

Camus, A. (1955) *The Myth of Sisyphus and Other Essays* (trans. J. O'Brien). New York: Vintage (original work published 1942).

de Beauvoir, S. (1991) *The Ethics of Ambiguity* (trans. B. Frechtman). New York: Citadel Press (original work published 1947).

Derrida, J. (1972) *Margins of Philosophy* (trans. A. Bass). Chicago: University of Chicago Press.

Descartes, R. (1979) *Meditations on First Philosophy* (trans. D. A. Cress). Indianapolis and Cambridge: Hackett (original work published 1641).

Dostoevsky, F. (1972) *Notes from Underground* (trans. J. Coulson). London: Penguin (original work published 1864).

Foucault, M. (1977) Nietzsche, genealogy, history (trans. D. F. Bouchard and S. Simon). In D. F. Bouchard and S. Simon (eds.), *Language, Counter-Memory, Practice – Selected Essays and Interviews by Michel Foucault*. Ithaca, NY: Cornell University Press (original work published 1971).

Freud, S. (1965) *New Introductory Lectures on Psychoanalysis* (trans. J. Strachey). New York: W. W. Norton (original work published 1933).

Gillespie, M. A. (1996) *Nihilism Before Nietzsche*. Chicago and London: University of Chicago Press.

Hegel, G. W. F. (1977) *Phenomenology of Spirit*. (trans. A. V. Miller). Oxford: Oxford University Press (original work published 1807).

Heidegger, M. (1962) *Being and Time* (trans. J. Macquarrie and E. Robinson). New York: Harper & Row (original work published 1927).

Husserl, E. (1962) *Ideas – General Introduction to Pure Phenomenology* (trans. W. R. R. Gibson). New York: Collier (original work published 1913).

Kant, I. (1951) *Critique of Judgment* (trans. J. H. Bernard). New York: Hafner (original work published 1790).

—— (1965) *Critique of Pure Reason* (trans. N. Kemp-Smith). New York: St. Martin's Press (original work published 1781; rev. edn. 1787).

Kierkegaard, S. (1941) *Concluding Unscientific Postscript* (trans. D. F. Swenson and W. Lowrie). Princeton, NJ: Princeton University Press (original work published 1846).

Marcel, G. (1960) *The Mystery of Being*, vol. I: *Reflection and Mystery*, vol. II. *Faith and Reality*. Chicago: Henry Regnery.

Maritain, J. (1956) *Existence and the Existent: An Essay on Christian Existentialism* (trans. L. Galantière and G. B. Phelan). Garden City, NY: Image Books (original work published 1947).

Merleau-Ponty, M. (1964a) The primacy of perception and its philosophical consequences (trans. J. M. Edie). In J. M. Edie (ed.), *The Primacy of Perception* (pp. 12–42). Evanston, IL: Northwestern University Press (original address given 1946).

—— (1964b) *Sense and Non-Sense* (trans. H. Dreyfus and A. Dreyfus). Evanston, IL: Northwestern University Press (original work published 1948).

Nietzsche, F. (1967) *The Birth of Tragedy* (trans. W. Kaufmann). New York: Vintage Books (original work published 1886).

—— (1996) *Beyond Good and Evil* (trans. W. Kaufmann). New York: Vintage Books (original work published 1886).

Pater, W. (1912) *The Renaissance: Studies in Art and Poetry*. London: Macmillan.

Sartre, J-P. (1948) *Existentialism and Humanism* (trans. P. Mairet). London: Eyre Methuen (original work published 1946).

—— (1956) *Being and Nothingness: A Phenomenological Essay in Ontology* (trans. H. Barnes). New York: Pocket Books (original work published 1943).

—— (1964) *Nausea* (trans. L. Alexander). New York: New Directions (original work published 1938).

St. John of the Cross (1991) The Ascent of Mt. Carmel (trans. O. Rodriguez). In *The Collected Works of St. John of the Cross*. Washington, DC: ICS (original publication date unknown).

Stolnitz, J. (1961) On the origins of aesthetic disinterestedness. *Journal of Aesthetics and Art Criticism*, 20(2), 131–43.

Central Concepts

15

The Concept of Authenticity

TAYLOR CARMAN

The concept of authenticity is one of the most important and fruitful ideas to emerge from the existential tradition in philosophy, especially in the works of Kierkegaard, Heidegger, and Sartre. Like the closely related but crucially distinct notions of sincerity, autonomy, and self-realization, all of which found early expression in the literary and philosophical writings of Jean-Jacques Rousseau, the idea of authenticity belongs to a cluster of ethical and psychological conceptions of individuality that stand in an uneasy relation to traditional norms of justice and the demands of morality. The concept of authenticity, however, also differs in crucial ways from Romantic and popular notions of uniqueness of character, individual integrity, and personal fulfillment.

It is tempting, as a rough approximation, to say that authenticity consists in somehow *being true* to oneself. One way to be true to oneself is to be honest with oneself, which is to say, inwardly sincere. This is neither easy nor common, in fact it arguably rose to the level of a genuine ethical value only fairly recently in the cultural history of the West. Earlier spokesmen of Christian virtue like St. Augustine aspired to a kind of radical honesty with themselves, but only by way of being fully candid and humble before God. Inner sincerity for its own sake requires no such reference to a transcendent moral authority, and its intrinsic moral value is not obvious. Indeed, there is a paradox about sincerity ordinarily conceived, namely, that it cannot thrive in one's inner self, but must at least on occasion be outwardly recognizable. To be sincere is not just to tell the truth about oneself willy-nilly, but to *present oneself* sincerely. That self-presentation must appear spontaneous and natural, however, for if one's efforts seem too deliberate, too calculated, they will also appear manipulative and so lose their claim to sincerity, even if what one says is true. This seems to suggest that sincerity requires subtlety and artifice. And yet, as Sartre observes, deliberate and artificial efforts to be sincere are self-defeating. In any event, ordinary social sincerity depends on a certain style of conduct, a kind of interpersonal performance we occasionally demand of others as a test of the putative underlying virtue.

Radical honesty with oneself is something different. With the possible exception of *Hamlet*, the first explicit articulation of such an ideal is probably Rousseau's *Confessions*, which opens with a proclamation in virtual defiance not only of the reader but of God himself to question or second-guess the sincerity of the autobiographical account that follows. Only Jean-Jacques, he lets us know, is in a position to judge Jean-Jacques.

Of course, such an overt declaration of inner sincerity is problematic and paradoxical in even more complicated ways than sincerity conceived as a social virtue. Authenticity, in any event, seems to lack the performative ambiguity bound up with the idea of sincerity, inner or outer.

Rousseau was also one of the principal sources of inspiration for Kant's conception of moral autonomy, and again it may be tempting to conceive of authenticity as a kind of self-governance, if not necessarily Kantian. What is crucial about the notion of autonomy, however, and what distinguishes it from the concept of authenticity, is precisely its reference to legislation and laws, which must be general, applying (more or less) equally to everyone. Authenticity, as we shall see, although it may be described as a kind of independence or self-reliance, stands in stark contrast to the universal applicability of moral laws essential to the Kantian concept of autonomy.

Finally, we have inherited from Rousseau and the Romantic tradition a less systematically articulated notion of self-fulfillment or self-realization, an idea still very much alive in popular ethical discourse. As soon as we try to define the idea more precisely, however, we find that it differs from the existential concept of authenticity in its implication of a self in principle capable of achieving a kind of metaphysical integrity, wholeness, completion, ultimate fulfillment. This normative ideal is what breathes life into familiar metaphors intended to describe the frailty of the human condition in terms of rupture, dissolution, fragmentation, alienation. The existential concept of authenticity is philosophically original and important for having transcended even this late modern conception of selfhood as integrated subjectivity. What follows is a brief sketch of the idea of authenticity as it figures in the work of Kierkegaard, Heidegger, and Sartre.

Kierkegaard

Although Kierkegaard makes no systematic use of (the Danish equivalent of) the term "authenticity," and although one must take care in ascribing views to him on the basis of books he wrote under pseudonyms, we can nonetheless identify in his major works a number of interconnected themes that, taken together, constitute an account of authentic selfhood. These include, above all, the account of religious faith in *Fear and Trembling* (1843; cited as Kierkegaard 1985), the discussions of subjectivity and inwardness in *Concluding Unscientific Postscript* and *A Literary Review* (1846; cited as Kierkegaard 1987 and Kierkegaard 2001, respectively), and the dialectic of selfhood in *The Sickness unto Death* (1849; cited as Kierkegaard 1989).

Religious faith, as Kierkegaard conceives it, is a form of unconditional individual commitment incommensurable with the universalistic demands of morality. Faith requires what he calls a "teleological suspension of the ethical," that is, a bracketing of general and impersonal moral requirements for the sake of a higher individual end, an end that cannot be counted among the objective values grounded in interpersonal relationships or social institutions. The paradigmatic exemplar of faith Kierkegaard offers for consideration is Abraham, whose seemingly unthinking obedience to God leads him to the very brink of killing his son Isaac in sacrifice, as God has commanded.

The pseudonymous author of *Fear and Trembling*, Johannes de Silentio, is anything but silent in his anxious ruminations about how Abraham could have been willing to kill Isaac, whom he loved more than anything in the world, and how such a horrific act could merit the admiration of all those who habitually praise Abraham as the father of faith. Johannes de Silentio is honest enough to admit that "while Abraham arouses my admiration, he also appalls me" (Kierkegaard 1985: 89). For unlike tragic heroes such as Agamemnon, Jephthah, and Brutus, who killed their children on ethical grounds (which is not to say rightly, but for the sake of duties prescribed by their respective social or institutional roles), Abraham can take no ethical comfort at all in losing Isaac. Abraham is no mere tragic hero, Johannes observes, and his worldly loss (if he goes through with it) will be total and evidently unredeemable.

The authorial structure of *Fear and Trembling* thus ingeniously underscores the very idea Johannes de Silentio himself is struggling to grasp, namely, that faith cannot in principle be an object of ethical or aesthetic admiration, for admiration must in effect assimilate actions and attitudes to standards that can be applied and assessed interpersonally and from multiple points of view. But not only are Abraham's motives opaque to any outside observer; his behavior also resists all reasonable ethical interpretation, even his own. It is hardly surprising, then, that Johannes de Silentio fails to understand Abraham; that, as he says, "when I have to think about Abraham I am virtually annihilated" (Kierkegaard 1985: 62). For Kierkegaard tells Abraham's story in such a way that it cannot be understood from any third-person point of view, not even that of Abraham's own ethical deliberations. In an ironic twist typical of Kierkegaard, the pseudonymous author of *Concluding Unscientific Postscript*, Johannes Climacus, describes the pseudonym Johannes de Silentio not as "an existing individuality," since real existing persons can never be captured in literary form, but as "a reflecting person who . . . continually bumps his head against the understanding, so to speak, while the lyric springs from the recoil" (Kierkegaard 1987: 261–2, translation modified).

Johannes de Silentio's failure to understand Abraham thus amounts to a literary representation of Kierkegaard's point about the nature of faith, namely its opacity to the third-person or observer's point of view and its recalcitrance to moral deliberation. Some aspects of my own actions and attitudes, perhaps in the end those most precious and crucial to my life, can be understood only from my own finite point of view, and even then not in reflective or conceptual terms. No one else can know what it means to be in my place, facing the choices I face, at what personal cost, for the sake of what ultimate ends, nor can I articulate them and make them explicit even to myself. Each of us is in this way singular and irreducible in our finite existence – not just de facto owing to the uniqueness of each particular situation, but formally, since the self's relation to itself is structurally different from its relation to another. Faith is something radically particular. Kierkegaard even goes so far as to say that if a true "knight of faith" such as Abraham were alive today, he would be outwardly indistinguishable from the tax collector, the shopkeeper, the bourgeois philistine (Kierkegaard 1985: 67–9).

The account of faith in *Fear and Trembling*, however, is far from Kierkegaard's final word on the subject. Indeed, there is some reason to suspect that the concept of faith elaborated there may be fatally unstable precisely because virtually nothing can be said about it from any point of view at all, even that of the subject whose faith it is. Indeed, for all Johannes de Silentio tells us, it seems to make no difference at all what specific content Abraham's faith has, or indeed if it has any. Faith, it seems, is a kind of affective attitude whose cognitive content is a matter of indifference: "Even if one were able to render the whole of the content of faith into conceptual form, it would not follow that one had grasped faith, grasped how one came to it, or how it came to one" (Kierkegaard 1985: 43). In any event, the account of faith advanced in *Fear and Trembling* plainly fails to capture what Kierkegaard himself regarded as distinctive and important about Christianity. As he later wrote in an unpublished reply to a critic, "according to the New Testament Abraham is called the father of faith, and yet it is indeed clear that the content of his faith cannot be Christian – that Jesus Christ has been in existence. But Abraham's faith is the formal definition of faith" (Kierkegaard 1987: Supplement, 164).

Kierkegaard's discussions of inwardness and subjectivity in *Concluding Unscientific Postscript* and *A Literary Review* reiterate the unique first-person structure of faith, but with less emphasis on its transcendent end or object and more on its social and psychological implications. Subjectivity or inwardness, in Kierkegaard's sense of those terms, constitutes a kind of truth incommensurable with objective truth, or truth as it would appear to an ideal observer. Kierkegaard argues that the theoretical standpoint has dominated philosophy since Socrates and now enjoys increasing prestige in virtually all areas of modern life, in our institutions, in the style of our practices, in our existence.

The observational point of view constitutes what Kierkegaard calls "reflection," a word whose connotations include deliberation, calculation, and dialectical complexity, as well as sheer exposure, visibility, and publicness. The standpoint of reflection is paradigmatic for the "present age," which is an age of reason, science, enlightenment, and the emerging public sphere of mass media and democratic practice. But reflection left to its own devices undermines passion, commitment, character, individuality, and selfhood. The triumph of abstract reflection over concrete personal commitment Kierkegaard calls the "leveling process," and its insidious effect is the creation of a social world dominated by an impersonal – indeed imaginary – normative authority governing our thoughts and actions, namely "the public."

Resisting the leveling process and renouncing the anonymous pseudoauthority of the public and public opinion means embarking on a project of becoming subjective, realizing inwardness, and becoming a true self. In *The Sickness unto Death* Kierkegaard again maintains that a self consists in an irreducible first-person reflexive relation to itself, and moreover that genuine selfhood involves a synthesis of three pairs of heterogeneous factors: finitude and infinitude, possibility and necessity, and temporality and eternity. Despair, or the loss of self, results from a failure to harmonize or integrate these aspects of ourselves. To sustain true selfhood, that is, our commitments must be holistic and yet concrete, they must open our horizons while at the same time fixing our identities, and they must be grounded realistically in the world even as we embrace them unconditionally. A self that could embark on such a focused, wholehearted commitment to something in this life, while nevertheless treating it as eternally valuable, would be a genuine or authentic self, exemplified according to Kierkegaard in the ideal of Christian faith.

232

Heidegger

Heidegger uses the term "authentic" (*eigentlich*) liberally throughout his magnum opus, *Being and Time* (1927; cited as Heidegger 1962), but in two different senses, one evaluative, the other merely descriptive.

On the one hand, what is "authentic" in the descriptive sense of the word is what is formally unique and particular to each individual human being. The *eigen* in *eigentlich*, like the *auth* in "authentic," means *own, proper,* or *peculiar*. What is authentic, then, is what is most my own, what is essentially most proper or peculiar to me. For Heidegger, then, as for Kierkegaard, authenticity has to do with the unique first-person structure of existence, what Heidegger calls its "mineness" (*Jemeinigkeit*). This notion of authenticity has no normative import, but merely indicates a formal distinction between the self's relation to itself and its relation to others. Authenticity in this sense is neither good nor bad, but has to do instead with my unique relation to myself in my existence, in contrast to my relations to others, or to myself regarded from a second- or third-person point of view.

So, for example, Heidegger maintains that *fear* is inauthentic, not because there is anything wrong with it, but because it is an intentional state directed at things outside oneself; fear is fear *of* something, or *for* someone. *Anxiety*, by contrast, is authentic, again not because it is somehow right or good, but because it has no external object, but relates immediately to one's own individualized being-in-the-world (see Heidegger 1962: §§30, 40). Nor is there in this merely descriptive sense any middle term between authentic and inauthentic, that is, between the reflexive and other-mediated dimensions of existence.

In many passages in *Being and Time*, on the other hand, and in spite of Heidegger's frequent protestations to the contrary, the term "authentic" obviously refers to something desirable, a choiceworthy way of life. Authenticity in this sense is clearly something *good*, inauthenticity bad. Indeed, regrettably, Heidegger muddies the waters by superimposing these evaluative notions on the descriptive distinction between authentic and inauthentic. For example, complicating the merely formal distinction between anxiety and fear as authentic and inauthentic, which is to say, self-directed and other-directed, respectively, he also refers to "cowardly fear" of death as a perversion of the "*courage for anxiety in the face of death*" (Heidegger 1962: 266, 254; all page references to Heidegger 1962 are to the marginal numbers). In this case, at least, the authentic attitude is obviously meant to be better than the inauthentic.

Moreover, in the normative sense of the words, authenticity and inauthenticity are not exhaustive categories, but lie at the ends of a spectrum, whose middle Heidegger describes as a kind of modal undifferentiatedness or "indifference" (*Indifferenz*) (Heidegger 1962: 232). That undifferentiated middle range, neither authentic nor inauthentic, is the "average everydayness" that serves as a neutral starting point for the hermeneutic phenomenology of Division I of *Being and Time* (Heidegger 1962: 43), while Division II goes on to focus more specifically on the authentic modes – anxiety, guilt, death – which Heidegger thinks afford deeper insight into the essential structures of human existence. Everydayness is the bland, undifferentiated state in which one's actions and attitudes are neither particularly authentic nor inauthentic, an indifferent condition in which one is neither especially owning up to oneself, one's situation, one's purposes, nor disowning oneself, evading one's unique situation, and fleeing into anonymous, generic forms of self-understanding.

Like Wittgenstein, but unlike any other major existential thinkers, Heidegger insists that all human conduct is informed by anonymous social norms and practices, which he designates with the nominalized impersonal pronoun, "the one" (*das Man*), as in "one doesn't do such things." Even the most authentic existence therefore presupposes some normative social background or other, whereas what characterizes the undifferentiated and inauthentic modes is their routine and desensitized conformity to the average understanding that happens to prevail in society.

Authenticity, understood as resisting conformism and coming into one's own, as we might say, in turn comprises two distinct elements: "resoluteness" (*Entschlossenheit*) and "forerunning" (*Vorlaufen*). Resoluteness is a rough equivalent to Aristotle's notion of practical wisdom (*phronêsis*), absent any implication that the insight it affords will necessarily be in harmony with the judgment of ethical experts and role models esteemed in the community (see Aristotle 2000: Book IV). To be resolute is to remain sensitive to the unique demands of the concrete "situation" (*Situation*), as opposed to subsuming it under generic rules and categories of thought, thus reducing it to a mere "general state of affairs" (*allgemeine Lage*) and responding with rigid, preconceived attitudes and behaviors (see Heidegger 1962: 300). Resolute agents, that is, maintain a subtle feel for the situations they confront and so are able to deal with them intelligently, skillfully, with finesse.

Forerunning, by contrast, is reminiscent of Kierkegaard's notion of subjectivity, wherein I take up my personal commitments as irreducibly my own, even though they may be incommensurable or irreconcilable with ethical norms applying to everyone, including me. More specifically, for Heidegger, forerunning means running up against or even *into* death, which means not literally expiring in the biological sense, but being continually exposed to the essential instability and vulnerability of my world and my identity. Forerunning into death, then, means being ready, willing, and able to embrace a particular and inherently fragile set of possibilities, even as they tend inevitably to fall apart under their own weight. Authenticity understood as "forerunning resoluteness" (*vorlaufende Entschlossenheit*) is thus a hybrid of Aristotelian *phronêsis* and Kierkegaardian subjectivity.

Finally, Heidegger maintains, authenticity has a crucial historical dimension since it necessarily involves the recovery, reappropriation, and renewal of a "heritage" (*Erbe*), or what he describes as "a *handing down to oneself* possibilities that have come down to one, though not necessarily *as* they have come down" (Heidegger 1962: 383; translation modified). Only by freely reappropriating a tradition and making it our own are we able to project resolutely into our utmost possibility as a kind of "fate" (*Schicksal*), or in the case of a community, a shared "destiny" (*Geschick*). Of course, Heidegger means *fate* and *destiny* not in their traditional metaphysical senses, but phenomenologically. A fate or destiny is not something objectively inevitable, that is, but rather something experienced as somehow deeply right and true in the opening up of possibilities. The complete evaluative concept of authenticity, then, is the notion of forerunning resoluteness and the reappropriation of a heritage for the sake of a freely inherited fate or destiny.

And yet, in spite of the richness and complexity of Heidegger's normative account of authenticity, it is arguably the formal, nonevaluative notion that figures most decisively in the overall argument of *Being and Time*. Beyond merely asserting the desirability of a life lived in responsiveness to the concrete situation and with a fateful commitment to one's projects in all their finitude and vulnerability, Heidegger's philosophical point is to show how such authentic attitudes and behaviors reveal the abiding and irreducible first-person structure of existence, my relation to my own existence being essentially asymmetrical with any relation in which I can stand to the existence of another.

Death is a crucial case in point, for death existentially understood, or what Heidegger calls "dying" (*Sterben*), is essentially mine in the way in which, for example, my body is mine, that is, *nontransferably*. Death, Heidegger says, is "nonrelational" (*unbezüglich*) and "unsurpassable" (*unüberholbar*). My own death is not just a future contingency that I might in principle prevent or defer indefinitely. Instead, it is constitutive of my existence. The death of another, by contrast, to which I stand in a merely external or third-person relation, is what Heidegger calls "demise" (*Ableben*). Demise is what we might call *biographical* death, that is, the concluding event or *dénouement* that occurs at the end of a life, drawing it to a close, rendering it a finished episode. It is no accident that I am excluded from understanding my own death under a merely biographical aspect, as others can and must; indeed, that asymmetry is precisely what defines death in its first-person dimension. Just as Merleau-Ponty observes that I would need a second body with which to perceive my own body as an object, so too I would need a second life from which to assess my own life from a biographical point of view.

And yet we typically lapse into an inauthentic understanding of death, in both a formal and an evaluative sense, by applying an undifferentiated notion of demise to ourselves as well as to others. "One dies," we say blandly. And while this is generically true, the very impersonal quality of the truth systematically obscures the non-relationality and unsurpassability my own death necessarily has for me. The popular idea that human existence has a narrative structure, with a beginning, a middle, and an end – birth, life, death – likewise blurs the distinction between the third-person perspective of a biographer and the first-person, existential perspective of the one whose existence is in question. "Authenticity," then, refers both to that first-person, existential point of view itself and to those styles of comportment that expose it and distinguish it from the generic concept of a person and the narrative notion of a life lived as a story.

Sartre

Sartre's early magnum opus, *Being and Nothingness* (1943; cited as Sartre 1956), is in large part an attempt to assimilate Heidegger's phenomenological-ontological interpretation of human existence, including his notions of authenticity and inauthenticity, into an explicit theory of consciousness, self-consciousness, subjectivity, and the drama of interpersonal interaction – themes Heidegger steadfastly avoids in *Being and Time*. As we shall see, however, owing to his competing loyalties to Heidegger and the

Cartesian tradition, Sartre's argument runs up against serious difficulties and raises questions about whether and how authentic selfhood is possible at all.

The *locus classicus* of Sartre's theory of subjectivity and authenticity is the chapter in *Being and Nothingness* on "bad faith" (*mauvaise foi*). Adapting terminology from Hegel, Sartre begins by drawing a sharp metaphysical distinction between "being-in-itself" (*l'être-en-soi*) and "being-for-itself" (*l'être-pour-soi*), the latter referring to the reflexive structure of self-awareness exhibited principally, perhaps exclusively, in human consciousness. Human agents are beings-for-themselves; mere physical objects are beings-in-themselves. Alongside this ontological distinction, Sartre also describes what he calls "the double property of the human being," two distinct aspects of being-for-itself, namely "facticity" and "transcendence" (Sartre 1956: 98). My facticity is that set of past and present facts about my body, my behavior, my character, and my social and physical situation, as they present themselves to a third-person point of view. My transcendence is the free, future-directed, first-person, conscious relation in which I stand to the world, including my own facticity. My facticity provides the setting and context of my transcendence, but my transcendence in turn determines what is important and salient for me in my facticity.

Bad faith, as Sartre conceives it, is a form of motivated irrationality in which I fail to coordinate these two aspects of myself, pretending either that I am not *responsible*, since my choices are determined by facts about my character and circumstances, or that I am not *committed*, since my possibilities always remain indefinitely open-ended. Sartre offers vivid examples of each form of bad faith. The overzealous French waiter seeks to evade responsibility for his choices by disappearing, as it were, into his stereotypical professional role. By contrast, a woman lets herself be seduced by denying to herself that letting the man hold her hand in the restaurant commits her to any kind of intimacy. The waiter wants to escape his transcendence, the woman her facticity. Both appear to be self-deceived, but Sartre argues that there is a paradox in the concept of self-deception, since deception ordinarily requires that the liar and the victim be distinct individuals. Indeed, Sartre seems to believe that self-deception is impossible, that is, that one can never really be the victim of one's own present lies. However, this does not imply that one cannot *lie* to oneself, only that one cannot *be deceived* by one's own lies. Bad faith is, in short, an *attempt* to lie to oneself by way of evading choice, an attempt Sartre thinks is doomed to fail.

Freudian psychoanalysis, by contrast, accepts the reality of self-deception and purports to explain it in terms of the dynamic interaction of conscious and unconscious subsystems within the mind. Sartre replies that all such explanations necessarily fail, for some crucial psychic mechanism must still somehow incorporate the contradictory intentions that gave rise to the paradox in the first place. If, for example, as Freud sometimes suggests, a kind of "censor" stands at the threshold of consciousness like a guard, blocking troublesome unconscious wishes from entering into a person's awareness, then the censor itself must simultaneously recognize the wish and yet try to repress it. But how is this possible? Why would the censor knowingly attempt to repress the wish? Indeed, if it knows what it's doing, Sartre asks, "What does this mean if not that the censor is in bad faith?" (Sartre 1956: 94).

Critics have complained that Sartre simply begs the question by taking for granted that all knowledge must be conscious. His point, however, has to do with the very intelligibility of supposedly unconscious psychic mechanisms as intentional systems. What Sartre's argument shows, then, is not that self-deception is impossible, but that the Freudian allegory fails to explain *how* it is possible, and that since the concept of bad faith is sufficient to describe many cases of motivated irrationality without making any appeal to unconscious attitudes, recourse to the idea of self-deception is unnecessary. Sartre does not prove that people never deceive themselves, then; he merely urges that we resist assuming so without first trying to understand their behaviors as fully conscious manifestations of bad faith.

Sartre insists, moreover, that bad faith "is an immediate, permanent threat to every project of the human being," and that "consciousness conceals in its being a permanent risk of bad faith." Nevertheless, he adds, it is possible to achieve "authenticity" (*authenticité*), which he defines, in the only passage in *Being and Nothingness* in which the word occurs, as "a self-recovery of being which was previously corrupted" (Sartre 1956: 116, 116n.). A positive account of authenticity, however, belongs to ethics, not ontology, and indeed no account of it appears in *Being and Nothingness*. Later in the text Sartre refers again to "the possibility of an ethics of deliverance and salvation," which "can be achieved only after a radical conversion," but again he defers this to consideration elsewhere (Sartre 1956: 534n.).

Why is all human conduct essentially subject to the threat of bad faith? Evidently because, for Sartre, ascriptions of intentional attitudes can never be literally true of us in the way predications of merely factual properties can be. It may be literally and unproblematically true that I was born forty years ago. But can I likewise literally and unproblematically believe that Pierre is my friend? Sartre insists that this cannot be true of me in the same way, or in the same degree: "Every belief is a belief that falls short; one never wholly believes what one believes" (Sartre 1956: 115).

Why not? One way to make sense of this paradoxical assertion is to say that Sartre construes intentional attitudes on the model of what Aristotle called "movement" (*kinêsis*), as opposed to "actuality" (*energeia*), or uncompleted as opposed to completed action (See Aristotle 1997: Book IX, 6; 2000: Book X, 4). Movements, or uncompleted actions, aim at goals outside themselves, so that in descriptions of them the imperfective does not imply the perfective: if I *am learning* French, it does not follow that I *have learned* it. Actualities, or completed actions, by contrast, are teleologically self-contained, so that the perfective implies the imperfective: if I *am sleeping*, I *have slept*.

If we regard intentional acts like *believing* as cases of uncompleted action, then it might seem that as long as I am, as it were, in the process of *believing* that Pierre is my friend, there is a sense in which I somehow haven't yet managed to believe it, since I haven't, so to speak, *finished* believing it. I could only be said to have *believed* it, with the same factual definiteness with which I could be said to be forty years old, if my believing came to an end, finally reaching its goal. But in that case I would be *done* believing and would no longer believe. For Sartre, that is, belief is an essentially self-transcending attitude and is therefore in a sense factically unrealizable. Indeed, Sartre seems to maintain that all intentional attitudes are strictly speaking factical impossibilities: "On no account can we say that consciousness is consciousness or that belief is belief." Rather, consciousness, or being-for-itself, is systematically elusive: "as soon as we wish to grasp this being, it slips between our fingers" (Sartre 1956: 122).

237

He even goes so far as to say that human reality is in general "a being which is what it is not and which is not what it is" (Sartre 1956: 100; cf. 28).

And yet, as Sartre acknowledges, "the for-itself *is*. It *is*, we may say, even if it is a being which is not what it is and which is what it is not." Consciousness is self-transcending and is therefore strictly speaking *nothing* in-itself. It is not nothing at all, of course; it *is* for-itself. To say that it *is*, then, is to affirm its *facticity*: "The for-itself *is*, in so far as it appears in a condition which it has not chosen" (Sartre 1956: 127). The *facticity* of the for-itself and being-*in-itself* are obviously different notions, and yet Sartre systematically conflates the two throughout his account. Facticity is a dimension of human existence, if only an artifact of the perspectival complexity of social self-consciousness; being-in-itself, by contrast, is a separate ontological category altogether, presumably inapplicable to consciousness, or human being. By running the two together, Sartre is able to draw dramatic but implausible conclusions about the ultimate futility of all our chosen endeavors – from believing that Pierre is my friend, to being a waiter, to being a hero or a coward. All such efforts are doomed to fail, Sartre infers, since they can only be efforts to be something *in-itself-for-itself*, an incoherent and impossible *ens causa sui*, "which religions call God. Thus the passion of man is the reverse of that of Christ, for man loses himself as man in order that God may be born. But the idea of God is contradictory and we lose ourselves in vain. Man is a useless passion" (Sartre 1956: 784).

But if Sartre's metaphysics implies the impossibility of even such things as believing and loving and being a waiter, then the implication is a *reductio ad absurdum* of the metaphysics. Indeed, the apparent paradox that consciousness "is not what it is and is what it is not" can be dissolved by insisting, as Heidegger does, that the very existence of human beings differs fundamentally from that of objects and artifacts, so that the criteria of success for their *being* anything definite differ as well. Unfortunately, unlike Heidegger, Sartre takes for granted a more traditional, homogeneous conception of being and supposes accordingly that if human beings can never be waiters or heroes in the fixed and determinate way in which a rose is a rose or a book is a book, then they can never really *be* waiters or heroes at all. But surely this is setting the bar too high, or rather in the wrong place. For people become waiters and heroes not by having either the fixed causal properties of objects or the functional attributes of tools, but by understanding themselves, and being understood, in socially conditioned ways as free, embodied agents.

As Sartre says, then, bad faith is a permanent threat to all human projects. But why is it not altogether inescapable? If all our projects essentially aim at a contradictory synthesis of the for-itself and the in-itself, how is avoiding bad faith and achieving authenticity even intelligible, let alone feasible? The concluding sentence of *Being and Nothingness* famously promises an ethics, in which one might expect to find Sartre's positive account of authenticity. The work never materialized, but Sartre's extensive notes on the subject, dating from 1947–8, were published after his death as *Notebooks for an Ethics* (Sartre 1992). He soon abandoned the project in favor of a Marxian ethic of social revolution, but the *Notebooks* confirm what is hinted at in *Being and Nothingness*, namely, that authenticity must consist in somehow keeping firmly in view the "double simultaneous aspect of the human project," that is, its transcendence and facticity, and in the end its arbitrariness and futility (Sartre 1992: 481). Whereas

"*Being and Nothingness* is an ontology before conversion," then the *Notebooks* describe a "new, '*authentic*,' way of being oneself, which transcends the dialectic of sincerity and bad faith" (Sartre 1992: 6, 474).

To transcend the dialectic of sincerity and bad faith is to escape at least one form of the self-defeating paradox seemingly entailed by the account of consciousness as uncompleted action in *Being and Nothingness.* Sartre still regards all projects as arbitrary and futile, but he now insists that in *doing* something we need not aim at *being* anything. Authenticity, he writes,

> leads to renouncing every project of being courageous (cowardly), noble (vile), etc. Because they are not realizable and because they all lead in any case to alienation. Authenticity reveals that the only meaningful project is that of *doing* (not that of being) . . . if the goal sought is *to be* courageous, the apparent and concrete end becomes a pretext for mystification . . . So, originally, authenticity consists in refusing any quest for being, because I am always *nothing.* (Sartre 1992: 475)

Rather than aspiring to *be* anything, the authentic self aims only at transcending itself in an immediate engagement with the world: "The only meaningful project is that of acting on a concrete situation and modifying it in some way" (Sartre 1992: 475). The authentic consciousness no longer strives to be God, then, but commits itself instead to "a radical decision for autonomy" (Sartre 1992: 478). Of course, *being* authentic in this sense will still mean *being* engaged and autonomous, but only as an aspect of one's facticity, not in-itself, not as a finally settled matter of fact to which one aspires self-consciously in transcending oneself toward the world.

References and Further Reading

Aristotle (1997) *Metaphysics* (trans. D. Ross). Oxford: Oxford University Press.

—— (2000) *The Nicomachean Ethics* (trans. R. Crisp). Cambridge: Cambridge University Press.

Heidegger, M. (1962) *Being and Time* (trans. J. Macquarrie and E. Robinson). New York: Harper & Row, 1962. Page references to the German edition (original work published 1927).

Kierkegaard, S. (1985) *Fear and Trembling* (trans. A. Hannay). New York: Penguin (original work published 1843).

—— (2001) *A Literary Review* (trans. A. Hannay). New York: Penguin (original work published 1846).

—— (1987) *Concluding Unscientific Postscript* (trans. H. V. Hong and E. H. Hong). Princeton, NJ: Princeton University Press (original work published 1846).

—— (1989) *The Sickness unto Death* (trans. A. Hannay). New York: Penguin (original work published 1849).

Sartre, J-P. (1956) *Being and Nothingness.* (trans. H. Barnes). New York: Philosophical Library. Page references to the Washington Square Press edition (original work published 1943).

—— (1992) *Notebooks for an Ethics* (trans. D. Pellauer). Chicago: University of Chicago Press (original work written 1947–8).

16

Affectivity

BÉATRICE HAN-PILE

Since fully covering the topic of affectivity in the short space allotted to this chapter is an impossible task, I have chosen to focus on three philosophers: Nietzsche, Heidegger, and Sartre. Of the three, only the latter was undoubtedly an existentialist – Heidegger explicitly rejected the categorization (in the *Letter on Humanism*), and there is disagreement among commentators about Nietzsche's status.[1] However, they have two major common points which justify my focusing on them: first, they uphold the primacy of existence over essence. Against the rationalist trend prevalent until the end of the eighteenth century, which saw human nature as determined *a priori* (as rational), all three authors consider human beings as living, self-interpreting entities, whose understanding of themselves is dependent on specific cultural and historical conditions. Given that this self-understanding is taken as constitutive of what it means to be human, it becomes impossible to define the essence of man independently of (let alone prior to) his existence. Secondly (and consequently), they reject the idea that philosophy can start from the study of man as a detached, disembodied consciousness primarily bent on knowing the world – or even that such a consciousness exists, except as a fiction propagated by rationalism.[2] Man is viewed as an *embodied* being, whose reason and cognitive powers are only the visible part of a much deeper and wider engagement with the world.

In turn, this rejection of the primacy of rationality and of consciousness explains the central part played by affectivity in our three authors' works. In all its forms,[3] affectivity is strongly tied to the body (although existentialist thinkers hold that it is neither identical to nor determined by physical reactions[4]): once the importance of embodiment has been recognized, an analysis of affectivity becomes necessary to understand the ways in which human beings relate both to themselves and to the world. Whereas the rationalist tradition mostly rejected affectivity,[5] either on moral grounds (as emotions interfere with self-mastery) or for epistemological reasons (because they supposedly cloud the clarity of mind required by knowledge), Nietzsche, Heidegger, and Sartre insist on rehabilitating it, mostly for two reasons: first, as it is constitutive of what it means to be human, affectivity just *cannot* be set aside – so the rationalist ideal to do away with emotions is unmasked as an illusion, the roots of which need to be investigated. Secondly, affectivity plays a crucial and potentially positive role in the constitution of the self and in our relation to the world.

240

In this chapter, I shall argue that Nietzsche considered affectivity primarily as a "psychologist" and as a *moralist*: this led him (a) to criticize his epoch as characterized by negative affects (nihilism as the "feeling of valuelessness"; Nietzsche 1968: 13) and more generally by the inability to feel properly; (b) to retrace genealogically the genesis of negative feelings (such as resentment or guilt); and (c) to sketch an analysis of the positive ways in which decadence could be overcome, and thus to establish a typology of positive affects. By contrast, both Heidegger and Sartre saw affectivity as *ontologists*: they were less interested in the moral distinction between positive and negative affects than in uncovering the deeper part played by affectivity in the disclosure of the world. This caused them (a) to refine the notion of affectivity by bringing to the fore the importance of moods (as opposed to feelings); and (b) to focus on moods that Nietzsche would have condemned as reactive (such as anxiety, boredom, or nausea, for example), the main reason for bracketing moral judgments being the high potential for ontological disclosiveness of such moods.

Nietzsche's diagnosis of the West is rather pessimistic: the modern type of person is decadent: "the diminution and leveling of European man constitutes *our* greatest danger . . . We see nothing today that wants to grow greater" (Nietzsche 1967c: 44). Central to this decline is the fact that affectivity has become sick. For Nietzsche, healthy types (exemplified by the pre-Socratics) had the instinctive ability to harmonize themselves, i.e., to both maintain and integrate inner conflicts by means of establishing a hierarchy among drives. While this harmony existed, we were attuned with ourselves, in the dual sense (a) that we could feel the smallest variations in our emotions (we were well tuned, so to speak); and (b) we instinctively knew which kind of emotions to avoid or favor, and how much of the latter we could tolerate.[6] But due to a "threatening anarchy among the instincts and [to] the fact that the foundation of the affects, which is called 'life', has been shaken" (Nietzsche 1989: 202), we have lost this inner harmony. As a result, we have also lost our ability to feel properly, i.e., in a balanced way which ultimately enhances our power. We have been deprived of our "power of resistance against stimuli and have come to be at the mercy of accidents . . . disintegration of the will" (Nietzsche 1968: 27): we have become passive, not so much in the sense that we cannot control what happens to us (not even the healthy type could), but in that we cannot integrate our emotional reactions in such a way that they make us stronger.[7]

Having become unable to deal with inner conflicts, we also have come to experience life as unbearably painful. We no longer understand that pain is necessary for life to expand, nor that happiness is not the avoidance of pain, but the ability to fully experience and overcome pain. Historically speaking, this triggered in us three apparently very different but deeply related strategies: waging a war against the senses (rationalism and Christian asceticism), trying to numb our sensibility (Buddhism), or drowning in an excess of passion (Romanticism). For Nietzsche, all three attitudes are deeply decadent in that they stem from the loss of our instinctive ability to regulate ourselves, and from the newly manifest desire to avoid pain at all costs. Thus, "those who suffer from the *impoverishment of life* . . . seek rest, stillness, calm seas, redemption from themselves through art and knowledge, or intoxication, convulsions, anaesthesia and madness" (Nietzsche 1974: 328).[8] As I have just suggested, the first twin forms taken by this search for "calm seas" are rationalism and asceticism. Both are motivated by the decadent type's inability to deal with inner conflicts and thus ultimately by fear: "fear of the senses, of the desires, of the passions, when it goes so far as to counsel us against them, is already a symptom of weakness: extreme measures always indicate abnormal conditions" (Nietzsche 1968: 408).

The first and perhaps most notable instance of such a reaction was Socrates, whom Nietzsche considers the father of rationalism:[9] being prey to a newly appeared internal tyranny of unbalanced instincts, Socrates sought to save himself by means of a "counter-tyrant", i.e., reason (Nietzsche 1997: 33). Unable to harmonize his emotions, he tried to eradicate them by becoming indifferent to his own desires and needs, and thus turned to the kind of ascetic practices attributed to him by Xenophon, such as fasting, sleeping in the snow, spending the night in the company of desirable boys without touching them, etc. At the theoretical level, he introduced the metaphysical division between the intelligible and the sensible worlds so as to depreciate the latter, and with it, the body and the senses (cf. Nietzsche 1978: the "Despisers of the body," 34–5). In doing so, he produced a deeply distorted and deleterious image of human beings as divided entities, torn between reason and affectivity (the chariot of the *Phaedrus*), and wrongly attributed to consciousness (for Nietzsche, the "small reason") the power of dominating the body (the "large reason"). As explained by the *Genealogy of Morals*, this conception of the human was taken up and made even more noxious by Christian asceticism (through the introduction of a feeling unknown to the Greeks, namely, guilt).[10] While the pre-Socratic, healthy type was "whole," "hewn out of stone" (Nietzsche 1924: 79; translation modified), the rationalist – and later the Christian – is hopelessly at war with his own affectivity.

But there is worse: whereas Socrates or the ascetic priest hoped to win this war, for Nietzsche the characteristic of our decadent age is that we have given up and only look for a peace born of exhaustion: "in an age of disintegration . . . human beings have in their bodies opposite, . . . drives that fight each other . . . Their most profound desire is that the war that they *are* should come to a rest. Happiness appears to them in agreement with tranquilising and thought" (Nietzsche 1989: 111–12). This is the second expression of the search for calm seas: not triumph over the senses, but the longing for nothingness of the Buddhist, for whom happiness "appears essentially as narcotic, drug, rest, peace . . . slackening of tension and relaxing of limbs, in short, *passively"* (Nietzsche 1967c: 38). This is an even worse form of decadence because it is more passive: whereas the rationalist prepared for battle against the senses, and thus intensified his will to power (although in a way that is ultimately self-detrimental), the Buddhist refuses to struggle altogether and hopes for extinction. Yet Nietzsche insists that it is only through conflict that life can grow – the most paradigmatic example of this is "great health," which is not the absence of illness but the ability to be stimulated by and to *overcome* sickness:[11] Buddhism is thus the worst way of treating affectivity, an "attempt to win for man an approximation to what in certain animals is *hibernation* . . . the minimum metabolism at which life still subsists without really entering consciousness" (Nietzsche 1967c: 131). At the heart of the Buddhist rejection of life there is, once more, fear – fear of suffering: "One longs for a condition in which one no longer suffers: life is actually experienced as the ground of ills; one esteems unconscious states, without feeling (sleep, fainting) as incomparably more valuable than conscious ones"[12] (Nietzsche 1968: 27).

Thus for Nietzsche both rationalism and Buddhism are two extremes that stem from the same origin, namely the loss of the pre-Socratic ability to harmonize the self. At the other end of the scale (but rooted in the same unbalance), there is the search for excitants exemplified by the Romantics, and by Wagner in particular. Such a quest is motivated by the same desire as that for calm seas: it seeks to escape a life become overly painful, this time by means of a constant drowning in an excess of passion meant to hide the background pain of existing: "'passion': a matter of nerves and wearied souls: like the delight in high mountains, deserts, storms, orgies, and horrors" (Nietzsche 1968: 826). Because we have become degenerate types that can't experience nuances or subtle feelings anymore (due to the loss of self-harmony made worse by centuries of rationalism and Christianity), we need ever stronger stimuli: yet this does not indicate strength, but weakness – "in romanticism: this constant *espressivo* is no sign of strength but of a feeling of deficiency" (Nietzsche 1968: 826). Thus "Wagner's art is sick. The problems he presents on stage – all of them problems of hysterics – the convulsive nature of his affects, his overexcited sensibility, his taste that ever required stronger spices . . . – all of this taken together represents a profile of sickness that permits no further doubt . . . Nothing is more modern than this total sickness, this lateness and overexcitement of the nervous mechanism" (Nietzsche 1967b: 5). Thus contrary to appearances, the Romantics' rejection of classicism, their emphasis on passion and self-expressivity, are just as unhealthy as the rationalist's attempt to squash emotions. In fact, they are the logical consequence of rationalism and asceticism: now that we can't feel anymore, unless we are to embrace the ascetic renunciation to life we must be *made* to feel – "Wagner represents a great corruption of music . . . His inventiveness is not inconsiderable in the art of goading again those who are weariest, calling back into life those who are half dead" (Nietzsche 1967b: 5).

However, all hope is not lost: "[man] gives rise to an interest, a tension . . . as if with him something were announcing and preparing itself, as if man were not a goal but only a way, an episode, a bridge, a great promise" (Nietzsche 1967c: 85). Although a return to pre-Socratic health is not possible (once reflectivity has settled in, it cannot be gotten rid of voluntarily – one cannot choose not to be conscious), Nietzsche gives some scattered indications of what restored health could look like for the "noble" type. The first thing to note is that it does not entail a rejection of affectivity: on the contrary, "noble mindedness" is a passion. "The passion that attacks those who are noble is peculiar . . . It involves the use of a rare and singular standard and almost a madness . . . the discovery of values for which no scales have been invented yet" (Nietzsche 1967c: 117).

However, the use of the singular here ("a passion") is significant: the noble type is governed by a "dominating passion, which even brings with it the supreme form of health: here the coordination of the inner systems and their operation in the service of one end is best achieved" (Nietzsche 1968: 408). Like the pre-Socratics, the noble type has inner harmony; however, because of the historical inheritance he is exposed to through his belonging to a later culture, he has much more to harmonize than the pre-Socratics. And because he has a much higher degree of self-awareness, such a harmonization cannot be fully instinctive: it needs "a real mastery and subtlety in waging war against oneself, in other words, self-control, self-outwitting" (Nietzsche 1989: 111). Thus Goethe, one of Nietzsche's models for the healthy individual, "carried the strongest instincts [of the eighteenth century] in him: sentimentality, idolatry of nature, the anti-historical, idealistic, unrealistic and revolutionary instincts" (Nietzsche 1997: 83). Yet faced with this inner diversity, greater than that confronted by any of the pre-Socratics, Goethe managed to unite himself through his passion for completeness: "what he wanted was totality: he fought against the separation of reason, sensation, emotion, and will . . . he disciplined himself into wholeness, he *created* himself"[13] (ibid.). Thus the healthy type does not deny his body or his senses; nor does he shrink in front of suffering. On the contrary, the ultimate proof that he is healthy lies in his ability to endure pain, and even to use it so as to further his strength. The more conflicts one can face and maintain in oneself without being destroyed by them, the richer and stronger the individual: "How much one is able to endure: distress, want, bad weather, sickness, toil, solitude . . . One stands forth as one was born, unbreakable, tensed, ready for new, even harder, remoter things, like a bow that distress only serves to draw tauter" (Nietzsche 1967c: 44).

Once health has been restored, one can experience affects and emotions in a fundamentally different way, the model for which is provided by artistic creation. Art is seen by Nietzsche as a fundamentally transformative process, whereby the artist both maximizes tensions and harmony within himself, and projects this newly acquired "perfection" onto his work: art is a transmutation of the self and of the world dependent on having the right ability to *feel*. Contrary to the rationalist and the Buddhist, the artist does not seek to deny or extinguish his emotions and feelings: quite the opposite, intoxication, by means of which the "system of emotions is excited and intensified" (Nietzsche 1997: 56), is viewed by later Nietzsche as a precondition for *all* artistic states (and not just Dionysian states, as in the early work[14]). Yet whereas romantic excesses were made necessary by a dulling of sensibility, intoxication generates the "extreme sharpness of certain senses, so they understand quite a different sign language – and create one" (Nietzsche 1968: 470). The artist's perceptions acquire the ability both to encompass the sublimely vast and to focus on the infinitesimally small: "Tremendous distances are surveyed and, as it were, for the first time apprehended . . . The refinement of the organs for the apprehension of much that is extremely small and fleeting; *divination*, the power of understanding with only the least assistance, at the slightest suggestion . . . All these climactic moments of life mutually stimulate one another" (Nietzsche 1968: 421). Yet whereas the Romantic would lose himself in this sea of new emotions, the Dionysian artist maintains his inner balance and sense of self throughout the creative process: "becoming more beautiful as the expression of a *victorious* will, of increased coordination, of a harmonizing of all the strong desires, of an infallibly perpendicular stress"[15] (Nietzsche 1968: 421). This higher openness to feelings is the sign of an increase in inner strength which feeds back into the perceptions themselves: "in this state, your own fullness leads you to enrich everything: whatever you see . . . you see as swollen, packed, vigorous, over-loaded with strength" (Nietzsche 1997: 56). Correlatively, the discharge of force in the creative process is seen as an attempt to harmonize the outside with the inside, i.e., to make the work the reflection of the artist's newly enhanced self: "In this state you transform things until they are the mirror of your own power – until they reflect your perfection. This *necessity* to transform things into perfection is – art" (Nietzsche 1997: 56).

As we have just seen, for Nietzsche the study of affectivity cannot be dissociated from a genealogical appraisal of decadence in the West, and is ultimately governed by his ethical concern for the part feelings play in the constitution of the self. By contrast, early Heidegger considers affectivity as an ontologist, and thus mostly in a non-ethical and *ahistorical* way:[16] rather than diagnosing the sickness of affectivity in the present age, he is interested in the relation between Dasein (i.e., an entity whose being involves an understanding of what it means to be) and its world. This leads him to inquire into the conditions of possibility for the disclosure of such a world. Among these, which he calls "existentials," affectedness (*Befindlichkeit*) and more specifically mood (*Stimmung*) play a major role, along with understanding (*Verstand*) and discourse (*Rede*). In §29 of *Being and Time*, Heidegger insists on three characteristics common to all moods: (a) they are indicative of Dasein's thrownness; (b) they "disclose being-in-the-world as a whole"; and (c) they make things matter to us. I shall examine them briefly in turn. Heidegger's first claim is that moods disclose thrownness as the "facticity of being delivered over" (Heidegger 1962: 136) to a world which we do not choose, nor constitute. "In affectedness Dasein is always brought before itself, and has always found itself . . . in the sense of finding itself in the mood that it has" (Heidegger 1962: 136). By insisting on the passivity and groundlessness inherent to our being thrown, moods indicate "a disclosive submission to the world" (Heidegger 1962: 137–8). Heidegger establishes against Husserl the impossibility of taking the subject as an autonomous and isolated starting point for phenomenological analysis: thus, "a mood assails us. It comes neither from the 'outside' nor from 'inside', but arises out of being-in-the-world, as a way of such being" (Heidegger 1962: 136). Dasein finds itself already in its mood and beyond itself, already attuned in ways that are beyond its control. It is not possible for it to attain the kind of mood-less state that Husserl thinks the epochê will provide: as Nietzsche had already seen, even the so-called objectivity of the scientist involves moods. Thus we are never free of moods" (Heidegger 1962: 136). The same desire to refute any solipsistic or internalist interpretation of moods governs Heidegger's insistence on their publicness: "publicness, as the kind of being which belongs to the 'One', not only has in general its own way of having a mood, but needs moods and 'makes' them for itself"[17] (Heidegger 1962: 139).

The second claim is that in revealing our thrownness, moods reveal being-in-the-world itself: thus, "in having a mood, Dasein is always disclosed mood-wise as that entity to which it has been delivered over in its being . . . which, in existing, it has to be" (Heidegger 1962: 134). Although our moods are changeable, the fact that we have moods is not: a mood-less Dasein would not be Dasein. Yet most of the time we do not *know* which mood we are in: "[in mood] Dasein is disclosed to itself *prior* to all cognition and volition, and *beyond* their range of disclosure"[18] (Heidegger 1962: 136). Moods are the very background on which both world and Dasein are disclosed, and from which only mental directedness toward objects is possible: "mood has already disclosed, in every case, being-in-the-world as a whole, and makes it possible first of all to direct oneself towards something"[19] (Heidegger 1962: 136). Moods are thus ontologically prior to any form of mental directedness: "Only because the 'senses' [*Sinne*] belong ontologically to an entity whose kind of being is being-in-the-world with a affectedness can they be 'touched' by anything or 'have a sense for' something in such

245

a way that what touches them shows itself as an affect" (Heidegger 1962: 138). This discovery explains the third characteristic of moods: the fact that entities can "matter" to it [Dasein] is grounded in one's affectedness" (Heidegger 1962: 138). We do not encounter neutral entities on which we would project subjective emotional qualities. On the contrary, we can only be affected by entities, and thus react to them or make decisions regarding them, if they have *already* been disclosed to us as attractive, fearsome, boring, etc., by the mood we are in. Heidegger gives the example of boredom: "[a book] can ultimately be boring only because the attunement already plays around it. It does not cause the boredom, nor does it receive it merely as something attributed by the subject. In short: boredom – and thus ultimately every attunement – is a hybrid, partly objective, partly subjective"[20] (Heidegger 2001: 88). So while being boring is a genuine aspect of the book, boredom is the background affectedness on the basis of which it is disclosed as boring.

While Dasein always has moods, some moods, however, are more fundamental than others in that they do not only disclose entities, but also the very structure of being-in-the world. This is particularly clear in the case of anxiety: "that in the face of which one has anxiety is not an entity-within-the-world" (Heidegger 1962: 186); on the contrary, it is "completely indeterminate" (ibid.). Contrary to fear, anxiety has no worldly object: "*that in the face of which one has anxiety is being-in-the-world as such*" (ibid.). Heidegger elaborates on this claim by indicating that in anxiety, the relevance for us of entities in the world disappears. The fact that they do not matter to us anymore allows the whole network of significance, which usually is both presupposed and covered up by our involvement with the world, to come forward. Thus, "on the basis of this *insignificance* of what is within-the-world, the world in its worldhood is all that still obtrudes itself" (Heidegger 1962: 187). The two slightly different claims ("the *world as such* is that in the face of which one has anxiety; Heidegger 1962: 186–7) and "*being-in-the-world itself* is that in the face of which anxiety is anxious"; Heidegger 1962: 187; emphasis added in both cases) are complementary. When our involvement with entities is absent, the world appears to offer us an infinite field of possibilities; however, this very infinity, joined with our temporary impossibility of practically engaging with worldly entities (or making decisions about them), reveals our "nullity," i.e., the groundlessness of being-in-the-world. If nothing matters to us, it also becomes clear that while many forms of involvement are possible, we have no ground for committing ourselves to anything. From this follows a third characteristic of anxiety: "Anxiety makes manifest in Dasein its *being towards* its ownmost potentiality for being – i.e. its *being free* for the freedom of choosing itself and taking hold of itself. Anxiety brings Dasein face to face with its *being free for*, the authenticity of its being" (Heidegger 1962: 188).

Thus Heidegger shows that while all moods can form the background of the disclosure of entities, some moods – anxiety in particular[21] – are especially disclosive in that they reveal the ontological lineaments of being-in-the-world. Sartre develops this idea by showing the part played by another mood, nausea, and by bringing to the fore an element which remains very embryonic in Heidegger's thought, namely, the connection between affectivity and embodiment. He identifies two fundamental moods: nausea and anxiety.[22] Each of them, when properly analyzed, reveals a fundamental aspect of consciousness's existence: nausea brings out its primordial relation to its body, and thus its contingency. Conversely, anxiety highlights consciousness's ability to transcend this contingency, and thus its freedom. While these assertions are clearly reformulations of Heidegger's first two claims about mood in §29 of *Being and Time* (respectively, they reveal thrownness and being-in-the-world), there are two important differences: first, whereas Heidegger thought that this was conjointly true of *all* moods, and especially true of anxiety, Sartre separates these disclosive aspects to refer each to a *specific* mood, and does not talk much about moods in general. Secondly, while Heidegger implicitly considered Dasein as a fairly disincarnated entity, Sartre's analysis of the two primordial moods is designed to emphasize consciousness's relation to its body.

This is particularly clear in the case of nausea. According to Sartre, nausea occurs when we are not aware of any particular pure affective quality: this unusual lack generates *a contrario* an awareness of the pure fact that we are embodied, and thus of our finitude as something indefinable and yet heavy and repellent: "coenaesthetic affectivity is then the pure . . . apprehension [*saisie*] of a contingency without colour, a pure apprehension of the self as *de facto* existence" (Sartre 1958: 338). In this case, we experience a "perpetual apprehension . . . of an *insipid* and distanceless taste": a "discrete and insurmountable nausea perpetually reveals my body to my consciousness" (Sartre 1958: 338, translation modified). Although Sartre's insistence on embodiment is not Heideggerian, there are three common points with Heidegger here: first, nausea is an ontological feature. Sartre underlines that far from being an empirical aversion, it is the transcendental condition of possibility for "concrete and empirical nauseas, in front of rotten meat, fresh blood, excrements, etc." (ibid.). Secondly, like anxiety, nausea has two modes of being: on the one hand, it constantly lurks in the background of our relation to the world and to ourselves, generating a vague feeling of unease and distaste. On the other, this impression can be thematized and become an acute awareness of our contingency (as Roquentin experiences in *Nausea*; Sartre 1969). Finally, nausea induces the kind of comportment described by Heidegger as falling. Sartre indicates that our non-positional awareness of embodiment may spur us to seek physical pain or pleasure, which consciousness can transcend within the framework of affective projects which then hide its own contingency from it. However (like anxiety), nausea is inescapable: "as soon as pain or pleasure are existed by consciousness, they in turn manifest its facticity and its contingency, and are uncovered on the background of this nausea" (Sartre 1958: 338, translation modified).

What anxiety discloses is not the burden of existing but human freedom. When I am anxious, I become aware of two things: (a) that nothing in the world can determine my choices because I am radically separated from the in-itself[23] by my nihilating activity (therefore nothing can act as a "cause" on me unless I construe it as such, thematically or non thematically); and (b) that nothing *in myself* can determine my choices either. Anxiety forces me to adopt the standpoint of pure reflection[24] and thus to abandon bad faith in order to realize that what I see as myself (the ego) is a construct to which I can't be identified.

A "nothingness has slipped into the heart of my relation to myself: I am not the one I shall be . . . because what I am is not the foundation of what I will be [in the sense that my present does not *determine* my future, the idea that the past is causally active is an illusion of impure reflection]. Finally, because no existing being can determine strictly what I am going to be. . . . *I am the self which I will be on the mode of not being it* . . . Anxiety is precisely the consciousness of being one's own future on the mode of not being it. (Sartre 1958: 31–2, translation modified)

Thus freedom is revealed by anxiety as the pure nihilating activity of consciousness: "for the for-itself, to be is to nihilate the in-itself which it is. Under these conditions, freedom can be nothing other than this nihilation" (Sartre 1958: 439). As far as the relation of original affectivity to the body is concerned, the two moods work in opposite ways: while nausea is the revelation of the inescapability of physical embodiment (because consciousness cannot fully transcend its body), anxiety shows that its being embodied does not determine consciousness (because the latter constantly transcends its corporeity, although the process is made infinite by the fact that it cannot be completed). Thus although it is less apparent, anxiety has no less relation to the body than nausea – in this regard, it is perhaps also significant that the starting point chosen by Sartre should be that of vertigo, which involves strong bodily sensations (although, of course, anxiety is not a physical or empirical form of vertigo).

While Nietzsche was mostly interested in the transformative part played by affectivity for the constitution of the self, and on establishing a typology of feelings and emotions, Heidegger and Sartre focused on the ontological disclosiveness of moods. Whereas Nietzsche's perspective was strongly influenced by his antagonism to Christianity, Heidegger's own views (in particular about anxiety) were partially shaped by his reading of Kierkegaard[25] and by his own Christian upbringing. There are also substantial differences between Sartre's and Heidegger's ontological assumptions (in particular regarding the status of consciousness and negation) which I have overlooked for the sake of brevity. Yet all three authors have a strong common point, which is that they have made it impossible for philosophers to ignore the central part played by affectivity both in the constitution of the self and in the disclosure of the world. They indicated research directions which more recent developments within the continental tradition explored further – in particular, Maurice Merleau-Ponty for embodiment and Michel Henry for the notion of original affectivity.

Notes

1 Some commentators, like Alexander Nehamas (1987) or Tracy Strong (1988), favor a so-called "existentialist" interpretation of key themes such as the Eternal Return; others, like Brian Leiter (2002), read Nietzsche as a naturalist.
2 The case is less clear for Sartre because of Husserl's influence on his philosophy. On the other hand, Sartre repeatedly criticized Husserl for failing to see that consciousness is always *engaged* in the world.
3 By "affectivity," I mean a generic term covering affects, emotions, feelings, passions, and moods. Owing to lack of space, I cannot expand here on the conceptual differences between these notions.
4 Perhaps the clearest rejection of this view can be found in Sartre 1971.
5 Roughly speaking, the trend started with Plato's famous claim (in the *Phaedo*) that the body is a tomb, *sôma sêma*. However, there are notable exceptions, such as Descartes (who

recognized the positive part played by some passions, such as generosity or admiration) and more extensively, Spinoza.

6   Thus the healthy type "has a taste only for what is good for him: his pleasure, his delight cease when the measure of what is good for him is transgressed" (Nietzsche 1967a: 224).

7   In Nietzsche's physiological terms, we have lost the capacity to "digest" events: our emotional reactions are overly quick and leave us at the mercy of whatever feeling rises in us (contrary to the healthy type, who "reacts slowly to all kinds of stimuli, with that slowness which long caution and deliberate pride have bred in him: he examines the stimulus that approaches him, he is far from meeting it halfway"; Nietzsche 1967a: 224.

8   Such a redemption has become necessary because the self is unbalanced. The (failed) attempt to redeem oneself through art is exemplified by Wagner, while Schopenhauer is the (equally flawed) model of redemption through knowledge.

9   This is a debatable point: for a contrary interpretation, see for example, Kaufmann 1974. My own reading of Socrates can be found in Han-Pile 2000.

10   Owing to lack of space, I cannot expand here on the genealogy of moral feelings. Apart from the *Genealogy of Morals*, the most relevant passages are in *Beyond Good and Evil* (Nietzsche 1989: in particular §§201, 260). The main difference with *The Genealogy of Morals* (Nietzsche 1967c) is that in *Beyond Good and Evil* (Nietzsche 1989), Nietzsche views the development of moral feelings as a reaction of the *herd* itself against the strong once a minimum of social stability has been achieved. The same aggressive drives that were praised for their usefulness against external dangers are "now experienced as dangerous" and "branded and slandered most" (Nietzsche 1989: 113). By contrast, *The Genealogy of Morals* puts a very strong emphasis on the part played by a specific type, the ascetic priest, in the genesis of moral feelings. The priest is responsible for such crucial (and detrimental) "inventions" as the soul and bad conscience (Nietzsche 1967c: II, §16) or guilt (Nietzsche 1967c: III, §20), as well as for the unleashing of resentment – which, interestingly, is not a new feeling: it was occasionally felt by the strong, but in such a way that it was not internalized and thus did not "poison" ("Resentment itself, should it appear in the noble man, consummates and exhausts itself in an immediate reaction, and therefore does not *poison*; on the other hand, it fails to appear at all on countless occasions on which it inevitably appears in the weak and the impotent", Nietzsche 1967c: I. 38). The priest is also the originator of a panoply of negative feelings, such as "love of the neighbour" (in fact grounded in fear of the neighbor; Nietzsche 1989: §201), pity (which weakens the strong by spreading suffering), altruism and self-sacrifice (fundamentally forms of self-gratification, the "petty pleasures" required to encourage the Christian to go on living his sick existence, Nietzsche 1967c: §18). To these, Nietzsche opposes the "pathos of distance" of the noble type (Nietzsche 1989: 201) or "love of the enemies" (Nietzsche 1967c: I. 38).

11   "For a typically healthy person . . . being sick can even become an energetic *stimulus* for life, for living *more*. This, in fact, is how that long period of sickness appears to me now: as it were, I discovered life anew, including myself; I tasted all good and even little things, as others cannot easily taste them – I turned my will to health, to *life*, into a philosophy" (Nietzsche 1967a: 224).

12   Cf. Nietzsche 1967c: 134: "The hypnotic sense of nothingness, the repose of deepest sleep, in short *absence of suffering* – sufferers and those profoundly depressed will count this as the supreme good, as the value of values."

13   See also: "to be classical, one must possess *all* the strong, seemingly contradictory gifts and desires – but in such a way that they go together beneath one yoke . . . to reflect a total state (of a people or of a culture) in one's deepest and innermost soul" (Nietzsche 1968: 446). On the question of the self-transformation potentially triggered by Nietzsche's own writings, see Solomon 2004.

14 In *The Birth of Tragedy* (Nietzsche 1995), Nietzsche distinguished between two main categories to think of art: the Apollonian and the Dionysian. The first, whose physiological analogon is dream, is referred to the principle of individuation and to self-mastery. The Apollonian artist (the archetype of which is Homer) serenely produces clearly individuated and luminous "dream images" (the heroes). By contrast, Dionysian states (exemplified by intoxication) are characterized by the loss of selfhood and self-control, and a return to primordial and violent forms of affectivity. Nietzsche mentions Archilochus as a paradigm of the Dionysian artist. A good example of this loss of self is provided by Sophocles' depiction of the maenads in the *Bacchae*.

15 This implicitly refers to what Nietzsche calls the "pathos of distance," i.e., among other things, the necessity for the higher type to distantiate himself not only from others, but also from himself. This creates a constant inner tension (as our natural impulse is to flow with our drives), also illustrated in Nietzsche's work by the metaphors of the yoke and of the bow.

16 After the "turn," Heidegger will change his approach and insist on the historical character of certain moods (in particular, wonder). See, in particular, Heidegger 1958.

17 This collective character of moods is particularly apparent in the case of strong moods – I remember being in Paris when France won the football World Cup. Even though I neither knew nor cared about football, I was swept away by an atmosphere of enthusiasm, pride, and optimism which lasted for days and transformed the most mundane activities, such as taking the subway, into a shared experience of slightly dazed happiness.

18 This is emphasized in another passage, which asserts that "the possibilities of disclosure which belong to cognition reach far too short a way compared with the *primordial disclosure belonging to moods*, in which Dasein is brought before its being as 'there'" (Heidegger 1962: 134; emphasis added).

19 Cf. also the following: "attunement is not something inconstant, fleeting, merely subjective; rather because attunement is the originary way in which every Dasein is as it is, it is not what is most inconstant, but that which gives Dasein *subsistence and possibility* in its very foundations" (Heidegger 2001: 64).

20 This third characteristic of moods commits Heidegger to a plurirealist view of the world: to paraphrase a famous passage of *Being and Time*, the bear we come across in the forest is not the same as that calmly studied by the naturalist. The first, being encountered in a specific environment (say, my walking alone and without any means of defense) and on the background of a specific mood (fear), is fearsome. The second, encountered on the background of a different mood (*theoria*, not as the absence of mood but as a mood of scientific detachment and impartiality; cf. Heidegger 1962: 138), is not.

21 Deep boredom, in which case "entities as a whole have become indifferent" (Heidegger 2001: 208), is another such mood. Heidegger 1993 offers a revised treatment of anxiety, which is now seen as disclosive of the "nothing of the world."

22 It could be argued that there is a third fundamental mood, namely, shame, if only because the latter discloses another fundamental dimension of consciousness's existence, i.e., intersubjectivity. However, Sartre explicitly refers to it as an "*emotional* attitude," not as a mood. As I do not have the space here to present a developed argument, I have left the issue aside entirely. Cf. Cabestan 1999.

23 In the introduction and first chapter of *Being and Nothingness* (Sartre 1958), Sartre distinguishes between two fundamental modes of being: the in-itself and the for-itself. The first is non-reflective and thus "opaque." It is the mode of being of things and objects. By contrast, the for-itself is a reflective mode of being typical of human beings. It is the spontaneous movement whereby consciousness separates itself not only from all its objects, but also from itself (as a content). Sartre expresses this by saying that the characteristic of the for-itself is negation. This distinction is seminal in that it allows Sartre (among other things) to

differentiate between pure and impure reflection, between consciousness and the ego, and here, between authenticity and bad faith.

24 For Sartre, the main characteristic of pure reflection has no content and is the true movement of consciousness: it is a reflection almost in the optical sense, as it is dependent on consciousness always having objects from which it separates itself by having a non-positional awareness (of) itself as intending them. Sartre puts it clearly in the following passage: "it is by means of that of which it is conscious that consciousness distinguishes itself in its own eyes and that it can be self-consciousness; a consciousness which would not be consciousness (of) something would be consciousness (of) nothing" (Sartre 1958: 173). Pure reflection is thus both transparent and elusive, due to the fact that consciousness can only appear to itself indirectly (non-positionally), as the self-negating activity whereby objects are intended: "pure reflection, the simple presence of the reflective for-itself to the reflected for-itself, is at once the original form of reflection and its ideal form (Sartre 1958: 155; translation modified). By contrast, impure reflection is "what gives itself primarily in everyday life" and explains the constitution of the ego: it "constitutes the succession of psychical facts or psyche ... Its motivation is within it in a twofold movement of interiorization and objectification: to apprehend the reflected as an in-itself in order to turn oneself into this in-itself which is apprehended" (Sartre 1958: 159–60; translation modified). As a result, the ego is not really identical to consciousness: it is "in-itself, not for-itself . . . It is always given as having been there before consciousness – and at the same time as possessing depths which have to be revealed gradually. Thus the ego appears to consciousness as a transcendent in-itself, as an existent in the human world, not as consciousness" (Sartre 1958: 103; translation modified).

25 In particular, Kierkegaard 1981.

References and Further Reading

Cabestan, P. (1999) Qu'est-ce que s'émouvoir? Emotion et affectivité chez Sartre (literal translation). *Alter* 7, 91–120.

Han-Pile, B. (2000) Nietzsche and the masters of truth: The Presocratics and Christ. In M. Wrathall and J. Malpas (eds.), *Heidegger, Authenticity, and Modernity* (pp. 165–86). Cambridge, MA: MIT Press.

Heidegger, M. (1958) *What is Philosophy?* (trans. J. T. Wilde and W. Kluback). New Haven, CT: College and University Press (original work published 1956).

—— (1962) *Being and Time* (trans. E. Macquarrie and J. Robinson). Oxford: Blackwell Publishing (original work published 1927). Pagination refers to page numbers given in the original German version and indicated by marginal denumeration in Heidegger 1962.

—— (1993) What is metaphysics? (trans. D. Krell). In D. Krell (ed.), *Basic Writings* (pp. 89–110). New York: Harper & Row (original work published 1929).

—— (2001) *Fundamental Concepts of Metaphysics* (trans. W. McNeill and N. Walker). Indianapolis: Indiana University Press (original work published 1929).

Kaufmann, W. (1974) *Nietzsche: Philosopher, Psychologist, Antichrist*. Princeton, NJ: Princeton University Press.

Kierkegaard, S. (1981) *The Concept of Anxiety* (trans. R. Thomte and A. Anderson). Princeton, NJ: Princeton University Press (original work published 1844).

Leiter, B. (2002) *Nietzsche on Morality*. New York: Routledge.

Nehamas, A. (1987) *Nietzsche: Life as Literature*. Cambridge, MA: Harvard University Press.

Nietzsche, F. (1924) *Early Greek Philosophy & Other Essays* (trans. M. A. Mügge). New York: Macmillan (original work written 1873).

—— (1967a) *Ecce Homo* (trans. W. Kaufmann). New York: Vintage (original work published 1888).

—— (1967b) *The Case against Wagner* (trans. W. Kaufmann). New York: Vintage (original work published 1888).

—— (1967c) *The Genealogy of Morals* (trans. W. Kaufmann). New York: Vintage (original work published 1887).

—— (1968) *The Will to Power* (trans. W. Kaufmann). New York: Vintage Books (original work published 1901).

—— (1974) *The Gay Science* (trans. W. Kaufmann). New York: Vintage (original work published 1882).

—— (1978) *Thus Spake Zarathustra* (trans. W. Kaufmann). New York: Penguin (original work published 1891).

—— (1989) *Beyond Good and Evil* (trans. W. Kaufmann). New York: Vintage (original work published 1886).

—— (1995) *The Birth of Tragedy* (trans. C. P. Fadiman). New York: Dover (original work published 1872).

—— (1997) *Twilight of the Idols* (trans. R. Polt). Indianapolis: Hackett (original work published in 1889).

Sartre, J-P. (1958) *Being and Nothingness* (trans. H. Barnes). London: Methuen (original work published in 1943).

—— (1969) *Nausea* (trans. L. Alexander). New York: New Directions (original work published 1938).

—— (1971) *Sketch for a Theory of Emotions* (trans. P. Mairet). London: Methuen (original work published 1939).

Solomon, R. (2004) *Living with Nietzsche: What the Great Immoralist Has to Teach Us*. Oxford: Oxford University Press.

Strong, T. (1988) *Nietzsche and the Politics of Transfiguration*, revised edn. Berkeley: University of California Press.

17

The Body

PIOTR HOFFMAN

In responding to the challenge of Cartesian dualism, Sartre and Merleau-Ponty seem to have adopted a very similar approach. The task of a phenomenological study of the body is to bring out a level of experience where the experiencing subject can be said to *be* its body. According to both philosophers, the mind–body dualism and its difficulties stem from an approach whereby the experiencing subject's body is viewed by the subject from a third-person standpoint, that is, as an object among other objects. Moreover, it is quite natural to adopt this "objective" attitude toward one's own body. Since the bodies of others are objects I encounter within the field of my perception and action, and since my body is an object the others encounter within the field of their perception and action, it is easy and tempting to apply *that* conception of the body within my understanding of my own body. The philosophical dualism is then all but inevitable, for I cannot understand how I as a subject of mental experiences could ever be united with my body-object. For both Sartre and Merleau-Ponty any hope of avoiding this outcome hinges upon our ability to show that our body (and not just our "mind") is accessible to us in the first-person experience and accessible to us in such a way that our conscious life appears *eo ipso* as embodied. By contrast, the conception of our body as an object should not be taken as primordial on the experiential level.

Yet even within this shared broad assumption significant differences between the two thinkers can be detected. For Sartre, the first-person status of my body (my body as a "being-for-itself") is not only "radically distinct," but even "incommunicable" with the status of my body as object (Sartre 1956: 304). Merleau-Ponty rejects such a radical separation between these two modes of experiencing one's own body. Take, for example, our sense of touch. For Sartre to touch (here the body functions as a subject) and to be touched (here the body is an object) represent two essentially different orders of phenomena. To be sure, when I am touching the floor with my leg, I can also, and at the same time, touch my leg with my hand; or, again, my hands can touch each other. But these experiences of the so-called "double sensation" are unessential to the for-itself status of the body and can have no significance within the phenomenological account of the first-person experience of our body (Sartre 1956: 358). This is not Merleau-Ponty's view even in *Phenomenology of Perception* (1945; cited as Merleau-Ponty 1962), to say nothing of the posthumously published *The Visible and the Invisible*

(1964; cited as Merleau-Ponty 1968). The hand as touching and the same hand as touched are not, as in Sartre, "radically distinct" and "incommunicable." The hand has an "equivocal status as touching and touched" (Merleau-Ponty 1962: 95); as I look at and touch my inert right hand, so far only a "bundle of bones and muscles" (Merleau-Ponty 1962: 93), I already "anticipate" (ibid.) the same hand as an exploring and touching power; and this double status of my hand as both a subject of exploration, a part of my "phenomenal body," *and* an object touched and explored, is by no means unessential to the first-person phenomenological account of my body (ibid.).

Still, although this particular difference between Sartre's and Merleau-Ponty's accounts of the body becomes of paramount importance in *The Visible and the Invisible*, in *Phenomenology of Perception* it is kept in the background. Both *Being and Nothingness* and *Phenomenology of Perception* are devoted mainly to the task of bringing out the primacy of the body as subject: of the "phenomenal body" in Merleau-Ponty, of the body as "being-for-itself" in Sartre. And it is precisely from within this common focus upon the body as subject that Merleau-Ponty advances a significant objection against the corresponding part of Sartre's theory. In *Being and Nothingness*, as readers of the work may recall, Sartre argues that this or that object within our world can emerge as an "obstacle" offering us a degree of "resistance" only in the light of certain free projects of human individuals. Even this may be saying too little; Sartre's point is not simply that what counts as an obstacle or resistance is interpreted in this way only in the light of our freely chosen ends, but that, in point of fact, the very *concept* of a resisting obstacle is meaningless outside of our human understanding of reality (Sartre 1956: 488). Sartre illustrates his theory with, among other things, an analysis of a rock apprehended as an obstacle by a potential climber (Sartre 1956: 482, 488–9). The rock is viewed as such an obstacle (as endowed with the *meaning* "non-scalable" rather than "scalable," as Sartre puts it), only given the free project of the climber to scale the rock. In the last chapter of *Phenomenology of Perception* Merleau-Ponty takes up this example and shows what he thinks are the shortcomings inherent in Sartre's account. "Whether or not I have decided to climb them, these mountains appear high to me because they exceed my body's power to take them in its stride" (Merleau-Ponty 1962: 440). Merleau-Ponty is here saying that I need not form the specific project of climbing these mountains to see that they (or a huge rock, for that matter) are beyond the power of my body " to take them in its stride" (*la prise de mon corps*); in this sense the mountains do have a meaning, but it is not a meaning attributed to them by a free project of my ends (Merleau-Ponty 1962: 441). According to Merleau-Ponty, here as elsewhere, the Sartrean absolute freedom of the for-itself must be anchored in a field of meaning already pregiven to it – in this case, in a field of meaning laid out by our phenomenal body.

Replying to this line of criticism of Sartre, Simone de Beauvoir has accused Merleau-Ponty of ignoring the role of *facticity* in Sartre's phenomenology; and, in pressing this point, Beauvoir has brought in, as the key support for her claim, a number of passages from Sartre's phenomenology of the body as experienced in the first person, in its "first ontological dimension," as Sartre has it. She draws our attention to the fact that for Sartre the for-itself is not only a free "surpassing" and "transcendence," but an inherently perspectival and "embodied" consciousness which thereby "loses itself" in the world just as much as it "surpasses" it (de Beauvoir 1998: 450–1).[1]

Is Merleau-Ponty's criticism of Sartre justified? And, if it is, what are the underlying differences in their accounts of the body as experienced in the first person, prior to its objectification in the third-person standpoint? In what follows I propose to shed some light on this issue.

Let us begin with the relevant features of Sartre's account. The body-for-itself is discovered as an item in the structure of our being-in-the-world; the two internally related poles of this structure – the world and the for-itself – indicate the essentially embodied character of consciousness.

To start with the world: in both perception and action the world is experienced as a perspectival and orientated field made up of objects ("instrumental-things," as Sartre calls them) ordered in terms of "right" and "left," "before" and "behind," and so on (Sartre 1956: 306). While the specific form of this ordering will vary to a lesser or greater degree, the presence of some such ordering of "instrumental-things" is their *necessary* feature. It is "not even *conceivable*" (ibid.) that a world stripped of these features could be experienced by consciousness; and since experience remains, in the last analysis, the ground of all meaning, the conception of such a world would be altogether meaningless. Now, this is simply another way of saying that the world refers, and necessarily so, to a *situated* agent and perceiver; the world refers to a conscious being endowed with a *point of view*. Thus, from the necessity of an orientation of instrumental-things we can infer that for the for-itself "to be is to be there" (Sartre 1956: 308), i.e., in a particular location in reference to which the presently experienced orientation of instrumental-things is determined. But to have that location – to be "there in that chair," "there at the top of that mountain," to take Sartre's examples (ibid.) – presupposes that the for-itself be embodied. Of course, there is a difference between this or that location my body happens to occupy and the body itself. The chair or the mountain *can* become objects within my perceptual field: I can get up from the chair, take a few steps to the left, and look at the chair from there; similarly, I can descend from the mountain and look at it from a viewpoint in the valley below. But I can perform no such feat with that privileged location offered to me by my body: I can't look at my body while being located somewhere else. The body *is* my point of view, but it is "the point of view on which I can't take a point of view" (Sartre 1956: 340).

Thus far, Sartre's account is quite in line with Merleau-Ponty's. For Merleau-Ponty, too, the world we experience is experienced in perspective and with an orientation; and for Merleau-Ponty too this perspectival and orientated character of the world refers to our body as to our permanent point of view upon the world (Merleau-Ponty 1962: 67, 70, 90–1). But does Merleau-Ponty understand this function of our body in the same way that Sartre does?

To bring this out we must take a closer look at the way in which the Sartrean for-itself experiences *itself* as the point of view upon the world. This experience is, in fact, a manifestation of an "ontological necessity" (Sartre 1956: 308) for the for-itself. All of the for-itself's perceptions of the world must represent a view from somewhere; all of the for-itself's actions must be undertaken given the location of the for-itself as their starting point. But this ontological necessity for the for-itself to exist as situated should not hide two contingencies: it is contingent that the for-itself exists at all, and it is contingent that it has this (rather than some other) point of view upon the world. For this reason, the body belongs to the *facticity* of the for-itself (Sartre 1956: 308) and it can be "defined" as "*the contingent form which is assumed by the necessity of my contingency*" (Sartre 1956: 309). Correlatively, the world can be shown to refer to the body as *so* defined: for while it is necessary that the world must have *some* order (i.e., some distribution of instrumental-things in terms of "left," "right," "before," "behind," etc.) it is contingent that it happens to have *this* particular order in a given person's experience.

Still more is involved in this notion of the body as the for-itself's point of view. Take our sight, for example. The visual field does show a certain orientation, and a certain perspective, of the items we see; and this orientation and perspective refer to our eye as to the point of view from which we look at the world. But how is the eye itself given to the for-itself in the body's "first ontological dimension"? In this mode, at least, the eye itself can't be an object of sight: the eye can't see itself as seeing (Sartre 1956: 304, 316). I can, of course, touch my eyeball, or scrutinize it in the mirror; and we can even imagine a living being whose one eye would be capable of gazing upon his other eye as the latter gazes upon the world – in all such cases, however, the eye would not be experienced *as seeing* (Sartre 1956: 304). But if our body as subject is thus "inapprehensible" (Sartre 1956: 328), aren't we left with something akin to Descartes's mere "thought of seeing," its perspectival character notwithstanding? Sartre thinks not. To be sure, the eye as seeing is indeed not given as an object of sensory experience; but still, the particular ordering of my visual experience (say, the street appears closer than the tree, which in turn appears to the left of the lake, etc.) includes an "abstract indication" (Sartre 1956: 317) of my eye as the "center" (ibid.) referred to by the present ordering of instrumental-things within my visual field. And at least this abstract indication points to my eye as to an "object" (ibid.), that is, to something "in the midst of the world" (ibid.). This, then, is how my eye is indicated to me as seeing.

But how are we to understand this "abstract indication" of my body by the perceptual field? It is at this point that we can begin to notice fundamental differences between Sartre's and Merleau-Ponty's understanding of the body as our point of view upon the world. Here, for example, is what Sartre writes about our perception of *distance*. "If the object gets smaller when moving away, we must not explain this by some kind of illusion in the observer, but by the strictly external laws of perspective. Thus by these *objective* laws a strictly *objective* center of reference is defined" (Sartre 1956: 317; my emphasis). The same type of explanation (in terms of some such "objective" laws) is said to be valid for all senses (Sartre 1956: 318–19).

Merleau-Ponty's account is very different. Consider again the case of our perception of distance: for example, the perception of a car resting in front of me and then driving away (Merleau-Ponty 1962: 256). On the various accounts Merleau-Ponty here criticizes, the perception of the increasing interval between myself and the car would be determined, above all, by the diminishing apparent size of the car and the changes in the convergence of my eyes. The car diminishing in size, the eyes and the changing degree of their convergence, the interval between myself and the car – all of this would be located in the objective world and, in that purely objective capacity, would be determining my perception of distance. But what kind of "determining" would this be? Here, as elsewhere, Merleau-Ponty criticizes the two competing "objective" accounts: the *causal* explanation of perception and the intellectualist reconstruction of it in terms of *judgments*. The causal explanation tells us nothing about our *experience* of distance.

The apparent sizes of the car, the changing convergence of the eyes, as well as the registration of these occurrences by the brain are, to be sure, the perception's "factual conditions" (Merleau-Ponty 1962: 258), but they do not suffice to account for the *experience* of distance, that is, for its "immanent significance" (ibid.). So far, however, Sartre would be in agreement with Merleau-Ponty. When Sartre speaks of those "objective laws" determining our perception of distance he does not simply mean some causal laws (of optics, physiology, etc.) conditioning our perceptual experience; indeed, any such supposition would be in principle unacceptable to Sartre. In general, there are no laws of consciousness; there is only consciousness of laws (Sartre 1956: lv). As far as perception is concerned, we cannot say that its factual conditions determine it causally, since it is consciousness itself which "determines itself as perception" (Sartre 1956: liv). This does not mean, of course, that consciousness is free to perceive anything it wishes, but it does mean – for Sartre just as much as for Merleau-Ponty – that the perceptual experience, like any other experience, can only be understood in its own terms.

On the other hand, the intellectualist account of our perception of distance – at least as reconstructed by Merleau-Ponty – is almost indistinguishable from Sartre's account. The experience of distance involves an *interpretation* of certain factual data (the apparent size of the car, the convergence of the eyes, etc.) as the "signs" of distance. This interpretation is itself "conditioned by my knowledge that there is a world of undistortable objects, that my body is standing in front of this world like a mirror . . . in other words by my inclusion of my eyes, body and the external world into one and the same objective space" (Merleau-Ponty 1962: 257). There is nothing here that departs from the general thrust of Sartre's own argument. Although, on this type of account, the perceiving body must be included in the objective space, it need not be itself *directly* perceived. Sartre's "abstract indication" of my body by the perceptual field (in this case, by the field which includes that car driving away from me) will do just as well in this respect; for, even if not directly perceived but merely indicated, the location of my perceiving body is "objectively defined" (Sartre 1956: 317) by the very same objective laws which determine my perception of the growing distance between myself and the car. Only this objective and law-like determination of the car's distance from myself is not a mere given, since it involves – as does everything else within our experience – the subject's own assessment. Whether or not this assessment is called "judgment" is a matter of secondary importance, just as long as the subject's determination of distance presupposes – as it does in Sartre – the subject's grasp of a purely *objective* relational system of which his own body is an element.

But any such account is repudiated by Merleau-Ponty. Those objective relations can't be constituted on the level of perception; quite the contrary, our grasp of those relations is derived from, and based upon, our prior perceptual grasp of distance (Merleau-Ponty 1962: 257). What, then, is the original and the specifically perceptual understanding of distance? The "increasing distance . . . expresses merely that the thing is beginning to slip away from the grip of our gaze . . . We shall define it then as we defined 'straight' and 'oblique' above: in terms of the situation of the object in relation to our power of grasping it" (Merleau-Ponty 1962: 261). Here Merleau-Ponty connects his analysis of the perceptual meaning of distance with his earlier demonstration (Merleau-Ponty 1962: 251–3) of how each perceived object has its own appropriate orientation – the orientation where we would be at our best when coping with that object in perception and action, the orientation giving us a "maximum sharpness of perception and action" (Merleau-Ponty 1962: 250) in relation to that object. But this perceptual "maximum" is not ascertained on the grounds of our assessment of some objective system of which our body is a part. Rather, it is an example (one among many of the perceptual "maxima" discussed in *Phenomenology of Perception*) of our body's ability to understand the perceptual field in terms of preobjective norms and meanings.

In the passage just quoted Merleau-Ponty also speaks of the object's "maximum sharpness" intended for our body's *actions*. So far, we have said nothing about Sartre's view (and its contrast with Merleau-Ponty's view) of the body's role in action. In this, we have followed the order of Sartre's own argument, for, as he tells us himself, his account of the body as the subject of perception must be taken as the "guiding thread" for understanding the body as a "center of action" (Sartre 1956: 320).

Once again, Sartre's initial moves look, on the surface at least, quite similar to those of Merleau-Ponty. In considering the active body in its for-itself mode we must avoid treating it as an ordinary object among other objects. Since we *are* our body when we act, the body can't be viewed as an instrument we manipulate and use when acting. But still, the body *is* used in action: my hand picks up the hammer to pound the nail into the wall, my foot presses on the car's brake, and so on. Thus, even though the body is not treated in action as being merely an instrument among other instruments, it does belong to the instrumental field to the extent to which it manipulates and uses other instruments: "the structure of the world implies that we can insert ourselves into the field of instrumentality *only by being ourselves an instrument*" (Sartre 1956: 324; my emphasis). Not only in perception, then, but in action as well, the body is "in-the-midst-of-the-world" (Sartre 1956: 325). The difficulty is obvious: how can we view the body as belonging to the instrumental field (indeed as *being* "an instrument") and yet remaining for-itself?

As in the case of perception, Sartre appeals here to his concept of "empty indication." The practical position of my body within the instrumental field is not given *directly*; in fact, it is "never given to me but only indicated by a sort of gap" (Sartre 1956: 323) or "a sort of hollow" (Sartre 1956: 327) within a given instrumental field. As I look at the wall I want to decorate, the wall refers me to the picture I just bought, which refers me to the nail and to the hammer; and this entire instrumental field calls upon *me* (this is the "gap" and the "hollow" within it defining for me the practical position and capacity of my hand) to perform certain actions needed to hammer the nail into the wall. But what is the nature of this "indicating"? Aside from its emptiness and indirectness it is just as *objective* as the relations of indication *within* the instrumental field. "The instrumental-things indicate other instruments or *objective* ways of making use of them: the nail is 'to be pounded in' this way or that, the hammer is 'to be held by the handle' . . . etc." (Sartre 1956: 322; my emphasis). Notice that the "indications" between the instruments (the hammer and the nail) and the indications between an instrument and the hand (the hammer is to be held by the handle) are here lumped together at least as far as their objectivity is concerned. The body may be a "center of action," but "this center is at once a *tool objectively defined* by the instrumental field which refers to it" (Sartre 1956: 324; my emphasis). Since instrumental-things have definite "properties" (Sartre 1956: 322) – thus the hammer's head is heavy, the nail is sharp, the wall is made of wood – there exist "definite rules" (Sartre 1956: 327) which determine the uses of such and such instrumental-things. But the very same rules indicate to me the practical position and capacity of my body: the instrumental-things' "dynamic order, whether it depends on my action or not, refers to it according to *rules*, and *thereby* the center of reference is *defined* in its change as in its identity" (ibid.; my emphasis). In both perception and action, then, the body is indicated, and defined, as an element of an objective system. And just as our perception of distance turned out to be determined (albeit not causally) in conformity with the objective laws of perspective, so too our bodily actions are viewed as either appropriate or inappropriate to the instruments and tasks at hand due to our understanding of the strictly objective relations between instruments and our active bodily members. Nothing could be further from Merleau-Ponty's view, where the body's perceptual and practical assessments of what it copes with are prior to, and independent of, our understanding of any such objective system.

To avoid possible confusion we must stress that for Sartre this objective system of which my body is an (emptily indicated) element is never displayed for me from the vantage point of "absolute objectivity" or "pure rationality" (Sartre 1956: 319). Within *such* a view my body would become one of the merely relative and equivalent centers of reference; and *such* a conception "destroy[s] the world's quality of being a world" (ibid.). For there to be a world, the (indicated) center of reference that my body is in its first-person, for-itself status, must remain a point of view on which I cannot take a point of view. Otherwise, the inherently perspectival and orientated character of the world, and hence also the world as world, would vanish. In this sense – but in this sense alone – the body escapes complete objectification and must remain merely "indicated" by other objects. Nevertheless, the *objectivity* of this indication is quite continuous with that absolute objectivity I can achieve at least in abstract thought: "all that is necessary is that my rational and universalizing thought should *prolong* in the abstract the indications which things give to myself about *my* sense" (Sartre 1956: 319; my emphasis). The shift is only from partial to total objectivity; in both cases (in the case of my body *experienced* as my point of view upon the world and in the case of my body *thought of* as a purely relative center of reference, equivalent with other centers) we are dealing with an objective and objectively determined system.[2]

We have said enough by now to conclude that Simone de Beauvoir's reply to Merleau-Ponty's criticism of Sartre was off target at least as far as the problem of body is concerned. It is not the case that Merleau-Ponty failed to appreciate how the body represents, for Sartre, the facticity of the for-itself. Rather, he saw it only too well and found Sartre's account wanting. We have now seen the reasons for it. Both Sartre and Merleau-Ponty reject the Cartesian approach. Both of them rediscover the necessarily embodied character of our conscious life by adopting the first-person approach to our body. But for Sartre, the body in its first-person status is itself an element of an objective system. The body's practical and perceptual position within that system – say, my body's distance from that car driving away, or what kind of motion of my hand is required in order to hammer that nail in the wall, etc. – is determined (if only by an "empty indication") by the strictly objective laws and rules. By contrast, in Merleau-Ponty's account our body's practical and perceptual relation to its environment is sustained by the body's own striving to understand things through the preobjective norm of a "maximum" articulation and sharpness. In this sense the body is *itself* a power of transcendence and surpassing: within the first-person experience of my body, "I am a body which rises towards the world" (Merleau-Ponty 1962: 75).

Unlike in Merleau-Ponty, in Sartre our "body's *nature-for-us*" is to be "perpetually the *surpassed*" (Sartre 1956: 326). And our body is the surpassed precisely in its capacity of the "center of reference" (ibid.) of our instrumental and perceptual field. But we have seen that as such a center of reference the body is only an element within a system defined by purely objective relations. Since *this* is what the body is for Sartre, the surpassing itself can only be attributed to the for-itself's individual projects. In an important passage Sartre puts together these two ideas: as a "center of reference" the body is "*already surpassed* . . . in each project of the For-itself, in each perception the body is there; it is the immediate Past in so far as it still touches on the Present that flees it . . . it is . . . a point of view, and a point of departure which I *am* and which at the same time I surpass towards what I have to be" (ibid.), that is, toward the freely chosen ends I pursue. On the one hand, then, there is the body as the purely surpassed element within an objective system and there is also, on the other hand, the surpassing itself identified with the individual's pursuit of his ends.

But this is precisely what separates Sartre's and Merleau-Ponty's competing accounts of the experience of that big rock, encountered as an obstacle. Sartre's analysis conforms to the general framework we have just brought out. To encounter the rock as an obstacle or not ("scalable" or "non-scalable"), two contributing factors must be brought to bear upon the situation. *First*, there must be the individual's "projected scaling" (Sartre 1956: 488). If I don't entertain such a project when looking at the rock (if, in Sartre's example, I am a "traveler" simply contemplating the rock), the rock will be neither "scalable" nor "non-scalable." *Second*, the rock manifests itself as "scalable" or "non-scalable" "only within an instrumental-complex which is already established" (Sartre 1956: 482). And this second condition is, we recall, determined by the purely objective laws and rules governing the "dynamic order" of instrumental-complexes in general, including my own body as the (emptily indicated) instrument that I *am*. To put it plainly, if my climbing equipment, as well as the objectively ascertainable condition of my body, is adequate to the task of scaling that rock, then, given my project of climbing, the rock will manifest itself as "scalable" rather than "non-scalable."

The individual's project plus his body as the surpassed center of reference within an objective system: this is Sartre's account, and this is why Merleau-Ponty finds Sartre's account unsatisfactory. Let us grant the obvious: given the individual's project of climbing and the instruments available to him, this particular rock may appear as scalable while that other (much bigger) rock may appear as non-scalable. But, according to Merleau-Ponty, we need not rely upon such individual projects (joined with the instruments available) to evaluate the potentialities of our environment. Whether I am the Sartrean climber or the Sartrean traveler just driving by, the mountain (and the same can be said of a huge rock) appears to me as exceeding my body's "power to take it in stride" (Merleau-Ponty 1962: 440). But this discovery of the mountain's significance is not the result of my project joined with my assessment of my body's position within an objective system. Like all perceptual meanings, this "autochthonous significance" (Merleau-Ponty 1962: 441) of the mountain is discovered on a preobjective level, where the body, far from being merely a "center of reference" emptily indicated by the world in conformity with strictly objective laws, appears *itself* as a movement of surpassing and transcendence organizing the world through its "spontaneous evaluations" (ibid.).

But, perhaps, even Merleau-Ponty's account needs to be taken one step further, for it often seems as if this bodily surpassing and transcendence were merely a general striving (a pure "*je peux*," to use Merleau-Ponty's term) to achieve the maximum grip upon the world. In this respect, Samuel Todes' phenomenology of the body (Todes 2001) supplies the much-needed completion of Merleau-Ponty's philosophical project. For Todes, also, the body is the active organizer of the experienced reality. But, unlike in Merleau-Ponty, in Todes the body exercises this function insofar as the body is, to use Todes' terms, a "material subject" endowed with a concrete structure and "thrown" into a material world. As such a material subject the body is, in the first place, inherently needy and dependent; and the body's striving to achieve a maximum grip upon objects is grounded in its activity to satisfy its needs. Second, the temporal quality of this striving, and indeed our very experience of time, are also due to the material structure of the body since, as Todes argues, the asymmetry between our body's forward and backward motions allows us to constitute the experience of temporal passage with its irreversible direction. Finally, the body's ability to determine a stable meaning of objects is grounded in their common "thrownness" into the gravitational field of the earth. In all these respects, the material structure and circumstances of our bodily activity are essential to the constitution of perceptual meanings.

Notes

1   Unfortunately, the meaning of one of the key passages quoted by Beauvoir has been lost in the standard English translation by Hazel Barnes of *Being and Nothingness*, from which it has been reproduced in the Zaytzeff translation of Beauvoir's article. Here is the original passage: "il faut se garder de comprendre que le monde existe en face de la conscience comme une multiplicité indéfinie de relations réciproques qu'elle survolerait sans perspective et contemplerait sans point de vue" (Sartre 1943: 368). And here is the English version of this passage: "we must be careful to remember that the world exists confronting consciousness as an indefinite multiplicity of reciprocal relations which consciousness surveys without perspective and contemplates without a point of view" (Sartre 1956: 306; Sartre 1956: 282 is the page number given by Zaytzeff from the Citadel Press edition) As will be noticed, the original meaning of the passage is the very opposite of what the English translation offers to the reader.

2   The function attributed by Sartre to the phenomena of "coenesthesia" only sharpens that fundamental difference between his own and Merleau-Ponty's account of the body. Why does Sartre think that such phenomena of "pure" or "original" affectivity (i.e., of affectivity prior to our intentions and projects, including even various affective projects) are necessary to account for the body's "first ontological dimension"? For, as Sartre notes, if we limit ourselves to the criterion of "indication," " we shall not be able to distinguish, for example, between the body and the telescope through which the astronomer looks at the planets" (Sartre 1956: 329). Similarly, "glasses, pince-nez, monocles, etc. . . . become, so to say, a supplementary sense organ" (ibid.). Consequently, what distinguishes my "real" organ from

such and similar devices is precisely the coenesthetic affectivity in which I "exist" the former, but not the latter. For example, when I am studying the stars and my eyes hurt, the pain is here the way in which I "exist" my eyes (but not the telescope); or, again, when I am walking and my foot hurts, the pain is now the way in which I "exist" my foot (but not the cane on which I also lean), and so on. Here we see very clearly that these coenesthetic experiences are called upon to single out our (proper and organic) body from among various devices which come close to being indistinguishable from it by the mere "indication" criterion. By this criterion alone, the body is only a part of an objective system within which we perceive and act.

Consequently, when Sartre attempts to offer some explanation of how we can be non-positionally aware of the spatial location of various parts of our body as experienced in the first-person mode, he can find no conceptual resources to construct a counterpart of Merleau-Ponty's "body image," endowed with its own spatiality. For example (Sartre 1956: 334), how can I be non-positionally aware of my eyes – as singled out from the rest of my body – when I am reading a book? First of all, Sartre appeals here, again, to his concept of "indicating." My body as a whole, he argues, is indicated to me by my entire perceptual and instrumental field, that is, by the world. Now, the book I am reading appears to me as the figure on the total ground of the world. And so just as the world indicates my body as my "total point of view" (ibid.), as the "corporal totality" (ibid.) that I am, so too the book singles out my eyes as a "functional specification of the corporal totality" (*ibid.*). Since none of this goes beyond the strictly objective laws of "abstract indication," all of this must be supplemented (for the reasons already mentioned) with some tonality of coenesthetic affectivity in which I "exist affectively" (*ibid.*) both the corporal totality and (perhaps in some different tonality) its specification in this or that organ as experienced in the first-person mode. Unlike in Merleau-Ponty, the spatial position of, say, my hand as a power of grasping and touching is either objectively indicated or affectively experienced; it is not part of the body image, endowed with its own spatial articulation.

References and Further Reading

de Beauvoir, S. (1998) Merleau-Ponty and pseudo-Sartreanism (trans. V. Zaytzeff). In J. Stuart (ed.), *The Debate Between Sartre and Merleau-Ponty*. Evanston, IL: Northwestern University Press (original work published 1955).

Sartre, J-P. (1943) *L'être et le néant* [Being and nothingness]. Paris: Gallimard.

—— (1956) *Being and Nothingness* (trans. H. E. Barnes). New York: Philosophical Library (original work published 1943).

Merleau-Ponty, M. (1962) *Phenomenology of Perception* (trans. C. Smith). London: Routledge & Kegan Paul (original work published 1945).

—— (1968) *The Visible and the Invisible* (trans. A. Lingis). Evanston, IL: Northwestern University Press (original work published 1964).

Todes, S. (2001) *Body and World*. Cambridge, MA: MIT Press.

18

Freedom and Responsibility

FREDERICK A. OLAFSON

The concepts of freedom and responsibility are central to any understanding of what a human being is. The contribution to this understanding that has been made by the tradition of thought we refer to as "phenomenology and existential philosophy" has been somewhat uneven. In its earliest phase, it showed no strong interest in either of these concepts. Later on, after phenomenology became existential philosophy, there was a marked uptake in the attention paid to freedom, but responsibility, at least in any ethical sense, never achieved a comparable prominence. The relation between the two concepts has also been neglected, even though freedom without responsibility sounds dangerous and responsibility without freedom is hard to imagine. A partial explanation for this pattern of attention and neglect can be gathered from the thought of Edmund Husserl, the founder of phenomenology. As he conceived this new discipline, it was not to be a broad philosophical anthropology or theory of human nature. Because the concept of a human being was not a primary focus of interest, the active and social life of human beings also tended to get rather short shrift. Since this is the rubric under which freedom and responsibility are most naturally discussed, they were never accorded an important place in Husserl's thought. The puzzle about this is why a philosophy centered on the concept of consciousness should have failed to make a larger place for matters that might well be thought to belong there. Husserl understood phenomenology as the study of "pure consciousness." "Pure" meant that all the metaphors used for describing consciousness that had been drawn from our experience of things and processes in the natural world have to be set aside. Indeed, for these purposes, even the existence of the world would have to be abstracted from or "bracketed," at least provisionally. This was to ensure that the models the natural world suggests would play no part in the description and analysis of pure consciousness and its functions. The concept of an "impression" is one such model and a good example of this kind of transfer to consciousness of notions borrowed from some physical process or other. In Husserl's view, the result of such transfers was always a seriously distorted conception of consciousness.

There is, evidently, a question here about where freedom and responsibility are to be accommodated within the scheme of things established by this distinction between pure consciousness and everything else. More concretely, are they to be assigned to what Husserl calls the "empirical ego" or, as one might have thought more likely, to the "transcendental ego" that is the individuated form of pure consciousness?

In trying to answer this question, the distinction between these two egos should not be confused with the more familiar one between the body and the soul or mind. The empirical ego is not simply the body as a physical system; it has psychological functions as well that are dependent upon the functioning of the body in its natural milieu. As an entity that forms part of the natural world, moreover, the empirical ego is an appropriate object of inquiry, as the transcendental ego is not, for various empirical sciences, among them psychology. But if freedom and responsibility belong to the empirical ego and phenomenology deals only with the pure or transcendental consciousness, we have to ask whether phenomenology can tell us anything about them that would be at all different from the story that is told by these empirical sciences. That is not likely to be very much. Because the relation of freedom and responsibility to the causal order of things is more than a little problematic, they do not figure at all prominently in the account these sciences give us of ourselves. The difficulty about this is that Husserl himself was an avowed opponent of the kind of naturalism implicit in this treatment of the empirical ego. Nevertheless, he assigns the great bulk of what we mean by "human nature" to just this kind of naturalistic treatment.

This paradox might be at least partly resolved if freedom and responsibility could be associated with the transcendental rather than the empirical ego. But how are we to conceive this transcendental ego, and what is its relation to its more humble empirical counterpart? On one interpretation, there would be only a conceptual difference between the two. The transcendental ego would be simply the empirical ego as conceived in abstraction from its entanglements in an organism and in the natural world. They would not be two different entities but one and the same entity conceived in different ways.

That does not, however, appear to have been the way Husserl understood the relation between these two egos. The transcendental ego was to be somehow prior to and the ground of the empirical ego. Its character was similar to that of the Cartesian (and Kantian) Cogito – the "I think" – that is supposed to be implicit in every positing of a world that transcends the consciousness that so posits it. It is a function rather than a thing, even an immaterial one. As such, it could be said to have a career – a history – although this would necessarily be a rather attenuated one that would be spelled out in terms of the continuity of its categorial functioning and not in those of a perduring substance. Even so, Husserl spoke of the transcendental ego as a "sphere of immanence" that contained what he called "hyletic data," or sensations. That made it sound very much like something more than a disembodied function and more like a new version of the mind or soul.

When we examine the passages in Husserl's writings in which he explicitly discusses freedom, it is plainly the freedom of the empirical ego that he is talking about. In *Ideas Second Book*, for example, the account of freedom forms part of a discussion of the "constitution" of, first, the natural world and then of the *geistige Welt* – the world of mind and thought (Husserl 1989). This is where the empirical ego is taken up. What Husserl says about it is that at least certain human actions are free. These actions are the ones that issue from the self and express its purposes and not simply the causal influence of something outside the self. This conception of freedom is similar to that of David Hume, who identified freedom with our being able to do what we want to do. On this definition, freedom does not require that there be alternative possibilities between which we choose or that human action resist subsumption under causal regularities. This would be consistent with Husserl's view that the empirical ego is part of the natural world. It also means that an empirical ego cannot be free in any sense that does not apply to at least some other living things. But if we are not free in the sense of being (and having been) able to act in either of at least two equally possible ways, in what sense can we be said to be responsible for what we do and have done?

Is the transcendental ego free in some stronger sense than the empirical ego is? One might be inclined to think so because it is not part of the natural world, where it would be subject to the action of other entities upon it. But in order to be free the transcendental ego would have to be able to act, and acting is normally understood as the effecting of a change in the world so that something in it is not what it would otherwise have been. But a transcendental consciousness that is pure in Husserl's sense does not even recognize that there is a world that is independent of it and in which such changes could be made. Nor could it have any motive for wanting to change anything in it.

There really is only one kind of action that the transcendental ego *could* perform, and that is the one that Husserl calls "constitution." Constitution is the central function of pure consciousness by which the original "bracketing" of all entities that transcend consciousness is at least partially reversed. It might have been thought that this would involve no more than a suspension of a suspension – the unbracketing of all the references to an actually existing body and world that were disallowed in the context of a phenomenological account of pure consciousness. The natural world would simply be readmitted to its former status once the true character of consciousness had been safeguarded. On this view, constitution would be a conceptual operation in which what is to count as an entity of a certain kind is delineated as well as everything else that defines its ontological status. Phenomenology, on this interpretation of constitution, would, in Wittgenstein's words, leave everything in the world unchanged, only a little neater.

Once again, that is not how Husserl understood constitution or phenomenology. It certainly involves the kind of conceptual delineation just described, although Husserl would have talked about essences that make things what they are and not about concepts. But the truly radical thesis associated with this notion of constitution is the claim that these meanings that make up the identity of any given object simply *are* that object. What this means is that the original reduction of the world to our consciousness of it has ontological and not just methodological import. The void left by that original operation is to be filled, but not by its former occupants which have been exposed as being merely notional. They are to be replaced by meaning-like entities – Husserl calls them "noemas" – that define the character of the something in question. The qualitative elements in these noemas are derived from the sense-data in the transcendental ego. For example, in constituting an ordinary perceptual object, a color sensation would be upgraded to the status of a property of that object. In this sense, Husserlian phenomenology is, as he declared it to be, a new version of idealism.

Is constitution in this sense an action and, if it is, is it a free action? Doubts about this may be suggested by the fact that neither the phenomenological reduction nor the kind of the reconstitution of the world that Husserl proposes appear to have any detectible reality in our lives, whether transcendental or empirical. *Pace* Husserl, we simply are not aware of any such operations as he describes, and our ability to withdraw from the world and then rebuild it as a tissue of meanings is more than a little dubious if it is supposed to be something that we *do*. Doubts may also be stimulated by the fact that an ordering of our experience and of the world has already been laid down in the languages we learn as children. Our relation to that ordering seems to be a pervasively passive one. If "constitution" is supposed to express a transformation of that passivity into something that amounts to an action on our part, it is likely that most of us will not be able to recognize the difference between an action of this kind and our normal passivity.

As far as this putative action being a free one is concerned, there is a further difficulty. It has already been pointed out that Husserl spoke of essences rather than of concepts, presumably because the latter term has such strong mentalistic connotations. However that may be, by virtue of what Husserl calls its "eidetic" intuition – its ability to identify things by their ontological type – the transcendental ego deals with essences rather than with spatio-temporal particulars. In ordering these properly, it really has no more alternatives than a mathematician does in dealing with the equally abstract objects he studies. Presumably, it can get things wrong but that would only mean that it has not done what it has to be assumed to "want" to do. What this comes to is the fact that the transcendental ego would be so tightly constrained by the character of the field in which it operates that the idea of alternatives and thus of freedom simply has no application to it.

In the matter of responsibility, Husserl's phenomenology does not even have as much to say as it does about freedom. About responsibility as an ethical relationship between human beings in which someone is responsible *for* something – a payment, a recommendation – *to* someone else, nothing at all is said. What Husserl does talk about is the responsibility that a human being takes upon himself in thinking philosophically. Normally, our whole stance as cognitive and ethical beings is derived rather uncritically from some tradition or institution with which we are affiliated. Husserl saw philosophical reflection, especially in its phenomenological mode, as an acceptance of the fact that we are, each of us, the judges of what is true and false and thus of what we should believe and do. For most of human history that responsibility has not been recognized by individual human beings who have, instead, assigned it to some superordinate authority. In this respect, as in others, Husserl was very much a Cartesian, and he regarded this kind of responsibility as marking the accession to full maturity as a human being. This appears, however, to be a responsibility that is owed only to oneself, or if it has a social meaning bearing on our relations with other human beings, it is not developed.

The deficiencies of Husserlian phenomenology to which attention has been drawn here did not pass unnoticed by the philosophers who studied his work and were influenced by it. Criticism was directed above all to Husserl's claim that our experience of the world has to be reduced to pure consciousness as well as to the distinction between an empirical and a transcendental ego that resulted. The goal of philosophers like Heidegger, Sartre, and Merleau-Ponty who set about developing a new kind of phenomenology was to work out a unitary concept of human existence. The word "existence" itself was reserved for human being and this new phenomenology was to be "existential" rather than transcendental. If the unquestioning, pre-philosophical acceptance of the existence of the world was, as Husserl had described it, "the natural attitude," then existential phenomenology was to be an analytical description of just that attitude and of the way it informs human nature as a whole. Even so, it is not altogether clear that these existential phenomenologists were able to deal more successfully with freedom and responsibility than Husserl.

Once they have been separated, bringing the transcendental and the empirical ego back together again in a unitary conception of human being is not an easy task. Even if it is in fact the right way to go, it is far from clear how it can be done. Simply saying, as some philosophers do, that human beings have *both* physical and mental properties will not help unless we are told what they are properties of and how they are related to one another. Martin Heidegger simply cut the Gordian knot by endorsing the common-sense view that we are entities that, without any bifurcation into transcendental and empirical parts, are in the presence of other entities in the world. What he did was to devise a new philosophical language in which this pre-philosophical understanding could be expressed. This new idiom replaced the old mentalistic apparatus of mind and consciousness and representative ideas. On this interpretation, human beings are entities that are in the world as the Cartesian soul was not, but they are in it in such a way that they transcend themselves toward other entities in the world they are in, other human beings among them.

Heidegger also laid great emphasis on the fact that these are active beings and that their way of disclosing things in the world is pragmatic in the sense that they are set in some context of use or avoidance. This distinctive way of being in the world also accounts for the freedom of these unitary beings. Heidegger strongly opposed any psychological account of freedom as freedom of the will. Instead, it is our way of being in the world that makes us free. One way of putting this would be to say that the "space" into which things emerge on being disclosed or "uncovered" is one with modal and temporal dimensions. Human beings transcend themselves not only toward other actual entities but also toward possibilities that they might try to actualize by their actions. In this sense, what is disclosed as actual by the openness of human being is always profiled against what is not actual but might possibly be, as well as against what has been the case but no longer is. That same openness bridges the distinctions between present, past, and future so that past events can be said to be present in absence and future events are present (in absence) in the mode of possibility.

Heidegger's conception of freedom has to be set in the context of his radical revision of the concept of the human subject. It is not the soul or the mind, and it does not operate on ideas or representations that mediate its relation to the world. It simply is the openness in which things in the world are disclosed to it – what Heidegger calls a "clearing." That disclosure can be expressed in statements of fact – "That car is black" or "There was a cat in this room" – and the world to which these things belong is accordingly a world of states of affairs or facts and not simply an aggregate of things. We cannot, of course, understand what it is for something to *be* something without implicitly pairing this fact with that something's *not* being whatever it is. The point here is that freedom is bound up with our being in the world in such a way that what is present to us might very well not be. We are thus confronted by alternative possibilities. Whether we are able to change what is presently the case is, of course, another matter. Freedom is not, however, a matter of actually having the strength or the resources required to accomplish some task successfully. It is being in a position to try, at least, to do either this or that, whether or not one succeeds. For Heidegger, being in that position defines the way we are in the world and it is that way that constitutes us as free beings.

When it comes to responsibility, it is much less clear that Heidegger has anything to say that really bears on our ordinary understanding of it. The chief virtue he recognizes as having an appropriately existential character is authenticity. Authenticity is like responsibility in that it requires that we acknowledge what we do and have done and that we not claim any auspices for our actions that relieve us of that responsibility. Heidegger never made clear whether being authentic in this sense was compatible with trying to justify one's actions to people affected by them. In the absence of clarifications on this point, it sounds as though authenticity were a virtue that does not have any social meaning because it carries no obligation *to* anyone else. But if that is the case, its affinity with responsibility in any familiar sense would be a decidedly narrow one. Somehow, in spite of some important insights, Heidegger never appeared to be willing to recognize the relation of one human being to another as having significant philosophical import. Much of the time we in fact live in a state of unthinking and anonymous conformity to the expectations of those around us who live in the same way. When we emerge into a more authentic individuality, we are indeed free, but Heidegger never explained what our relations to other such beings would be.

In Heidegger's later writings, the original pragmatic character of the way we disclose entities in the world is almost entirely eclipsed and, with it, anything that at all resembles human freedom. No more is heard of authenticity and nothing that more closely resembles responsibility puts in an appearance either. Heidegger's original interest in the active lives of human beings and their relations with one another gave way to a conception of being as such as shaping the destinies of human beings and their societies.

In France, the influence of Husserl's thought remained very strong and almost sixty years passed before Heidegger's principal work, *Being and Time*, was translated into French (Heidegger 1962). Nevertheless, Sartre's first major work, *Being and Nothingness* (Sartre 1956), was heavily derivative of Heidegger's *Being and Time*. It was also very different from Heidegger's thought in several respects. Although it abandoned the idea of a phenomenological reduction á la Husserl, it retained the concept of consciousness and tried to combine it with the Heideggerian conception of being-in-the-world. Even more significantly, Sartre greatly enlarged the place assigned to freedom in his account of the human subject. The non-being that Heidegger had made a dialectical component of his concept of being was straightforwardly identified with consciousness by Sartre. From this bold assimilation, he drew the consequence that freedom constitutes the human essence. We are, as he put it, "condemned to be free" by the fact that we are always in situations that present alternatives, and so our lives have to be understood in terms of the choices we have to make, even if it is only by doing nothing. What is most distinctive of Sartre's conception of freedom is its absolute character. There is nothing local about it in the sense of our effective alternatives being confined to those expressible in the terms handed down to us in some historical tradition. Instead, it is as though every choice we make was made from a complete array of all the logically possible options in a given situation. Sartre was, after all, an admirer of Descartes who conceived the freedom of God as being so absolute that it included the ability to make even the basic truths of arithmetic different from what they are now.

An essential adjunct to his theory of human freedom is Sartre's thesis about the unwillingness of human beings to acknowledge their being radically free in his sense. This thesis is best known as an indictment of the "bad faith" that is implicit in the various stratagems by which we try to avoid any such acknowledgment. We insist, for example, that we "have no choice" when we obviously do, no matter how inconvenient it may be for us. We also talk about ourselves as though we were all of a piece, endowed with some "nature" from which all our actions, no matter how objectionable they may be to others, flow as if by some unchallengeable logic of necessity. If there is any existential virtue implicit in Sartre's account of these matters, it is one based on the avoidance of bad faith and the open acknowledgment that we are in fact choosing when we might otherwise be tempted to claim that we are not, and that matters are somehow beyond our control.

Is this a concept of responsibility? In a way it is because it clearly rules out the kinds of fraudulent justifications we so often offer to people we have offended or injured in some way. In another respect, however, it falls short as a statement of what responsibility involves. Responsibility is not just a kind of ultimate candor that acknowledges what one has done without any excuses or bogus justifications. That might serve the purposes of a rather bizarre vanity that sets honesty, in abstraction from all other considerations, above every other good one might care about. As such, however, it would be altogether self-regarding and unconcerned about the effect on others of the actions about which one is being so candid. Responsibility is not a solipsistic exercise of this kind; it is being answerable *to* someone *for* something. That means that the agent shares at least some understandings with the person(s) affected by his action. Not only does he or she care about the same things someone else cares about; the fact that someone else cares in this way means something to him that can motivate his action. There is no hint of any of this in what Sartre has to say about responsibility. It is apparently assumed that avoidance of bad faith will be enough to ensure the moral quality of one's actions. But in the famous dialogues in Thucydides' history of the Peloponnesian War, the Athenians are perfectly candid in giving the reasons why the people of Melos who are resisting them must perish. They were, therefore, not in bad faith, but that did not make them "responsible" in any sense that carries moral implications.

The other great figure in French phenomenology was Maurice Merleau-Ponty. Although he was a friend and colleague of Sartre, he took issue with many of the stands, philosophical and political, that Sartre took and above all with his conception of freedom. Merleau-Ponty's philosophical stance and its contrast with that of Sartre are perhaps best expressed in his statement that before we can say "No," we have to learn to say "Yes." What this means is that a human being is not simply the kind of absolute negativity that Sartre postulates. We are also "invested" in the world and that investment, with the complex relations with other human beings it carries with it, is a presupposition for the revisionary choices we make.

In the background of this conception of freedom there is a more general account of the relation of consciousness to things in its world, including the human body, that is

269

very different from that of Sartre. The body as Merleau-Ponty conceives it is not the body of neurophysiology, nor is it just another object that consciousness "constitutes." It is the expressive body whose movements anticipate the character of the objects and situations to which they are addressed. Merleau-Ponty, like Sartre, still uses the concept of consciousness, but he comes very close to replacing it as the proper unit for existential analysis with the Heideggerian notion of the human being as a whole.

The main point Merleau-Ponty makes in his critique of Sartre's conception of human freedom is that freedom as pure negativity has to have an analogue in the world. Otherwise, a slave or a prisoner in irons would be just as free as anyone else. What this means is that freedom expresses itself by bringing into being a situation for itself in the world that is at least compatible with a meaningful exercise of human powers. Perhaps even more significant is Merleau-Ponty's acknowledgment of what he calls the "aura of generality" that surrounds an individual life and the actions in which it issues. "Generality" here means that the import of a situation and of an action taken in it figures in many lives, not just in mine. This is very different from the Sartrean position that precludes anything like a recognition of the equivalence of other lives with my own and thus of the very possibility of a "We" based on a reciprocal recognition of one another as human beings. These elements in Merleau-Ponty's position also offer at least the rudiments of a conception of responsibility. It is not expressed in terms that directly announce its moral character, but it certainly makes a place for the justification of an action to those affected by it that was missing from the Sartrean account. Merleau-Ponty was always rather skittish about invoking recognizably moral ideas because he was deeply convinced that a true morality based on reciprocal recognition had still to be brought into being. It was, as he said, "à faire," and most definitely not a given. What is very plain, however, is the fact that the human world in which we live – he described it as a "knot of relations" – is saturated with intersubjectivity and with the ethical implications it carries with it.

On balance, the most important contribution these philosophers made to our understanding of freedom and responsibility was Heidegger's non-psychological conception of freedom as a function of our way of being in the world. That conception was taken up, although not necessarily fully understood, by Sartre and Merleau-Ponty. It was not, however, satisfactorily integrated with a concept of responsibility and, as a result, a conception of the ethical basis of a human society never emerged in this tradition of thought. The thought of Merleau-Ponty was the one probably best adapted to this purpose, but it was tragically cut short.

References and Further Reading

Heidegger, M. (1962) *Being and Time* (trans. J. Macquarrie and E. Robinson). New York: Harper & Row (original work published 1927).

Husserl, E. (1989) *Ideas Second Book* (trans. R. Rojcewicz and A. Schuwer). Dordrecht: Kluwer (original work published 1952).

Sartre, J-P. (1956) *Being and Nothingness* (trans. H. E. Barnes). New York: Humanities Press (original work published 1943).

19

Absurdity

DAVID SHERMAN

"Absurdity," or, alternatively, "the Absurd," generally refers to the experience of groundlessness, contingence, or superfluity with respect to those basic aspects of "the human condition" that seem as if they should be open to rational justification. Although first coined by Kierkegaard, the father of existentialism, and largely associated with a select group of existential philosophers, novelists, playwrights, and poets, the philosophical problem to which absurdity refers arose with modern philosophy and has continued to persist beyond the existentialist moment proper.

By most accounts, what underlies the modern philosophical project (historically, if not also conceptually) is the so-called "philosophy of subjectivity." Sartre's claim that "subjectivity must be the starting point" (Sartre 1957: 13), which clarifies his basic definition of existentialism (i.e., "existence comes before essence"), thus hearkens back to Descartes, who turned philosophy inward by making subjectivity the foundation of indubitable knowledge. Descartes' emphasis on the well-distributed power of reason, "the natural light" within each person that would impel him to "accept nothing as true which [he] did not clearly recognize to be so" (Descartes 1998: 11), represents a crucial moment in the gradual movement away from a Church-based worldview to a humanistic one. Consequently, although nominally relating to narrow epistemological concerns, Descartes' dualism of mind and matter, which is the result of estranging consciousness from the world to ground its knowledge of it, is a decisive sociocultural phenomenon – and, moreover, a portent of absurdity. This omen was not lost on his contemporary, Pascal, who cried that "the eternal silence of these infinite spaces frightens me" (Pascal 2003: 61). Momentarily bracketing this existential repercussion, however, the objective certainty that Descartes sought was gotten on the sly, as the rationality that he put into question by methodically doubting everything at the start of his *Meditations* was then used to prove the existence of God, who mediates the relation between mind and matter, and thus permits Descartes' contemporaries to trust their perceptions, as well as the meaningfulness of their (now less solidly grounded) Church-based worldview.

After Hume delivered a devastating blow to the Cartesian project by showing that truths about the world could not have the same sort of ironclad necessity as the truths of mathematics and logic, Kant upped the subjective ante with his recourse to transcendental idealism, which, he stated, made good the truths of empirical realism. For

Kant, in other words, there is a necessity with respect to our empirical truths (and, most of all, the truths of the natural sciences) because these truths are made good by the nature of our own minds, which provide the template for what can count as objective truths *for us*. How the world is "in itself," however, is beyond the bounds of our reason. Even with respect to objective matters, then, Kant, like Sartre, thinks not only that "subjectivity must be the starting point" but also that there is a limit to reason, which Kant turns into a virtue by arguing that reason's limitations make room for faith. It is when Kant moves from theoretical to practical philosophy, however, that the specter of absurdity arises. Although the belief in such things as God, freedom, and the immortality of the soul can find no place in Kant's theoretical philosophy, in his practical philosophy they are needed as regulative ideas – or, as he articulates it, "postulates of pure practical reason" – because without them his moral philosophy, based on necessity, would collapse in the face of the world's contingence. This suggests not only that faith can begin only where theoretical reason ends but also that faith is the very condition of the possibility of pure practical reason. Yet, although Kant's faith itself is not rationally grounded, as his attacks on the sundry proofs for God's existence attest, it is of such a nature that it does not provoke the experience of absurdity.

With his articulation of the paradoxical notion of "subjective truth" and, specifically, its relation to religious faith, it is Kierkegaard who first broaches absurdity. In the *Concluding Unscientific Postscript*, he declares: "Instead of the objective uncertainty [of believing in God's existence], there is here a certainty, namely, that objectively it is absurd; and this absurdity, held fast in the passion of inwardness, is faith" (Kierkegaard 1992: 210). Although opposed to the basic tenets of enlightenment reason, this notion of absurdity – crystallized, for Kierkegaard, in the paradox that Christianity's eternal truths have a historical becoming with God's Incarnation in the personage of Christ – is a product of it. Kierkegaard's distinctive form of Protestantism, with its emphasis on the subjective inwardness of a believer who passionately confronts God in a "vertical relation," is a result of the enlightenment promise that individual subjectivity has a right to its satisfaction, a promise that both he and his nemesis Hegel seek to make good. And his rejoinder to Hegel's emphasis on a rationally structured ethical totality – that is, a "horizontal relation" that subsumes everything within it, including the absolutely "other" that is God – must be understood as an attempt to vindicate this right against Hegel's totalizing "System."

However, as Kierkegaard relates in *Fear and Trembling* (1843; cited as Kierkegaard 1986), even believing in the absolutely "other" that is God, which makes clear to the believer his infinite nature, is only the last stage on the way to true faith. Still operating from the standpoint of the understanding, these believers (of whom Kierkegaard counts himself one) are only "knights of resignation" for whom the world's privations empty life of all hope, joy, and meaning. It is only by embracing the absurdity that is part and parcel of true faith that one becomes a "knight of faith" who can joyfully partake of life, since with meaning conferring faith hope springs eternal: all things, including – indeed, perhaps, especially – those that are not amenable to reason, are possible. Despite the subjective bounty to be had by the individual of faith, then, Kierkegaard believes that he cannot rationally argue for Christianity but rather must "seduce" his reader into it. And, indeed, it is not even Kierkegaard *qua* Kierkegaard who is doing the seducing, because out of respect for the individual's right to self-determination he writes pseudonymously: by undermining the authority of the authorial position, Kierkegaard gives his reader the room to make an uncoerced choice about whether to subjectively embrace the objective absurdity that is the Christian faith.

Kierkegaard's vital insight, however, is that absurdity is not limited to the paradoxes of religious faith. He is perhaps the first to see that all "existential" choices – that is, fundamental orienting choices made by an individual about how he is to be in the world (which determines what counts as a subjective truth for that individual) – are really a matter of faith. In explicating his "existential dialectic," which is a deliberate refashioning of Hegel's historical dialectic along individual lines, Kierkegaard says, in essence, that every choice of oneself is ungrounded. Thus, in opposition to what he takes to be the ultimate convergence of thought and being in Hegel's dialectic, in which there seems to be a rational necessity with respect to the movement from one (collective) "form of consciousness" to another, Kierkegaard sees thought and being as riven. As a result, although he explicitly privileges the notion of being an "existing" individual – that is, an individual for whom there is a higher-order commitment that coherently delineates the ultimate rules by which he will live – he can only implicitly privilege the "religious," as opposed to "ethical" or "aesthetic," sphere of existence. In other words, there can be no reason for choosing to live by the rules of a particular sphere of existence, for it is the wholly ungrounded choice of a sphere of existence that brings anything that can count as a reason into existence as an initial matter. Even in a wholly secular sense, then, choosing to be an existing individual by choosing to live in conformity with the rules of one sphere of existence as opposed to another involves nothing more than a "leap of faith."

That absurdity (whether understood in a secular or religious fashion) is part and parcel of enlightenment humanism, which is distinguished by its emphasis on subjectivity, is illustrated by the fact that Heidegger, who explicitly rejects enlightenment humanism, sees absurdity mostly as a derivative problem rather than as a problem in its own right. Endeavoring to get beneath the protracted history of enlightenment subjectivism to recover "the meaning of Being," Heidegger calls human beings "Dasein" (literally "being-there") to emphasize that we are not fundamentally disengaged subjects who "re-present" the world of our experience as disconnected objects but rather are situated beings who are part of an interconnected whole. And if a "leap of faith" is needed in order to engender existential meaning, as is the case for Kierkegaard, it is because our collective self-understanding is mistakenly predicated on the "subject–object" model, in which subjectivity has been artificially cleaved from its preexisting world of collectively constituted practices (i.e., the "there" that is inextricably a part of Dasein) which delineate what counts as "meaningful," existentially or epistemologically. In Heidegger's terms, the shared practices of this always already existing world constitute a "fore-structure" of implicit understandings that. when interpreted, provide meaning, and at this juncture the problem of existential meaning or absurdity does not even arise as an issue for Dasein.

Heidegger knows that his "paradigm shift" away from enlightenment subjectivism alone does not ultimately resolve the problem of absurdity, but just pushes it back a step. The meaning conferring world of shared practices collectively engendered by Dasein itself – "only Dasein can be meaningful or meaningless" – can, of course, be

273

called into question, which raises anew the problem of absurdity. Thus, in terms of the always already existing fore-structure of Dasein, Heidegger admits, "there would still remain the question, 'why?'" (Heidegger 1962: 192) – a question that, Camus will later argue, outstrips any possible answer. For Heidegger, however, although the understandings that constitute the fore-structure of Dasein are themselves ungrounded presuppositions that prejudge what will come to count as "meaningful," the circularity that this implies is actually part and parcel of the very nature of understanding itself. Moreover, the scientific approach to understanding that would summarily reject this circularity because it is ungrounded is only a form of understanding that derives from it. Thematizing "objects" in a supposedly presuppositionless way is "only a sub-species of understanding" that takes its cue from the existential conditions that give rise to it as an initial matter.

Nevertheless, Heidegger does carve out a space for his own particular notion of absurdity in *Being and Time*: "That which is unmeaning can be absurd. The present-at-hand, as Dasein encounters it, can, as it were, assault Dasein's being; natural events, for instance, can break in upon us and destroy us" (Heidegger 1962: 193). For Heidegger, the "present-at-hand" is the more objectifying approach to worldly entities that takes place when our basic non-cognitive way of dealing with them (as "ready-to-hand") breaks down, and his point seems to be that natural events – "natural" because non-natural or historical events would, presumably, already be saturated with meaning – might not yet have presented themselves in such a way as to have been assimilated into our collective understanding, and therefore can strike us as absurd. For the most part, however, since virtually all natural events that might strike us as absurd are ones that have either already occurred or we could foresee occurring, they have already been reposited within our fore-structure, which means that their occurrence, although perhaps devastating, would not be absurd. Furthermore, Heidegger speaks of anxiety in *Being and Time*, an "individualizing" mood characterized by Dasein's experience of the ultimate groundlessness of its world: "Anxiety brings it back from its absorption in the 'world.' Everyday familiarity collapses" (Heidegger 1962: 233). Such a mood would surely seem to augur absurdity. Yet, for Heidegger, this mood does not close down further inquiry but rather opens it up, for it is privileged in that it reveals to Dasein that it is not the measure of all things. It is in this way that Dasein is opened up to Being, whose primordial meaning not only transcends our pedestrian reason (which initially raises the specter of absurdity) but is, crucially, ontologically (and, implicitly, ethically) privileged with respect to it. And, indeed, even when Heidegger comes to fear in later writings, such as *What is Metaphysics?* (1929; cited as Heidegger 1998), that we are consigned to "oblivion" with respect to Being, anxiety testifies not to absurdity but to loss.

Conversely, for the French existentialists, who qualifiedly retain the Cartesian dualism of mind and matter but without even the higher-order unity that Descartes's God provided, absurdity is a basic aspect of human reality. Beyond this similarity, however, Sartre and Camus, who are most commonly associated with the notion of absurdity, differ with respect to the way in which they understand it. And to make matters somewhat more complicated, with the evolution in his philosophical thought from a more or less exclusively neo-Husserlian position to one that was also mediated by Heidegger and Hegel, Sartre's understanding of absurdity tacitly changed.

In *Nausea*, a philosophical novel published in 1938, when Sartre was still substantially under the influence of Husserl, he characterizes absurdity as a quality of all existing objects (and, more broadly, the material world as a whole), regardless of the stance that human beings might take with respect to them. Because Sartre sees consciousness as wholly external to the objects that it perceives, his protagonist, Roquentin, is totally estranged from the world of his experience, which – in a twist on the Cartesian problematic – leaves the justification for his own existence, if not his actual existence itself, in doubt: "I am, I am, I exist, I think, therefore I am; I am because I think, why do I think? I don't want to think any more, I am because I think that I don't want to be, I think that I ... because ... ugh! I flee" (Sartre 1964: 100–1). Set off from the world of objects, Roquentin comes to see not only that his own existence, as he recognizes it, is based on purely contingent thought, but also that the external reality perceived by language encrusted thought bears only a contingent relation to the objects themselves, which are actually "divorced" from the words that we use to either name or describe them: "The world of explanations and reasons is not the world of existence." And, finally, as to the objects "themselves" – that is, their brute existence – there is, once again, just contingence: all is "superfluous." Thus, "the essential thing is contingency. I mean that one cannot define existence as necessity. To exist is simply *to be there*" (Sartre 1964: 131). It is this brute contingency – in *Nausea* the occasion for this revelation is the gnarled root of a chestnut tree – that Roquentin refers to as the "fundamental absurdity," which, he says, is the "the key to existence."

Accordingly, although Sartre's basic philosophical orientation in *Nausea* originates with Husserl and, ultimately, Descartes – crudely, there is consciousness on one side of the divide and the objects of its perception on the other – his conclusion that "the essential thing is contingency" is wholly at odds with the commitment to necessity that Husserl and Descartes share. Indeed, in critical respects, Sartre's conclusion in *Nausea* is similar to Hume's skeptical broadside on the Cartesian project. Hume's argument that "matters of fact" (truths about the world) cannot have the same iron-clad necessity as "relations of ideas" (the truths of mathematics and logic) because relations of ideas are "discoverable by the mere operation of thought, without dependence on what is anywhere existent in the universe," while "the contrary of every matter of fact is still possible," is summarily expressed by Roquentin: "A circle is not absurd [because] it is clearly explained by the rotation of a straight segment around one of its extremities, [b]ut neither does a circle exist, [while] this root, on the other hand, existed in such a way that I could not explain it" (Sartre 1964: 129). And, indeed, Hume's consequent argument to the effect that the laws of the natural sciences are the result of inferential processes predicated on custom or habit rather than reason finds perfect expression in Roquentin's exclamation that "I see it, I see this nature ... I know that its obedience is idleness, I know it has no laws: what they take for constancy is only habit and it can change tomorrow" (Sartre 1964: 158). The crucial difference between Sartre and Hume here is that Hume is still dealing in the third-person perspective of purely theoretical philosophy. As Hume puts it, he can escape the "philosophical melancholy and delirium" by leaving his study, dining, and playing backgammon with friends, which enables him to see how "cold, strained, and ridiculous" his philosophical speculations actually are. Sartre's Roquentin, conversely, is perpetually assaulted by this "philosophical melancholy and delirium," which is the phenomenon of absurdity when taken up from the first-person perspective of a practical philosophy shorn of postulates and other guardrails.

Indeed, the stark, decontextualized way in which Sartre's Roquentin sees worldly objects has the feel of Husserl's "phenomenological reduction" – that is, a methodological approach in which the "natural attitude" toward the object being contemplated is bracketed to discern the way in which transcendental consciousness necessarily experiences it – but, unlike Husserl, Sartre's Roquentin never comes back to the "natural attitude." By 1943, when Sartre publishes *Being and Nothingness*, however, this approach all but disappears. Now as powerfully influenced by Heidegger and Hegel as he is by Husserl, Sartre no longer sees consciousness as standing over and against the world of its experience, as Husserl's epistemologically oriented commitments had previously inclined him to do, but rather as inextricably intertwined with it. By virtue of Sartre's continuing commitment to subjectivity, however, the problem of absurdity does not go by the wayside for him, as it largely does for Heidegger, but takes on a different form. Because consciousness is always already immersed in a world within which it must concretize itself by constructing a "self" – "the self" is a publicly verifiable, fluid construct born of the interaction between consciousness, certain brute givens (for e.g., my physiology and history) and other people – the contingent material world (now "being") itself is no longer absurd. (One possible exception to this, more or less synonymous with Husserl's phenomenological reduction, occurs when consciousness undergoes an exceedingly rare "purifying reflection," which fleetingly puts a person's self and world up for grabs.) Rather, what comes to be absurd is the contingent nature of the self (which, based on its constitution, might *choose* to see the material world as absurd).

Because consciousness has an awareness of its awareness of objects, the most central of which is the self, it is, in a crucial sense, always already beyond the self that it nevertheless has a substantial hand in constructing. And, for Sartre, the ineradicable nature of this "beyond" – i.e., of consciousness's inexorable transcendence with respect to the empirical self – is the source of our ineradicable freedom. Thus, consciousness and the empirical self are of a different logical order, and for this reason they can never be identical. But, according to Sartre, all of our projects in the world, and finally the self that we choose to be ("in the mode of not being it," given this fundamental non-identity), emanate from what he calls "the fundamental project," which is "the desire to be God." And this project, in short, is the desire to establish the very identity between consciousness's freedom and the self's concretion that is ontologically off limits to mere mortals. Accordingly, while God is both absolutely free and absolutely self-identical, which makes Him a necessary being (who is adequate to His concept), human beings are contingent, both in terms of the unjustified choices of self that they make and the sociohistorical contexts into which they've been contingently "thrown" (to use Heidegger's phrase), which provide the very stuff of these choices. This absurdity, which defines the human reality, is graphically characterized by Sartre: "Picture an ass drawing behind him a cart. He attempts to get hold of a carrot which has been fastened at the end of a stick which in turn has been tied to the shaft of the cart. Every effort on the part of the ass to seize the carrot results in advancing the whole apparatus and the cart itself, which always remains at the same distance from the ass" (Sartre 1956: 277–8). Sartre's point is that human beings, who can never become identical with themselves, are (by virtue of what they are) compelled to seek this self-identity, and although the futile pursuit itself engenders meaning, the pursuit, more broadly, is meaningless, or, more to the point, characterized by absurdity. And, in sharp contrast to Heidegger, there is no higher-order "meaning of Being" that can trump the problem because, for Sartre, "being" in *Being and Nothingness* is, in its brute inexplicable givenness, only the condition of the possibility of human conferring meaning.

If Sartre's notion of absurdity shifts from one focused on the contingency of the object (i.e., the superfluousness of the material world) to one focused on the contingency of the subject (i.e., the fruitless pursuit of self-identity), Camus's naïve experience of absurdity arises from the unmediated relation between subject and object itself – that is, from the irreparable split between human reason and what he refers to as an indifferent universe. Arising directly out of Descartes's problematic, Camus's absurdity is the practical analogue to skepticism, the theoretical quandary with which Descartes would have been left if, after establishing the *cogito*, he had seen that he was not justified in using reason to prove the existence of God, who (because He is adequate to His concept) basically underwrites the veracity of our sense perceptions. Like skepticism, which presupposes God's vacant throne, since the skeptical problem seems to be based on a notion of truth that corresponds to the "God's-eye view" or "view from nowhere," absurdity, as Nietzsche would put it, arises "in the shadow of God." And the question under this circumstance, Camus asserts, is whether we can "live and create in the very midst of the desert" – or, what amounts to the same thing, whether we can "live without appeal."

In *The Myth of Sisyphus*, Camus asserts that Sisyphus, who was condemned by the gods to eternal, futile labor (namely, interminably pushing a boulder to the top of a mountain only to watch it fall back again) is "the absurd hero," as well as the prototype of the modern individual: "Rising, streetcar, four hours in the office or the factory, meal, streetcar, four hours of work, meal, sleep, and Monday, Tuesday, Wednesday, Thursday, Friday, and Saturday according to the same rhythm . . . But one day the 'why' arises and everything begins in that weariness tinged with amazement" (Camus 1955: 10). Because "the why" will outstrip any answer that we might give it – that is, because all of our endeavors will be deemed meaningless as there is no transcendent meaning that exists to justify them – the "one truly serious philosophical problem," Camus declares, is suicide. After giving a rather weak argument for why we might not opt for suicide (i.e., "the only condition of my inquiry is to preserve the very thing that crushes me"), he goes on to suggest that there are two ways in which life might be made palatable, both of which Sisyphus manifests: his scorn of the gods ("There is no fate that cannot be surmounted by scorn") and his immersion in his life (He makes "his rock his thing").

Both of these alternatives are, in some sense, indebted to Nietzsche, who himself was no absurdist. Quite the contrary, although no philosopher has recognized the limits of reason more clearly than Nietzsche, he would have interpreted absurdity as a manifestation of a psychological illness rather than a metaphysical or ontological condition – and, indeed, according to Nietzsche, metaphysics and ontology are themselves indicative of a psychological illness. Camus's scorn, in particular, is cut from the very same cloth as the *ressentiment* that Nietzsche took to be part and parcel of what he called "slave morality." And, at least in his literary works, Camus himself sees that this negative emotion is not an adequate answer to absurdity. In different ways, both *Caligula* (a play written around the same time as *The Myth of Sisyphus* and *The Stranger*) and *The Fall* (which was written years later) testify to the ultimate futility of this approach, as the major protagonists in both live (at best) empty lives. It is only by immersing ourselves in our lives that we might find meaning, and then only *within* them, for it is only within our lives that meaning might be generated. And, indeed, it is life itself that is the ultimate source of value for Camus, which, on occasion, leads him to privilege the brute quantity of experience, without any qualitative distinctions whatsoever: "On the one hand the absurd teaches that all experiences are unimportant, and on the other hand it urges toward the greatest quantity of experiences," or more simply, "what counts is not the best living but the most living." Nevertheless, much as is the case for Nietzsche himself, the commitment to life itself does provide the basis for making normative distinctions, and although Camus says when speaking of Sisyphus that "the absurd man says yes and his effort henceforth will be unceasing," this is not the yea-saying of Nietzsche's ass in *Thus Spake Zarathustra*. Thus, Ivan Karamazov's "'everything is permitted' does not mean nothing is forbidden" (Camus 1955: 50), and perhaps the best illustration of Camusian ethics in the face of absurdity is to be found in his novel *The Plague*, an allegory of the Nazi occupation.

At the start of this chapter, I indicated that absurdity has survived the existentialist moment proper, a fact amply demonstrated by the relatively recent turn in Derridean deconstruction. For many years, deconstruction seemingly eschewed the politico-ethical, ostensibly on the grounds that any position staked out would capitulate to the pernicious fiction of "self-presence." Since the late 1980s, however, deconstruction has turned away from its more objectivistic deportment, which grew out of the structuralist moment that had supplanted existentialism in France, to one oriented toward the politico-ethical, and, specifically, the problematical nature of politico-ethical decision-making. According to Derrida, such decisions are "impossible," for there is no factual situation or set of reasons that can determine the decision in advance, lest the decision itself lose its ethical bona fides. Thus, self-consciously mimicking Kierkegaard, he contends that a "leap of decision" is needed in which all prior reasoning is bracketed, for all truly responsible decisions are "radically incommensurable" – or, in other words, they are absurd.

References and Further Reading

Camus, A. (1955) *The Myth of Sisyphus and Other Essays* (trans. J. O'Brien). New York: Vintage (original work published 1942).

Descartes, R. (1998) *Discourse on Method* (trans. D. A. Cress). Indianapolis: Hackett (original work published 1637).

Heidegger, M. (1962) *Being and Time* (trans. J. Macquarrie and E. Robinson). New York: Harper & Row (original work published 1927).

—— (1998) What is metaphysics? In *Pathmarks*, ed. W. McNeill (pp. 82–96). Cambridge: Cambridge University Press (original lecture delivered 1929).

Kierkegaard, S. (1986) *Fear and Trembling* (trans. A. Hannay). New York: Penguin (original work published 1843).

—— (1992) *Concluding Unscientific Postscript to Philosophical Fragments: Volume I* (trans. H. V. Hong and E. H. Hong). Princeton, NJ: Princeton University Press (original work published 1846).

Pascal, B. (2003) *Pensées* (trans. W. F. Trotter). Mineola, NY: Dover (original work published 1670).

Sartre, J.-P. (1956) *Being and Nothingness* (trans. H. E. Barnes). New York: Philosophical Library (original work published 1943).

—— (1957) *Existentialism and Human Emotion* (trans. B. Frechtman). New York: Philosophical Library.

—— (1964) *Nausea* (trans. L. Alexander). New York: New Directions (original work published 1938).

20

Death

DAVID COUZENS HOY

In view of the genocidal wars and the slaughter of millions of noncombatants in the last hundred years, it is not surprising that death is a crucial issue for twentieth-century continental philosophers. Martin Heidegger's *Being and Time* (1927; cited as Heidegger 1962) provokes a fascination with death that continues to be a central preoccupation of existentialism. However, when Heidegger in his "Letter on Humanism" (1947; cited as Heidegger 1993) repudiates Jean-Paul Sartre's existentialist reading of *Being and Time*, he opens the door to philosophical reactions against existentialism.

In addition to Heidegger, however, these existentialist and phenomenological ruminations about death are unimaginable without Hegel. Hegel's *Phenomenology of Spirit* (1807) is the story of shapes of consciousness undergoing dialectical transformations. The transitions from one shape to another involve a form of logical suicide or "dialectical negation" whereby a shape of consciousness discovers incoherence between what it thinks it can know and what it does know. In the transition from consciousness to self-consciousness, for instance, death takes on a central philosophical importance when Hegel makes it one of two conditions – the other is work – for the emergence initially of *self*-consciousness and eventually of *free* self-consciousness. Death has this role because it is only by seeing one's entire life negated that one comes to have a sense of one's life as a whole. Without this grasp of the whole of life, Hegel suggests that a being could be neither self-conscious nor free. At the same time, however, Hegel's analysis may be open to the objection that one could not be aware of one's death unless one were already self-conscious. This problem elicits different reactions from philosophers as twentieth-century continental thought takes on different shapes. Heidegger's phenomenology and Sartre's existentialism, which are the topic of this chapter, represent crucially different moments in the history of "death" in twentieth-century philosophy.

Martin Heidegger on Being-toward-Death

In *Being and Time*, Heidegger maintains that a distinguishing feature of human existence, or what he calls Dasein, is that it is an issue for itself. Dasein can call itself into question and take a stand on itself. However, Heidegger expressly avoids beginning his analysis of Dasein with the isolated, reflective individual standing at a distance from worldly affairs. Dasein is neither a Cartesian cogito whose contents are transparent to itself nor an existentialist tragic hero who stoically resists the social pressure to conform. Instead, Dasein is to be understood from its immersion in everyday activities. Whereas the existentialist picture views everydayness negatively, for Heidegger our ability to get around in the world and to cope with its demands is a skill. Although he says that everydayness involves "falling," he is not using this term pejoratively. However, when he also describes everydayness as "fleeing," the suggestion of evasion and self-deception is evident. We find ourselves always already "fallen" into a situation that we did not create and that we cannot entirely control. When we are unable to face up to the situation, which includes human mortality, we flee into doing what everyone else would do. Although Heidegger does not express it this way, the difference between falling and fleeing is much like the difference between acculturation and conformism. Acculturation is how people acquire their preferences. Conformism turns these preferences into patterns of thought and action that everyone is expected to display. Acculturation gives us the possibilities in terms of which we understand our lives. Conformism reifies these possibilities into a single set of necessary norms that then becomes the only recognized and sanctioned way that one should comport oneself.

Insofar as functional acculturation or falling can turn so readily into dysfunctional conformism or fleeing, Heidegger needs to explain how Dasein can resist the conformist pressures of society and establish its unique identity or "authenticity." An antecedent for his account of how this resistance is possible is the poet Rainer Maria Rilke, who had already seen death as the key to this problem. In his one prose work, *The Notes of Malte Laurids Brigge* (1910; cited as Rilke 1990), Rilke distinguishes between the great death and the small death. His character, Malte, anticipates not only Sartre's protagonist in the novel, *Nausea* (1938), but also Heidegger's distinction between my own death and the death of others. Rilke's Malte, who is destitute and despondent in Paris, writes:

> The desire to have a death of one's own is becoming more and more rare. In a short time it will be as rare as a life of one's own . . . You come, you find a life, ready-made, you just have to slip it on. You leave when you want to, or when you're forced to: anyway, no effort: *Voilà votre mort, monsieur.* You die as best you can; you die the death that belongs to the sickness that you have (for since all sicknesses are well known, it is also known that the various fatal endings belong to the sicknesses and not to the people; and the sick person has, so to speak, nothing more to do). (Rilke 1990: 9)

Death is experienced uncomfortably and is covered up in elaborate but discreet funerals where, as Thomas Mann suggests, one can blink at death and not see it. Heidegger, Rilke, and Mann make the point that in refusing to recognize death, one refuses to recognize life.

In *Being and Time*, Heidegger maintains that the everyday evasion of my own death happens by taking my own death as if it were the death of another. Death is not really encountered when another dies insofar as one lives on. Furthermore, although one suffers a loss when another dies, it would be a mistake to equate that loss with the loss that the dying person experiences. When the other dies, for the survivors there is just one less person in the world, whereas the dying person loses everything. As an example (not Heidegger's), consider grief for a stricken loved one. Profound grief is not simply

for the objective loss of the person or for the resulting restrictions on one's own continuing possibilities. Instead, a more authentic form of grief would be over the other
person's own sense of the loss of any continuing possibilities.

This sense of loss is misconstrued by typical ways of thinking about death as an end,
such as when a curtain comes down at the end of a play. Heidegger deconstructs such
clichés about death, which mistakenly treat the end of life as the end of a present-
at-hand object or a ready-to-hand tool. Death is not equivalent to the fullness of the
moon because Dasein always includes what is *not yet*. Even when faced with immediate execution, Dasein still has a bit of the "not yet" left. Death is also not comparable to
the ripening of fruit because Dasein does not necessarily end in fulfillment, or it may
have long passed its ripeness. Death is also not similar to the rain stopping, the road
ending, or the bread running out. When the road ends in a construction zone, for
instance, it is simply unfinished or incomplete, which Dasein never is. Dasein is always
entirely itself at every moment precisely because of its relation to its death. Dasein's
death is always impending, even if not in the same way that a storm or the arrival of a
friend impends. In these latter examples life continues, whereas "the death which
impends does not have this kind of Being" (Heidegger 1962: 294). In death, what is
impending is more radically the absence of any impending at all. Heidegger therefore
characterizes death as "the possibility of the absolute impossibility of Dasein" (Heidegger
1962: 294). Heidegger's point is that the idea of death as an end that completes life is
an inappropriate characterization of Dasein's dying.

There are many inauthentic ways of covering up my own death. Publicly, the other
always dies, not oneself. Dying is "leveled off" so that it only happens to nobody in
particular, and "'in no case is it I myself'" (Heidegger 1962: 297). The ambiguity of
idle talk conceals the nonrelational (*unbezügliche*) or the not-outstrippable (*unüberholbare*)
character of my own death. The fact that death is not to be outstripped means that it is
unavoidable and necessary. Death is nonrelational because I must die my own death.
The "temptation" is to go into what we now call denial and conceal our own deaths
from ourselves. People try to "tranquilize" the dying by telling them that they will
be fine again soon. Heidegger believes that the living are really trying to convince
themselves that death is not a problem. Watching people die becomes so uncomfortable that an actual death is taken as a serious social inconvenience, and even a display
of "downright tactlessness" (Heidegger 1962: 298).

On the existentialist reading of *Being and Time*, Heidegger is sometimes interpreted
as dwelling on anxiety in the face of death because he wants to encourage both a stoic
indifference to death and an aristocratic superiority over death. This criticism misreads
Heidegger's text, for he describes this attitude of indifference toward death as the
inauthentic alienation from death. This alienation is produced by two evasions. First,
there is the evasion of turning anxiety about the impending death into a fear of the
event itself. Fear is of an object in the world, whereas anxiety is about the world as
such. Collapsing anxiety into fear makes a concern for death into a weakness. This
concern about being weak leads to the second evasion whereby one then has to prove
one's superiority and indifference to one's own death. However, it is important to
realize that Heidegger is not advocating this attitude of superior indifference. Instead,
he sees such an attitude as another instance of inauthentic "alienation" from the
inevitability of one's own death, and as an attempt to blink at death by trying not to

care about it. Although Heidegger does not put the point exactly in these words, his analyses imply that this attitude fails insofar as the effort involved in the attempt to control death shows how much one really does care about one's mortality. At least, this interpretation is suggested by Heidegger's examples of trying to control death by "brooding" over it all the time or by "expecting" it at any moment, both of which in effect represent the attempt to put death off as long as possible (Heidegger 1962: 305). Even an air of "untroubled indifference" toward the uttermost possibility of existence masks a deeper concern where Dasein's ownmost potentiality-for-Being is "constantly an issue for Dasein" (Heidegger 1962: 299). At one level, Heidegger is suggesting that the attempt to appear indifferent to and untroubled by death is likely to be merely feigned. At a deeper level, his point is that being-toward-death is not just a matter of "thinking about death," but that it pervades a much broader spectrum of everyday comportment.

For Heidegger, facing up to instead of fleeing my own mortality becomes the key to authentic life. Heidegger believes that my own death has priority over the death of others (a claim that Sartre disputes). Death is uniquely mine, Heidegger says. He adds that dying is the one thing that nobody else can do for me, and that I cannot do for someone else: "*No one can take the Other's dying away from him*" (Heidegger 1962: 284). Just as for Hegel, for Heidegger the possibility of death first makes it possible to see one's life as a whole. This vision would also include a projection of the "not yet" that is still outstanding in one's life. Given the immersion in the multitude of demands placed on one in everydayness, the possibility of rising above these demands and seeing life as a whole would seem unlikely. Only the possibility of death and of the withdrawal of all these everyday demands gives rise to a sense of life as a whole, even if simply in the negative sense of all that would no longer be the case. Mortality is behind our sense of our finitude, and the recognition of finitude is what first makes some things matter more than others.

The authentic relation to death involves not being in denial, but instead, recognizing the *certainty* of death. What Heidegger calls the *anticipation* of the certainty of death "shatters *all* one's tenaciousness to whatever existence one has reached" (Heidegger 1962: 308; emphasis added). In this sense, anticipatory being-toward-death "individualizes" Dasein (Heidegger 1962: 310). Anticipation frees up Dasein from inauthentic everydayness and from the anonymous other (*das Man*) so that it can act "of its own accord" (Heidegger 1962: 308). To individualize is not to subjectivize, however, and Heidegger does not mean to cut Dasein off from the world and leave it with inner subjectivity as the only source of commitment. To subjectivize Dasein in this way is the mistake made by the existentialist misreading of Heidegger. That is at least the view of Heidegger in the "Letter on Humanism," where he writes: "Man is never first and foremost man on the hither side of the world, as a "subject," whether this is taken as "I" or "We." Nor is he ever simply a mere subject which always simultaneously is related to objects, so that his essence lies in the subject–object relation" (Heidegger 1993: 252).

Although death could come at any moment, insofar as it is not here just yet, it is *indefinite*. The constant indefiniteness as to "when" the utter impossibility will become possible is the "constant *threat*" held open in anxiety (Heidegger 1962: 310). Heidegger draws together the certainty and the indefiniteness of death in what he calls "anticipatory resoluteness." Insofar as death is certain, one must anticipate it rather than cover it up. However, insofar as death is indefinite, and one does not know when it will happen, one finds oneself pushed into taking action. In taking action not haphazardly, but resolutely and with determination, Dasein "frees itself for its world" and is "nothing else than *Being-in-the-world*" (Heidegger 1962: 344). By a "being-in-the-world," Heidegger means that Dasein is a committed agent, who is situated in a worldly context, and not a disengaged subject, whose place in the world cannot be located. Resoluteness, explains Heidegger, "does not detach Dasein from its world, nor does it isolate it so that it becomes a free-floating 'I'" (Heidegger 1962: 344). To detach Dasein from its engagement in the world and to make it an alienated and isolated subject is the (existentialist) error that is due to what the "Letter on Humanism" describes as "the dominance of the modern metaphysics of subjectivity" (Heidegger 1993: 222–3).

Of course, we are still cultural beings and resoluteness will draw on the way the world is, including the way the anonymous other (*das Man*) configures it for us. Even when I determine my own commitments and others no longer determine my commitments for me, I am not disconnected from others because my commitments will involve understanding the others' potentiality as well as my own. The authentic Dasein can only ever start from possibilities inherent in its Situation. Heidegger does not think that resolve comes down to empty advice such as *carpe diem* ("seize the day"). However, he also says that "even resolutions remain dependent on the 'they' [*das Man*] and its world" (Heidegger 1962: 345–6). As an example, consider that in deciding one's career, one has to choose from what is available. However, the choice of becoming a teacher or a doctor or a sculptor is not authentic resoluteness insofar as these slots are there already. Authentic resoluteness would involve how one configured one's career to one's own potential and made one's activity distinctive.

Resoluteness does not create the concrete Situation, but only puts Dasein into it (Heidegger 1962: 347). Through the encounter with the limit-Situation of being-toward-death, anticipatory resoluteness allows us for the first time to *disclose* the concrete Situation authentically as our own, even if it is not our creation. In anticipatory resoluteness, the deeper, ontological being-toward-death is thus no longer simply about death in Rilke's "ontic," everyday sense of the moment of dying. Instead, being-toward-death involves reconfiguring life after the realization that at the limits choices have no transcendent grounding or justification. By showing that there is no authority for action other than one's own accord, authentic anticipation leads Dasein to give up commitments that it no longer sees as binding. Authentic resoluteness then involves thinking and acting so differently as even to transform the world and to change history. Ontologically interpreted, *Being and Time* therefore does not see authenticity as the psychological result of a private subject choosing its inner attitude toward the world. On the contrary, authenticity is a function of Dasein's efforts to bring about genuine change in the social and historical world.

Jean-Paul Sartre's Critique of Heidegger

In *Being and Nothingness* (1943; cited as Sartre 1966), the quintessential work of existentialism, Jean-Paul Sartre offers a different account of the finitude of existence, one that draws on the structure of choice rather than on the inevitability of death. For Sartre, one's death has little relevance to one's life. "It is the Other who is mortal in his being," Sartre asserts, and "there is no place for death in being-for-itself" (Sartre 1966: 699). Sartre recognizes that humans are finite beings, but he thinks that this finitude is not to be found in a future death that awaits me so much as from the present need to choose a course of action. Finitude and the irreversible direction of time come from the temporal necessity of choosing one thing before another and being unable to reverse this sequence. To argue for radical freedom and to prove that death is of no importance, Sartre wants to undermine the analysis of death in *Being and Time*. One must remember, however, that his criticisms often depend on an existentialist misreading of Heidegger. In particular, subjectivity for Sartre must be the point of philosophical departure and Sartre thinks that Heidegger goes wrong at the start by trying to avoid the Cartesian cogito. An initial critical move is to reject Heidegger's claim that dying is the only thing that no one else can do for me. Sartre maintains that no one else can love for me either, or do any number of other things for me. Furthermore, because subjectivity is already required if I am to be able to recognize death as mine, death does not individualize. Sartre also argues that death could not be awaited. "Live each moment as if it were the last" is bad advice, from Sartre's point of view, because it loses sight of the need for consistent action in a life that looks to the future. Sartre insists that I cannot experience my own death, because when I am dead, I cannot experience anything. Therefore, when I try to adopt an attitude toward my own death, what I am really doing, according to Sartre, is trying to view myself from the point of view of the other. *Contra* Heidegger, then, because I cannot experience my own death, Sartre concludes that death is merely a contingent brute fact. As such, my own death has no meaning for me.

However, at this point a close reader of Heidegger will want to insist that Sartre appears to be overlooking some central points of Heidegger's analysis that anticipate and avoid these criticisms. In particular, Heidegger's distinction between "perishing," "demise," and "being-toward-death" must be taken into account. "Perishing" and "demise" both suggest in ordinary language the ending of a life. "Perishing" is the ending of anything that lives. However, Dasein does not simply perish. Unlike lower forms of life, ending matters to it and is a feature of life itself, not merely a point at which life ends. Moreover, Dasein cannot perish. Insofar as Dasein never experiences its end, only the organism perishes. If "perishing" does not apply to one's own sense of existence, it also does not apply to the death of others. Human burial practices would not be as elaborate as they are if others were thought simply to perish. When loved ones die, cultural practices do not treat them as having simply ended. Instead, elaborate rituals are constructed to show that they continue to matter to us. If Sartre were right, a human corpse would be simply a lifeless thing. For Heidegger, in contrast, as something that has lost life, a human corpse deserves continued respect. Cultural burial practices confirm this claim.

Heidegger goes beyond ordinary language, therefore, and uses the term "demise" specifically for the ending of Dasein, which involves more than merely perishing: "Dasein too can end without authentically dying, though on the other hand, *qua* Dasein, it does not simply perish" (Heidegger 1962: 291). He also distinguishes demise from being-toward-death, even if ordinary language does not. Demise is the ending of a human life. However, "demise" is not coextensive in meaning with "being-toward-death," which is a feature of every moment of Dasein's life, not merely of the last moment. Being-toward-death involves a way to be, and specifically, a way to be *toward* the end, which Heidegger distinguishes from being *at* an end. "Being-toward-death" is a phenomenon of *life*. Heidegger says explicitly, "The 'ending' which we have in view when we speak of death, does not signify Dasein's Being-at-an-end [*Zu-Ende-sein*], but a *Being-towards-the-end* [*Sein zum Ende*] of this entity. Death is a way to be, which Dasein takes over as soon as it is" (Heidegger 1962: 289). Heidegger grounds his claim in a citation handed down from antiquity through Seneca: "'As soon as man comes to life, he is at once old enough to die'" (Heidegger 1962: 289).

Even if these distinctions obviate some of Sartre's criticisms of Heidegger, Sartre has other disagreements with him about the structure of human life and the direction of temporality. For Sartre, death can only remove meaning from life. A senseless death makes life senseless as well. This claim has several corollaries. Death cannot be the completion of life insofar as the individual does not freely determine death. Waiting for death would undercut all my other projects insofar as it would be the project of not having a project. Rather than death being the key to individualization, it cannot individualize because it is radically impersonal. In short, Sartre connects death to the existentialist notion of the absurd.

Sartre also disagrees with Heidegger about death as the source of temporal direction in the connectedness of life. Because death comes from the outside and is not an event that I can do anything about, it is not even one of my possibilities but is instead a pure fact, a brute datum. Sartre even goes so far as to say that at bottom death is "in no way distinguished from birth" (Sartre 1966: 698). This claim echoes the Roman philosopher Lucretius, who maintained that insofar as no one finds the eternity before one's birth disturbing, no one should fear the eternity after one's death. However, from Heidegger's point of view, this argument is off target because his notion of being-toward-death is concerned with what goes on *between* birth and death, not before birth or after death. Moreover, Lucretius and Sartre ignore the temporal asymmetry between birth and death. Most people feel strongly averse to their death, but not to their birth. There is a good reason for this aversion. As the contemporary analytic philosopher, Thomas Nagel, has argued in a way that supports Heidegger, "The direction of time is crucial in assigning possibilities to people or other individuals" (Nagel 1979: 8). Nagel maintains that the difference between birth and death is that death *deprives* one of life, whereas the time before birth does not represent a *loss* of life. To die earlier would represent a loss of possibilities. To have been born earlier would make one a different person entirely.

Finally, Sartre presses a charge derived from Alexandre Kojève's reading of Hegel's dialectic of the master and the slave, which Sartre generalizes into an account of the relation of self and other. Sartre says that death is "the triumph of the Other over me" (Sartre 1966: 697). The only way to prevent myself from being looked at and reduced to an object with no freedom is, on Sartre's account, to look back at the other and reduce it to an object. When I am dead, according to Sartre, I lose the ability to look back, and thus my death makes me the future prey of the living. This charge again depends on the existentialist assumption of an inner subjectivity that is isolated and alienated from others. Normally, however, one does not expect one's family or acquaintances to experience one's death as their triumph. Loved ones are also unlikely to think of the deceased as their prey. Sartre's counterintuitive claim follows only from his pessimistic view that social relations are essentially antagonistic. As one of his characters says in the short play, *No Exit* (1944; cited as Sartre 1989), "Hell is – other people."

Making these philosophical interpretations of death explicit is not a morbid enterprise. On the contrary, these philosophers' reflections on death are intended to help people live fuller lives. These phenomenological and existentialist debates are not about how to die, but about how to live. Correspondingly, from the social and historical perspective, philosophy's goal in the twenty-first century should be to ensure that the carnage of the twentieth century is not covered up and forgotten. By remembering the victims, philosophy now has a better chance of realizing its greatest hope and overcoming its deepest fear. The hope is that in the new century the record on life and death will be better. The fear is that it could turn out to be even worse.

References and Further Reading

Heidegger, M. (1962) *Being and Time* (trans. J. Macquarrie and E. Robinson). New York: Harper & Row (original work published 1927).

—— (1993) Letter on Humanism. In D. F. Krell (ed.), *Basic Writings* (pp. 213–66). San Francisco: Harper (original work published 1947).

Nagel, T. (1979) *Mortal Questions*. Cambridge: Cambridge University Press.

Rilke, R. M. (1990) *The Notebooks of Malte Laurids Brigge* (trans. Stephen Mitchell). New York: Vintage (original work published 1910).

Sartre, J-P. (1966) *Being and Nothingness* (trans. H. E. Barnes). New York: Washington Square Press (original work published 1943).

—— (1989) No Exit *and Three Other Plays* (trans. S. Gilbert). New York: Vintage Books (original work published 1944).

Part III

Contemporary Issues in Phenomenology and Existentialism

21

Emotions in Phenomenology and Existentialism

ROBERT C. SOLOMON

The realm of emotions is rich and promising territory for phenomenologists, although Edmund Husserl himself neither expressed nor exemplified much interest in the "affective" dimension of human life. In existentialist phenomenology, in particular, the emotions – or, in an older and more dramatic terminology, the passions, play a central role, in part as a pivotal concept in the opposition to traditional rationalism in philosophy. The two ancestral figures of existentialism, Søren Kierkegaard and Friedrich Nietzsche, both celebrated the life of the passions and, not surprisingly, developed some precocious phenomenological insights about them. Martin Heidegger, who was indebted to both Kierkegaard and Nietzsche, pursued some of these insights in a highly original thesis concerning the vital role of *moods* in human life, the various ways we "tune in" to the world and the way some of them, notably *angst* and boredom, prompt us to think "ontologically" about our lives and the meaning of our mortality. Other phenomenologists who have "existential" leanings, notably Max Scheler, Emmanuel Levinas, Jean-Paul Sartre, Maurice Merleau-Ponty, Gabriel Marcel, and Paul Ricoeur, also defended and explored the role of emotions, moods, and passions in life. Their many different projects and goals (ethical, interpersonal, religious, political) might be roughly suggested in Max Scheler's stunning expression, *"the emotional a priori,"* the idea that in emotions as in knowledge, there are basic structures of human existence that demand our attention and can be fruitfully explored. The emotions are as essential to our being as our rationality, and understanding them is just as necessary to understanding ourselves.

In this chapter, I want to spend only a modest amount of space and time reviewing the contributions of the classic phenomenologists and existentialists from Husserl and Heidegger to Sartre and Merleau-Ponty and instead try to do what they were doing, by way of an "original" project of phenomenological investigation and description. Needless to say, much of this will be greatly influenced if not outright parasitic on their work and their insights, and in that sense, let me first say that phenomenology is not and should not try to be a-historical. What we "see" and describe in our experience (even our allegedly "immediate" experience) is mediated by historically conditioned concepts and categories. The essential structures of emotional experience, as the essential structures of human experience more generally, are dependent on historical and social context and on the evolution of language. As Heidegger noted, there is no reason to suppose that the experience of the ancient Greek was comparable or even commensurable – much less identical – to ours. (Heidegger wryly commented that the Greeks did not *have* experiences.) The medieval Christians did not share an emotional world with the pagans, and we no longer share the world with our various puritan, Victorian, and tribal ancestors. Whether or not there is some core of "basic" emotions, now defined in terms of universal neurophysiological "affect programs" that humans share with many "higher" animals, there is no a priori reason to suppose that the emotional lives of different peoples or even of different individuals is essentially – "basically" – the same.

The very idea of "basic emotions," however, suggests that the phenomenology of emotions might be a superfluous or even grossly mistaken enterprise. If an emotion is essentially a physiological state, then any experience associated with it is merely incidental. There are many researchers in emotion theory who have suggested just this, insisting that an emotion is (essentially) a neurophysiological state or process and any distinctive experience is epiphenomenal (or "icing on the cake," as one recent researcher put it (Le Doux 1996)). William James set the stage here. Although he insisted that an emotion is essentially a kind of experience he also insisted that it was a specific, phenomenologically impoverished experience, a sensation or set of sensations registering physiological disturbances (e.g., the feeling of being flushed, or being agitated, of one's hair standing on end). So, too, a recent theorist, Antonio Damasio, has speculated that an emotional feeling is a "marker" of what is going on in the brain (Damasio 1999). To be sure, it has now been established beyond question that the emotions have an interesting life in the brain, that there are specifiable brain states or processes which seem to be the *sine qua non* of particular emotions (and of emotions in general).

One might argue that, nevertheless, our *concept* of emotion (and emotions) does not include this causal substratum, and though it may be demonstrable that the brain is causally necessary to emotion, it is surely not conceptually necessary that emotions have their substance in the brain. It is often noted, in this regard, that Aristotle had a remarkably clear understanding of *pathé* without having the foggiest idea of what the brain did. But I think that this argument (which for many years I prosecuted myself) misses the point. First, it presumes an essentialism about psychological concepts, that psychological concepts do not change with increased awareness of (what may once have been) extraneous knowledge. Whether or not one wants to go so far as the "eliminative materialists"[1] of our own day, there is every reason to think that our concept of emotion is rapidly changing with the burgeoning literature on neurology. (And also, I would add, on computers and artificial intelligence. A moment's thought brings to mind all sorts of computer images and metaphors, "program," "input," "circuits," "delete button," etc., that now function in the vernacular of talk about emotions.) As historical fact, our present concept of emotion – that is, the use of "emotion" (in English) to encompass a very wide and varied group of phenomena, is only a century and a half old (see Dixon 2003). Second, the argument misses the important point that the emotions have almost always been considered (including by Aristotle) *bodily* phenomena and the physiological (as opposed to the specifically neurophysiological) has always been part and parcel of the phenomenology of emotion.

This, in turn, raises the question of whether emotions really are "essentially" any-thing at all, and thus whether they have essential structures as well as whether they are essentially experiential. There is still considerable debate and disagreement as to whether Husserl's phenomenology was or was not essentialist, but it became quite clear in his footsteps – in Heidegger and Merleau-Ponty, especially – that essentialism was not essential to phenomenology. One can describe the seemingly most significant features or structures of one's experience without supposing either that these are universal features of (human) experience or that they are strictly necessary features of (one's own or any) experience. So I propose the following modification: that our psychological concepts (our concepts of emotion in particular) change, and there is nothing strictly essential (in the Aristotelian sense of logically necessary and sufficient conditions) about them. Nevertheless, one can describe particularly significant and stable structures and features, and I will continue to use the adjective "essential" in this much weakened condition. Thus our concepts of emotion change (and with that, our emotions), and so do their "essential" (in the weakened sense) features.

I should also say that while I will continue to use the "Cartesian" language of "expe-rience" and "consciousness," I do not mean to imply any ontological commitment of the sort that is at stake, most notably, in the dispute between Husserl and Heidegger. In other words, I want to imply nothing about consciousness as a "realm," as a special kind of being ("for-itself"), or as an aspect of the Cartesian worldview. Nor do I mean to commit myself to a sense of "experience" such that an experience is strictly mental, or private, or "privileged," nor do I want to legislate whether experiences can be shared and public. All I need is the plausibility of a first-person viewpoint, or what one con-temporary philosopher (Thomas Nagel) is fond of calling "what it's like to be." An emotional experience, accordingly, can be described as "what it is like to have that emotion," as distinct from "what one does when having that emotion," or "what happens in the brain of someone having that emotion."

Our emotions (as we now conceive of them) involve different aspects or dimensions, two of which are the bodily (broadly conceived) and the experiential (also broadly conceived). Whether or not either of these aspects or dimensions in turn has anything like essential structures, they both surely have well-confirmed central attributes, the involvement of the brain, for one, certain kinds of experience for another. This leaves considerable room for counter-examples and theoretical revision, but it does not give up the quest for understanding in terms of notably significant structures and features. For example, one of the central attributes of emotional experience is *intentionality*: an emotion has an object. Intentional objects can be any number of sorts of things, people, people's behavior, states of affairs, and so on, but the idea that emotions are directed toward (or, I would rather say, engaged with) the world (including oneself) is an idea that has been well confirmed even by theorists who set out to challenge it (see Zajonc 1980; Prinz 2004b). There are moods and other emotional phenomena (dread, anxiety, joy) that seem to violate this claim, but rather than give up the claim, which seems to me essential to understanding emotion (and why emotions are not, for instance, mere physiological affect programs), we are invited to rethink the nature of intentionality (and the range of emotions) in a more creative way. Is the object of an emotion necessarily determinate (a specific person, event, state of affairs)? Or are there indeterminate objects ("the Unknown," "the world of the depressed man")? Are all emotional phenomena necessarily emotions, or should we make the latter category more restrictive and broaden the former? So, too, the common claim that emotions are (essentially) bodily. It may well be that many emotions have their characteristic physiological expressions, including spontaneous facial expressions and other such behavior. But surely there are some that do not, for instance aesthetic emotions and certain moral emotions (what Hume called "the calm passions"). So should we take rage and panic as paradigms of emotion because of their obvious physiological symptomatology, or should we hold out for a broader, more inclusive category of the emotional as "what we care about"? In which case, the bodily manifestations of emotion, in at least many cases, are pretty much beside the point. To end this introduction on a purely tautological note, from the phenomenological point of view, the essence of an emotion is its phenomenology.

The Phenomenology of Emotions: A Historical Sketch

Long before phenomenology, there were insightful analyses of emotion. With a bit of hindsight and reinterpretation, we can understand at least some of these analyses as precocious phenomenological descriptions. Aristotle, notably, gave us a detailed and deeply insightful analysis of emotions in his *Rhetoric* (*c.* 350 BCE), focusing especially on anger. He made only passing mention of the feelings involved in emotion (and, in *De Anima* – *c.* 350 BCE – hypothesized a physiological description in terms of the boiling of the blood around the heart). But the core of his analysis was very much a piece of social phenomenology: anger is the perception of a slight and the accompanying desire to avenge oneself. Whether or not he had any concept of intentionality (see Caston 1992), Aristotle clearly acknowledged that the proper description of an emotion focused first of all on what it was about and thus made emotion kin to perception. But he also added that emotion is essentially tied to intention, desire, and action (or rather, joining some contemporary theorists, we should say action tendencies) and, we should note, judgments of value and appropriateness (in today's terms, "appraisal").

After Aristotle, the Stoics in particular developed a rich set of theories about emotion, focusing on their "cognitive" aspects (emotions as evaluative judgments), distinguishing between physiologically based but distinctively felt "first movements" and the emotion proper, which involved judgment and "affirmation." Seneca's wonderful but somewhat verbose treatise on anger (*De Ira, c.* 50; cited as Seneca 1928), for example, is an excellent example of phenomenological analysis made 1,850 years before Husserl gave that discipline its name. St. Augustine, of course, described his tumultuous emotions in considerable detail, as did everyone who later took the "subjective" turn in philosophy. Thus Descartes devoted a significant portion of his career to analyzing the emotions, and his best book, in my mind, is his treatise on the *Passions of the Soul* (1649). Descartes was concerned about emotions first of all because they stood in a particularly awkward position straddling the two Cartesian "substances" of mind and body. But in addition to his speculations about the brain, the well-placed pineal gland, and the "animal spirits" that pulsed with the blood through the body, Descartes found himself inevitably describing the phenomenology of emotions as well, for instance, "love is the desire to be with the beloved object" (Descartes 1989: Article XXX). So, too, Spinoza, despite his off-putting geometrical-deductive style and seeming rejection of the subjective perspective, undertook a catalog of the emotions, reduced for the most part to one-sentence phenomenological descriptions, some of them surprisingly poignant.

In the empiricist camp, David Hume provided us with an elaborate quasi-phenomenological description of several emotions, struggling with the idea of intentionality ("an original connection"), and making it clear that the phenomenology of emotion was complex, not simple. An emotion consists of two different sorts of distinct but causally linked phenomena: impressions (sensations) and ideas. The intentional object of pride, for instance, is one's Self, but the self in two different guises (ideas), one the Self as the author of some accomplishment, the second the Self as such. And although Hume sticks with the common idea that the emotion is essentially only a sensation (in the case of pride a distinctively pleasant sensation) and thus "contains not any representative quality," his analysis makes it perfectly clear that emotions necessarily have a conceptual structure and that this is what defines them (Hume 1973: 415).

Hume was also one of the "moral sentiment theorists," and, with his friend Adam Smith, he undertook a somewhat detailed (and not entirely consistent) analysis of "sympathy." Smith expanded on Hume's analysis considerably, and he made it clear that not only was sympathy (or, rather, what we would now call "empathy") essential to morality but to human nature as such. Without sympathy for/with the emotions of others, it is doubtful that we could have social relations at all.[2] But the analysis of sympathy in Smith pays considerable benefits in terms of the phenomenology of emotions in general, as sympathy (empathy) turns out not to be a single emotion but a vehicle for understanding, from the first-person point of view, any number of emotions ranging from disgust and repulsion to compassion and concern. It is worth noting here that virtually all of these theorists, not only Hume and Smith but Aristotle, Augustine, and Spinoza took the analysis (phenomenology) of emotions to be an essential part of *ethics*. In their view, a value-free phenomenology of emotion would have been a pointless academic exercise. With the turn toward scientific philosophy, including Husserl's own insistence on rigorous and scientific phenomenology (*als Wissenschaft*), this essentially ethical orientation would tend to get lost.

I have already credited Kierkegaard and Nietzsche for their sometimes profound if unsystematic observations on both the nature of emotion and on specific emotions (for instance, *ressentiment* and *angst*), and by the time we approach genuinely phenomenological territory a good deal of the terrain has already been mapped out. Franz Brentano is of particular importance here, not only because he directly influenced Husserl and Max Scheler (who were more or less his students), but because he himself elaborated a proto-phenomenological theory ("descriptive psychology") of love and hate and rejected the more traditional views of Descartes and Hume, in particular, and the idea that emotions are essentially sensations. He also deserves mention among the moral sentiment theorists, but greatly improves on their analysis by insisting on intentionality as the essential feature of emotions. Thus emotions are not merely subjective and can be "correct," as judgments are correct. He only sketched analyses of such emotions as fear, hope, and dread, which he insisted were "extraordinarily complex," but he urged subsequent theorists to take up such an investigation. And some of his students did just that.

William James, despite his physiological bent in his analysis of emotion, gave a powerful prod to phenomenology. His overall philosophy, after all, was all about *experience*, and though he tends to treat emotion as a species of unthinking instinct his more general analysis of sensation and perception in his classic *Principles of Psychology* (1950) is first-rate phenomenology, as are some of his analyses in *The Varieties of Religious Experience* (James 1902).[3] In the *Principles*, James makes clear that all sensation and perception are conceptual and, though he tends to avoid the term, intentional. If only he had extended this analysis to the emotions, he would rate as one of the most import-ant phenomenologists of emotion, instead of serving in a very different role as the target of Sartre's critique and the butt of several generations of philosophical emotion theorists in the twentieth century. Freud, another student of Brentano, embraced the idea of intentionality even if, like James, also a physician, he tended to medicalize his analysis and attempt to ground it in physiology and "instinct." Thus Freud dis-tinguishes between "idea" and "affect," much like Hume before him, and, as in Hume, the distinction causes him considerable grief (see Freud 2001). But intentionality soon emerges as the very core of any adequate analysis of emotions, and this is Brentano's and Husserl's invaluable contribution to the phenomenology of emotions.

The Phenomenology of Emotions: The Existential Turn

Phenomenology proper begins with Edmund Husserl, but Husserl displayed little interest in the emotional side of life. Brentano, as mentioned, embraced the phenom-enological approach without calling it such, but his other student, Max Scheler, was both a phenomenologist and very interested in emotions. He elaborated Brentano's moral sentiment theory in great detail, focusing especially on the nature of sympathy as well as on Brentano's own interests in love, hate, pity, and resentment. Like the earlier moral sentiment theorists, Scheler defended such feelings of sympathy, kind-ness, generosity, and sincerity as the essential moral values of actions. This set him on a collision course with a philosopher he greatly admired, Immanuel Kant, and Scheler's *Formalism in Ethics and Non-formal Ethics of Values* is essentially a rejection of Kant's formalism in favor of "value-feelings" (Scheler 1973). Echoing Brentano and anticip-ating Heidegger, Scheler insists that our primary awareness of the world consists of our emotional responses, not affect-less knowledge. Thus he, too, rejects the Cartesian–Humean analysis of emotion in terms of sensation or, as he put it, "blind feeling." He defends a strongly cognitive theory of emotions, an analysis in terms of "intentional feeling" rather than "feeling states" with this. Following his own interpretation of Pascal's "the heart has its reasons . . . ," he attempts to transcend the traditional distinction between emotion and reason. Rationality includes – it does not stand in opposition to – emotional appraisal of the world.

Martin Heidegger's role in history of the existential phenomenology of emotion is both central and problematic. To begin with the problems, Heidegger wrote about moods, not emotions, he refused the label "existentialist," and it is highly debatable whether he remains a phenomenologist even through the opening chapters of Part I of *Being and Time* (Heidegger 1962). But I think that these problems are superficial and irrelevant for our purposes here. Whether or not Heidegger continued to con-sider himself a phenomenologist as he was writing *Being and Time* (it is clear that he gave it up afterward) is of little importance in understanding his important contributions to the phenomenology of emotion. He clearly adopted his teacher's conception of intentionality, however radically his understanding of that concept may have shifted (for instance, in his insistence that the primary object of our awareness is the world and in his rejection of Husserl's idea that the immediate object of perception is something other than the world). He vehemently rejected the Cartesian framework that Husserl presupposed, but the idea that "being-in-the-world" is a "unitary phenomenon" is an important breakthrough in the analysis of emotional experience (though Heidegger, of course, would never use such a phrase). It also updates and improves upon Scheler's insight about the "objectivity" of [some] emotions and his rejection of the idea that emotions consist of subjective feelings as opposed to a direct apprehension of the world. As for Heidegger's rejection of the label "existentialist," we need only say that he was not the only one to do so (Camus, for one, also rejected it, and, at first, Sartre and de Beauvoir did as well.) We need not delve into the complex question just what that label means, but it is enough to say that it gives a nod to Kierkegaard and Nietzsche, both important influences on Heidegger's own philosophy, and it points to an emphasis on "*existenz*," a sense of one's possibilities (which I will make no attempt to explicate here). For Heidegger, as for Kierkegaard, it is enough to say that *existenz* is one of the essential features of Dasein and, with particular reference to emotions, encompasses the insight that many if not most of our emotions are concerned with possibilities for the future (including our understanding and response to the past).[4]

Of particular significance is the fact that Heidegger wrote about moods, not emotions. This makes particularly good sense if it is the world, and not particular things or events, that is their primary object. Moods are usually distinguished from emotions on the basis of the specificity of the object, although the nature of the distinction often varies, sometimes radically. For instance, it is said that while emotions are intentional and are directed toward a (more or less specific) object, moods are *not* intentional and are not directed toward anything at all. Thus, in an important sense, emotions are "objective" and moods are merely "subjective," rather like transient mental weather ("cloudy this morning, becoming sunny in the afternoon"). I think that this is wrong and Heidegger gets it right. Moods are directed toward *the world*, and, on this view, one might think of all emotions as the narrowing of the scope and focus of a mood. On the other hand, some psychologists treat moods as more durable, rather like psychological traits, and emotions as short-term immediate responses.[5] Or, perhaps, we might think of emotions as directed toward a (more or less) specific object while moods are directed toward a more general object, namely the world, or as indeterminate, directed toward any number of objects, or as indiscriminate, directed toward any objects that happen to come along. Consider sadness, for instance. In a sad mood, the world itself may seem a let-down, disappointing, a poor excuse for a world. Or, in a sad mood, *everything* seems sad. Or, in a sad mood, whatever topic one brings up seems sad, now the political situation, now one's romantic life, now the state of education in America or the unpreparedness of one's own students. But, in any case, emotions and moods are tightly linked and differ mainly in the specificity of their objects, not in their essential structure. Thus what Heidegger says of moods I think we can fairly extrapolate to at least those emotions with some sort of global import, not petty anger, perhaps, but certainly Kierkegaardian dread and Nietzsche's resentment.

And what Heidegger says about moods (emotions) is dramatic. First and foremost, they are our ways of being "tuned" to the world (a notorious pun in German: *Stimmung*, mood; *bestimmen*, tuning). We can appreciate the (unacknowledged) debt to Scheler here, but whereas Scheler was primarily concerned with those emotions such as love and hate that define our personal relationships with other individuals, Heidegger is concerned with those moods that have a special role in prompting our becoming "ontological," that is, reflective of what is essential and important in our lives. Thus *angst* is a mood, initiated (knowingly or not) by our sense of our own impending death, that prompts us to self-reflection, self-understanding, and "authenticity" (*eigentlichkeit*). Thus moods (and at least some emotions) do not only allow us to find out about the world but to find out about ourselves and spur us to life-changing resolutions. (This is the existential dimension in Heidegger's philosophy, if anything is.)

Jean-Paul Sartre is the first of the existential phenomenologists to attempt a theory of emotions as such, taking on such psychologists as William James and Sigmund Freud. Sartre's short 1938 essay, *Emotions: A Sketch of a Theory* (Sartre 1948), part of a (discarded) longer work on "the psyche," begins with a long critique of James and ends with a sketch of Sartre's own theory of emotions as "magical transformations of the world." Against James, Sartre scores two important points. First, he points out that James has ignored the essential structure of emotional experience, namely, intentionality. An emotion, Sartre insists, is about the world. Second, Sartre insists that emotions have "*finalité*," that is, purposefulness. They are not only functional and occasionally advantageous, nor are they just the fortuitous residue of fickle evolution, but emotions are *in themselves* strategic and political. To put it differently and somewhat controversially, emotions do not just "happen" to us, as the whole language of "passion" and "being struck by" would suggest. They are, with some contentious stretching of the term, activities that we "do," strategies that work for us.

Sartre here makes a bold step onto treacherous territory. Not that he is without his illustrious predecessors. The ancient Stoics, in particular, insisted that emotions are judgments that we choose to make about the world, and even where they are spontaneous (and we "find ourselves" making them), we can choose not to "assent" to them. Some of the Medievals insisted that we have a lot more control over our passions than we allow ourselves to believe, and, accordingly, sins are not just afflictions but matters of will and responsibility. Sartre would say (although he had not coined this phrase yet) that believing that we cannot control our passions is just another strategy of "bad faith" (*mauvaise foi*), a way of denying our responsibility for who we are, what we do, and what we feel. Like the Stoics, and like his more immediate predecessors Scheler and Heidegger, Sartre thinks that our emotions are not only ways of knowing the world but ways of transforming the world and ourselves.

Sartre's phrase, "magical transformations of the world," means just this, that we alter our perceptions of the world in order to reorient ourselves and set in motion a different way of understanding the world and its difficulties. (The word "magical" does at least double duty for Sartre. First it marks a distinction between changing the world and "non-instrumentally" altering our perceptions of the world. Second, it refers to the ability to alter our bodily states, by way of "incantation," to further our emotional strategies, for instance – to take an extreme example – by fainting or making oneself otherwise incapacitated.) Unfortunately, Sartre follows through this promising analysis by losing heart. The only purpose of emotion he specifies is "escape behavior" which avoids a difficult situation. He further gives up ground by admitting that emotions are "degradations of consciousness" in which we "entrap" ourselves, thus falling back into the old prejudices against emotions and neglecting the most exciting promise of *finalité*, namely the many ways in which we *use* our emotions to inspire and further our projects in life. (This is a correction which becomes apparent in his later, greater work, *Being and Nothingness*; 1943; cited as Sartre 1954).

Against Freud, Sartre initiates his soon to be familiar arguments against "psychic determinism" and against the very concept of "the unconscious." Sartre's insistence on freedom as the essence of human consciousness means that nothing in our psyches is simply "determined," and what he describes (in good Cartesian fashion) as the "trans-lucency" of consciousness means that nothing can hide or be hidden in consciousness. Thus there can be no "Unconscious" mind. But Sartre explains many Freudian phe-nomena by insisting that emotions tend to be "pre-reflective" (rather than "reflective") and in place of Freudian "defense *mechanisms*" there is the pre-reflective *refusal* to admit or acknowledge certain facts about oneself. Indeed, Sartre follows Freud quite energetically, however harsh his words about Freud's theories, in the pursuit of an effective psychoanalytic therapeutic technique. But it is an "existential psychoana-lysis," and it suggests the potential practical value of a phenomenology of emotions. Describing the structures of our emotions is not just a matter of self-understanding. It can be a matter of self-transformation as well.

Finally, a word about Sartre's younger existentialist partner (and co-editor of the journal *Les Temps Modernes*, founded in 1945), Maurice Merleau-Ponty. Merleau-Ponty is important for the phenomenology of emotions – a subject that he barely broached – mainly because of his ingenious and much-needed shift from intentionality to motility, creating a distinctively bodily perspective for phenomenology. The Husserlian notion of intentionality focuses primarily on the object of emotion and its significance to the subject, and only secondarily on the "act" of intending. Even then, this act is almost wholly disembodied, an act of pure or "transcendental" consciousness. It includes nothing by way of reference to the body (except insofar as the body itself might be the object of the emotion). But the body, insists Merleau-Ponty, is the *subject* of the emo-tion. The intentions of the body are not merely subsequent or secondary to the sorts of intentions discussed by Husserl, Scheler, and Sartre. (Heidegger clearly does not en-dorse the Cartesian "mind–body" split on which all of this is based, but neither does he talk about the body as an important aspect of our existential structures.) What Merleau-Ponty brings to the center of our attention is a new appreciation of the ancient and Jamesian sense that the emotions are essentially bodily, but without the neglect of phenomenology that this realization usually encourages. The phenomenology of emo-tion is, in part, a phenomenology of the body and bodily movement, and any analysis that neglects this cannot possibly provide an adequate analysis of emotion.

The Phenomenology of Emotional Experience – Intentionality

The phenomenology of emotions is the investigation of the essential structures of emotional experience. The most important of these structures, I have suggested, is *intentionality*, but with a nod toward Merleau-Ponty, something like *motility* as well. For many years, I have argued that emotions are structured by judgments and thus thoroughly permeated by concepts (see Solomon 1993, 2003). I have even argued, following the Stoics, that emotions *are* judgments. I would now rather say that *emotions are engagements with the world*, a more Sartrean formulation that avoids the common criticism of "judgment" as too intellectual and not a describable aspect of experience. Nevertheless, I would continue to argue that emotions are structured and thoroughly permeated by judgments and concepts, and I reject the neo-Jamesian presumption that the experience of emotion is nothing more than the sensations that accompany the relevant bodily changes. Emotional experience is much more and much richer than this. To insist that emotions have a structure, and to insist that the most important structure of emotions is (something like) intentionality, is to insist that an emotional experience is primarily an experience of the world. It may well include experiences of one's own body (including the autonomic reactions that James dwells on) and experiences of action-preparedness (the warrant for the Merleau-Pontean shift toward bodily motility), but these experiences, too, for the most part, are directed toward and engaged with the world. (In Peter Goldie's nice phrase, they have "borrowed intentionality.") They are neither the products of "introspection" nor internal bodily "markers." An emotional experience is the experience of a fully embodied and active engagement with the world.[6]

A phenomenology of emotions is a description of the experience of the many distinctive engagements that define the various emotions, which vary enormously in their specificity and scope, from the cloying irritations of petty anger to the global aspects of joy, *angst*, and depression. But because of this enormous variety, we should be cautious about trying to describe the fundamental nature of the engagements that constitute emotion as such. There may be no such uniformity or "essence" to emotion "as such." The general class of emotions may be a quite heterogeneous collection of phenomena, at best a matter of family resemblances and not a "natural kind" at all.[7] But this should be an open question. A phenomenology of emotion might well attempt a general description that will apply to all emotions, but any such attempt must be filled with particular examples of emotions, and very different emotions, to see if the general description holds. An analysis of the small family of "basic" emotions, for example, fear, anger, sadness, and such, might lead us to think that emotions all involve something like "arousal" (or other bodily change) and distinctive facial expressions (which subtly register in our experience).[8] On the other hand, if we focus just on the social, interpersonal, and self-reflective emotions – anger, shame, pride, and embarrassment, for example – we may well be led to the conclusion that emotion is a social category and emotions are "socially constructed" or "socially constituted." The phenomenology of particular emotions or emotion-types, by contrast, avoids the temptation to generalize, but at the risk of suggesting that there are no general structures of emotion as such to be described. Thus the phenomenology of emotion and the phenomenology of emotions are interdependent disciplines and the dialectic between the two enriches both of them.

The phenomenology of emotion is also complicated by the fact that every emotional experience involves a number of aspects or dimensions, including the distinctively bodily, the judgments that structure the experience, the experience of the object of the emotion, and the social context of the experience. Different theorists focus on one or another of these dimensions, and not surprisingly the theories look very different as well (Jamesian, cognitivist, social constructionist, respectively). But there is no given priority among these various dimensions, and so the question is how they can be ordered and organized in a phenomenological description. What will not do is to separate them out into distinct categories. (Thus my discomfort in even using the terms "dimensions" and "aspects," and I have long opposed "components" talk in the analysis of emotions. An emotion is not an assemblage.) An emotional experience is just that, *an emotional experience*, and while we should not assume that it will be singular and unified, we certainly should not rule that out in our mode of description. (The story of the blind Persians and the elephant comes to mind here.) One can, perhaps, describe one's physiological responses while angry to the exclusion of everything else that is experienced, but what is noteworthy is the effort this kind of abstraction requires. The experience of anger does not consist of tensing up, getting flushed, squinting one's eyes, tightening one's fists, *and also* seeing one's antagonist as offensive and wanting to hit him. The changes in one's body, seeing one's antagonist as offensive, and wanting to hit him constitute a single complex experience.

The idea that an emotional experience is a *unitary phenomenon* is Heidegger's important contribution to the phenomenology of emotion (although he does not discuss it explicitly in this context). This is most important when we go back to the traditional notion of intentionality, the idea of an emotion being directed toward an object. It is all too tempting to then start talking about the emotion as one phenomenon, its object another. Husserl gave into this temptation when he insisted that any number of "acts" could be directed at the same intentional object, and the same "act" could be directed at various intentional objects, although he rather desperately insisted that act and object are "essentially related to one another" (Husserl 1931: 117; 4: 41).[9] In the realm of emotion, this at first seems evident enough. We love, then get angry at, then feel guilty toward, the same person. In an angry mood, driving along the Interstate in rush-hour traffic, we first get angry at driver A, then at B, then at C, and so on. But even without going back to the Cartesian framework presupposed by this distinction – between emotion (as an "act of consciousness") and the object (as a thing or person in the world) – we can recognize that our phenomenology has gone awry. Is the person who is the object of our love indeed *the same* person who is the object of our anger? Is my anger at driver A in fact *the same* as my anger at driver B? Common-sense ontology certainly says yes, and is baffled by such questions. *Of course* it is Sally who is the object of both our love and our anger! *Of course* my anger stays constant although the drivers might be different! But we're not talking ontology here, but phenomenology, and the question is not whether the real-life person remains the same over time (however an ontologist might analyze that) but whether the objects of the emotional experiences of love and anger are the same.

An emotional experience is primarily an experience of the object of emotion, from the peculiar perspective of that emotion. That much is very right about the intentionality thesis. Thus the object of anger is different in kind from the object of love, even if the person who is the target of both emotions is ontologically one and the same. (One might object to this distinction between ontology and phenomenology as still overly Cartesian, and I would agree with this, but I do not want to get off into this more abstract question here.) The object of anger is experienced as infuriating. The beloved is experienced as lovable. Thus the traditional empiricists (including, with many qualifications, William James) made a serious error in their assumption that an emotion is some sort of self-contained, "internal" perception, a sensation of some kind. An emotion is first of all a way of experiencing and engaging with the world. But it is not as if the emotion and object are two "components" of the emotion complex, nor is it as if the emotion is one thing, the (non-intentional) feeling, but it is distinguished by the ideas, which are intentional and identify the object of the emotion. (This was Hume's brave thesis, trying to somehow wrest the notion of intentionality from the causal associationism that his theory demanded.) An emotional experience is a unitary experience defined by one's engagement in an emotional world, which is sometimes a world of anger, sometimes of love, or of grief, or of embarrassment, or, sometimes, of an incoherent mix of several of these.

An emotion defines its object, just as the object defines the emotion. The connection – which is why Hume had such difficulty – is a logical connection, not a causal one. The full description of the emotion requires a description of its object – as the object of that emotion. The description of the object of an emotion, *as* the object of that emotion, presumes the perspective of that emotion. Thus it is (more or less) contingent that one's beloved is five foot four (although perhaps it is not contingent that she is not over six feet tall). It is not contingent that one's beloved is lovable (and I want that to sound as tautological as possible). The scholastics referred to this non-contingent description of the object as the "formal object" of an emotion. Recent work by Anthony Kenny and Ronald de Sousa retains this usage (Kenny 1963; de Sousa 1987). The idea is that the object of a particular emotion (or, rather, emotion-type) has certain *necessary* features, whatever the details. We can argue about the specifics, of course, but love requires something or someone beloved, anger requires an offense or, as Aristotle insisted, a "slight," sadness requires a loss, and so on. I should add, of course, that all of these are "subjective" or "as perceived." Thus Aristotle quickly qualifies "slight" as "real or imagined." One can experience a serious loss when, in fact, no loss has been suffered, and, sadly, one can deeply love someone who is not (from other peoples' perspectives) lovable at all. But it is clear that the necessity of the formal object description only holds as a description of the object of the emotion, not of the object described independently of the emotion.

We all know the old cliché, "beauty is in the eye of the beholder." So now the philosophical question: is the quality *beautiful* in the object (the beloved), or is it rather only in the mind of the subject? The properties of the beloved are just these factual features that might be recorded by a police sketch artist (a certain shape of nose, eyes, mouth, ears, hair), but it is only by way of appraisal by the lover that these features take on aesthetic or romantic value. But then what happens to Scheler's "objectivity" of values? Is Sartre correct in his early suggestion that emotions are merely "magical" transformations rather than intentional vehicles for changing the world? How does either of these views jive with what we have called Heidegger's important contribution to the phenomenology of emotions, his insistence on the unity of the emotional phenomenon?

We have been through all of this before, in Plato, in John Locke and the early empiricists, in all of those philosophers who have raised the question about "primary and secondary qualities," those supposedly in the object and those supposedly in the mind of the subject. (Color has long been one of the favorite examples.) But what phenomenology has taught us is that such a debate is misplaced, the very distinction between what's in the object and what's in the mind, what's "outside" and what's "inside," is itself a misunderstanding of the nature of perception. Nevertheless, Husserl's carefully qualified distinction between the phenomenological act and the intentional object tends to hold onto this problematic distinction, and lends itself to the debate over the distinction between the having of an emotion and the object of that emotion. But it seems to me that the fate of empiricism and the mind–body distinction more generally ought to dictate the nature of phenomenological analysis of emotion as well, namely, that (in Heidegger's terms) the emotion and its object form a "unified phenomenon." From a phenomenological point of view it makes no sense to try to pry the merely "subjective" contributions of the subject from the "objective" features of the object. In terms of the non-phenomenological approach of psychology and cognitive science to emotion, this means that it may also be a mistake to think of emotions in terms of "components," the psychological aspect of an emotion versus its object or, worse, its "stimulus."

Emotional Experience and Consciousness

I said that the experience of having an emotion is first of all an experience of the world, understood as the "unitary phenomenon" of *emotionally-experiencing-the-world*. But our experience is not just one-dimensional, an unreflective experience of emotionally-experiencing-the-world. We are self-conscious and reflective ("ontological") creatures, and consequently we are aware not only of the world (or our *emotionally-experiencing-the-world*) but of ourselves *in* the world. We are also aware of our awareness of the world and we can label it ("I am angry," "I am ashamed"), reflect on it ("should I really be angry?" "Does he really deserve it?"), and try to control it ("I've got to calm down – I'm going to lose my job."). Few nonhuman animals, one might argue, are capable of such reflection or, with some notable exceptions, self-consciousness.[10] But that means that the emotional experience described by phenomenology needs to include both self-consciousness and experience due to reflection as well as unreflective emotional experience. A phenomenology of emotion should describe the ways in which self-consciousness and reflection shape, enter into, and alter emotion and emotional experience.

It is all too common for emotion researchers, particularly in the social and neurological sciences, to define emotion in such a minimalist way that both self-consciousness and reflection are necessarily something over and above emotion and thus not part of the emotional experience at all.[11] But emotions are much more than neurological responses or "affect programs" and can be complex and long term – lasting even for years or a lifetime and occupying several levels or dimensions of consciousness. They are ways of experiencing and engaging with the world, and insofar as emotional experience is structured by judgments and deeply conceptual (as opposed to consisting of what Scheler calls "blind" feelings), then the reflective overlay of emotions becomes part of the emotional experience itself. In one sense, this is a *logical* consequence: if emotions are structured by judgments then judgments *about* these judgments (even including something so simple as supplying an identifying label) logically entail some alteration in the original emotion. If I am angry but then come to recognize *that* I am angry, my anger changes. If I am angry and come to question the warrant for my anger, my anger radically changes, and with it my experience. It becomes far more complex. My anger is mixed with and to some extent undermined by doubt and perhaps also by shame. But it is not as if there are distinct "layers" of emotion, corresponding to "levels" of consciousness, with pre-reflective anger at the base, reflective anger on top of that, with doubt and perhaps shame yet another level above. Experience is not so neatly stratified but constitutes a (more or less) coherent whole. Confusion and perplexity may, of course, be part of that complex whole, and with shifts of attention (and intentional objects) one experience may replace another in fairly rapid succession. But the complex phenomenology of emotional experience has yet to be adequately described or analyzed, although there are hopeful signs of interest in the psychological literature.[12]

Self-consciousness is not so complex as reflection and its vicissitudes, perhaps, but it also admits of considerable variation which easily lead to confusion. To begin with, some emotions are by their very nature self-referential and so might be called, in one sense, self-conscious. Shame and pride, for instance, are about the self and take the self as object, in the first case by way of a recognition of disgrace, in the second by way of accomplishment. But shame and pride clearly occur in a non-reflective mode; one need not even be aware that he or she feels either emotion. (It may be evident to others in the way that one walks or holds one's head, in self-demeaning or self-aggrandizing comments, with no sign that the subject recognizes one's own emotion.) On the other hand, becoming self-conscious of one's emotion, in the sense that one becomes reflectively aware *that* one has that emotion, is clearly self-consciousness of a very different sort. It requires not only self-reference but articulate self-recognition. And articulate self-recognition has its own consequences. One can imagine becoming defiant as one recognizes one's shame, or, perhaps, becoming even more ashamed. One can imagine becoming ashamed as one recognizes one's pride, especially if he or she has been raised to believe that pride is a "deadly" sin, for instance. At this juncture, self-consciousness and reflection come together, but they nevertheless, in general, should be distinguished. (Sartre, I think, tends to collapse them.) Self-consciousness, in general, does not require language. Animals and very young children display self-consciousness and emotions that involve self-consciousness. But reflection, many would argue, does require language, and one of the knottier problems of phenomenology remains Merleau-Ponty's concern about the relationship between pre- and post-linguistic experience and whether the former can ever be adequately grasped by linguistic creatures such as ourselves. This has special poignancy for the phenomenology of emotion, as it has long been pointed out that at least some emotions are evident in pre-linguistic animals and infants, and the question (now raised to crisis level by many neuroscientists) is how we should understand the relationship between those pre-linguistic emotions and the more sophisticated emotions of adult human life.

The Phenomenology of Emotional Experience – Feelings

Joseph Doux distinguishes between the "low road" followed by such primitive emotions as fear and the "high road" that brings such emotions to consciousness (Le Doux 1996).

So, too, Paul Griffiths distinguishes between the "affect programs" of primitive emotions and the "higher cognitive emotions" that are typical of most social and relatively sophisticated situations (pride, shame, guilt, love, etc.) (Griffiths 1997).[13] But the tendency remains to downplay the higher cognitive features and emphasize the primitive "hard-wired" aspects of emotion, and with this move the concept of emotional experience is once again reduced to (more or less) simple sensation, the "feelings" consequent to the firing of this or that neurological affect program. Thus Damasio writes about "the feeling of what happens" in the brain, and philosopher Jesse Prinz argues that "emotions are perceptions (conscious or unconscious) of patterned changes in the body" (Prinz 2004a: 221–40). It is all an update of the theory that William James proposed more than a hundred years ago, now bolstered by fifty years of very sophisticated neuroscience research. But our emotions, I have argued, are not so primitive, and emotional experience is much more than perceptions of changes in the body.

Nevertheless, it would be a mistake to err in the opposite direction (as I did for many years) and simply dismiss the neurological and the feelings that follow as irrelevant or secondary to emotion, leaving an account of emotions that is too cerebral to do justice to the phenomena. As Michael Stocker has protested for years, affect is essential to emotions, and if James and his successors oversimplified by reducing affect to bodily feelings, feeling is nonetheless the sine qua non of emotion, which is to say something more than just that an emotion is an experience. But what are the feelings that are so central to emotional experience? How are they related to intentionality? (Decades ago, Anthony Kenny distinguished emotions among the variety of feelings by insisting that emotions are intentional, feelings are not (Kenny 1963)). Can the feelings essential to emotion ("affect") be described or are they, as Stocker and many others often suggest, "ineffable"?

Here is where Merleau-Ponty's great insight becomes particularly valuable to us. Even if we grant that the source of most feelings is the body, it does not follow that it is the body in its physiological aspect, the firing of nerves, the release of hormones, the prickling of skin, an increase in heart rate, or the shifts in circulation of the blood through the body. Merleau-Ponty's notion of "motility" gives us a good clue as to where else we should look, to what some recent psychologists have called "action-readiness" (Frijda 1968: 69–70), and at least one contemporary psychiatrist-philosopher has called "bodily micro-practices" (Downing 2001).[14] The phenomenology of feeling is by no means a hopeless matter, because the feelings essential to emotion are by no means "ineffable." ("Affect," I would argue, is just another word for ineffable feeling and serves us no good at all.) That is not to say that one can simply identify and describe as such the complex of sensations that accompany even the simplest muscle movement, but one can readily specify "the feeling you get when you tense your brow muscles" or "the feeling you get when you clench your fists."

I would suggest that emotional experience consists in part of a variety of different kinds of feelings, some of them physiological, to be sure – sensations following the various operations of the autonomic nervous system in particular (speed of the heart and pulse, the contraction and expansion of blood vessels, release of hormones and their various effects), but others that depend on the voluntary musculature. Among these voluntary muscle movements and their accompanying sensations will be some "spontaneous" and more or less "hard-wired" muscular responses, in particular the facial expressions of emotion that have been studied in such admirable detail by Paul Ekman and others (see Ekman and Friesen 1971; Ekman 1999). Other sensations will be the effects of preparations for action, such as the tensing of the fist muscles for a punch, the clenching of teeth for a bite, the tensing of leg muscles to run. As Darwin pointed out in 1876, some of these movements are "vestigial," residues of "once serviceable traits." It is only the most primitive among us who actually follows through on the urge to bite, other than symbolically. ("Do you bite your thumb at us, sir?" asks Abram, a Capulet servant. Sampson, the offending Montague, answers, "No sir, I do not bite my thumb at you, sir. But I bite my thumb, sir" (Shakespeare 1969: I.i. 42–8). (Evander Holyfield can attest to the real effects of such unbridled emotional expression.[15]) Such tensions and their accompanying sensation may be conscious or unconscious in the sense that the subject may or may not be aware of them and recognize them for what they are, but of course they will be conscious in a simpler sense, the sense in which every sensation is, if it is a sensation at all.

But much of our action-preparedness is, at least potentially, real. It is intended (whether or not consciously) to result in action. At this point intention (in the usual sense) meets intentionality, and the feelings that are part of emotion signal both an intention to act and something about the world, that is, something to be done. Thus, as Aristotle argued long ago, revenge is not just the consequence of anger; it is an essential aspect of that emotion. Flight is not just the consequence of fear. It is part of what that emotion is about. And the complex feelings that accompany those intentions and the actions they prepare for are an essential aspect of the experience of emotion. Thus we might say, with Peter Goldie and against Anthony Kenny, that these feelings have "borrowed intentionality" (Goldie 2001: 54–7). They take as their object the object of the emotion, and it makes perfectly good sense to say that I *feel* angry with him as well as I *am* angry with him. Not that those feelings as such, out of the context of emotion or as stimulated by some drug or other, would be intentional (Schachter and Singer 1962). But as an aspect of emotion, this does make sense and thus it also makes sense to say that I *feel* angry with him.

Downing's idea of bodily micro-practices owes much to Merleau-Ponty. It is an apt way of bringing in not only the essential role of the body in emotion, but also the Sartrean idea that we use our bodies in emotion to serve our purposes. Again, this is an idea with ancient roots. Aristotle taught that we cultivate our emotions, and with them our virtues and our characters. Downing's idea is that in part we cultivate our emotions by way of cultivating our bodily responses and expressions, what he calls "bodily micro-practices." Needless to say, most of this cultivation and these practices are unconscious. Over the years, a person takes on the posture of defeat, or arrogance, the look of anxiety, the softness of loving. But calling one's attention to such postures and habits works wonders, as Downing has found in his therapeutic practice. To recognize the bodily roles that one plays is to be in a position to alter those roles. And to recognize that the feelings one has are in part the voluntary if incremental feelings of a certain stance in the world may be just as essential to understanding our emotional experience and just as valuable an outcome of a phenomenology of emotion as recognizing that we really are in love or furious with our father.

This is to say that our emotional experience is primarily *practical*. It is this that is wrong, or in any case misleading, to say that emotions are "cognitive." (I say this despite the fact that this is how my own theory has often been categorized.) An emotion is not primarily a matter of knowing, or, better, phenomenologists since Heidegger have long argued that a relatively small store of human knowledge is of the form "knowing that." Philosophers, of course, are naturally concerned with such knowledge and that leads them not unnaturally to the prejudice that only such knowledge, propositional knowledge, is important. Not that they deny the need for all sorts of nonverbal skills of the "knowing how" variety, but these typically ignored in philosophical analysis, first, perhaps, because there may be nothing distinctively human about them (animals display such nonverbal skills at least as impressively as humans) and second, because it is well known that "knowing how" cannot be reduced to any number of "knowing that"-type propositions. But it is a distortion of cognition and consciousness to suggest that "knowing that"-type propositional knowledge is prior to or independent of "knowing how." As I have insisted that emotional experience concerns our ways of engaging the world, it more or less follows that the primary questions for a phenomenology of emotions concern describing *how* we do this rather than knowing *what* it is that we are emotional about.

Conclusion

The phenomenology of emotions is the study of the essential structures of emotional experience. But these structures are enormously varied, from the more or less primitive feelings that result from the firings of our autonomic nervous system to the very sophisticated and self-conscious plots and plans through which we express and act out many emotions. To reduce emotional experience to anything less is to fail to appreciate the complexity and richness of our emotional lives, but to appreciate the complexity and richness of our emotional lives is to further enrich them as well as to further complicate them. Thus the practical pay-off of a phenomenology of emotions. In phenomenology, we do not always leave that which is described as it is.

Notes

1   For instance, Paul Churchland and Richard Rorty in an earlier incarnation.
2   I have defended this in Solomon 2005.
3   I find it particularly revealing that James juxtaposes his chapter on "Emotions" in his *Principles* (vol. 2) just after the chapter on "Instinct" and not with his chapters on perception and cognition. See James 1950.
4   On this point, see the very analytic treatment of emotions with reference to possibility in Gordon 1987.
5   For instance, see Izard 1974.
6   By "active" engagement I do not mean to deny that a great many emotional reactions seem to us passive in nature, or that the circumstances that provoke emotion often *happen to* us, or that the mode of emotional expression (and therefore emotional experience) is often passive, as in passive-aggressive behavior.
7   See, for instance, Griffiths 1997. For an impressive rebuttal, see Charland 2002.

8   This is the family of emotions and the set of characteristics defined, for example, by Paul Ekman in his very influential writings on the subject (see Ekman 1994, 1999). Ekman goes on, however, to define "emotion" in terms of just this class.

9   See also Gurwitch 1966.

10 Debates about the self-consciousness of "higher" animals and the very meaning of "self-consciousness" have been ferocious and frequent, beginning with the Stoics and then at least since Descartes (and Sartre) denied that animals were capable of developing such capacities. In contemporary ethology, animal behavior researchers have generally attributed self-consciousness to chimpanzees and dolphins, some have extended this to elephants, gorillas, dogs, and cats, but a few have broadened the concept such that it applies not only to domestic animals but, at the far reaches, any creature that is capable of orienting itself in the world. (Lewis Thomas suggests that even slime molds have self-consciousness in that they recognize those that are or are not themselves, that is, the result of their own asexual reproduction).

11 In the article referred to above, Carroll Izard defines emotion as a "brief . . . response" (Izard 1974: 248). Joseph Le Doux similarly insists that an emotion as such is only the distinctive neurological (amygdala) response and not at all the intellectual (cerebral) subsequent activity (Le Doux 1996).

12 For example, Marcel and Lambie 2002.

13 The phrase "affect program" comes from Sylvan Tompkins but was popularized by Paul Ekman in his work on "basic emotions."

14 The main psychologist in question is Nico Frijda (see Frijda 1986). The psychiatrist-philosopher is George Downing (see Downing 2001).

15 Thanks to John Deigh for this Shakespearean reminder.

References and Further Reading

Brentano, F. (1969) *The Origin of our Knowledge of Right and Wrong* (trans. R. Chisholm and E. Schneewind). London: Routledge (original work published in 1889).

Caston, V. (1992) Aristotle on Intentionality. Dissertation, University of Texas at Austin.

Charland, L. (2002) The natural kind status of emotion. *British Journal for the Philosophy of Science*, 53, 511–37.

Damasio, T. (1999) *The Feeling of What Happens*. New York: Harcourt Brace.

Descartes, R. (1989) *Passions of the Soul* (trans. S. H. Voss). Indianapolis: Hackett (original work published 1649).

de Sousa, R. (1987) *The Rationality of Emotion*. Cambridge, MA: MIT Press.

Dixon, T. (2003) *From Passions to Emotions: The Creation of a Secular Psychological Category*. Cambridge: Cambridge University Press.

Downing, G. (2001) Emotion theory revisited. In M. Wrathall and J. Malpas (eds.), *Heidegger, Coping, and Cognitive Science: A Festschrift for Hubert Dreyfus, vol. 2* (pp. 245–70). Cambridge, MA: MIT Press.

Ekman, P. (1994) All emotions are basic. In P. Ekman and R. J. Davidson (eds.), *The Nature of Emotion* (pp. 15–19). Oxford: Oxford University Press.

——(1999) Basic emotions. In T. Dalgleish and T. Power (eds.), *The Handbook of Cognition and Emotion* (pp. 46–60). New York: John Wiley.

Ekman, P., and W. V. Friesen (1971) Constants across cultures in the face and emotion. *Journal of Personality and Social Psychology*, 17, 124–9.

Freud, S. (2001) The unconscious. In J. Strachey (ed.), *The Standard Edition of the Complete Psychological Works of Sigmund Freud, vol. 14*. New York: Random House (original work published 1915).

Frijda, N. (1986) *The Emotions*. Cambridge: Cambridge University Press.

Goldie, P. (2001) *The Emotions: A Philosophical Exploration*. Oxford: Oxford University Press.

Gordon, R. (1987) *The Structure of Emotions*. Cambridge: Cambridge University Press.

Griffiths, P. E. (1997) *What Emotions Really Are*. Chicago: University of Chicago Press.

Gurwitch, A. (1966) On the intentionality of consciousness. In A. Gurwitch (ed.), *Studies in Phenomenology and Psychology*. Evanston, IL: Northwestern University Press.

Heidegger, M. (1962) *Being and Time* (trans. J. Macquarrie and E. Robinson). New York: Harper & Row (original work published 1927).

Hume, D. (1973) *A Treatise of Human Nature*, 2nd edn. (ed. L. A. Selbe-Bigge). Oxford: Oxford University Press (original work published 1739).

Husserl, E. (1931) *Ideas: A General Introduction to Pure Phenomenology* (trans. G. W. R. Boyce). London: Macmillan (original work published 1913).

Izard, C. (1974) Emotions, human. In *Encyclopedia Britannica*, 15th edn., vol. 18, 248–56.

James, W. (1902) *The Varieties of Religious Experience: A Study in Human Nature*. New York: Longmans, Green & Co.

—— (1950) *The Principles of Psychology*, 2 vols. New York: Dover.

Kenny, A. (1963) *Action, Emotion, and Will*. London: Routledge & Kegan Paul.

Kierkegaard, S. (1944) *The Concept of Dread* (trans. W. Lowrie). Princeton, NJ: Princeton University Press (original work published 1844).

Le Doux, J. (1996) *The Emotional Brain: The Mysterious Underpinnings of Emotional Life*. New York: Simon & Schuster.

Marcel, T., and Lambie, J. (2002) The varieties of emotional experience: A theoretical framework. *Psychology Review*, 109(2), 219–59.

Nietzsche, F. (1967) *On the Genealogy of Morals* (trans. W. Kaufmann). New York: Random House (original work published 1887).

Prinz, J. (2004a) Emotions embodied. In R. C. Solomon (ed.), *Thinking about Feeling* (pp. 44–60). Oxford: Oxford University Press.

—— (2004b) *Gut Reactions*. Oxford: Oxford University Press.

Sartre, J-P. (1948) *Emotions: Sketch of a Theory* (trans. B. Frechtman). New York: Citadel (original work published 1939).

—— (1954) *Being and Nothingness* (trans. H. Barnes). New York: Philosophical Library.

Schacter, S., and Singer, J. (1962) Cognitive, social, and physiological determinants of emotional state. *Psychological Review*, 69, 379–99.

Scheler, M. (1954) *The Nature of Sympathy* (trans. P. Heath). London: Routledge (original work published 1913).

—— (1973) *Formalism in Ethics and Non-Formal Ethics of Value* (trans. M. Frings and R. Funk). Evanston, IL: Northwestern University Press (original work published 1913).

Seneca. (1928) *De Ira*, in *Seneca: Moral Essays*, vol. 1 (trans. John W. Basore). Cambridge, MA: Harvard University Press (original work published c.50).

Shakespeare, W. (1969) *Romeo and Juliet*. In A. Harbage (gen. ed.). *William Shakespeare: The Complete Works*. New York: Viking.

Solomon, R. C. (1993) *The Passions*. Indianapolis: Hackett.

—— (2003) *Not Passion's Slave: Emotions and Choice*. New York: Oxford University Press.

—— (2005) Sympathy for Adam Smith. In C. Fricke and H-P. Schuett (eds.), *Adam Smith as Moral Philosopher*. Berlin: de Gruyter.

Zajonc, R. (1980) Feeling and thinking: Preferences need no inferences. *American Psychologist*, 35, 151–75.

22

The Egological Structure of Consciousness: Lessons from Sartre for Analytical Philosophy of Mind

MANUEL BREMER

1 Using Sartre

According to a well-known account, phenomenology and analytic philosophy have a common origin in the attempt to found and defend the objectivity of logic and philosophy against psychologism, a tradition of anti-pyschologism going back ultimately to Bernhard Bolzano. The respective founding fathers (Edmund Husserl and Gottlob Frege) differ in their methods and points of departure, so that – so the story is told (see Dummett 1988) – at last analytic philosophy was more successful in that language as intersubjectively shared turned out to be the better foundation of objectivity than the realm of pure phenomenology, where phenomenologists disagree and cannot establish an intersubjectively valid method of *eidetic reduction*. Analytic philosophy of mind also shares with phenomenology the fundamental interest in intentionality. Accounting for intentionality – in terms of propositional attitudes – turned out not only to be successful, but became (in the guise of functionalism) the very paradigm of the philosophy of mind and the cognitive sciences. What is missing in that philosophy of mind – as its main proponents like Jerry Fodor readily admit (see Fodor 1975) – is an account of consciousness *as experienced* by someone. Others in the analytic camp have offered theories of consciousness focusing on phenomenality and so called *qualia* (see Chalmers 1996). What is mostly and strikingly missing in these theories are (sub-)theories or models of the egological structures of consciousness (i.e., a theory of the subjectively experienced or theoretically to be assumed agents/egos in consciousness). There are mostly reflections on the use of the personal pronoun "I" and an undifferentiated notion of a/the "self." It is here, I think, that the analytic philosophy of mind should revisit phenomenology. The egological structures of consciousness have been a – or even *the* main – topic of Kantian, Idealistic, and phenomenological theories of consciousness.

I have chosen Jean-Paul Sartre as my point of departure, since I believe that he has an advanced theory of these structures, and that some of his insights are congenial to theses in the analytic philosophy of mind. Sartre develops this theory in *The*

Transcendence of the Ego (Sartre 1937), the introduction to *Being and Nothingness* (Sartre 1943), and his lecture "Self-Awareness and Self-Knowledge" (Sartre 1948).

There are positive and negative lessons to be taken from Sartre:

*Taking up some of his ideas one may arrive at a better model of consciousness in the analytic philosophy of mind; representing some of his ideas within the language and the models of a functionalist theory of mind makes them more accessible and integrates them into the wider picture.

*Sartre, as any philosopher, errs at some points, I believe; but these errors may be instructive, especially inasmuch as they mirror some errors in some current theories of consciousness.

This chapter, therefore, is not a piece of Sartre scholarship, but an attempt at a "friendly takeover" of some ideas I ascribe to Sartre into current models in the philosophy of mind.

2 Ordinary Language and the Self

Talking of the self or an ego is often ridiculed by analytic philosophers by pointing out that sentences like

(1*)   I came around and I brought (with me) my Self.
(2*)   She visited Frank and my I was there, too.

are ungrammatical. They are ungrammatical, if they are, in the sense of running against the meaning of the expression involved, i.e., their common usage. This is, however, a very weak argument. The strangeness of (1*) might be accounted for by a proponent of a Self in noting the inseparability of person and self, so that it is no more strange than

(3?)   I came around and I brought (with me) my body.

This may not work for all constructions; (2*) may be an example of real deviance. Such deviance, nevertheless, does not show much. Starting from ordinary usage, sentences like

(4)   Near heavy bodies space is curved.
and
(5)   All full explanation has to consider the color of the quarks.

are nonsensical as well, since there is nothing, according to our pre-scientific understanding of space and before redefining the notion, against which it can be curved; and subatomic particles simply have no colors. Once it is conceded that scientific language may deviate from ordinary and pre-scientific usage, there is no exception with the philosophy of mind. Maybe "the I," different sorts of "Egos," and "the Self" are theoretical posits. Given a background theory, sentences like

(6)   The I unites experiences to present the Self to us.

may no longer sound strange.

The deviance from ordinary usage may be considered a special problem for philosophy inasmuch as it is assumed to merely work with our intuitive understanding of ourselves and the world. Although this is partially right, this poses no real problem. On the one hand this complaint cannot be brought forward by analytic philosophers, who – especially in the cognitive sciences – stress the continuity of scientific and philosophical methods. On the other hand, the problem may be due to the intricate character of the distinctions involved. There are enough other concepts and distinctions introduced by philosophers to reconstruct our ordinary understanding of ourselves and our access to reality (e.g., the terminology of "possible world" semantics, the vocabulary of epistemic appraisal and confirmation, like "falsifiable," "simplicity," keeping "indirect" and "direct" duties apart, and so on).

3 Self-Denial in the Analytic Philosophy of Mind and in Sartre

Another criticism has focused on "the" Self as a supposed *object* we encounter in self-awareness. The deeper – even if philosophically somewhat shallow – reason that self-awareness is neglected as a topic by many analytic philosophers may just be that it is understood as being the awareness of a self as an object. If it is excluded that self-awareness might be more, and given the dubious character of "the Self" as an object, self-awareness drops out of consideration as being a mere byproduct (a secondary construction) of more interesting and fundamental mental events.

Nevertheless, there is something to this criticism. Marvin Minsky (1985) sees the self as a construct: Thoughts are outputs of the cognitive systems, where several agencies, each of which doing only its job, work in the background being involved in perception, association, and memory access and where several information states compete for the access to consciousness; some of the information states model control states that work on lower states; from these states a *self-image* of the system is built up; this construct is the self, seen as the agent who has the thoughts in question and who is responsible for the actions of the system; the self is not some *additional agent* inside you looking at the performance of the other agencies; the self is a *representation*; the self is ascribed properties that are essential to give the system's self-representation unity; so the self develops as a *narrative* in which language is used to describe an entity with coherent properties.[1]

Interestingly, this opinion is not far off from Sartre's. The me is, for Sartre, a posited transcendent object (see Sartre 1937: 70, 76). The self – called "ego" by Sartre here – is something brought *before* consciousness, is an object and not that which is intentionally directed at this object. The self is "an object," not something active. The self is posited *as* the origin of acts and *as* their unifying principle: "[C]onsciousness projects its own spontaneity into the ego-object in order to confer on the ego the creative power which is absolutely necessary to it. But this spontaneity, *represented* and *hypostatized* in an object, becomes a degraded and bastard spontaneity" (Sartre 1937: 81). So we may understand the Self[2] as representing the whole "society of mind" (with all its processes and agencies) as a single agent. With the concept of "the Self" we represent the whole system/architecture. This is not wrong inasmuch as that system is us, and is acting. It is misleading inasmuch as we might start a search for that *agent* Self that is not among the agents of the mind. The Self is nevertheless *phenomenally real* and can be described in its features. The self represents the unification process within the cognitive system, including the occurrence of deliberate (verbal) control states. Other features of the Self may correspond to hidden cognitive agents, and so again the Self as construct is not inadequate. It is, therefore, misleading to say that by positing the Self we are victims of an illusion.[3] The decisive point is to see the Self not as the agent in control but as a (narrative) construct.

Having thus downsized the Self one has to avoid overdoing the deconstruction. Overdoing the rejection of supposed entities in the vicinity of self-awareness loses the phenomenon itself. The crucial distinction that is often overlooked, and which is at the center of this chapter, is that between the Self and – at least one – I, which both have to be kept apart from the person that I am. Sartre clearly sees that there is a question of the *Ego* to be considered after having kept apart the Me. Several questions are put to us either as a phenomenologist or a cognitive scientist by the phenomena.

4 A Short Phenomenology of Some Distinctions

There are a couple of basic observations concerning my knowledge and experience of myself.

Phenomenon I

"I" is a singular term. Singular terms are used in statements to refer to objects which are said to have some property, which is referred to by the predicate (the general term):

(1)   The table in lecture hall 3F is white.

Statement (1) is true if one has identified by the description (or its meaning) an object and discerns (by the meaning of "is white") that it has the corresponding property. Singular terms serve to identify objects. Identification need not be successful: "the headless rider" is a singular term, but refers to nothing.

The meaning of "I" is usually given as "the one speaking." That seems reasonable: If somebody uses the term "I" we (the hearers) know that she is talking of herself. Can "I," however, be employed to characterize self-awareness? It seems not. Self-awareness cannot have the structure of the following statement:

(2)   I see a white table in lecture hall 3F.

The question of identifying the referent (i.e., the question generally associated with singular terms) does not arise: I need not identify myself for myself. I am immediately present to myself.

Furthermore, there is no chance of misidentification here. I am present in my consciousness and no one else whom I could mistake for the referent of "I" or whom I could mistake for myself. Further on I have to know myself as the one who does the identification in every act of identifying – even if I am not doing this in inner speech (i.e., I am not using the pronoun "I") *I* have to be aware of the act of identifying. And to identify *myself* I have to know myself already![4]

These phenomena throw a bad light on a propositionalist theory (employing the pronoun "I" to account for the structure of self-awareness).

Phenomenon II

I am a person. I can refer to that person, for example, by the description "the one who is lecturing on December 18, in lecture hall 3F at 4: P.M." The description refers to me and I know that. I can describe myself in several ways, but not all ways of referring to myself as a person are dependent on a description. Some famous anecdotes highlighting my peculiar knowledge of myself make this clear: Jon Perry, with his trolley in the supermarket, follows a trail of sugar to draw the attention of the customer responsible to his defective sugar bag. After a while he realizes that he himself has laid the trail of sugar with the defective sugar bag in his trolley (see Perry 1979). How can one describe this case?

Jon Perry had at some time, t (when he started his search), an opinion with respect to the customer he sought. At this time, t, Perry is *de facto*, although he does not know it, this very customer. Perry has, at this time, *de facto* a belief about himself, only he does not recognize this. At a later time, t*, Perry recognizes that he himself is the customer looked for. Now he still has *de facto* a belief about the customer, but additionally he now has a belief *de se* with respect to *himself* (in an emphatic sense of "himself" which points to the self-access to be explained here).

This phenomenon shows that there is a difference between beliefs/attitudes in which I am referred to by a description and such in which *I* know about *myself*.

Phenomenon III

"The I/the *Ego*" sounds peculiar, echoing philosophical traditions out of fashion. With the first phenomenon, however, we have already seen that to know about some objects involves knowing in some way about myself as the one who knows the objects. There is obviously in any conscious mental event – if we stick to individual mental acts for the moment – something that attributes that very act to itself as the thinking "thing." And this I is not a modification that sometimes occurs, as the anecdotes in phenomenon III may make you believe, but is present in *every* conscious episode. (The anecdote is telling by being an instance of misdescribing myself using a description, although I am immediately given to myself without using a description.) Even if I am not engaged in inner speech (processing thoughts in public language), but looking absentmindedly out of the window – nevertheless I know that it is *me* who is looking out. I do not have to use the pronoun "I" for this; I am just having my thoughts. There is no question as to who is having these thoughts. I am immediately given to myself (I am "at"/"by" myself). There are mental events (e.g., in phonetic decoding) which are not conscious, but if some act is conscious I am present. In *this* sense human consciousness is self-awareness (knowing oneself as thinking) – whatever forms of consciousness there might be in the animal kingdom (see Bremer 2005). It is not the case that we first have consciousness and then – in some additional act? – there comes self-awareness. Whatever I know of consciously I know as known by me. Whatever content I am thinking I know about me. Mental content is content for somebody. This somebody (the I) is (phenomenological) the same, whereas the content changes. Although the content or the scene before my eyes changes, I am still there. We experience a continuous agent of thinking while the content varies. The I does not fall on the side of mental content (in the sense of the observed scene, the sentence thought, etc.). The I might be the agent I experience within my mental acts as the one who does the thinking (the supposed actor of the acts of thinking). Is it not the case that *I* am thinking – and not that thinking happens to me?[5]

Phenomenon IV

There is, however, a further distinction to be made with respect to the just mentioned role of the *Ego*. Sometimes, although the question does not arise whose acts these are, I am absorbed in whatever I am doing. I am only looking at the cat playing with the cork, I am absorbed in the book I am reading. Then – without any effort – immediately I can become aware that *I* am looking at the cat, that I am reading. Now I am *explicit* about the subject of the act; no longer is only the content I was absorbed in presented.[6] This shift is almost imperceptible. It is not that I consciously *intend* now to focus on myself or set out to see who is doing the thinking. It just happens that from one moment to the next I realize my *Ego* as being the subject of my acts. If there is some reflection involved here, it does not take place as explicit reflecting by some of my *acts* on *another* of my *acts*. If this shift toward the I is a reflection it has to be modeled in some other fashion.

Phenomenon V

We have to add a phenomenological remark on (some) representations: Suppose you hear a bear humming. By the humming we refer to the bear as its source. We represent the bear *as* humming. The humming sound represents the bear in some fashion (including pitch, frequency, etc.). The humming *itself*, however, by pain of a vicious regress, is not represented "as" itself. To hear the humming is nothing besides or above the fact of having some representation. Expressed as a general observation:

(F)   There are representations with respect to which it is the case that their being tokened is accompanied by a phenomenal quality.

By tokening such a representation some quality is given in consciousness.

Several distinctions have to be made in the light of these phenomena:

1 "The Self" is that vague complex of biography and biographical knowledge, discussed in §3, that together with some body defines an individual person; names and descriptions refer to that person as known by me and others; the Self falls on the side of *content* of conscious states.

2 "The I/the *Ego*" is my I that, although in fact related to an individual Self, contains the structural functions which are shared by conscious beings (e.g., in the acts of perception mentioned above); let us call it the *Ego* or the *functional I*; in the light of phenomenon IV we will have to distinguish two components here, depending on whether (2a) the focus is on the I itself or (2b) on the objects that I am aware of.

3 "The implicit I" is the functional correlate of the functional I within the realm of tacit knowledge or mental events that are *not* conscious, but nevertheless are processed (e.g., in memory or pre-conscious association) as being self-attributed states.

4 The set of conditions necessary for consciousness to be possible at all, to arise in the first place, are not present in consciousness itself; in correlation to the talk of the *Ego* as present in consciousness one might talk of a "transcendental *Ego*" here, but this analogy to an agent as we know it from consciousness may be simply mistaken.[7]

A theory of the logical structure of my knowledge of myself (including the *de se* theory of self-awareness introduced in section 6) deals mainly with the functional I and secondarily with its relations to the other two instances. It does not deal primarily with biographies or the Self. The talk of a transcendental unity of consciousness has been transformed within cognitive science into the talk about the architecture of a cognitive system that may give rise to consciousness. Keep in mind the fact (F) about representations.

Sartre's theory also distinguishes between the Self/Me as a biographical construct and the functions of self-awareness. His distinction between a pre-reflexive and a reflexive *cogito* may mirror the distinction between (2b) and (2a).

5 Sartre's Conception of the Pre-Reflexive *Cogito*

Sartre, in his way, defends the thesis that consciousness cannot be separated from self-consciousness, as was alluded to phenomenologically in section 4. It is in this context that his introduction of a pre-reflexive *cogito* is crucial. It is a necessary condition for being conscious of some object to be conscious of being conscious, since an unnoticed consciousness is an absurdity (see Sartre 1943: 18). Consciousness presents itself (to itself). This cannot be another intentional act on pains of a regress of presupposed or required acts of consciousness. Thus the accompanying consciousness of oneself is no additional act besides the intentional act, and it is not a reflexive act having the intentional act as object: "[T]his consciousness of consciousness . . . is not *positional*, which is to say that consciousness is not for itself its own object. Its object is by nature outside of it, and that is why consciousness *posits* and *grasps* the object in the same act" (Sartre 1937: 40–1). This pre-reflexive *cogito* is within one and the same act that is a conscious act presenting some intentional object. Neither does it come *after* there being some intentional act already, nor is it vacuously present to be filled then with content. There is only the one (unified) conscious state representing an object in which

I am also (non-positionally) aware of myself (see Sartre 1943: 21). My being conscious of myself falls *not* on the side of the content of my conscious acts. It is responsible both for the content being conscious for me, although I do not focus on me, and is the pre-condition for the reflexive *cogito*. In having then a reflexive *cogito* I once again have a pre-reflexive *cogito* for the act of reflection being a conscious act.

Note for the following paragraph that that I which we call pre-reflexive *cogito* is not an *object* of thought as long as it is active in accompanying other content. It is related to but not phenomenally identical to the I brought into focus by reflection. The latter, in addition, has to be kept apart from the Self. The pre-reflexive *cogito* does not have itself as an object, so we may model it along the line of fact (F) as some peculiar representation that with its mere occurrence has its crucial features. Since the pre-reflexive *cogito* is no act, it cannot be phenomenologically brought into focus itself, although the immediacy of any conscious act may be claimed as evidence *for it*. Its characteristic is only given negatively, in terms of what it isn't. For a theory of self-awareness we need a working model. Here we turn to some help from theories developed within the analytic philosophy of mind.

6 *De Se* Theories of Self-Awareness

In the analytic philosophy of mind *de se* theories of self-awareness have been proposed by Roderick Chisholm (1981) and David Lewis (1979). Within the philosophy of mind we can distinguish between phenomenological and psychological theories. A psychological account, say, functionalism, refers to the role the state has with respect to other states or the system's behavior. Within such an explanation it might be important that it "is like something" to be in that state, but not all psychological accounts of some states require that is feels like something to be in such a state. A psychological theory need not account for (all) phenomenological features of mental states. Therefore one and the same psychological theory is compatible with different phenomenological descriptions. A complete functionalist theory of self-awareness comprises:

1 The identification of self-awareness by giving criteria for is being ascribed and by explaining its causal role.
2 The specification of the format of representation of mental content, which explains its inferential structure and its causal efficacy.

One and the same answer to (1) can be coupled with different answers to (2). The non-propositionalist account of self-awareness discussed here (a *de se*-theory) is an answer to (2). The *de se*-theory, therefore, is at least in part a phenomenological theory. The basic alternative is a propositionalist account in which all states of self-awareness (including the states/aspects enabling self-awareness) have to be propositional if not also sentential.

De se-theories (in short: DST) were developed by Roderick Chisholm (1981) and David Lewis (1979). I will not explain their theories, but take a few of Chisholm's considerations as a starting point for some systematic explorations. Both theories are embedded in peculiar ontologies that need not concern us here.

Chisholm puts the basic theses of a *de se*-theory as follows (see 1981: 1):

(A1)   There are attitudes which are not propositional but self-attributions of properties.

The objects of these attitudes does not belong to their content, as §4 said, so that the content consists just of the properties the supposed object is considered to have:

(A1′)   (i) Some contents of attitudes are properties.

Instead of *propositional attitudes* DST speaks of attitudes in a more general way. Propositional attitudes are secondary with respect to the basic non-propositional self-attributions. (A1) is the fundamental structural axiom of DST. It uses the two *relata* properties and I (see (A1′) (ii) below). The fundamental relation is the relation of self-attribution which involves direct self-reference. (A1′) contradicts the thesis of the propositionalist who claims that the content of an attitude can be given only by a proposition or a sentence. In a proposition or sentence properties are ascribed, but the referent (or its description) is part of the content. According to (A1) the object of some attitudes is descriptionless and, therefore, contentless. This object is, according to Chisholm, the I:

(A1′)   (ii) The I does not belong in/to the content of some attitudes.

To be justified is the following thesis:

(T1)   The primary form of reference is direct self-reference.

This thesis should be justified by defining the ordinary ways of referring (usage of statements, singular terms, beliefs, perceptions . . .) with the use of the concept of direct self-reference.[8]

Thus it has to be shown that the following generalizations are true:

(T2)   The primary form of belief is the self-attribution of properties.
(T3)   The I is the primary object of my attitudes.

These basic ideas are taken up here. Of course it has to be made clear *which* I is the one relate of conscious acts, considering Sartre's distinction between a pre-reflexive and a reflexive *cogito*. Sartre and the DST seem to agree that the subject of consciousness does not belong to the side of the content. Whether the reflexive *cogito* has to be taken as propositional, as one may take it in Sartre, is not that clear. The pre-reflexive *cogito* certainly cannot be on pains of the well known regresses – here Sartre and the DST agree. Further on the talk of "object" in the DST, say in (T3) should either not be taken in the sense in which Sartre denies that the pre-reflexive *cogito* is the object of a conscious act, in which case (T3) would be false for it, or the talk of "object" should be taken as in Sartre and then there will be a distinction between the reflexive I, for which something like (T3) holds, and the pre-reflexive *cogito*.

318

7 A Synthesis of the Pre-reflexive *Cogito* with a *De Se* Theory of Self-Awareness

De se theories and Sartre's conception share the crucial axiom that the I responsible for being also aware of myself in being aware of something else is not part of the content of my thought proper. Self-awareness – and thus any consciousness, since the two phenomena cannot be brought apart – has two components: my knowledge of myself (not to be understood as a second act) and my attitude (believing, wishing, seeing . . .) to some content.

In this paragraph I try to build a synthesis of Sartre's idea of a pre-reflexive *cogito*, the distinction to reflexive consciousness, and a *de se* model of representation. As a means of presentation I use symbols like "☺," "☺," "☹," and others, alluding to the *Language of Thought* hypothesis (Fodor 1975).[9]

Suppose there is a *Language of Thought*, then also to thoughts not rendered in inner speech there is a chain of corresponding LOT-symbols. Taking some pictograms and capitalization as representation of LOT-symbols we may have, for example,

(1)   ☎ RED

as the representation that a (specific) telephone is red.

The structures of the *Language of Thought* are the structures of intentionality. We refer to some property by using or tokening the corresponding LOT-symbol (or some symbol of ordinary language). Someone tokens a LOT-symbol if he produces a token of it (in his brain or "belief box"). To refer to some property is nothing else than tokening the LOT-symbol. Using the LOT-model we can try to make the representational structure of non-propositional consciousness plausible. If self-awareness was propositional it would have to have the structure:

(2)   A believes that p.

Believing would be a relation to a sentence or proposition p. Put thus, the difficulty is that with the believer a subject seems to be presupposed with respect to which we can ask whether it is aware of itself (see §4). If it is self-aware, the propositional structure adds nothing. If it is not self-aware, self-awareness had to arise by believing some special sentences/propositions, taking believing as such as not involving self-awareness. Which sentence/proposition should be able to achieve that? Take a sentence like:

(3)   I am F.

The meaning "the one who is speaking" secures by the use of the pronoun "I" self-reference which is pragmatically immediate with the tokening of (3). This self-reference can also have a special functional role. The processing of "I" can be explanatory for behavior. The combination of (3) and (2) in third person reports like

(4)   A believes "I am F."

319

could be explanatory for A's self-directed behavior. What this functional role, however, has to do with *phenomenal* self-awareness is not clear. It seems to be an addition to (3). In case of the first person one would say

(5)   I believe I am F.

If (5) is the *relatum* of my belief it seems that I am (as the agent of the thought) opposite or besides (5). If (5) was the structure of my self-ascriptions it would have to be made certain that "I" refers to me, and that both uses of "I" refer to the *same* entity. The relatum of my believing, if (5) was the structure of my thought, would be (3) again. The pronoun "I" can secure infallible self-reference, but phenomenal self-awareness might not *arise* thus.

If we have to presuppose phenomenal self-awareness, the processing of "I" is not necessary, even if "I" has a special causal role. I am given to myself and directly attribute myself (without a further act of self-reference) to have property F. The content of such an ascription is the property only, as (A1) of the DST in §6 says.

Now it seems that even in such self-attribution I *refer* to myself, however immediately. I know myself. The representation of this self-reference cannot be a symbol of a natural language, which by its meaning allows a referent to identify itself, since the meaning of the symbol looked for cannot be intersubjective, the supposed meaning being my self-apprehension of myself. Subjective meanings are a *contradictio in adjecto*. Even claiming that to the public expression "I" there correspond different subjective contents does not help, since this content, because of it being content *for me*, had to be my self-apprehension, but we were trying to explain this whole self-apprehension by postulating the *processing* of the (meaning of the) pronoun "I." So we had a second self-representation as the content of a part of the first self-representation (by using "I") leading us into a vicious regress. The representation of my self-reference can, therefore, have no meaning (as meaning is usually understood). Let us suppose instead that "☺" is the LOT-symbol of immediate self-reference (the I-symbol). Self-attributions have then the structure:

(6)   ☺ F

where "F" either is a general term of a natural language or the LOT-representation of a property. "F" stands within the scope of "☺." (6) models an act of consciousness the content of which is F. So "☺" is not part of the content; it is the awareness of oneself that accompanies the awareness of some content. It is Sartre's pre-reflexive *cogito*. The pre-reflexive *cogito* has the same role in Sartre's theory as my unmediated knowledge of myself has in a *de se*-theory of awareness. The self-access given with Sartre's pre-reflexive *cogito* and that given with tokening of "☺" is *part* of the one conscious state, not a further positional reflexive act.

Thinking (6) as a whole has a propositional structure, but this should not be confused with the claim that the content of the thought would be propositional. "☺" is not part of the content of my thought. If my self-apprehension consisted in representing "☺" to myself there would be a difference between my processing of "☺" (analogous to hearing a word) and my understanding the content of "☺" (analogous to understanding the word). So we would have two processes taking place. These two acts are not in my consciousness, neither do I *meet* a self-symbol or the like. Therefore my self-apprehension *is nothing else* than tokening "☺." Remember the fact (F). As content of my belief I only experience "F" or the property referred to by "F." Between me and my self-reference no symbol intervenes. The symbol is not for me; I am it. In section 4, Phenomenon III we said the I is not within the content. The I-symbol is not for me, but I am self-aware in virtue of tokening the I-symbol. "☺" is not perceived or apprehended from some point of view within me. The pre-reflexive *cogito* is not apprehended itself. "☺" does not "stand for" something, but with its tokening self-awareness is presented.[10]

So we have a correspondence of our awareness with a LOT-sentence like

(7) ☺   SEE   ☎ RED
     ↓_ mode of the act ← (percept of) a red telephone
     such that I am conscious of it

What this modeling does for Sartre's theory is gives it a working theory background that cashes in, in terms of a semi-formal model, the talk of a non-propositional pre-reflexive *cogito*. The LOT-hypothesis – and the funny-looking symbols like "☺" – provide a model of mechanisms connecting the workings of a cognitive system with the occurrence of consciousness. What the appeal to Sartre's pre-reflexive *cogito* does for the DST is gives further backing to the fact that one has to comprehend the being aware of oneself as distinct from the contents of consciousness, as something not be thought of as in the (propositionalist) higher-order model of self-awareness.

8 Unity of Consciousness and Reflexive Assent

Given the basic features of DST this paragraph takes up related problems:

(a) Accounting for the assent from pre-reflexive *cogito* to *presenting* an I to myself
(b) Accounting for the *unity* of consciousness on its different levels.

(a)

Sartre goes wrong, I believe, in identifying the object given in a self-presentation with the Me (and so finally rejecting the *epoché*).[11] Even though what we experience in our self-awareness is ourselves as the individual we are, there is the distinction between the Self/Me and the self-representation of the agent of consciousness, since the assent to this self-representation is functionally distinct from object-centered consciousness, and the operation of assent can be characterized generally without paying attention to any involvement of biographic knowledge (as would be distinctive of an involvement of the Self).

The reflexive assent should not be modeled simply in the traditional way as one act having as object another act, as Sartre himself mostly does.[12] The LOT-hypothesis gives as the means to model the assent as the relation and modification of I-symbols.

321

"☺" works as an operator and has to be distinguished from a further LOT-symbol for me, say "☻," which can occur within the scope of "☺." Consider, for example, a reflexive thought having me not only as the agent of the thought, but also as an object; this objectification could be done by something like "☻." "☻" in fact is the reflected *cogito*. "☻" stands for the *Ego*, that arises with the almost imperceptible shift of focus mentioned in phenomenon IV in §4. With the tokening of "☻" we have the presentation of an I to ourselves. The thought has a structure like

(1)   ☺ THINK ☻ SEE ☎ RED

being the thought that it is me who sees that the telephone is red. We can model the shift from being absorbed into seeing the red telephone to being aware that it is me who sees the red telephone as the shift from

(2)   ☺ SEE ☎ RED

to (1). The operation that is responsible for the shift can be described as a rule:

(R1)   Whenever "☺" is put into the scope of another "☺," then the left most "☺" within the scope is changed into "☻."

That only the left most "☺" is changed is necessary, since there is just *one Ego* and not a nesting of *Egos* in consciousness, even if there are higher-order thoughts like

(3)   I believe that I want that I believe that dogs are green, but they just aren't.

As mentioned already, we need another self-representation for mere self-representation, i.e., not as tokening either the pre-reflexive or the reflexive *cogito*. This self-representation is needed for such nested occurrences like in (3) and at the level of sub-doxastic processing in the cognitive system. We take "⊗" as the corresponding symbol of the LOT. The LOT-rendering of (3) then becomes something like

(4)   ☺ BELIEVE (☺ WANT ⊗ BELIEVE ALL:[{ [🐕]} → GREEN]) & NOT(ALL:[{ [🐕]} → GREEN])

where I have an explicit thought about me.[13]

"☻" is not the Self (as biographical construct), but the *Ego* experienced, although posited as a representation in the scope of "☺," as the agent of the acts, giving them unity. This objectification "☻" of "☺" has the function as *presenting* to me myself *focused* as the subject of my acts. This function is independent from the biographical narrative surrounding the Self needed, e.g., in claims of responsibility and understanding ourselves *as persons*.

"☻" and "☺" are *not the same*; thus, as Sartre says (1937: 44), the occurrence of the *Ego* is not due to the fact that one and the same entity – beneath the level of the whole cognitive system – is reflected *in itself*, as some Neo-Kantians claim.

(b)

The question of the unity of consciousness appears either as the question of what unites some content into a consciousness of something or the question of what unites several acts into a unified consciousness. The first question is the topic of Kant's theory of the transcendental unity of apperception or a theory of the conditions for consciousness to arise. The second question is closer to the role of the *Ego* within the conscious acts. Sartre denies that we need the *Ego* to unite consciousness, since the temporal structure of consciousness (including retention and protention) and the holism of mental content would suffice for that (see Priest 2000: 36–42); but this may seem questionable, since temporal or intentional unification seems to presuppose that there *are* several acts within *something* waiting to be unified. Given the DST, however, we can formulate a simple rule of unification of content:

(R2)   ☺ F & ☺ G ↔ ☺(F & G)

This means that on some level of information processing a conjunction principle within the scope of "☺" applies. A similar rule may apply for "☻" and "☹." The rule is no deep explanation of the unity of consciousness, but merely a description of an architectural constraint. On the other hand, there is nothing in it that commits us to conclude from the fact that some *cogito* (the fact that some content occurs within the scope of some I-symbol) is responsible for unification that it is not the pre-reflexive *cogito* that is central for self-awareness.

9 Where Do Higher-Order Theories of Consciousness Go Wrong?

The DST model is not a higher-order theory of consciousness (HOT) as they are widely held in the analytic philosophy of mind (see Carruthers 1996; Rosenthal 1995), but it has some of its features. The *Ego* only appears after a modification of awareness that resembles reflection (see §8). This bringing the *Ego* into focus, nevertheless, was not modeled as involving propositions or even sentences of a natural language, as a HOT would have it.

Is Sartre's conception of self-awareness compatible with a propositionalist rejoinder to the DST?

There is one obvious point of reply for a HOT, which is also the most fundamental: A theory of the logical structure of knowing oneself has to keep – for the sake of the unity of a functionalist account of the mental – the connection between the functional I of awareness with the implicit I of mental processing. A propositionalist theory can do this more systematically than a *de se*-theory, since in the propositionalist theory both levels have the same logical format. The basic claim of the propositionalist is:

(P)   Any propositional attitude, any information processing explicit or tacit, but cognitively penetrable,[14] has the form: I (ATTITUDE) SENTENCE.

For example,

(1) I believe that it is Monday.

(2) I see that the audience is falling asleep.

and so on.[15]

The "I" as LOT-symbol "☺" or as a symbol of a natural language has, according to the propositionalist, the meaning "that which is tokening this very sentence" and, therefore, is immune from failure of reference. It refers to the thinking person. This "I," still the propositionalist speaking, does *not* yield phenomenal awareness immediately. "☺" is not the representation for this. Fact (F) does *not* apply to "☺." Phenomenal self-awareness – even if it does not occur as explicit (inner) speaking – occurs only if *in the scope* (that is in the sentence within the structure defined by (P)) an I-symbol is tokened (be it one of a natural language or an according symbol of LOT like "☺"), like we had in (R1). For the propositionalist the unity of the levels of mental processing requires that mental events on different levels (i.e., some of which are conscious, some of which are *not*) be within the scope of an I-symbol, whereas only those yield self-awareness where an I-symbol gets into the scope of an I-operator. What happens by bringing "☺" into the scope of "☺" is the *decisive* step from tacit processing to phenomenal self-awareness. This differs from the DST, where the mere presence of the pre-reflexive *cogito* (alias ☺) gave rise to awareness. Whereas DST is a "first-order" theory (self-awareness arising by tokening a special symbol), the propositionalist account is a higher-order theory (only by some representation being represented or being brought into the scope of another does self-awareness arise). The corresponding cognitive architectures or models of inferential roles might vary accordingly. Nevertheless, the general idea of accounting for self-awareness by a process of tokening some LOT-symbol is kept also in the propositionalist theory. A radical version of a propositionalist theory could even claim that the I-symbol that matters is the pronoun "I" of a natural language. It helped to build up the structures that matter for a functional architecture with consciousness.[16] A less radical version could admit the secondary role of the pronoun "I," and might agree to denying a speaker meaning to "I," but would still see the structure (P) as the defining structure of self-awareness.

Furthermore, the fundamental role which attitudes *de se* have according to Chisholm need not be denied; the propositionalist just sees this fundamental role for *de se* propositions. The only thing left over from DST then will be the claim of the direct attribution of properties. This claim was motivated by phenomenological considerations how we know of ourselves within our states and as *not* being part of *the content* of the states which we experience. Can this phenomenology be undermined? Can the arguments given in §§4–7 be circumvented? In fact, the justification given there depends on the analysis of the sentences

(3) I am F.

and

(4) I believe I am F.

It was claimed that these sentences cannot express the phenomenal content of self-awareness, since the agent believes these sentences would occur "on the other side" of this content. If these sentences are the content of my thoughts, where am I? It seems that I am the one thinking the content, i.e., being related to the content and therefore distinguished from it. The analysis operates with a principle which could be expressed thus:

(E)   That which is experiencing is not itself an experienced object in that act.

Now *suppose* it is the defining and peculiar characteristic of the I that it knows itself and *at the same time* is presented as part of the content of consciousness. The I-symbol then would instantiate my knowledge of myself and at the same time be part of the represented sentence. Why should it be impossible that I know myself as the continuous agent representing content and at the same time represent *that very agent* (not only myself in the manner of *another* representation like "☺") as that object to which some properties are attributed? This would have to be done by a *single* representation to avoid the problem of identifying the referents of the symbols.[17]

Phenomenologically it is not that clear, as §4 made us believe, whether self-awareness is non-propositional: Since I always am aware of myself when I am attributing myself – directly, since I do not have to identify myself – a property (like "☺ LookOutOfTheWindow"), this very knowledge has to be part of the content of what I am thinking. Where else should it be? What I know – even if it is knowledge of myself – seems to be mental content. If we put this knowledge into the processing of the I-symbol we are back at the prepositional structure of (3) in §7! But putting it there is more than dubious for the reasons given in §7, and merely saying that (E) might be false, as in the beginning of the preceding paragraph, does not give us a model of how this might be. For Sartre giving up (E) and thus going back to a propositionalist account in which the *cogito* in every case is part of the content is unacceptable; the pre-reflexive *cogito* is *defined* as being non-positional. It is thought of as a non-thetic consciousness, and thus cannot be modeled in the propositionalist fashion. Further on, what would become to the shift between being absorbed in the content, although being conscious, and being aware that I am thinking these contents? This focusing on oneself simply does not seem to have that higher-order reflexive structure the propositionalist assigns to it. Thus Sartre's theory of consciousness appears to be congenial to a DST account.

Conclusion

One major shortcoming of the analytic philosophy of mind seems to be keeping insufficiently apart the Self as constructed biographical object from the *Ego* as the subject of our conscious acts. Even if the *Ego* is an aspect/is tied to a Self, its functions and phenomenology require a theory of its own. Narrowing the attention to the Self downsizes self-awareness to an awareness of an object "Self." A motivation to avoid a theory of the *Ego* may have been the fear of being committed to extravagant metaphysics. Keeping Self and *Ego* apart, however, allows the substantiation of the thesis that all awareness of something is at the same time awareness of oneself. Sartre's version of this thesis, using the pre-reflexive *cogito*, helps here. It can be synthesized with a *de se* account of self-awareness. Both parts may shed light on each other and come closer to saving the phenomena.

Notes

1 Similar accounts of the self as (narrative) construction can be found in Dennett 1991 and Metzinger 1995.

2 I have capitalized the Self, the Me, and the Ego to highlight that we are dealing with philosophically reconstructed/defined (concepts of) entities here.

3 Sartre may come close to this (see also Priest 2000: 124–6), Metzinger (1995) really claims that; but the mere fact that the Self is a representation does not make it a misrepresentation. If the Self is a representation of the whole cognitive system its referent really does what it is described as doing. Even our narrative of the Self reenters memory and so influences our further acts. For the phenomenology and structural modeling of self-awareness it is indeed important to see that the Self as representation is not the agent of the act. *Here* a hypostatization would block the view on the pre-reflexive structures of consciousness and the *Ego*. This does not come, however, as sensational revelation.

4 This is a variant of "Fichte's original insight" that self-awareness cannot *come into existence* by reflection or higher-order thought, because a vicious regress ensues (see Pothast 1971). The phenomenology is systematically developed here, but the phenomena have been recognized, of course, in the mentalist tradition – otherwise they could not be basic phenomena. Fichte writes in the *Nachgelassenen Schriften*: "Das Ich setzt sich *schlechthin*, d.h. ohne alle Vermittlung. Es ist zugleich Subjekt und Objekt. Nur durch das sich selbst Setzen wird das Ich – es ist nicht vorher schon Substanz – sondern sich selbst setzen als setzend ist sein Wesen, es ist eins und ebendasselbe; folglich ist es *sich seiner unmittelbar selbst bewusst*" (Fichte 1967, vol. 2: 352).

5 That self-awareness is no *addition* to consciousness is expressed by Hegel as follows: "Ich bin beim Sehen, Hören einfach bei mir selbst, und es ist nur eine Form meiner reinen Durchsichtigkeit und Klarheit in mir selbst" (Hegel 2000: §350). The fact that the I cannot be taken to be part of *the content* is expressed by (the Neo-Kantian) Paul Natorp in his *Einleitung in die Psychologie nach kritischer Methode*: "Ich-Sein heißt nicht Gegenstand, sondern allem anderen gegenüber dasjenige sein, dem etwas Gegenstand ist" (Natorp 1912, §4).

6 Sartre himself (1937: 46–9) uses the example of reading or looking at a picture. Sartre (1948: 42–5) expresses the phenomenon as being at the same time at myself (because of the pre-reflexive *cogito*) and detached from myself (since it is *only* a pre-reflexive *cogito*, reflecting breaking the immediacy to the object).

7 One might – as Kant did – also speak of the transcendental synthesis or unity of apperception. I will not discuss this topic here. In Sartre it is clear that one should not confuse such conditions with the *Ego* as experienced by me. Sartre (1937) may be taken as accusing Husserl of confusing his talk of a transcendental *Ego* with Kant's talk of a transcendental *Ego*. I will neither discuss whether this interpretation of (Sartre 1937) is right, nor whether Sartre himself represents Husserl's theory appropriately. Husserl (1913, 1969) is in his distinction between the empirical Me as a transcendent object and the *Ego*, which remains after the *epoché*, closer to the model advanced here. Husserl, however, takes that *Ego* as not being part of the content of acts, since he neither endorses a pre-reflexive *cogito*, nor is he as explicit as Sartre about the distinction between being absorbed in the intentional objects and focusing on oneself as having these intentional objects; see §8.

8 A topic that does not concern us here. See Chisholm 1981, belaboring the point.

9 The thesis (henceforth LOT) will only be used in a vague or general sense, since so it will be easier to understand the psychological reality of the fundamental relation of self-attribution used in DST. Not much is said about the inferential role of such an I-symbol

within a LOT-model of self-awareness. That these symbols are looking funny should not be confused with the serious intent of the presentation. The use of these symbols circumvents some problems with keeping the different *Egos* apart linguistically, and avoids using expressions that carry heavy connotations in the history of philosophy (such as "transcendental *Ego*," etc.).

10 That "☺" is not part of mental content does not mean that "☺" does not contribute to the inferential role that representations like (6) have. (6) taken entirely has sentential structure. A fully-fledged LOT-theory should be able to specify inferential roles accordingly. Even if "☺" was an atomic symbol, this does not exclude its having a central role in processing – according to Fodor, quite a few LOT-symbols are atomic. The characterization of *de se* attributions given is compatible with a functionalist account of the peculiar way I am to myself (i.e., of "☺"). "☺" has by its syntax a causal role, as all LOT-symbols do. The DST tries to explain the structure of acts in which "☺" occurs and their relation to the other attitudes and attitude reports in natural language using *inter alia* the pronoun "I"; something I do go not into here (see Chisholm 1981 for details). The fact (F) for ordinary representations – that the appearance does not appear itself again, as Husserl said – can now be reduced to "☺" possessing this crucial feature; other representations behave according to fact (F) inasmuch as they are the content of some state introduced by the symbol "☺."

11 See Sartre's way of equating "I" and "Me" (Sartre 1937). If there is an *Ego* apart from the Self/Me then after the *epoché* not all egological structures are gone in favor of Sartre's "pure field of consciousness." A problem of the *epoché* is that by cutting of the objects as real one turns from being at the objects to focusing on *act content*, thus easily getting into a reflexive state. But then – in virtue of being in a reflexive state – there is this persisting I, its ubiquity being due to the *epoché*.

12 See, e.g., Sartre 1937: 45; but maybe in contrast to Sartre 1948: 42, 85.

13 This account of the phenomenality of myself experiencing myself is not that of the original DST in Chisholm (1981). Chisholm's theory works by kind of "self-representing" properties. What these properties are and how they work seems to me to be part of Chisholm's arabesque ontology. The appeal to "self-representation" in properties either is only a title to the problem or has to appeal to something like (F). Since there are different *Egos* to be coordinated, however (see §4), we need also an account of their relation. An appeal to something like (F) is not enough at this crucial point of the theory. Chisholm also uses a relation of "considering" that one has such a property. This brings his account dangerously close to a higher-order theory of self-awareness (see §9).

14 For this notion, see Pylyshyn 1989: 130–45). Pylyshyn and Fodor are two of the main proponents of a propositionalist theory.

15 The thesis that all conscious events are propositional is compatible with the claim that some contents of conscious acts are non propositional representations (example: "I see this: ☺," in which a picture follows the colon). Perceptual scenes can be embedded in sentential frames.

16 Carruthers (1996) is a proponent of such a strong version of propositionalism.

17 Remember Fichte's "original insight" which was mentioned in §4. Self-awareness cannot arise by one I reflecting on *another*. The second I-symbol in (4) must not be a mere *objectivation* of the I, however that might be possible. The traditional opinion that subject and object are "one" or "united" here is a mere redescription of the problem. The traditional thesis (in Schelling or Natorp) that the acting I cannot be completely objectified does nothing to account for the mechanism by which that very agent is incompletely objectified.

References and Further Reading

Bremer, M. (2005) Animal consciousness as a test case of cognitive science. Some theses. In *Bewusstsein: Interdisziplinäre Perspektiven*. Munich: forthcoming.

Carruthers, P. (1996) *Language, Thought and Consciousness*. Cambridge: Cambridge University Press.

Chalmers, D. (1996) *The Conscious Mind*. New York and Oxford: Oxford University Press.

Chisholm, R. (1981) *The First Person. An Essay on Reference and Intentionality*. Minneapolis: University of Minnesota Press.

Dennett, D. (1991) *Consciousness Explained*. Boston: Little, Brown.

Dummett, M. (1988) *Ursprünge der analyischen Philosophie*. Frankfurt am Main: Suhrkamp.

Fichte, J. G. (1967) *Gesamtausgabe. Reihe II: Nachgelassene Schriften*. vol. 2: *Nachgelassene Schriften 1791–1793* (ed. R. Lauth and H. Jacob). Stuttgart, Bad Cannstatt: F. Frommann.

Fodor, Jerry (1975) *The Language of Thought*. New York: Crowell.

—— (1994) Jerry Fodor. In S. Gutenplan (ed.), *Companion to the Philosophy of Mind* (pp. 292–300). Oxford and Cambridge, MA: Blackwell.

Hegel, G. W. F. (2000) *Enzyklopädie der philosophischen Wissenschaften im Grundrisse* [Encyclopedia of the philosophical sciences in outline]. *Gesammelte Werke* vol. 13. Hamburg: Felix Meiner (original work published 1817).

Husserl, E. (1913) *Ideen zu einer reinen Phänomenologie und phänomenologischen Philosophie*. Mohr: Tübingen.

—— (1969) *Cartesianische Meditationen* (ed. E. Stroker). Hamburg: Meiner (original work published 1931).

Kenevan, P. (1981) Self-consciousness and the ego in the philosophy of Sartre. In P. A. Schilpp (ed.), *The Philosophy of Jean-Paul Sartre*. La Salle, IL: Open Court.

Lewis, D. (1979) Attitudes *De Dicto* and *De Se*. *Philosophical Review*, 88, 513–43.

McCulloch, G. (1994) *Using Sartre. An Analytical Introduction to Early Sartrean Themes*. London and New York: Routledge.

Mererk, P. (1988) *Sartre's Existentialism and Early Buddhism*. Bangkok: Buddhadhamma Foundation.

Metzinger, T. (1995) Faster than thought: Holism, homogeneity and temporal coding. In T. Metzinger (ed.), *Conscious Experience* (pp. 425–63). Lawrence, KS: Allen Press.

Minsky, M. (1985) *The Society of Mind*. New York: Simon & Schuster.

Natorp, P. (1912) *Allgemeine Psychologie nach kritischer Methode*. Mohr: Tübingen.

Perry, J. (1979) The problem of the essential indexica. *Nous*, 13, 3–21.

Pothast, U. (1971) *Über einige Fragen der Selbstbeziehung*. Frankfurt am Main: Klostermann.

Priest, S. (2000) *The Subject in Question. Sartre's Critique of Husserl in the Transcendence of the Ego*. London and New York: Routledge.

Pylyshyn, Z. (1989) *Computation and Cognition: Toward a Foundation for Cognitive Science*, 5th edn. Cambridge: Cambridge University Press.

Rosenthal, D. (1995) Multiple drafts and facts of the matter. In T. Metzinger (ed.), *Conscious Experience* (pp. 359–72). Lawrence, KS: Allen Press.

Sartre, J-P. (1937) La transcendence de l'ego: Esquisse d'une description phénoménologique. *Recherches Philosophiques*, VI; quoted in the English edition, *The Transcendence of the Ego* (trans. F. Williams and R. Kirkpatrick). New York: Noonday Press, 1962.

—— (1943) *L'être et le néant. Essai d'ontologie phénoménologique*. Paris: Gallimard.

—— (1948) Conscience de soi et connaissance de soi. *Bulletin de la Société Francaise de Philosophie*, XLII, quoted in the German edition, *Bewußtsein und Selbsterkenntnis*. Reinbek bei Hamburg: Rowohlt, 1973.

23

Phenomenology, Neuroscience, and Intersubjectivity

MATTHEW RATCLIFFE

There is considerable current interest in the potential for fruitful interdisciplinary exchange between cognitive neuroscience and phenomenology.[1] One popular view is that specific phenomenological descriptions can be extricated from their philosophical context and then explained scientifically. The goal of the explanation is to *naturalize* the phenomenology. This chapter explores the interplay between phenomenology and neuroscience with respect to intersubjectivity and the recent discovery of "mirror neurons." These are cells in the premotor cortex of humans and monkeys, which discharge when one performs certain actions and are also active when one observes the same or similar actions being performed by others. Since their discovery in 1996, mirror neurons have attracted considerable philosophical and scientific attention, due largely to their possible implications for theories of intersubjectivity. Some of the focus has been on whether they cast light on current debates between "theory" and "simulation" theories of interpersonal understanding. However, some interesting parallels can also be drawn between the mirror system and the claims of phenomenologists such as Husserl, Merleau-Ponty, and Scheler. In what follows, I will explore these parallels and show that the two fields of enquiry can indeed interact and complement each other in several ways, generating some novel claims concerning the structure of intersubjectivity. However, the result is not a naturalization of phenomenology but a retreat from certain epistemological and metaphysical assumptions that are constitutive of mainstream naturalism.

Phenomenology and Naturalism

A way of thinking about the interaction between phenomenology and neuroscience is set out by Roy, Petitot, Pachoud, and Varela (1999), who focus on Husserl's phenomenology and suggest that: "when provided with adequate characterizations such as those conducted along the lines of Husserlian phenomenology, phenomenological data can be adequately reconstructed on the basis of the main tenets of Cognitive Science, and then integrated into the natural sciences"[2] (Roy et al. 1999: 48). Hence Husserlian phenomenology is to be "naturalized." The term "naturalism" is applied to several different doctrines. In its broadest sense, it may amount to no more than the premise that philosophical theories should not appeal to anything irrevocably mysterious. However, it has also acquired a more specific meaning, which incorporates both epistemological and metaphysical theses:

1   Epistemological: The standpoint and method/s of empirical science comprise the best way to acquire knowledge of every aspect of the world, including ourselves.
2   Metaphysical: The world is comprised solely of the kinds of objects, properties, and causal relations posited by scientific theories.

Acceptance of these two theses fuels the project of exhaustive "naturalization." Understanding something is identified with integrating it into the scientifically described world. Anything that exists but does not appear to fit requires reinterpretation in objective, physical, and scientific terms. It is this kind of conception that Roy et al. adopt, where to be "naturalized" means to be "integrated into an explanatory framework where every acceptable property is made continuous with the properties admitted by the natural sciences" (Roy et al. 1999: 1–2). Thus, in so far as there are "phenomenological data," they need to be reinterpreted and integrated into an objective, scientific view of the world that makes no ultimate appeal to the irreducible character of experience (Roy et al. 1999: 48). In order to incorporate the demand for "naturalization," naturalism must involve some quite rigid metaphysical and epistemological assumptions. It is not just that the world consists of *whatever science ultimately reveals*. The demand for reinterpretation and integration into a scientific view is only compelling if the current "scientific worldview" is taken to be metaphysically authoritative. And this can only be accepted on the grounds that (a) current science *does* reveal the world to be that way and (b) certain kinds of epistemic process, characteristic of scientific enquiry, are privileged over others.[3] Hence, when I refer to "naturalism" in what follows, I have in mind a doctrine incorporating contestable assumptions about the nature of science and the way the world is, which legitimate the goal of "naturalization." This is different from the more general and open view that philosophy should in some sense be continuous with science, a version of which I will support.

"Phenomenology," broadly construed, encompasses many different approaches, whose aim is to describe the structure of experience, much of which is ordinarily tacit. Phenomenologists offer very different methods for charting that structure, which yield different descriptions of experience. However, there is general consensus amongst phenomenologists that, in studying the structure of experience, one discovers that empirical scientific knowledge does not comprise our most fundamental understanding of the world. For example, Husserl (1970) proposes that science draws its meaning from a presupposed experiential "lifeworld" [*Lebenswelt*] of social purposes and practices. The empirical sciences, according to Husserl, are to be interpreted instrumentally, as sets of concepts and methods that organize the lifeworld in such a way as to enhance our practical negotiation of it in various contexts. They will always presuppose the lifeworld because their intelligibility depends upon it. Naturalism, Husserl claims, rests on a misinterpretation of the relationship between scientific theories and the lifeworld; the latter is quietly forgotten and the former are taken as our most fundamental descriptions of reality. It amounts to a "surreptitious substitution of idealized nature for prescientifically intuited reality" (Husserl 1970: 48–9).

330

A similar view is suggested by Merleau-Ponty. Like Husserl, he regards naturalistic interpretations of science and the world as confused, in failing to acknowledge that objective scientific descriptions are not all-encompassing or fundamental. According to Merleau-Ponty, restricting one's enquiry to the methods and discoveries of empirical science involves a failure to recognize their grounding in a more fundamental experiential disclosure of the world. In "The Primacy of Perception," he construes perceptual experience as a context of intelligibility for all thought, scientific or otherwise, the source of "all rationality, all value and all existence" (Merleau-Ponty 1964b: 13). It is an "openness to *something*," which is presupposed by the meaningfulness of scientific thought.

Such themes do not entail that phenomenology is anti-*scientific*. Indeed, Merleau-Ponty makes extensive use of neuropsychological case studies in *Phenomenology of Perception* (1945; cited as Merleau-Ponty 1962) and Husserl, in the *Crisis of European Sciences* (1937; cited as Husserl 1970), takes one of his central tasks to be the *clarification* of natural science. Science still has a place in phenomenology, despite the rejection of naturalism. Science does not contain its own interpretation and naturalism is not sewn into its structure. However, whether phenomenological claims *can* be developed into a legitimate case against naturalism is another matter. The question therefore arises as to how the interaction between phenomenology and science should be conceived. Should phenomenology surrender to naturalism, or can it go some way toward repudiating naturalism? Roy et al. adopt the former view. They suggest that, although Husserl's overall phenomenology is resolutely anti-naturalistic, it is possible to extract some of his numerous phenomenological insights from their philosophical context and put them to good use in a naturalistic cognitive science. Phenomenology comprises a rich archive of intricate, accurate, and insightful descriptions of various aspects of experience. Furthermore, there is considerable similarity between some of Husserl's phenomenological descriptions and recent findings in neurobiology. So Husserlian phenomenology can supply explananda for cognitive science. The job of the science is then to provide objective, naturalistic models of cognitive processes in order to explain the phenomenology. Roy et al. construe their project as a "reciprocal movement" between Husserlian phenomenology and cognitive science (Roy et al. 1999: xiii). Phenomenological descriptions are fed into cognitive science and reinterpreted in the process, so as to accord with naturalism.

This conception does not incorporate the possibility of the naturalist's ontology or epistemology undergoing significant reappraisal and reinterpretation through the interaction between phenomenology and science. Instead, a fairly orthodox conception of "naturalization" is assumed, according to which phenomenological properties are to be rendered non-mysterious through their "reconstruction" and integration into an objective, scientific description (Roy et al. 1999: 48–9).

In what follows, I will employ the example of "mirror neurons" to argue that such assumptions are unwarranted. I will assume that science can utilize phenomenological descriptions, without accepting phenomenological methods or phenomenological accounts of the nature and role of science, but will show that this does not lead to naturalism. The relationship between phenomenology and science is not simply a matter of one being put to work to serve the other. It is an ongoing process of *mutual* reinterpretation, which is not legitimately constrained by inflexible metaphysical and epistemological assumptions about the nature of science that are imposed in advance of empirical enquiry.

Mirror Neurons and Intersubjectivity

The cells known as "mirror neurons" were first discovered in area F5 of the ventral premotor cortex of monkeys, by means of electrophysiological studies (Gallese et al. 1996; Rizzolatti et al. 1996) and have since been found in other cortical areas (Rizzolatti et al. 2002: 37). There is also strong evidence for the existence of a mirror system in humans. Although direct recording of individual neurons is not an option with human subjects, studies have been conducted using magnetoencephalography (MEG), transcranial magnetic simulation (TMS), and positron emission tomography (PET).[4] Mirror neurons have both perceptual and motor properties. In monkeys, they discharge when another monkey is seen performing a hand action. They do not discharge when the target object is observed but the action is not and response is also significantly diminished or absent when a tool, rather than the hand, is employed to manipulate the object.[5] Responses are variably specific to "kinds" of action. Some cells are tuned to general categories of action, such as "grasping, manipulating, tearing, holding objects," whereas others are also receptive to the *manner* in which an object is grasped or held (Fogassi and Gallese 2002: 16).

In addition to these perceptual properties, mirror neurons discharge during the performance of certain kinds of action and "match" observed actions with actions performed. For example, a cell that responds during the perception of another monkey reaching for food may also respond in the same way when the observer reaches for food. This matching between action and perception of action is variably refined. "Strictly congruent" neurons match quite specific similarities between perception and performance, such as "firmly grasping an object." Broadly congruent neurons are sensitive to less specific similarities, such as just "grasping." There are also broadly congruent neurons that match sequential actions. For example, in monkeys, some cells will discharge when an experimenter places food in front of the monkey and then when the monkey reaches for it (Fogassi and Gallese 2002: 15–19).

Interestingly, these cells do not appear to be tuned to *movements*, characterized as physical changes in posture. They are receptive to *actions* and to the differences between kinds of action. Observation of an action being mimicked in the absence of a target object results in a substantially weakened or absent response, suggesting that it is goal structure, rather than physical behavior, that is important. That mirror neurons are selective to the teleological structure of action, rather than to the physical structure of behavior, is also illustrated by the difference between strictly and broadly congruent cells. Broadly congruent neurons pick up on the goal structure of an action, such as grasping an object, whereas strictly congruent ones are also receptive to the "style" of the action, the way in which that goal is achieved (Rizzolatti et al. 2002: 37).

It is likely that the mirror system in humans has additional properties. For example, we routinely employ our bodies to make communicative gestures, which do not have target objects, and there is evidence that the human mirror system is receptive to these (Rizzolatti et al. 2002: 41). We also employ an elaborate range of facial expressions when communicating, and it has been suggested that there is a specialized mirror system for matching the facial expressions of others with one's own (Studdert-Kennedy 2002). Of further interest is the observation that monkey F5 is homologous to Broca's area in humans, which is associated with linguistic ability. So the possibility arises that our mirror system plays some role in facilitating verbal communication (Rizzolatti et al. 2002: 42–3). Humans also differ from monkeys in their ability to imitate, which may play a considerable role in the development of communication. And it has been suggested that the mirror system could well support this ability. For example, Wohlschläger and Bekkering (2002) claim that the human mirror system is a necessary though not sufficient condition for imitative abilities. That "children perceive goals and intentions from a very early age on" (Wohlschläger and Bekkering 2002: 103) indicates that imitation does not involve the complicated cognitive task of observing behaviors and then working out how to do something similar. Given a "direct perceptual-motor mapping" (Wohlschläger and Bekkering 2002: 101) of the sort that the mirror system might facilitate, one can *see what to do*.

Much of the current philosophical and scientific interest in mirror neurons is concerned with their implications for our understanding of intersubjectivity. When we observe another person, we do not ordinarily explicitly infer an action interpretation from observation of a perceived series of mechanical movements. Behavior is *perceived* as goal-directed and purposive. Mirror neurons provide a possible explanation of how action perception can be precisely *perception* and not *implicit inference* or *tacit theorizing*. An inter-modal link between perception of others and activation of one's own motor system constitutes the basis for a perceptual appreciation of others, not as mere objects that causally interact with a world but as agents, like oneself. Elaborate theorizing is not required:

> What we would like to emphasize is that when "reading the mind" of conspecifics whose actions we are observing, we rely *also*, if not mostly, on a series of explicit behavioral signals, that we can detect from their observed behavior. These signals are intrinsically meaningful to the extent that they enable the activation of equivalent inner representations on the observer/mind-attributer's side. (Fogassi and Gallese 2002: 30)

It has been suggested that mirror neurons shed light on current debates between "theory" and "simulation" theories of interpersonal understanding. Most versions of both positions assume that an ability to assign intentional states to other agents, in order to interpret, predict, and explain behavior, is central to intersubjectivity. According to the "theory" view, this is achieved through deployment of a largely tacit, systematic body of knowledge, which may be largely innate (e.g., Carruthers 1996) or learned (e.g., Gopnik 1996). Simulation theories take interpersonal understanding to be a matter of practical know-how rather than theoretical knowing. In order to explain and predict others, we somehow put ourselves in their position (either their environmental situation or their psychological state), run our own cognitive processes "off-line" to ascertain what we would do in their predicament and attribute the output to them.[6]

Gallese and Goldman suggest that mirror neurons are a precursor to mature intersubjective abilities and that their presence supports the simulation theory over the theory theory: "The activity of mirror neurons, and the fact that observers undergo motor facilitation in the same muscular groups as those utilized by target agents, are findings that accord well with simulation theory but would not be predicted by theory theory" (Gallese and Goldman 1998: 493). Theory theory implies that intersubjective understanding is a matter of detached contemplation, which does not require *sharing* the mental states of others. As Stone and Davies (1996: 126–7) put it: "according to [theory theory], other people are objects in our environment, and the task of understanding them is no different, in principle, from the task of understanding the behavior of other, more inert, objects." Given the theory view, one would not expect to find a system matching action observation with action performance. But simulation points to just such a mapping. The mirror system "seems to be nature's way of getting the observer into the same "mental shoes" as the target – exactly what the conjectured simulation heuristic aims to do" (Gallese and Goldman 1998: 497–8).

However, it is doubtful that mirror neurons can be incorporated into the simulation theory in this way. As Gallagher (2001a) points out, the idea of simulation suggests that another person is perceived and *then* simulated. But evidence from mirror neurons does not point to a two-step process: "perception of action is already an understanding of the action; there is no extra step involved that could count as a simulation routine" (Gallagher 2001a: 102). You do not see a person and *then* use your mind as a model with which to interpret her as an agent. You just *see her as an agent.* So even if simulation and/or theory are to be invoked to explain some aspects of interpersonal understanding, it seems that they both presuppose the kind of understanding that a mirror system might facilitate. They pass over the question of how we are initially aware of another person as a locus of experience and agency, which we might then theorize about or simulate in a certain way. Thompson (Thompson 2001b: 12) suggests that this presupposed awareness of others as *others* consists in a "pre-reflexive couplings of self and other at the level of the lived body." It is therefore something that mirror neurons, a bridge between sensory and motor modalities, can help to illuminate.

Of course, mirror neurons alone do not add up to a comprehensive explanation of our sense of others. In fact, they do not even account for the differentiation between self and other. That X discharges when I perform action A and also when you perform action A does not explain how I experience one action as "mine" and the other as "yours." But they do show how a *perceptual* grasp of agency is possible, thus challenging the assumption that action interpretations need to be *inferred* from perception of behavior. The problem of understanding others is perhaps not that of surmounting a perceptual gulf between two distinct and hidden mental lives but of distinguishing between them, given an undifferentiated perceptual-motor awareness of agency. That the starting point for intersubjectivity is just such an awareness is suggested by Gallese's "shared manifold" hypothesis: "When we enter in relation with others there is a multiplicity of states that we share with them. We share emotions, our body schema, our being subject to pain as well as to other somatic sensations" (Gallese 2001: 44–5). Although Gallese associates such ideas with the simulation theory, a "shared manifold" is something that is presupposed by an ability to simulate. In order to simulate effectively, one must already be able to appreciate that another being is relevantly similar to oneself. Mirror neurons, if they facilitate an inter-modal bridge between perception and action, show how an understanding of others can rest upon a shared, practical, bodily, affective togetherness. They thus point to a kind of interpersonal connection that much recent work on intersubjectivity ignores or quietly presupposes. Gallese and others go some way toward explicating this but the idea is developed much further in the writings of certain phenomenologists (as noted by Petit 1999; Gallagher 2001a, 2001b; and Thompson 2001b).

Perceiving Others

Phenomenological approaches attempt, in various ways, to make explicit and clarify the structure of intersubjective experience. In so doing, phenomenologists have argued that theoretical cognition, inference, analogy, and simulation do not constitute the basic awareness of others upon which all interpersonal understanding and interaction rests. Instead, the emphasis is placed upon perceptual and affective awareness of others as animate organisms, an awareness that is not detached or theoretical but inextricable from bodily interactions between self and other.[7] This kind of understanding is not appropriately characterized in terms of the perception of others as external objects, followed by the positing of internal mental states as causes of behavior. The agency of others is somehow experienced rather than inferred. For the phenomenologist, "bodily behaviour is meaningful, it is intentional, and as such it is neither internal nor external, but rather beyond this artificial distinction" (Zahavi 2001: 153). In this section, I will show how phenomenology and neuroscience converge on a conception of intersubjectivity as a kind of presupposed "togetherness," rather than the traversing of a gulf between people.

Perhaps the most intricate phenomenological discussion of intersubjectivity is that of Husserl in his Fifth *Cartesian Meditation* (Husserl 1960). Husserl rejects the view that an awareness of others is achieved through inference or analogy. Such views assume that another person is first encountered as a kind of object, distinct from oneself, with which one then comes to identify in certain ways. However, Husserl claims that any experience of an objective world already has an appreciation of other experiential subjects incorporated into it. An objective world is just a world that is "there for everyone, accessible in respect of its Objects to everyone" (Husserl 1960: 91). So any grasp of others as objects *within a world* presupposes an appreciation of them as experiential subjects. To articulate the nature of this appreciation, Husserl attempts to formulate a transcendental theory of "empathy," a description of the foundational apprehension of others as *like me and yet distinct from me* that is presupposed by the intelligibility of all intersubjective understanding. His phenomenological method incorporates what he calls a reduction to the "sphere of ownness." This procedure involves discarding all experiential structures that incorporate or presuppose a sense of others. What is left is a peculiar experiential world, an "abstraction" devoid of the meaning "another person," or, as Husserl puts it, a world from which *"all constitutional effects of intentionality relating immediately or mediately to other subjectivity"* have been extracted (Husserl 1960: 93). It is unclear whether this procedure is proposed as a sort of thought experiment or whether it is an experiential state that one is invited to achieve. However, setting aside methodological concerns, it is instructive to consider what Husserl claims to discover through the procedure. In explicating the various layers of experience that differentiate this sphere of ownness or "primordial sphere" from fully enriched intersubjectivity, Husserl aims to make explicit the structure of our most basic awareness of others. He envisages this project as an exercise in *static* phenomenology, a description of the layers that are present in fully developed, adult intersubjective experience. However, his descriptions may also apply to developmental accounts, given that that the more foundational levels will, presumably, arise first. As Smith (2003: 235) puts it: "what is foundationally first is also genetically first."

Although a sense of others has been removed from the primordial sphere, Husserl claims that some kind of pre-objective realm of experience remains, constituted by perception and kinesthesia. He takes this as the starting point from which to address the question of how an appreciation of other experiential subjects, distinct from oneself, can be built up from it.

Husserl suggests that the first step out of solipsistic experience must be an awareness of the other's body as an animate organism like oneself. This requires some kind of "*apperceptive transfer from my animate organism*" (Husserl 1960: 110). He proposes that a pre-reflective, non-inferential "analogizing apperception" is involved, which somehow links perception of the other organism with one's awareness of oneself as a locus of experience (Husserl 1960: 111). This "analogizing" is not a process that relates distinct objects of experience. The bond between self and other is experienced rather than inferred. And this is achieved through a passive "pairing" of certain aspects of self and other: "*ego* and *alter ego* are always and necessarily *given in an original 'pairing'*" (Husserl 1960: 112). Just as a knife and fork are passively grouped together in an experiential Gestalt, so too one's own body and that of the other must be somehow associated, allowing the other's body to "appropriate from mine the sense: animate organism" (Husserl 1960: 113). Once this foundational bond between self and other is explained, Husserl suggests that building up the higher strata of intersubjectivity and culture, which involve various differentiations between self and other, is comparatively easy.

Husserlian phenomenology and research on mirror neurons can interact and complement each other in several ways. Husserl's account rests on an intersubjective achievement whose nature is unclear. What could a pre-objective bodily analogizing actually consist of, aside from the *judgment* that the another's body is relevantly like one's own, which is precisely what Husserl rejects? Work on mirror neurons can lend some support to Husserl, by illustrating what such a relation might consist of and how it is possible. As Gallagher (2001b: 95–6) notes, the problem concerns just which aspect of the other's body Husserl thinks we pair with our own and how. Mirror neurons, Gallagher argues, constitute part of the solution, in showing how an intermodal link between proprioception and perception of *action* might be possible. Hence neuroscientific findings can provide support for Husserl and can also be integrated into the interpretation of phenomenological descriptions, by clarifying the kind of relation described and showing how it need not be something mysterious or even impossible. Similarly, Husserl's claims can complement recent work on mirror neurons, by peeling back the layers of intersubjectivity to reveal a foundational sense of others, the existence and nature of which is largely ignored in the recent theory of mind literature. He provides a phenomenological framework in which the role of mirror neurons can be conceptualized, interpreted, and explained.

Such a marriage may require some reinterpretation of Husserl. For example, Smith (2003: 239) suggests that Husserl's *Fifth Meditation* is "over-intellectualized," in emphasizing relations between stationary bodies rather than mobile, interacting agents. He goes on to discuss Husserl's unpublished work,[8] which places a more explicit emphasis on the role of instincts, drives, and behaviors in the constitution of intersubjectivity. It is certain patterns of *movement*, rather than bodily *appearance*, which are paired.[9] However, it is doubtful that Husserl, even in *Cartesian Meditations*, envisages a pairing between *static bodies*. For example, he claims that "the experienced animate organism of another continues to prove itself as actually an animate organism, solely in its changing but incessantly harmonious behavior" (Husserl 1960: 114). It is through perception of movement that the analogizing between self and other occurs, perhaps through a sequence of movements being harmoniously matched with a coherent sequence of motor patterns. Neuroscience and phenomenology thus complement each other in postulating a foundational, perceptual, practical and self-engaging sense of other agents.

The descriptions of aspects of experience supplied by various other phenomenologists also complement work on mirror neurons. For example, Scheler (1954) claims that we have a pre-theoretical, perceptual experience of others as animate organisms. He considers cases of having fellow-feelings or pitying someone and argues that empathetic and sympathetic experiences of this nature presuppose a more basic appreciation of others as experiential subjects. One does not understand someone *by* pitying her; that she is a possible object of one's pity is already understood. It is this presuppositional sense of others that Scheler attempts to make explicit:

> One may look at the face of a yelling child as a merely physical object, or one may look at it (i.e., in the normal way) as an expression of pain, hunger, etc., though without therefore pitying the child; the two things are utterly different. Thus experiences of pity and fellow-feeling are always additional to an experience in the other which is already grasped and understood. (Scheler 1954: 8)

Before any transference of feeling between self and other, before any attribution of states to the other, any theorizing, analogy, or inference, she is already given as *one like me*. She is not an internal consciousness that inhabits a perceivable body; she is *perceived as* a locus of experience. Her expressions and movements are not external clues to inner states. Experience presents itself in her visible expressions and is grasped with a kind of immediacy. The body as a mere *object* is an abstraction from the perceived meaningfulness of expressive phenomena: "that 'experiences' occur there is given for us *in* expressive phenomena – again, not by inference, but directly, as a sort of primary 'perception'. It is *in* the blush that we perceive shame, *in* the laughter joy" (Scheler 1954: 10). This "primary givenness" of others, Scheler claims, is the basis of other interpersonal abilities, such as imitation. Imitation presupposes an understanding of the meaningfulness of gestures, an understanding which is not achieved by inferring underlying mental states from behavior but through perception; "the impulse to imitate only arises when we have already apprehended the gesture *as* an expression of fear or joy" (ibid.). Thus Scheler's view also requires some kind of inter-modal link between perception and activity, allowing perceived phenomena to be perceived *as* expressions. "The relationships between expression and experience

have a fundamental basis of connection" (Scheler 1954: 11). This connection constitutes the "primitive givenness of 'the other'" (Scheler 1954: 31), which underlies all
intersubjective experience. It is seldom recognized or articulated, and so the problem
of intersubjectivity is misconstrued as that of connecting two entities that start off
experientially cut off from each other. In contrast, Scheler claims that the appreciation
of others as animate forms always incorporates "some degree of undifferentiated identification" (Scheler 1954: 31); one does not fully distinguish oneself from others.

Merleau-Ponty similarly claims that others are encountered perceptually, without
the need for inference or analogy. Like Scheler, he rejects the idea of a gulf between
internalized subjects, to be bridged by inference from behavior to agency. Merleau-
Ponty claims that the meaning of behavior is perceptually evident in a sense that is
prior to any intellectualized divide between subjects that philosophers might impose
(Merleau-Ponty 1964b: 17–18). My own body is a sense-giving orientation through
which all experience is structured, as opposed to a mere object with which I am uniquely
familiar. And the bodies of others are not encountered as objects either:

> Just as my body, as the system of all my holds on the world, founds the unity of the objects
> which I perceive, in the same way the body of the other – as the bearer of symbolic
> behaviors and of the behavior of true reality – tears itself away from being one of my
> phenomena, offers me the task of a true communication. (Merleau-Ponty 1964a: 17–18)

But how is a body apprehended as a locus of agency and experience, rather than a
mere object in motion? In "The Child's Relations with Others," Merleau-Ponty ven-
tures a developmental account of the experiential structures that enable intersubjective
understanding. He rejects the commonplace assumption that: "since I cannot have
direct access to the psyche of another . . . I must grant that I seize the other's psyche
only indirectly, mediated by its bodily appearances" (Merleau-Ponty 1964c: 114), and
suggests that young infants' responsiveness to facial expressions and ability to imitate
them cannot be based upon inference or analogy. The infant could not have a sufficiently developed perceptual appreciation of its own body to map others' actions onto
its own. Hence the ability to imitate must have its source in some kind of direct mapping between perception and proprioception.[10] Merleau-Ponty asks: "have we the means
of systematically comparing the body of the other as seen by me with my body as
sensed by me?" He claims that this is indeed the case and that the other's agency is
directly apprehended in his behavior; "it is in his conduct, in the manner in which the
other deals with the world, that I will be able to discover his consciousness" (Merleau-
Ponty 1964c: 116–117). The foundational understanding of others incorporates,
Merleau-Ponty claims, a link between the perception of others and the goal-oriented
potentialities of one's own body: "If I am a consciousness turned toward things, I can
meet in things the actions of another and find in them a meaning, because they are
themes of possible activity of my own body" (Merleau-Ponty 1964c: 117). Like Scheler,
he indicates that intersubjectivity is founded on an undifferentiated awareness of
agency, through which self and other emerge as separate beings. It is just such a link
between perception and action that mirror neurons are taken to indicate. While
Merleau-Ponty was unable to supply an account of how the link could be innate,
mirror neurons provide a resource with which to do so (Gallagher and Meltzoff 1996).[11]

Wriggling out of Naturalism

I have indicated a number of ways in which phenomenological descriptions and neurophysiological findings can complement each other. Phenomenology provides rich and insightful descriptions of intersubjective experience, thus indicating just what it is that scientific accounts are required to explain.[12] These descriptions can serve as a directive and interpretative framework for scientific enquiry. How we think about intersubjectivity will influence the kinds of processes we look for and shape the framework of problems to which we relate various experimental findings. Conversely, neuroscientific findings can provide support for phenomenological descriptions. The discovery of an inter-modal link between perception and action illustrates how the kind of non-inferential bond postulated by Husserl and others might be possible. Furthermore, in emphasizing perception of *action*, neuroscience can aid phenomenological interpretation, clarifying the *nature* of the achievements that phenomenologists describe. So mutually enlightening interaction between the two is certainly possible. Phenomenological descriptions constitute a context for the interpretation of scientific findings, which feed back into phenomenological interpretations, clarifying notions such as "analogizing apperception."

In discussing these relationships, I have assumed throughout that neuroscience need accept neither phenomenological methods nor phenomenological accounts of science. Does this then entail that specific phenomenological insights should be pillaged in the service of scientific naturalism? I suggest not. If one rejects the imposition of phenomenology as an inflexible a priori framework for the interpretation of science, it does not follow that naturalism, as conceived of in the first section, is the only viable alternative. In fact, the interplay between phenomenology and neuroscience undermines certain epistemological and ontological assumptions that are integral to mainstream naturalistic thinking.

Naturalism depends upon assumptions concerning the nature of our cognitive processes. The world, as disclosed through a particular epistemic standpoint, is taken to be ontologically privileged or indeed exhaustive. Hence one is committed to the assumption that processes exist which *do* disclose the world in such a way, and which also constitute *the best way* of disclosing it. If naturalism is to be coherent, our understanding of cognition will be vulnerable to revision, as cognitive processes are not just a means whereby science is accomplished but also an object of scientific inquiry. Scientific findings could well prompt us to revise our conception of what certain cognitive achievements consist of and of the processes via which various aspects of the world are understood. A possible outcome of this is that the kind of epistemic standpoint taken as basic by naturalism turns out not to be characteristic of the way in which we encounter certain phenomena:

1   Naturalism takes processes of type A to be universally epistemically privileged.
2   A-type processes disclose the world as fundamentally X.
3   But empirical research suggests that B-type processes carry the primary burden of disclosing some aspect of the world. A-type processes impede this disclosure.
4   B-type processes reveal that aspect of the world to be Y and not X.

The question then arises as to why Y should be reinterpreted, so as to conform to the limitations of a naturalistic standpoint. Unless a compelling case can be formulated, we have:

5   There is no good argument for the primacy of A.
6   Reinterpretation of Y as X is therefore not warranted.
7   That A and X are all-encompassing is a premise of naturalism.
8   Therefore naturalism should be rejected.

If naturalism is not fallible in the above sense, then it is a transcendent doctrine, which imposes a metaphysic and epistemology upon science that is neither drawn from science, revisable in the light of science, nor necessarily compatible with what science reveals about the world. Such a position would explicitly contradict the aim of naturalism, which is to integrate everything into the scientifically described world. If science can tell us about epistemic processes, it must surely incorporate the possibility of significant metaphysical revision, given that claims concerning how the world most fundamentally is are mortgaged on claims concerning the structure of our epistemic capacities, and vice versa. There is an ongoing hermeneutic between the discoveries and metaphysical presuppositions of science.

Now it might be argued that, even if epistemology and ontology are revisable, as naturalism suggests, the result is still the worldview adopted by most naturalists, according to which an objective, physical world, best surveyed from a theoretical standpoint, is metaphysically complete. Naturalism is not a rigid epistemological and metaphysical doctrine; it only puts forward its claims about the world and how it is known as a contingent product of current science.

However, I suggest that a specific version of the general argument against naturalism outlined above can be formulated with respect to intersubjectivity, given the picture of our intersubjective accomplishments that I have drawn from phenomenological findings and recent work on mirror neurons. In our everyday interactions with the world, we experience things through all sorts of standpoints. Naturalism incorporates an epistemological assumption to the effect that the world is best disclosed from a standpoint of theoretical detachment, through which it is resolved as a collection of objective entities, processes, properties, and relations, extricated from one's own concerns and practical engagements. But other people are disclosed through a very different standpoint. It is through an inter-modal link between perception and proprioception, incorporating pre-reflective activation of one's own motor system, that others are *perceived*. This "personal stance" is essentially self-engaging, rather than detached. If an objective, detached stance could be adopted toward others, it would serve to mislead, revealing them to be objects rather than others like oneself.

Nevertheless, the assumption that others are understood through a detached, objective stance is commonplace in the literature on intersubjectivity. It is simply assumed by theory theories and by some simulation theories. As Thompson (2001b: 12) puts it, "the presupposition both theories share is that mind-reading is primarily a 'spectatorial' process of explanation and prediction." Thus the epistemic standpoint *supposedly* characteristic of science is taken as primary. One adopts a detached perspective, through which things appear as distinct objects, to be predicted and explained.

However, assuming the universal applicability of a detached, spectatorial stand-point eclipses that fact that people are not ordinarily experienced as complex objects. Intersubjective experience and understanding depend upon a perceptual, practical, interactive process, which engages one's own sense of agency, rather than detached theorizing. Consider two people dancing together, the engaged spectator at a football match, or the intricate interplay of complementary gestures that characterizes all healthy interpersonal interaction. The majority of interpersonal relations do not involve one person adopting a theoretical stance toward an observed "he," "she," or "it." Others are disclosed as *what they are* through an *interactive, practical orientation.* This insight is developed by Gallagher (2001a), who reflects on the extent to which our understanding of others can be accommodated by a direct, perceptual, bodily and interactive grasp of each other, of just the sort that mirror neurons are hypothesized to facilitate. He develops this into an argument against mainstream philosophical and scientific approaches to intersubjectivity. Adopting Trevarthan's term "primary intersubjectivity" (Gallagher 2001a: 87), Gallagher argues that "primary" embodied practices are not just developmentally prior to theory, inference, and simulation. They remain primary in adulthood. In other words, almost all interpersonal relations can be interpreted as direct, perceptual, pragmatic understanding through interaction. Spectatorial stances toward others, which involve inferring hidden mental states, are unusual and peripheral. What's more, assuming in one's scientific theorizing that a theoretical explanation-prediction stance is central to intersubjectivity serves to obfuscate both the way in which others are encountered and what they are encountered as. Others are perceptually disclosed *as agents,* through an orientation that differs substantially from the kind of detached perspective that is generally regarded as primary to world-disclosure. Given this, I suggest the following:

1   Phenomenology and neuroscience together suggest that other people are disclosed perceptually, through a self-engaging, practical stance.
2   A theoretical stance toward others is secondary and peripheral.
3   If taken as primary, a theoretical stance obfuscates the disclosure of others.
4   Others are not ordinarily disclosed as objects.
5   *Others like oneself* are experienced with a kind of immediacy as members of a distinct *ontological* category.

Therefore:

6   The assumption that epistemic detachment is the means through which the way things are is disclosed should be rejected when it comes to understanding other people, as should the assumption that all knowing reveals objective entities.

Hence phenomenological descriptions, in conjunction with neuroscientific findings, can call into question the epistemic practices and objective ontology presupposed by the project of naturalization. Naturalism, in taking an objective ontology and theoretical detachment as primary, incorporates assumptions concerning the manner in which the world appears to us. However, other people don't appear to us like this at all. Of course, one might argue that a theoretical stance and the world of inanimate objects it discloses have a more general or ultimate priority. So intersubjectivity will eventually be accommodated into such a picture and what I have described is just a hurdle en route. However, there is a troubling circularity here:

> Why should certain cognitive processes have authority?
> Because the world is like that.
> Why is the world like that?
> Because those processes reveal it to be.

The possibility of breaking out of this loop should be accommodated.[13] Why assume that what a "personal stance" reveals is ultimately better revealed in a very different way through a detached, impersonal, objective stance? As Goldie (2000: 181–2) observes, "the impersonal stance, whatever might be its merits for scientific inquiry, is not the stance of commonsense psychology." And, contrary to naturalism, it need not be the only legitimate stance for scientific enquiry. There are insufficient grounds for assuming that the impersonal, objective stance is the only one through which things are adequately revealed and there may be much that a personal stance discloses which cannot be encompassed by an objectivist standpoint. Psychology could quite conceivably incorporate interaction between "objective" and "personal" standpoints, without one being ultimately reducible to the other.

Science is part of our everyday experience and understanding. In order for the aim of "naturalization" to make sense, a substantial assumption is required to the effect that this aspect of our experience and practice somehow discloses the world in such a way as to warrant the integration of everything else into its sphere. But the nature of science and of the world it reveals are surely themselves open to significant reinterpretation in the light of enquiry. Hence the interaction between phenomenology and neuroscience should not be constrained by inflexible metaphysical and epistemological doctrines.

Acknowledgments

For helpful comments on previous drafts of this chapter, I am grateful to Hubert Dreyfus, Dan Hutto, Darrell Rowbottom, Mark Wrathall, and audiences at the University of Hertfordshire, the Institute of Psychiatry (London), and the conference "Continental Philosophy and the Sciences," University of Warwick, 2003.

Notes

1   The level of interest in the relationship between phenomenology and cognitive science is exemplified by the arrival of a new journal *Phenomenology and the Cognitive Sciences* in 2002.

2   The term "cognitive science" is employed in a very general sense, which encompasses various projects in neuroscience, rather than just the attempt to explain the psychological in information-processing terms.

3   It is not always clear what the metaphysical commitments of naturalism actually are. However, they at least incorporate the view that the world can be comprehensively characterized in objective, physical terms. The critics of metaphysical naturalism are often clearer about its nature than are its proponents. See, for example, Craig and Moreland 2000.

4   See Rizzolatti et al. 2002: 40–2 for a discussion of the evidence for mirror neurons in humans.

5   They therefore differ from "canonical neurons," which are the other class of visuo-motor neurons in F5. These discharge during action and also when an object congruent with that same kind of action is perceived (Fogassi and Gallese 2002: 15).

6   The emerging consensus seems to be that theory and simulation accounts are not antagonists and that a comprehensive theory of interpersonal understanding will incorporate aspects of both. See Carruthers and Smith 1996 for various theory, simulation, and hybrid accounts.

7   See Zahavi 2001 for a survey of various phenomenological approaches to intersubjectivity.

8   Petit 1999 and Thompson 2001b also discuss Husserl's unpublished later work on intersubjectivity and movement.

9   Smith points out that Husserl's conditions for empathetic pairing need to be fairly abstract, given the achievement of intersubjectivity in cases of sensory deprivation. If the link between perception and kinesthesis were specific to visual perception, it could not be foundational to intersubjectivity, given intact intersubjective abilities in congenitally blind people. The same point can be applied to mirror neurons. If they are an indispensable constituent of intersubjectivity, they cannot be exclusive to the visual modality. Perhaps there are mirror neurons that match sounds with patterns of motor activation? I do not know of any studies that answer this question.

10 Zahavi 2001: 164 discusses neonate studies that support some of Merleau-Ponty's claims.

11 Although I restrict my discussion to Husserl, Scheler, and Merleau-Ponty, similar themes do occur in the work of other phenomenologists. For example, Sartre suggests that "the original bond with the Other first arises in connection with the relation between my body and the Other's body" (Sartre 1989: 361).

12 These descriptions are a considerable improvement on the brief allusions to "*qualia*" that pervade the recent literature on consciousness.

13 See Gallagher 2004 for an account of hermeneutics and cognitive science that challenges the presupposition of objectivism.

References and Further Reading

Carruthers, P. (1996) Simulation and self-knowledge: A defence of the theory-theory. In P. Carruthers and P. K. Smith (eds), *Theories of Theories of Mind* (pp. 22–38). Cambridge: Cambridge University Press.

Carruthers, P., and Smith, P. K. (eds) (1996) *Theories of Theories of Mind.* Cambridge: Cambridge University Press.

Craig, W. L., and Moreland, J. P. (2000) *Naturalism: A Critical Analysis.* London: Routledge.

Fogassi, L., and Gallese, V. (2002) The Neural correlates of action understanding in non-human primates. In M. Stamenov and M. Gallese (eds), *Mirror Neurons and the Evolution of Brain and Language* (pp. 13–35). Amsterdam and Philadelphia: John Benjamins.

Gallagher, S. (2001a) The practice of mind: Theory, simulation or primary interaction? In E. Thompson (ed.), *Between Ourselves: Second-Person Issues in the Study of Consciousness* (pp. 83–108). Thorverton, UK: Imprint Academic.

—— (2001b) Emotion and intersubjective perception: A speculative account. In A. Kaszniak (ed.), *Emotion, Qualia and Consciousness*. (pp. 95–100). London: World Scientific.

—— (2004) Hermeneutics and the cognitive sciences. In D. Zahavi (ed.), *Hidden Resources* (pp. 162–4). Exeter: Imprint Academic.

Gallagher, S., and Meltzoff, A. (1996) The earliest sense of self and others: Merleau-Ponty and recent developmental studies. *Philosophical Psychology*, 9, 213–36.

Gallese, V. (2001) The "shared manifold" hypothesis: From mirror neurons to empathy. In E. Thompson (ed.), *Between Ourselves: Second-Person Issues in the Study of Consciousness* (pp. 33–50). Thorverton, UK: Imprint Academic.

Gallese, V., Fadiga, L., Fogassi, L., and Rizzolatti, G. (1996) Action recognition in the premotor cortex. *Brain*, 119, 593–609.

Gallese, V., and Goldman, A. (1998) Mirror neurons and the simulation theory of mind-reading. *Trends in Cognitive Sciences*, 2, 493–501.

Goldie, P. (2000) *The Emotions: A Philosophical Exploration*. Oxford: Clarendon Press.

Gopnik, A. (1996) Theories and modules: Creation myths, developmental realities and Neurath's boat. In P. Carruthers and P. K. Smith (eds.), *Theories of Theories of Mind* (pp. 169–83). Cambridge: Cambridge University Press.

Husserl, E. (1960) *Cartesian Meditations: An Introduction to Phenomenology* (trans. D. Cairns). The Hague: Martinus Nijhoff (original work published 1931).

—— (1970) *The Crisis of European Sciences and Transcendental Phenomenology* (trans. D. Carr). Evanston, IL: Northwestern University Press (original work published 1937).

Merleau-Ponty, M. (1962) *Phenomenology of Perception* (trans. C. Smith). London: Routledge (original work published 1945).

Merleau-Ponty, M. (1964a) *The Primacy of Perception. And Other Essays on Phenomenological Psychology, and Philosophy of Art, History and Politics* (ed., trans., and intro. J. M. Edie). Evanston, IL: Northwestern University Press (original work published 1946).

—— (1964b) The primacy of perception (trans. J. M. Edie). In *The Primacy of Perception* (ed., trans., and intro. J. M. Edie) (pp. 12–42). Evanston, IL: Northwestern University Press (original work published 1946).

—— (1964c) The child's relations with others (trans. W. Cobb). In *The Primacy of Perception* (ed., trans., and intro. J. M. Edie).(pp. 96–155). Evanston, IL: Northwestern University Press (original work published 1946).

Petit, P. (1999) Constitution by movement: Husserl in light of recent neurobiological findings. In J. Petitot, F. J. Varela, B. Pachoud, and J. M. Roy (eds.), *Naturalizing Phenomenology: Issues in Contemporary Phenomenology and Cognitive Science* (pp. 220–4). Stanford, CA: Stanford University Press.

Petitot, J., Varela, F. J., Pachoud, B., and Roy, J. M. (eds.) (1999) *Naturalizing Phenomenology: Issues in Contemporary Phenomenology and Cognitive Science*. Stanford, CA: Stanford University Press.

Rizzolatti, G., Craighero, L., and Fadiga, L. (2002) The mirror system in humans. In M. Stamenov and V. Gallese (eds.), *Mirror Neurons and the Evolution of Brain and Language* (pp. 37–59). Amsterdam and Philadelphia: John Benjamins.

Rizzolatti, G, Fadiga, L., Fogassi, L., and Gallese, V. (1996) Premotor cortex and the recognition of motor actions. *Cognitive Brain Research*, 3, 131–41.

Roy, J. M., Petitot, J., Pachoud, B., and Varela, F. J. (1999) Beyond the gap: An introduction to naturalizing phenomenology. In J. Petitot, F. J. Varela, M. Pachoud, and J. M. Roy (eds.), *Naturalizing Phenomenology: Issues in Contemporary Phenomenology and Cognitive Science* (pp. 1–80). Stanford, CA: Stanford University Press.

Sartre, J-P. (1989) *Being and Nothingness* (trans. H. E. Barnes). London: Routledge (original work published 1943).

Scheler, M. (1954) *The Nature of Sympathy* (trans. P. Heath). London: Routledge (original work published 1913).

Smith, A. D. (2003) *Routledge Philosophy Guidebook to Husserl and the Cartesian Meditations*. London: Routledge.

Stamenov, M. I., and Gallese, V. (eds.) (2002) *Mirror Neurons and the Evolution of Brain and Language*. Amsterdam, Philadelphia: John Benjamins.

Stone, T., and Davies, M. (1996) The mental simulation debate: A progress report. In P. Carruthers and P. K. Smith (eds.), *Theories of Theories of Mind* (pp. 119–37). Cambridge, Amsterdam, and Philadelphia: Cambridge University Press and John Benjamins.

Studdert-Kennedy, M. (2002) Mirror neurons, vocal imitation, and the evolution of particulate speech. In M. Stamenov and V. Gallese (eds.), *Mirror Neurons and the Evolution of Brain and Language* (pp. 207–27). Amsterdam and Philadelphia, PA: John Benjamins.

Thompson, E. (ed.) (2001a) *Between Ourselves: Second-Person Issues in the Study of Consciousness*. Thorverton, UK: Imprint Academic.

Thompson, E. (2001b) Empathy and consciousness. In E. Thompson (ed.), *Between Ourselves: Second-Person Issues in the Study of Consciousness* (pp. 1–32). Thorverton, UK: Imprint Academic.

Wohlschläger, A., and Bekkering, H. (2002) The role of objects in imitation. In M. Stamenov and V. Gallese (eds), *Mirror Neurons and the Evolution of Brain and Language* (pp. 101–13). Amsterdam and Philadelphia, PA: John Benjamins.

Zahavi, D. (2001) Beyond empathy: Phenomenological approaches to intersubjectivity. In E. Thompson (ed.), *Between Ourselves: Second-Person Issues in the Study of Consciousness* (pp. 151–67). Thorverton, UK: Imprint Academic.

24

The Intrinsic Spatial Frame of Reference

SHAUN GALLAGHER

We need an absolute within the sphere of the relative . . .
– Merleau-Ponty 1962: 248

The absolute in the relative is what my body brings to me.
– Merleau-Ponty 2003: 75

In one of Colin Dexter's British detective stories, Inspector Morse finds a solitary limb – an arm and hand – in a canal in Oxford. Morse can tell a number of things from this body part; not only about the nature of the foul play that resulted in a dismembered body, but about the victim, including his or her gender, possibly race, and definitely DNA. Morse can use forensic science to discover many things about the victim. There is one thing, however, that is absolutely apparent about the hand; something that, for Kant, was thought to be important in regard to the very foundations for our successful use of science. The one thing that would be immediately apparent upon discovering the isolated hand is that it is either a right hand or a left hand. Kant took this important fact about hands to be part of a proof for the absolute nature of space – which he and Newton understood to form part of the stable framework or foundation for scientific knowledge.

Kant proposes that space is absolute, and the proof of this is close to hand, or to be precise, the proof is in your hands. Try putting a right-handed glove on your left hand and you will see immediately that hands are incongruent counterparts.

> It is apparent from the ordinary example of the two hands that the shape of the one body may be perfectly similar to the shape of the other, and the magnitudes of their extensions may be exactly equal, and yet there may remain an inner difference between the two, this difference consisting in the fact, namely, that the surface which encloses the one cannot possibly enclose the other. (Kant 1992: 370).

Kant, however, takes this insight some distance further with the following thought experiment: "imagine that the first created thing was a human hand. That [hand] would have to be either a right hand or a left hand" (Kant 1992: 370).

346

That is, imagine that there is only one thing in the universe. A hand. Without anything else to relate to this object, the hand has some spatial properties that make it either a left hand or a right hand. Accordingly, space cannot be relational, as Leibniz would have it.

> Suppose that one were to adopt the concept entertained by many modern philosophers, especially German philosophers, according to which space simply consists in the external relation of the parts of matter which exist alongside each other . . . [Since] there is no difference in the relation of the parts of the hand to each other, and that is so whether it be a right hand or a left hand; it would therefore follow that the hand would be completely indeterminate in respect of such a property. In other words, the hand would fit equally well on either side of the human body; but that is impossible. (Kant 1992: 370–1)

Does this argument go all the way through to prove that space is absolute? I am going to leave that metaphysical question aside and focus on a more modest phenomenological issue. Is there a first-person, experiential spatial frame of reference that is absolute? Kant himself recognized the importance of an experiential spatial frame of reference, albeit a relative one. Thus:

> the most precise map of the heavens, if it did not, in addition to specifying the positions of the stars relative to each other, also specify the direction by reference to the position of the chart relative to my hands, would not enable me, no matter how precisely I had it in mind, to infer from a known direction, for example, the north, which side of the horizon I ought to expect the sun to rise. The same thing holds of geographical and, indeed, of our most ordinary knowledge of the position of places. Such knowledge would be of no use unless we could also orientate the things thus ordered, along with the entire system of their reciprocal positions, by referring them to the sides of our body. (Kant 1992: 367–8)

Merleau-Ponty, like Kant,[1] recognized that there is something special about our own bodies, and that they play a specific role in the institution of spatial frames of reference. In spatial terms we treat our body differently from any other object.

> If my arm is resting on the table I should never think of saying that it is *beside* the ash-tray in the way in which the ash-tray is beside the telephone. The outline of my body is a frontier which ordinary spatial relations do not cross. This is because its parts are interrelated in a peculiar way: they are not spread out side by side, but enveloped in each other. (Merleau-Ponty 1962: 98)

In this chapter I want to explicate the way the body helps to generate spatial frames of reference, which in turn, however, do not cross the frontier of the body itself. In addition I want to show that within the envelope of the body itself we find a spatial frame of reference that is absolute.

Spatial Frameworks

Traditional discussions in philosophy of mind refer to two spatial frames of reference: egocentric and allocentric. The *egocentric* framework is defined relative to a perceiver,

Figure 24.1

or to the body of a perceiver. An object may be located to my right or to my left; it may be above me or below me; in front of me or behind me. But if I change position, or if I simply turn around, some of this changes. What is to my right and before me, is suddenly to my left and behind me when I turn 180 degrees. The object itself can remain relatively in the same position, but the egocentric specifications of where that object is in relation to my body change. Egocentric space is first-person, and relative, although, from Kant to contemporary psychology, it is often thought to be innate (Miller and Johnson-Laird 1976, Wang and Spelke 2002).

Allocentric spatial frameworks can be defined in a number of ways. We can specify how one object is related to another in terms of third-person categories – that is, categories defined independently of any perceiver. A good example would be the global positioning system. We can specify the longitude and latitude of any object; or in a less technological mode, we can say that the fork (in Figure 24.1) is to the north of the spoon; the spoon is south of the fork. This description does not change from one perceiver to another, and is not relative to a perceiver's body. The perceiver might be east of the spoon or west of the fork, or north or south of both. But the fork does not change its location relative to the spoon, and no matter where the perceiver stands she can say that the fork is north of the spoon. An allocentric framework is a third-person, objective framework. The global positioning version of it appears to be absolute in either Cartesian or non-Euclidian space; the compass-directional version – north, south, east, and west – however, is ultimately relative within the larger framework of the solar system – and may even be so on our own globe, since recent science suggests that our compasses would have pointed south during some period in the distant past, and may do so again if there is a global magnetic shift.

Majid et al. (2004) have recently complicated the conceptions of spatial frames of reference by showing that they are culturally relative, and more specifically, linguistically determined. Rather than the egocentric framework being an innate structure of perception, it appears to be an option that some cultures simply do not use. While some cultures code position based on reference to the perceiver's body (my glasses are to the left of the telephone as I face it), others will employ allocentric frames (my glasses are to the telephone's right; or they are northeast of the telephone). Allocentric frameworks can involve object-centered or "intrinsic" coordinates (the telephone's right) or what Majid et al. consider to be "absolute" (north, south, east, west). Thus they distinguish between Relative (i.e., egocentric), and two allocentric spatial frameworks: Absolute and Intrinsic.

> English speakers use two different FoRs [frames of reference] to describe spatial relation-
> ships in table top space: they say either "the fork is to the left of the spoon" (Relative FoR)
> or "the fork is beside the spoon" (Intrinsic FoR). They do not say "the fork is to the north
> of the spoon"; they restrict their use of the Absolute FoR to large-scale, geographical
> descriptions. However, speakers of Guugu Yimithirr (Australia) use only the last kind of
> description; they do not have available either a Relative or an Intrinsic FoR. The Absolute
> FoR is used even to describe the location of an object on a body part – a Guugu Yimithirr
> speaker would say "There's an ant on your south leg." (Majid et al. 2004: 108–9)

The *intrinsic* framework is an allocentric one relative to the object. This frame of
reference, in English, is determined in one of two ways: parsed in terms of an "oriented
template" (front, back, side), or a functional mapping (the front of a building is the side
that has the primary entrance). But how intrinsic space is parsed differs from one
language to another. For example, one could determine front, back, side on the basis
of geometric or volumetric characteristics (as in the Tzeltal language of Mexico).

Majid et al. now make what I take to be a controversial claim: "There is a tight
connection between the Relative [i.e., egocentric] FoR and the Intrinsic FoR: it seems
that you cannot have a Relative FoR without an Intrinsic FoR [13,17]. Like the
Intrinsic FoR, the Relative FoR requires 'parsing' of objects – most importantly, a parsing of the self into front, back, left and right" (Majid et al. 2004: 109). The claim, then,
is that the egocentric spatial framework is derived from an intrinsic frame of reference
applied to the perceiver's own body. On this view, the body, like any other object, is
allocentrically parsed into front, back, left, and right. And, by implication, this can be
done according to different criteria – via oriented mapping, functional mapping, or
geometric mapping. This gives a certain priority to the intrinsic framework – which
is an allocentric frame of reference – over the egocentric framework, and makes all
spatial frameworks relative to conventions of language and culture. On this view, the
egocentric frame of reference is not innate, but a projection of the intrinsic frame of
reference, which itself is a matter of convention.

> This [intrinsic] parsing [of one's own body] is then projected into space, so that objects
> can be to my left and right side even when I am not in contact with them. However, if
> I say "the fork is on the left" or "the fork is in front of me," meaning in the space adjacent
> to my left side or my front side, this is not the Relative [i.e., egocentric] FoR, but still the
> Intrinsic FoR. This is because only a binary relation is being coded: the relationship
> between myself and the fork. (Majid et al. 2004: 109)

That is, "the fork is on the left" means the fork is to my body's left, in the same way
that we could say the fork is to the spoon's left – in which case the frame of reference
would be intrinsic to or centered on the spoon. "It [becomes] a Relative [egocentric]
FoR when a ternary relationship is encoded; for example, 'the fork is to the left of the
spoon' or 'the fork is in front of the spoon': now the relationship between the fork and
the spoon is encoded from the perspective of a third participant, the viewer" (ibid.).

Now, for reasons that will become clear, I will substitute the term "object-centered"
for what Majid terms "intrinsic." This is precisely what Majid means, in any case, and
I want to use the term "intrinsic" in a different way. In summary, according to Majid
et al., an object can be spatially experienced, or located in four different ways:

349

1   According to my own object-centered frame of reference (that is, taking my body as the object around which things are arranged) objects can be located to my left or right, etc.; or

2   According to the Relative (egocentric) frame of reference an object can be located to the left or right of some other object, where left and right are defined relative to me;

3   According to an object (not my body)-centered frame of reference, an object can be located to the left or right, where left and right are defined relative to the landmark object – so, object B is to object A's left; or finally,

4   According to the "absolute" frame of reference, an object can be located north of another object.

An Intrinsic, Innate, and Absolute Bodily Frame

Setting aside the fact that what Majid calls an "absolute" frame of reference may be in some sense relative (because of shifting magnetic fields), and setting aside the fact that what he distinguishes from the "relative" frame of reference as the object-centered frame of reference is itself relative, I want to argue that Majid misses an important frame of reference that truly is both absolute and *intrinsic*. This frame of reference is the spatiality of the body that Merleau-Ponty describes as involving a unique law that is anterior to the spatial organization of the surrounding world: "the spatiality of the body must work downwards from the whole to the parts, the left hand and its position must be implied in a global bodily *design* and must originate in that design" (Merleau-Ponty 1962: 99; translation modified). Merleau-Ponty, however, cautions that this description is inadequate insofar as it remains tied to a static geometrical perspective. He suggests we flesh it out in terms of pragmatic action: since my body is geared toward existing or possible tasks, its spatiality "is not, like that of external objects or like that of 'spatial sensations', a *spatiality of position*, but a *spatiality of situation*" (1962, p. 100). We could also call this a pragmatic spatiality. In this regard, Merleau-Ponty's insights are quite consistent with contemporary neuroscientific accounts of perception in the service of motor action, and the spatial aspects that are implicit in such processes (see, e.g., Jeannerod 1997). In his lectures at the Collège de France in the mid-1950s, for example, he describes perception in this context in the following terms.

> When I perceive an object, I am aware of the motor possibilities that are implied in the perception of this thing. The thing appears to me as a function of the movements of my body . . . My body is the absolute "here." All the places of space proceed from it . . . The Absolute in the relative is what my body brings to me. (Merleau-Ponty 2003: 74–5)[2]

Specifically, I want to argue that in connection with perception and action, there is an intrinsic spatial frame of reference that is innate and absolute. It is neither allocentric nor egocentric, but primarily, and in the most original sense, it is what Thomas Brown called the "bodily frame," a frame of reference that applies to the lived body as perceiver and actor, in a first-person perspective (Brown 1820: 505). In precise terms, it is the proprioceptive frame of reference. Let me try to map this out, and then return with some comments on Majid et al.

In some sense, as Merleau-Ponty had already indicated, the body is the source of phenomenally experienced spatiality: "far from my body's being for me no more than a fragment of space, there would be no space at all for me if I had no body" (Merleau-Ponty 1962: 102). One of the important functions of the body in the context of perception and action is to provide the basis for an egocentric (or body-centered) spatial frame of reference. The fact that perception is egocentrically spatial (for example, the book appears to my right or to my left, or in the center of my perceptual field) is a fact that depends precisely on the spatiality of the perceiving body. If one accepts the premise that sense perception of the world is spatially organized by an implicit reference to our bodily position, the basis for that implicit reference cannot itself be an egocentric frame of reference without the threat of infinite regress. This point is closely tied to the notion of the experiential transparency of the body, and is accurately stated by Merleau-Ponty. "I observe external objects with my body, I handle them, examine them, walk around them, but my body itself is a thing which I do not observe [in action or in the act of perception]: in order to be able to do so, I should need the use of a second body which itself would be unobservable" (Merleau-Ponty 1962: 91).

This is just the problem with Majid's notion of an object-centered frame of reference in which I take my body to be the landmark object. This frame of reference is not at all intrinsic, because it requires me to take an observational stance toward my own body. I say that object A is to my right, in the same way that I might say that object A is to the right of object B. It's just that object B in this case is my body. But in this observational perspective, I have to judge which side is right and which is left, in the same way that I would do so for object B when object B is not my body. The question is, when I make this observational judgment, from where do I make it? Of course, I might say, *I am standing in my own body.* But that odd way of putting it points to the problem. The point is that as a perceiver and actor, I do not have observational access to my body in perception or in action. I neither stand outside of my own body, nor inside of my own body – indeed, whatever inside and outside mean in this case, they depend on me being my body. Although I do not have observational access to my body in action, I can have non-observational proprioceptive and kinesthetic awareness of my body in action. Proprioception is the innate and intrinsic position sense that I have with respect to my limbs and overall posture. It is literally innate insofar as proprioception develops prenatally.

What kind of spatial framework is involved in proprioceptive awareness? As Brian O'Shaughnessy notes, with proprioception "we encounter a unique situation . . . the revealed (material object) [the body in the case of proprioception] constitutes the very system of ordering/individuation/differentiation of the revealer (bodily sensations [and their proprioceptively determined locations])" (O'Shaughnessy 1995: 191). He attributes this to the immediacy of proprioception: the fact that proprioceptive awareness does not attentively mediate the perception of the body; for if it did, it would have an ordering system, a spatial frame of reference that would have to be independent of the body. Generally speaking, the proprioceptive spatiality of the body is not framed by anything other than an intrinsic framework that belongs to the body itself. In other words, proprioception involves a non-perspectival (non-egocentric) awareness of the body in an *intrinsic* spatial frame of reference.

351

In contrast, the perceptual spatiality of a perceived object is framed by something other than the perceived object, namely, it is framed in reference to the perceiving body. As Bermúdez points out, this is not the case for proprioception: rather, there is a "fundamental disanalogy between the bodily space of proprioception and the egocentric space of perception and action . . . In contrast with vision, audition, and the other canonically exteroceptive modalities, there are certain spatial notions that do not seem to be applicable to somatic proprioception" (Bermúdez 1998: 152–3). Specifically he mentions distance and direction. That is, we can ask about the distance and direction of a perceived object in terms of how far away it is, and in what direction. But these spatial parameters are meaningful only in relation to a frame of reference that has an origin. This does not apply to proprioception. Proprioceptive awareness does not organize the differential spatial order of the body around an origin. Whereas one can say that this book is closer to me than that book over there, one cannot say that my foot is closer to me than my hand.

Although it is possible to read both egocentric and allocentric registers into the body, and to say that bodily sensation A is to the left of bodily sensation B, or that sensation A is farther away from sensation B than is sensation C, proprioceptive spatiality is not equivalent to either egocentric or allocentric spatial frameworks. Left, right, center, and distance are spatial parameters that are completely relative in egocentric spatial perception. What is to my right may be to your left. And what is to my right now will be to my left if I turn 180 degrees. But intrabodily parameters are absolute in the proprioceptive register. What is proprioceptively on the right side of my body is just so, whether my right side is located to your left, or whether I turn. If I move my left hand to touch my right shoulder, it does not become a second right hand. If sensation A is just this distance from sensation B, I cannot make them closer on the proprioceptive map even if I contort my body to make them objectively closer.

Perception organizes spatial distributions around an egocentric frame of reference that is implicitly indexed to the perceiving body, and things appear near or far, to the left or to the right, and so forth, only in relation to the body. In contrast, proprioception follows the contours of my body, but not from a perspective. Proprioception, even as it contributes to the establishment of an egocentric spatial framework for perception, operates in a non-perspectival, intra-corporeal spatial framework that is quite different from the egocentric structure of action and exteroceptive perception, and yet essential to establishing that structure. Thus, as Merleau-Ponty puts it, "The word 'here' applied to my body does not refer to a determinate position in relation to other positions or to external co-ordinates, but the laying down of the first co-ordinates, the anchoring of the active body in an object, the situation of the body in face of its tasks" (Merleau-Ponty 1962: 100). The proprioceptive register is thus not independent of the subject's experience – that is, it is not a matter of third-person, objective, or allocentric mappings in Cartesian coordinates. The grid of a global positioning system might map out my body as I lie in the sun at Cocoa Beach, but this is not the system I use when I need to scratch my foot; nor do I have to figure out whether my foot is to the east or west of my hand, even if in some languages I would have to figure out whether the foot was on my south leg. But I'll return to this issue, namely, how I know which leg is my south leg.

We have described a bodily spatial frame of reference that is intrinsic, innate, and neither egocentric nor allocentric. What I'm calling intrinsic here, clearly, is different from what Majid et al. define as intrinsic, that is, different from an allocentrically object-centered and relative frame of reference. So it is important to offer some clarifications in regard to their analysis, and we return to that now.

Spatial Projections

Majid et al. suggest that we project the egocentric spatial frame of reference found in perception and action on the basis of a parsing of our own body according to an allocentrically object-centered system. "This [object-centered] parsing [of one's own body] is then projected into space, so that objects can be to my left and right side even when I am not in contact with them" (Majid et al. 2004: 109). That this object-centered frame is relative is clear from their example. If I say "the fork is on my left," all I have to do is turn 180 degrees and the object-centered registration changes – the fork will be on my right. So for Majid, the object-centered frame of reference is just as relative as the egocentric one.

Furthermore, in their terms, these spatial frameworks are parsings or projections. I seemingly parse my own body, taken as an object, in the object-centered framework – although where I stand to do this parsing is unclear. Then I extend this object-centered (i.e., body-centered) framework to things around me, and further project an egocentric framework for perception and action. How do I move from these relative frames of reference to the absolute (allocentric) frame of reference?

> The computations required if you use an Absolute FoR in all situations, from table-top space to geographic, are of a quite different kind. For example, you must know at all times and in all locations where your conventional fixed bearings are . . . To do this, you must run a "mental compass", a constant background computation of direction. You must code all percepts that you might later want to talk about in terms of such fixed bearings, so you can say (or for that matter, think) "I must have left my glasses to the north of the telephone". You need to maintain mental maps correctly oriented so that you can calculate the bearing between any two points you might want to talk about. You also need to dead-reckon your current location so that you can correctly describe where unseen points are from the current location. (Majid et al. 2004: 109)

Majid et al. ignore the question of how this knowledge is possible, or precisely how one "dead-reckons" their current location. What does it mean to maintain mental maps so that you can reckon north, south, east, and west?

The problem is that we are not global positioners who live in allocentric, absolute space. If you ask me where north is, I will only be able to say that north is "that way" (pointing in front of me) or "this way" (pointing behind me), or "over that way" (pointing in some other direction). The direction of north, and all directions, can only be dead-reckoned from the "here" of my lived body in relation to some landmark. Directions are always directions away from *me*, here, where I define the "first coordinates." Phenomenologically, I triangulate north, pointing to it from here, with some implicit or explicit reference point of which I know the relative location. As I stand facing New

York, the coast is to my right, so north is straight ahead. One's bearings must implicitly start from one's body – even if they explicitly start from some other landmark.

Imagine placing a speaker of Guugu Yimithirr asleep in a dark forest, waking him up and asking which way north is. Unless he first got his bearings relative to some landmark, he would not be able to say where north was. North is not built into the body. It is not the case, and here I must dissent from Merleau-Ponty's suggestion, that "I know where my hand and my body are, as primitive man in the desert is always able to take his bearings immediately without having to cast his mind back, and add up distances covered and deviations made since setting off" (Merleau-Ponty 1962: 100). Primitive humans, as well as contemporary speakers of Guugu Yimithirr, may not have to cast their minds back to calculate their location. But something different is involved than in knowing where one's hands are. Normally, in regard to the latter, I can't get lost. How do I know whether the foot I want to scratch is on my south leg or my north leg? I have to determine whether my right leg is to the north or south of my left leg, and to do that I first have to know whether the northerly direction is to my right or to my left. Knowing my right from my left, my right hand from my left hand, my right leg from my left leg, is only possible within the intrinsic and absolute spatial frame of reference that constitutes the first coordinates.

As Merleau-Ponty points out, the same is true of up and down, on top of or underneath, etc.: "When I say that an object is on a table, I always mentally put myself either in the table or in the object, and I apply to them a category which theoretically fits the relationship of my body to external objects" (Merleau-Ponty 1962: 101).

The spatial frames of reference that Majid et al. identify as culturally relative are nonetheless mapped onto a spatial frame of reference that is the natural one of my body. "Stripped of this anthropological association, the word on is indistinguishable from the word 'under' or the word 'beside'." Thus for the meanings of these words we need to "look beneath the explicit meaning of definitions for the latent meaning of experiences" (Merleau-Ponty 1962: 101–2).

The order of projections, then, always runs back to the body of the perceiver/actor. And right there, at the experiential center of things, you find an absolute – the intrinsic spatial framework from which one reckons the egocentric frame of reference, and the object-centered frame of reference (in this case, I think, simply by putting ourselves in the place of the object and saying what is on its right or left), and even the purely allocentric positioning of things.

The issues I have addressed here do not concern metaphysical questions about objective space – questions about the absolute or relative nature of space. These are questions that are suspended within the phenomenological investigation of how we experience space. Whatever Kant thought about these questions, however, I want to suggest that when he pointed to the incongruent counterparts of the left and right hands, he offered an important clue about the absolute spatial frame of reference that is intrinsic to the body itself. And this is the right starting point, as Merleau-Ponty tells us:

> for us to be able to conceive space, it is in the first place necessary that we should have been thrust into it by our body, and that it should have provided us with the first model of those transpositions, equivalents and identifications which make space into an objective system and allow our experience to be one of objects, opening out on an 'in itself'. (Merleau-Ponty 1962: 142)

Thus the intrinsic spatial frame of reference in which we live and through which we experience the surrounding world is "the ultimate court of appeal, according to Kant himself, of all knowledge connected with space" (Merleau-Ponty 1962: 244).

Notes

1 Merleau-Ponty is influenced by Brunschvicg's (1922) reading of Kant on these matters. Specifically in regard to the notion of space, he favors the early Kant, as Brunschvicg interprets him. On this view, space is *inhabited* rather than a pure form of intuition, and as such, Brunschvicg suggests that action engenders space (see Merleau-Ponty 2003: 27–8). "Our body is the instrument of work by which we order the horizon of our daily life, and it remains the center of reference in relation to which the fundamental dimensions of space are determined" (Brunschvicg 1922, cited by Merleau-Ponty 2003: 28).

2 Again, the influence of Brunschvicg's reading of Kant is apparent here: "if we are condemned to an unsolvable alternative of absolutely absolute space and absolutely relative space, it is first of all because we have pulled space out of the coordinating activity, which human being is probably capable of extending to infinity, but that has its origin in the organism, its center of perspective. Space is relative to our body, and relatively to this body, it is a given" (Brunschvicg 1922, cited by Merleau-Ponty 2003: 28).

References and Further Reading

Bermúdez, J. L. (1998) *The Paradox of Self-Consciousness*. Cambridge: MIT Press.

Brown, T. (1820) *Lectures on the Philosophy of the Human Mind*. Edinburgh: Bell & Bradfute.

Brunschvicg, L. (1922) *L'expérience humaine et la causalité physique* [Human experience and physical causality]. Paris: Alcan.

Jeannerod, M. (1997) *The Cognitive Neuroscience of Action*. Oxford: Blackwell.

Kant, I. (1992) Concerning the ultimate ground of the differentiation of directions in space. In D. Walford & R. Meerbote (eds.), *The Cambridge Edition of the Works of Immanuel Kant. Theoretical Philosophy, 1755–1770* (pp. 365–72). Cambridge: Cambridge University Press.

Majid, A., Bowerman, M., Kita, S., Haun, D. B. M., and Levinson, S. C. (2004) Can language restructure cognition? The case for space. *Trends in Cognitive Sciences*, 8(3), 108–14.

Merleau-Ponty, M. (1962) *Phenomenology of Perception* (trans. C. Smith). London: Routledge & Kegan Paul (original work published 1945).

—— (2003) *Nature: Course Notes from the Collège de France* (trans. R. Vallier). Evanston, IL: Northwestern University Press (original work published 1995).

Miller, G. A., and Johnson-Laird, P. N. (1976) *Language and Perception*. Cambridge, MA: Harvard University Press.

O'Shaughnessy, B. (1995) Proprioception and the body image. In J. Bermúdez, A. J. Marcel, and N. Eilan (eds.), *The Body and the Self* (pp. 175–203). Cambridge, MA: MIT Press.

Wang, R. F., and Spelke, E. S. (2002) Human spatial representation: Insights from animals. *Trends in Cognitive Sciences*, 6, 376–82.

25

Action, the Scientific Worldview, and Being-in-the-World

CRAIG DELANCEY

The nature of action becomes a special problem for philosophy in the modern era, largely as a result of the influence of the sciences. In a modern scientific view of nature, each event is the unique causal product of past events. This appears incompatible with a view of human beings as purposeful agents, whose actions have meaning. Causal events have no direction, but rather are pushed along by necessary laws. Purposeful events seem to be aimed at some end; their past matters less than where they are going and if they arrive there. In analytic philosophy, where some kind of scientific naturalism is usually assumed, this clash of perspectives is particularly acute, and has led to a number of perplexing and resistant difficulties. In the tradition of existential phenomenology these difficulties have not arisen. In part this has sometimes been a matter of focus; Heidegger, for example, is concerned foremost with ontology, and is not sympathetic to scientific naturalism, and so did not often stray into these questions. In part this has sometimes been a matter of stipulation; for Sartre (1956), the *for-itself*, the kind of being of human beings, must act, and is unconstrained in its action. Free action is a primitive feature of such beings. But in part this is also sometimes a matter of insight. The notion of being-in-the-world, which plays its most prominent role in the thinking of Heidegger and Merleau-Ponty, forms the principal element of an attempt to break radically with the modern divisions that lead to some of the most difficult problems of action.

In this chapter, my goal is to show how the notion of being-in-the-world is not only a break with modern views of the subject that solves epistemological problems, but by offering an alternative to the subject/object division it can solve, or more often escape, some of the central problems of the philosophy of action. This is done through the attempt not to reduce a purposeful consciousness (in this context, subjectivity) to a deterministic world of objects and their causal interactions (objectivity), nor vice versa, but rather to find something more fundamental which underlies both and makes them possible. On such grounds, kinds of activity might be possible which are neither a *sui generis* feature of an isolated subject, nor solely a product of external and purposeless laws.

I proceed as follows. First, I review some dominant themes of action theory, using action theory in the analytic philosophical tradition as my example, and identify what I believe are the central problems, including a neglected problem, for these approaches.

356

Second, I consider these problems from the perspective of the early Heidegger, with some brief exploration of how these themes develop in Heidegger's later work. Third, I argue that the problems are avoided, but in a different way, in the work of Merleau-Ponty. I conclude with a brief observation of the continuing insight that existential phenomenology and the notion of being-in-the-world offer to contemporary action theory.

Scientific Naturalism and the Problems of Purposeful Activity

The nature of human action becomes most acute as a phenomenon in need of philosophical explanation with the modern division between a free and rule-following mind and a mechanical world, a division most clearly articulated in the philosophy of Descartes. The need is older than this division, however, arising as the early sciences displace a teleological view of nature with a view that nature follows deterministic causal laws. In such a nature, human actions, which appear to have meaning and goals, and thus in some sense to be fundamentally teleological, seem to have no place. There is both a challenge of explaining how such actions are possible, and also explaining how they differ from other kinds of events, including behaviors of nonhuman animals. These challenges have been most extensively addressed in analytic philosophy, where a scientific naturalism is typically assumed, and many philosophical questions are approached from the perspective of reconciling potential solutions with the presumptions of a general scientific outlook. As such, analytic action theory provides many of the clearest examples of the difficulties involved. My discussion, however, will seek to remain more general than in most contemporary action theory, since it is possible to identify underlying common presuppositions across a range of seemingly incompatible views.

Consider three events, *prima facie* of three different kinds:

1   After Jones trips on a crack in the sidewalk, she falls down.
2   Jones blinks.
3   Jones announces her plan to balance her checkbook, adds up the total value of the checks she has written, and writes down this sum.

The first appears to be a *mere event*. The second appears to be *behavior*, something distinct from mere events, but of a kind with behaviors seen across the animal kingdom. The third kind of event appears to be a special kind of behavior, unique in the terrestrial sphere to humans: an *action*.

A successful science of mechanics allows us to describe the first kind of event with great accuracy. If we know the mass of Jones, the mass of the earth, her height, her center of mass, the rigidity of her legs as she falls forward, and so on, we can compute a trajectory for her and describe such things as how long it will take her body to fall to the Earth, and how much energy (heat) will dissipate when she impacts the sidewalk. This prediction depends upon a description of a current state of affairs, and the application of natural laws to this description to derive some future state of affairs. Here the past, and lawlike relations over time, determine the future. There is no need to

357

describe, as Aristotle might have done, some *telos* to the events, such as a natural inclination for the body to seek the earth. The things which occur are not going toward some goal, but rather they are pushed along.

The second event appears special because *prima facie* it has a purpose. Jones blinks, even unconsciously, *in order to* moisten her eye, or to remove some irritant. The third kind of event has not only a purpose, but it seems plausible that there is something special about this purpose. It may be conscious and in some sense under volitional control, for example. Also, in this example, the accomplishment of this purpose requires the following of explicit logical rules that Jones could explain to us if she needed to do so. It appears that only humans, or at most humans and other complex animals, are capable of such actions. We describe such events in a terminology of intentions or intentional states. We say Jones balanced her checkbook because she *desires* to know the remaining balance, or because she *fears* that she may make an overdraft. Such terminology of beliefs, knowledge, desires, fears, and other mental states is distinct from the kind of analysis a mature predictive science like physics offers of more simple events.

The first task for a theory of action, the *basic task*, is to distinguish between mere events (events of type 1) and behaviors (events of types 2 and 3). Given the success of some sciences in explaining some mere events, this task would also seem to require that we explain where, if anywhere, purposive behavior fits in a scientific worldview. In practice, analytic philosophy of action has neglected the question of what distinguishes behavior from mere events, and generally tried to distinguish mere events from actions (that is, distinguish events of type 1 and 3), ignoring the other kinds of behavior. Most accounts hold that actions are distinguished either by special mental states or special kinds of descriptions.[1] There are many problems with these approaches, which have resisted solution and have spawned a vast literature.[2] However, as a group they share, even if only implicitly, the goal to explain how such purposeful behavior can be reconciled with a strong form of scientific naturalism that forms a background assumption for these discussions. This naturalism typically includes the conviction that science will ultimately yield sufficient causal explanation of all events.

Given this conviction, one might argue that purpose is a superfluous notion, and that in principle we could eliminate from our discourse talk of purposeful behavior.[3] The effects of sincerely adopting such a view are unknown but appear to be potentially devastating, since most, perhaps all, of our social conventions depend upon our view of ourselves as purposive agents. Furthermore, it seems that such a view is practically impossible at this time; we cannot make sense of ourselves and our world without conceiving of each other as purposeful agents. If such an eliminativism is rejected, an explanation of action appears to require either proof that we can explain purposes in terms of causes in the causal theory (this is to reduce purpose to elements in our scientific discourse), or proof that purposes are irreducible and survive somehow alongside the mechanical explanation.

These two options dominate contemporary discussion of the basic task of action theory. Some philosophers are trying vigorously to reduce purposes to mechanical explanations (e.g., Millikan 1984). Others have argued that purposes are irreducible: Donald Davidson's highly influential paper "Actions, Reasons, and Causes" (1963), posits various irreducible mental states that cause actions.[4] A long-standing alternative is that irreducible purposes are not causes but rather kinds of explanations; this is a view inspired by the work of the later Wittgenstein, and has been developed, for example, by Wilson (1989). But for any of these approaches, it remains vexing that the faith of those committed to the scientific worldview is that a physical explanation will provide sufficient explanations of all events, including human behaviors. But if this were so, purposes, whether reducible or irreducible, whether explanations or causes, would be superfluous. The central difficulty was well stated by Norman Malcolm, a student of Wittgenstein. Comparing the view that purposes are irreducible because they are a different kind of explanation, with an assumption of a sufficient scientific view, he observes:

> It is true that the two kinds of explanation employ different concepts and, in a sense, explain different things: but are they really independent of one another? Take the example of the man climbing a ladder in order to retrieve his hat from the roof. This explanation relates his climbing to his intention. A neurophysiological explanation of his climbing would say nothing about his intention but would connect his movements on the ladder with chemical changes in body tissue or with the firing of neurons. Do the two accounts interfere with one another? . . . I believe there *would* be a collision between the two accounts if they were offered as explanations of one and the same occurrence of a man's climbing a ladder. We will recall that the envisaged neurophysiological theory was supposed to provide *sufficient* causal explanations of behavior. Thus the movements of the man on the ladder would be *completely* accounted for in terms of electrical, chemical, and mechanical processes of his body. (Malcolm 1968: 52–3)

The basic task of action theory is to explain what distinguishes purposeful behavior from mere events. Coupled with an assumption of scientific naturalism, this gives rise to the *basic problem* of contemporary action theory: the role of purpose in human being appears certain to be superfluous, but it is purpose that makes certain events behaviors or actions.

It is not clear that an explanation satisfying this basic task will also distinguish simpler purposeful behaviors from rich human actions (events of type 2 and type 3). Common sense seems to find that something separates the automatic or limited behaviors of many other kinds of animals, or some human automatic behaviors, from certain complex behaviors of which humans alone appear to be capable. A spider builds a web, a fly moves toward the light, and a human blinks – these are behaviors, they have purposes, but they appear of limited flexibility. In contrast, actions might be behaviors that fulfill a plan, or are motivated by conscious and complex cognitive states, or are guided by explicit rational rules. Jones blinks often without being aware of it, and sometimes without being able to stop it or otherwise control it even if she tries. A fly moves toward light, we assume, without any kind of deliberation or choice. But it would seem that Jones can also decide not to add together a list of numbers, or not to write them down. Jones has some kind of control over some behaviors, and perhaps she has a special experience of deliberation also when she undertakes them. The notion of control is mysterious, but we can identify some indications of it. For example, in some cases Jones can say, "I will (not) do this," and then (not) perform the behavior. Since action theorists have tended to suppose that what distinguishes actions from both mere events and mere behaviors is that actions are *intentional* (i.e., they are caused or partly constituted or best described by intentional states of the

359

appropriate kind), this leaves the distinction between behaviors and mere events mysterious, and few have addressed this distinction.[5]

The difficulty of distinguishing behavior from action can be illustrated by consideration of a kind of situation that is an important part of the discussion of action in the tradition of existential phenomenology, although it is largely ignored or denied in the analytic tradition.[6] A difficulty for the view that actions require some special mental state (such as volition, will, conscious or direct awareness, plans, or explicit rules) is that many of the most uniquely human activities, which demonstrate our greatest skills, are themselves activities that we seek to make, in some sense, automatic. In seeking to make them automatic, it seems that we seek to make these behaviors independent of such special mental states. I will appropriate an example from Merleau-Ponty to which we will return. Suppose that Jones is an organist of some note. She has just received the sheet music for an experimental new composition that she will debut. The piece is difficult, and also includes a number of unusual directions. As Jones sits down to practice, she reads the music over and reads the special instructions. She makes a number of decisions, such as which portions she will practice first, and how she will perform certain additional actions required. At this point, Jones is conscious of what she is doing, she could describe it to us at any time if she were interrupted, she could justify her actions using rational arguments, and in fact if we had asked her to think aloud and describe her actions to us as she prepares her study, we can expect that she would have come to the same conclusions in roughly the same way (which is to say, her ability to justify her actions is plausibly not just an interpretation added on after the actions). Her actions appear to be guided by a plan, and to have a conscious goal that she could describe for us (this goal is to master the music for the performance). Thus, her activity up to now will satisfy any of the standard criteria for being action.

Suppose that Jones now acts on her plan. She practices the music as she intended to do, until she masters it. What is mastery? It amounts to being able to play the piece correctly and *automatically*. What the expert seeks, what typically constitutes expertise, is the acquisition of capabilities which have all the characteristics of mere behaviors: they do not require deliberation, they are fast, we cannot accurately report upon each step of the behavior, there is no reason to believe the behaviors are in any simple sense governed by plans or discrete rules or rational norms, and the behaviors can be resistant to conscious control. The athlete, the musician, and the craftsperson all seek to acquire their most important capabilities as expert skills that do not require the kind of capabilities that many philosophers posed as necessary for action. In fact, what distinguishes the expert from the amateur is the progression from behavior that fulfills the leading and diverse criteria for action, to behavior that appears not to do so. This phenomenon is one studied in contemporary psychology and neural science, where there is now recognized a clear and measurable difference between explicit declarative memory, and a non-declarative "implicit memory" that amounts to the acquisition of skills.[7] Jones's practice develops special learning for the acquisition of implicit memories for skills, and it appears that distinct regions of the brain are dedicated to the acquisition and storing of these skill programs. This seems to lead to the paradoxical conclusion that the master organist is engaged in mere behavior, of the kind we might attribute to a nonhuman animal, whereas the amateur is the paragon of free activity.

360

Thus, although there is significant initial plausibility to many of the candidate explanations for the distinction between action and behavior, a new look at the phenomenon reveals a problem. The assumption that conscious control, or some similar standard, is the distinguishing factor between action and behavior does not cut in any clear way between the blink of the eye and the mastery of an organist. In fact, it would seem that on most such views, only amateur activity is capable of being action. Once we have mastered a task, its performance lacks many of the features that seem to distinguish actions from mere behaviors. But this contradicts the basic motivation for the distinction: that there is something special to human action in contrast to mere behaviors of a kind we share with other species of animals. The second task for action theory, to distinguish between actions and mere behaviors, should also address a second problem: it should either explain how the mastery of skills by humans is still an action, or explain away our common-sense prejudice that things like playing the organ are uniquely rich human actions.

Action raises then at least two special problems for contemporary philosophy. A commitment to a sufficient scientific naturalism appears to render notions of purpose superfluous. A commitment to distinguishing action from behavior (by way of being caused or explained by one or more of a range of candidates for uniquely human mental states) faces substantial difficulties, including that most candidates for such states are inconsistent with the actual practice of expertise.

Action and Heidegger's Critique of the Subject/Object Distinction

Martin Heidegger's *Being and Time* (1927; cited as Heidegger 1962) provides the most extensive and radical attempt in recent philosophy to find an alternative to the division we inherit between a causal and objective external world and a purposeful and subjective inner world. For this reason, Heidegger's existential phenomenology provides not only the possibility of reformulating the classical problems of epistemology, but also of action. These opportunities arise as corollaries of his more general task: Heidegger's goal is to seek to formulate and answer the question of the meaning of Being. As a first step toward accomplishing this task, Heidegger reformulates phenomenology in the direction that we can call existential phenomenology: he focuses upon an analysis of the everyday activity and experience of human being, or Dasein, with the goal of discerning how an understanding of beings and Being is possible for Dasein. This analysis requires him to deconstruct many of our prejudices, and to attempt to develop more radical alternative explanations of Dasein and its understanding. These alternatives allow us to formulate a distinct perspective on action. However, it must be stressed that explaining action in the sense of contemporary action theory is never Heidegger's concern; nor is Heidegger ever concerned to reconcile our view of ourselves with any form of scientific naturalism.

Dasein, Heidegger observes, is fundamentally *being-in-the-world*. As such, Dasein cannot be separated from the world, and the world cannot be separated from Dasein: "Self and world belong together in the single entity, the Dasein. Self and world are not two beings, like subject and object, or like I and thou, but self and world are the basic determination of the Dasein itself in the unity of the structure of being-in-the-world"

361

(Heidegger 1988: 297). Here *world* is a technical term, and does not mean the collection of physical objects in space. Rather, for a particular Dasein, world is the system of purposes that determines the actual and potential interactions this particular Dasein can have with things or other Dasein, and also the actual or potential interactions this Dasein can understand. Dasein is "in" this world by acting appropriately for these purposes. Describing world more fully is difficult, and at first the concept is elusive. World is neither occurrent nor extant, that is, it is not the kind of thing that is an object of scientific theory. For this reason, it cannot be fully defined or described. But Heidegger believes he can *indicate* what it is, since by way of phenomenology he can observe it, partially describe it, and so help us observe it.

The notion of world, and of being-in-the-world, provides a bold way to avoid the traditional problems of the subject/object division. The most obvious such problems are epistemic: if the world is out there, external to me, and communicated to me by way of some kind of representations or other sensory data, then there is always a remove of myself from the world. As a result, I can always doubt that my knowledge of the world is accurate. I can even rightly doubt that there is any external world. But Heidegger asserts that world in this sense of extant, present objects external to me is derivative from world in the sense of being-in-the-world. World in the sense of being-in-the-world is not external, but includes essentially the interaction of myself with things, and I am essentially defined by these interactions, as are the things with which I interact. There is no gulf to cross, no wall between two worlds that requires a window.

The classical epistemic problems are closely related to the problems of action. Many of us have inherited a superficial theoretical belief that we have both an experience of a causal natural world external to ourselves, and a purposeful world of consciousness internal to ourselves. In breaking down this distinction, Heidegger finds something more fundamental that allows for a new perspective on action. Here again, being-in-the-world is the guiding concept. As world is in part encountered in terms of the things with which we interact, revealed first and most often through the ways in which we interact with them, world is the *horizon* of possibilities for Dasein. This is a feature that is ultimately to be explained in terms of Dasein's temporal nature. Dasein projects itself onto its possibilities. Unlike a stone or a magnetic field, Dasein can question what it is. It inherits its past, but the future is present for it as a range of possible ways of being. With this characterization of Dasein's potential, Heidegger works to avoid either a notion of Dasein as a passive object, like a scientific object pushed along by laws, or a totally free subject, spontaneously choosing options. He seeks to indicate something else: Dasein is confronted with possibilities and it is the very nature of Dasein to be aware of these possibilities in some sense, and to realize some of them and reject others. This is not, however, solely a way of choosing options, but rather the actual constitution of Dasein: "the projection is the way I *am* the possibility" (Heidegger 1988: 277).

This projection into possibilities, which are themselves the future, is part of what Heidegger calls *transcendence.* Since Dasein is not, like a Cartesian subject, removed from the world and observing it as through a window, Dasein is out in the world encountering beings. Being-in-the-world literally means that Dasein is, compared to the traditional idea of the internal subject, outside. This transcendence of being-in-the-world makes possible intentionality. But "Transcendence, being-in-the-world, is never to be equated and identified with intentionality" (Heidegger 1992: 168). Rather, Heidegger introduces a new term, *comportments*, for this way that Dasein is mixed with and directed toward its possibilities, which typically means directed toward beings (objects). Mental states like knowing are comportments, but comportments need not be mental states of a subject, and some comportments make possible mental states by preceding them and grounding them. For example, comportments might include perceptuomotor skills – "automatic," but important ways we have of interacting with our environment that in turn are essential to many other capabilities that we have. World is essentially revealed and so constituted through Dasein's comportments. These comportments arise because of the temporal nature of Dasein: Dasein cannot, as it were, sit still, but must interact. It is thrown into the world from its past, into its future, and this makes it possible for Dasein to have comportments.

This projection into possibilities of Dasein in turn makes possible *understanding*, and this includes also activity: "Understanding as the Dasein's self-projection is the Dasein's fundamental mode of *happening*. As we may also say, it is the authentic meaning of action" (Heidegger 1988: 277). Dasein has activity,[8] its being-in-the-world depends upon Dasein being concerned, or directed in a "toward-which," with the world. This way of viewing Dasein breaks down the cause/purpose division traditionally associated with object and subject. The projection of Dasein upon its possibilities is a fundamental feature of Dasein, which actually makes it what it is. Thus, Heidegger attempts to reappropriate the notion of freedom: "we also have to remove freedom from the traditional perspective where emphasis is placed on self-initiating spontaneity, *sua sponte*, in contrast to a compulsive mechanical sequence" (Heidegger 1992: 191). This notion of freedom is meant to escape the problems that arise when freedom is defined as an alternative or even denial of (physical) determinism. By defining freedom as an essential part of Dasein's projection upon its possibilities, Heidegger can claim that "Being-in-the-world is accordingly nothing other than freedom, freedom no longer understood as spontaneity but as defined by the formulation of Dasein's metaphysical essence" (Heidegger 1992: 192). This freedom cannot be escaped. Even when we give into a kind of passivity, we are really realizing a possibility that Dasein is projected upon:

> The essence of freedom, which surpasses every particular factic or factual being, its surpassing character, can also be seen particularly in despair, where one's own lack of freedom engulfs a Dasein absorbed in itself. This completely factical lack of freedom is itself an elemental testimony to transcendence, for despair lies in the despairing person's vision of the impossibility of something possible. Such a person still witnesses to the possible, inasmuch as he despairs of it. (Heidegger 1992: 193)

Heidegger's notion of freedom can perhaps be made more compelling by way of an analogy with the analytic notion of agent causation. We have noted that when we presuppose the eventuality of a sufficient scientific theory of behavior, we are confronted with the difficulty of finding a place for purposeful action in a world that presumably will be sufficiently described in terms of purposeless causes. One approach to this challenge is to suppose that some causes either are, or can be described as, intentions. When analytic action theory is concerned with freedom, the problem is redoubled, because such causes, if they are fully explained by natural laws and past events, are explained ultimately by events that occurred before I was even born. Such causes seem, in some sense, not to be *mine*. Some have argued that what is needed to explain human action and also human freedom is the idea of *agent causation*, of causes that are essentially identified with the agent (examples include Chisholm 1976, Taylor 1966). The idea is compelling: if the agent is a cause of some action, then we can say the agent was the source of her actions, and we may even say that she was "free" in her actions. If the agent has some prior cause, this does not change the fact that her agency is her own. That is, it seems plausible that we can retain something of what we mean by saying the agent caused an action when the causes in question are *constitutive of who and what the agent is*, and so cannot be made alien to the agent. Even if these actions can be explained by prior events, it would seem that these actions are owned by the agent because they are literally identical with (part of) the agent. For Heidegger's Dasein, something analogous to this is argued here. Dasein *is* its projection upon its possibilities. As such, it is free and an agent in the sense that this projection is not outside of or something other than Dasein.

Heidegger's approach to action partly eludes, partly asserts the basic problem of action theory. Dasein has activities essentially, as part of its projection upon its possibilities. When we look at Dasein in its most fundamental understanding of Being and beings, we see this freedom that precedes all other kinds of understanding. Dasein is not a scientific object, a thing occurrent or present-at-hand, which appears both purposeful and also amenable to scientific reduction. Rather, Dasein is revealed in a radical critique of what makes other views of the world even possible, including the scientific view. In part, this means that what distinguishes the activity of Dasein from mere events is that the activity of Dasein is part of what it is to be Dasein, and mere events have no such ownership (but this can be a deceptive way to put the distinction, since from the perspective of some phenomenological analyses of Dasein's everyday experience, we may not see mere events). Heidegger then does not reduce Dasein to being a physical object, nor posits irreducible intentions that are had by a subject (which he would see as just another kind of object), but rather he claims that the scientific worldview is derivative of a more fundamental relationship between Dasein and Being. A scientific explanation of how bodies act should then not be expected to reduce, eliminate, or otherwise conflict with a view of human being as purposeful. However, the basic problem of action theory is not solved by this move: we are surely able to see our bodies as occurrent, extant objects, which can be described by science. As such, these bodies may present a scientific challenge to us – we may describe organisms and their organs as having purposes (e.g., the purpose of the heart is to pump blood), while maintaining a conviction that a causal theory will ultimately sufficiently explain these objects. This is no doubt a problem for the scientific worldview. But when we look at the human organism in this way, we are *not observing Dasein*. That is, in taking the scientific worldview, we are taking a derivative perspective which already excludes an understanding of Dasein in its essential nature as free and having activity. Such a worldview may ultimately be sufficient for its own purposes, and Heidegger later (1977c) seems to suggest that there is a real danger that we will come to see ourselves solely in this way, but this view can never be *complete*.

This points us toward how Heidegger answers the question of the difference between what I have called mere behaviors and more complex purposeful human action. A brief discussion of the beings we encounter in the world is required first. In its world, Dasein tends to encounter beings as available equipment, as ready-to-hand objects (*Zuhandenheit*). These are beings understood as elements of the ongoing projects of the Dasein. The hammer is experienced not normally or first as an external object, but rather via the role it plays in the activity of hammering, which in turn is understood in terms of the role it plays in building a home, and so on. These different roles together are aimed at what Heidegger calls a for-the-sake-of-which (1962: 118/86ff.). However, Dasein sometimes encounters objects as external, independent, even recalcitrant objects, as things occurrent or present-at-hand (*Vorhandenheit*). This can happen, for example, when a tool breaks. We look at the hammer with the cracked handle, and suddenly it is set before us as something other than us, an object that we can describe with objective features, perhaps even find a little strange.

These two ways that beings can be revealed to Dasein are part of Heidegger's recasting of the distinction between a subjective and objective world. In first and most typically encountering things as *pragmata*, practical objects (Heidegger 1962: 96/68), these things are revealed to us as they fit into our projects. Again, this leaves no gulf to be crossed between subject and object. It is tempting to read Heidegger as suggesting that seeing the beings of our world as equipment is in some sense a more accurate way that Dasein encounters its world, and that when we encounter the beings of the world as occurrent or present-at-hand we are somehow deceived or confused or at least seeing these beings in a reduced way. If we could resist the theoretical attitude, we would, for example, avoid the problems of action, since the causal worldview would not intrude into our experience of ourselves as purposeful. The way Heidegger describes these matters in *Being and Time* can encourage such a reading,[9] but his later clarifying comments show that he was eager to reject this kind of reading. In his 1929–30 lectures *The Fundamental Concepts of Metaphysics*, Heidegger is explicit:

> I attempted in *Being and Time* to provide a preliminary characterization of the *phenomenon of world* by interpreting the *way in which we at first and for the most part move about in our everyday world*. There I took my departure from what lies to hand in the everyday realm, from those things that we use and pursue, indeed in such a way that we do not really know of the peculiar character proper to such activity at all, and when we do try to describe it we immediately misinterpret it by applying concepts and question that have their source elsewhere . . . It never occurred to me, however, to try to claim or prove with this interpretation that the essence of man consists in the fact that he knows how to handle knives and forks or use the tram. (Heidegger 1995: 177)

If our view of beings as occurrent is not wholly deceptive, then there must be some truth to the view of, say, our bodies as occurrent things, perhaps fully determined in their behavior by causal laws. Here Heidegger's discussion of the difference between human being and the being of nonhuman animals, and therefore of the difference between action and mere behavior, arises.

Nonhuman animals have purposeful behavior, but, as noted, it seems that they lack the ability for some kinds of complex behaviors. Heidegger accepts this common-sense observation:

> The *specific manner* in which man *is* we shall call *comportment* and the *specific manner* in which the animal *is* we shall call *behavior*. They are fundamentally different from one another . . . Being capable of ____ means being capable of behavior. Capability is instinctual, a driving forward and maintaining oneself in being driven toward that which the capacity is capable of, toward a possible form of behavior, a drivenness toward a performance of a particular kind in each case. The behavior of the animal is not a *doing and acting*, as in human comportment, but a *driven performing*. (Heidegger 1995: 237)

So far, this seems a rather simplistic acceptance of the common-sense idea of nonhuman animals driven along by instincts, and of humans having something more than instinct. But Heidegger's analysis turns out to be more subtle than that. He argues that nonhuman animals can, in one sense of "world," be said to have a world, but that these animals are *world poor*. He draws here upon the ideas of the biologist Jakob von Uexkull, who argued that organisms have a lifeworld, or worldview, that reflects their capabilities (von Uexkull 1926). What then makes our world complete or rich, and the world of the nonhuman animal poor – or, put differently, in what sense of "world" do nonhuman animals lack a world? Heidegger's answer is striking. The bee, for example, "is not governed by any recognition of the presence or absence of that which it is driven to engage with . . . the bee does *not comport itself* toward the blossom *as something present or not present*" (Heidegger 1995: 243). This lack of such comportment arises because the nonhuman animal is incapable of interpreting beings. Ultimately, this means that the nonhuman animal is incapable of understanding beings as occurrent, as present-at-hand. Its relation to beings "is *not* an apprehending of something *as something*, as something present at hand" (Heidegger 1995: 247), thus "The behavior of the animal, contrary to how it might appear, does not and never can relate to *present-at-hand* things singly or collectively" (Heidegger 1995: 255).

Heidegger does not formulate a distinction in human activities between mere behaviors and actions, but he does tell us what makes a human world different from the nonhuman animal's "world," and thus shows how our activities can have something lacking to nonhuman animals even though both human and nonhuman animal behavior are purposeful. Our world is in part constituted by our ability to encounter beings as occurrent, as present-at-hand objects. But I argued above that the view of beings as occurrent is consistent with a scientific worldview, where we might suppose that a causal explanation will be sufficient. When we look at a human body as occurrent, for example, we cannot see in it Dasein or Dasein's being-in-the-world. Is Dasein, or the world, in the sense of being-in-the-world, then nothing? Heidegger would say that in fact Dasein must be able to confront this possibility of conceiving of its own nothingness, and that the world can slip away from us. This is because Dasein must be capable of seeing its purposes as tentative – as, from a certain perspective, evaporating. This is one of his points in the elusive 1929 lecture "What is Metaphysics?" where Heidegger describes the "nihilation" that occurs in severe anxiety, when "All things and we ourselves sink into indifference . . . We can get no hold on things" (Heidegger 1977e: 103). Anxiety can reveal the world as threatening to become all alien objects, fully occurrent and lacking any availableness. Such a world threatens to become meaningless for us, and thus threatens to be in this sense *nothing*.

This insight into a perspective under which meaning threatens to disappear under-lies Heidegger's notion of authenticity. For Dasein to be authentic, it must choose resolutely its own possibilities. To do this means that Dasein must recognize that there is no absolute grounding to its choices among its possibilities. Viewed from, say, a faith in a complete or sufficient causal scientific worldview, Dasein's possibilities may dis-appear, they may be nothing, they may be seen as purposeless. Resoluteness arises when we confront such a way of seeing ourselves. We are authentic when we recognize that there is no way to secure our purposes from all doubt, no way to finally ground our purposes so that they cannot ever threaten to be meaningless, to be nothing. Heidegger thus in part casts the distinction between action and behavior not in terms of some special causes, but rather in terms of the ability to confront the otherness of beings, including even some aspects of our own being (such as our bodies), and confront their potential to be resistant to us and even be purposeless and absurd, and still undertake activity.

This way of distinguishing action is consistent with t' e case described of the organ-ist. When Jones first began to study the organ it would be a strange and recalcitrant object, occurrent for her, resisting her. As she masters it, she acquires a thing available as equipment, something ready-to-hand. When she is confronted with a new musical piece, the same thing happens: if the piece is difficult, she may have to reflect on it, make choices about it, and she may see it as frustrating and question the purposes of the composer. As she masters the piece, she will no longer see it as occurrent. But one thing that distinguishes her expertise from the behavior of nonhuman animals is that she can always turn to any decision of the composer, or any decision she makes in performing, and see it *as something*, and this means that she can also possibly see the composer's choices as *nothing* (that is, as arbitrary). This also holds out the possibility for authenticity. She can ultimately recognize that she cannot absolutely secure the purpose of her choices – each could always appear nearly meaningless or purposeless. In practice, she strives to make her performance automatically live up to very high standards she has adopted. But she can at all times look at what she is doing and see that there is ultimately no standard which cannot be questioned, which cannot be seen as arbitrary. To play the organ this way and not that way comes down ultimately to something like, this is just how others have done it or others think it should be done. As a master organist, she strives for perfection, but if she is authentic in this activity, she sometimes recognizes that there is no absolute standard for perfection. She has then chosen, resolutely, her standards. Human activity is distinguishable from mere behavior not in the nature of its causes, but in the possibility that it can be questioned and accepted.

This view of action that we can reconstruct from Heidegger's early work is com-pelling but not fully complete. Heidegger did not develop a complete analysis – or, perhaps it would be better to say, he did not develop as complete an analysis as he aimed to provide – of the nature of our understanding. As a result, we do not have a complete analysis of activity. We may well wonder, for example, how our experience of being-in-the-world will stand against the progress of human sciences, or how it might answer concrete questions about responsibility and freedom in contexts such as legal proceedings. In his later work, after the *Kehre* or turn toward more radical methods and concerns that occurred in the 1930s, this incompleteness is more explicit. In his "Letter on Humanism," Heidegger in part responds to Sartre's brief paper, "Existentialism is a Humanism" (1946; cited as Sartre 1988). Heidegger begins the essay with the statement

> We are still far from pondering the essence of action decisively enough. We view action only as causing an effect. The actuality of the effect is valued according to its utility. But the essence of action is accomplishment. To accomplish means to unfold something into the fullness of its essence, to lead it forth into this fullness – *producere*. (Heidegger 1977e: 193)

In the new terminology here and in other later works, Heidegger increasingly speaks of the activity of Dasein in more passive terms. This is also part of his growing focus upon Dasein's historical role. This surely is a change of focus for Heidegger, but it is one that is arguably a natural outgrowth of his implicit views on Dasein and its activity in his earlier work, especially in terms of Dasein's freedom and its facticity. As we saw, Heidegger's notion of Dasein's freedom is meant to resist the notion of Dasein as acting spontaneously. But our tradition, and our common-sense view of ourselves, encourages us to interpret all talk of freedom and activity in such terms. In exploring the nature of Dasein's projection upon its possibilities, Heidegger may have felt that he failed to reveal sufficiently the understanding he asserts of a kind of being between passivity and spontaneous activity. His later work can be seen, then, in part, as returning to the projection of Dasein upon its possibilities, its activity, with the goal of revealing them in a more original light.

Heidegger does this in at least two ways. First, Heidegger identifies thinking as a kind of action. This is first clear in the "Letter on Humanism," where he argues that thinking is the most important kind of action that Dasein can undertake. We do not typically consider thinking as exemplary of action; we even distinguish, for example, a "man of action" from a "thinker." Second, Heidegger struggles for a terminology that sounds less spontaneous and is more concerned with a letting happen. Examples of this occur throughout his later works. I will cite just a few examples. In "On the Essence of Truth," Heidegger argues that truth requires freedom, but now describes freedom differently: "Freedom for what is opened up in an open region lets beings be the beings they are. Freedom now reveals itself as letting beings be" (Heidegger 1998: 127). In "The Question Concerning Technology," Heidegger describes the "highest dignity of the essence" of human beings, which may allow humans to escape the dangers of an all-consuming technological worldview: "This dignity lies in keeping watch over the unconcealment – and with it, from the first, the concealment – of all coming to presence on this Earth" (Heidegger 1977e: 313). Also during this period he frequently uses the term "releasement," explaining "Releasement lies – if we may use the word lie – beyond the distinction between activity and passivity" (Heidegger 1966: 61). In his last interview, Heidegger concluded despairingly that the being of Dasein was in danger, and that "only a god can save us," but said that we can actively wait for this god, and "awaken the readiness of expectation" (Heidegger 1991: 107). In all of these cases, a charitable reading is that Heidegger strives for a poetic way of asserting the freedom of Dasein in a manner that moves away from notions of spontaneity by using increasingly passive language, but without asserting ever that Dasein is passive.

Merleau-Ponty and a Concrete Being-in-the-World

Heidegger's view of action rests upon a critique of understanding that is both radical and highly abstract. Furthermore, he had neither sympathy for, nor interest in, scientific naturalism. As such, his views seem to have little immediate bearing upon the confrontation of the scientific worldview with a view of action as purposeful. In the work of Merleau-Ponty, the notion of being-in-the-world offers a solution to the problems of action, but does so in a philosophy that seeks to integrate science with a phenomenological understanding, and which sees human being as essentially bodily. For these reasons, Merleau-Ponty's views on action are of special relevance to contemporary theory of action.

Merleau-Ponty's philosophy has several important features that distinguish it from Heidegger's. Heidegger believes that an analysis of Dasein of a highly general and abstract kind is possible, and seems open to the possibility that there can be other kinds of Dasein, even perhaps Dasein without a physical body. Merleau-Ponty is instead not engaged in any abstract or general kind of analysis, but is concerned specifically with human beings. Heidegger rarely discusses the body, and appears to see it as a factical contingency of Dasein, akin to other features of the inherited situation that a particular Dasein finds itself in. Merleau-Ponty sees humans as essentially bodily – they are their bodies – and he believes being-in-the-world is only possible through a body. This more concrete focus of Merleau-Ponty has an important consequence regarding science. Heidegger does not suggest that science without phenomenology will somehow fail. He seems to consider it possible that we could become fascinated by what technological science can do, and ourselves fail to see – perhaps even get ourselves into a situation where we are unable to see – where such science is incomplete. Merleau-Ponty, instead, identifies or predicts concrete failures in science caused by false beliefs that really are prejudices arising from a failure to undertake phenomenology. These failures can be identified, even scientifically demonstrated, and also they can be overcome with the right phenomenology. For example, in the opening of his magnum opus, *The Phenomenology of Perception*, Merleau-Ponty writes concerning perception:

> Inevitably science, in its general effort towards objectification, evolved a picture of the human organism as a physical system undergoing stimuli which were themselves identified by their physicochemical properties, and tried to reconstitute actual perception on this basis, and to close the circle of scientific knowledge by discovering the laws governing the production of knowledge itself, by establishing an objective science of subjectivity. But it is also inevitable that this attempt should fail. (Merleau-Ponty 2002: 12)

Merleau-Ponty makes the same assertion about action (see Merleau-Ponty 2002: 127ff.). Since phenomenology can reveal these failures, there is a direct interaction possible between phenomenology as he practices it and science. For this reason, his claims about action are particularly relevant to contemporary action theory.

For Merleau-Ponty, being-in-the-world is the unreflective skills and experience of human being that ground all knowledge, including scientific knowledge. Merleau-Ponty does not seek something so radical as an understanding of the meaning of the question of Being, but rather he is concerned to explain how we perceive, understand, and act. Furthermore, he is not concerned with perception, understanding, and action in the abstract – he would doubt that they could be studied abstractly. He specifically addresses concrete examples of human perception, human understanding, and human action (and of the failure of these capabilities in illness and disability). Each of these is essentially related for Merleau-Ponty. "Perception" is his term not only for our usual notion of perception, but more specifically for our experience of the world pretheoretically – that is, the experience of being-in-the-world. Perception and intentionality are essentially related to action: we perceive things not in terms, say, of a construction of sense data, but rather as opportunities for action.

The abilities of human being rest, then, on skills and on experiences that come before knowledge. Because scientific knowledge both characterizes our age, and is the paradigm of theoretical knowledge, Merleau-Ponty is particularly concerned to assert that science depends upon this experience. Phenomenology describes, or points out to us, this experience: "To return to things themselves is to return to that world which precedes knowledge, of which knowledge always *speaks*, and in relation to which every scientific schematization is an abstract and derivative sign language, as is geography in relation to the country-side in which we have learnt beforehand what a forest, a prairie or a river is" (Merleau-Ponty 2002: x).

Merleau-Ponty's first major work, *The Structure of Behavior* (1942; cited as Merleau-Ponty 1983), addresses the problems of both distinguishing behavior from mere events, and actions from behavior. Merleau-Ponty reviews numerous scientific results, with the goal of showing the inadequacy of both the causal "realist" view of the phenomena, and of idealistic alternatives. Throughout his review of scientific results from psychology and ethology, Merleau-Ponty discovers that scientific approaches to the phenomena of learning always take for granted some of the purposes of the organism as a whole. For example, organisms often will achieve a task that we can recognize as the same kind of task they learned to achieve before, but which they perform in different ways. To choose a simple case: "A cat, trained to obtain its food by pulling on a string, will pull with its paw on the first successful trial but with its teeth on the second" (Merleau-Ponty 1983: 96). A scientist studying such a phenomenon might be pleased to say the cat learned the task, a fact that can be measured (the cat pulls the string). But of course, there is no one kind of series of causal events shared by two such behaviors. If we were to track out a physical explanation in terms of neurons, and muscles, and so on, it would be very different in the two cases. What makes them the same? Although there is something measurable here (the pulling of the string), the scientist surreptitiously recognizes that the cat is behaving with this as a purpose, and grants that these are the same kind of behavior because of this purpose (the scientist, for example, would not count the cat as pulling the string if it became entangled in it and fell).

Another example includes the developments of what Merleau-Ponty calls "habits," and what above I described as implicit memory of skills. In habits, Merleau-Ponty claims, we acquire a skill that moves from being a conscious undertaking to being part of our pre-reflective or unconscious background of skills. "Habit expresses our power of dilating being-in-the-world, or changing our existence by appropriating fresh instruments" (Merleau-Ponty 2002: 166). There is no need for reflection or interpretation in habitual action, but rather it relies upon the more fundamental background of understanding that we have and which is not any kind explicit knowledge; the formation of a habit shapes and alters this background of understanding. Habit is thus, "knowledge in the hands, which is forthcoming only when bodily effort is made and cannot be formulated in detachment from that effort" (Merleau-Ponty 2002: 166). This latter claim is particularly important: Merleau-Ponty is not just asserting that the background skills of being-in-the-world are unconscious but otherwise like our conscious actions; rather, they cannot be formulated as a declarative set of plans or instructions because they are qualitatively different. Presumably the skills so exercised cannot be correctly formulated as embodying any of the standard criteria for being actions (caused by intentional states, fulfilling represented plans, etc.).

Returning to an example that he first used in *The Structure of Behavior*, Merleau-Ponty describes in *The Phenomenology of Perception* the skill of an organ player. This organ player, when asked to play on a new organ, is quite capable. "It is known that an experienced organist is capable of playing an organ which he does not know, which has more or fewer manuals, and stops differently arranged, compared with those on the instrument he is used to playing" (Merleau-Ponty 2002: 167–8). This organist may have to practice for a short while to determine the placement of the pedals, or of the stops, but is otherwise able to exercise his capability fully. This reveals something of great importance. For although the player's ability is surely in some sense nothing more than an ability for kinds of movements, these have to be understood dynamically, as a whole, with their specific purpose in mind. A very naïve understanding of motion, for example, of the kind we find in early work in AI, might take the skill of playing the organ to amount to the ability to move this limb to this place at this time. But if that were so, one would develop the skill to only play on one particular token of one kind of instrument. But as Merleau-Ponty observes, we know that you can move the stops and pedals, put the keys higher and farther apart, and the organist can still play. The motor ability is therefore a whole dynamic capability, and the actual specific movements are malleable. We will need therefore to understand action, including complex habits, as whole capabilities, which in turn only can be understood in terms of their purposes.

To explain behavior, Merleau-Ponty argues, we must recognize what actually *looking* at the phenomenon will reveal: that there is a form or structure to behavior that is not reducible to causal discourse. These irreducible forms include essentially an observation of the purposes of the organism, purposes which we attribute to the organism as a whole autonomous entity, and which are evident to us as we watch the organism as a body interacting with the world. This is Merleau-Ponty's answer to the first and primary question of action theory: the difference between behaviors and other kinds of events is that behaviors cannot be recognized or explained without reference to their form. To even identify a behavior as a kind – feeding, fleeing, seeking a mate – we must recognize the organism as a whole with purposes. In his later work, this idea of the irreducible form of behavior is subsumed into the idea of being-in-the-world, but although he expands on the view of *The Structure of Behavior*, it remains unchanged.

About his convictions that we must understand activity as a dynamic whole, Merleau-Ponty is indisputably correct. His more general claim, that we see this dynamic whole as an irreducible form, is more debatable, but progress in the study of behavior has so far been consistent with this conviction: in contemporary sciences concerned with organisms, there is simply no avoiding teleological talk. The doctor must speak of the heart as having the purpose of pumping blood. The ethologist describes a particular call as serving to warn other organisms. A neural scientist describes the activity of ion channels as opening so that a neuron may fire. And so on. Of course, we can construct an experiment and our discourse about one particular kind of biological event in such a way that we avoid such talk, but Merleau-Ponty's claim is that this is never more than an incomplete effort artificially restricted to a small, reduced domain, where our understanding of form or being-in-the-world is pushed back until we can pretend our understanding in the case is not dependent upon the pre-theoretic understanding we have of what is happening.[10] In part by drawing upon these very insights of Merleau-Ponty, Hubert Dreyfus was able to provide a strikingly prescient critique of traditional AI (Dreyfus 1972) that has remained relevant to this day in an otherwise rapidly changing technical field.

Merleau-Ponty also addresses in *The Structure of Behavior* the differences between behavior and more complex kinds of action. He does this by distinguishing three kinds of behavior: syncretic, amovable, and symbolic (Merleau-Ponty 1983: 104ff.). Syncretic behaviors are the simplest. Although they can be difficult to distinguish from more complex forms of behavior, they are behaviors triggered by some complex of stimuli and result in simple behaviors. Amovable forms of behavior are the most complex behaviors that we see in other kinds of animals. They include learning, and flexible uses of different kinds of behavior to achieve the same end. Their only distinction from those most special cases of human intelligence is that they are not symbolic. Symbolic behavior appears to be unique to humans. In such behavior, the systematic nature of a behavior can become evident through our explicit recognition that there is a kind of isomorphism between the understanding that underlies our practice and the world itself: "The true sign represents the signified, not according to an empirical association, but inasmuch as its relation to other signs is the same as the relation of the object signified by it to other objects" (Merleau-Ponty 1983: 121–2). This allows us to recognize ourselves and objects and abstract away from our situation, in order to conceive of different perspectives or situations.

> It is this possibility of varied expressions of a same theme, this "multiplicity of perspective," which is lacking in animal behavior . . . In making possible all substitutions of points of view, it liberates the "stimuli" from the here-and-now relations in which my own point of view involves them and from the functional values which the needs of the species, defined once and for all, assign to them. (Merleau-Ponty 1983: 122)

In contrast, nonhuman animals that are capable only of syncretic and amovable behaviors are limited by what Merleau-Ponty calls the "*a priori* of the species." Because of our ability for symbolic behavior, in which we can see a skill from different perspectives, we have additional power to act. There is not some special mental state that distinguishes action from behavior, but rather we have capabilities that give us profound additional flexibility and thus enable us to undertake special kinds of activities. The exercise of an expertise, what Merleau-Ponty calls a habit, is therefore as capable of being symbolic activity as is any other kind of human behavior. In symbolic activity, we can consider different possibilities, and chose among them. The organist, for example, can reflect on the relationships between the activities he undertakes in playing the organ, and the relationships between the sounds he makes, and so consider transcribing the music for different instruments. Since for Merleau-Ponty our perceptions, and so our world, are determined by the capabilities of our bodies for action, this means symbolic behavior is a recognition of alternatives for action. But, conversely, since our abilities for action shape perception, which is how we experience being-in-the-world, our abilities for symbolic action make us capable of, to some degree, changing our world and what we are in that world.

Merleau-Ponty presents a bold theory of action. He is open to the results of scientific naturalism, but he asserts that we can demonstrate that when applied to animal behavior, including human behavior, such naturalism is demonstrably insufficient. As a result, he claims, we must accept what phenomenology reveals: that our being-in-the-world provides us with irreducible structures or forms of behavior. Explaining the behavior of humans and other animals requires essential reference to purposes had by the organism as a whole. In light of contemporary philosophy, especially contemporary analytic philosophy of action, this view remains a little-pursued path. It is all the more remarkable, however, that so far Merleau-Ponty has been right: the science of behavior today must always refer to irreducible actions, attributed to the organism or organs being studied as a whole, and it remains only a matter of faith of the stronger forms of scientific realism that such references will eventually be reduced away.

An Opportunity

Action theory as an independent endeavor, practiced with the presumption that a causal scientific account of events will be sufficient, is confronted with a number of apparently intractable problems concerning the distinction between behavior and events, and action and behavior. This suggests that there are fundamental problems lurking in the presuppositions of this philosophical discipline, which, if ignored, shall cause continued stagnation. The concept of being-in-the-world, essential to existential phenomenology, offers an important alternative to the dominant formulations of the problems of human action. Heidegger's conception of being-in-the-world is part of a radical alternative to scientific naturalism that can allow us to reflect upon the presuppositions of contemporary philosophy. Merleau-Ponty's conception of being-in-the-world presents a concrete, apparently even falsifiable, set of alternative presumptions about the sciences of behavior. Both alternatives have been insufficiently explored in the theory of action.

Acknowledgment

I owe special thanks for Ingo Farin and Mark Wrathall for helpful comments.

Notes

1 For example, philosophers have struggled with the question of what makes some kinds of behavior *intentional*, arguing that this is sufficient to characterize action. A range of answers have been proposed: that intentions are other kinds of states (beliefs and desires) which cause actions (Davidson 1963); that there are states which can be identified as intentions (through logical analysis) and which partly constitute the action (Searle 1983); that intentions appear to be causes but are convenient fictions which explain human action (Dennett 1971); or that intentions arise in intentional explanations, which as explanations are explicitly not physical states that act as causes (Wilson 1989).

2 Most discussed have been concerns of wayward causation (see Chisholm 1964): if actions are caused by special kinds of mental states, such as intentions, it is easy to conceive of situations where a causal chain gets diverted, but the sought goal is still realized. In such cases, the causal explanation breaks down, but the purpose seems satisfied. Describing causal accounts in such a way that this problem is avoided has proved difficult for many of the existing approaches to action theory. Other concerns include identifying the ontology of events, so that one can distinguish actions from other things. When we imagine a subject that generates intentional states which cause actions, we imagine a chain of causes from this mental state through a series of events. It becomes natural to ask questions like, "If Jones acts to kick the ball, is the neural message from her brain or spinal cord to her muscles an action, or is the contracting of her leg muscles an action, or just the impact of her foot with ball, or all of these, or is something else the action?" Every answer to this question has proved to give rise to challenges of its own.

3 I know of no one who explicitly endorses such an approach, although Daniel Dennett can be interpreted as offering a variation on it (Dennett 1971; see Stitch 1983: 242ff.).

4 Davidson's irreductionism is complex, and illustrative of the difficulties involved in reconciling the scientific causal view with one of purposeful agency. Davidson argues that the mental states of an agent can in fact only be recognized from a perspective of interpreting the agent as a purposeful agent, and as such these mental states are irreducible, but these mental states are otherwise physical (1970, 1974). He supports this view by arguing that mental states, including the causes of intentional actions, are not *type reducible*, although they are token identical with physical events. For those unfamiliar with this position known as *anomalous monism*, Davidson is claiming that although each individual mental state is some physical (e.g., brain) state, there is no neat correlation between a kind of mental state and a kind of physical state. Roughly, not all fears of a particular kind, for example, will be instantiated in a recognizable fear structure in the brain.

5 Exceptions occur largely in the philosophy of mind, and include Millikan 1993 and Dretske 1988.

6 An important exception is Searle, whose notion of the background of skills seems to address the seemingly-automatic nature of expert skills (1983). Searle denies that expert skills require self-aware mental states, but he otherwise characterizes them as like other kinds of actions, including the most obvious cases of the kind contrasted below with expert behaviors. (A valuable discussion of these issues is to be found in Searle 2000 and Dreyfus 2000.) This leaves it unclear, however, whether there is a difference between mere behaviors and actions, and if so, what such a difference is.

7 Some dramatic early evidence for this distinction came from a famous patient, HM, who as part of a treatment for epilepsy had portions of both temporal lobes removed. HM could form no new declarative memories, but he acquired motor skills like a normal person (Scoville and Milner 1957; Penfield and Milner 1958).

8   I follow Dreyfus (1991: 57) in using "activity" as a neutral term to avoid confusion with the formal notion of action described above. As such, the term includes behaviors, but could also refer to events described in alternate ways where the distinction between behaviors and mere events may not arise.

9   Another temptation encouraging such a reading, especially for American readers, is to interpret Heidegger as a kind of American pragmatist, since the pragmatists are the preeminent figures of English language philosophy who stressed the primacy of activity. However, in this regard it is important to recognize that there were other traditions that singled out the control of bodily activity as significantly distinct from other kinds of mental activity. Bergson, to pick one example, promoted in his 1911 book *Matter and Memory* (Bergson 1919) a unique dualism in which bodily activity was controlled by the physical body, and perception was essentially a relation to possible activity, but certain forms of conceptual understanding required some secondary kind of explanation not reducible to physical explanation. This work is also notable as a potential influence on existential phenomenology for its struggle to avoid the options of idealism and materialism by way of positing a space and time of experience that is distinct from the space and time posited by science.

10 Just as Merleau-Ponty argues that the logical empiricist project of assembling perception out of sense data atoms is always possible in a very limited case, but only because we have pushed back the pretheoretical understanding that we depend upon: "the empiricist can always build up, with psychic atoms, near equivalents. But the inventory of the perceived world will increasingly show it up as a kind of mental blindness" (2002: 29).

References and Further Reading

Bergson, H. (1919) *Matter and Memory* (trans. N. M. Paul and W. S. Palmer). New York and London: Macmillan and George Allen & Unwin (original work published 1911).

Chisholm, R. (1964) The descriptive element in the concept of action. *Journal of Philosophy*, 61, 613–25.

—— (1976) The agent as cause. In M. Brand and D. Walton (eds.), *Action Theory* (pp. 199–211). Dordrecht: Reidel.

Davidson, Donald (1963) Actions, reasons, and causes. *Journal of Philosophy*, 60, 685–700.

—— (1970). Mental events. In L. Foster and J. Swanson (eds.), *Experience and Theory*. Boston: University of Massachusetts Press.

—— (1974) Psychology as philosophy. In S. C. Brown (ed.). *Philosophy of Psychology*. New York: Macmillan.

Dennett, D. (1971) Intentional systems. *Journal of Philosophy*, 68, 87–106.

Dretske, F. (1988) *Explaining Behavior: Reasons in a World of Causes*. Cambridge, MA: MIT Press.

Dreyfus, H. (1972) *What Computers Can't Do*. New York: Harper & Row.

—— (1991) *Being-in-the-World: A Commentary on Heidegger's Being and Time, Division I*. Cambridge, MA: MIT Press.

—— (2000) Reply to Searle. In M. Wrathall and J. Malpas (eds.), *Heidegger, Coping, and Cognitive Science: Essays in Honor of Hubert L. Dreyfus, Volume 2* (pp. 323–37). Cambridge, MA: MIT Press.

Heidegger, Martin (1962) *Being and Time* (trans. J. Macquarrie and E. Robinson). New York: HarperCollins (original work published 1927).

—— (1966) *Discourse on Thinking* (trans. J. M. Anderson and E. Freund). New York: Harper & Row (original work published 1959).

—— (1977a) *Basic Writings* (ed. D. Krell). New York: Harper & Row.

—— (1977b) Letter on Humanism (trans. F. A. Capuzzi). In *Basic Writings* (pp. 193–242) (original work published 1947).

—— (1977c) What is metaphysics? (trans. D. F. Krell). In *Basic Writings* (pp. 95–112) (original work published 1967).

—— (1977d) The question concerning technology (trans. W. Lovitt). In *Basic Writings* (pp. 287–317. (original work published 1954).

—— (1988) *Basic Problems of Phenomenology* (trans. A. Hofstadter) (revised edn.). Bloomington Indiana University Press (original lectures delivered in 1927).

—— (1991) Only a god can save us: *Der Spiegel*'s interview with Martin Heidegger. In R. Wolin (ed.), *The Heidegger Controversy* (pp. 91–116). New York: Columbia University Press) (original interview conducted in 1966 and first published (trans. M. P. Alter and J. D. Caputo) in *Philosophy Today* (1976), 20, 267–85).

—— (1992) *Metaphysical Foundations of Logic* (trans. M. Heim). Bloomington: Indiana University Press (original lectures delivered in 1928).

—— (1995) *The Fundamental Concepts of Metaphysics: World, Finitude, Solitude* (trans. W. McNeill and N. Walker). Bloomington: University of Indiana Press (original lectures delivered in 1929/ 30).

—— (1998) On the essence of truth. In *Pathmarks*, ed. W. McNeill (pp. 155–82). Cambridge: Cambridge University Press (original work published 1943).

Malcolm, N. (1968). The conceivability of mechanism. *Philosophical Review*, 77, 45–72.

Merleau-Ponty, M. 1983) *The Structure of Behavior* (trans. A. Fisher). Pittsburgh, PA: Duquesne University Press (original work published 1942).

—— (2002) *The Phenomenology of Perception* (trans. C. Smith). London: Routledge (original work published 1945).

Millikan, R. (1984) *Language, Thought, and Other Biological Categories*. Cambridge, MA: MIT Press.

—— (1993) What is behavior? A philosophical essay on ethology and individualism in psychology, part 1. In *White Queen Psychology and Other Essays for* Alice. Cambridge, MA: MIT Press.

Penfield, W., and Milner, B. (1958) Memory deficits induced by bilateral lesions in the hippocampal zone. *American Medical Association Archives of Neurological Psychiatry*, 79, 475– 97.

Sartre, J-P. (1956) *Being and Nothingness* (trans. H. Barnes). New York: Washington Square Press (original work published 1943).

—— (1988) Existentialism is a Humanism (trans. P. Mairet). In *Existentialism from Dostoyevsky to Sartre* (pp. 345–68). New York: Plume (original work published 1946).

Scoville, W. B., and Milner, B. (1957) Loss of recent memory after bilateral hippocampal lesions. *Journal of Neurology and Neurosurgical Psychiatry*, 20, 11–21.

Searle, J. (1983) *Intentionality: An Essay in the Philosophy of Mind*. New York: Cambridge University Press.

—— (2000) The limits of phenomenology. In M. Wrathall and J. Malpas (eds.), *Heidegger, Coping, and Cognitive Science: Essays in Honor of Hubert L. Dreyfus, Volume 2* (pp. 71–92). Cambridge, MA: MIT Press.

Stitch, S. (1983) *From Folk Psychology to Cognitive Science*. Cambridge, MA: MIT Press.

Taylor, R. (1966). *Action and Purpose*. Englewood Cliffs, NJ: Prentice-Hall.

von Uexkull, J. (1926) *Theoretical Biology* (trans. D. L. Mackinnon). New York: Harcourt, Brace (original work published 1920).

Wilson, G. (1989) *The Intentionality of Human Action*. Stanford, CA: Stanford University Press.

Wrathall, M. and J. Malpas (eds.) (2000) *Heidegger, Coping, and Cognitive Science: Essays in Honor of Hubert L. Dreyfus, Volume 2*. Cambridge, MA: MIT Press.

26

Phenomenology in Artificial Intelligence and Cognitive Science

DANIEL ANDLER

Fifty years before the present volume appeared, artificial intelligence (AI) and cognitive science (Cogsci) emerged from a couple of small-scale academic encounters on the East Coast of the United States. Wedded together like Siamese twins, these nascent research programs rested on some general assumptions regarding the human mind, and closely connected methodological principles, which set them at such a distance from phenomenology that no contact between the two approaches seemed conceivable. Soon, however, contact was made, in the form of a head-on critique of the AI/Cogsci project mostly inspired by arguments from phenomenology. For a while, it seemed like nothing would come of it: AI/Cogsci bloomed while the small troop of critical phenomenologists kept objecting. Then AI and Cogsci went their separate ways. AI underwent a deep transformation and all but surrendered to the phenomenological critique. Cogsci meanwhile pursued the initial program with a far richer collection of problems, concepts, and methods, and was for a long time quite unconcerned by suggestions and objections from phenomenology. The last decade and half has seen a remarkable reversal: on the one hand, a few cognitive scientists have been actively pursuing the goal of reconciliating Cogsci, whether empirically or foundationally, with some of the insights procured by phenomenology; on the other, many cognitive scientists and philosophers of mind who think of themselves as, respectively, mainstream and analytic, and have no or little acquaintance with, and often little sympathy for, phenomenology, have been actively pursuing research programs geared toward some of the key issues identified by phenomenological critics of early AI/Cogsci. It might seem, then, as if those critics were now vindicated. But while these new directions are undoubtedly promising, it is not yet clear that phenomenology and Cogsci can be truly reconciled. Some suspect that Cogsci must distort beyond recognition those phenomenological themes it means to weave into its fabric, while phenomenology may be losing touch with its roots by tuning onto the logic of Cogsci which is, after all, an empirical science. To the present writer, it is far too early for anything like a verdict, as the task of clarifying the issues and gaining a much deeper understanding of the issues on both sides has barely begun. But whatever emerges from this exploration will probably have deep consequences for both Cogsci and philosophy.

A Phenomenologically Inspired Critique of Early AI

In a book which appeared in 1972 and went through two further, augmented, editions (Dreyfus 1972), Hubert Dreyfus provided a massive set of interrelated arguments against AI. This seminal work, together with subsequent writings by Dreyfus and his followers, provides the backdrop to a large part of the discussion which has been developing since then. Dreyfus attempted to show that (1) contrary to heretofore unchallenged claims by its proponents, AI was not making significant progress toward creating intelligent artifacts; (2) to a large extent, this lack of success was due to erroneous assumptions about the mind; (3) AI was ignoring dimensions of the mind which are critical to intelligent, adaptive behavior.

Before the most central and enduring ideas are summarized, three remarks are in order. First, Dreyfus's approach is not aprioristic: he fights AI on its own turf, like a naturalistic philosopher of science who conceives of science and philosophy as continuous. The naturalistic spirit of his approach is also made manifest in his rejection of any form, overt or covert, of dualism: not for him, stirring appeals to consciousness, emotions, freedom, norms and values, or the Subject; not a thought directed against science or technology; no attempt to downplay the causal powers of the brain; no reliance on interpretive or other nonrealistic views of mind or psychology. This straighforward naturalistic stance explains the otherwise unexpected efficacy of the Dreyfusian line of thought in penetrating the culturally hostile world of AI and Cogsci. It also shows the profound inadequacy of the analytic/continental distinction in accounting for the commerce of ideas in the case at hand: in fact, themes and theses originating in continental traditions are increasingly deployed and refined most ably by analytically trained philosophers. What may be called Dreyfus's methodological naturalism, on the one hand, and the analytic co-opting of (aspects of) continental philosophy, on the other, raise interesting philosophical and meta-philosophical issues which cannot be pursued here.

Second, Dreyfus aims at a moving target, and a target which he himself helps to displace for the reasons just mentioned. The several components of his attack on AI form a cohesive "long argument" (somewhat in the way Darwin viewed *On the Origin of Species*) in the context of early AI. The general structure of the argument is something like this: AI aims at explaining human intelligence by building intelligent machines, and to this end it takes on board a set of hypotheses (H) regarding the essential nature of the mind. But the assumptions in (H) are mistaken, and further, the mind exhibits a set of properties (P) which seem to account for, or be constitutive of, intelligence, and which AI ignores. The falsity of (H) and the reality and importance of (P) result in part from independent considerations, in part from an inference to the best explanation (of AI's persisting difficulties and of the patterns they follow). Unlike Darwin's object of study, however, Dreyfus's has been rapidly changing: AI has developed new models, based on different assumptions, and it now sees it as an obligation to account for at least some of the properties in (P); unsurprisingly, the clinical tableau presented by this new AI (actually, by the variety of new paradigms in AI) is different from that of early AI (also known as GOFAI: Good Old-Fashioned Artificial Intelligence; see Haugeland 1985). Thus it would seem that Dreyfus's long argument would need at least a thorough revision, or perhaps be archived among the minutes of successful pleas against reformed or extinct culprits. Sorting out those parts of the argument which can be safely shelved, those which need adjustment, and those which remain essentially valid as is, has in fact been a task for Dreyfus and for those who were convinced by the argument or at least took it seriously.

Third, however closely connected, the considerations gathered here under (2) – the mistaken assumptions (H) – and (3) – the ignored dimensions (P) – were distinct and met with unequal degrees of approval. Dreyfus's rejection of a view of the mind as an information-processor is at the heart of (2), and to this day is deemed inconclusive by many thinkers, including some who are fully sympathetic to part (3). The latter, on the other hand, revolves around such issues as the role of common sense, embodiment, engagement, and context, which now figure among the core issues of the field. A crucial question therefore is the extent to which one can honor (3) without siding with (2).

Let us now briefly review the main tenets of Dreyfus's analysis. Regarding the difficulties which beset GOFAI (the "Wagnerian phase of AI research" in Jerry Fodor's phrase; Fodor 1983: 126; also often dubbed "Promethean AI"), little needs to be said here: this variety of AI is essentially defunct (according to one of its founding fathers, Marvin Minsky,[1] it has been "brain dead" since the early 1970s – by which he presumably means that although apparently alive and well, it had suffered internal theoretical injury from which it was not to recover).

By contrast, some of the basic assumptions underlying the defunct research program are shared by many working scientists and philosophers today; thus Dreyfus's objections retain most of their relevance. Intelligence (insufficiently distinguished, at the time, from "mindedness," the property of having a mind or exhibiting the essential functions of the human mind) was hypothesized to be a property of information-processing systems such as suitably programmed computers. This implied that (1) mental processes operate on a uniform basis of discrete units of information; (2) the units are carried by material vehicles whose causal powers are in principle independent from the entities about which they carry information; (3) thinking results from, or rather, is nothing but, the performance of computations on symbolic "representations" built up from elementary bits of context-independent information; (4) the ability of a system to produce true, rational, or adaptive thinking is due to its possessing the requisite facts and a truth-preserving inference engine, i.e., a computational routine for drawing logical conclusions from the stored facts. An intelligent system placed in an environment is made up of three compartments or modules, one for the perceptive intake of transient information; another for the computation of the appropriate inferences about the state of the world and the required action; the third, for the motor control of the actions to be effected. The central module is thus insulated from the world (a property sometimes referred to as the formality condition, or, indirectly, as methodological solipsism): it "communicates" only via informational transducers, somewhat like a military command center sunk deep in the ground so as to escape any (directly) physical contact. It operates on a set of explicit propositions which together form a "data base," a theory which serves as "model" of, or "represents," the (appropriate parts of the) world, and is limited to applying explicit formal rules to its "data base."

Dreyfus objected to this conception of the intelligent mind on a variety of grounds. He faulted it for being unmotivated; incoherent; wildly implausible from the most elementary phenomenological standpoint; vulnerable to collapse in real-world situations. At the same time, he claimed that AI was nothing but a zealous follower of the rationalistic tradition in Western philosophy. Uncovering its fatal flaws was therefore not as simple a task as might first appear; however elementary, the phenomenological stance deployed against AI's theoretical framework was rooted in the deepest sources of phenomenology in the historical sense.

Out of this vast set of considerations, three will be briefly explained. The first concerns the positing of context-free units of meaning, or primitives. With his colleague, John Searle, Dreyfus co-invented the amusing and now popular game of finding examples showing that even the simplest sentences, the most obvious pieces of behavior, could have radically different meanings, and call for radically different responses, according to the context in which they appear. The project of reducing this context-sensitivity to a mere matter of differences in collateral information (itself assumed to be context-independent) is, according to Dreyfus, doomed to fail, and the claim that somehow it must succeed, if we are to provide a naturalistic account of intelligence, mere question-begging. Heidegger, says Dreyfus, was the first to pinpoint the fallacy of what he called the "metaphysical assumption," which consists in viewing the background as simply extra information which merely needs to be made explicit.

Another problem Dreyfus raised concerns the idea of intelligent behavior as resulting from the application of formal rules to the information at hand. One objection has since then become familiar from discussions about rule-following initiated by Wittgenstein's skeptic argument: what rule must one deploy to determine which rule, or in which case a given rule, should be applied? (The regress had already been noticed by Lewis Carroll.) But Dreyfus also undermined the reasons given by the rationalistic tradition up to and including AI, for thinking that rational behavior *must* result from rule application. First, he argued that from the fact that the trajectories of cognitive systems, like those of all physical systems exhibiting some regularity, are rule-*governed*, it is fallacious to infer that these trajectories causally follow from the system's (conscious or unconscious) *observance*, in the psychological or information-processing sense, of some rules. When I ride my bicycle, my trajectory "obeys" a complicated system of differential equations, but there is no reason to suppose that I am "unconsciously" computing the solutions and using them to apply to the handlebar the angle appropriate to my negotiating the turn without falling. Second, Hubert and Stuart Dreyfus (1986) developed a model of skill acquisition which, if accurate, undermines the argument from learning. Many skills are, in fact, taught initially by inculcating a set of context-free rules; isn't it obvious then that, as the learner's proficiency improves, she is "automating" those rules and still applying them, albeit now "mindlessly," whenever a particular move or gesture is requires? Isn't this in fact the paradigm of "knowledge acquisition," and hence the very basis of the process by which a (presumably) essentially unintelligent newborn becomes in due course an intelligent adult? Now on the Dreyfus's model, based on a combination of phenomenological observations and results from experimental psychology, the rules given the beginner are not pushed down under the threshold of consciousness, ready to be unconsciously activated when needed; rather, they are discarded like training-wheels on toddlers' bicycles. Fluid, expert performance rests on entirely different principles, those of "skillful coping."

The third target which Dreyfus aims for is the assumption which AI was led to make explicit regarding common sense, understood as what enables any normal human being to negotiate familiar and novel situations effortlessly, with rare and usually benign mistakes, and that even sophisticated and lightning-fast computers seem to lack, leading them to catastrophic breakdowns and wildly improper behavior. AI's assumption is that this common sense is made up of a gigantic mass of propositional knowledge about the various realms of common activity, ranging from the taxonomy and behavior of middle-sized physical objects and substances to the basics of human interactions. In order for a computer to become truly intelligent, in the human sense of the word (and in particular useful outside its usual range of applications), it is obvious, according to AI, that it needs to have access to all the banal facts which a human being knows about the way the ordinary world works in ordinary circumstances. Dreyfus sees two seemingly unsurmountable, and to this day unsurmounted, problems with this proposal. The first is that there seems no end in sight for the task of collecting the "facts" which together purportedly make up common-sense knowledge. The conjecture that with about 10 million items a computer should at last achieve common sense, floated today by some diehard "factualists," is a wild guess. But even supposing that these millions of items were actually at hand, and conveniently stored in a database, the second and even harder problem is that of relevance: how does a rational, rule-governed computer retrieve, among its millions of facts, the few which are required to solve the problem at hand? One answer which has been proposed in various guises and at various moments is to divide up the big bundle into smaller, more manageable bundles. But this won't do, for two reasons at least. One is a matter of simple arithmetic: the bundles are individually more manageable only if they are smaller than the whole thing by several orders of magnitude, in which case the system will run into the problem of discovering in less than astronomical time which is the right bundle to exploit. The other reason is that human situations don't invariably involve just one domain. Interferences happen all the time, and intelligence at a quite ordinary level requires, indeed in large part consists in, dealing at least adequately, in all but perhaps the most extreme circumstances, with interferences. Flirting behavior in a restaurant ceases when the courted one chokes on a fishbone, or when a racist remark is made by a customer sitting at a neighboring table; etc., to any degree of embedding. Life, not just knowledge or belief fixation or the interpretation of utterances, is "Quinean" in Fodor's sense (see Fodor 1983: 107): at any moment, anything might turn out to be relevant in any situation. (One form of the relevance problem has gained fame in the AI literature under the label of the *frame problem*.)

But then, *how* do humans achieve intelligence? This is the question which the constructive part of Dreyfus's program attempts to answer, by bringing out the features or dimensions of the mind which AI has been oblivious to, and which may precisely hold the key to intelligence. Dreyfus proposes an account of intelligent behavior which sits somewhere between description and explanation. According to the perspective one adopts, one will tend to think of what follows as part of the *explananda* or part of the *explanantia*. The explanatory function of the account consists in redescribing the phenomena so as to make apparent, first, that, once the redescription is achieved, a large part of the mystery of intelligence dissolves, and second, that an explanation of these phenomena will in all likelihood call on principles radically different from those propounded by AI. But although, as will shortly be seen, Dreyfus has exploited his own suggestion by proposing that connectionist networks go some way toward providing the desired solution, thus showing how the initial problem – the elucidation of the material basis of human intelligence – might be solved, the most enduring contribution he makes in this part of his work consists in drawing attention to what he regards as *fundamental* abilities of the human mind and which have been either completely ignored by the classical rationalist tradition, or categorized as sophisticated and derived from more basic powers.

"Abilities" is not quite the right word for what Dreyfus points us to. Rather, he invites us to think of the mind not as a set of abstract functions of an autonomous organ, the brain, but rather as a complex of emerging properties of something considerably more inclusive. This enlargement goes through three phases. First, what is traditionally attributed to the solitary, cogitative or computational mind, Dreyfus, drawing on Merleau-Ponty, assigns to the entire body. The body is no puppet manipulated by the brain; rather, the body relies on its various organs, with their characteristic shapes and subject to their proprietary constraints (knees don't bend backward, arms are less than a mile long, eyes don't pop out of their sockets to check what's behind our backs, etc.) to generate appropriate responses to the situation at hand. This "skillful coping," however elaborate and complex it would appear as a performance of a computational-representational device, is for humans (and presumably for other animal species) a basic, primitive ability, regardless of the way it becomes part of their repertoire. In brief, the mind is *embodied*.

The second stage of the enlargement brings in the physical environment. Combining insights from Merleau-Ponty and the American psychologist J. J. Gibson (1904–79), Dreyfus suggests that objects and relations in visual space are not identified from a neutral perspective on the basis of their computationally salient features. Instead, they are grasped as "affordances" (see Gibson 1979), as "in order to's" (Heidegger); they are holistically perceived as potentials for action. The mind is not initially disconnected from the physical environment; it leans on it from the very beginning and is engaged in an uninterrupted interaction, somewhat in the way a fish moves about in the water ("*immersion* in daily activity" is a phrase which comes up frequently in this discussion). Physical space is not a homogenous repository of objects, it is a structured realm of possible trajectories, tools, and doings, and it is in this strong sense that the mind must be regarded as *physically embedded or situated*.

In the last stage, the intrinsically social nature of the mind is brought to light. Human activity is responsive to social practices and to the particular individuals we are, directly or indirectly, connected with. Foremost among social practices is language, but the most ordinary tools and pieces of equipment are permeated with socially determined uses and purposes: as Heidegger stresses, equipment invariably is equipment-for. Paths are both to-be-treaded-on-by-me and historical traces of social activity projecting backward and forward. The mind is now seen as *socially and culturally embedded or situated*.

So finally, according to Dreyfus, we are beginning to comprehend the full implications of Merleau-Ponty's somewhat cryptic claim that "[t]he life of consciousness – cognitive life, the life of desire or perceptual life – is subtended by an "intentional arc" which projects round about us our past, our future, our human setting, our physical, ideological and moral situation" (Merleau-Ponty 1962: 136; quoted by Dreyfus in Wrathall and Kelly 1996).

But *how* does the embodied, embedded, and multiply situated mind actually accomplish the remarkable feats it is credited with? This is not a question to which Dreyfus or any of his followers claim to have an answer: it is the job of science to uncover the material basis of these capacities. However, there is a proposal which goes some way toward bridging the gap. Intelligent behavior, the proper comportment in a given situation, may result from an ability to match the situation to one sufficiently and relevantly similar among a stored repertory of previously encountered situations. Much more needs to be said about this, but space allows us to do no more than stress the priority given in this conjecture to active perception and pattern matching. Provided this intermediary level of description is phenomenologically and conceptually secured, the question then arises of how to connect it with a causally more basic level. One possibility is to move directly to the neural level and search for the processes in the brain responsible for the abilities in question. Another is to construct intermediate models, systems which are in turn realizable in the neural tissue: such is strategy of (a certain brand of) connectionism, as we will see presently.

In the end, the traditional intellectualist view of the mind, culminating in classical AI, is seen to be, as Merleau-Ponty says, not so much utterly false as abstract. In fact, the claim is that it gets things exactly backward: first comes the engaged body, tuned to its environment through constant adjustments involving perception–action arcs, skillfully coping with situations in a world which it inhabits and shares with others; second come a series of disengaging procedures which gradually make space for a detached intellect reflecting on context-independent facts in order to discover, by deliberate and conscious search, a solution to a given problem and to implement this solution through an appropriate sequence of actions. Far from being the more basic mode, reflective problem-solving is an advanced elaboration, requiring the deployment of sophisticated cognitive tools and techniques such as a logically-reformed language use, record-keeping, writing, calculating, etc. But further, the traditional account of such cogitative processes is no more than a rational reconstruction, a "model" of the competence deployed, not a phenomenologically true description of the performance, nor a scientific-psychological account of it. In the accomplishment of abstract intellectual tasks, our skills for coping are brought to bear, whether in the analytical set-up of the problem to be solved, in the application of the rules most likely to uncover candidate solutions, or in the final decision to select and apply one of them: it takes a distinctive know-how to put knowings-that to good use (or to any use at all, for that matter).

A Methodological Interlude. Threesomes

It may seem at this juncture that the issues are fairly clearly delineated, and that it only remains for AI/Cogsci to draw the lesson by making the required adjustments in its assumptions and the scope of its empirical investigations (or else show that the phenomenological accounts are, wholly or partly, mistaken). In fact, as hinted in the introduction, this is not at all the way things are going. The problem situation is vastly more complicated. The main reason is that what, in the context described above, appeared as forming a unity, has come apart and turned out to be a plurality.

Dreyfus correctly saw in GOFAI a technological venture aiming for intelligent computing systems, as well as a research program within scientific psychology, and to boot a set of foundational assumptions amounting to a doctrine in the philosophy of mind. But while even then AI was only notionally or programmatically, in the eyes of its more ambitious and articulate proponents, technology, science, and philosophy rolled into one, it gradually transpired, in the 1970s and 1980s, that there were in fact three distinct areas with admittedly active exchanges between them as well as border regions. This is perhaps not always clearly perceived outside the concerned areas, due in part to a variable and misleading terminology, in part to an objective historical evolution.

Terminology first. "Cognitive science" took hold gradually, beginning in the mid-1970s, and stabilized to its present, still somewhat uncertain, definition, only a decade later. Initially, it was barely distinguishable from "cognitive psychology," itself a very recent creation (1967). Cognitive psychology was understood then as the new, computational-informational approach in the psychology of cognitive processes, themselves construed in a restricted sense as those which subtend the formation and treatment of knowledge (and more generally, belief). Cognitive psychology was thus more than just a part of psychology (on a par with such branches of scientific psychology as clinical or social or differential psychology): it was a research program, or, in Kuhn's sense (Kuhn 1962), a "paradigm" or a "disciplinary matrix" within psychology, and the Siamese twin of (early) AI. Actually, by the time the locution had been coined, cognitive psychology had begun to separate from AI, and reidentified some of its roots in previous traditions within psychology (from Vygotsky to Piaget, and including, in fact, parts of behaviorism). Similarly, cognitive science in the beginning was restricted to a (slightly broader) paradigm, what might be called an "interdisciplinary matrix": it referred to the study of mental processes conducted in the framework of the computational-representational theory of mind, also known, thanks to John Haugeland, as "cognitivism." Although psychology occupied the center of this new program, it crucially involved linguistics, as well as AI, the brain sciences (not yet dubbed "neuroscience"), philosophy, and some tidbits from the social sciences. For the purposes of the present chapter, let us call this program Cogsci-1, so as to clearly distinguish it from the construal most current today, labeled here Cogsci-2, which is like Cogsci-1 but with no commitment to cognitivism. Whether it is conceptually unproblematic to proceed in this way (which implicitly appeals to such precedents as physics, biology or geology, which don't come, on the face of it, with strings attached to any particular "physicalism," "biologism," or "geologism") is a genuine issue which cannot be discussed here. *De facto*, many practitioners of Cogsci-2 regard cognitivism as no more than a school, a set of assumptions to be accepted or rejected piecemeal *ad libitum*, or again as a cohesive paradigm within their discipline, but in no way a condition of its existence.

Historical changes now. AI has undergone a profound overhaul. First, it has shed its "Promethean" ambition, or rather, it has ceased making it an official goal. The new frontier within AI now concerns "intelligent" cognitive prostheses, aids for the human agent, and falls under the wider label of applied cognitive science. Part of the old AI is indistinguishable from software engineering; the remainder is divided between applied logic and natural language processing and is a province of Cogsci. The Promethean inspiration has moved to Artificial Life and more recently to Artificial Consciousness, with very limited effect on Cogsci. Finally, AI has taken on board connectionism (see Rumelhart et al. 1986; Smolensky and Legendre 2005), and tries to federate all the new modeling techniques useful in Cogsci; unfortunately for the new AI, the most powerful methods are wielded by physicists, who tend to deal directly with the neuroscientists, with whom they share the intuition that modeling the brain is a safer bet than simulating the mind.

Cogsci-2 is opportunistic, as mature sciences are wont to be. It has broadened its scope to include not only just about every respectable topic in scientific psychology, including "hot" cognition (emotions, motivation, etc.), consciousness, animal cognition, and the origins of mind, but also entirely novel themes.

Finally, philosophy of mind has expanded enormously; it follows Cogsci opportunistically, but also pursues an agenda of its own, which makes room for every conceivable ontological option, including dualism. There is no trace left of its former role of handmaiden to cognitivism.

Thus, instead of one doctrine uniting the efforts of philosophers and scientists (somewhat like the mechanical philosophy around Descartes's and Galileo's time), the camp which was challenged by Dreyfus and his followers from the mid-1960s to the late 1980s has split up into three disciplines, each of which has diversified and expanded beyond recognition. Inspiration, penetration, or critique by phenomenology will thus take on different forms according to the particular disciplinary or doctrinal province of the cognitive "galaxy" one is concerned with.

On the side of phenomenology, in contrast with the Dreyfus line strongly moored in the works and intentions of the original movement, there are at present, besides extensions and variations of this authentic inspiration, two diluted varieties at work in the field of cognition. Phenomenology-1 is no more than the consideration of consciousness, *qualia*, and the first-person reports of introspection, the structure of intentional states, etc.; it demands no connection at all with philosophical phenomenology; in fact, one can claim to be in that sense a phenomenologically inclined philosopher of cognition or cognitive scientist without having read a line of Husserl, Heidegger, or Merleau-Ponty. Phenomenology-2 consists in attempts to domesticate typically phenomenological themes in the cognitive culture; for example, embodiment, or concern, or shared intention, or equipment, with some of their attendant properties, might be designated as requiring sustained attention, without the need being felt to attend to these phenomena in the style and with the tools of phenomenology. Phenomenology-3, finally, is the approach illustrated originally by Dreyfus, and pursued with increasing intensity by the current which he created and by some more recently formed schools.

To a first approximation, the three shades of phenomenological interventions correspond to three kinds of effects on Cogsci. Phenomenology-1 is a *heuristic* device for Cogsci: it merely suggests the inclusion of new phenomena to the agenda. Phenomenology-2 brings in *constraints*: insofar as it suggests not only some phenomenon, but a requirement that its central aspects be taken into account, a phenomenological-2 contribution will typically impose on the cognitive-scientific

385

accounts involving the phenomenon the obligation to take care of its phenomeno-logical properties. Finally, the sense of a phenomenological-3 intervention is to pro-pose, or impose, ontological or metaphysical options. Admittedly, the boundaries are fuzzy and permeable; still, there are clear-cut differences between central cases. But the massive influx of phenomenology-1 and -2 may be in the process of inducing in Cogsci changes of a magnitude such that the effects are no less than what one would expect from a successful phenomenological-3 therapy. Perhaps, if this turns out to be the case, one should conclude that cognitive scientists will have rediscovered on their own some of the guiding intuitions of the great phenomenologists. On the other hand, such an outcome raises the question of the internal consistency of Cogsci thus revised: will it not require serious readjustments, the reexamination of some of its results, and the abandonment of some of its classical tenets? This would be reminiscent of what physics underwent during the nineteenth century, when it had finally to shed the remains of the mechanistic philosophy which had kept developing during the eight-eenth century side by side with Newtonianism. But this "new Cogsci" will not likely resemble anything like a pure natural science, and may be something like a morphed interpolation of brain science and phenomenology, within which what we now still think of as scientific psychology will have undergone a complete transformation. This remains, however, quite speculative, and the remainder of the chapter will be devoted to ongoing, documented developments.

A Sample of Phenomenologically Inspired Interventions in Cognitive Science

Phenomenology-1

A list of themes which have recently made it to the top of Cogsci's agenda would include consciousness, emotions, culture and distributed cognition, and social cogni-tion. On all of these, save occasionally the first, there is no visible trace of an influence from phenomenological writings, vocabulary, or style of inquiry.

Consciousness in this context is approached mostly in functional or operational terms, with heavy emphasis on neuroscientific studies. There are many "theories" and "models" of consciousness on the market, few if any of which include anything like a careful phenomenological examination of the phenomena. On the other hand, there is an abundant literature on "phenomenal" consciousness, the "explanatory gap" which seems to separate it from any conceivable scientific account, and the "hard problem" this raises.

Emotions has also been an explosive topic, with contributions from conceptually as well as empirically minded philosophers, evolutionary biologists, anthropologists, and neuroscientists. The important insight procured is that emotions should not be seen as a set of phenomena separate from cognitive processes or faculties, but an integral part of the mind, so that even the seemingly plausible divide between "cold" and "hot" cognition should be abandoned.

Individual cognitive processes are increasingly seen as highly dependent, or even derivative, on populational phenomena. Cognition is thought to be in part, or for some authors in essence, a distributed process, involving entire populations of individual minds (or perhaps one should say people, or organisms) and things, whether culturally enrolled natural objects and processes or artifacts. The radical view here is that all cognition is intrinsically social (see Hutchins 1995); the moderate view is that there is an important family of processes which constitute an integrated realm of socially supported cognition.

Social cognition also refers to the bases, in individual minds, of the perception and understanding of people as agents; in more traditional language, one wants to understand what in the mind of individuals makes them capable of supporting intersubjectivity. The field began with the realization that social interactions among apes, or other creatures without language such as infants, heavily depend on the ability of an individual A to attribute to a conspecific B views, i.e., beliefs, desires, and intentions, of its own, in particular, of holding about a given state of affairs beliefs which differ from A's. Without such a "theory of mind," it is said, the social life of individuals is quite limited (as in the case of apes), or impaired (as in the case of autistic children). Recently, the basis and resources of this "naïve psychology" (as this ability or set of abilities is also known) have been further explored. Of particular interest is the discovery of "mirror neurons" in macaque premotor cortex (Rizzolatti et al. 2001), and the postulation of similar "mirror systems" in humans, which are seen by some as providing the neurophysiological basis for the identification of a conspecific's intentions, and possibly of one own's intentions, no longer considered to be known on the basis of an incorrigible first-person report or intuition. Another line of inquiry is pursued by Michael Tomasello (1999), whose conjecture is that the basis of intersubjectivity is the much more powerful faculty of identifying, and participating in, *shared* intentions – an instance of the general trend of seeing action as more basic for cognition than knowledge or belief.

Phenomenology-2

Action is indeed a key idea, perhaps the single most important factor in the renewal of Cogsci. It seems that sheer reflection has oriented many analytic philosophers, and subsequently or in parallel some cognitive scientists, toward the rejection of the modular view propounded by GOFAI and cognitivism, according to which action is nothing but the result of a planned sequence of motor episodes accomplished by mindless effectors under instructions from Central Control. Actionist views, whose roots plunge in the past of physiology and medicine, but were also adumbrated by Piaget and Merleau-Ponty, among others, are now occupying center stage. What justifies their inclusion under "phenomenology-2" is the fact that, while acknowledging no direct indebtedness to phenomenology in the historical sense (with some exceptions, as we shall see), they start with detailed, unprejudiced examinations of the structure of action, and only then ask how Cogsci can accommodate the phenomenological data thus acquired.

Some examples of currrent action-based research programs are theories of "active perception" (O'Regan and Noë 2001); the "new robotics" (Brooks 2002); theories of motor control (Jacob and Jeannerod 2003). They all lead directly to deep and controversial questions about four related topics of central philosophical significance, which space unfortunately does not permit me to discuss here. One is whether we should continue to think of representations as playing a role in, or (as cognitivism holds), quite simply defining, cognition. Antirepresentationalism has for many years been a rallying cry of nay-sayers and rebels of all stripes, and constitutes a common ground for thinkers coming from phenomenology, and insiders to AI and Cogsci. Unfortunately, nobody could agree, for a long time, on exactly what this amounted to. Somewhat like antipsychologism at the turn of the nineteenth century, of which every proponent (there were many) kept accusing the others of being insufficiently firm in their conviction, of still being in the grips of the fatal mistake, antirepresentationalism has been something of a flag over whose possession the rival chapels have been fighting over. Recent developments in empirical Cogsci afford a much better chance to treat the issue in a less ideological manner. The second, very closely related, general issue, bears on the notions of non-conceptual content of thought and thought without language. The third question, also in the immediate vicinity, is that of the body. *Embodied* cognition is another program, research topic, and rallying cry for many. Analytic philosophers and mainstream cognitive scientists by the hundreds are working at spelling out the implications of the idea that cognition is a property *of* a body *for* a body, and brush shoulders with "professional" phenomenologists as well as roboticians and "ALifers" (specialists of Artifical Life). "Virtual reality," a tool for investigating perceptual and motor capacities in unnatural environments, is also a means to ask questions about "presence," something to do with a property of objects and persons over and above any of their attributes. The fourth issue concerns autonomy, and the related themes of self-organization and selfhood. On all of these issues, empirical and philosophical inquiries feed one another and in some estimates are profoundly changing the state of play.

We have just listed, under the headings of phenomenology 1 and 2, a rather over-whelming array of new themes, directions, and proposals. It then becomes an issue whether these sometimes connected, sometimes disparate ways of breaking away from the cognitivist tradition can be integrated into a common vision. This is a challenge which has not gone unmet. There are on offer quite a number of proposals for an integrated account, or at least for programs aiming at providing such an account. For the sake of exposition, they can be grouped under three headings: philosophy, science, models.

Philosophical treatments proceed by identifying a master theme to which all or most of the proposals found acceptable can be related. The most popular theme is externalism: philosophers have been arguing for a long time, and from various types of consideration, in favor of (sometimes restricted) versions of externalism (also labeled "anti-individualism"), contrasted with "solipsistic" conceptions of the mind. The new perspectives reported in this chapter plead in favor of a generalized form of externalism. One example of a global philosophical treatment along the externalist line is McClamrock (1995). This work sits on the borderline between type 2 and type 3 phenomenological interventions: developed almost in its entirety in purely cognitive-scientific analytic style, it concludes with a brief section in which the historical phenomenological sources are quoted. It also shares with phenomenology a sensitivity to the interplay between ontology (how the world is cut up in regions) and naturalistic epistemology (how the embedded subject becomes acquainted with, by makes himself at home in, the world). This show of genuine phenomenology is typical of the synthetic attempts described here: (historical) phenomenology can hardly be totally ignored by someone trying to bring all these proto-phenomenological attempts under one roof. Another synthesis, this one inspired by philosophy of science as well as a generally ecological perspective, it that of Sunny Auyang (2001).

The best-rounded synthesis is that by Andy Clark (1997), a philosopher well-versed in Cogsci and not so interested in foundational issues. Clark provides a sketch of what Cogsci might look like if enough of the promises made are kept, and enough overall consistency is maintained. One theme which he weaves in, and which space does not allow me to develop in this chapter, is the contribution of neuroscience. It raises foundational problems which are left wide open by Clark, and to which there are today no agreed-upon solutions. Another synthesis straddling philosophy and Cogsci/AI, and taking as its unifying theme the emotions, is DeLancey (2002).

On the AI-modeling side, there are three broad directions of integrative research. The oldest and best-established, connectionism (or neural-net modeling, sometimes also called neurocomputation), grew out of a tradition (see Anderson and Rosenfeld 1989), with no direct links with phenomenology, and in response to phenomenological-2 considerations, but has been greeted by Dreyfus, among others, as a partial fulfillment of the constraints brought to light by (genuine or strict) phenomenological inspection. Neural nets are essentially plastic perception machines which learn by exposure to specific cases, and do not rely on rigid rules; they exhibit a number of properties, such as context-sensitivity and graceful degradation (their performance does not degrade catastrophically, like classical AI programs, when the circumstances of the problem at hand begin to drift away from the normal conditions, those of the learning phase). They are not "mentalistic" in that they do not rely on the classical notion of representation, they are devoid of anything like a central control unit, they proceed in a massively parallel fashion, and they exhibit a degree of self-organization. However, Dreyfus notes that their disembodiment (they are, after all, nothing other than programs implementable on a regular computer) stands in the way of their ever becoming true analogs of human intelligence.

This is exactly the objection which the "new robotics" program associated with Rodney Brooks and his collaborators at the MIT AI Lab (2002) intends to crush in the egg, by starting with a body (the robot) with primitive sensors and effectors, and inviting it to learn and pick up novel, emerging cognitive capacities by interacting (in "flesh") with the world. Unsurprisingly, Brooks advertises a radical antirepresentationalism; with other ecologically oriented thinkers such as O'Regan and Noë, he credits Dreyfus with the insight he is working out: the (real) world is its own "best model." There is no argument there against anything which has a claim on being a *serious* representationalist view, but the emphasis on real-time, in-flesh interaction has both biological and phenomenological plausibility.

Finally, we come almost the full round by returning to AI. AI was under intense pressure to reform: it wasn't working, and Dreyfus has given reasons why it shouldn't. Unlike science and unlike philosophy, a technology cannot survive defeat for very long. Many researchers realized that the mind they were trying to emulate was too impoverished for the models it inspired them to be of any use in the "real world." As a result, there were a number of attempts to build models with "consciousness," "emotions," "involvement," etc., and this is still going on. But the more interesting current is the one initiated by Terry Winograd and Fernando Flores (1986), who took their inspiration directly from Dreyfus's phenomenological account and to some lesser extent from Searle's theory of speech acts, which has a strong actionist component. The "existential AI" advocated by Winograd and Flores is realistic enough to forego the pretension of building self-sufficient intelligent artifacts, and is content to aim for "intelligent", i.e., adaptive, useful, interfacing tools for working communities. In this endeavor, they put phenomenological descriptions of engagement, thrownness, commitment, equipment, etc., to interesting use: a suitably programmed computer is first and foremost a piece of equipment, and an understanding of tool-use is a prerequisite, it would seem, for the manufacture of useable tools ("usability" has indeed become a central concern of computer and communication technologies). There is, however, the shadow of a possible paradox here: if the lesson from existential phenomenology is that theory is not the royal route to practices (and surely kayaks, hammers, pubs, and even guns did not result from better theories), perhaps theorizing about the right sort of software is not the right way to get it. There is a mirror-image to this apparent paradox: when von Neumann was told that there was something wrong with his machine, he rhetorically asked to know *exactly* what was missing (the obvious implication being that with this information in hand, the machine could be fixed). It is far from obvious that there is a way out of these dual conundrums.

Phenomenology-3

As we near the end of this chapter, we come to what some would regard as the philosophical core of its topic: what can (genuine, historical, strict) phenomenology contribute *today* to Cogsci, and in virtue of which of its features? As a very partial answer, complementing the first part of the chapter, some directions of inquiry pursued within a European school of "naturalized phenomenology" in the spirit of Husserl rather than Heidegger will be briefly presented (see Petitot et al. 1999).

The first is formal ontology. This project of Husserl's (see Chapter 2) is being revived by scholars of Austrian philosophy before and beyond Husserl, and incorporates themes from ecological vision (Gibson 1979) as well as Gestalt psychology. Mereology is a central part of the project (see Smith 1982), but it turns out that there are many domains, such as places (Casati and Varzi 1999), sounds (Casati and Dokic 1994), holes (Casati and Varzi 1994), shadows (Casati 2003), objects . . . which are in need of a formal characterization. The immediate applications concern semantics and perception, and the possible relation between them.

Another project takes up directly from Husserl, and attempts to enroll the tools of contemporary mathematical physics to show that Husserl's objections to the naturalization of eidetic contents were based on an outdated stage of scientific development, and that physics has now the means to detect the objective morphological structures in the natural processes subtending perception which alone can be put in correspondence with the eidetic contents. The optic flux is not an amorphous sheaf of energy; it possesses enough structure to allow the visual system to "interpret" the "sense data," and today's mathematical physics can provide an objective account of this interpretative process.

However, the most popular route from Husserl and Merleau-Ponty to Cogsci, within this school of thought, goes through the analysis and examination of the various modes and levels of intentionality. Here are a couple of examples of what Gallagher (1997) calls, after Varela et al. (1991), "mutual illumination" between Cogsci and phenomenology. Sean Kelly examines Merleau-Ponty's account of "motor intentionality" and the body's tendency toward maximum grip as an experiential equilibrium, and shows how it supports, and is in turn supported by, the account of visual perception by cognitive neuroscientists such as Milner and Goodale, and such dynamic brain models as Walter Freeman's, which involve chaotic attractors. The second example is the parallel which Ron McClamrock draws between Husserl's conception of the relation between noesis and noema and Cogsci's intuitions about multiple realizability (several physical processes filling the same cognitive function) and context-dependence (one physical process filling different cognitive functions). Another example is Tim van Gelder's account of time consciousness based on second-hand summaries of Husserl's work (in Petitot et al.1999). Such attempts raise a couple of questions about the possibility and meaning of "naturalizing" Husserl against his own expressed intentions. One is whether such an enterprise is coherent; whether it really is possible to peel apart the side of Husserl's thought which can be put to use in Cogsci from his anti-naturalistic arguments. The second concerns the chances of success of a naturalized version of Husserl. On this last point, opinions differ: Petitot et al. disagree with Dreyfus's cognitivist-representationalist interpretation of Husserl. On the first question, there are other disagreements: here Petitot and Dreyfus find themselves in the same camp, together with (to some extent and under proper reading) Daubert, Merleau-Ponty, Aron Gurwitsch, Ervin Straus, or Roger Chambon, facing opposition by what remains to this day a vast majority of Husserl scholars.

However, these issues concern phenomenology more than they do Cogsci, whose sole interest is to take clues anywhere it can find them to make progress in its quest for scientific advances. And this leads to a final question, which concerns the weight of phenomenological reports as prima facie, defeasible evidence to which Cogsci is bound, pending countermanding instructions from psychology or neuroscience. Considering the plain fact that every cognitive scientist starts with some rudimentary form of phenomenological account, is it not a case of misplaced methodological perfectionism to bar more refined accounts from the scientific process?

Note

1 This statement was made in a speech at MIT (see http://www.wired.com/news/technology/0,1282,58714,00.html).

References and Further Reading

Anderson, J., and Rosenfeld, E. (eds.) (1989) *Neurocomputing: Foundations of Research.* Cambridge, MA: MIT Press.

Andler, D. (2000) The normativity of context. *Philosophical Studies,* 100, 273–303.

Andler, D., ed. (2004) *Introduction aux sciences cognitives.* Paris: Gallimard.

Auyang, S. Y. (2001) *Mind in Everyday Life and Cognitive Science.* Cambridge, MA: MIT Press.

Baars, B. J., Banks, W. P., and Newman, J. B. (eds.) (2003) *Essential Sources in the Scientific Study of Consciousness*. Cambridge, MA: MIT Press.

Bechtel, W., and Graham, G., eds. (1998) *A Companion to Cognitive Science*. Oxford: Blackwell.

Bermúdez, J. L. (2003) *Thinking Without Words*. Oxford: Oxford University Press.

Bermúdez, J. L., Marcel, A., and Eilan, N. (eds.) (1995) *The Body and the Self*. Cambridge, MA: MIT Press.

Berthoz, A. (2000) *The Brain's Sense of Movement*. Cambridge, MA: Harvard University Press (original work published 1997).

Block, N., Flanagan, J., and Güzeldere, G., eds. (1997) *The Nature of Consciousness: Philosophical Debates*. Cambridge, MA: MIT Press.

Brooks, R. (2002) *Flesh and Machines. How Robots Will Change Us*. New York: Vintage Books.

Carruthers, P., and Smith, P. K. (eds.) (1995) *Theories of Theories of Mind*. Cambridge: Cambridge University Press.

Casati, R. (2003) *The Shadow Club*. New York: Knopf.

Casati, R. and Dokic, J. (1994) *La philosophie du son*. Nîmes: Chambon.

Casati, R. and Varzi, A. (1994) *Holes and Other Superficialities*. Cambridge, MA: MIT Press.

—— (1999) *Parts and Places: The Structures of Spatial Representation*. Cambridge, MA: MIT Press.

Chambon, R. (1974) *Le Monde comme perception et réalité*. Paris: Vrin.

Clark, A. (1997) *Being There. Putting Brain, Body, and World Together Again*. Cambridge, MA: MIT Press.

Davidson, R. J., Scherer, K. R., and Goldsmith, H. H. (eds.) (2003) *Handbook of Affective Sciences*. Oxford: Oxford University Press.

DeLancey, C. (2002) *Passionate Engines. What Emotions Reveal about the Mind and Artificial Intelligence*. Oxford: Oxford University Press.

Dennett, D. C. (1991) *Consciousness Explained*. Boston: Little, Brown.

Dreyfus, H. L. (1972) *What Computers Can't Do. A Critique of Artificial Reason*. New York: Harper & Row. Revised edn. 1979, augmented edn. 1992, *What Computers Still Can't Do*. Cambridge, MA: MIT Press.

Dreyfus, H. L. (ed.) (1982) *Husserl, Intentionality and Cognitive Science*. Cambridge, MA: MIT Press.

Dreyfus, H. L., and Dreyfus, S. E. (1986) *Mind over Machine. The Power of Human Intuition and Expertise in the Era of the Computer*. Glencoe, IL: Free Press.

Fodor, J. A. (1983) *The Modularity of Mind*. Cambridge, MA: MIT Press.

Freeman, W. J. (1999) *How Brains Make Up Their Minds*. London: Weidenfeld & Nicolson.

Gallagher, S. (1997) Mutual enlightenment: Recent phenomenology in cognitive science. *Journal of Consciousness Studies*, 3, 195–214.

Gibson. J. J. (1979) *The Ecological Approach to Visual Perception*. Boston: Houghton Mifflin.

Griffiths, P. (1997) *What Emotions Really Are*. Chicago: University of Chicago Press.

Gurwitsch, A. (1966) *Studies in Phenomenology and Psychology*. Evanston, IL: Northwestern University Press.

Haugeland, J. (1985) *Artificial Intelligence. The Very Idea*. Cambridge, MA: MIT Press.

Haugeland, J. (ed.) (1981) *Mind Design*. Cambridge, MA: MIT Press.

Hutchins, E. (1995) *Cognition in the Wild*. Cambridge, MA: MIT Press.

Jacob, P., and Jeannerod, M. (2003) *Ways of Seeing: The Scope and Limits of Visual Cognition*. Oxford: Oxford University Press.

Kuhn, T. (1962) *The Structure of Scientific Revolutions*. Chicago: University of Chicago Press.

Levine, J. (2004) *Purple Haze: The Puzzle of Consciousness*. Oxford: Oxford University Press.

McClamrock, R. (1995) *Existential Cognition*. Chicago and London: Chicago University Press.

Mele, A. (1992) *Springs of Action: Understanding Intentional Behavior*. Oxford: Oxford University Press.

392

Merleau-Ponty, M. (1962) *The Phenomenology of Perception* (trans. C. Smith). London: Routledge & Kegan Paul (original work published 1945).

Neisser, U., Fivush, R., and Hirst, W. (eds.) (1999) *Ecological Approaches to Cognition: Essays in Honor of Ulric Neisser*. Mahwah, NJ: Lawrence Erlbaum.

O'Regan, J. K., & Noë, A. (2001) A sensorimotor account of vision and visual consciousness. *Behavioral and Brain Sciences*, 24(5), 939–1011.

Petitot, J., Varela, F. J., Pachoud, B., and Roy, J-M. (eds.) (1999) *Naturalizing Phenomenology: Issues in Contemporary Phenomenology and Cognitive Science*. Stanford, CA: Stanford University Press.

Port, R. F., and van Gelder, T. (eds.) (1995) *Mind as Motion: Explorations in the Dynamics of Cognition*. Cambridge, MA: MIT Press.

Pylyshyn, Z. (1984) *Computation and Cognition. Toward a Foundation for Cognitive Science*. Cambridge, MA: MIT Press.

Rizzolatti, G., Fogassi, L., and Gallese, V. (2001) Neurophysiological mechanisms underlying the understanding and imitation of action. *Nature Neuroscience Reviews*, 2, 661–70.

Rumelhart, D, McClelland, J., and PDP Research Group (1986) *Parallel Distributed Processing. The Microstructure of Cognition*, 2 vols. Cambridge, MA: MIT Press.

Searle, J. (1983) *Intentionality: An Essay in the Philosophy of Mind*. Cambridge: Cambridge University Press.

Smith, B. (ed.) (1982) *Parts and Moments. Studies in Logic and Formal Ontology*. Munich: Philosophia.

Smolensky, P., and Legendre, G. (2005) *The Harmonic Mind*, Cambridge, MA: MIT Press.

Tomasello, M. (1999) *The Cultural Origins of Human Cognition*. Cambridge, MA: Harvard University Press.

Varela, F., Thompson, E., and Rosch, E. (1991) *The Embodied Mind. Cognitive Science and Human Experience*. Cambridge, MA: MIT Press.

Weiskrantz. L. (1988) *Thought Without Language*. Cambridge: Cambridge University Press.

Winograd, T., and Flores, F. (1986) *Understanding Computers and Cognition. A New Foundation for Design*. Norwood, NJ: Ablex (repr. Reading, MA: Addison-Wesley, 1987).

Wittgenstein, L. (1953) *Philosophical Investigations*. London: Macmillan.

Wrathall, M., and Kelly, S. (eds.) (1996) *Existential Phenomenology and Cognitive Science*, special issue, *Electronic Journal of Analytic Philosophy*. http://ejap.louisiana.edu/EJAP/1996.spring

Wrathall, M., and Malpas, J. (eds.) (2000) *Heidegger, Coping, and Cognitive Science, Essays in Honor of Hubert L. Dreyfus*. Cambridge, MA: MIT Press.

27

Phenomenological Currents in Twentieth-Century Psychology

FREDERICK J. WERTZ

In this chapter, we will first discuss the historical development of phenomenological and existential approaches in psychology. We will describe the contributions of seminal philosophers and the early European schools that were conversant with the movement. We will detail the impact of phenomenological thought in psychiatry. Then we will discuss the growing breadth of phenomenological work across diverse psychological subject matters. We place particular stress on the development of qualitative research methods for psychology by phenomenologically oriented psychologists.

A Brief Historical Narrative

Psychology traces its modern origin to the founding of the first psychological laboratory by Wilhelm Wundt in Leipzig in 1879. This development was prepared by the psychophysicists Gustav Fechner and Hermann Helmholtz, who initially applied the quantitative methods of natural science to psychological phenomena in the search for universal laws. This event is also celebrated as the moment when psychology broke away from philosophy, became a separate discipline, and took its place among the positive sciences. Currently, ambiguity and debate remain concerning psychology's identity, but the discipline is widely recognized as a science that tests hypotheses or explores relationships among variables by using quantitative analysis.

Historians of psychology have been giving increasing attention to the discipline's lack of univocality. Wundt himself did not believe that the experimental method was appropriate for all psychological subject matter and developed other methods for such "higher" processes as language in his "folk psychology" (see Wundt 1916). However, largely due to the work of his student Edward Titchener, Wundt's experimental psychology, called "structuralism," was imported to the United States and spread widely through American Universities (though some phenomenological work did take place in Titchener's Cornell lab, e.g., Edmonds and Smith 1923). Generations of American psychologists learned the history of psychology through an influential textbook written by Titchener's student, E. G. Boring. Boring viewed the entire field from the vantage point of experimental psychology. As a result, he neglected much of Wundt's work and considered such early "functionalist" American psychologists as William James and John Dewey only in light of the trajectory of the dominant natural scientific psychology as it evolved through the study of conditioned reflexes and operant conditioning in the school of behaviorism, an approach which ignored subjectivity (methodological behaviorism) or asserted that mental life does not exist (radical behaviorism). As the mental testing movement and applied quantitative procedures developed in the United States, such alternative European approaches as psychoanalysis and Gestalt psychology were downplayed or ignored. The dialogue between psychology and philosophy remained dormant in mainstream American psychology until the late 1970s, and even today it remains a concern of only a small minority of psychologists. The most common view that psychology is an empirical science on a par with biology and its applied field of medicine has yielded considerable social status and competitive, economic advantage.

European psychology, in contrast, did not wholly identify with physical science. Some philosophers, such as Wilhelm Dilthey (1833–1911), insisted on the *difference* between disciplines that focus on human phenomena and those that study nature. One of the leading competitors to Wundt's structuralism was the "act psychology" of Franz Brentano (1838–1917), who insisted that mental life does not resemble physical objects and that a genuine psychology would have to be based on an understanding of its irreducibly unique characteristics, such as intentionality and meaning. One of Brentano's most well known and productive students, Sigmund Freud, did just that. Freud's psychoanalytic movement grew, changing through the twentieth century, and generated vast resources of psychological knowledge. This knowledge, however, was passed on to new generations in the field of psychiatry and in postgraduate institutes. Psychoanalysts have largely been practitioners, psychotherapists engaged in scholarship outside of academic psychology, which identified the movement with its theories and occasionally tested them, with mixed results, using the same methods that were universally required in the "legitimate science" of academic psychology. Moreover, psychoanalytic theorizing itself borrowed uncritically from the natural sciences rather than explicitly challenging psychology's natural scientific orientation and developing a formal alternative to its established research methodology. Psychoanalysis did not acknowledge its rootedness in Brentano's tradition, recognize itself as offering an alternative conception of human science, or carry on a conversation with twentieth-century philosophers until recently.

The other generative student of Brentano, Edmund Husserl (1859–1938), originally a mathematician, began his philosophical career around the turn of the century as both a response and a contribution to the institution of Western science. Husserl explicitly called for broadening the enterprise of science beyond the concepts and methods of the physical sciences and for a psychology that does not reify mental life. Psychology occupied a special place in Husserl's work, from his first *Logical Investigations* (1970), through his more mature *Ideas* (1962) and *Phenomenological Psychology* (1977), to his posthumously published *Crisis of European Sciences and Transcendental Phenomenology* (1954), in which he approaches the mother philosophical discipline of transcendental phenomenology through the science of psychology. Husserl formulates scientific methods that, in contrast to those borrowed from natural science, are uniquely fashioned to investigate the intentionality and meaning-structures of subjectivity and human experience.

The key features of Husserl's phenomenological science of experience, which he recognized as crucially important for psychology, are its being descriptive, reflective, and eidetic. The psychology that has evolved in this tradition abstains from naturalistic and hypothetical thought of all kinds (by employing the epoché of the natural sciences) and describes experience as it is concretely lived, that is, according to its meanings and the subjective performances that constitute those meanings (by employing the epoché of the natural attitude). Psychologists learned from Husserl that in order to grasp what is distinctive about their subject matter, the procedures of deduction and induction as well as any fact gathering and mathematization would be insufficient. Psychological science must be informed by eidetic intuition, that is, a grasp of the essential qualities of mental life, by employing the method of free imaginative variation. For instance, in the study of anger, a psychologist would begin with an example of a person being angry and imaginatively vary its features, noting those without which anger is no longer present, in order to determine the essential qualities of anger. It might be recognized that anger involves an intention to oppose an unjust and unnecessary situational threat to something valued by the self. The most fundamental essential quality of mental life, according to Husserl, is its "intentionality," its self-transcendence. As Husserl described consciousness, it is always consciousness *of something* (beyond itself), a quality utterly lacking in physical nature. By carrying out intentional analyses of numerous subject matter such as perception, imagination, emotion, action, and judgment, Husserl opened up the vast realm of experiences whose meanings and the subjective performances giving rise to them could be rigorously known. In these analyses, Husserl gained the important insight that consciousness cannot be reduced to its actualities but includes potentialities. The "I can" is a fundamental structure of lived experience: My possibilities are present as objective virtualities of my surroundings. Although much of Husserl's work aimed at philosophical, transcendental issues, he descriptively articulated such psychologically relevant themes as the lifeworld, embodied subjectivity, meaning, empathy, intersubjectivity, and generativity.

Husserl's work engendered a tradition of twentieth-century philosophy whose multifaceted impact on psychology and psychiatry has been elaborated by Spiegelberg (1982, 1972). The philosophers Max Scheler (1874–1928), Martin Heidegger (1889–1976), Jean-Paul Sartre (1905–80), Maurice Merleau-Ponty (1908–61), Alfred Schutz (1899–1959), Emmanuel Levinas (1906–95), and Paul Ricoeur (1913–2005), to name a few, have made extensive contributions to psychology and influenced psychologists working in all subfields. There emerged in Europe, during the first half of the twentieth century, numerous schools of psychology following and conversant with the philosophical, phenomenological movement, but they were disrupted by World War II and did not continue in Europe, where American positivistic psychology has dominated since the post-war reconstruction (Giorgi 2004). Phenomenological and existential currents in Continental thought remained alive, however, in the work of European psychiatrists, whose work crossed the ocean and captured the attention of American clinical psychiatry and psychology around the mid-twentieth century.

Although a few isolated scholar/researchers in mainstream academic psychology, such as Robert McLeod, began to develop a phenomenological approach at the grassroots level, it was not until the Dutch Adrian Van Kaam emigrated to the United States and founded a doctoral program in Phenomenological Psychology at Duquesne University that the institutionalization of that approach began to play a role in psychology proper (Cloonan 1995). The most significant development of the American phenomenological movement came though the formulation of research methods for psychology by Amedeo Giorgi, for this enabled empirical, scientific (in an expanded phenomenological sense) research to address the full spectrum of psychological subject matter. Although phenomenological and existential approaches remain a small minority viewpoint in contemporary psychology, a number of graduate schools and individual researchers have adopted the approach. Their contributions to the growing pluralism in psychology have included from the start, a close collaboration with phenomenological philosophers.

Contributions of Philosophers

There is probably no movement in philosophy that has produced more significant psychological works than that of existential phenomenology. Beyond Husserl, Martin Heidegger did not himself engage in psychology, but his thinking has been highly influential. Heidegger's early opus, *Being and Time* (1962), is a work in phenomenological ontology. However, its methodical tack – namely, to address the question of the meaning of Being by investigating the Being of the entity questioning Being, *Dasein* – requires and delivers an extensive analysis of *Existence*. As such, Heidegger has provided psychologists with a rich and elaborate, non-Cartesian conceptualization of the character and fundamental dimensions of human existence. In Heidegger's description, Dasein is neither an isolated thing nor even a consciousness but is Existence itself, that is, an intricately structured Being-in-the-world including the ready- and present-to-hand spatiality, sociality, moodedness, understanding, discourse, and temporality, all of which make up a holistic structure whose essence is *Care*. This vision of the "person" has been seized by psychologists studying the full spectrum of the field's topics. For instance, Heidegger teaches us that although our human lives are basically anonymous and collectively structured, we also have the potential to be uniquely individual, and, in our directedness to our finitude and death, our lives – through our engagement in spatiality, sociality, and temporality – can become more authentically our own. In addition, Heidegger's articulation of "the hermeneutic circle," as a phenomenological research method applied in his interpretation of existence, has demonstrated how studies of human being can overcome preconceptions and gain fresh, grounded knowledge. Heidegger's later works on poetry, thought, and technology have also served as a resource for psychologists.

Jean-Paul Sartre, besides being a philosopher and author of fiction, conducted numerous seminal psychological studies. His early Husserlian works of eidetic psychology (Sartre 1948a, 1948b), on the imagination and the emotions, are classics in the field of phenomenological psychology. Sartre finds in the imagination an actualization of human freedom par excellence, in its ability to project the unreal. His study highlights the magical character of the emotional transformation of the world as an alternative to practical action. His early opus, *Being and Nothingness* (1956), a work in phenomenological ontology, includes analyses of many topics that have close bearing on psychology, such as concrete relations with others, the gaze, love, indifference, arrogance, masochism, and human freedom. This work contains a seminal critique of the psychoanalytic concept of "the unconscious" and of any psychology that reifies human subject matter. It culminates in the elaboration of a proper approach to psychology, based on Sartre's ontology, called "existential psychoanalysis." Sartre carried out this program for "personality psychology" in later works on Baudelaire, himself, Flaubert, and Jean Genet. The lives of human beings, Sartre shows, involve original choices or projects that are freely undertaken and may be modified in the course of existence. His later opus, *The Critique of Dialectic Reason* (1976), though not itself psychological, elaborates a "progressive-regressive" method that has influenced psychologists in their attempt to come to terms with the apparent contradictions between social, material conditions and human freedom.

Maurice Merleau-Ponty began his philosophical career in dialogue with all the various schools of psychology in his time, including the psychologies of neurophysiology, behavior, sensation, perception, personality, social relations, language, development, thinking, psychopathology, and the unconscious. Merleau-Ponty (1962, 1963) demonstrated how Cartesian – idealistic and realistic – assumptions have led to unresolvable problems and have hampered psychological analysis. By employing fresh descriptive methods, Merleau-Ponty made contributions to all of the above mentioned areas of psychology. His holistic conceptualization of human behavior as requiring a new concept of the *body-subject* highlights the body that *can*, the body *I am* in contrast to the body I have that is grasped by others. In his study of practical, embodied ways of living toward situations, Merleau-Ponty has helped psychologists overcome the fallacies of mentalism and has provided analyses and conceptual tools that describe the embodied modes of psychological life in which the achievements of human thought and science are rooted. Beyond his early analyses of behavior, perception, neuropathology, and language, while occupying the Chair of Child Psychology at the Sorbonne (later succeeded by Jean Piaget), Merleau-Ponty investigated the child's acquisition of language, the phenomenon of imitation, the development of personality and self, and psychopathology. Merleau-Ponty's posthumously published *Visible and Invisible* offered the psychologists such notions as "flesh" and "the chiasm," that enabled them to even more radically transcend the antinomy of the mental and the physical and to describe human phenomena more faithfully (Merleau-Ponty 1968).

Philosophers in the phenomenological movement who have contributed directly to psychology and the works of psychologists are many, but at least a few more must be mentioned. Max Scheler (1954, 1971) was the first philosopher to relate phenomenology to psychopathology, in works on self-deception and *ressentiment*, and to address psychoanalysis in his study of sympathy. Scheler's contributions were diverse and centered on his study of the emotions. Although primarily concerned with metaphysics, Gabriel Marcel has offered fresh methods and descriptions of psychological phenomena such as hope, having, the body, participation, availability, commitment, and family relations. Marcel cogently argued that the human being cannot be reduced to any theoretical system and stressed the necessity of probing first-person description and reflection on concrete life events in order to conceptualize human existence faithfully. Paul Ricoeur introduced and advocated the hermeneutic or narrative turn along with analyses of volition, symbolism, respect, sympathy, and an extensive dialog with psychoanalysis. Gaston Bachelard has analyzed the psychological significance of the material world in his studies of basic elements such as fire, water, and air as well as of lived space, reverie, and the poetic and scientific imaginations (Bachelard 1964a, 1964b, 1999). Among Emmanuel Levinas's (1969) numerous contributions to psychology is his insistence that ethical treatment requires the recognition of the irreducible difference and fundamental unknowability of the Other in relations with the self. Martin Buber's (1878–1965) distinction of I–it and I–Thou relationships has been a perennial reference point for psychologists who draw upon the existential phenomenological tradition.

The Early European Schools of Psychology

In the first half of the twentieth century, psychology throughout Europe was quite conversant with the emerging phenomenological movement. Influences ranged from direct contacts between psychologists and philosophers to secondhand contact through students and publications. Some psychologists independently adopted phenomenological procedures and later found reinforcement among the originators of and those formally schooled in the approach (Spiegelberg 1972). For instance, in Germany there were numerous holistic schools of psychology: Wilhelm Stern's (1871–1938) personalistic psychology, the *Verstehen* psychology of Eduard Spranger (1882–1963) (a follower of Dilthey), the experimental phenomenological work of David Katz (1889–1953), and Gestalt psychology (the Berlin school). Many German psychological researchers distinguished description from introspection, believed that the proper methods for psychology are phenomenological, employed the full spectrum of those methods (often stopping short of the transcendental reduction), embraced insights originated by philosophers, and contributed breakthroughs that in turn influenced philosophers including Husserl himself. For instance, William Stern, who insisted on the primacy of description and eidetic analyses, used phenomenology in his studies of apperception and his "personalistic" approach to personality (Stern 1938). The concept of *Präsenzzeit* from his study of the apperception of "change" was quoted, discussed, and utilized by Husserl in his studies of time (Spiegelberg 1972: 37). Stern's student Gordon Allport was later to become a champion of qualitative research in American psychology and to introduce students at Harvard, including Rolf Von Eckartsberg, to phenomenology. Even in Leipzig, where Wundt had reigned, Felix Krüger established his psychology of wholeness (*Ganzheitspsychologie*) and phenomenological thought took root in the new Leipzig school. Holistic, qualitative psychology that distinguished itself from natural science approaches pervaded Europe in many forms.

Göttingen psychologists, led by Georg Elias Müller, were inspired and influenced by their personal contact with Husserl. Erich Jaensch (1830–1940) researched eidetic imagery, personality, and the perception of space. David Katz produced classic works on color (Katz 1935) and on a psychology of touch perception (Katz 1930). He described a phenomenological method for psychology in detail (Katz 1950) and was the first to use the approach in the study of animals and comparative psychology (1937). Katz studied the enjoyment of music by the deaf and suggested the sense of vibration, between that of touch and hearing, as a new modality. Edgar Rubin (1886–1951), an active experimental researcher employing phenomenological methods in the Göttingen group, is best known as the originator of the concept of figure and ground in perception – the differentiation, in the perceptual field, of something from its background – that he studied extensively, including the phenomenon of figure-ground reversibility. Géza Révész (1878–1955) also focused on the world of touch and delved into investigations of acoustic and optic space. Wilhelm Schapp (1884–1969) carried out concrete studies of the perception of things in everyday life and demonstrated the role of the interrelations of sensory modalities in the constitution of such elementary perceptual qualities as "hardness" and "fluidity."

The Würzberg school, led by Oswald Külpe, focused on "higher" psychological processes such as thinking, language, will, and meaning. In studies on the comparison of weights, the concept of *imageless thought* (*Bewusstseinslage*) was introduced into the psychological literature. August Messer (1867–1937) critiqued sensationalistic theories of perception, made extensive use of Husserl's idea of intentionality, and argued for the compatibility of phenomenology and experimental psychology. Karl Bühler (1879–1963), carrying phenomenological methods into the areas of language and development and argued for the centrality of the concept of meaning in overcoming the fragmentation of the discrepant schools of psychology of his time. Albert Michotte (1881–1965), a Belgian who later established his own school in Louvain, received his exposure to phenomenology in Würzberg and integrated phenomenological description and analysis into his experimental work, yielding insights into the perception of causality, object permanence, and illusion (Michotte 1963).

The Gestalt psychology of Wertheimer (1880–1943), Köhler (1887–1967), and Koffka (1885–1941) was, according to Spiegelberg (1972), a parallel movement to phenomenology in its early years in Europe, where Husserl's approach had become part of a general atmosphere in which they shared the same liberating new approach to reality. The Gestaltists had more direct interchange with phenomenologists proper after they emigrated to the United States. In Wertheimer's breakthrough study of the *phi phenomenon* (apparent movement) and his analysis of thinking, holistic descriptions of the organization of experience go beyond reductive atomistic theories. Wertheimer emphasized the precedence of the whole over the parts in perception, which cannot be reduced to mechanically effective stimuli or sensations, and in human thinking, which can creatively reorganize the situation in many different ways in order to solve problems. Koffka, more philosophical, explicitly acknowledged Gestalt psychology's commitment to phenomenological descriptive methods in its emphasis on the phenomenal field, as he distinguished the Gestalt approach from introspectionistic psychology on one hand and behavioristic psychology on the other. Köhler demonstrated the presence of insight in apes, who used tree branches to extend their reach for food. According to Spiegelberg (1972), Wolfgang Köhler went farthest in giving open support to phenomenological philosophy, joining the editorial board of *Philosophy and Phenomenological Research* after 1941. Another noteworthy area of application is Köhler's demonstration of the role of *values* in human experience (Köhler 1938). Karl Dunker, well known for his psychology of problem solving, applied his extensive knowledge of phenomenology to original analyses of how the usual uses of objects (functional fixity) may be transcended by employing an object for novel uses, as one does when covering one's head with a cardboard box in a rainstorm. The seminal work of Kurt Lewin and Fritz Heider, who was familiar with Scheler, Sartre, Merleau-Ponty, and Schutz, moved from research on perception and causality to the field of interpersonal relations, extending the common intellectual paths of phenomenology and the Gestalt school.

Socio-historical forces involved in the emergence of Nazism and eventually World War II had a devastating effect on this European tradition (Giorgi 2004). Individual psychologists in Europe, such as Albert Wellek, Philipp Lersch, C. F. Graumann, J. Linschoten, Hans Kunz, and Wilhelm Keller have contributed to the post-war literature in phenomenological approaches to psychology, but research in reconstructed Europe followed mainstream American psychology for the most part. It is unlikely that the *Ganzheitzpsychologie* of Kruger, who was a Nazi, will ever be given attention. Many phenomenologically oriented European psychologists fled Europe and emigrated to the United States, where they often held positions at exclusively undergraduate colleges. Elements of their theories were absorbed into mainstream, positivist psychology without their underlying philosophy and research methods having any impact. Dutch phenomenologists such as F. J. J. Buytendijk shed light on the human meanings of the psychophysiological functions of sleep, breathing, digestion, sexuality, and pain and studied animal experience. Stephan Strasser (1969, 1977) developed a phenomenology of affectivity and stressed the need for a dialogical model in psychological research, which would approach participants as full partners in the acquisition of scientific knowledge rather than known objects. However, these works of isolated individuals have not established schools in which generations of researchers learn and apply phenomenological methods to psychological subject matter in post-war Europe.

Phenomenological Influences on Psychiatry and Clinical Psychology

European psychiatrists read the texts of Dilthey, Husserl, and Heidegger with great care. Halling and Dearborn-Nill's (1995) history of phenomenology in psychiatry and psychotherapy highlights multiple sources and influences that undergird, complement, and permeate traditional and mainstream approaches. Karl Jaspers (1963), influenced by Dilthey's idea of a *Verstehende Psychologie* (psychology based on *understanding* rather than explanation) and Husserl's *Logical Investigations*, also drew on Kierkegaard and Nietzsche as he developed the first general phenomenological psychopathology that offered a descriptive knowledge of hallucinations, delusions, dreams, expressions, motor activity, and gestures, as well as a comprehensive approach to characterology and "the person as a whole" that still today provides guidance, provocation, and inspiration for contemporary mental health researchers and practitioners.

The work of Husserl and Pfaender found its way into the psychiatric writings of Binswanger (1881–1966) (1963), Minkowski (1970), and von Gebsattel (1958). Heidegger's (1962) analytic of human Dasein gave psychiatry its most radical reorientation by providing a new anthropology for understanding both the human person and the pathologies of existence. Paramount in Heidegger's contribution was his insistence on the *structural unity of Dasein*, which has introduced into phenomenological clinical psychology a framework for interpreting psychopathological

401

phenomena within the context of the person's being-in-the-world as a whole, a scope scarcely approached in academic psychology. In other words, phenomenological psychologists now use philosophical resources to move beyond the description of more or less isolated mental states to the Gestalt "existence" (see Binswanger 1963; Boss 1963; Spiegelberg 1972). This *existential* phenomenology had impact in America on such psychologists as Rollo May, Carl Rogers, Viktor Frankl, Erich Fromm, Clark Moustakas, and James Bugental. Existential concepts of freedom, alienation, the facticity of death, estrangement of self from other, the falling into "inauthenticity," the possibility of becoming an "authentic self," ontological guilt, and the experience of nothingness were incorporated into clinical psychology and into critical analyses of modern Western culture. This conceptual appropriation was more for the sake of human service than formal research. Its representatives devoted themselves to healing the men and women of the mid-twentieth century, who had lost touch with themselves, their fellow-man, their sense of wonder at existence, their freedom to make meaning, and their creative courage (see May 1953, 1996; Frankl 1962). Let us turn to existential phenomenological psychiatry in more detail.

Husserl's turn-of-the-century publication *The Logical Investigations* quickly caught the attention of European psychiatrists. Karl Jaspers saw Husserl's "return to the things themselves" as an opportunity to discard biasing medical assumptions and to study mental illness with a new openness, publishing his classic *General Psychopathology* in 1913 in an attempt to bring the "whole person" in biographical context into psychiatry. Heidegger's existential and interpretive phenomenology inspired the work of such psychoanalytically trained psychiatrists as Ludwig Binswanger and Medard Boss, who published numerous case studies, analyses of mental disorders, and dream interpretation. Psychiatry, hitherto dominated by biological paradigms, became fundamentally historical and temporal, interpersonally oriented, and affirming of human freedom. Boss (1963) interpreted the various forms of psychopathology ranging from the neuroses to personality disorders, schizophrenia, psychophysiological illnesses, and sexual perversions as distinctive constrictions of Dasein's openness. The therapy he developed, an emancipatory praxis of dis-closure, aimed to restore the patient to a full existence.

Consistent with these broadening horizons of psychiatry, Von Weizsäcker demonstrated how camaraderie between physician and patient is necessary in order to engage the patient as an agent and full partner in psychotherapeutic change, in contrast to traditional medicine, in which an expert physician treats a passive patient in an impersonal manner. Viktor von Gebsattel attempted to *respirit* clinical practice and restore the fundamental mystery of the person. Along similar lines, his student Igor Caruso reinstated in therapy the moral and religious dimensions of patients' lives. Eugene Minkowski (1970), in *Lived Time*, presents a phenomenological study of depression based on his experience hosting a patient in his own home for an extended period and sharing in the patient's life on a daily basis. He identified the core of depression in the collapse of the futural dimension of existence. Erwin Straus (1966) grounded his psychopathology of disorders involving hallucination, amnesia, depression, compulsion, and catatonic stupor in a broad-based psychology of normal life, including analyses of the phenomena of posture, action, sensing, expression, awakeness, remembering, and relations with others. For instance, whereas normal sensory experience involves an integration of active and passive modalities (e.g., touching and being touched), hallucination involves pure passivity and therefore lacks spatial localization; whereas one feels one's way around spatially situated objects in normal touching, the hallucinating schizophrenic is assailed, for instance, by burning fire or electricity – being touched but not able in turn to touch, grasp, locate the phenomena of hallucination among the world-transcendent things.

Clinical phenomenological psychology shows a trend toward increased ecological focus, moving from elementary abnormal experiences to their existential ground in the person's overall world-situatedness, narrative biographical transformations, society, culture, and history (Foucault 1987). R. D. Laing's studies of schizophrenia in *The Divided Self* (1962) and *Sanity, Madness, and the Family* (Laing and Esterson 1963) draw respectively on the early and later philosophy of Sartre. In the former work, Laing utilizes hermeneutic and narrative methods to delineate one general way that some people become schizophrenic. By using deliberate efforts to protect themselves from the terrors of "ontological insecurity," these persons intentionally engage in a disembodied and socially isolated forms of experience that lead to disorganization and non-being on the part of the self. In the later work with Esterson, Laing uses multiple interviews with schizophrenic women and their families and finds that symptoms having no meaning when viewed as precipitates of an impersonal disease process become intelligible in the context of the person's social praxis and the family's interpersonal processes. J. H. van den Berg (1972) provided a systematic general description of the modifications in the spatial, social, and temporal dimensions of existence in psychopathology. Investigating clinical phenomena in ever-larger contexts, van Den Berg (1961) also developed a new discipline of metabletics – historical psychology, in which he demonstrates that discoveries and theories of different historical eras reveal actual changes in the nature of human experience that have taken place over time. For instance, van den Berg (1974) demonstrates that "neurosis," "the unconscious," "multiple selves," "developmental crises," and even "pain" are relatively recent and have come to pass with the complexities and pluralism of modern social existence.

The European existential phenomenological psychiatrists extricated research on psychopathology from the confines of the disease-medical model, in which human experience is reified, reduced to symptoms, and explained by impersonal forces. They carefully described the lived meanings of abnormal experiences in the context of persons' biographical trajectories and holistic relations with their world. In this way psychopathology became a fully human phenomenon, patients were raised to the full status of persons, and mental disorders were placed in existential, life-historical contexts, becoming meaningful and understandable ways of existing with their own forms of bodily selfhood, spatiality, sociality, temporality, and historicality.

This work began to come to the attention of American psychologists in the 1930s through Robert McLeod, later through Gordon Allport, who had studied in Europe, and through Europeans immigrating to the United States such as the Gestalt psychologists Kurt Koffka and Wolfgang Kohler, Paul Tillich, and Erwin Straus. Other European-born and European-trained psychologists such as Andreas Angyl, Adrian Van Kaam, and Henri Ellenberger, already in the United States, contributed to the growing interest. Halling and Dearborn-Nill (1995) cite Martin Buber's participation in the William Alanson White Memorial Lectures in 1957 and the publication of

Existence (May et al. 1958), a collection of previously untranslated papers including those of many of the above-mentioned authors, as the two pivotal events that created an unexpected upsurge of interest in the European movement on the part of American psychotherapists. American-born mental health scholars and practitioners such as James Bugental, Eugene Gendlin, and Irving Yalom joined and broadened an American movement (Halling and Dearborn-Nill 1995) that has continued through to the present, for instance, in the work of George Atwood and Robert Stolorow (1984). However, this interest was without academic institutionalization until Duquesne University undertook to educate new generations of researchers in a systematic existential phenomenology that addresses all areas of psychology.

Phenomenologically Based Research Methods and Contributions to General Psychology

In 1961, Adrian Van Kaam, founding editor of the *Review of Existential Psychiatry and Psychology*, wrote convincingly that all psychology, not just clinical psychology, must acknowledge existential foundations (Van Kaam 1966). He had conducted descriptive, empirical research on "feeling really understood" (1959), delineated an existential style of thought ("comprehensive theorizing") that brings unity to the fragmented discipline, and set up a program at Duquesne University that aimed to apply phenomenological methods to the full spectrum of psychological subject matter. Amedeo Giorgi, trained in the experimental research on perception, played the key role of articulating the need for a "human science" foundation for the entire discipline of psychology and in developing empirical research methods that have been applied to a broad range of subject matter (Giorgi 1970, 1985). Diverse phenomenological research has taken place at Duquesne using Giorgi's empirically based procedures as well as hermeneutic, dialogical, narrative, and progressive-regressive methods. Although little of the early European work had been translated, these psychologists studied the works of Husserl, Heidegger, Sartre, Merleau-Ponty, Schutz, Ricoeur, and Levinas with such leading phenomenological philosophers at Duquesne as Andre Schewer, John Sallis, Alphonso Lingis, John Scanlon, and Lester Embree. Modeling the "human science" approach to various subject matter, faculty's work includes Giorgi's on learning (1975, 1985); William Fischer's studies of emotions, anxiety, and self-deception (1970, 1974, 1985); Rolf Von Eckartsberg's work in social psychology (1975); Anthony Barton's analyses of the psychotherapies (1974), Constance Fischer's individualized psychological assessment (1985), and Edward Murray's writing on imagination and language (1986).

Beginning in 1970, Giorgi developed empirically based research methods using phenomenological principles and addressed general methodological issues such as the legitimacy of using verbal descriptions in psychological research, reliability, and validity. The research conducted by Giorgi and his colleagues and students have included many types of participants, expressive and descriptive forms of data collection, analytic procedures, and ways of presenting findings. Early on, established experimental paradigms were replicated "with a twist," that is, collecting and qualitatively analyzing descriptions from the points of view of experimental participants. For instance, in one traditional paradigm in which participants memorized nonsense syllables, phenomeno-logical descriptions revealed a host of creative cognitive strategies that facilitated learning in order to supplement the quantitative findings of previous research. In other projects, researchers approached established experimental problems by selecting naturally occurring situations in the life-world that would allow contextually sensitive access to the processes under investigation. For instance, descriptions provided by golfers while putting on greens were collected and analyzed in order to study the perception of horizontal lines in a setting more natural than the laboratory "rod and frame" test offered. In other projects such as Giorgi's on learning, research moved beyond traditional conceptions of subject matter by asking participants to choose situations from their own lives that related to the research topic. Giorgi asked par-ticipants to "describe a situation in which you learned something" in order to achieve a psychology of learning that captures the full diversity and complexity of learning as it occurs in the lifeworld.

Giorgi (1989) has indicated that this research is phenomenological in that it (1) describes lived experience; (2) utilizes the phenomenological reductions; (3) invest-igates the intentional relationship between persons and situations; and (4) provides knowledge of psychological essences (that is, the structures of meaning immanent in human experience) through imaginative variation. Much attention has been devoted to delineating the procedures of qualitative data analysis whereby reflection on everyday descriptions provides general knowledge of the meaningful structures of psychological life (Giorgi 1985; Giorgi and Giorgi 2003; Wertz 1983a). These same qualitative analytic procedures have been identified throughout the broad movements of existential phenomenological psychology (Wertz 1983b) and of psychoanalysis (Wertz 1993), leading to the conclusion that the method Giorgi systematized char-acterizes any and every qualitative method in genuinely psychological research (Wertz 2005).

The reflective development and formal explication of broadly applicable methods for empirically based research has given rise to a wide diversity of projects, including over 250 psychological dissertations at Duquesne on a range of topics including perception, language, thought, problem solving, imagination, memory, emotion, life-cycle develop-ment, interpersonal relations, roles, attitudes, group processes, community, health, sexuality, psychopathology, psychotherapy, psychopharmacology, morality, cross-cultural issues, and spirituality (Smith 2002). The Duquesne Circle edited and pub-lished four volumes of *Duquesne Studies in Phenomenological Psychology* featuring qualitative research, with Giorgi as lead editor, in 1971, 1975, 1979, and 1983. For prototypic and exemplary research, see Colaizzi (1973), W. Fischer (1970, 1974, 1985), Giorgi (1975, 1985), Giorgi et al. (1971, 1975, 1979, 1983), von Eckartsberg (1975), Wertz (1982, 1987), Jager (2001), Valle and King (1978), Aanstoos (1984), Valle and Halling (1989), and Valle (1998).

Since the early 1970s, Giorgi and other human science psychologists have intro-duced the phenomenological approach to mainstream psychology through their active leadership in the American Psychological Association's Society for Theoretical and Philosophical Psychology and the Division of Humanistic Psychology, which continue to welcome and encourage phenomenologically based work in their journals and convention programs. The Human Science Research Association, a multidisciplinary international organization which has held annual conferences for over twenty years, has been spearheaded by Giorgi and other North American phenomenological psychologists. American phenomenological psychologists have led the qualitative research movement in their field. Rennie, Watson, and Monteiro (2000) analyzed the rise of qualitative research in psychology and found that the *Journal of Phenomenological Psychology*, founded by Giorgi in 1970, has been the leading venue for qualitative research in psychology since the 1970s.

Contemporary work in phenomenological psychology draws on many historical sources in the movement. Although the expanded ecological scope including literary, societal, cultural, and historical analyses continues to inform research, the psychological description of the lived experience of individual persons remains the defining focus of scholarship. One qualitative action-research program addressing schizophrenia and chronic mental illness from a Husserlian perspective, led by Duquesne graduate Larry Davidson, is underway at Yale University Medical School. In a study designed to contribute to a reduction of rehospitalization of chronic schizophrenics, Davidson et al. (2001) analyzed the post-discharge experience of former patients. They set aside the assumption that training in strategies for coping with symptom-recurrence was ineffective in preventing the rehospitalization of former patients. They found instead that in the context of post-discharge social isolation, a shrinkage of possibilities for employment, and a hopeless view of the future, the hospital was experienced as a haven where one gains interpersonal understanding, respectful sociality, and a sense of empowerment directed toward the future. By addressing patients' problems in living outside the hospital holistically, through the establishment of meaningful communities, the cultivation of agency, and the construction of an open future, rehospitalization was dramatically decreased (see also Davidson 2004).

The study of existential phenomenological psychology is currently available in the psychology departments of Duquesne University, Seattle University, West Georgia University, the University of Dallas, the University of Tennessee, Sonoma State University, Brigham Young University, Fordham University, the University of Quebec in Montreal, and Sheffield University in the UK, as well as in graduate institutes: the Saybrook Institute, the Center for Humanistic Studies, the Union Graduate Institute, the Fielding Institute, and the Pacifica Graduate Institute. Led by Howard Pollio, the experimental psychology program at the University of Tennessee has generated many phenomenological dissertations (Henley and Meguiar 1988) focused on the meanings of situations encountered in everyday life. A sampling of the Tennessee program's research has been widely disseminated (Pollio et al. 1997; Register and Henley 1992; Adams-Price et al. 1998).

The Future of Existential-Phenomenological Psychology

The phenomenological movement has been present throughout the history of twentieth-century psychology, contributing unique methods and knowledge that describe human experience contextually and bring to light its "lived" realities. Phenomenological trends remain a small, minority perspective in this field, where most researchers continue to embrace a natural scientific, hypothetico-deductive approach that isolates variables and relies on measurement and quantitative analysis. Most practitioners subscribe to variants of the medical model. The broad "postmodern" critique of science and technology has created a small but intellectually hearty receptivity to alternative ways of knowing in psychology. This growing pluralism has been bolstered by the political forces of feminism and multiculturalism as well as convergent intellectual trends in psychoanalysis, the humanities, and other social sciences. These developments have introduced new ideas and increasing growth in the area of qualitative research, especially in practice-related specializations. Phenomenological approaches to psychology are a vital force and resource in this broader movement.

Despite the presence of a significant body of scholarship on which psychology can build in the new century, the future of existential phenomenology in this field is uncertain. Because it is typically not represented in academic curricula, students have limited opportunities for exposure. Students must discover the approach on their own or at the suggestion of a faculty member who at most offers opportunities for independent study. Graduate education in phenomenological approaches to psychology is limited to a handful of institutions, most of which focus primarily on orthodox approaches or, like Duquesne, have broadened their scope to include other non-mainstream approaches in the field. Phenomenological philosophy remains a lively and growing movement, and phenomenological psychologists continue to draw on its transcendental, existential, hermeneutic, dialogical, and narrative developments. The *Journal of Phenomenological Psychology*, now published by Brill Academic Publishers, draws interest in its focus on philosophical issues, theoretical criticism and innovation, empirically grounded research, and continuing dialogue with mainstream psychology, psychoanalysis, and the humanities. Research continues to be conducted by individuals and in a handful of generative groups, which now find numerous publication outlets hospitable to phenomenological work in psychology. Their hope is that the very nature of psychological subject matter, which demands the kind of critical perspective and descriptive research initiated by phenomenological, existentially oriented psychologists, will motivate the development of this approach in the present century as it has throughout the last.

References and Further Reading

Aanstoos, C. M. (ed.) (1984) *Exploring the Lived World: Readings in Phenomenological Psychology*. Carrollton: West Georgia College.

Adams-Price, C., Henley, T. B., and Hale, M. (1998) Phenomenology and the meaning of aging to young and old adults. *International Journal of Aging and Human Development*, 47, 263–77.

Atwood, G. E., and Stolorow, R. D. (1984) *Structures of Subjectivity: Explorations in Psychoanalytic Phenomenology*. Hillsdale, NJ: Analytic Press.

Bachelard, G. (1964a) *The Poetics of Space* (trans. E. Gilson) Boston: Beacon (original work published 1958).

—— (1964b) *Psychoanalysis of Fire* (trans. A. C. M. Ross) Boston: Beacon Press (original work published 1938).

—— (1999) *Water and Dreams: An Essay on the Imagination of Matter* (trans. E. Farrell). Dallas, TX: Pegasus Foundation (originally work published 1942).

Barton, A. (1974) *Three Worlds of Therapy: An Existential-Phenomenological Study of the Therapies of Freud, Jung, and Rogers*. Palo Alto, CA: National Press.

Binswanger, L. (1963) *Being-in-the-World* (ed. J. Needleman). New York: Basic Books.

Boss, M. (1963) *Psychoanalysis and Daseinsanalysis*. New York: Basic Books.

—— (1979) *Existential Foundations of Medicine and Psychology* (trans. S. Conway and A. Cleaves). New York: Jason Aronson (original work published 1971).

Brentano, F. (1973) *Psychology from an Empirical Standpoint* (trans. A. C. Rancurello, D. B. Terrell, and L. L. McAlister). New York: Humanities Press (original work published 1874).

Buber, M. (1970) *I and Thou*. New York: Schribners.

Buytendijk, F. J. J. (1973) *Prolegomena to an Anthropological Physiology*. Pittsburgh, PA: Duquesne University Press.

Cloonan, T. F. (1995) The early history of phenomenological psychological research methods in America. *Journal of Phenomenological Psychology*, 26(1), 46–126.

Colaizzi, P. F. (1973) *Reflection and Research in Psychology: A Phenomenological Study of Learning*. Dubuque, IA: Kendall/Hunt.

Davidson, L. (2004) Phenomenology and contemporary clinical practice: Introduction to the special issue. *Journal of Phenomenological Psychology*, 35(2), 149–57.

Davidson, L., Stayner, D. A., Lambert, S., Smith, P., and Sledge, W. S. (2001) Phenomenological and participatory research on schizophrenia: Recovering the person in theory and practice. In D. L. Tolman and M. Brydon-Miller (eds.), *From Subjects to Subjectivities: A Handbook of Interpretive and Participatory Methods* (pp. 163–82). New York: New York University Press.

Dilthey, W. (1977) Ideas concerning a descriptive and analytical psychology (1894) (trans. R. M. Zaner). In W. Dilthey (ed.), *Descriptive Psychology and Historical Understanding*. The Hague: Martinus Nijhoff (original work published 1924).

Edmonds, E. M. and Smith, M. E. (1923) The phenomenological description of musical intervals. *American Journal of Psychology*, 24, 287–91.

Fischer, C. (1985) *Individualizing Psychological Assessment*. Monterey, CA: Brooks/Cole.

Fischer, W. F. (1970) *Theories of Anxiety*. New York: Harper & Row.

—— (1974) On the phenomenological mode of researching "being anxious." *Journal of Phenomenological Psychology*, 4, 405–23.

—— (1985) Self-deception: An existential-phenomenological investigation into its essential meanings. In A. Giorgi (ed.), *Phenomenology and Psychological Research* (pp. 118–54), Pittsburgh, PA: Duquesne University Press.

Foucault, M. (1987) *Mental Illness and Psychology* (trans. A. Sheridan). Berkeley: University of California Press (original work published 1954).

Frankl, V. E. (1962) *Man's Search for Meaning; An Introduction to Logotherapy* (trans. I. Lasch). Boston: Beacon Press (original work published 1946).

Gendlin, E. (1962) *Experiencing and the Creation of Meaning*. Chicago: Free Press.

Giorgi, A. (1970) *Psychology as a Human Science: A Phenomenologically Based Approach*. New York: Harper & Row.

—— (1975) An application of phenomenological method in psychology. In A. Giorgi, C. Fischer, and E. Murray (eds.), *Duquesne Studies in Phenomenological Psychology (Volume II)* (pp. 82–103). Pittsburgh, PA: Duquesne University Press.

Giorgi, A. (ed.) (1985) *Phenomenology and Psychological Research*. Pittsburgh: Duquesne University Press.

—— (1986) Theoretical justification for the use of descriptions in psychological research. In P. Ashworth, A. Giorgi, and A. deKoning (eds.), *Qualitative Research in Psychology* (pp. 3–22). Pittsburgh, PA: Duquesne University Press.

408

—— (1988) Validity and reliability from a phenomenological perspective. In W. J. Baker, L. P. Mos, H. V. Rappard, and H. J. Stam (eds.), *Recent Trends in Theoretical Psychology* (pp. 167–76). New York: Springer-Verlag.

Giorgi, A., Barton, A., and Maes, C. (eds.) (1983) *Duquesne Studies in Phenomenological Psychology: Volume IV*, Pittsburgh, PA: Duquesne University Press.

Giorgi, A., Fischer, C. T., and Murray, E. L. (eds.) (1975) *Duquesne Studies in Phenomenological Psychology (Volume II)*. Pittsburgh, PA: Duquesne University Press.

Giorgi, A., Smith, D., and Knowles, R. (eds.) (1979) *Duquesne Studies in Phenomenological Psychology (Volume III)*. Pittsburgh, PA: Duquesne University Press.

Giorgi, A., Von Eckartsberg, R., and Fischer, W. F. (eds.) (1971) *Duquesne Studies in Phenomenological Psychology (Volume I)*. Pittsburgh, PA: Duquesne University Press.

—— (1989) Some theoretical and practical issues regarding the psychological phenomenological method. *Saybrook Review*, 7, 71–85.

—— (1992) Description versus interpretation: Competing alternative strategies for qualitative research. *Journal of Phenomenological Psychology*, 23, 199–35.

Giorgi, A. P. (2004) Critical history of psychology: A phenomenological perspective. Invited address at Fordham University, New York City, October.

Giorgi, A. P., and Giorgi, B. M. (2003) The descriptive phenomenological psychological method. In P. Camic, J. E. Rhodes, and L. Yardley (eds.), *Qualitative Research in Psychology* (pp. 242–73). Washington, DC: American Psychological Association.

Halling, S., and Dearborn-Nill, J. (1995) A brief history of existential-phenomenological psychiatry and psychotherapy. *Journal of Phenomenological Psychology*, 26(1), 1–45.

Heidegger, M. (1962) *Being and Time* (trans. J. MacQuarrie and E. Robinson). New York: Harper & Row (original work published 1927).

Henley, T. B. and Meguiar, T. M. (1988) Phenomenology at the University of Tennessee. *Humanistic Psychologist*, 16, 358–60.

Husserl, E. (1954) *The Crisis of European Sciences and Transcendental Phenomenology* (trans. D. Carr). Evanston, IL: Northwestern University Press (original work published in 1939).

—— (1962) *Ideas: General Introduction to Pure Phenomenology* (trans. W. R. B. Gibson). New York: Collier Books (original work published 1913).

—— (1970) *Logical Investigations* (trans. J. N. Findlay). New York: Humanities Press (original work published 1900).

—— (1977) *Phenomenological Psychology: Lectures, Summer Semester, 1925* (trans. J. Scanlon). Boston: Martinus Nijhoff (original work published 1925).

Jager, B. (2001). Introduction to the special issue: Psychology and literature. *Journal of Phenomenological Psychology*, 32(2), 103–17.

Jaspers, K. (1963) *General Psychopathology* (trans. J. Hoenig and M. W. Hamilton). Chicago: University of Chicago Press (original work published 1913).

Katz, D. (1930) The vibratory sense and other lectures. University of Maine Studies, Second Series, No. 14. *Maine Bulletin*, 32, 1–163.

—— (1935) *The World of Color* (trans. R. B. McLeod and G. W. Fox). London: Kegan Paul (original work published 1911).

—— (1937) *Animals and Men* (trans. H. Steinberg and A. Summerfield). New York: Longman.

—— (1950) *Gestalt Psychology* (trans. R. Tyson). New York: Ronald Press (original work published 1944).

Köhler, W. (1938) *Place of Values in a World of Facts*. Philadelphia: Liveright.

Laing, R. D. (1962) *The Divided Self*. New York: Pantheon Books.

Laing, R. D., and Esterson, A. (1963) *Sanity, Madness, and the Family*. New York: Penguin Books.

Levinas, E. (1969) *Totality and Infinity: A Study in Exteriority* (trans. A. Lingis). Pittsburgh, PA: Duquesne University Press (original work published 1961).

May, R. (1953) *Man's Search for Himself*. New York: Norton.

—— (1996) *The Meaning of Anxiety*. New York: Norton (original work published in 1950).

May, R., Angel, E., and Ellenberger, H. F. (eds.) (1958) *Existence: A New Dimension in Psychiatry and Psychology*. New York: Simon & Schuster.

Merleau-Ponty, M. (1962) *Phenomenology of Perception* (trans. C. Smith). London: Routledge & Kegan Paul (original work published 1945).

—— (1963) *The Structure of Behavior* (trans. A. Fisher). Pittsburgh, PA: Duquesne University Press (original work written 1942).

—— (1968) *The Visible and the Invisible*. Evanston, IL: Northwestern University Press (original work published 1964).

Michotte, A. (1963) *Perception of Causality* (trans. T. R. Mills and E. Mills). London: Methuen.

Minkowski, E. (1970) *Lived Time: Phenomenological and Psychopathological Studies*. Evanston, IL: Northwestern University Press.

Murray, E. L. (1986) *Imaginative Thinking and Human Existence*. Pittsburgh, PA: Duquesne University Press.

Pollio, H. R., Henley, T. B., and Thompson, C. J. (1997) *The Phenomenology of Everyday Life*. New York: Cambridge University Press.

Register, L. M. and Henley, T. B. (1992) The phenomenology of intimacy. *Journal of Social and Personal Relationships*, 9, 467–91.

Rennie, D. L., Watson, K. D., and Monteiro, A. M. (2002) The rise of qualitative research in psychology. *Canadian Psychology*, 43(3), 179–189.

Sartre, J-P. (1948a) *The Emotions: Outline for a Theory* (trans. B. Frechtman). New York: Philosophical Library (original work published 1939).

—— (1948b) *The Psychology of Imagination* (trans. B. Frechtman). New York: Philosophical Library (original work published 1940).

—— (1956) *Being and Nothingness: An Essay on Phenomenological Ontology* (trans. H. Barnes). New York: Washington Square Press (original work published 1956).

—— (1976) *Critique of Dialectical Reason* (trans. A. Sheridan-Smith). London: New Left Books (original work published 1960).

Scheler, M. (1954) *The Nature of Sympathy* (trans. P. Heath). New Haven, CT: Yale University Press (original work published 1913).

—— (1971) *Ressentiment* (trans. W. H. Holdheim). New York: Free Press (original work published 1915).

Smith, D. L. (2002) *Fearfully and Wonderfully Made: The History of the Duquesne University's Graduate Psychology Programs (1959–1999)*. Pittsburgh, PA: Simon Silverman Phenomenology Center of Duquesne University.

Spiegelberg, H. (1972) *Phenomenology in Psychology and Psychiatry*. Evanston, IL: Northwestern University Press.

—— (1982) *The Phenomenological Movement*, 3rd edn. The Hague: Martinus Nijhoff.

Stern, W. (1938) *General Psychology from the Personalistic Viewpoint*. New York: Macmillan.

Strasser, S. (1969) *Dialogal Phenomenology*. Pittsburgh, PA: Duquesne University Press.

—— (1977) *Phenomenology of Feeling: An Essay in the Phenomena of the Heart*. Pittsburgh: Duquesne University Press.

Straus, E. (1966) *Phenomenological Psychology: Selected Papers* (trans. E. Eng) New York: Basic Books.

Valle, R. (ed.) (1998) *Phenomenological Inquiry in Psychology: Existential and Transpersonal Dimensions*. New York: Plenum.

Valle, R. S., and Halling, S. (eds.) (1989) *E-P Perspectives in Psychology: Exploring the Breadth of Human Experience*. New York: Plenum.

Valle, R. S., and King, M. (eds.) (1978) *Existential-Phenomenological Alternatives for Psychology.* New York: Oxford University Press.

van den Berg, J. H. (1961) *The Changing Nature of Man: Introduction to Historical Psychology.* New York: Norton.

—— (1972) *A Different Existence: Principles of a Phenomenological Psychopathology.* Pittsburgh, PA: Duquesne University Press.

—— (1974) *Divided Existence and Complex Society.* Pittsburgh, PA: Duquesne University Press.

Van Kaam, A. (1959) Phenomenal analysis: Exemplified by a study of the experience of really feeling understood. *Journal of Individual Psychology,* 15, 66–72.

—— (1966) *Existential Foundations of Psychology.* Pittsburgh, PA: Duquesne University Press.

von Eckartsberg, R. (1975) The eco-psychology of motivational theory and research. In A. Giorgi, C. T. Fischer, and E. L. Murray (eds.), *Duquesne Studies in Phenomenological Psychology (Volume II)* (pp. 155–80), Pittsburgh, PA: Duquesne University Press.

von Gebsattel, V. E. (1958) The world of the compulsive. In R. May, E. Angel, and H. F. Ellenberger (eds.), *Existence: A New Dimension of Psychiatry and Psychology* (pp. 170–90). New York: Basic Books.

Wertz, F. J. (1982) The findings and value of a descriptive approach to everyday perceptual process. *Journal of Phenomenological Psychology,* 13(2), 169–95.

—— (1983a) From everyday to psychological description: Analyzing the moments of a qualitative data analysis. *Journal of Phenomenological Psychology,* 14(2), 197–241.

—— (1983b) Some components of descriptive psychological reflection. *Human Studies,* 6(1), 35–51.

—— (1987) Abnormality from scientific and prescientific perspectives, *Review of Existential Psychology and Psychiatry,* 19(2 & 3), 205–23.

—— (1993) The phenomenology of Sigmund Freud. *Journal of Phenomenological Psychology,* 24(2), 101–29.

—— (1999) Multiple methods in psychology: Epistemological grounding and the possibility of unity. *Journal of Theoretical and Philosophical Psychology,* 19(2), 131–66.

—— (2005) Phenomenological research methods for counseling psychology. *Journal of Counseling Psychology,* 52(2), 167–77.

Wundt, W. (1916) *Elements of Folk Psychology: Outlines of a Psychological History of the Development of Mankind* (trans. E. L. Schaub). New York: Macmillan (original work published 1912).

28

Medicine

FREDRIK SVENAEUS

Apart from the attention it has received within psychiatry (Spiegelberg 1972), the phenomenology of medicine is a field that remains largely uninvestigated. The main areas of interest for phenomenologists, outside the realm of "pure" philosophy, have been the arts, the humanities, and the social sciences, rather than medicine. Consequently, a great deal of phenomenological work remains to be done on the core experiences and concepts of medical practice and science. At the same time, quite a few of the central themes of phenomenological research – themes central to the development of the tradition during the twentieth century – are applicable to the world of medicine; the works carried out on these themes can therefore be said to have explored the phenomenology of medicine in an indirect manner. A few important examples are phenomenological investigations of the concepts of self, intersubjectivity, the body, feeling, action, gender, death, life, nature, ethics, science, and technology.

In any case, when "applied" to a certain domain of our experiences, phenomenology always remains loyal to the peculiar brand of reflection that is essential to all phenomenological work. Doing phenomenology of regional ontologies always implies situating one's project in a larger fundamental ontology; for the particular phenomena one is exploring (medical phenomena, for example) are embedded in a general horizon of phenomenological concepts and investigations. One such concept, particularly relevant in the case of medicine, is "facticity": that is, the attempt to elucidate the meaning of everyday life without falling prey to either scientific reductionism or transcendental idealism. In the preface to his authoritative exposition of phenomenological methodology, *Phenomenology of Perception*, Merleau-Ponty writes:

> Phenomenology is the study of essences; and according to it, all problems amount to finding definitions of essences: the essence of perception, or the essence of consciousness, for example. But phenomenology is also a philosophy which puts essences back into existence, and does not expect to arrive at an understanding of man and the world from any starting point other than that of their "facticity". (Merleau-Ponty 1962: vii)

Rather than being a survey of books and articles written in the field of the phenomenology of medicine (see Toombs 2001), the present chapter will develop a line of inquiry, the goal of which is to seek out the essences of illness and health – the subject and the aim of medical science and practice – by way of the facticity of the medical realm. Though many key works of medical phenomenology will be mentioned, the most important references in the text will be to the central figures of the phenomenological tradition, from whose works we will excavate themes for further analysis. My main sources of inspiration will be the philosophies of Heidegger and, to some extent, Gadamer, but I believe the same themes could also be approached from the perspective of Husserlian phenomenology, or with the help of the heterogeneous French tradition.

The Phenomenological Concept of Meaning

By way of introduction, phenomenology might be described as the attempt to found a conceptual apparatus that, in contrast to the disembodied theories and investigations of empirical science, is based on lived experience. The starting point is everyday life, as viewed and investigated from a certain perspective, the phenomenological attitude. What is focused upon in this attitude is often called the *meaning* of experience. Lived experience, on the one hand, and the theories and results of science, on the other, are meaningful in entirely different ways; suffering from the ravages of an illness, for example, is something altogether different from coldly cataloging the characteristics of a disease. (In what follows, the terms "illness" and "disease" will be used in accordance with the distinction made in the fields of medical philosophy, psychology, and sociology between personal experience, on the one hand, and biological processes, on the other.) Science, as a human activity that strives to solve puzzles and produce results, is no doubt meaningful, but the manner of explanation particular to science, with its focus on causal relations within nature, is not directly tied to the everyday world. The demonstration that a previously unknown virus is responsible for chronic fatigue syndrome (CFS) might become meaningful for me, particularly if I suffer from an illness diagnosed as CFS; however, in that case, it becomes meaningful primarily because it finds a place in my life as something that matters to me and my future projects (for instance, the discovery may lead to a new treatment for CFS). The meaningfulness for me of the discovery of the virus will in other words depend on whether or not I, or somebody close to me, suffer from the associated illness. The discovery is meaningful if it plays a role in my everyday world.

Yet the discovery of the virus could also be said to be meaningful in the sense that the scientific hypotheses and experiments involved in its discovery are understood by me. The discovery may allow me to understand the workings of this virus in relation to the workings of other biological entities – to understand a little bit more of the complex causal network of nature, which is the subject of scientific explanations and predictions. But this meaningfulness is different from that in the first scenario, in which the discovery of the virus was connected to the problems and prospects of my everyday life. The meaningfulness of the second scenario is the peculiar meaningfulness of the natural sciences – enterprises that, despite their origins in human culture, approach nature as something *independent* of human patterns of understanding. Exactly how skeptical we are about the possibility of attaining a scientific understanding of nature

413

that is wholly independent of our culture will depend on which position we endorse in the philosophy of science, constructivism or realism (Hiley et al. 1991).

The meaning that phenomenology investigates is not found within the causal patterns of the world studied by science. The phenomenologist does not want to suppress the subjectivity of the subject, in order to investigate the object as it "really is"; on the contrary, she wants to ground her analysis in the relationship between subject and object, in the patterns of meaning that bind them together and make the object appear to the subject in a certain manner. The object's manner of appearing constitutes its meaning – its manner of making sense to the subject. In Husserl's phenomenology, this relation between subject and object is termed intentionality; his successor Heidegger called it "being-in-the-world."

In our own lives, however, we direct ourselves, not only toward *objects* such as chairs, but also toward *concepts* spelled out in *propositions* such as "the chair is yellow"; we see *that* the chair *is* yellow. Upon this "is," which cannot appear on its own, but only when something is seen *as* something, rests the famous ontological difference between being and beings (*Sein und Seiende*) in Heidegger. The main sources of Heidegger's "question of being" appear to be Husserl's analysis of categorial intuition in the *Logical Investigations* (Husserl 2001) (Watanabe 1993), and the practical philosophy of Aristotle in the *Nicomachean Ethics* (Aristotle 2002) (Volpi 1996), although quite a few other influences are also found in the lecture courses that preceded the publication of *Being and Time* in 1927 (Heidegger 1996).

What does it mean that something appears as something for a subject? How can an object appear as a chair, for instance? Heidegger's explanation in *Being and Time* is that the objects we encounter in our lives are *interconnected* through a pattern of meaning; it is on the basis of this interconnectedness that the objects make sense to us. A chair never appears in isolation; it always appears within a horizon of human projects, where it is used in a variety of activities. The meaningfulness of the chair, its being *as* a chair, can only be understood if we focus on its place in a context of practice. In *Being and Time*, Heidegger describes such contexts as "totalities of relevance" – as settings in which objects assume the roles of tools (*Zeuge*) used to attain specific goals (Heidegger 1996: 66 ff.). To sit on the chair at the table eating one's lunch with knife and fork would be one example; to sit on the chair listening to a lecture at a conference would be another. The chair thus inhabits different totalities of relevance, which in turn are all bound together by what Heidegger calls "the world" (Heidegger 1996: 72 ff.). Accordingly, the world of phenomenology is not the world of nature (a collection of natural objects presented to a subject), but rather the world of culture (a structure of interconnected tools). But culture here must be construed in a very basic sense, as the myriad ways in which we bestow the world with meaning. A tool in Heidegger's phenomenology need not be an artifact; it could just as well be what we would normally consider a natural phenomenon that is "at hand" for us in our everyday doings. The forest would be a forest of harvestable timber; the wind would be a favorable wind in the sails of a boat, and so on (Heidegger 1996: 70).

One should note here that the "is" of Husserl's categorial intuition is present in its basic form as soon as we encounter the chair as chair – that is, as soon as we use it as such a thing. I do not have to make any explicit statements about the chair being yellow, heavy, or uncomfortable, in order to experience its meaningfulness, to address its way of being (Heidegger 1996: 153 ff.). What's crucial is that, as part of the task of making sense, I accord it a place in the world, in its capacity as tool. "As" is consequently construed by Heidegger in the sense of "in order to": to bestow meaning on the chair as chair means to assign it a place in a context in which it is used to attain specific goals by virtue of my being-in-the-world.

Thus, according to Heidegger, meaning and understanding do not rest solely on thinking, watching, and speaking, but also on the silent understanding of the body in action. The world of the lived body, as is well known, is the main focus of the philosophy of Merleau-Ponty, and not that of Heidegger. Yet, already from the outline of the world as a world of tools, found in the third chapter of section one of *Being and Time*, it is clear that, in any analysis of the ways in which human being (what Heidegger calls "Dasein") inhabits the world, the body (*Leib*) must be a central source of meaningfulness (Heidegger 1996: 108; see also Heidegger 2001). It is important to emphasize at this point, however, that the phenomenology of *Being and Time* is intended to surpass not only the naturalism of empirical science and the idealism of a disembodied mind, but pragmatism as well. "Da-sein" means a "being there" in the world constituting meaning through actions in using tools, but it also means "to be" in the manner of a being which strives to understand its *own* manner of existing; this is the overarching existential goal of Heidegger's analysis (Heidegger 1996: 41 ff.).

Illness as Meaninglessness and Alienation

I would now like to advance Heidegger's analysis beyond the interests and investigations of *Being and Time*, while proposing that a phenomenology of illness should focus upon the concept of otherness and its relation to meaningfulness. In the case of illness, otherness is a peculiar experience of incomprehensibility, which permeates the life of the ill. As we will see later, a further specification of otherness in illness can be found in the concepts of unhomelikeness and alienness.

Human Dasein – being there, existing – is, according to Heidegger, open to the world; it is disclosed (*erschlossen*), in that it makes itself *at home* in the world (Heidegger 1996: 54). This openness is a form of hospitality toward the world – a constant striving to find a place for new phenomena in the meaning pattern, in order to make sense of them:

> Since understanding and interpretation constitute the existential constitution of the being-there (Da sein), meaning must be understood as the formal, existential framework of the disclosedness belonging to understanding. Meaning is an existential of Dasein, not a property which is attached to beings [of the world], which lies "behind" them or floats somewhere as a "realm between." Only Dasein "has" meaning in that the disclosedness of being-in-the-world can be "fulfilled" through the beings discoverable in it. *Thus only Dasein can be meaningful or meaningless (sinnvoll oder sinnlos).* This means that its own being and the beings disclosed with that being can be appropriated in understanding or they can be confined to incomprehensibility.
>
> If we adhere to this interpretation of the concept of "meaning," which is in principle ontological-existential [phenomenological], all beings whose mode of being is unlike Dasein must be understood as *unmeaningful (unsinnig)*, as essentially bare of meaning as such.

415

> "Unmeaningful" does not mean here a value judgment, but expresses an ontological determination. *And only what is unmeaningful (unsinnig) can be absurd (widersinnig).* Objectively present things encountered in Dasein [in its being-in-the-world] can, so to speak, run against its being, for example, events of nature which break in on us and destroy us. (Heidegger 1996: 151–2; translation slightly modified)

What I would like to focus upon here is the meaninglessness (incomprehensibility) human Dasein experiences in its being-in-the-world whenever it encounters something that is not only unmeaningful (*unsinnig*) but also absurd (*widersinnig*). The example given by Heidegger is the encountering of "events of nature which break in on us and destroy us." I think what he has in mind here is something like a natural catastrophe – an earthquake or tornado – but wouldn't the same hold for a disease? A disease, at least if severe, is undeniably something that breaks in on us and destroys us. According to Heidegger, such phenomena are totally devoid of meaning; they even offer resistance against our attempts to find a place for them in the meaningful totality of our life. They afflict us, as something entirely unfamiliar that threatens our existence.

Now, it could be said that there is a way of making sense of diseases – namely, the explanation of their causes by science, which can also devise practical means for interfering with the disease process and curing the person whose body has been affected by it. The same could possibly be said of tornadoes and earthquakes, to the extent that it is possible to predict their occurrence and protect oneself against them using meteorology, geology, and construction technology. But this way of dealing with events of nature – rendering them unmeaningful rather than absurd, in Heidegger's terminology – does not mean that the phenomena smoothly assume their place in the everyday world of Dasein. They are still a source of meaninglessness and resistance, since they are hard to incorporate into the totalities of relevance that constitute the everyday (in contrast to the natural-scientific) meaningfulness of human being. They remain a threat to the homelike being-in-the-world of Dasein in their radical and dreadful otherness.

There is another aspect of disease, and of the illness it brings about, that augments, not only its absurdity and meaninglessness, but also its *alien* nature – namely, that it appears as something other *within me*. This is what makes the disease alien: in contrast to the earthquake, it appears in me as something other than me. Thus, the tendency of nature to resist our quest for meaning can crop up either "outside" of us or "inside" of us. We must be careful here in our use of spatial metaphors, however, since the phenomenological point of view, especially that of Heidegger, stresses that the self and its surroundings can only be studied and understood as a synthesis of meaning – a "da-sein," or being-*in*-the-world.

In the phenomenologies of illness attempted so far – particularly the works of Richard Zaner, Drew Leder, and Kay Toombs – the otherness of illness has been depicted precisely as an otherness of one's own *body*. In *The Context of Self*, Zaner writes of the alien and uncanny quality of the body in illness (and also, to some extent, in health) (Zaner 1981: 47 ff.). Leder, in *The Absent Body*, describes this otherness as the "dys-appearance" of the body in illness – as a process whereby the body manifests itself as an independent creature that resists the will and understanding of the ill person (Leder 1990: 69 ff.).

Finally, Toombs, in *The Meaning of Illness*, develops a four-stage model whereby the body in illness is gradually objectified: it ceases to be something lived by me and instead becomes the biological organism researched by science (Toombs 1992: 31 ff.). Scientific and technological representation and objectification of the body, according to Toombs, threaten to aggravate the alienation experienced when the body becomes a source of pain and an obstacle to my everyday projects – threaten to make the reattainment of a state of being at home with one's body even more difficult. On the other hand, of course, medical science and technology can provide remedies for this alienation, as when they devise treatments that alleviate suffering. Although the main points of departure for these American philosophers are the philosophies of Husserl (Zaner), Merleau-Ponty (Leder), and Sartre (Toombs), they are also inspired by the work of European medical phenomenologists of lesser renown, including F. J. J. Buytendijk, Hans Jonas, Herbert Plügge, and Erwin Straus (Spiegelberg 1972).

Body, World, and Time

The lived body is clearly the central domain of the totality of tools making up the world of Dasein, but the alienated body can only be thought of within the patterns of a self that attains its meaning from a being-in-the-world shared with others (what Heidegger calls *Mitsein*). No lived body is disconnected from the world in which it acquires and bestows meaning. Since my life and identity are built up in relation to my world, the alien character of illness shows itself within this entire domain, making the entire being-*in*-the-world unhomelike. This unhomelikeness is therefore inextricably bound both to the experience of the body as a vehicle of meaning and to life with others. Phenomenologically oriented psychiatrists, such as Ludwig Binswanger and Medard Boss (Spiegelberg 1972), were aware of the importance of the whole being-in-the-world of the patient for the understanding of mental illness; yet the phenomenological approach to the loss of meaning experienced in illness rejects the dualistic cleavage of mind from body, conceiving of illness as neither entirely "mental" nor entirely "somatic."

A central aspect of the unhomelikeness experienced in illness is its attuned quality (Svenaeus 2000). Alienating meaninglessness is experienced as a breakdown of understanding, which manifests itself concretely as pain, fatigue, nausea, anxiety, and so on. Feelings, especially moods, are basic to our being-in-the-world, since they open up the world as having significance for Dasein (Heidegger 1996: 134 ff.). They are the basic strata of our facticity – of Dasein's being "thrown" into the world where it makes itself at home. We find ourselves *there*, always already engaged in activities that *matter* to us, and this "mattering to" rests on an attunement, a mood quality, which the being-in-the-world always already has. Moods need not be powerful, or even consciously attended to, but they form a necessary condition of Dasein's being-in-the-world. Indeed, as Heidegger points out, we do not choose our moods freely; they come over us and cannot easily be changed. Illness is a striking example of this.

Heidegger's phenomenological outline describes a curious trajectory in *Being and Time*: it moves from the worldliness of Dasein to its temporality as the ultimate horizon of meaning. The analysis of the temporality of Dasein, in section two of the book, provides the structure necessary for an understanding of Dasein's being-in-the-world as a whole – as a "taking care" of its own existence. What about the place of illness in this context? How does the temporal character of the life of illness differ from that of the healthy life? Are there any important differences to be found at the phenomenological level? We are talking here about lived time, of course, and not about the measurable clock time of the natural sciences. It would not be difficult to detect differences scientifically, since diseases lead to the destruction and death of the biological organism: statistically, the diseased life is usually shorter than the healthy life.

Death is also present in Heidegger's phenomenology, though not as the end of the biological organism, but rather as a privileged, "authentic" possibility for understanding the meaningfulness of life in its relation to time. Death at the phenomenological level is not the ending of life (since it is clearly never experienced as such), but rather the utmost possibility of human existence. Death is the possibility that is always present and yet impossible to realize; it is *pure* possibility. The next moment could always be the last, and death as this overreaching possibility affects our way of receiving meaning from and giving meaning to our existence, which is thus a being-*toward*-death (Heidegger 1996: 247 ff.). When death is acknowledged by Dasein on the phenomenological level (which is made possible, in *Being and Time*, through existential anxiety), the finitude of human existence comes to permeate our way of making sense of life. Life matters because the possibilities realized in our being-in-the-world are finite and dependent on a future approached on the basis of our factual past. In this sense, Dasein is not *in* time, but rather *is* temporal in itself: it projects the possibilities of the future, on the basis of the pattern of meaning constituting its past, as a means of constructing its present. In Heidegger's words, "The totality of being of Dasein as care means: ahead-of-itself-already-being-in (a world) as being-together-with beings encountered in the world" (Heidegger 1996: 327).

If one compares accounts by people suffering from illnesses – in, for example, biographies, fiction, or medical case studies – one thing stands out: an accentuated focus on the present, amid a shrinking away of the past and the future. This focus on the present may be brought on by intense pain, but also by other ailments; in fact, it seems to be a typical feature of the life of illness, at least in the case of a serious illness that forces one to change one's life in crucial ways. Based on my interpretation of illness above, I propose that the temporal structure of illness can be conceptualized as an *alienation* of past and future, whereby my past and future appear alien to me, compared with what was the case before the onset of illness. Illness ruptures my life, to the point that the past and the future appear in a new light – or perhaps a new darkness – in which they acquire a strange quality of being, simultaneously, mine and yet no longer mine.

Two paths open up here for a phenomenology of illness to explore. The first path pertains to the temporality of the body in relation to the temporality of Dasein. One way of understanding the alienating character of illness is that nature, as the temporality of our bodies, ceases to obey our attempts to make sense of phenomena: the time of the body no longer fits into the time of the self. This experience is alienating, since the body, as part of the realm of nature, is also at the center of my own existence – a "my-thing," which I need to fit into the temporality of being-in-the-world.

In chapter six of the second section of *Being and Time*, Heidegger acknowledges that nature plays a crucial part in the temporality of Dasein: day and night, summer and winter, and so on, structure the world of possibilities opened up to human being in its taking care of things (and in its taking care of itself). Yet here again (as above), Heidegger's discussion is limited to the nature "outside" of us (Heidegger 1996: 412 ff.). The earth's movement around the sun forms the basis of both world time (the calendar) and public time; in both the original temporality of Dasein is forgotten and concealed. Eager to stress that Dasein temporalizes, rather than being temporalized (is *as* time, rather than *in* time), Heidegger fails to mention the anonymous temporal process at the heart of our own nature – the time of the body; but this inner world time of the body is just as crucial as outer world time for an understanding of Dasein's temporality. We live in time cycles of breathing, digesting, sleeping, and so on; in women, this "natural temporality" is particularly evident in the case of phenomena such as menstruation and pregnancy (Leder 1990: 89 ff.).

The second path to be explored by a phenomenology of illness with regard to temporality is the path of narrativity. When we make sense of the present, in relation to our future and past, we do so in a special manner – namely, by structuring our experiences in the form of stories (Ricoeur 1992). Illness breaks in on us as a rift in these stories, necessitating a retelling of the past and a re-envisioning of the future, in an effort to address and change their alienated character. The use of narrative as a way of approaching the world of illness is the subject of a growing field in the medical humanities – a field that has contributed many insights to medical ethics and other fields of medical philosophy (Zaner 2004).

Phenomenology at this point becomes acutely hermeneutic in its emphasis on language as the medium of life stories. But these stories never allow us to leave the silent otherness of our bodies behind. They are stories nurtured by the time of nature at the heart of our existence – by a temporality we try to make our own, but which resists these attempts. Stories of illness are haunted by an alien experience at the core of our existence – an experience we try to make our own, or, alternatively, cover up, in order to be able to go on living (Frank 1995).

Medicine: Practice, Science, and Technology

In addressing the alien life of the body in stories of illness, we are approaching a situation in which illness is not only experienced by the suffering person, but also discussed with and examined by the expert in terms of health and disease (Svenaeus 2001: 119 ff.). The idea that medical practice is not only an application of medical science and technology but also an instance of *interpretation* at a phenomenological-hermeneutical level is developed in a late work by Gadamer entitled *The Enigma of Health* (1993; cited as Gadamer 1996).

In several of the papers collected in this volume, Gadamer returns to Aristotle's philosophy (the other main source of inspiration for Heidegger's phenomenology, along with Husserl's philosophy) in his attempts to characterize the essences of health and the clinical encounter. Gadamer's discussions of Aristotelian themes and concepts in this work are similar to those found in his earlier works, with one exception: he now explicitly addresses *medicine*, and not only the humanities, as a form of interpretation and practice. Gadamer makes the point that, in the original meaning of *praxis*, we

419

hear the call for *phronesis* (practical wisdom) in medicine, and not merely the call for technical skill (*techne*) or the applied knowledge of science (*episteme*) (Gadamer 1996: 125 ff.). The goal of medical practice is health, but health cannot be produced by the doctor using technical and scientific skills; rather, it must be *re-established*, as something that has been lost, by helping the patient heal himself. Health is a self-restoring balance, and the doctor provides the means by which a state of equilibrium can re-establish itself on its own power:

> Without doubt it is part of our nature as living beings that the conscious awareness of health conceals itself. Despite its hidden character, health nonetheless manifests itself in a kind of feeling of well-being. It shows itself above all where such a feeling of well-being means that we are open to new things, ready to embark on new enterprises and, forgetful of ourselves, scarcely notice the demands and strains which are put upon us . . . Health is not a condition that one introspectively feels in oneself. Rather it is a condition of being there (Da-Sein), of being in the world (In-der-Welt-Sein), of being together with other people (Mit-den-Menschen-Sein), of being taken in by an active and rewarding engagement with the things that matter in life . . . It is the rhythm of life, a permanent process in which equilibrium re-establishes itself. (Gadamer 1996: 112–14; translation modified)

Health, in contrast to the alien meaninglessness of illness, effaces itself in an enigmatic way. It seems to be the absence of alienness – the state we are in, the process we undergo, when everything is flowing smoothly. Here, the conceptual backdrop for Gadamer's analysis of health is undoubtedly Heidegger's phenomenology of everyday human being-in-the-world, which has served as the general point of departure in this chapter. Health and illness, on the phenomenological level of everyday meaningfulness, are thus contrary tendencies, opposite ends of a continuum. They are homelike and unhomelike ways of orienting ourselves in the world and striving to make sense of our way of being. On the temporal level, the being-at-home of health takes on a rhythmic quality, tied to the temporality of the lived body; it is thus inscribed in the overarching temporality of being-in-the-world – in the projecting of the future, out of the past, that gives rise to the present.

But medicine is not only *phronesis*, which in *The Nicomachean Ethics* means the practical wisdom of how to encounter the other and deal with normative matters of life – i.e., ethical-political knowledge of what is vital to human flourishing (Aristotle 2002). Modern medical practice makes use of theories and technologies developed by the natural sciences in its attempts to understand and alter the biological organism. Such theories and technologies have changed the essence of medicine during the past 200 years in revolutionary ways, making it possible to interfere with pathological processes by way of biological therapies. Such therapies (antibiotics, for instance) help nature heal itself, and the doctor must know how and when to use them. Gadamer's point would not be that the doctor should eschew a biological approach; rather, the doctor must be both a scientist and a phronetic craftsman – and, in his capacity as the latter, a phenomenologist as well, in the sense of an interpreter of the meaning patterns of the patient's life (Svenaeus 2003). According to this perspective, the body is not only a biological system of causal relations, but also a vehicle of meaning, a being-in-the-world, which is lived by the person afflicted with illness in the manner of a life narrative.

The success story of medical science threatens to legitimize a pragmatic approach in which the phenomenology of health and illness – the phronetic-hermeneutic aspect of medical practice – is forgotten and the patient is regarded *exclusively* as a biological organism. The rebirth of medical ethics, since the mid-1970s, as a vital part of the medical enterprise is a clear acknowledgment of this threat: the questions of modern medicine are not reducible to what *could* be done with biological knowledge and technology, but rather to what *should* be done with them. Medical science today makes it possible to control the processes of life in astonishing ways – ways that sometimes have little to do with the re-establishing of health. Consider ventilators, psychotropic drugs, plastic surgery, and the new molecular-biological technologies, for example. Isn't modern medicine today redrawing the border between health and disease, rather than facilitating the reestablishment of a basic equilibrium? This is an urgent question, not least from the phenomenological perspective.

Let us return to the question of what kind of knowledge and activity (medical) science represents, in contrast to the meaningfulness of everyday life. The realist answer would be that science discovers nature as it really is, making it possible to manipulate nature through interfering with the causal processes of the basic stuff of reality. The constructivist answer, on the other hand, would be that science not only *discovers*, but also *constructs* reality, through the concepts of scientific theories. As is the case with other forms of human understanding, scientific theory represents the meaning pattern in which science lives. Husserl, in his late works, increasingly stressed that the natural sciences must anchor their concepts in the meaning patterns of the life world (the being-in-the-world) from which they have originated (Husserl 1970). Nevertheless, science – provided it doesn't fall prey to naturalism, forgetting its origin in the life world – represents, in Husserl's view, a liberating *telos* of humanity that is an alloy of philosophy and phenomenology, as different expressions of a general *theoria*.

Heidegger, in works such as *The Question Concerning Technology* (Heidegger 1977), a speech first delivered in 1953, and Gadamer, in *The Enigma of Health* (Gadamer 1996: 6 ff.), are more critical than Husserl of modern science and technology. Technoscience is held to be an enframing worldview (*Gestell*), in which nature is made invisible and turned into an energy resource in a scientific-economic calculus (the modern power station exploiting the River Rhine is Heidegger's main example in the essay). As a contrast to this enframing pattern of technoscience, Heidegger, in *The Question Concerning Technology*, sees a possibility for nature to show itself out of itself – an original *poiesis* of *physis*, in Greek terms. This breaking forth of nature, according to Heidegger, can actually be upheld and sustained with the help of human constructions, such as the old wooden bridge over the Rhine, which lets the river be a river and not just a source of energy.

This approach to nature and technology is of crucial importance for our phenomenological interpretation of health and medical science. In many ways, *The Question Concerning Technology* represents a more nuanced account of the constitution of meaning than *Being and Time*, since the former work assigns distinct places and functions

421

to both nature and technology within the tool-based pattern of human being-in-the-world (Dreyfus 1992; Fell 1992). In *Being and Time*, pure nature is conceptualized as merely unmeaningful or absurd, whereas in *The Question Concerning Technology*, it becomes obvious that nature can become meaningful for human beings in the form of an *autonomous* self-showing – a *physis*. But the self-disclosure of nature would not only be a part of the "outer" world of Dasein, it would also be the basic element of health as a self-establishing rhythmic process at the heart of our bodies – the process Gadamer describes in *The Enigma of Health*. Just as the bridge helps the Rhine disclose itself, medical practice can help the nature of our bodies to make itself at home in the culture of our being-in-the-world.

But what is the difference really, in Heidegger's analysis, between the old wooden bridge and the modern power station? In the terminology of *Being and Time*, they are both tools, both nodal points of the practical meaning pattern of Dasein's being-in-the-world. Why does the bridge, but not the power station, let the nature of the river shine through? Why does the power station, but not the bridge, transform the river into something manipulated in the course of human projects? Heidegger's answer to the second question in *The Question Concerning Technology* is that the enframing of modern technology is not a human project at all, but rather a meaning pattern whereby we understand things in the world as merely economic and physical resources. The goal of modern technology is not determined by humans; rather, it is a meaning pattern in which we cease to be human, in the sense of beings dwelling in the world, and are transformed into materials and numbers ourselves. For even if Heidegger's example of modern technology as an enframement limits itself, in *The Question Concerning Technology*, to nonhuman examples of nature, such as rivers and forests, the *Gestell*, as our modern *Geschick* (destiny), will ultimately enframe, not only plants and animals, but human beings as well. Nuclear physics has today been surpassed by molecular biology as the leading force of modern science, and evolutionary biology is determining the patterns of the twenty-first-century *Gestell*. As Michel Foucault has pointed out in many seminal works, since it assumed its modern forms around the year 1800, medical science has framed the patterns of normality, not only by discovering new diseases, but also by directly determining, on a political level, the meaning patterns of the normal and abnormal life. The biopolitics of Foucault fits perfectly into the Heideggerian analysis of modern technology, and in both cases we can trace the influence of a Nietzschean genealogy of ethics and science.

Let us return to the first question above. Why doesn't the wooden bridge enframe the river in the same way as the power station? Lest our answer simply reflect a romantic preference for pre-modern tools, I think we must stress the extent to which the wooden bridge is constitutive of a world that is still within the reach of *phronesis*. But such constitutiveness might also be said to be a feature of many modern technological apparatuses, such as the computed-tomography scanner, used to visualize brain tumors, or the cochlear implant, used to improve hearing. The important questions are the following: Is the scientific-technological examination or therapy enveloped in a pattern of phronetic understanding? Or is it let loose to operate independently, in the form of an objectifying pattern of scientific-technological powers and forces – a *techne* that is no longer the *techne* of human *praxis*, but rather that of technoscience itself?

422

Concluding Remarks: Being-with-Nature and Being-with-the-Other

We are, from the outset, together with other human beings in our being-in-the-world, and this being-with-the-other, just like being-with-nature, contains the basic potentiality of otherness and difference. The otherness of the other, however, is not usually an experience of meaninglessness, but rather a reserve of new meaning waiting to be developed. Being with the other is not unhomelike or alienating in itself in the way illness is. However, nor is nature in itself alienating. On the contrary, being-with-nature (in the sense both of being embodied and of encountering nature in one's everyday doings) is most often a source of meaningfulness and belonging. It must consequently be emphasized that neither the otherness of nature nor the otherness of culture are alienating in themselves; rather, they *become* alienating in illness.

In this chapter I have chosen to analyze illness and health primarily from the viewpoint of the alienness of nature at the heart of our being. But being-with-nature is always already a being-with-the-other, since we are thrown into the meaning structure of worldliness. The alienness of the other (i.e., the alienness of culture) must be acknowledged and understood by medical phenomenology, particularly in cases of "mental illness" (i.e., within psychiatry). At this point in my argument, two questions arise, which I (for lack of space) have omitted above, but which need to be addressed phenomenologically: In what sense do the healthy life and the life of illness differ from the good life and the miserable life? And to what extent do they differ from, or overlap with, what Heidegger calls authentic and inauthentic existence? Although I have offered preliminary answers to these questions elsewhere (Svenaeus 2001: 90 ff., 2003), I am convinced that much remains to be said. Alienness is a key concept, not only in the case of illness, but also in the case of authenticity.

References and Further Reading

Aristotle (2002) *Nicomachean Ethics* (trans. S. Broadie and C. Rowe). Oxford: Oxford University Press (original publication date unknown).

Dreyfus, H. L. (1992) Heidegger's history of the being of equipment. In H. L. Dreyfus and H. Hall (eds.), *Heidegger: A Critical Reader* (pp. 173–85). Oxford: Blackwell.

Fell, J. P. (1992) The familiar and the strange: On the limits of praxis in the early Heidegger. In H. L. Dreyfus and H. Hall (eds.), *Heidegger: A Critical Reader* (pp. 65–80). Oxford: Blackwell.

Frank, A. W. (1995) *The Wounded Storyteller: Body, Illness and Ethics*. Chicago: University of Chicago Press.

Gadamer, H-G. (1996) *The Enigma of Health: The Art of Healing in a Scientific Age* (trans. J. Gaiger and N. Walker). Stanford, CA: Stanford University Press (original work published 1993).

Heidegger, M. (1977) *The Question Concerning Technology and Other Essays* (trans. W. Lovitt). New York: Harper & Row (original work published 1954).

—— (1996) *Being and Time* (trans. J. Stambaugh). Albany: State University of New York Press (original work published 1927; references in this chapter refer to the standard German pagination found in the margins of the English translation).

—— (2001) *Zollikon Seminars: Protocols, Conversations, Letters* (trans. F. Mayr and R. Askay). Evanston, IL: Northwestern University Press (original work published 1987).

423

Hiley, D. R., Bohman, J. F., and Shusterman, R. (eds.) (1991) *The Interpretive Turn: Philosophy, Science, Culture*. Ithaca, NY: Cornell University Press.

Husserl, E. (1970) *The Crisis of European Sciences and Transcendental Phenomenology: An Introduction to Phenomenological Philosophy* (trans. D. Carr). Evanston, IL: Northwestern University Press (original work published 1954).

—— (2001) *Logical Investigations* (2 vols.) (trans. J. N. Findlay). London: Routledge (original work published 1900–1).

Leder, D. (1990) *The Absent Body*. Chicago: University of Chicago Press.

Merleau-Ponty, M. (1962) *Phenomenology of Perception* (trans. C. Smith). London: Routledge (original work published 1945).

Ricoeur, P. (1992) *Oneself as Another* (trans. K. Blamey). Chicago: University of Chicago Press (original work published 1990).

Spiegelberg, H. (1972) *Phenomenology in Psychology and Psychiatry*. Evanston, IL: Northwestern University Press.

Svenaeus, F. (2000) Das Unheimliche: Towards a phenomenology of illness. *Medicine, Health Care and Philosophy*, 3, 3–16.

—— (2001) *The Hermeneutics of Medicine and the Phenomenology of Health: Steps Towards a Philosophy of Medical Practice*. Dordrecht: Kluwer.

—— (2003) Hermeneutics of medicine in the wake of Gadamer: The issue of *phronesis*. *Theoretical Medicine and Bioethics*, 24, 407–31.

Toombs, S. K. (1992) *The Meaning of Illness: A Phenomenological Account of the Different Perspectives of Physician and Patient*. Dordrecht: Kluwer.

—— (2001) Introduction: Phenomenology and medicine. In S. K. Toombs (ed.), *Handbook of Phenomenology and Medicine* (pp. 1–26). Dordrecht: Kluwer.

Volpi, F. (1996) Dasein as *praxis*: the Heideggerian assimilation and radicalization of the practical philosophy of Aristotle. In C. Macann (ed.), *Critical Heidegger* (pp. 27–66). London: Routledge.

Watanabe, J. (1993) Categorial intuition and the understanding of being in Husserl and Heidegger. In J. Sallis (ed.), *Reading Heidegger: Commemorations* (pp. 109–17). Bloomington: Indiana University Press.

Zaner, R. M. (1981) *The Context of Self: A Phenomenological Inquiry Using Medicine as a Clue*. Athens: Ohio University Press.

—— (2004) *Conversations on the Edge: Narratives of Ethics and Illness*. Washington, DC: Georgetown University Press.

29

Realism, Science, and the Deworlding of the World

PETER ELI GORDON

Strangest is their reality.
their three-dimensional workmanship:
veined pebbles that have an underside,
maps one could have studied for minutes longer,
books we seem to read page after page.

If these are symbols cheaply coined
to buy the mind a momentary pardon,
whence this extravagance?

From "Dream Objects," by John Updike (Updike 1988: 55)

Introduction

The classical thinkers of the phenomenological tradition – Husserl, Heidegger, and Merleau-Ponty – were deeply divided as to what should count as "world" and "reality." Generally speaking, the phenomenological view is that the world is the horizon of disclosure: it is the field that permits phenomena to show themselves. And reality is the transcendent realm of entities as they exist independent of the world. But this raises a wealth of intriguing problems: What, more precisely, is the relation between world and reality? Is reality external to the world? If so, doesn't this transform the category of world into a subjective condition, such that phenomenology becomes a species of subjective idealism? If not, if reality shows up only as it is disclosed in the world, doesn't this mean that there is no hope of describing what reality itself is "actually" like? A decisive question in this debate is whether one holds that metaphysical reality is equivalent to what scientists call "nature." The variety of responses to this question reveals a great deal not only about phenomenological methods, but also about the often negative image of natural science that has informed phenomenology over the twentieth century.

This chapter has four parts. First, I offer a brief excursus on the concepts of world and reality in Husserl's transcendental phenomenology. My aim is twofold, to stress a continuity between Husserl and Heidegger, insofar as both of them conceived of the world as the transcendental horizon for phenomena, but also, to emphasize a discontinuity, insofar as Husserl's way of conceptualizing the world left him vulnerable to the charge of subjective idealism, a charge Heidegger believed he could evade. Second, I provide a more detailed discussion of Heidegger's existential notion of "worldhood." Here, I will pay special attention to the *spatial* character of worldhood, in order to cast some light on Heidegger's strong distinction between existential spatiality and natural-scientific space. Third, I will address Heidegger's more controversial claim that, whereas worldhood is dependent upon practices and interpretative schemes, the scientific-realist conceives of entities as "deworlded." This claim, as I will show, raises a variety of problems for Heidegger in the debate over realism and idealism. Heidegger's position in this debate, as I shall explain, might be considered a version of "quietism." Fourth and finally, I offer some broader, more critical reflections on the place of scientific realism in phenomenology. Here I will suggest that Heidegger's image of the scientist as confronting a realm of deworlded entities is philosophically unhelpful and inconsistent. Indeed, such an image of deworlded scientific reality is a remnant of anti-scientism, and is best dispensed with, for reasons Heidegger's own philosophy would seem to support.

To anticipate, this chapter supports the view that reality, even scientific reality, is always disclosed within an interpretative world. This is a view the early Heidegger did not unambiguously endorse and only came to accept in his later writings. For the early Heidegger, reality as it is disclosed by natural science is a deworlded realm of entities lacking in significance. But, if Heidegger himself was right that Dasein "always" projects a world, then this view cannot be sustained. For as post-Kuhnnian philosophers and historians of science have tried to show, scientific reality is itself disclosed only within communities of practice and horizons of "care." And, more importantly, the way those entities are disclosed *bears on the understanding of Being that we ascribe to those entities:* they are not the deworlded or "non-interpretive" entities the early Heidegger took them to be. The thrust of my argument, then, will be that we need to adopt a more consistently Heideggerian view: (1) We can affirm Heidegger's doctrine that Dasein always projects a world, and we can also affirm his commitment to metaphysical realism, i.e., the doctrine that there is a "reality" independent of the worlds that disclose that reality. And (2) we can also affirm Heidegger's scientific realism, i.e., the doctrine that scientific practice investigates entities that are in some way independent of those practices. But (3) we should dispense with Heidegger's own misunderstanding of science as a practice that discloses entities *just as they are* independent of those practices. For if science is one kind of practice alongside others, then the scientific image of deworlded entities is itself *an interpretation of the Being of those entities.* Science does not enjoy a special access to deworlded reality.

This argument has broad consequences for how phenomenologists conceive of the relation between science and the world. For once the scientific conception of reality is seen as merely one world among others, the longstanding conflict between the *Kulturwissenschaften* and the *Naturwissenschaften* can no longer be construed as a quarrel between interpretive and non-interpretive modes of knowing. And so, the romantic fear that science brings "disenchantment" – a deworlding of the interpretive world – must yield before the more inclusive view that science has an interpretive world of its own.

426

Husserl, World, and the Problem of Metaphysical Realism

What did Husserl mean by "world" and "reality"? For Husserl, the attempt to describe the "stream of experience" must begin with what he called the "real events" of the natural world. Phenomenology, as he conceives it in *Ideas I*, could only develop by means of a decisive mental shift from the attitude of involved, everyday understanding to that of disengaged, mental awareness. To be sure, it must take as its point of departure the so-called "natural standpoint" and the understanding of reality that belonged to everyday consciousness of the "man on the street." Now Husserl claims that such an everyday understanding of reality depends upon the "natural thesis" (or, alternately, the "general thesis"), according to which "the real world about me is at all times known not merely in a general way as something apprehended but as a fact-world *that has its being out there*" (Husserl 1931: 108).

But Husserl is not content to remain with this understanding of reality. If phenomenology is to be a "rigorous science," it must perform a mental bracketing of the existential commitment as it is expressed in the natural thesis. For only then can we discover that region of pure consciousness which is alone the concern of phenomenological inquiry. Husserl emphasizes that nothing about this mental shift actually called into question the "reality" of the natural standpoint:

> We do not abandon the thesis we have adopted, we make no change in our conviction . . . And yet the thesis undergoes a modification – whilst remaining in itself what it is, *we set it as it were "out of action,"* we *"disconnect it," "bracket it."* It still remains there like the bracketed in the bracket, like the disconnected outside the connexional system. We can also say: The thesis is experience as lived (*Erlebnis*), *but we make "no use of it."* (Husserl 1931: 108)

Crucial to Husserl's method of disconnection is that our everyday belief in reality remains undoubted – here Husserl dissents from Descartes – but it simply plays no further role in phenomenological inquiry. And Husserl is also emphatic that, because *all of the empirical sciences* involve this commitment to reality, the bracketing of existential conviction puts all such sciences equally out of play, for the sake of an altogether distinctive kind of a priori science of consciousness:

> The whole world as placed within the nature-setting and presented in experience as real, taken completely "free from all theory," just as it is in reality experienced, and made clearly manifest in and through the linkings of our experiences, has now no validity for us, it must be set in brackets, untested indeed but also uncontested. Similarly all theories and sciences, positivistic or otherwise, which relate to this world, however good they may be, succumb to the same fate. (Husserl 1931: 111)

Husserl's bracketing technique implies a two-tiered theory of knowledge, and it poses a stark choice between the natural attitude and attitude of transcendental phenomenology: We may concern ourselves with either (a) any one of a number of richly textured investigations of empirical reality, the plenum of both everyday experience and the natural sciences, and all of these empirical sciences necessarily rely upon the

427

"natural thesis" and its existential commitment to a mind-transcendent reality; or, (b) we can concern ourselves with the "a priori" investigation of mental "sense" as it falls within "transcendental subjectivity," and, in doing so, attempt a unique science of our own mind-immanent sphere. This sphere itself contains the grounds for all possible experience and which is therefore the condition *for* the first kind of empirical inquiry.

The first attitude directs our attention to "reality," and the latter to the "world," in its technical, phenomenological sense of that term. The well-known consequence of this dualistic contrast is that the second option, once established, seems in conflict with the very commitment to metaphysical realism that the natural attitude had presupposed. Instead, the very presence of the world to consciousness is revealed – in Merleau-Ponty's phrase – as something "paradoxical":

> Reflection does not withdraw from the world toward the unity of consciousness as the world's basis; it steps back to watch the forms of transcendence fly up like sparks from a fire; it slackens the intentional threads which attach us to the world and thus brings them to our notice; it alone is consciousness of the world because it reveals that world as strange and paradoxical. (Merleau-Ponty 1962: xiii)

But if the phenomenological reduction thus makes "intentional threads" available to analysis, it also means that the "world" takes on a wholly immanent meaning. Indeed, the reduction seems to forbid any intelligible talk of a mind-transcendent reality. This result is especially evident in Husserl's most idealist work, the *Cartesian Meditations* (first written in 1929):

> Every imaginable sense, every imaginable being, whether the latter is called immanent or transcendent, falls within the domain of transcendental subjectivity, as the subjectivity that constitutes sense and being. The attempt to conceive the universe of true being as something lying outside the universe of possible consciousness, possible knowledge, possible evidence, the two being related to one another merely externally by a rigid law, is nonsensical. They belong together essentially; and, as belonging together essentially, they are also concretely one, one in the only absolute concretion: transcendental subjectivity. If transcendental subjectivity is the universe of possible sense, then an outside is precisely – nonsense. (Husserl 1973: 84)

This claim is remarkably idealistic. And Husserl only strengthens its idealistic tone with his further, clarificatory remark that the "world" is itself immanent to consciousness:

> That the being of the world "transcends" consciousness . . . and that it necessarily remains transcendent, in no wise alters the fact that it is conscious life alone, wherein everything that is transcendent becomes constituted, as something inseparable from consciousness, and which specifically, as world-consciousness, bears within itself inseparably the sense: world – and indeed, "this actually existing" world. (Husserl 1973: 62)

For Husserl, then, "world" is something constituted *within* transcendental subjectivity. And it is our conception *within* consciousness *of any mind-transcendent reality* that is a condition *for* our actual experience. Whether Husserl found a way to avoid the undesirable idealist implications of this world-concept has been explored elsewhere

(Kelly 2003). Here it is relevant only to note that Husserl expressly defines his world-theory *as a species of idealism*. Phenomenology, he claims, "is *eo ipso* 'transcendental idealism,'* though in a fundamentally and essentially new sense." For, "this is not a produce of sportive argumentations, a prize to be won in the dialectical context with 'realisms.'" Instead, it is an investigation of "the constituting intentionality itself," and "an explication of my ego as subject of every possible cognition, and indeed with respect to every sense of what exists, wherewith the latter might be able to *have* a sense for me, the ego" (Husserl 1960: 86). In sum, Husserl recasts the "world" as an intentional horizon immanent to consciousness, and then welcomes the suggestion that this represents a kind of idealism. And, finally, he suggests that without this consciousness-immanent "world," there can be no sensical talk of a mind-transcendent "true being." Whether Heidegger managed to evade this idealistic theory of the world remains to be seen.

Heidegger and the "Worldhood of the World"

Let us now turn to Heidegger, and to his analysis in *Being and Time* of the existential category he terms "worldhood of the world" (Heidegger 1962: §§14–24). To properly grasp the importance of this analysis, we should recall that Heidegger's larger task in the first half of *Being and Time* is to lay the grounds for the ultimate inquiry, the so-called *Seinsfrage*, or question of Being. This question is directed at the "sense of Being," or *Sinn des Seins*, a terminological choice that signals Heidegger's continued allegiance to phenomenological technique. Briefly, if reference is the *meaning* one intends, then sense is one's *way* of intending that meaning. To recall Frege's own example, "the Morning Star" has an identical reference as "the Evening Star," while their sense is nonetheless distinct (Frege 1970). The investigation of sense rather than reference marks a crucial way-station toward the phenomenologist's theory of intentionality, since sense is the specific modality by which consciousness intends, or is directed toward, its object (Lafont 2000). The "sense" of Being, then, is that transcendental condition in virtue of which the object of one's intention is said "to be" at all.

Heidegger's question of Being is thus an inquiry into the sense of Being that belongs to the intentional horizon. Like Husserl, Heidegger believed the constitutive features of this horizon might be described without recourse to the possibly prejudicial concepts and methods of the philosophical tradition. Phenomenological description is supposed to begin with an analysis of phenomena simply as they "show themselves" to be and as they present themselves in experience. But here Heidegger departs from his teacher Husserl: Whereas Husserl developed a method of phenomenological bracketing, or *epoché*, so as to isolate the purely transcendental features of intention, Heidegger wished to develop a phenomenology of the "natural attitude." That is, he wished to explore the intentionality – the route of intention opening upon the world – insofar as this is manifest in the "everydayness" of human existence. In sum, against the quasi-Cartesian project of Husserl's "transcendental" analysis which sought to investigate the a priori structures of transcendental consciousness, Heidegger proposed an "existential" analysis of human being-in-the-world.

The difference between Husserl and Heidegger as to their point of departure should not be exaggerated, and recent scholarship has shown that in his later lectures Husserl anticipated or came to share many of Heidegger's own views (Zahavi 2003). Still, it seems clear that Heidegger at least rejects Husserl's bracketing-technique. Indeed, for Heidegger, the metaphysical-realist commitments of the natural thesis cannot be held in suspension. For, by defining human existence as "being-in-the-world," Heidegger wishes to grant in advance that the human being's existence is bound up with the existence of the world. And this has an important consequence that any anti-realist challenge to the independence of the external world would *already* be a challenge to the reality of the human subject, as I shall explain later on.

Heidegger's analytic begins with the claim that the human way of being can claim as its core identity nothing else besides its existence. There is no mysterious or transcendental "essence" which lies behind the various expressions of human activity as their unmoved mover or point of origin. We "are" nothing more than our unfolding existence itself. Heidegger terms this unfolding identity "Dasein," and he then offers a provisional definition of Dasein as "being-in-the-world." The entirety of division one in *Being and Time* amounts to a kind of anatomical portrait that serves to deepen our appreciation of the various facets of this essentially holistic structure. It aims to disclose that pre-philosophical yet constitutively necessary "sense of being" that belongs to and serves as the ultimate horizon for our being-in-the-world. The guiding assumption of this interpretation is that Dasein "is" only insofar as it is "ontological." Human life, in other words, exhibits, in its very *way of being*, a rudimentary understanding of what it means to be. It is this, Dasein's ontological understanding, that Heidegger contrives to examine in the existential analytic, and he proposes to do so by breaking it down into each one of its elements. These include: the social quality of "being-with," the interpretative structures of "understanding" and "being-in" as such, and the so-called "worldhood of the 'world.' "

The analysis of worldhood as it is set forth chiefly in the third chapter of *Being and Time* introduces the distinctively "existential" theme of spatial relation that bears directly on Heidegger's broader conceptions of world and reality. In what follows, I will first reconstruct some of his basic claims about spatial relation, and then move on to his more general conceptions of worldhood and reality.

Heidegger begins by warding off a possible misunderstanding, that the "world" to be analyzed is that of objective "nature" enjoying ontological independence from Dasein. The world should not be construed as what-is-*not*-Dasein, since the aim is precisely to examine that "worldhood" which is a constitutive part of Dasein's own intentional structure. Thus "worldhood" (*Weltlichkeit*) is itself, in Heidegger's terminology, an "existentiale," or existential category (Heidegger 1962: §14).

What does it mean to say that worldhood is an existential? Here the comparison to Kant is helpful, since an "existential" is analogous in some respects to a Kantian category. It is an *a priori*, constitutive condition for possible experience, although, unlike Kant, it is not a mentalistic condition for possible representations. On the contrary, Heidegger does not wish to prejudice his analysis in favor of cognitivism or representationalism. But he believes this prejudice has become so deeply ingrained in the way we habitually relate to the world that it passes already for the common-sense metaphysics of everyday life. Accordingly, it would be unwise to begin by describing the "entities"

430

(*Seiende*) within-the-world, since any such description would necessarily presuppose the existential horizon we need to examine. We always risk falling back without notice upon a particular ontological interpretation of these entities as "things," as objective and extended substances (*res extensa*) that are somehow "out there" and "beyond" the subjective mind (*res cogitans*) that wishes to know them. This is an interpretation, Heidegger tells us, that we have inherited from the metaphysical tradition, chiefly from Descartes. Heidegger takes great pains to ward off this interpretation, since he believes it misses the ontological character of "worldliness" that informs Dasein's own self-understanding as a being whose manner of being is being-in-the-world.

Similarly, Heidegger wants to avoid the misinterpretation that Dasein's way of "being-in" the world is just like that of extended things. The "being-in" of two sub- stances, say, a ball in a box, is something altogether different from the "being-in" which accompanies Dasein's ontological understanding. Properly speaking, merely extended things are merely co-present, and "they can never 'touch' each other, nor can either of them, '*be*' *alongside* the other," in the special way that touching, or being- alongside, is possible for beings who exist in and through their interpretative relation to the world. Unlike the ball in the box, then, "Being-in . . . is a state of Dasein's Being; it is an existentiale. So one cannot think of it as the Being-present-at-hand of some cor- poreal Thing . . . 'in' an entity which is present-at-hand" (Heidegger 1962: 54). Heidegger's attempt to reject the philosophical picture of Dasein as a metaphysically independent entity "in" or "alongside" the world has important consequences for his views on the debate between idealists and realists, as I shall explain later.

Heidegger's own analysis of worldhood takes as its point of departure that sense of one's practical surroundings that belongs to human ontological understanding: This, he writes, is "that world of . . . Dasein which is closest to it," namely, the "*environ- ment*," or *Umwelt* (Heidegger 1962: 66). While Heidegger warns us that the prefix "*Um*," or "aroundness" should not be construed in a literally *spatial* sense, he nonethe- less devotes much effort later in the chapter to distinguishing between the spatiality most customarily associated with the Cartesian, physical-scientific understanding of the world as nature and his own understanding of the world as environment.

The analysis of "environmentality" begins, however, not with environmental spatiality but with our practical relation *to* that environment, which Heidegger – using the same prefix, "*Um*" – calls our involvements or "dealings" (*Umgang*). He explains: "The kind of dealing which is closest to us is . . . not a bare perceptual cogni- tion, but rather that kind of concern which manipulates things and puts them to use; and this has its own kind of 'knowledge.'" The basic and pre-philosophical interpreta- tion of environmental entities therefore construes them not as "things" independent of us but rather as things-in-use, as "equipment" (*Zeug*), an interpretation captured in the term "*pragmata*." Heidegger's claim is that the human relation to worldly entities is primarily a relation of skillful "coping" (Dreyfus 1991a). We understand them not as objects of theoretical analysis, but rather only as they first appear within the context of practice, in and through our involvement. To reinforce this idea, Heidegger here introduced his famous distinction between the ready-to-hand (*zuhanden*) status of entities when understood as equipment, as against the present-at-hand (*vorhanden*) understanding of entities as they show themselves in perceptual cognition. The ready- to-hand is how entities show themselves in our "everyday" and pre-philosophical

431

experience. It is, moreover, the "primordial" way entities are for us. Entities only show up as present-at-hand conditional upon a theoretical *dissociation* from our equipmental involvement.

Given the pragmatic relationship to the world as described above, Heidegger suggests that entities are interpreted in advance according to a teleological network, where each facet of the environment enjoys its most basic significance only because it is assigned a purpose in relation to the whole. An environmental entity is thus a "something 'in-order-to'" (*etwas um-zu*), and this significance immediately implies its purposive interconnection with the other entities of the world. Indeed, Heidegger points out that this interconnection belongs to the very essence of equipment, since each entity is assigned its place only in reference to something else. Consequently, there is no such thing as "an equipment," since discrete entities are understood in advance according to a referential totality of assignments. The totality thereby assumes a transcendental function, in that it is a condition for the possibility of understanding any one of its parts. The world as thus encountered is already a "totality of equipment" (Heidegger 1962: 68).

The environment, then, is a holistic structure of concern, in which entities are *always* practically understood in advance of any discrete or explicit knowledge. To underscore this point, Heidegger coins an additional term of art that captures the mode of understanding which accompanies our environmental relation: As against theoretical "vision," or *Sicht* we understand in a mode of implicit sight, or *Umsicht*. Accordingly, we should not think of "dealings" as explicit "tasks" that we understand theoretically in advance and then go on to complete in practice. As Heidegger explains, most of our dealings "have already dispersed themselves into manifold ways of concern" (Heidegger 1962: 95). A future-oriented intention is built in to human understanding, and this implies that our practical relation to things is best understood, not as an instrumentalist one that aims to fulfill some specified goal, but instead as a kind of implicit investment in how things turn out and how our life-involvements as a whole are going to unfold.

As this exposition may suggest, Heidegger believed that Dasein's own sense of spatial relatedness in-the-world – "existential spatiality" – is itself conditional upon Dasein's equipmental context. Existential spatiality, or *"Räumlichkeit,"* is thus unlike the Cartesian notion of extension or a Newtonian idea of space as a container. The latter make sense only in reference to present-to-hand objects. They do not apply to a being whose primary relation to the world is one of involvement. Heidegger's point, in other words, is that picking out discrete "concepts" of things and relating them to one another is only possible once things have first been conceived as "present-at-hand," that is, as matter or "substance" in Cartesian space. But to conceive of entities in this way is to "break" from the equipmental context which constitutes the true ground of human understanding. It follows, however, that we must develop a notion of existential spatiality that is consistent with our involvement, and we must take care to dis-tinguish between Dasein's spatiality and the "Cartesian" space of present-to-hand things. Spatiality is different from space (Malpas 2000; Dreyfus 1991a: 43).

The spatiality of Dasein is the sense of orientation which emerges out of the equipmental totality of Dasein's world. The ready-to-hand has its own spatiality insofar as equipment requires placement within the totality of assignments. This sort of placement implies an understanding of something ready-to-hand as being "close" (*in der Nähe*), but it is not closeness in the sense of measurable distance. It is more a matter of an item's "belonging-somewhere" (*Hingehörigkeit*) within the context of involvement itself. And this sense of proper fit is what first lends the context its specific orientation: Everything within the context is thus assigned a certain position, a "there" or "yonder" (" *'Dort' und 'Da' "*), and the entire context accordingly appears as a spatial "region" (*Gegend*). Unlike the three-dimensional, coordinate system of Cartesian space, which possesses neither left nor right, neither up nor down, the spatiality of Dasein's involvement first lends our world a definite orientation (Heidegger 1962: 103).

The spatiality attending the equipmental context of the ready-to-hand is thus irreducible to Cartesian space. The strength of this contrast is most noticeable when one reflects upon the fact that Cartesian space always places things at a measurable distance, whereas Dasein's spatiality determines distance in terms of its own context of significance. This is true already, Heidegger suggests, insofar as bodily orientation and directionality attend our involvement in the world. Stated more broadly, our sense of what is near is a function of significance rather than measure: The soles of one's feet, for example, tend as a rule to vanish into the inconspicuousness of the ready-to-hand, while the person encountered while walking is brought to the fore, even while she may remain at a great measurable distance. To clarify this peculiar feature of Dasein's existential constitution, Heidegger introduces the term *"Entfernung,"* or deseverance, to indicate the "undoing-the-far" which accompanies our orientation within the equipmental context (Heidegger 1962: 138–9). It is important to note that such deseverance is not the result of an interpretative action: it is not as if things lying at some measurable distance were brought close as a result of subjective imposition. As Heidegger explains, "de-severance" is an *existential*, and this means that Dasein's world is first *constituted* with this existential-spatial structure: "*In Dasein,*" he concludes, "*there lies an essential tendency towards closeness*" (Heidegger 1962: 105).

This observation is important because one might otherwise believe that Dasein's spatiality were a kind of interpretation overlaid upon a pre-existent given Cartesian space. On the contrary, Heidegger wants to argue that existential spatiality is the precondition for Dasein having a world at all, and the scientific conception of space *presupposes* existential spatiality. But this raises the question of how Dasein could ever effect what Heidegger terms a "deworlding" of the world.

Deworlding the World

As the above exposition of existential spatiality makes plain, it is characteristic of Heidegger's overall manner of thinking to posit a sharp break between existential worldhood and natural-scientific observation. Whereas Cartesian space is that of measurable distance, existential spatiality is a horizon that "brings close." And whereas Cartesian space is a world of pure dimensionality that nonetheless lacks any determinate sense of orientation, existential spatiality "with regard to right and left" is itself based upon the "*a priori* of Being-in-the-world," and yet "lacks the pure multiplicity of the three dimensions" (Heidegger 1962: 110). Moreover, existential spatiality is the

433

precondition for our understanding of Cartesian space, since the former is an existential condition for understanding at all. It follows that whatever formalized structures of measurement we may create in our attempt to better negotiate our surroundings, such structures are themselves merely a way of "thematizing" the spatiality of Dasein's everyday environment. From this, Heidegger derives the noteworthy conclusion that there is no such thing as a "breakthrough" from existential spatiality to space:

> As Being-in-the-world, Dasein maintains itself essentially in de-severing. This de-severance – the farness of the ready-to-hand from Dasein itself – is something that Dasein can *never cross over*. Of course the remoteness of something ready-to-hand from Dasein can show up as a distance from it, . . . [and] Dasein can subsequently traverse the "between" of this distance, but only in such a way that the distance itself becomes one which has been desevered. So little has Dasein crossed over its de-severance that it has rather taken it along with it and keeps doing so constantly; for *Dasein is essentially de-severance.* (Heidegger 1962: 142–3)

Heidegger does not deny that it is possible to develop a purely mental representation of formalized, Cartesian space. But he denies that this representation puts one in touch with something more "real" or objective than Dasein's spatial world. While he does not develop the point at length, the following passage clearly accords with Heidegger's more general view that existential contexts are constitutively *prior* to the conceptual schemes of science:

> Space . . . can be studied purely by looking at it, if one gives up what was formerly the only possibility of access to it – circumspective calculation. When space is "intuited formally," the pure possibilities of spatial relations are discovered. Here one may go through a series of stages in laying bare pure homogenous space, passing from the pure morphology of spatial shapes to *analysis situs* and finally to the purely metrical science of space. (Heidegger 1962: 147–8)

Here Heidegger reinforces the thought that existential spatiality is prior to, and a condition for, scientific space. But what then can it mean to "give up" an existential condition in one's passage toward abstractly "metrical" categories? An existential condition, by definition, is constitutive and cannot be abandoned. As Heidegger himself notes earlier on, it is not possible to somehow "cross over" the interpretative horizon by which Dasein brings close the equipment of its world. The order of connection is ostensibly a "series of stages," a term that seems to indicate a process of advance (Carman 2003: 195–9). But if this remark appears momentarily to assign scientific conceptualization a status of greater sophistication in human understanding, the suggestion is just as quickly withdrawn in dramatic language that implies not progress but loss:

> When space is discovered non-circumspectively by just looking at it, the environmental regions *get neutralized to pure dimensions*. Places – and indeed the whole circumspectively oriented totality of places belonging to equipment ready-to-hand – *get reduced to* a multiplicity of positions for random Things. The spatiality of what is ready-to-hand within-the-world *loses its involvement-character*, and so does the ready-to-hand. The world *loses its*

specific aroundness; the environment becomes the world of Nature. The "world," as a totality of equipment ready-to-hand, becomes spatialized to a context of extended Things which
are *just present-at-hand and no more*. The homogenous space of Nature shows itself only
when the entities we encounter are discovered in such a way that it has the character of
a specifically *Deworlding* [*Entweltlichung*] of the worldliness of the ready-to-hand. (Heidegger
1962: 147)

The importance of this passage should not be underestimated. One of the core issues in
Heidegger's fundamental ontology is whether the world-conditions he describes are
analogous to Kantian conditions, in the precise sense that one might distinguish
between reality "in itself" and the existential world that is projected by human understanding. If this distinction is tenable, Heidegger has left himself open to the charge
that the existential world is merely ideal, since, however deep its constitutive role, one
might nonetheless appeal, if only counterfactually, to a realm of things present-at-
hand, i.e., entities metaphysically independent of Dasein's world.

The danger of this idealistic reading, however, is considerable, for it conflicts with
the fundamental premises of Heidegger's metaphysical anti-naturalism: According to
Heidegger, philosophy since Plato has remained captive to a metaphysics of "presence," i.e., the notion that the "Being" by virtue of which "there is" intelligible reality
can only be understood as occupying some kind of metaphysical precinct beyond that
reality, since only then could it serve as its self-sufficient ground. This notion of Being,
however, takes its cue from the idea that time is a series of "nows," such that Being
itself would naturally appear as an eternal present. It is this conception which then
seems to warrant the rationalist's view that one can describe what ultimate reality
itself is like in some incorrigible and non-interpretive way. Moreover, it is a notion that
tends to posit a sharp break between the knower and the known: By disengaging from
the world, one can ostensibly achieve a position of complete neutrality and lay bare
what Bernard Williams called "the absolute conception of reality" (Williams 1978).

But it is just this aspect of metaphysical realism that Heidegger wants to combat.
A basic insight of Heidegger's thinking is that the urge to identify one and only one
"ultimate reality," even the reality as scientific realists would describe it, is symp-
tomatic of the error he ascribes to the metaphysical tradition. And this error must be
vigorously combated on behalf of the "post-metaphysical" insight that Being is itself
grounded in time. It follows, however, that philosophers are mistaken if they lay claim
to an unmoved and ultimate reality such as "God," "Reason," or "Nature." But such a
claim is possible only if there is a "view from nowhere." And that is precisely the kind
of vantage point that Heidegger believes human beings cannot achieve if they are the
interpretive beings he claims they are.

Modern natural science thus confronts Heidegger with a serious challenge. If
science knows what is "real," then existential categories would appear to be merely
subjective. It is important to realize that Heidegger himself was uncertain as to how best
to cope with this difficulty, as his remarks on the "neutralization" of world conditions
clearly illustrate: Once the structures of involvement are consigned to the status of
human-dependent "interpretation," the way is open for science to declare as its own
domain the world as it is disclosed *without* interpretation, and so to proclaim that only
through scientific "objectivity" can one gain access to what is metaphysically real.

435

Kant himself, of course, believed he had inoculated his own doctrine against this subjectivist reading, with the assertion that not only is transcendental idealism compatible with empirical realism, it in fact underwrites whatever passes for "reality." Scientific objectivity is, for Kant, correlative with the structures of understanding. For Heidegger, however, this solution is not available: By insisting that scientific reality was itself disclosed to Dasein as the present-at-hand, Heidegger's transcendental–existential conditions – unlike Kant's conditions – appear to be merely subjective and, indeed, contingent. By Heidegger's own logic it seems possible to break free of those conditions so as to encounter the scientist's field of merely "given" reality.

How does Heidegger address this problem? As I shall explain, Heidegger wants to sustain his commitment to metaphysical realism especially as concerns the entities that are revealed through scientific practice. But he is ambivalent about just how far that realism should carry him. His image of science as a practice for deworlding the world goes too far, I will claim, by conceding that the entities of science are revealed precisely *as* they are independent of our revealing them.

To clarify this point, let us look further at how Heidegger tries to resolve the debate between realism and idealism. There is much controversy over Heidegger's position in this debate (as summarized by Hubert Dreyfus in Dreyfus 2001). A strong case has been made for the view that Heidegger was a transcendental idealist (Blattner 1994, 1999). But there are also grounds for calling Heidegger a realist, though one must take care to note which kind of realism is meant (Cerbone 1995; Dreyfus 1991a). I want to argue here that Heidegger tries to propose a conciliatory or "quietist" answer, by dismantling the metaphysical picture that first makes the debate between realism and idealism possible. But, as I will explain, Heidegger's idea of deworlding the world comes very close to resurrecting that metaphysical picture and returning us to Husserl's contrast between world and reality.

First, note that most of his remarks on the debate suggest that, like Husserl, Heidegger cleaved to a position one might plausibly call "idealist." In *Being and Time*, for example, he writes:

> As compared with realism, *idealism* . . . has an advantage in principle, [since] [i]f idealism emphasizes that Being and Reality are only "in the consciousness," this expressed an understanding of the fact that Being cannot be explained through entities . . . If what the term "idealism" says, amounts to is the understanding that Being can never be explained by entities but is already that which is "transcendental" for every entity, then idealism affords the only correct possibility for a philosophical problematic. (Heidegger 1962: 251)

In *Basic Problems of Phenomenology*, Heidegger concludes: "The world is not the sum total of extant entities [*die Summe des Vorhandenen*]. It is, quite generally, not extant at all. It is a determination of being-in-the-world, *a moment in the structure of Dasein's mode of being*. The world is, so to speak, Dasein-ish [*Daseinmäßiges*]" (Heidegger 1982: 166; emphasis added). At first glance it may seem tempting to call this a variety of subjective idealism. Indeed, one might want to charge Heidegger's conception of the world with the same idealistic tendencies that afflict Husserl's conception (as it was presented above). But Heidegger is quick to note that the classical opposition between idealism and realism rests upon a falsely metaphysical picture of Dasein as a subject set over and against reality as a set of Cartesian, present-at-hand entities. That distinction should be overcome, Heidegger suggests, because Dasein itself is already "projected outward" though its practical engagement with reality. There is a Wittgensteinian flavor to Heidegger's idea that we revise the underlying metaphysical description that got us into our philosophical dilemma. But, even we grant Heidegger's therapeutic solution, the subjective idealist charge still seems to more or less correct, as he admits:

> The world is something "subjective," presupposing that we correspondingly define subjectivity with regard to this phenomenon of world. To say that the world is subjective is to say that it belongs to the Dasein so far as this being is in the mode of being-in-the-world. The world is something which the "subject" "projects outward," as it were, from within itself. But are we permitted to speak here of an inner and an outer? What can this projection mean? Obviously not that the world is a piece of myself in the sense of some other thing present in me as in a thing and that I throw the world out of this subject-thing in order to catch hold of the other things with it. Instead, the Dasein itself is as such already projected. *So far as the Dasein exists a world is cast forth with the Dasein's being.* (Heidegger 1982: 168)

Heidegger claims that the conventional distinction between idealism and realism is misleading, since it posits a "subject-thing" on the one hand and a "world-thing" on the other, and then asks whether the latter depends on the former for its existence. Heidegger grants that the "world" depends on Dasein. But this is only because he has proposed what has recently been dubbed a "quietist" response: i.e., he has revised the metaphysical picture of the human subject in such a way that the debate between realism and idealism is not so much solved as it is simply *dissolved* (McDowell 1994; Rosen 1994; van Fraassen 1980).

But if the "world" is dependent on Dasein, then what happens to the metaphysical realist commitment that normally goes along with the scientific conception of "nature"? The answer is that Heidegger wants to be an idealist about the existential world, but he also wants to be a realist about the entities scientists find in nature. For example, in the 1925 lectures, *History of the Concept of Time*, Heidegger grants that "nature" is "encountered 'in' the time which we ourselves are." And this means that our mode of access to "nature" is the existential-horizon of Dasein's world. But this does not mean that the entities that are found in nature are *themselves* dependent upon Dasein. As Heidegger notes in *Basic Problems*: "being within the world does not belong to the *being* of nature." In other words, "nature" as such remains what it is independent of its possible disclosure: "Nature can also be when no Dasein exists" (Heidegger 1982: 169–70). Heidegger makes a similarly realist point in his account of truth in *Being and Time*. He first proposes a distinction, between the "original truth" which is relative to Dasein's existential world, and the traditional concept of truth as correspondence, which, he claims, is dependent upon original truth. But that means that "scientific truth" is dependent on Dasein, even while the *entities* that scientific truth describes are *themselves* metaphysically independent:

> *"There is"* truth only in so far as Dasein *is and so long as* Dasein *is*. Entities are uncovered only *when* Dasein *is*; and only so long as Dasein *is*. Newton's laws [for example] . . . are true

only so long as Dasein *is*. Before there was any Dasein, there was no truth; nor will there be any after Dasein is no more . . . Before Newton's laws were discovered, they were not "true"; it does not follow [however] that they were false, or even that they would become false. To say that before Newton his laws were neither true nor false, cannot signify that before him there were no such entities as have been uncovered and pointed out by those laws. Through Newton the laws became truth; and with them, entities became accessible in themselves to Dasein. Once entities have been uncovered, they show themselves precisely as entities which beforehand already were. (Heidegger 1962: 269)

Heidegger is trying to suggest that, although the Being of scientific objects is contingent upon Dasein's existential horizon, the entities thus disclosed are themselves robustly realist and, therefore, "already" there prior to Dasein's disclosure of them. As Hubert Dreyfus has suggested, this means that Heidegger thinks that our scientific practices reveal entities that are independent of those practices (Dreyfus 2001). In this way, Heidegger can insist that while there is no "world" without Dasein, the entities disclosed in science would retain their reality even if the world were lost.

Heidegger, then, is a realist about the entities of science. But there remains a crucial ambiguity in Heidegger's conception of nature. For even while Heidegger grants the Dasein-independent status of nature, he is uncertain whether our scientific practices for deworlding the world permit our access to something like brute, non-interpretative reality. In *History of the Concept of Time*, Heidegger writes:

Nature is what is in principle explainable and to be explained because it is in principle unintelligible *(unverständlich)*; it is *the unintelligible pure and simple*, and it is the unintelligible because it is the *deworlded world*, if we take nature in this extreme sense of entities as they are uncovered in physics. (Heidegger 1985: 298; Carman 2003: 197)

One may detect an idealistic strain in this passage. Indeed, it seems reminiscent of Husserl's idea, cited above, that we must dismiss the very notion of an "outside" to the phenomenological world as "nonsense." Heidegger's own notion of deworlding the world implies that science confronts the metaphysically real entities of the universe as devoid of meaning: the scientist deworlds Dasein's world and then seeks to explain the Dasein-independent entities that have been revealed as "unintelligible." But there is a crucial ambivalence in this image of science. It implies that the scientist has special, non-interpretative practices, i.e., practices of deworlding, that reveal nature to Dasein *in just the way it actually is independent of the practices that revealed it.* This is more than a commitment to scientific realism. It is also a commitment to the popular image of science as providing "objective" and "clear-eyed" access to the real. But this further claim is obviously inconsistent with Heidegger's own exposition of Dasein's interpretive way of being. If Heidegger is right that science deworlds the world and gets to an "unintelligible" nature, this means that *Dasein has achieved, via science, a uniquely non-interpretative vantage upon reality.* But this obviously conflicts with Heidegger's basic thesis that *Dasein is essentially an interpretative being,* i.e., that Dasein "is" only insofar as it casts forth a world. Heidegger's apparent inconsistency on this point thus seems to require that he dispense with one of his two premises: either he must admit that Dasein does not always cast forth a world (and thereby concede that the world is merely contingent, an interpretative scheme only sometimes imposed upon reality), or, Heidegger must insist that Dasein does in accordance with its very essence cast forth a world, and he must accordingly dispense with his conception of science as a practice for deworlding the world so as to discover a brute, non-interpretative nature.

Phenomenology and the Nature/World Debate

How is Heidegger best rescued from this impasse? A basic dogma of Heidegger's existential analytic is that Dasein's interpretive and practical world can break down into meaningless bits of occurrent data which are then available to formalistic observation. And this distinction – between *Zuhandenheit* and *Vorhandenheit* – seems to correspond to another sort of contrast, between, on the one hand, the various interpretative activities that we pursue on a daily basis, whether in work or culture, and, on the other hand, the ostensibly non-interpretive activities that fall under the rubric of objective science. For Heidegger, then, culture and nature are ontologically distinct. Whereas science observes world-independent (metaphysically real) entities, our cultural or historical life is concerned with objects whose very Being is world-dependent. Heidegger calls these world-dependent objects "historical":

> There are beings, however, to whose being intraworldliness belongs in a certain way. Such beings are all those we call *historical* entities – historical in the broader sense of world-historical, all those things that the human being, who is historical and exists historically in the strict and proper sense, creates, shapes, cultivates: all his culture and works. Beings of this kind *are* only or, more exactly, arise only and come into being only *as* intraworldly. Culture *is* not in the way that nature is. (Heidegger 1982: 169)

Furthermore, when Heidegger suggests that scientific truth "depends" on Dasein, he seems nonetheless to think that scientific knowledge has dispensed with the interpretative dimension of Dasein's world. Recall, for example, Heidegger's claim that space can be studied "purely by looking at it" (Heidegger 1962: 147). This requires a complete deworlding of the ready-to-hand: "The homogenous space of Nature shows itself only when the entities we encounter are discovered in such a way that it has the character of a specifically *deworlding* [*Entweltlichung*] of the worldliness of the ready-to-hand" (Heidegger 1962: 146).

The later Heidegger reinforced this view: In his essay, "Science and Reflection," for example, he suggests, first, that science is "the theory of the real." And, he further explains that with the scientific conception of reality, the "subject–object" relation "attains its most extreme dominance," because "everything real is recast in advance into a diversity of objects for the entrapping securing [*nachstellende Sicherstellen*]" (Heidegger 1977: 173, 168). I take this to mean that the natural-scientific attitude is not compatible with existential involvement. Heidegger seems to believe instead that only complete breakdown or deworlding of Dasein's interpretive world is sufficient to yield the scientific image of mathematized and fungible nature. Incidentally, the negative quality of the later Heidegger's characterization of science is especially evident once we recall that the term "*nachstellen*" can be used figuratively to mean "to

439

persecute." The question we must now ask is whether this is in fact an accurate characterization of natural-scientific understanding.

I would like to suggest that Heidegger's conception of science as deworlding is inaccurate. Specifically, it does not capture the distinctive, world-shaping practices that first enable the scientist to pursue an investigation of nature. Since Thomas Kuhn and post-Kuhnian scholarship in the philosophy and sociology of science, it has been persuasively argued that science too, no less than other human activities, is a mode of practice that requires richly interpretive "worlds" or "paradigms." For Heidegger, if science confronts a "pure" space of "nature," it is because it deworlds Dasein's practical worldliness. For Kuhn and his followers, however, this image of science is a myth: "No more in the natural than in the human sciences," he writes, "is there some neutral, culture-independent, set of categories within which the population – whether of objects or of actions – can be described" (Kuhn 2000: 220).

According to Kuhn, scientists who explain nature in incommensurable paradigms actually live in "different worlds" (Kuhn 1996: 150). Of course, one might take such remarks as hyperbole. But one can plausibly read his notion of world-constitution as endorsing the phenomenologists' conception that the world is a subject-dependent context of disclosure. And, as noted above, that theory is compatible with scientific realism about the entities that are so disclosed.

But the early Heidegger did not share a Kuhnian view of science as a world-constitutive activity. Instead, he believed that to view real entities in the scientific manner required deworlding, i.e., it demands that one "give up" one's world-shaping practices, that they be "neutralized," "reduced" or, more dramatically, "lost" (Heidegger 1962: 147). But there is no good reason to see science as deworlding and to confine the phenomenological concept of world merely to the objects of history and culture. If the post-Kuhnian view is right, then science, too, is a kind of world-disclosure with its own richly interpretative manner of representing and intervening with its entities. Indeed, a proper description of scientific practice would seem to suggest that our engagement with nature is just as thickly interpretative as our engagement with culture.

We should find it surprising, I think, that Heidegger neglected to include science along with the other world-constitutive practices he analyzed. In fact, this inclusive view of science would be more consistent with Heidegger's own philosophical finding that Dasein *always* "casts forth a world." For if Dasein's very existence necessarily involves worldhood, then scientific inquiry as one possible mode of Dasein's existence must presuppose a world. Indeed, what I have called Heidegger's "quietistic" response to the debate over idealism and realism would seem to suggest that Dasein is *never not* disengaged from the world: Heidegger evades the debate by claiming that it rests upon an illusory picture of the human subject as a metaphysically real thing standing apart from another, equally real object. Quarrels over dependence or independence only make sense if we hold on to that picture. But Heidegger himself lapsed into that picture when he suggested that natural science takes a "pure" and disengaged stance toward metaphysical reality, while he should have argued that no such stance is possible for an interpretive, thrown being like Dasein.

I am suggesting, then, not that Heidegger was mistaken or too daring in his conception of worldhood, but that he conceived of worldhood in a needlessly re-strictive way, and he should have applied that conception more broadly. But, if the phenomenological theory of worldhood should be taken in the inclusive sense, then it would appear that there can be no such thing as a complete "breakdown" of worldhood. The very notion of piercing through our interpretative practices of "giving up" existential worldhood to get to brute reality conflicts with the inclusive thesis that Dasein always projects a world.

Why did Heidegger cleave to this strong distinction between nature and culture? A plausible answer is that his concept of deworlding may reflect anxieties about scientific "mechanism" that were fairly widespread in early twentieth-century German thought (Harrington 1996). Here it may be helpful to compare Heidegger's idea of "*die Entweltlichung der Welt*" (deworlding the world) to Max Weber's nearly contemporaneous notion of "*die Entzauberung der Welt*" (the disenchantment of the world). In his 1918 speech, "Science as a Vocation," Weber suggested that the rise of modern rationalism entails a "disenchantment" of the natural environment and a corresponding loss of meaning:

> Who – aside from certain big children who are indeed found in the natural sciences – still believes that the findings of astronomy, biology, physics, or chemistry could teach us anything about the *meaning* of the world? . . . If [the] natural sciences lead to anything . . . they are apt to make the belief that there is such a thing as the "meaning" of the universe die out at its very roots. (Weber 1946: 155)

There is a notable similarity between Heideggerian "deworlding" and Weberian "disenchantment." For Weber as for Heidegger, the natural sciences are bereft of all significance because the latter has to do with cultural constructs alone. It has nothing to do with the region that is revealed to us when we break out of those constructs and just "look" at the way natural objects "really" are. Weber's condescending tone suggests that those who still long for meaning in nature are just refusing to abandon their premodern and infantile wishes and are not facing up to the hard truth of disenchanted reality. Heidegger's judgment is more subtle, but perhaps more nostalgic: scientific deworlding for him is "reduction," and even "loss." But, as I have tried to suggest, this image of science is inaccurate. As recent contributions to "science studies" have shown, there are good reasons for thinking that, while science deals with nature, it is no less a practice than other practices, all of which, regardless of domain, entail a culture and richly normative criteria of interest and significance. Science studies is a growing and diverse discipline and is frequently divided on the realism question. It sometimes takes a "debunking" view, as if noting the interpretive conditions for scientific discovery were sufficient to refute metaphysical realism. Needless to say, the antirealist conclusion about the metaphysical existence of entities hardly follows from descriptions of their context of discovery. But the important lesson to take from such studies is that science cannot provide deworlded access to entities in themselves (Papineau 1988; Pettit 1988). If these studies are right, then science is far from requiring the kind of breakdown in contexts of significance that both Weber and Heidegger associated with scientific modernity.

Of course, this image of science as a "culture" may not capture the self-image that actually governs natural-scientific practice. Some scientists may think that the scientific "world" cuts nature at its joints, i.e., they conceive of scientific practice as *non*-interpretive, as providing a clear window upon metaphysical reality. But this has little bearing on the *philosophical* question of whether scientific practice *in fact* presupposes an interpretive world. Indeed, from a Heideggerian view, we might say that the image of deworlding is just part of the *self-interpretation* that accompanies scientific activity. What is puzzling is that the early Heidegger should have mistaken that self-interpretation for a correct description of scientific practice. The later Heidegger seems more on target: "Scientific representation is never able to encompass the coming to presence of nature; for the objectness of nature is, antecedently, only *one* way in which nature exhibits itself. Nature thus remains for the science of physics that which cannot be gotten around" (Heidegger 1977: 174). For the later Heidegger, *all* worlds are sustained by interpretations that cannot be dispensed with (or "gotten around"). And the scientific world is sustained by the interpretation that reality just *is*, and *is nothing other than*, nature.

As Hubert Dreyfus has argued, Heidegger might be called a "plural realist" insofar as he claimed that all entities are disclosed only on the basis of a world (Dreyfus 1991a). But we also need to explain why Heidegger seems often to prioritize different types of worlds. Especially in his later writings, he seemed to believe that the "world worlds" (*Welt weltet*) more fully in works of art than in science: "The work," he tells us, "holds open the Open of the world" (Heidegger 1971: 44–6). In other words, a work of art permits us to experience the *simultaneous* concealing and revealing that makes the world the site of disclosure. In "setting up a world and setting forth the earth," a work of art thereby reveals the very *difference* between a world and the reality it discloses. But then, what really distinguishes the world as revealed by science from the world as revealed by art? The difference is *not* that science alone deworlds the world and opens upon the field of meaningless entities, whereas art opens up a realm of significance. Both are practices that disclose worlds. Science and art are different *only* because the scientific world does not let its own worldhood come into clear view, and it can thus take itself to be a non-interpretative encounter with reality.

Some historians of philosophy have observed that the "analytic" tradition took shape at the beginning of the twentieth century with an inflationary and ultimately unhelpful devotion to natural-scientific models. But one might also note that the "continental" tradition has frequently betrayed the correlative, *de*flationary view of natural science. And this, too, has spawned its own share of invidious philosophical debate, concerning, e.g., the differences between the *Naturwissenschaften* and the *Kulturwissenschaften*, the relative merits of scientific reductionism as against cultural constructivism, and so forth. I have tried to suggest that that there are good reasons to overcome Heidegger's restricted thesis that nature lies somehow "outside" the world, and I have argued, instead, that the phenomenological concept of world deserves the broadest possible application, in the natural sciences as well as in cultural life. The naïve discussion as to whether something is *either* "nature" *or* "culture," for example, appears to be partially dissolved once we recognize that we cannot, in Heidegger's words, "cross over" our own existential world. The investigation of nature is itself, therefore, a cultural activity, deeply imbricated with meaning and interest. But this claim should not be understood as a strike against the authority of science. It is, rather, a mark of its humanity.

Note

This chapter is dedicated to my father, Professor Emeritus of Biochemistry at the University of Washington (Seattle), on his 75th birthday, February, 2005.

References and Further Reading

Blattner, W. (1994) Is Heidegger a Kantian idealist? *Inquiry*, 37, 185–201.

—— (1999) *Heidegger's Temporal Idealism*. Cambridge: Cambridge University Press.

Carman, T. (2003) *Heidegger's Analytic: Interpretation, Discourse, and Authenticity in* Being and Time. New York: Cambridge University Press.

Cerbone, D. R. (1995) World, world-entry, and realism in early Heidegger. *Inquiry*, 38, 401–21.

Dreyfus, H. (1991a) *Being-in-the-World: A Commentary on Heidegger's* Being and Time, *Division I*. Cambridge, MA: MIT Press.

—— (1991b) Heidegger's hermeneutic realism. In D. Hiley, J. F. Bohman, and R. Shusterman (eds.), *The Interpretive Turn: Philosophy, Science, Culture* (pp. 25–41). Ithaca, NY: Cornell University Press.

Dreyfus, H. (2001) How Heidegger defends the possibility of a correspondence theory of truth with respect to the entities of natural science. In T. R. Schatzki, K. Knorr Cetina, and E. von Savigny (eds.), *The Practice Turn in Contemporary Theory* (pp. 151–62). London: Routledge.

Frege, G. (1970) On sense and reference (trans. P. Geach and M. Black). In P. Geach and M. Black (eds.), *Translations from the Philosophical Writings of Gottlob Frege* (pp. 56–78). Oxford: Blackwell (original work published 1892).

Harrington, A. (1996) *Reenchanted Science: Holism in German Culture from Wilhelm II to Hitler*. Princeton, NJ: Princeton University Press.

Heidegger, M. (1962) *Being and Time* (trans. J. Macquarrie and E. Robinson). New York: Harper & Row (original work published 1927).

—— (1971) The origin of the work of art (trans. A. Hofstadter). In A. Hofstadter (ed.), *Poetry, Language, Thought* (pp. 15–86). New York: Harper & Row (original work published 1935–6).

—— (1977) Science and reflection (trans. W. Lovitt). In W. Lovitt (ed.), *The Question Concerning Technology and Other Essays* (pp. 155–82). New York: Harper & Row (original work published 1954).

—— (1982) *The Basic Problems of Phenomenology* (trans. A. Hofstadter). Bloomington: Indiana University Press (original lectures delivered 1927).

—— (1985) *History of the Concept of Time* (trans. T. Kisiel). Bloomington: Indiana University Press (original lectures delivered 1925).

Husserl, E. (1931) *Ideas: General Introduction to Pure Phenomenology* (trans. W. R. Boyce Gibson). New York: Macmillan (original work published 1913).

—— (1973) *Cartesian Meditations: An Introduction to Phenomenology* (trans. D. Cairns). The Hague: Martinus Nijhoff.

Kelly, S. D. (2003) Edmund Husserl and phenomenology. In R. C. Solomon and D. Sherman (eds.), *The Blackwell Guide to Continental Philosophy* (pp. 112–42, esp. 122–7). Oxford and Malden, MA: Blackwell.

Kuhn, T. (1996) *The Structure of Scientific Revolutions*. 3rd edn. Chicago: University of Chicago Press.

—— (2000) The natural and the human sciences. In J. Conant and J. Haugeland (eds.), *The Road Since Structure* (pp. 216–23). Chicago: University of Chicago Press.

Lafont, C. (2000) *Heidegger, Language, and World-Disclosure* (trans. G. Harman). Cambridge: Cambridge University Press (original work published 1963).

Malpas, J. (2000) Uncovering the space of disclosedness: Heidegger, technology, and the problem of spatiality in *Being and Time*. In M. Wrathall and J. Malpas (eds.), *Heidegger, Authenticity, and Modernity. Essays in Honor of Hubert L. Dreyfus*, vol. 1 (pp. 205–28). Cambridge, MA: MIT Press.

McDowell, J. (1994) *Mind and World*. Cambridge, MA: Harvard University Press.

Merleau-Ponty, M. (1962) *Phenomenology of Perception* (trans. C. Smith). New York: Routledge & Kegan Paul (original work published 1945).

Papineau, D. (1988) Does the sociology of science discredit science? In R. Nola (ed.), *Relativism and Realism in Science* (pp. 35–50). Dordrecht: Kluwer.

Pettit, P. (1988) The strong sociology of knowledge without relativism. In R. Nola (ed.), *Relativism and Realism in Science*. Dordrecht: Kluwer.

Rosen, G. A. (1994) Objectivity and modern idealism: What is the question? In M. Michael and J. O'Leary-Hawthorne (eds.), *Philosophy in Mind: The Place of Philosophy in the Study of Mind* (pp. 277–319). Dordrecht: Kluwer.

Taylor, C. (1985) Interpretation and the sciences of man. In *Philosophy and the Human Sciences, Philosophical Papers II* (pp. 15–57). Cambridge: Cambridge University Press.

Updike, J. (1988) Dream objects. In *Midpoint and other Poems*. New York: Alfred A. Knopf.

Weber, M. (1946) Science as a vocation (trans. H. H. Garth and C. Wright Mills). In H. H. Gerth and C. Wright Mills (eds.), *From Max Weber: Essays in Sociology* (pp. 129–56). New York: Oxford University Press (original work published 1919).

Williams, B. (1978) *Descartes: the Project of Pure Enquiry*. Hassocks: Harvester Press.

van Fraassen, B. (1980) *The Scientific Image*. Oxford: Oxford University Press.

Zahavi, D. (2003) *Husserl's Phenomenology*. Stanford, CA: Stanford University Press.

30

Environmental Philosophy

IAIN THOMSON

Introduction: Uncovering the Conceptual Roots
of Environmental Devastation

Since the 1970s, an interdisciplinary movement has been gaining momentum at the intersection of phenomenology and environmental philosophy (Brown and Toadvine 2003b: 239–48).[1] *Eco-phenomenology* is inspired and guided by the idea that uprooting and replacing some of modern philosophy's deeply entrenched but environmentally destructive ethical and metaphysical presuppositions can help us to combat environmental devastation at its conceptual roots. This *radical* or *deep ecological* approach is moving from the margins to the center of the environmental movement, thanks both to its inherent philosophical appeal and to the unhappy recognition that, although environmental destruction continues to accelerate, "[p]hilosophy has yet to find an effective voice in our struggle with the environmental crisis" (Brown and Toadvine 2003a: x). On the basis of recent UN and WorldWatch reports, Erazim Kohák, a leading neo-Husserlian eco-phenomenologist, assesses the stakes of our environmental crisis starkly: "our civilization – originally European, then Euro-American, today global – appears to be well on its way to self-destruction" (Brown and Toadvine 2003a: 19). Christian Diehm summarizes a few of the disturbing statistics: "More than half of the earth's forests are gone, and they continue to be leveled at the rate of sixteen million hectares [or 39.5 million acres] per year, accompanied by an anthropogenic extinction rate nearing one thousand times the natural or 'background' rate" (Diehm 2003: 171). Many eco-phenomenologists maintain a desperate optimism despite this massive erosion of global biodiversity, believing we now have not only the correct diagnosis of, but also the necessary treatment for, our environmental crisis. This radical ecological diagnosis holds that "environmental destruction and crisis are caused by core beliefs within our worldview that sanction, legitimate, and even encourage the domination and technological control of nature," while the eco-phenomenological cure suggests that these core beliefs can be changed, since "the

This is a shortened and revised version of Iain Thomson, "Ontology and ethics at the intersection of phenomenology and environmental philosophy," *Inquiry*, 47,4 (2004), pp. 380–412. By permission of Taylor & Francis.

insights of eco-phenomenology hold the promise of bringing about a dramatic shift in our current understanding of ourselves and of our place in the natural world" (Brown and Toadvine 2003a: xiii, xx–xxi).

Why should phenomenologists feel particularly called upon to respond to our environmental crisis? Because the anti-environmental assumptions most frequently singled out are mind/world dualism and the fact/value divide, and the phenomenological tradition has been working for over a century to help us think beneath and beyond these conceptual dichotomies entrenched in our habits of thought.[2] Mind/world dualism and the fact/value divide seem obvious when one is theorizing from within the modern tradition (where they have functioned as axioms since Descartes and Hume at least), but phenomenologists argue that these conceptual dichotomies fundamentally mischaracterize our ordinary experience. By failing to recognize the integral entwinement of self and world basic to our experiential navigation of the lived environment, modern philosophy effectively splits the subject off from objects (and other subjects), thereby laying the conceptual groundwork for the modern worldview in which an intrinsically meaningless objective realm ("nature") is separated epistemically from – and so needs to be mastered through the activities of – isolated, self-certain subjects. This worldview functions historically like a self-fulfilling prophecy, its progressive historical realization generating not only the political freedoms and scientific advances we cherish, but also unwanted downstream consequences such as our escalating environmental crisis. Although environmental devastation is a predictable side effect of our collective historical effort to master an ostensibly meaningless world of objects, we tend to ignore the conceptual connections between our modern worldview and the environmental crisis. This is not only because the modern worldview is so deeply entrenched that it usually passes unnoticed, but also because modernity's definitive divorce of mind from world creates a number of irresolvable pseudo-problems (including most species of skepticism) which distract philosophers, diverting our intellectual efforts away from pressing real-world problems such as our mounting environmental crisis.[3]

The phenomenological critique of modernity just sketched remains controversial, of course, but eco-phenomenology is not primarily a critical movement, content to uncover environmental devastation's conceptual roots. Its more important, positive aim is to undercut and replace them. How do eco-phenomenologists seek to uproot the mind/world and fact/value dichotomies inherited from modern philosophy? First, phenomenological approaches seek to begin from – and so return us to – the experience of a pre-differentiated, mind–world unity. By thus methodologically undercutting mind/world dualism, phenomenology hopes, second, to recognize the reality of environmental "values," the alleged "fact" that certain pro-environmental values are "always already in the world" and so simply await the appropriate phenomenological approach in order to be discovered and made the basis of a new environmental ethics. How, then, are we to understand and evaluate such radical claims, which seek to undercut and replace views near the core of the modern philosophical tradition? What kinds of arguments can be given in support of these eco-phenomenological views, and what problems do they bring in their wake? How significant are their different formulations in competing eco-phenomenological approaches? These difficult and interesting issues will be our primary focus in what follows.

446

From Ontological Method to Eco-Phenomenological Ethics

Eco-phenomenology seeks to get the *mentalism* out of environmentalism. By recognizing a pre-theoretical level of experience in which we do not yet distinguish ourselves
from our worlds (a dimension of practical, everyday experience eclipsed by the modern
tradition's emphasis on detached, theoretical contemplation), and attempting to do
justice to this fundamental layer of experience by incorporating it into their methodological points of departure, phenomenologists seek to undercut and transcend the dualistic mind/world divide. Indeed, such methodological points of departure as Husserl's
"life-world," Heidegger's "being-in-the-world," Merleau-Ponty's "motor-intentionality"
(and later, "flesh"), and Levinas's "*il y a*" (the "anonymous" existing not yet differentiated into an individual "existent" and its "existence" or world) were formulated precisely in order to capture and express a mind/world unity, a basic level of experience at
which mind and world remain integrally enmeshed. This is precisely the point (to take
the most influential of the above examples) of Heidegger's recognition that a human
being is always a "being-in-the-world." For, in Heidegger's famous formulation, "in"
signifies pragmatic involvement rather than spatial inclusion ("being-in-the-world"
means "being-in[extricably involved with]-the-world"), and "world" refers not to the
totality of physical objects, but rather to the holistic nexus of intelligibility organized
by our identity-constituting life-projects (a sense of "world" conveyed in such expressions as "the world of the parent," "the runner's world," or "the world of the tree-
sitter").[4] There are, of course, important differences and disagreements between the
competing approaches that constitute the phenomenological tradition (Langer 2003:
106). Indeed, Heideggerians argue that phenomenologists such as Husserl, Sartre,
and Levinas still presuppose the concept of "subjectivity," and thus that their methodologies tend to ramify rather than undermine Cartesian dualism. The fact that most
contemporary Husserlians, Sartreans, and Levinasians would take such an argument
as a *criticism* suggests, however, that the eco-phenomenological claim that this broad
methodological agreement obtains across the phenomenological tradition is probably
as uncontentious as any substantive generalization concerning a broad and diverse
living tradition is likely to be.

If eco-phenomenology's methodological principle concerning phenomenological
approaches to the environment is thus relatively uncontroversial (at least for
phenomenologists characterizing their own schools), the same cannot be said for
the eco-phenomenologists' competing "ethical" principle, which represents a more
original development of the phenomenological tradition. This ethical principle, stated
broadly, holds that phenomenological approaches undercut the fact/value dichotomy,
enabling eco-phenomenologists to recognize the non-subjective reality of environmental "values" (see, e.g., Marietta 2003: 121–4; Llewelyn 2003: 57; Langer 2003: 112–
14; Embree 2003: 40–1). In order not to beg questions concerning the metaphysical
baggage attendant on the concept of "value," however, let us instead specify that eco-
phenomenologists are all committed to some type of *ethical realism*. I say "some type,"
because we can discern a significant disagreement within the eco-phenomenological
movement concerning how best to articulate and defend the ethical realist view, a disagreement which – reactivating preexisting fault lines within the tradition – implicitly

447

divides the eco-phenomenological movement into two different, competing approaches. Put simply, and so perhaps controversially (but by way of anticipation of the rest of this chapter), we could say that Nietzscheans and Husserlians gravitate toward a *naturalistic* ethical realism, in which "good" and "bad" are ultimately *matters of fact* (hence their *naturalism*), and our "values" should be grounded in and reflect these proto-ethical facts (hence their *ethical realism*). (One may have difficulty recognizing *Husserl himself* in any *naturalistic* ethical realism, given his notorious antipathy to "naturalism" as he understood it; nevertheless, we will see that this moniker aptly describes *neo*-Husserlian eco-phenomenological approaches.) Heideggerians and Levinasians, on the other hand, articulate a *transcendental* ethical realism, according to which we can indeed discover what really matters (hence *ethical realism*) when we are appropriately open to the environment, but what we thereby discover is neither a "fact" nor a "value" but rather a transcendental source of meaning that cannot be reduced to facts, values, or entities of any kind (hence *transcendental* ethical realism). As we examine these two eco-phenomenological species of ethical realism, moreover, we will notice that they generate two importantly different kinds of *ethical perfectionism* (by which I mean views that hold that ethical flourishing, broadly conceived, is best served by identifying, cultivating, and developing the significantly distinctive traits or capacities of the entities under consideration), and that these competing views have conflicting practical implications. The naturalistic ethical realism leads to an *eco-centric* perfectionism which stresses the need to acknowledge and develop *universal* traits of nature, even at the expense of human concerns, while transcendental ethical realism is capable of generating a more *humanistic* perfectionism, one which emphasizes the cultivation of *distinctive* traits of *Dasein*, and so, I will suggest, yields more acceptable ethical consequences.

The Meaning of the Earth

In order to understand these two eco-phenomenological approaches to ethical realism, as well as the roots and implications of their differences, let us trace these differences back to an ambiguity implicit in the eco-phenomenological motto, *"Back to the Earth Itself."* This is, of course, a clever twist on the famous battle cry of Husserlian phenomenology – "Back to the things themselves!" (*Zu den Sachen selbst!*) – in which the crucial *Sache*, the phenomenological "heart of the matter" or "sake" (Llewelyn 2003: 59), has been replaced by "earth." This substitution, a specifying instantiation that delimits the horizon of phenomenological concern, implies both that *the earth* is the heart of the matter for eco-phenomenology and that eco-phenomenology is for the sake of the earth. "Earth" is problematic as a singular term, however, because eco-phenomenologists are not simply referring to the third planet from the sun in our solar system. Rather, "earth" is a philosophical term of art for both Nietzsche and Heidegger, although the term has almost completely opposed senses for the two thinkers. Indeed, the basic divergence in the eco-phenomenological movement can be traced back to and illuminated in terms of this basic philosophical disagreement between Nietzsche and Heidegger over the meaning of "the earth."

In Nietzsche's *Thus Spoke Zarathustra*, Zarathustra repeatedly urges his audience to *"Remain true* [or *"faithful,"* Treu] *to the earth."* The precise meaning of "earth" in

Nietzsche's slogan can best be understood from the term with which it is contrasted: "otherworldly" (*überirdischen*, literally "overearthly"), meaning that which is above or beyond the earth, or *meta-physical* (Nietzsche 1954: 125). In Nietzsche's conceptual vocabulary, the *otherworldly* is something impossible for human beings to attain, our vain desire for which leads us to consider even the best we can achieve insufficient and unsatisfying. Nietzsche's main examples of the otherworldly are the Platonic "forms" (according to which, for instance, nothing we ever encounter or create in this world will be as beautiful as the perfect "form" of beauty) and the Christian "heaven" (conceived as a place some will go to after this life, compared with which our world is a mere "veil of tears"). According to Nietzsche, this unfulfillable desire for the otherworldly generates the nihilism of "resentment" (*Ressentiment*). The exact inverse of the "sour-grapes" phenomenon (in which something desired but out of reach is deemed undesirable), nihilistic resentment denigrates what we living human beings can attain in the name of something we cannot; our "earthly" aspirations are devalued by comparison to unfulfillable "otherworldly" dreams. It is precisely in order to root out this source of nihilism that Zarathustra will "beg and beseech" his audience:

> Remain faithful to the earth, . . . serve the meaning of the earth . . . Do not let your giftgiving love and knowledge fly away from earthly things and beat with their wings against eternal walls. . . . Lead back to the earth the virtue that flew away, as I do – back to the body, back to life, that it may give the earth a meaning, a human meaning. (Nietzsche 1954: 188)

"Remain true to the earth" is, in other words, a *naturalistic* slogan. Nietzsche calls for us to aspire to that which is attainable (albeit attainable in principle, not easily attainable). His philosophical goal, stated simply, is to *revalue* the world (that is, to give it new values and, in so doing, restore its value) by recognizing and (in a post-Kantian, neo-Darwinian spirit) embracing the limits of possible human knowledge. We "remain true to the earth," then, by maintaining ourselves within the bounds of the knowable.

For Heidegger, to put the contrast sharply, "earth" refers to something cognitively unattainable, something that can never really be *known*. In his famous essay on "The Origin of the Work of Art" (1935; cited as Heidegger 1971), Heidegger maintains that for a great artwork to *work*, that is, for it to "gather and preserve" a meaningful "world" for its audience, it must maintain an essential tension between this *world* of meanings and something he calls "earth." *Earth*, on his analysis, both sustains this meaningful world and resists being interpretively exhausted by it, thereby allowing the artwork quietly to maintain the sanctity of the uninterpretable within the very world of meanings it conveys. "Earth," in other words, is one of Heidegger's names for that which gives rise to our worlds of meaning without ever being exhausted by them, a dimension of intelligibility we experience primarily as it recedes from our awareness, eluding our attempts finally to *know* it, to grasp and express it fully in terms of some positive content. Heidegger contends, nevertheless, that we can get a *sense* for the "earth" from great works of art such as Van Gogh's painting of the peasant shoes, where, in the worn opening of one shoe and in the hole in the sole of the other, thick, dark paint conveys the insides of the shoes, interior spaces we cannot see because they are hidden by what the painting conveys: not just the visible exterior of these shoes, but the entire *world* of the peasant. Admittedly, Heidegger's rather poetic way of putting these crucial points makes them easy to miss:

> From out of the dark opening of the worn insides of the shoes the toilsome tread of the worker stares forth . . . In the shoes vibrates the silent call of the earth, its quiet gift of the ripening grain [i.e., "earth" makes "world" possible] and its unexplained self-refusal in the fallow desolation of the wintry field [i.e., it is also constitutive of "earth" that it resists "world"]. (Heidegger 1971: 33–4)

On Heidegger's reading, Van Gogh's painting teaches the very "truth" of the work of art, the essential tension in which "earth" simultaneously makes possible and resists being fully expressed by "world." This notion of earth is thus very close to the later Heidegger's central conception of "being as such" (*Seins als Solche*), a phenomenological "presencing" (*Anwesen*) that makes historical intelligibility possible without ever being exhausted by it. (These are difficult notions, obviously, but ones which, I will show, remain crucial for any eco-phenomenological appropriation of Heidegger.)

In sum, then, Nietzsche's conception of "earth" leads in a *naturalistic* direction, while Heidegger's points toward his phenomenological understanding of the *transcendental* condition of historical intelligibility (and so of all meaning and, more broadly, all *mattering*). This difference, we will now see, makes itself felt in the two different approaches implicitly competing within the eco-phenomenological movement.

Naturalistic Ethical Realism in Eco-Phenomenology

We can recognize the influence of Nietzsche's conception of earth on those eco-phenomenologists who tend toward a naturalistic ethical realism by adopting an ecological framework within which the good is ultimately a matter of fact to be discerned by the appropriate phenomenological approach. Thus neo-Husserlian eco-phenomenologists such as Charles S. Brown contest the scientistic divorce of "the Good" from "the Real" and instead seek to renaturalize ethics by recognizing the non-subjective reality of the good. For, when we abandon the idea that there are moral facts of the matter to be discovered and realized, Brown complains, procedural issues in ethics take the place of substantive ones, and "the good" thereby becomes "secondary to the right" (Brown 2003: 9). Brown thus rejects the long-standing trend by which ethics has become an increasingly formal, proceduralist endeavor (such that, reversing the old consequentialist slogan, *the means come to justify the ends*); he protests that "the Good has been so conceptually severed from the Real that goodness itself is often dismissed as an empty concept reflecting only personal preference" (ibid.: 7). To avoid such ethical relativism, neo-Husserlian eco-phenomenologists suggest we must recognize an important dimension of "lived moral experience" in which we discover our "prereflexive axiological consciousness," the fact that "[w]ithin our pre-reflective experiences, we regularly find the world and the things within it to be infused with value" (ibid.: 9–11).

Now, within the phenomenological tradition, there are at least two ways to take the claim that, as Lester Embree puts it, "the world in which one finds oneself is always already fraught with *values*" (Embree 2003: 39). Taken as an *ontic* claim (concerning our everyday experience of entities), the idea is that, for example, ripe apples show up looking *good* to us, clear-cut forests looking *bad*. Taken as an *ontological* claim (concerning what such ontic facts reveal about the structure by which reality is disclosed to "Dasein," that entity whose being is an issue for it), the idea is rather that entities only show up for us at all because we *care* about them in some way (as Heidegger argues in *Being and Time* (1927)). This latter, ontological claim complicates the ethical realism assumed by the former, ontic one, however. For, if entities only show up within the horizons of my concerns, then unless there is some universal concern, the values entities possess when encountered pre-theoretically cannot be made the basis for a non-relativistic ethics. The ripe apple, for example, may not look good to someone who has eaten too much, or who simply dislikes the taste of apples, and Brown himself maintains that "[c]lear-cutting large tracks of old-growth forest may appear as good from the perspective of business and profit" (Brown 2003: 11). Thus, although entities and events show up within our worlds as already mattering to us in various ways (our pre-reflexive experience is always already infused with "value," if you will), appealing to these "pre-given values" will not help us escape the charge of ethical relativism unless these values are both universal and substantive. There may be "no separation of factual information from meaning and value" in our ordinary experience of the lifeworld (Marietta 2003: 122), but among the values that show up in this "pre-thetic" lifeworld, we still need to be able to distinguish between the entrenched sedimentations of pernicious traditions, on the one hand, and truly universal values (if there are any) on the other. Given the *conflicting* values embedded in our lifeworld, and the fact that pre-reflexive experiences are often shaped by, and so tend to reinforce, all manner of preexisting *prejudices*, Brown's own faith that the ethical wisdom "pre-given" in the lifeworld will eventually resolve all of our conflicts seems rather optimistic. The next two questions, then, are, first, whether there are any universal horizons of concern, and thus any "values . . . that actually do hold for all subjects" (Embree 2003: 40), and if so, second, whether these universal "values" are substantive enough to ground an eco-phenomenological ethics.

The neo-Husserlian eco-phenomenologists try to answer "Yes" to both questions. What makes their *naturalistic* ethical realism so interesting is their further contention that our pre-given world of "background values" can itself be peeled back to reveal "an axiological transcendental" (Brown 2003: 13), that is, a proto-ethical substrate of nature they believe can function as the ground for a new eco-phenomenological ethics. For such naturalistic eco-phenomenologists as Kohák, Brown, Diehm, Ted Toadvine, and David Wood, the very notion of something's being "good" is ultimately rooted in the objective conditions required to sustain and enhance the life of an organism, while the "bad" comes from those conditions which diminish or eradicate such life. As Kohák influentially maintains, "good and evil does have an ontological justification: some things sustain life, others destroy it" (Kohák 1993: 31). Brown suggests how one might develop Kohák's view of the intrinsic value of life into a full-blown ethics: "Why are we so sure that dishonesty, fraud, rape, and murder are evil? Because they each, although in different ways, retard and inhibit the intrinsic purposes and desires of life" (Kohák 2003: 14). It is easy to understand why a naturalistic environmentalist might find such a view attractive. Yet, one need not believe the "rape is in our genetic interest" view some sociobiologists defend in order to be skeptical of the claim that what we in the West take to be ethically good (or bad) is what serves (or undermines) the "intrinsic purposes and desires of life" – even assuming, *concessio non dato*, that we can make adequate sense of that phrase, something Kohák does only by making "Husserl's phenomenology an anticipation of evolutionism in sociobiology" (Kohák 2003: 28).[5] The sociobiology literature is replete with less controversial studies of behaviors we would condemn as immoral among humans that seem to have been advantageous from the perspective of Dawkin's "selfish gene." (Perhaps that should only surprise the prudish; as Freud explained in *Totem and Taboo* (1913), societies do not morally prohibit acts no one wants to commit.) Indeed, both Nietzsche and Freud argue that Western civilization is premised on the repression and sublimation of the very innate purposes and desires of life to which the naturalistic ethical realists appeal, and that ethics functions, at least in part, to codify and enforce this very repression.

So, instead of assuming that our core values are natural (which would be to *mystify* rather than to *naturalize* the ground of ethics), we should admit that, insofar as we can articulate an ethics in conformity with the "intrinsic purposes and desires of life" (which Nietzsche too called for), the resulting *naturalistic* ethics is likely to differ significantly from the core value system we have inherited from the Judeo-Christian-Kantian tradition, with its familiar proscription of "dishonesty, fraud, rape, . . . murder", and so on (and its defense of pity and compassion for the weak, Nietzsche would add). Naturalistic eco-phenomenologists thus seem more forthright when they suggest, for example, that an ethics that does justice to "life" may require not only "an attitude of moral regard and respect for some nonhuman others" (Brown 2003: 10), but even – and as one of its "basic principles" – "that the human population needs to be reduced by several billion" (Embree 2003: 47). If we cannot expand our core value-system to accommodate such differences, they may render the adoption of a naturalistic eco-phenomenological ethics unlikely, undesirable, or both. At best, Marietta may be correct to see in this ethics a "rejection of humanistic ethical concerns – which thinkers of our day are not ready to accept, but at which thinkers in the future might not blanch" (Embree 2003: 125).

To turn to our second question, is the notion of the "intrinsic purposes and desires of life" sufficiently substantive to ground an ethics? Insofar as it is, should we adopt this ethics? Nietzsche argues that a naturalistic *ethics of life* will not resemble our Judeo-Christian-Kantian value system; some will go further and worry that it may not justify any value system at all. This worry about the *indeterminacy* of an ethics of life is suggested by the fact that, the more specific the values that are supposed to follow from "the intrinsic purposes and desires of life," the more dubious their derivations seem. To add another example: when Kohák asserts that the human attachment to a "homeland" is justified by the fact that we are embodied entities (Kohák 2003: 28), it sounds as if he is rationalizing a politically disastrous and thus ethically suspect attachment. We are not salmon, after all. The underlying worry here is that the "axiological transcendental" (which holds that ultimately the objective conditions that generate life are *good* while those which diminish it are *bad*) is too general to be of much help in resolving real-world environmental disputes, especially once we have made room at the ethical bargaining table for nonhuman organisms, as the view suggests we must when it posits life in general as its fundamental value (see Thomson 2004). It was, more-over, just such an emphasis on the fundamental value of life itself that led Nietzsche to his controversial doctrine of the "superman" (or "trans-human," *Übermensch*), his neo-Darwinian idea that evolution is not over, since humanity too "is something that shall be superseded" (Nietzsche 1954: 124; Richardson 2002). Nietzsche's own pursuit of a naturalistic ethics of life, in other words, brought him to the conclusion that if what we most value is the continuing survival of life itself, then humanity not only will but *should* be superseded.

Nietzsche's conclusion brings out what may be the most serious objection to the naturalistic ethical realism we have been examining. What if a rigorous ethical observance of the underlying conditions that sustain and enhance life actually ends up undermining what human beings prize most highly: art, literature, religion, culture, and the like? Here the naturalistic eco-phenomenological perspective, true to its Nietzschean roots, threatens to degenerate into a defense of the "post-human" (see Foucault 1973: 386–7; Pearson 1997; Fukuyama 2002). For, insofar as naturalistic ethical realism generates an eco-centric ethical perfectionism in which the preserva-tion of life in general is the highest value, it cuts against a more humanistic perfection-ism, according to which what matters ultimately is that we cultivate the distinctive talents and capacities which have thus far been associated almost exclusively with the human species. Thus, a perspective that gains much of its appeal from its attempt to put other forms of life on an equal footing with the human species risks losing that appeal by devaluing the highest achievements of humanity, even advocating the over-coming of the human as such – whether through continued evolution or technolo-gical innovation (or the latter understood as the former). The human fear of such a *coup d'état* by our technology (given popular expression in the *Terminator* and *Matrix* series) is not groundless (as these examples drawn from science fiction might suggest), but reflects a growing anxiety about the place of technology in our lives, an anxiety best understood in terms of the Heideggerian critique of technology appropriated and disseminated by transcendental eco-phenomenologists such as myself.

Transcendental Ethical Realism in Eco-Phenomenology

It is no coincidence that, "[o]ver the past decades, environmentalists have consistently focused more on Heidegger than on any of the other phenomenologists" (Langer 2003: 112). Heidegger's "later" (post-1937) philosophy in particular has proved an incompar-ably rich source of phenomenological reflection for ecologically minded philosophers, thanks to both his incisive philosophical critique of, and his suggestive treatments for, the nihilistic worldview underlying phenomena such as environmental devasta-tion.[6] As I argue (in Thomson 2005a), the later Heidegger's ontological critique of "enframing" (*Gestell*, our nihilistic, "technological" understanding of the being of entities) builds upon the idea that we Dasein implicitly participate in the making-intelligible of our worlds, indeed, that our sense of reality is mediated by lenses inherited from metaphysics. Here Heidegger historicizes Kant's *discursivity thesis*, which holds that intelligibility is the product of a subconscious process by which we spontaneously organize and so filter a sensibly overwhelming world to which we are fundamentally

453

receptive. For Heidegger, however, this implicit organization is accomplished not by historically fixed categories, but rather by a changing historical understanding of what and how entities *are* (an *ontotheological* understanding of both their essence and existence, to take the most famous example), and this "understanding of being" is supplied by the metaphysical tradition. Metaphysics, as ontotheology, temporarily secures the intelligible order both ontologically (from the inside out) and theologically (from the outside in), thereby supplying the most basic conceptual parameters and ultimate standards of legitimacy for each of history's successive "epochs" or constellations of intelligibility. We late-moderns, for example, implicitly process intelligibility through the ontotheological lenses inherited from Nietzsche's metaphysics, and so we ultimately understand the being of entities as eternally recurring will-to-power, that is, as forces coming together and breaking apart with no goal other than their own unlimited self-augmentation. The result is an unnoticed "enframing" of reality, by which we tend to reduce every entity we encounter to the status of an intrinsically meaningless "resource" (*Bestand*) merely to be *optimized* as efficiently as possible, leveling all attempts to say what matters to us down to empty optimization imperatives (such as the ubiquitous: "Get the most out of your potential!"). Thus we come to treat even ourselves (modernity's vaunted "subject") in the terms underlying our technological refashioning of the world, as just another resource to be optimized, ordered, and enhanced with maximal efficiency. Now, to take but one telling example, for every individual who goes out for a nature hike in the United States, thousands drive to indoor gyms in order to "get their exercise" on a treadmill, seeking to optimize their health by going nowhere fast, often while watching television or otherwise diverting their attention through technological means.

While many eco-phenomenologists recognize Heidegger's ontological critique of technology as a deeply revealing understanding of the precise metaphysical roots of our worsening environmental crisis, others ignore it and so, unknowingly, fatally reinscribe Nietzsche's metaphysics into their environmentalism. Indeed, the very naturalistic eco-phenomenological view we examined seeks to ground the "intrinsic value" of living organisms in an implicitly Nietzschean understanding of life as "a spontaneous, self-maintaining system, sustaining and reproducing itself, executing its program" (Toadvine 2003: 140), thereby failing to recognize that this ontological understanding of life as a self-reproducing program clearly is borrowed from, and so inevitably reinforces, our nihilistic Nietzschean ontotheology. Of course, however insightful and revealing Heidegger's critique of technology is, if he gave us only this diagnosis with no reason to hope for a cure, his critics would be right to accuse him of fatalistic quietism. Fortunately, the later Heidegger's influence on environmental philosophy stems from a second source as well, namely, his complementary efforts to elaborate a positive philosophical treatment for the nihilism that results from the fact that we implicitly interpret intelligibility through the lenses of our age's reigning Nietzschean ontotheology. This treatment includes Heidegger's calls for such ecologically suggestive phenomenological comportments as "dwelling" (*wohnen*) and "releasement toward things" (*Gelassenheit zu den Dingen*), to which we will return shortly.

Michael Zimmerman, a leading neo-Heideggerian environmentalist, is best known for persuasively connecting Heidegger and deep ecology (Zimmerman 1993a). This is rather ironic, however, since he quickly reconsidered his advocacy of this connection

(Zimmerman 1993b; Zimmerman 2003). Zimmerman's reversal can be explained in part by the fact that his own important work on the "Heidegger controversy" (Zimmerman 1990) made him acutely aware of the political risks of enlisting a philosopher maligned as an "unrepentant fascist" as the prime philosophical ally for a radical environmental movement similarly accused of "eco-fascism," risks which presumably would only be heightened if it were widely known that (as Zimmerman 1997 shows) the development of the environmental movement itself was intertwined with the rise of Nazism. I have argued that Heidegger joined the Nazi party in 1933 in order to attempt to enact his own long-developed philosophical vision for a radical reformation of the university (Thomson 2005a). It seems likely, however, that Heidegger's stunningly naïve belief that the Nazi "revolution" could be led to a "second, deeper awakening" in which it would discover its own "inner truth and greatness" was reinforced by the misleading sense of Nazism he absorbed from the German youth movement, a movement pushing for educational reform which drew a great deal of its strength from the student hiking associations, which in turn were rooted philosophically in German Romanticism. Indeed, the great Romantic poet Friedrich Hölderlin became, in effect, an exemplary hiker, thanks to the way in which his legendary, heartbreaking walk back home to Germany through the French countryside captured the imagination of subsequent generations. Nietzsche, an early admirer of Hölderlin and a passionate proponent of the culturally restorative powers of youth, frequently celebrated hiking as a stimulus to philosophical innovation. Nietzsche, in turn, inspired the Stephan George circle, one of whose members, Norbert von Hellingrath, brought to light Hölderlin's later poetry, the very poetry which (taking us full circle) proved formative for Heidegger's own philosophical vision of a spiritual revolution, first of Germany, then, later, of the world. Although such romantic influences on environmentalism deserve careful study, the fact that the historical rise of environmentalism is permeated by the politically dangerous dream of philosophical revolution does not allow either simply to be dismissed (Thomson 2003, 2005b).

Of course, Zimmerman's dramatic reversal of his own well-known case for taking Heidegger as the prime philosophical ally for the deep-ecological movement cannot be understood simply as the politically prudent strategizing of a leading philosophical environmentalist. Philosophically, it turns rather on Zimmerman's adoption of Thomas Sheehan's (Sheehan 2001) contention that the later Heidegger never meant to disseminate an understanding of "being as such" (*Seins als Solche*) that was any different from his own earlier understanding of the "being of entities" (*Sein des Seienden*). Yet, Heidegger himself admits that his own earlier failure to recognize precisely this difference was "disastrous" philosophically (Heidegger 1989: 250), and those of us who believe Sheehan is wrong on this crucial point will also think it a serious mistake for Zimmerman to follow him here. Deprived of the central notion of "being as such," Heidegger's later thought would indeed suffer from many of the problems Sheehan and Zimmerman diagnose – and numerous others. (For instance, Heidegger could not account for "historicity," the vertiginous fact that our bedrock understanding of what is changes with time, and, most seriously, his later positive project would lose much of its force and appeal.)[7] Hermeneutic generosity alone thus suggests we recognize the notion of "being as such" at work in Heidegger's later thought and see what follows for eco-phenomenological appropriations of his work, rather than claim that he lacks this crucial notion and then enumerate the resulting problems for taking him as an ally of environmentalism.

The main reason the later Heidegger became dissatisfied with (and so mostly stopped using) the word "being" (*Sein*) is that it is ambiguous between "being as such" and "the being of entities." This ambiguity proved "disastrous" not only because it allowed Heidegger to mistake the "being of entities" for "being as such" in his early work (leading him to believe he could "recover" a "fundamental ontology" from beneath history, a false belief which fueled his political ambitions (Thomson 2005a)), but also because the ambiguity obscures three connected insights central to his later thought: first, that "being as such" makes possible the historical succession of different metaphysical understandings of the "being of entities"; second, that metaphysics, as "ontotheology," systematically obscures and forgets "being as such"; and thus, finally, that metaphysics systematically elides its own condition of possibility (which means that the metaphysical tradition can be deconstructed by immanent critiques that help reveal "being as such" and so point beyond this tradition). The later Heidegger thus abandons the locution "being" as disastrously misleading, but he nevertheless makes clear that the notion of "being as such" must be understood as implicit in his later concept of the "fourfold." Indeed, this fourfold of "earth, heavens, mortals, and divinities" simply unpacks the four quadrants of "being" when it has been "crossed-through," and so is meant by Heidegger as another way of developing and conveying his post-metaphysical insights into "being as such" (Heidegger 1958: 81–5). Because "releasement to things" is the later Heidegger's name for a phenomenological comportment receptive to this fourfold, and "dwelling" is another (slightly earlier) name for a comportment open to "being as such," these eco-phenomenologically suggestive comportments simply cannot be understood without recognizing the role of "being as such" in his later thought.

Here we encounter the transcendental ethical realism the later Heidegger pioneered, according to which we discover what really matters when we are appropriately open to the environment, but what we thereby discover are neither facts nor values but rather "being as such," a transcendental source of meaning that cannot be reduced to facts, values, or entities of any kind (Dreyfus and Spinosa 1997). For, as Zimmerman sees, "letting things be" means "allowing them to manifest themselves in terms of their own inherent possibilities" (Zimmerman 2003: 79), while the "fourfold" poetically names the interwoven horizons of this phenomenological self-showing, the "presencing" which Heidegger understands as made possible by all the grounds (including the past) which bear us up us without being completely within our control ("earth") as well as the projects which open the future ("heavens"), and which can thus matter most deeply ("divinities") to we finite and so reflexive entities ("mortals").[8] Similarly, to "dwell" means to be at "home" with "being as such," albeit an *unheimlich* dwelling in which one is outside any metaphysical understanding of the being of entities (*pace* Langer 2003: 114), attuned to that temporally dynamic phenomenological "presencing" metaphysics both presupposes and elides. These comportments will thus be crucial to any deep eco-phenomenological appropriation of the later Heidegger. For, when we adopt these comportments, and so become attuned to the phenomenological "presencing" whereby "being as such" manifests itself, we come to understand entities as being richer in meaning than we are capable of doing justice to conceptually, rather

456

than taking them as intrinsically meaningless resources awaiting optimization. Such transformative experiences, in which we recognize entities as being more than resources awaiting optimization (and so learn to approach them with care, humility, patience, gratitude, even awe), can become microcosms of, as well as inspiration for, the revolution beyond our underlying ontotheology Heidegger thinks we need in order to set our world aright.

Wood suggests that, in order to transcend the nihilistic metaphysics of our age, eco-phenomenologists "*need a model of the whole as something that will inevitably escape our model of it*" (Wood 2003: 217), which is what both Heidegger and Levinas give us with their respective understandings of "being as such" and "alterity." Given the proximity of Heidegger and Levinas on this crucial matter, it is revealing to observe that the same refusal to recognize the notion of "being as such" in Heidegger's later thought helps motivate the popular move beyond Heidegger to Levinas in pursuit of the "ethical" perspective Heidegger is supposedly missing. This too is ironic, since Levinas's ethics is essentially a sensitivity to alterity ("ethics is the other; the other is ethics," as Levinas told Derrida), and Levinas's notion of alterity (as a radical other who issues aporetic commands both necessary and impossible to obey) is much closer to the later Heidegger's understanding of "being as such" (as a temporally dynamic presencing that simultaneously elicits and defies conceptual circumscription) than most Levinas scholars acknowledge. Of course, these Levinasians are simply following Levinas himself, whose notorious animosity toward Heidegger (an extreme instance of Bloom's "anxiety of influence") distorted his own understanding of the profound conceptual debts he owed to Heidegger's thinking. Nevertheless, as Wood pointedly observes: "If you're going to be a Levinasian" (that is, someone who practices a Levinasian ethics of reading), then "you couldn't possibly read Heidegger in the way Levinas reads Heidegger" (Wood and Dalton 2002: 12).

Levinas, Heidegger, and the Ethical Question of Animality

Rather than endlessly restaging the old debates between the masters, however, we do better to follow the spirit of the eco-phenomenological movement by working creatively to appropriate their thinking for ourselves. In this spirit, Christian Diehm (2003) makes a noble attempt to rehabilitate Levinas's notion of alterity, purging it of its anthropocentrism so that it can serve the cause of animal rights. Edward Casey, however, points out insurmountable textual obstacles to this well-meaning hermeneutic endeavor, stemming from Levinas's (barely secularized) belief that only the face of the other human *person* can grant us access to alterity (albeit a para-doxical mode of access in which alterity is "manifest" but "non-apparent"). Levinas did well to ask himself, "*Can things have a face?*" Unfortunately, as Casey shows, "Levinas himself would doubtless have to conclude that either there is nothing like a face in the environment . . . or the face is all over the place: in which case, its meaning will be so diluted as to risk losing any ethical urgency. Otherwise put, ethics is human or it does not exist at all" (Casey 2003: 192–3). Casey's sharp critique of Levinas is convincing on this point, but Diehm does well nonetheless in what I take to be an attempt to show that the conceptual resources of a great philosopher often exceed the

457

narrow conclusions that philosopher, as an idiosyncratic individual, actually drew from them.

We could use the same strategy to ally Heidegger (more convincingly than Levinas) with the animal rights movement, building on John Haugeland's "unorthodox" argument that "Dasein" and "human being" are not coextensive, since the reference of "Dasein" is, in principle, broader. Haugeland (Haugeland 1982, 1992) argues that corporations, for example, could qualify as "Dasein," but I would suggest extending the term to (at least some) nonhuman animals. In my view, *Being and Time*'s revolutionary conception of the self not as a thinking substance, subject, ego, or consciousness, but as a *Dasein* (a "being-here," that is, a temporally structured making-intelligible of the place in which I happen to find myself) promises us a philosophically defensible, non-speciesist way of beginning to draw the ethically crucial distinctions between (something like) "lower" and "higher" forms of life missing from the eco-centric views considered above (as well as from more famous non-speciesist ethical views like Peter Singer's sensation-centered consequentialism). Without such distinctions, these positions tend to generate anti-human consequences that render their widespread acceptance extremely unlikely, leading to a practical dead-end in which even as creative a philosopher as Wood is willing to suggest a seemingly "eco-fascist" solution to the global environmental crisis, in which benevolent eco-centric dictatorships temporarily abrogate decision making from less rational, democratic states (Wood 2003: 231). Yet, such antihuman implications and antidemocratic conclusions can be avoided, and without falling back into illegitimate, speciesist reasoning, if we understand "rights" (with the progressive strand of the liberal tradition) as political protections owed to *all* agents capable of reflexively pursuing life-projects, since the pursuit of such life-projects gives one the kind of world that both desires and deserves protecting (Tooley 1972). The suggestion, put provocatively, is that eco-phenomenologists should answer the question "Which entities deserve intrinsic rights?" with: "All Dasein," that is, all entities whose being is an issue for them, and only these entities (although other entities could, of course, deserve rights instrumentally, in virtue of their relations to Dasein, including relations of eco-systemic interdependence).

On this neo-Heideggerian eco-phenomenological view, what counts (in contrast to the naturalistic, neo-Nietzschean and Husserlian positions considered earlier) is not life *per se*, but rather a life that has a temporally enduring world that matters to it explicitly. Heidegger did well to escape the gravity of his age far enough to recognize that being a Dasein is not an all-or-nothing affair, since there are degrees of "having a world." Still, as Llewelyn observes, "Heidegger's phenomenology . . . does not entail this . . . thinking of the non-human other. It only enables it" (Llewelyn 2003: 58, 62). The simple tripartite distinction Heidegger famously proposes in *The Fundamental Concepts of Metaphysics* between the "worldless" rock, the "world-poor" animal, and the world-disclosing "Dasein" really only inaugurates the more difficult labor of drawing fine-grained distinctions on a much fuller continuum. We might imagine such a *continuum of Dasein* as stretching, for example, from:

(1) "worldless" inorganic matter; to (2) similarly "worldless" invertebrate organisms (lacking a nervous system and so physiologically incapable of sensation); to (3) simple vertebrate organisms (possessing the capacity to experience pleasure

and pain, and so somewhere between being "worldless" and "world-poor"); to (4) "world-poor" entities like the lizard on the rock and cow in the field (sentient but not reflexive, apparently permanently immersed in perceptual immediacy); to (5) the "near-Dasein" of such entities as the chimpanzee (whose self-awareness is demonstrated, for example, by a remarkable capacity to incorporate an explicit understanding of its role in a complex social group into a creative plan to accomplish difficult, temporally distant goals); to (6) the partial Dasein of such entities as gorillas (who conveniently demonstrate their possession of a world by learning our languages); to (7) the potential Dasein of young children (who combine capacities like (6) with the potential for (8)); to (8) the "rich world" of full Dasein (including not only normal adult human beings but also whatever other entities – be they organic, android, or alien – possess a reflexive self-understanding making them capable of experiencing not merely pleasure and pain but also immense suffering and sublime elevation, and of developing and pursuing a self-understanding which gives meaning to their lives from within); and, perhaps, to (9) entities with even richer worlds than human Dasein – who could deny the possibility?

This suggested elaboration of a graded "continuum of Dasein" remains too simplistic and speculative, of course, and perhaps its implicit hierarchy is marked by a residual anthropocentrism. But the same "criticisms" hold even for extreme, eco-centric perspectives, which yield such anthropomorphizing confusions as Klaver's belief that a stone can have "being-in-the-world" (Klaver 2003: 159–62) and Diehm's idea that, in all organisms, "the horizon opened by need is, minimally, a horizon of self-concern, an openness to experience," such that mere "being alive . . . is appropriately . . . characterized as being-for-itself" (Diehm 2003: 181). Such implicitly anthropomorphic descriptions – which seek to bestow upon simple organic (and even inorganic) entities reflexive capacities such as "self-concern," "being-for-itself," and even "being-in-the-world" (in other words, *Dasein*) – generate a hyperbolic, neo-Levinasian extension of ethical concern in which (as Casey argues) ethical duties, multiplied to infinity, become uselessly "diluted."

Moreover, although Marietta's claim that "we are no more able than the ape to transcend the biological realities that affect our lives" (2003: 129) is false (since it ignores the transformations made possible by our scientific and medical technologies), the continuum I sketch may err in assigning a lesser degree of Dasein to chimpanzees, for example; certainly we should not precipitously foreclose that important empirical question, or others like it, which we should be able to address more precisely as we perfect techno-empirical means (such as fMRI and PET scans) allowing us to share more directly in the experiences of others, thereby opening up new domains for ethno-anthropological exploration (enabling us to work to cross the inter-species line, rather than expecting other animals to do so, for example, by learning sign language). While we struggle to decide which entities are sufficiently Dasein-like to deserve *intrinsic* political rights (again, other entities may deserve such rights *instrumentally*, in virtue of their relations to Dasein – including relations of eco-systemic interdependence), however, the burden of proof should be on the side of higher primates, elephants, dolphins, and other species we reasonably suspect might possess Dasein-like capabilities. The practical consequences of even this fairly minimal expansion of our current

459

conception of rights would be immense, and would surely be recognized by the naturalistic eco-phenomenologists as an enormous step in the right direction. The point of the continuum, then, is simply to suggest that we could articulate "degrees of Dasein" with more subtlety than Heidegger himself ever did, and thereby work toward a non-speciesist way of distinguishing between different kinds of life, as in fact we must if we are ever to find equitable ways of resolving the inter-species ethical dilemmas that will inevitably arise in a universe of scarcity, where life continues to live on life.

In the end, the contrast between the naturalistic and transcendental eco-phenomenological approaches comes down to two different understandings of what it is about life that makes it most worth living – in other words, to two competing versions of ethical perfectionism. Naturalistic ethical realism, we have seen, generates an eco-centric perfectionism that emphasizes the flourishing of life as such, even at the expense of the human, and so courts the charge of eco-fascism. Transcendental ethical realism yields a more humanistic perfectionism, yet avoids speciesism by seeking to protect the cultivation and development of those importantly distinctive traits and capacities belonging, by right, to all Dasein. I suggest that eco-phenomenologists should prefer this Heideggerian version of the transcendental approach, not only because it reveals serious problems with the naturalistic approach (including eco-fascism, the call for a post-human condition, and the reification of Nietzschean nihilism), but also because (as we saw in the case of animal rights) the neo-Heideggerian approach promises to help us draw nearer to the loftier eco-centric goals of the naturalistic approach while avoiding its problems.

Notes

1 This chapter is a significantly shortened and revised version of Thomson 2004.
2 Leading analytic philosophers have recently set their sights on the same dichotomies; see, e.g., McDowell 1994 and Putnam 2002.
3 Heidegger's first law of phenomenology, the law of proximity or "distance of the near" (Heidegger 1992: 135), states that what is closest to us in our everyday worldly environment, like the prescription on the glasses through which we see (or Poe's purloined letter), is furthest from us in terms of our ability to attend to and comprehend it explicitly.
4 On Heidegger's radical challenge to Cartesian dualism, see Guignon 1983; Richardson, 1986; and Dreyfus 1991.
5 On the debate over the sociobiological account of rape, cf. Thornhill and Palmer 2000 and Travis 2003.
6 Dreyfus (1992) shows, moreover, that Being and Time's claim that entities reveal themselves most fully when encountered as "hands-on" (zuhanden) equipment in contexts of practical use makes the early Heidegger look (from the perspective of the later Heidegger) to be caught up in the penultimate stage of the increasingly nihilistic "history of being" that culminates in "enframing."
7 Once Heidegger abandoned his earlier quest for a "fundamental ontology" (that is, a transhistorically binding understanding of "the meaning of being in general"), he could no longer appeal to such a notion in order to explain what makes possible Western history's succession of epoch-grounding understandings of "the being of entities" (a succession that, in the early work, he conceives of as a retrogressive falling-away from an originally complete "fundamental ontology"). I suspect Sheehan is misled by passages in which Heidegger

seems to *equate* "being as such" with "enowning" (*Ereignis*), but this is not Heidegger's considered view, and passages can be found alongside these that more carefully distinguish these two key terms of his later thought (put simply, *Ereignis* is how "being as such" takes place), as I show in Thomson 2003.

8   As this sketch implies, the middle and later Heidegger's conceptions of "earth" are different; most importantly, the ineffability of the middle concept of "earth" passes to "being as such," which is conveyed by the entire later fourfold. For a lucid, literal reading of Heidegger's "fourfold," see Wrathall 2003.

References and Further Reading

Brown, C. S. (2003) The real and the good: Phenomenology and the possibility of an axiological rationality. In C. S. Brown and T. Toadvine (eds.), *Eco-Phenomenology: Back to the Earth Itself* (pp. 3–18). Albany: State University of New York Press.

Brown, C. S., and T. Toadvine (2003a) Eco-phenomenology: An introduction. In C. S. Brown and T. Toadvine (eds.), *Eco-Phenomenology: Back to the Earth Itself* (pp. ix–xxi). Albany: State University of New York Press.

—— (2003b) Bibliography in eco-phenomenology. In C. S. Brown and T. Toadvine (eds.), *Eco-Phenomenology: Back to the Earth Itself* (pp. 239–48). Albany: State University of New York Press.

Casey, E. S. (2003) Taking a glance at the environment: Preliminary thoughts on a promising topic. In C. S. Brown and T. Toadvine (eds.), *Eco-Phenomenology: Back to the Earth Itself* (pp. 187–210). Albany: State University of New York Press.

Diehm, C. (2003) Natural disasters. In C. S. Brown and T. Toadvine (eds.), *Eco-Phenomenology: Back to the Earth Itself* (pp. 171–85). Albany: State University of New York Press.

Dreyfus, H. L. (1991) *Being-in-the-World: A Commentary on Heidegger's* Being and Time. *Division I.* Cambridge, MA: MIT Press.

—— (1992) Heidegger's history of the being of equipment. In H. L. Dreyfus and H. Hall (eds.), *Heidegger: A Critical Reader* (pp. 173–85). Oxford: Blackwell.

Dreyfus, H. L., and C. Spinosa (1997) Highway bridges and feasts: Heidegger and Borgmann on how to affirm technology. *Man and World*, 30(2), 159–77.

Embree, L. (2003) The possibility of a constitutive phenomenology of the environment. In C. S. Brown and T. Toadvine (eds.), *Eco-Phenomenology: Back to the Earth Itself* (pp. 37–50). Albany: State University of New York Press.

Foltz, B. V. (1995) *Inhabiting the Earth: Heidegger, Environmental Ethics, and the Metaphysics of Nature.* Atlantic Highlands, NJ: Humanities Press.

Foucault, M. (1973) *The Order of Things: An Archeology of the Human Sciences.* New York: Vintage Books (original work published 1966).

Fukuyama, F. (2002) *Our Posthuman Future: Consequences of the Biotechnology Revolution.* New York: Picador.

Glazebrook, T. (2001) Heidegger and ecofeminism. In N. J. Holland and P. Huntington (eds.), *Feminist Interpretations of Martin Heidegger* (pp. 221–51). University Park: Pennsylvania State University Press.

Guignon, C. B. (1983) *Heidegger and the Problem of Knowledge.* Indianapolis: IN: Hackett.

Haugeland, J. (1982) Heidegger on being a person. *Nous*, 16, 6–26.

—— (1992) Dasein's disclosedness. In H. L. Dreyfus and H. Hall (eds.), *Heidegger: A Critical Reader* (pp. 27–44). Oxford: Blackwell.

Heidegger, M. (1958) *The Question of Being* (trans. W. Kluback and J. T. Wilde). London: Vision Press (original work published 1955).

—— (1971) The origin of the work of art. In *Poetry, Language, Thought* (trans. A. Hofstadter). New York: Harper & Row (original lectures given in 1935–6).

—— (1989) *Beiträge zur philosophie (vom Ereignis)*, *Gesamtausgabe*, vol. 65. Friedrich-Wilhelm von Herrmann (ed.), Frankfurt: V. Klostermann (original work written in 1936–8).

—— (1992) *Parmenides* (trans. A. Schuwer and R. Rojcewicz). Bloomington: Indiana University Press (original work published 1982).

Klaver, I. J. (2003) Phenomenology on (the) rocks. In C. S. Brown and T. Toadvine (eds.), *Eco-Phenomenology: Back to the Earth Itself* (pp. 155–70). Albany: State University of New York Press.

Kohák, E. (1993) Knowing good and evil . . . (Genesis 3:5b). *Husserl Studies*, 10(1), 31–42.

—— (2003) An understanding heart: Reason, value, and transcendental phenomenology. In C. S. Brown and T. Toadvine (eds.), *Eco-Phenomenology: Back to the Earth Itself* (pp. 19–35). Albany: State University of New York Press.

Langer, M. (2003) Nietzsche, Heidegger, and Merleau-Ponty: Some of their contributions and limitations for "environmentalism." In C. S. Brown and T. Toadvine (eds.), *Eco-Phenomenology: Back to the Earth Itself* (pp. 103–20). Albany: State University of New York Press.

Llewelyn, J. (1991) *The Middle Voice of Ecological Responsibility*. New York: St. Martin's Press.

—— (2003) Prolegomena to any future phenomenological ecology. In C. S. Brown and T. Toadvine (eds.), *Eco-Phenomenology: Back to the Earth Itself* (pp. 51–72). Albany: State University of New York Press.

Marietta, D. E., Jr. (2003) Back to earth with reflection and ecology. In C. S. Brown and T. Toadvine (eds.), *Eco-Phenomenology: Back to the Earth Itself* (pp. 121–38). Albany: State University of New York Press.

McDowell, J. (1994) *Mind and World*. Cambridge, MA: Harvard University Press.

Naess, A. (1973) The shallow and the deep, long-range ecology movement: A summary. *Inquiry*, 16(1), 95–100.

Nietzsche, F. (1954) *Thus Spoke Zarathustra* (trans. W. Kaufmann). In W. Kaufmann (ed.), *The Portable Nietzsche*. New York: Penguin (original work published 1891).

Pearson, K. A. (1997) *Viroid Life: Perspectives on Nietzsche and the Transhuman Condition*. New York and London: Routledge.

Putnam, H. (2002) *The Collapse of the Fact/Value Dichotomy and Other Essays*. Cambridge, MA: Harvard University Press.

Richardson, J. (1986) *Existential Epistemology: A Heideggerian Critique of the Cartesian Project*. Oxford: Clarendon Press.

—— (2002) Nietzsche contra Darwin. *Philosophy and Phenomenological Research*, 65(3), 537–75.

Sheehan, T. (2001) *Kehre* and *ereignis*: A Prolegomenon to *Introduction to Metaphysics*. In R. Polt and G. Fried (eds.), *A Companion to Heidegger's* Introduction to Metaphysics (pp. 3–16). New Haven, CT and London: Yale University Press.

Taylor, C. (1995) Heidegger, language, ecology. In *Philosophical Arguments* (pp. 100–26). Cambridge, MA: Harvard University Press.

Thomson, I. (2003) The philosophical fugue: Understanding the structure and goal of Heidegger's *Beiträge*. *Journal of the British Society for Phenomenology*, 34(1), 57–73.

—— (2004) Ontology and ethics at the intersection of phenomenology and environmental philosophy. *Inquiry*, 47(4), 380–412.

—— (2005a) *Heidegger on Ontotheology: Technology and the Politics of Education*. Cambridge: Cambridge University Press.

—— (2005b) Deconstructing the hero. In Jeff McLaughlin (ed.), *Comics as Philosophy*. Jackson: University Press of Mississippi.

Thornhill, R., and C. T. Palmer (2000) *A Natural History of Rape: Biological Bases of Sexual Coercion*. Cambridge, MA: MIT Press.

Toadvine, T. (2003) The primacy of desire and its ecological consequences. In C. S. Brown and T. Toadvine (eds.), *Eco-Phenomenology: Back to the Earth Itself* (pp. 139–54). Albany: State University of New York Press.

Tooley, M. (1972) Abortion and infanticide. *Philosophy and Public Affairs*, 2, 37–65.

Travis, C. B. (2003) (ed.) *Evolution, Gender, and Rape*. Cambridge, MA: MIT Press.

Wood, D. (2003) What is eco-phenomenology? In C. S. Brown and T. Toadvine (eds.), *Eco-Phenomenology: Back to the Earth Itself* (pp. 211–33). Albany: State University of New York Press.

Wood, D., and Dalton, J. (2002) The art of time: An interview with David Wood. *Contretemps*, 3, 2–23.

Wrathall, M. A. (2003) Between the earth and the sky: Heidegger on life after the death of God. In M. A. Wrathall (ed.), *Religion After Metaphysics* (pp. 69–87). Cambridge: Cambridge University Press.

Zimmerman, M. (1990) *Heidegger's Confrontation with Modernity: Technology, Politics, and Art*. Bloomington: Indiana University Press.

—— (1993a) Heidegger, Buddhism, and deep ecology. In C. Guignon (ed.), *The Cambridge Companion to Heidegger* (pp. 240–69). Cambridge: Cambridge University Press.

—— (1993b) Rethinking the Heidegger–deep ecology relationship. *Environmental Ethics*, 15(3), 195–224.

—— (1997) Ecofascism: A threat to American environmentalism? In R. S. Gottlieb (ed.), *The Ecological Community* (pp. 229–54). New York: Routledge.

—— (2003) Heidegger's phenomenology and contemporary environmentalism. In C. S. Brown and T. Toadvine (eds.), *Eco-Phenomenology: Back to the Earth Itself*. Albany: State University of New York Press.

31

Ontology, Pragmatism, and Technology

SHUNSUKE KADOWAKI

1 Preliminaries

Whereas Heidegger in his later writings characterizes technology as the dismal fate of the West, Dewey describes it as a method of constructing "a fortress out of the very conditions and forces which threaten" human beings (Dewey 1929a: 3). For Heidegger a "danger in the highest sense" (Heidegger 1977: 28), technology for Dewey is no less than the way in which the world is made more secure. In this apparent disagreement, do these two thinkers offer opposing understandings of a central driver of the modern age, or do they rather only seem to address the same subject while speaking incommensurable languages?

The first reading of the disagreement might be developed as follows. If Heidegger's conception of technology and Dewey's conception of pragmatism share the idea that technology is no mere means, but rather the way in which everything is defined as something that is directed toward furthering something else, Heidegger sees technology as the last stage of the Western ontology wherein the real has lost its primordial condition to become standing-reserve for further exploitation; Dewey, in turn, sees in "art" the sole hope for coping with luck without resorting to dualistic metaphysics.

Richard Rorty evidently pursues such a reading. His interpretation of Heidegger's history of Being identifies American pragmatism with modern technological thought as at the bottom of the downward escalator of Being. In relation to this identification, Rorty illuminates a tension inherent in Heidegger's appraisal of technology, the tension between (a) a sense of contingency shared by Heidegger and Dewey that results from the destruction of mainstream ontology and the possibility it affords of recapturing what has been neglected as fragile and transitory, and (b) a nostalgia for the age of pre-Socratic Greek thinkers, before the launch of the Platonic project that would culminate in the total dominance of technology; in contrast, Rorty understands Dewey to put "technology in its proper place, as a way of making possible social practices . . . which will form the next stanza of Being's poem" (Rorty 1991: 47), while remaining grateful for what is disclosed by one's words and practices – that is, while retaining a sense of contingency.

The view that Heidegger and Dewey's understandings of technology are incommensurable, the second reading – which most serious defenders of Heidegger would

464

presumably support – emphasizes the clear contrast between Heidegger's ontological vocabulary and the metaphysical vocabularies that are redescribed by Heidegger's vocabulary, but that, asymmetrically, cannot redescribe it in turn. In terms of later Heideggerian ontology, the pragmatic conviction that the perils and contingencies of the real world can be overcome by developing new technologies can be convincingly interpreted as the most degraded form of the Nietzschean "Will to Power." Yet this interpretation is beyond the reach of pragmatists, who are trapped in a circle laid out by the infinite human desire for control over nature and the self.

According to another version of Heidegger and Dewey's incommensurability vis-à-vis technology, those who are troubled by the disagreement fail to grasp the difference between the "ontological" and the "ontic." Heidegger focuses solely on the "essence of modern technology" called Enframing (*Ge-stell*), an ontological structure that makes possible our peculiar way of encountering the physical environment as means and resources to be manipulated, and that regulates our age. Yet Heidegger demonstrates none of the pragmatists' concern for characterizing what kinds of devices contribute to greater happiness or "democratize technology" (Feenberg 1999), ontic issues circumscribed by the essence of modern technology.

Those who view Heidegger and Dewey's incommensurability in terms of this point attend so closely to Heidegger's abstraction of the "ontological" that they disregard the ontological assumptions that determine Dewey's pragmatism. However, Dewey is fully aware of the ontological turn of the modern age:

> When the things which exist around us, which we touch, see, hear and taste [through ordinary perception] are regarded [in modern experimental science] as interrogation for which an answer must be sought (and must be sought by means of deliberate introduction of changes till they are reshaped into something different), nature as it already exists ceases to be something which must be accepted and submitted to, endured or enjoyed, just as it is. It is now something to be modified, to be intentionally controlled. (Dewey 1929a: 100)

It thus seems quite unlikely that the ontic issue in technology is untouched by pragmatist ontology; if the conception of nature which implies its naive acceptance has already been lost – and both Heidegger and Dewey would agree that it has – how can nature be recovered from its state of exploitation other than through the technological devices and arts that our age has developed?

Yet the view that Heidegger and Dewey's understandings of technology are incommensurable is nonetheless incisive insofar as it focuses upon the translatability of ontological vocabularies. The real struggle between Heidegger and Dewey, to the extent that there is one, lies not in the conflict between the totalizing theory of Being and the liberation of ordinary practice from contemplation, but rather in the conflict over which vocabulary yields irrevocable gains in ontological intelligibility. However, one suspects that inferring the above-mentioned asymmetry between the thinkers' vocabularies from Heidegger's deconstructing story may be rash, and this suspicion deepens upon reflecting that a full understanding of Heidegger's Being (*Sein*) depends upon one's making recourse to such pragmatist conceptions as skills, practices, and interactions between agent and environment. Hence, it may be

465

the case that Dewey's ontological vocabulary clarifies the more obscure vocabulary of Heidegger.

I prefer the first reading to the first version of the second reading in the hope that a "free relationship" can be obtained between Heidegger and Dewey's respective theories of technology. Still, there remains an issue to be worried over in this reading: if an equivalent of pragmatism can be found in Heidegger, and an equivalent of philosophy of technology in Dewey, must not pragmatism and Heideggerian technological thought be reconsidered in depth? To put it differently, if pragmatism and Heideggerian technological thought are necessarily embedded in the ontologies of both thinkers, must not the reconsideration of these ontologies yield completely different understandings of pragmatism and technological thought in each?

This chapter presents in particular a consideration (in Sections 2 and 3) of how Heidegger's so-called "pragmatism" and theory of technology are shaped by his ontology, and in light of this inquiry, a reconsideration of Dewey's pragmatism; in light of this discussion, the chapter also offers (in Section 4) a brief exploration of the kind of articulation of technology these considerations might engender.

2 Ontology and Pragmatism

In *Being and Time* (1927), Heidegger systematically attempts to answer the following two questions, which have been central to ontological inquiry since Aristotle:

(1) How does one distinguish between what really is, and what is not, but only appears to be in dependence on what really is?
(2) What is the cause of entities (where "entities" include events, material things, human minds, and other things)?

With regard to the first of these questions (1), modern philosophy has transformed the question of "what really is" into an inquiry into the relationship between the human mind, or mental representations as modes of the human mind, and material things. The ontological procedure at the heart of the debate over the mind/body problem goes roughly as follows: first, one establishes the most general categorical framework, such as substance/property or event-relationship, and then one decides what kind of status mental and physical phenomena have within that framework, for which decision one refers to the certainty of consciousness, mental causation, and other criteria. Heidegger does not subscribe to this procedure. The three ontological categories he identifies in *Being and Time* – Dasein, availableness (*Zuhandenheit*), and occurrentness (*Vorhandenheit*) – are rather derived from the role that contextuality plays in each category: Dasein is context-forming Being, availableness is context-conforming Being, and occurrentness is context-annihilating Being. To understand the manner in which contextuality is significant requires that the cause of being in Heidegger's philosophy be addressed.

First, in answering the second question (2) raised above, Heidegger subscribes to Kant's idea of the "conditions of possibilities": that natural causation, whether it be event causation or Aristotelian generation, is not sufficient to explain the fact that an object of our experience appears as it does; to encounter an object of our experience as it appears, certain prior conditions of possibilities for the appearance of that object are required. Kant introduces the conditions of possibilities as a new candidate for the cause (in the broad sense of *aitia* in Plato and Aristotle) of being, insofar as these conditions are supposed to apply not only to possible knowledge but also to every object that can be encountered. In a different context, Michael Friedman distinguishes between two distinct senses of "*a priori*" – "necessary and unrevisable, true for all time, on the one hand, and 'constitutive of the concept of the object of [scientific] knowledge,' on the other" (Friedman 2001: 72); it is through the second of these conceptions of "*a priori*" that Kant develops his idea of conditions of possibilities.

In Heidegger, the famous ontological difference (*ontologische Differenz*) between Being (*Sein*) and entities (*Seiendes*) can be understood as a claim that the Being of entities constitutes the *a priori* conditions of the possibilities of encountering the entities. In his analysis of the available, Heidegger illustrates this ontological difference as that between a tool that Dasein currently encounters and the whole nexus of equipment that makes such an encounter possible. The term "*a priori*" in this context refers to the ontological dependence of such an entity on the whole nexus; if any single entity within the whole preceded this whole, that is, if it showed up independently of this whole, it would have no being within the practical nexus.

The holistic structure is not formal in the sense that the value of a constituent within the whole is determined by the configuration of the whole, as in the case of the configuration of chess pieces. Rather, it is embedded in two interdependent and inextricable directions of practical understanding: the world-understanding and the self-understanding. Consider the understanding of a female Japanese office worker who is carrying a tray from which she will serve tea to her male colleagues. Her comportment as she carries the tray is informed by her understanding of a local context (the culture of Japanese companies) in which carrying the tray makes sense. This world-understanding circumscribes tray-carrying skills, the necessary circumspection for employing these skills properly, the understandings that carrying a tray is assigned to serving tea and that serving tea is assigned to playing the role of a woman employee, and so on. Heidegger calls this world-understanding "involvement" (*Bewandtnis*). Within and inextricably connected to this world-understanding is self-understanding, which for the female office worker includes the skill to guide herself to her destination, avoiding obstacles with tray in hand, as well as acceptance of the possibility of playing the role of a female employee who is expected to serve tea. World-understanding, which comprises what it is to be a thing or tool by locating the thing or tool within a suitable local context, cannot be constituted without the self-understanding that opens the situation by playing one's role in the world.

These interrelated understandings of the practical whole – the understanding of the world and that of the role played by the agent in the world – might be termed "the understanding of context." Thus, the contextuality that constitutes the conditions of the possibilities of encountering the available makes the category "availableness" possible. The Being of the available is context-conforming, insofar as a tool appears as it is only within the context opened up by an agent's self-understanding; the Being of Dasein is context-forming, insofar as Dasein commits herself to certain roles and possibilities in opening up, and in accordance with a relevant context. In contrast to the available, the occurrent are objects of theoretical contemplation. Insofar as they are

467

not entities that function within a practical whole, in other words, they are stripped of their context – they show themselves as what they really are. Thus the occurrent, among which categorical frameworks such as substance/property, event-relationship, or other so-called building blocks of the world are counted, is context-annihilating.

On the basis of this conception of contextuality, *Being and Time* can be read as asserting a version of pragmatism. The tradition of Western philosophy has accorded to theoretical contemplation the privilege of having access to reality, and in accordance with this partiality to theoretical contemplation, reality has been narrowed down to what theoretical contemplation is supposed to grasp, that is, to the occurrent. The task of philosophy in Heidegger's view is to recover what is primordially experienced but has been passed over in the tradition: the world which is opened up by acting Dasein and which provides the context of the available.

Yet this conception of contextuality also reveals crucial differences between Dewey's pragmatism and Heidegger's version of it. First, let us recall that Dewey's pragmatism follows from an original situation or insecurity disclosed by his attenuated naturalism and its ontology. As Dewey puts it, "Man finds himself living in an aleatory world; his existence involves, to put it baldly, a gamble. The world is a scene of risk; it is uncertain, unstable, uncannily unstable. Its dangers are irregular, inconstant, not to be counted upon as to their times and seasons" (Dewey 1929b: 41). Living in a world that is uncertain, uncontrollable, and hazardous, the human being tries to safeguard himself against the uncertain character of the world.

In the genealogical manner of Nietzsche, Dewey argues that diverse philosophies can be viewed as "different ways of supplying recipes for denying to the universe the character of contingency" (Dewey 1929b: 46). That is, traditional metaphysics in Dewey's view identified reality with what is sure, regular, and so completely established as to render further inquiry unnecessary – what philosophers wished existence to be. Even after the triumph of modern scientific naturalism, the quest for certainty, *a priori* principle, or other secured realms continued within the domestic circle of philosophy.

Dewey's harsh criticism of the Western philosophical tradition and its inherent intellectualism follows not only from the pragmatist claim that human beings can change the world through action, but also from his ontological conviction that matter, life, and mind do not represent separate kinds of being, but rather that the distinction between them is "one of levels of increasing complexity and intimacy of interaction among natural events" (Dewey 1929b: 261). From the perspective of this attenuated naturalism, characteristic interactions can be found between human agents and environmental conditions much as can interactions characteristic of physical events. Interactions between human agents and environmental conditions are continuous with natural organic behavior in the sense that human beings experience an object or an event only within an interconnected whole – a process analogous to the stimulus-response process of an organism interacting with its environment. The whole is comprehensible only to human inquiry or problem-solving that is analogous to the efforts of an organism to restore its equilibrium.

Heidegger's main target is neither the metaphysical dualism that strives to separate the immutable from the empirical, nor the intellectualism that promises a direct approach to the immutable; for Heidegger, both dualism and intellectualism are only corollaries to the context annihilation of the philosophical tradition. Modern naturalism is still loyal to this misguided tradition for Heidegger, though for Dewey it affords liberation from both metaphysical dualism and intellectualism. Although it is obvious from the discussion thus far that Heidegger and Dewey agree on the importance of the role played by the context in which something matters to an agent, what Heidegger ascribes to contextuality differs fundamentally from what Dewey would ascribe to it in view of his naturalism; Heidegger's contextuality cannot be interpreted as the aspect of natural biological processes Dewey describes. The way in which one understands a practical whole so as to be able to encounter a tool is not the same as the way in which one aspect of the environment, such as a tool, a perception, or some other aspect, performs its function as an instrument for certain ends. Functionality, the pivot of Dewey's biological holism, does not require an agent to understand the functional whole as a background for understanding something, but the contextuality of Heidegger's conception does require background understanding of the whole.

Let us return to the example of the female Japanese office worker carrying a tray of tea. Her comportment as she carries the tray is informed by her understanding of a local context in which carrying the tray makes sense. This context includes not only the place in which the interaction between her skills and the environment transpires, but also the standards and norms by which her grasp of the world is judged. Her understanding of the tray is appropriate only if it is located in relevant situations. She comports herself appropriately only if she acts in accordance with the way in which she is expected to comport herself. She does not follow the standards and norms as lawlike ones, but she is familiar with them. John McDowell's view of virtue as "a reliable sensitivity to a certain sort of requirement that situations impose on behaviour" (McDowell 1979: 51) affords insight into this familiarity, which provides a reason for acting in accordance with standards and norms. It is noteworthy that the term "reason" applies here because an agent can interpret or misinterpret his/her situation. The female employee may rightly tell us that her behavior maintains the society that prescribes the destiny she has accepted, or she may (perhaps mistakenly) interpret her behavior as manifesting laudable virtue that will be shared by every generation to come. Were it not for such interpretations of the norms with which we are familiar, we would be unable to deal with the possible breakdown of the background understanding of norms that makes a local context intelligible: interpretation sustains the familiarity of norms, defending them from criticism, restoring them from disorder, and establishing them over and over again.

Though interpretable, however, background understanding is not codifiable in practical syllogisms or other forms, because propositional representations cannot provide the relevancy needed for ignoring what ought to be ignored under a wide variety of circumstances. With its limited resources, the mind cannot deal with what its environment imposes by means of syllogistic mental representation. Background understanding, furthermore, cannot be explicit. Heidegger calls the mode of ordinary "being-in-the-world" – another name for interrelated understandings of the self and the world – "absorbed concern" in the normative holistic nexus which is constitutive of the available, about which he says, "any concern is already as it is, because of some familiarity with the world" (Heidegger 1990: 107). Implicitness in this familiarity is an indispensable prerequisite for encountering the available in the world:

If, in our everyday concern with the "environment", it is to be possible for equipment available to be encountered in its "Being-in-itself", then those assignments and referential totalities in which our circumspection "is absorbed" cannot become a theme for that circumspection any more than they can for grasping things "thematically" but non-circumspectively. If it is to be possible for the available not to emerge from its inconspicuousness, the world must not announce itself. (Heidegger 1990: 106)

If this background understanding constitutes the contextuality of being-in-the-world, and if it ceases to function when it becomes logically calculable and thematically controllable, that which provides the *a priori* conditions of possibilities of encountering entities turns out to have original *contingency* built in (the term "contingency" here denoting every aspect of what is devoid of necessity, including incalculability, unpredictability, uncontrollability, and unavailableness). It is in this regard that Heidegger discusses the uncanniness of the world that anxiety reveals: "being-in-the-world which is tranquillized and familiar is a mode of Dasein's uncanniness, not the reverse . . . the "not-at-home" must be conceived as the more primordial phenomenon" (Heidegger 1990: 234).

Whereas contingency is *internal* to the contextuality that Heidegger finds constitutive of the Being of entities, it is *external* to the functionality of Dewey's naturalistic pragmatism. For Dewey, contingency remains in the threats and perils emanating from outside of an organism; it has meaning only as something to be surmounted. That this idea is deeply rooted in Dewey's thought is supported by the following passage from an early essay:

> Both [contingency and necessity] are teleological in character – contingency referring to the separation of means from end, due to the fact that the end having been already reached the means have lost their value for us; necessity being the reference of means to an end which has still to be got. Necessary means needed; contingency means no longer required – because already enjoyed. (Dewey 1893: 96)

Here a dichotomy arises: either contingency vanishes if what is supposed to give birth to the contingent has been integrated into a (teleologically) functional whole, or it remains external to the whole. This dichotomy resonates in Dewey's conception of technology, which for Dewey means legitimately extended science, while modern science means a generalized adoption of the point of view of the useful arts – pragmatic insights with which Heidegger would cordially agree. Technology is not extraneous application to science, but rather application *in* science – the expansion of operative interactions between science and nature. "Application in something," says Dewey, "signifies a more extensive interaction of natural events with one another, an elimination of distance and obstacles" (Dewey 1929b: 162). Such technologies as those of engineering, medicine, and the social arts reveal previously hidden potentialities, and realize new, previously unrealized means–end relationships. In this way, the technology of Dewey's conception deals with contingency in nature; in the unpredictable process of completion, technology tames the contingent that appears as "distance and obstacles" into a new functional whole.

However, this conception of technology disregards the internal contingency of what makes this technological whole possible. Not endorsing this dichotomy, Heidegger

470

proposes a different conception of technology based on what he has elucidated by defending his version of pragmatism, as discussed briefly in the following section.

3 Heidegger's Ambiguity on Pragmatism and Technology

The possibility of *interpreting* background understanding reveals that a mechanism of disguise dwells in the understanding of Being.

Heidegger harshly criticizes the reliance of the philosophical tradition on the ontological category of occurrentness, which leaves behind contextuality. However, this does not mean that for Heidegger, natural and human sciences that focus exclusively on occurrentness do not entail the understanding of context. Hubert Dreyfus calls Kuhn's "disciplinary matrix" to mind in addressing a similar point: "scientists need shared theoretical and technical assumptions, explicitly entertained as well as embodied in shared laboratory practices" (Dreyfus 1991: 202).

Analogously, Heidegger's criticism of occurrentness based on the concept of availableness does not necessarily prove everyday Dasein absorbed in the available to be innocent of the context-annihilation that is distinctive of occurrentness. If everyday Dasein is asked in the cases of coping with a breakdown of a tool, or of expressing what it is doing to interpret its dealings with the available, the Being of the available, and its being-in-the-world, it is inevitably inclined to offer its interpretation in terms of what manifests itself explicitly and thematically, that is, in terms of what is attainable, respectable, and controllable both theoretically and practically. This inclination might be explained in reference to our having been entrapped within a tradition that has excluded contextuality from ontology. But another, and for Heidegger deeper, reason for this inclination is that the very mode of everyday Dasein's absorption in the available restricts Dasein's view of what makes the available possible, that is, its view of our background understanding of the world and the self; background understanding requires one to interpret it specifically in terms of what it offers one proximally, and in such a manner that the interpretation leaves it untouched and passed over. For Heidegger, the mechanism of disguise, an analog of which Dewey discovers at the level of philosophical theory, functions in the self-interpretation of the ordinary practical concern with the available.

Thus, we face ambiguity in the pragmatism of *Being and Time*: on the one hand, the contextuality that for Heidegger constitutes (the understanding of) the Being of Dasein and the available affords liberation from the intellectualism and dualism of the philosophical tradition; on the other, the understanding of contextuality tends to conceal and even erase contextuality itself, such that availableness is equated with utility, and comes to be interpreted in categories of occurrentness including functionality and instrumentality. This ambiguity is reflected in Heidegger's ambiguous discussion of the "everydayness" of Dasein: although the average everydayness of Dasein that has been passed over in the tradition exhibits essential structures of being-in-the-world, and although Heidegger provides his most substantial descriptions of contextuality in explicating it, he regards average everydayness as an inauthentic mode of Dasein in which Dasein is dominated by a leveled way of interpretation, and is closed off to the understanding of the world in context and Dasein's own unseen possibilities.

This ambiguity of pragmatism is transferred to the concept of technology in later Heidegger in an isomorphic manner. In "The Question Concerning Technology," Heidegger argues that "the essence of technology is in a lofty sense ambiguous" (Heidegger 1977: 33), describing one aspect of the essence of technology as follows: "Enframing [the essence of technology] challenges forth into the frenziedness of ordering [*Bestellen*] that blocks every view into the coming-to-pass of revealing and so radically endangers the relation to the essence of truth" (Heidegger 1977: 33). The understanding of ordering (Dasein's essential way of dealing with entities in the technological age) as arbitrary humane control over objects does not fully capture the concept. Rather, ordering encompasses the ongoing synchronized activities that assign equipment a role within a functional whole and tightly fit equipment into that role. An airliner, for example, reveals itself as an airliner on the runway, inasmuch as it is ordered (*be-stellt*, literally, given its place) to ensure the possibility of transportation; the possibility of transportation in turn makes sense within a whole in which movement from one place to another contributes to some other purpose. Enframing is the supreme danger in the sense that every mode of understanding of Being is at risk of being restricted to regulating and securing what is encountered within a total system of ordering, and this restriction brings about self-interpretation which strengthens the essence of technology.

Let us consider the meaning of Heidegger's assertion that Enframing "endangers the relation to the essence of truth." By "essence of truth," Heidegger means the way the conditions of possibilities of entities guarantee a passage to the entities. This essence, which Heidegger calls the "clearing [*Lichtung*]," involves the aforementioned make-up that the conditions of possibility have original contingency built in, as Heidegger suggests in the following notoriously obscure passage:

> We believe we are at home in the immediate circle of beings. That which is, is familiar, reliable, ordinary. Nevertheless, the clearing is pervaded by a constant concealment in the double meaning form of refusal and dissembling. At bottom, the ordinary is not ordinary; it is extra-ordinary, uncanny. The nature of truth, that is, of unconcealedness, is dominated throughout by a denial. (Heidegger 1975: 54)

The "concealment" or "denial" inherent in the essence of truth can be rendered in the terms of *Being and Time*: "refusal" refers to the noncodifiability and implicitness of the background understanding that is constitutive of contextuality, and "dissembling" refers to the mechanism of disguise that is immanent in the interpretation of this background understanding. One might well claim that the danger of technology is *cognitive*: Enframing decisively furthers our ignorance of what is concealed, and even justifies it.

The essence of technology, however, has another aspect:

> Enframing comes to pass for its part in the granting that lets man endure – as yet unexperienced, but perhaps more experienced in the future – that he may be the one who is needed and used for the safekeeping of the coming to presence of truth. Thus does the arising of the saving power [*das Rettende*] appear. (Heidegger 1977: 33)

Defenders and even opponents of Heidegger have been puzzled by this mysterious turning of the tables. How can technology bring about a saving power? I will not meddle in the disputes of partisans, but Heidegger points a direction for dispelling uneasiness about this problem: even if Enframing tends to erase background understanding and our inclination is to secure entities exclusively within the framework of utility or functionality, total erasure will never occur and the technological securing of entities will remain embedded in background understanding. Heidegger argues: "it is precisely in Enframing . . . that the innermost indestructible belongingness of man within granting may come to light" (Heidegger 1977: 32) – "granting [*das Gewärende*]" here means roughly the conditions of possibility. The technological network which allows the Rhine to appear as a dammed-up source of electrical power rather than as the river of Hölderlin's hymn "The Rhine" presupposes the noncodifiable and implicit in functioning as it does.

Now let us suppose that the hydroelectric power plants along the Rhine break down due to the carelessness of operators, because the transmission of banal skills between older and younger operators, which has been taken for granted, has been interrupted; the explosion at the nuclear fuel reprocessing plant in Tokai-mura in eastern Japan on September 30, 1999 exemplifies this process, as subsequent investigations have shown. Granting that background understanding does not concern every possible cause of such breakdowns in technological networks, a distinction can still be drawn between two sorts of factors: internal factors that are understood implicitly and interpreted into some articulation, and external factors located beyond the scope of the understanding. This line of thought is obviously what has been taken over from the ontology that determines the pragmatism of *Being and Time*.

Saving power in the epoch of modern technology comes from the still-remaining dependence of the total system of ordering on the background that it cannot control, and the conspicuousness of this dependency, which has emerged precisely in this epoch. In the epoch of Greek craftsmanship – that is, of *techné*, which Heidegger describes as revealing and accepting its context without endangering the implicit relationship with what is concealed – *techné* and its context were so tightly fitted together that there was no sense of this dependency, no danger of its being neglected, and hence no possibility of a saving power. This epoch, if it ever occurred, has been irretrievably lost. Heidegger suggests not a return from the epoch of modern technology to one in which there is no such danger, or to any utopia of this sort, but rather that we retain a sense of the contingency and danger that are inherent in our background understanding as we make use of modern technology.

Heidegger argues: "we let technical devices enter our daily life, at the same time leave them outside, that is, let them alone, as things which are nothing absolute but remain dependent upon something higher" (Heidegger 1969: 54). One might well ask what kind of transformation of cognition and attitude this engenders. Though the question is puzzling, I suggest that Heidegger's ontological views on the essence of technology provide a basis for reorganizing our vocabulary of technology. If we remain unconscious of the essence of technology, this vocabulary will be bound by the dichotomy of contingency discussed above. Along the Heideggerian views on the essence of technology, for example, an evaluative use of the term "unpredictability" in relation to technology is no mere projection of subjects with limited resources onto the world, but rather makes reference to what is technological in itself. Along the thought of dichotomy, the term indicates either the incompetence of the subject exploiting technology, or external hazards threatening technological devices. This line of thought in some cases affords startling successes, but in others does not, especially in cases that concern technological matters that are deeply dependent upon background understanding, such as wars against colonized countries, the design of Artificial Intelligence, and aide for "developing" nations.

4 Articulating Technology

If technology depends on background understanding of being-in-the-world, and the danger of technology makes us aware of this dependency, the manner in which we talk about technology should be analogous to the way in which we make background understanding explicit.

As I have already suggested, we cannot be perfectly aware of background understanding, for background understanding is neither logically determinable nor thematically controllable. Yet neither can we be simply unaware of it, in that it comprises the interrelated understandings of the world and the role played by the agent in the world; we are familiar with it, and capable of interpreting it, as illustrated by the case of our female employee trying to make explicit sense of her behavior. Charles Taylor calls the process of bringing that with which we are implicitly familiar into explicit awareness "articulating" (Taylor 1993: 326), a markedly different process than describing independent realities, whether physical or psychological. Our female employee's articulation of her behavior does not recapitulate what has already been formulated either in her own or her colleagues' minds, for her background understanding of social norms is something she possesses in her nonrepresentational direct dealings with things and persons, and her articulation develops what has to be articulated into a new form of interpretive words. Nor does she freshly discover in articulation what has been unknown to her, constructing completely new vocabularies for making sense of her social reality independently of her pre-understanding of what it is to negotiate that reality, for undeniably she has a sensitivity to requirements imposed by social situations. The fact that background understanding is incalculable and uncontrollable, in our terminology, it has original contingency built in, is reflected in the impossibility of complete articulacy that Taylor explains in the following passage:

> The short answer to why complete articulacy is a chimera is that any articulation itself needs the background to succeed. Each fresh articulation draws its intelligibility in turn from a background sense, abstracted from which it would fail of meaning. Each new articulation helps to redefine us, and hence can open up new avenues of potential further articulation. The process is by its very nature uncompletable, since there is no limit on the facets or aspects of our form of life that one can try to describe or of standpoints from which one might attempt to describe it. (Taylor 1993: 328)

The Heideggerian understanding of how background understanding is to be articulated, moreover, leads to what is constitutive of *articulating technology*. At least three features distinguish the Heideggerian articulation of technology, each of which requires elucidation.

(1) Enframing, the essence of technology, implicitly dominates the understanding of Being by virtue of its securing what is encountered within a total system of ordering. Yet it would be misguided to understand this domination by picturing Enframing as a simplifying conceptual apparatus through which every dimension of modern social and intellectual activity is rashly reduced to an aspect of the modern West as a totalizing system. Indeed, the following comments of Heidegger on Enframing seem to suggest a contrary understanding of this domination:

> Enframing [Ge-stell] means the gathering together of that setting-upon [stellen] which sets upon man, i.e., challenges him forth, to reveal the real, in the mode of ordering [Bestellen], as standing-reserve. Enframing means that way of revealing which holds sway in the essence of modern technology and which is it self nothing technological . . . The word [stellen] should preserve the suggestion of another Stellen . . . which, in the sense of poiesis, lets what presences come forth into unconcealment . . . Physics, indeed already as pure theory, sets nature up to exhibit itself as a coherence of forces calculable in advance. (Heidegger 1977: 20–1)

As these comments suggest, Heidegger's "Enframing" does not exclusively designate the setting-upon – i.e., the making possible of revealing entities dependently upon the background – that pertains to *modern* technology, but also connotes other modes of setting-upon, including modes that preserve the suggestion of revealing archaic *techné* and modes that co-function with modern technology as well. Enframing is not a uniform essence; rather, it allows plural modes of revealing to relate to each other, synchronically or diachronically, within itself.

Is it only a technological network, for example, that makes hydroelectric power plants along the Rhine appear to be things that exploit the Rhine? More generally, is implicit background understanding presupposed only in the mode of modern technology? Certainly not, insofar as we do not confuse the modern mode of revealing, in which the understanding of Being is restricted to ordering, with the specific mode of technological revealing, in which this restriction manifests itself most conspicuously. A technological network has to coordinate with other modes of revealing network for equipment to be assigned a role within a functional whole. The hydroelectric power plants along the Rhine can only be encountered as they are within a social network that prescribes the way members of society play roles integrated into a world in which working as a plant engineer and behaving as an electricity consumer make sense. Articulating the domination of Enframing amounts to discerning between plural modes of revealing and defining the interplay between them.

(2) Technology stands in a twofold cognitive relationship with background understanding: it furthers our ignorance of background understanding, yet at the same time it remains implicitly dependent upon it. This twofold relationship engenders two questions, furthermore, that we confront in articulating technology: how does modern technology and its self-interpretation, in other words, "technology as ideology," conceal the intrinsic relation of technology to background understanding, and in what manner (and upon what occasion) can the background be disclosed and illuminated?

475

Jürgen Habermas has offered prominent answers to these questions. To the first, Habermas responds (to put it simply) that the context of lifeworld in which the process of communication is always embedded is, in the period of the late capitalism, supplanted by "steering media" [*Steuerungsmedien*] such as money and power, and is deprived of its communicative resources for constituting normativity; he calls this process the "technicizing of the lifeworld" (Habermas 1989: 183). To the second, Habermas responds that the lifeworld will be liberated from the oppression of the steering media, and its communicative resources will reappear, when as denizens of the lifeworld we change our ways of life so as to develop fully our communicative rationality, which is capable of establishing idealized democratic discourse but which we have not yet separated from modern instrumental rationality.

Heidegger would agree with Habermas that background understanding, as an analog (but not as the exact equivalent) of the context of the lifeworld in Habermas, suffers from the "colonization" of systems that lie outside reasonable control, and that this colonization specifically concerns the possibility of a cognitive approach to background understanding. However, the view that these systems lie outside reasonable control arouses deep concern. If they are uncontrollable because of external factors that causally dominate the basis of communication, their dominance does not penetrate the core of cognitive and communicative meaning and hence is not relevant to the lifeworld.

Habermas seems to respond to this concern with his claim that the dominance of such systems has arisen from the enlargement of modern instrumental rationality. However, this simply displaces the concern to the questions of how enlarged instrumental rationality covers up the basis of communication, and of how we can free ourselves from this covering up and reappropriate that basis. Heidegger would contend that to whatever extent one enlarges or complicates instrumental rationality, instrumental rationality alone cannot regulate the lifeworld, because as a bundle of rules in the form of propositional contents (as it is conceived by Habermas), it cannot provide the relevancy needed for its application without background understanding; Heidegger would further argue that our communicative rationality alone is not capable of resisting the dominance of instrumental rationality, because explicit open dialogue among equally qualified participants does not provide the resources needed to thaw the functional whole that is implicitly backed up by contextuality with intrinsic contingency – a change in background understanding is also required. Thus, for Habermas, it is only through legal institutions that dominating technological systems are anchored in the lifeworld (Habermas 1989: 366).

(3) The complete articulation of technology is impossible, not only because the essence of technology has plural modes of revealing, but also because, as Taylor has remarked, each new articulation introduces a new context from which to begin again. Articulation, a kind of which I described as the interpretation of norms with which we are familiar, can play diverse roles by making background understanding explicit, roles such as those of defending or criticizing ways of life handed down to us, redefining what it is to live in an epoch, and adjusting old norms to new situations. Such interpretations in turn open up new situations for further articulation. In this manner, the articulation of technology contributes to the redefinition of the background understanding that technology presupposes and at the same time conceals. The extravagant praise of futurists for modern technology, if widely accepted, may significantly

reorganize the vocabulary and ways of life of a society, whereas unfavorable interpretations of technology by ecologists, if deeply influential in a society, may provide a new context for approaching nature. Heidegger's theory of technology, doing justice to background understanding, is itself such an articulation; nonetheless, we still lack the profound confidence to divine what kind of new context this articulation will engender.

References and Further Reading

Dewey, J. (1893) The superstition of necessity. *Monist*, III, 362–79. Reprinted in L. A. Hickman and T. M. Alexander (eds.), *The Essential Dewey, Vol. 2, Ethics, Logic, Psychology* (pp. 91–110). Bloomington and Indianapolis: Indiana University Press, 1998 (page reference is to reprint edition).

—— (1929a) *The Quest for Certainty: A Study of the Relation of Knowledge and Action.* New York: Minton, Balch, & Co. Reprinted as a Perigee Book. New York: G. P. Putnam's Sons, 1980 (page references are to paperback edition).

—— (1929b) *Experience and Nature*, 2nd edn. La Salle, IL: Open Court. Reprinted as a Dover Book. New York: Dover Publications, Inc., 1958 (page references are to paperback edition).

Dreyfus, H. L. (1991) *Being-in-the-World: A Commentary on Heidegger's Being and Time, Division I.* Cambridge MA: MIT Press.

Feenberg, A. (1999) *Questioning Technology.* London: Routledge.

Friedman, M. (2001) *Dynamics of Reason.* Stanford, CA: CSLI Publications.

Habermas, J. (1989) *The Theory of Communicative Action, Volume 2, Lifeworld and System: A Critique of Functionalist Reason* (trans. T. McCarthy). Boston: Beacon Press (original work published 1981).

Heidegger, M. (1969) Memorial address. In M. Heidegger, *Discourse on thinking* (trans. J. M. Anderson and E. H. Freund). New York: Harper & Row (original work published 1959).

—— (1975) The origin of the work of art (trans. A. Hofstadter). In A. Hofstadter (ed.), *Poetry, Language, Thought* (pp. 15–86). New York: Harper & Row (original work presented 1935/6).

—— (1977) The question concerning technology (trans. W. Lovitt). In W. Lovitt (ed.), *The Question Concerning Technology and Other Essays* (pp. 3–35). New York: Harper & Row (original work published 1954).

—— (1990) *Being and Time* (trans. J. Macquarrie and E. Robinson). Oxford: Basil Blackwell (original work published 1927).

McDowell, J. (1979) Virtue and reason. *Monist*, 62, 331–50. Reprinted in J. McDowell, *Mind, Value, and Reality* (pp. 50–73). Cambridge MA: Harvard University Press, 1998 (page reference is to book edition).

Rorty, R. (1991) Heidegger, contingency, and pragmatism. In R. Rorty, *Essays on Heidegger and Others: Philosophical Papers Volume 2* (pp. 27–49). Cambridge: Cambridge University Press.

Taylor, C. (1993) Engaged agency and background in Heidegger. In C. Guignon (ed.), *The Cambridge Companion to Heidegger* (pp. 315–36). Cambridge: Cambridge University Press.

32

The Lived-Body and the Dignity of Human Beings

ANDREAS BRENNER

Respect for people's dignity requires that we look on human beings as ends in themselves and not regard them as things. Forbidding us to regard them as things goes back to Kant, who regarded autonomy as the foundation of dignity. Kant's concept of dignity divided human beings into two parts, a physical and a moral being. This division is not a good basis on which to found dignity. Instead of the term "autonomy" this chapter uses the term "authenticity," which is located in the human lived-body (*Leib*). Our lived-bodily nature gives us an original term of the self. From this point of view it is possible to deduce dignity from the self's lived-body which makes it superfluous to follow the route of transcendence, taken by Kant. To make this point clear we can regard the emotion of shame as strong evidence of dignity.

1 Point of Departure

Human dignity is accorded a position of paramount importance in philosophical and political literature. Political writings, and above all the documents of the United Nations, grant conceptual preeminence to the theme, whose special rank they indicate by naming human dignity in the preamble of all their great declarations.[1] In doing so, they allot to it an acclamatory function, which ostensibly is able to build on the self-explanatory content of this set phrase. This also appears to be correct in two respects: on the level of an everyday phenomenal consciousness, there appears to be almost no doubt about what dignity is. Or, to rephrase it *ex negativo* (which also in this case represents the more accurate approach), there seems to be almost no doubt when one's dignity as a human being is injured. It is maintained that this leads, in an everyday phenomenological manner, to a broadly supported knowledge which can, in case of doubt, get advice and assistance from the philosophical literature.[2] On the level of justification, the question of laying the foundation of the concept of dignity also appears to be conceived according to an analogous pattern, which promises to guarantee a wide dissemination and recognition: it is scarcely questioned in everyday phenomenology why dignity is due – at least to humans. They simply inherit it at

---

Originally published in German as "Des Menschen Leib und Würde," *Studia philosophica*, 63 (2004).

birth, and it therefore must not be "taken" from them. Or, we are to see to it that the bearer of dignity is taken as an end in itself and consequently is not instrumentalized. This very influential argument, which was constructed by Kant, (2) will be subjected to criticism in what follows (2); in its stead an alternative proposal will be made (3); and in conclusion, the breadth of the alternative's horizons will be indicated (4).

2 Kant's Concept of Dignity

In his moral philosophy and in his anthropology, Kant develops an idea of dignity which still today shapes political and judicial discussions of dignity, as well as the everyday understanding of a dignified life.

An end and never merely a means

Kant connects the position and fate of dignity with his moral philosophy, the central factor of which forms the distinction between ends and means. To draw this distinction is a question of reason. Reason grounds not only the distinction between ends and means, but also, based on the competence to establish one's own law that Kant calls "autonomy," the Categorical Imperative. The Categorical Imperative offers a sure orientation in the moral chaos of heteronomic influences that otherwise threatens us. The second formulation of the Categorical Imperative accordingly postulates the treatment of "humanity, whether in your own person or in the person of any other, in every case as an end and never as a mere means" (Kant 1974: BA67). The reason for this imperative does not lie in the immediate significance which one accords to oneself or to another person; what is represented by our intuitive understanding tells us that one will not be just to others or oneself as long as one merely respects others, as well as oneself, out of ulterior motives, and not for their own sake. By contrast, the Categorical Imperative utilizes a justification which is at the same time more demanding and poorer than that of the intuition we have described. It is more demanding because it has recourse to a person's will, which is regarded as establishing universal law by virtue of its orientation to reason. The autonomy of persons, their capacity to establish universal law, transforms them into ends in themselves and lifts them above every price befitting to a mere means. Therefore, the following holds for Kant: "Autonomy is the basis for dignity" (Kant 1974: BA69). This conception of dignity is more demanding than that of the intuition we took in mind, inasmuch as it binds dignity to the fundamental prerequisite of reason and to the autonomy that is connected to it. By contrast, the conception of dignity appears poorer when it expressly abstains from "feelings, impulses, and inclinations" and sets in their place the relationship of "rational beings to one another" (Kant 1974: BA67). The Kantian position is "poorer" insofar as it suppresses the multiplicity of the concept of self, as it appears in the call to respect everyone for his or her own sake. This multiplicity is considered by the Kantian position to be an accidental characteristic which disguises the significance of the community of rational beings and therefore distracts the gaze from the capacity for self-legislation as the basis of dignity. From Kant's explanatory perspective, this position is not seen as poorer. Instead it appears purer than those which refer to empirical characteristics. Kant does not deny the existence of these unique individual characteristics. Instead, he considers them insufficiently qualified for the act of giving oneself a universal law. This demand turns out to be significant for the concept of autonomy: in not recognizing the importance of unique individual characteristics for autonomy, autonomy attains a degree of universality, which appears indispensable if one is to retain autonomy's morally constitutive function. However, the costs of proceeding this way are very high indeed, both for autonomy itself, as well as for dignity as its foundation: the individual does not acquire universality in his autonomy through his unique characteristics, but rather through his capacity to recognize that which is universal and to make it his own, thereby overlooking the individual unique characteristics for the process of giving oneself a universal law. This process lays down the concept of the self which directs the legislation to its transcendental sense. Another, non-transcendental, concept of the self has no independent place alongside the transcendental concept of the self. On the contrary, a somewhat empirical concept of the self – Kant speaks of the "physical man" – finds itself in the dependent roll. This self feels "compelled to revere the (moral) human being within his own person," which compensates him with the "feeling of his inner worth (valor), in terms of which he is above any price (pretium), and possesses an inalienable dignity (dignitas interna)" (Kant 1977: A96). If one here accepts as unproblematic the division of the self that Kant works out, still the coercion which the "physical man" experiences through the "moral man" proves to be problematic: for the autonomy which, as we have already mentioned, is taken as the ground of dignity and consequently as the occasion for the uplifting feelings that correspond to it – this autonomy remains foreign to the "physical man." The establishing of universal law, which demands obeisance, is consequently not its own, and so autonomy proves to be heteronomous for the "physical man." This connection also affects dignity: It can apparently only be saved if it likewise is ascribed solely to the transcendental Self, and remains "untouched" by the physicality of the physical man. The idea of the human beings as ends in themselves – the idea sketched out at the beginning and disseminated in the political-philosophical literature – is thought to constitute our dignity as human beings, which is then injured when a human being is instrumentalized as a means to accomplish some other purpose. This idea consequently suffers from the perspective of positing ends which, although designated as autonomous, contains a heteronomous element in its orientation to an external perspective. By contrast, we will propose in the third section a concept of dignity that is oriented to the lived-body (*Leib*). It shall also become clear in the following section that Kant himself maintained a certain distance from the transcendental concept of dignity.

Servility is undignified

With the idea of human beings as ends in themselves, Kant provided the foundation for a concept of dignity that remains decisive to this day in the political-philosophical discussion. Under the title "On Servility" (Kant 1977: A92ff.), he furnished illustrative material for a widespread, everyday phenomenological notion of dignity and, by the same token, for its self-violation. In this article, Kant makes an appeal for human dignity, which forbids any form of self-humiliation. The dignity of human beings goes along with a bearing which commands self-respect, which is insurmountable and which, as Kant demonstrates, shows certain forms of religious reverence in particular to be undignified, as also in general is every form of "bowing and scraping" in which one "makes oneself into a worm" (Kant 1977: A98f.). These descriptions, which, as has been noted, are marked by a understanding of dignity *ex negativo* that is still widespread today, are clearly distinguished from the comments on the autonomy-based understanding of dignity in that they do not repeat the division of the self that we have observed earlier. Hence the attitude which detests servility can also be characterized as one in which the respective self tries to preserve the unity by remaining "itself." With this we have gained an understanding of dignity appropriate to human being, which would have proved itself to be capable of defending itself not only against self-injury, but also against exterior assault. Because such a road is closed off by Kant's understanding of autonomy, we will go another way in what follows.

3 The Dignity of the Lived-Body

In his critique of servility, Kant sketched out a conception of dignity which considers more closely its possessor and which furnishes not just a metaphorical way of speaking about bowing down, but also the test whether someone has preserved or distorted his dignity. By locating dignity in the immediate proximity of its possessor, however, Kant does not preserve his double division of a human being into a physical being and the moral being it reveres. This appears to be indispensable, however, precisely in the focus on dignity, because otherwise one can neither preserve the unity of the Self nor hinder the reifying demands made by third parties. Therefore, one can only satisfy the corresponding expectation if it is possible, first, to preserve the unity of human being, which, second, experiences its dignity in immediate self-realization, and not in detours, albeit detours one walks oneself, through a transcendental concept of self-legislation. There are presumably grounds for the supposition that these demands for a concept of the lived-body can be met. One can count toward the grounding of this presumption an everyday phenomenological determination that the gravest injury to dignity is an injury to "life and limb." For another thing, the opposition to every form of dualism, an opposition which identifies theories of the lived-body, calls one's attention to the expectation that the unity of human being, with corresponding consequences for its dignity, can be preserved in a special way through an idea of the lived-body. But what is the lived-body?

The lived-body embodies ("der Leib leibt")

Bodies (*Körper*) and lived-bodies (*Leib*) are not identical. The human body is in fact corporeal in the sense of being something three-dimensional. The lived-body, however, is more than merely a three-dimensional thing. Speaking about a lived-body is a question of perspective. For example, walking along Oxford Street in London, I see plenty of bodies, but there is – for me – only one lived-body – that is mine. And, vice versa, there are plenty of people who see me only as a body and identify their own body as a lived-body. This distinction has had no importance in the history of political ideas; there, lived-bodies have been totally ignored. One of the first documents of human rights, the act of habeas corpus, looks at people's bodies in merely their corporeal sense.[3]

To feel one's body as one's own body constitutes it as a lived-body. The lived-body is a sensation. Everyone can demonstrate this for himself by touching a part of his body with another body part. Edmund Husserl, who called our attention to this, describes what is felt in such cases as a "double sensation" (Husserl 1973: 297, 1952: 147). Touching the left hand with the right hand, for example, is impossible without this double sensation. In touching, the double sensation lets what is touched emerge: the hand constitutes itself consequently in tactile perception. In this perception, the hand is lifted out of the sphere of mere corporeal things to become a part of our lived-body. What is true for this body part is naturally also true for the lived-body as a whole. The Husserlian discourse gives the impression, however, that this can be experienced only through exterior touch. It is not so. Rather, it is always already perceived before every touch. Accordingly, these touches – by which is meant primarily the self-touch – can serve to reassure one of one's own bodily nature. Additionally, these touches allow one to attend to one's own body, whose existence threatens to sink and disappear easily into a diffuse variety of perceptions that are all mixed up and on top of each other. The insight gained from the example of the hands touching each other is also important for understanding the perception of the body: that the body first constitutes itself in perception;[4] consequently a lived-body that is not perceived is not a lived-body – that is, it is a mere corporeal thing and not a lived-body.

The being of the lived-body (*Leibsein*) reveals itself, therefore, in its embodying (*Leiben*) (Heidegger 1994: 112). Embodiment is the only mode of being for the body. This mode of being is, first and foremost, accessible to the possessor of the lived-body, which distinguishes the lived-body as the subjective constitution of perception from the objectively present and accessible corporeality, and is oriented on the other hand exclusively to self-perception, which is valid independently of the content of perception of the foreign. The therapy of "basal stimulation" serves to clarify the understanding of the lived-body and to indicate the practical significance of this understanding that is oriented exclusively to the perception of the self. Basal stimulation is successfully used in the treatment of comatose patients and other apparently perceptually handicapped persons (see Bienstein and Fröhlich 1991; Fröhlich 1998). This therapeutic method supports or at least allows a perceptive process in two directions: to the patients, sensations of themselves are conveyed which, without the stimulation, remain concealed in a deadened, dormant present. But the therapists also become aware of the perceptions of their patients by means of the basal stimulation and their own lived-bodily sensation, which for its part is stimulated through the practice of basal stimulation. With this begins a bodily communication, which differs only in its subtle and demanding nature from the stronger conventional forms of communication. The therapeutic form of basal stimulation, which relies implicitly on a theory of the body that emanates from the double sensation, has a wide-reaching ethical consequence: it suspends, finally, the concept of "unconsciousness"[5] and demands respect for a mode of being, which is conspicuous only because of its own, that is to say the observer's, cognitive deficiency. It thereby blocks an objectification of the concept of the lived-body.

A result of an objectification – from the perspective of this therapy, something to be prevented – is the contraction of the range of the phenomenon of the lived-body and of the circle of recognized possessors of a lived-body, who not only have at their disposal a corresponding self-perception, but also would be able to articulate it in intersubjectively valid ways. The ownness of the bodily nature would thereby be lost, however. That would not be without consequence for the concept of dignity which guides us here. The preceding arguments have made it clear that the lived-body turns itself away from objectification by the strength of self-preservation, and avows itself to radical subjectivity. The lived-body knows no alternative, it is subjective or not at all. Merleau-Ponty sums it up in this way: "But I am not in front of my body, I am in it, or rather I am it" (Merleau-Ponty 2002: 150).

By the way, Kant was not all that far removed in his pre-critical phase from this claim about the self's containment in a body. In the *Träumen eines Geistersehers* (*Dreams of a Spirit Seer*) Kant uses, it is true, the concept "corporeal body" (*Körper*), which is derived from the Latin *corpus* instead of the term "lived-body" (*Leib*). But at the same time he includes under that term an idea which comes quite close to the modern understanding of the lived-body when he says:

> No one has direct awareness of any specific place within his own body; one is conscious only of a place which one occupies as a human being in regard to the world external to oneself. I would therefore cling to my common experience and reply for the time being: I am there where I have sensations. I am just as much in my fingertips as in my head. I am the same person who feels a pain in my heel, and whose heart beats with emotion. (Kant 1976: A19/38–9)

As is generally known, Kant's philosophy distanced itself from this position in its further development and thereby also positioned dignity outside of the bodily nature of human being. In connection with that, foreign influences flow into the concept of dignity and accordingly dilute it.

Dignity is bodily

The dignity of human beings is damaged through every sort of instrumentalization, through making them into objects and through failing to preserve them as subjects. The definition of dignity that is here fundamental, exquisitely put in the self-as-an-end formulation of the categorical imperative (Kant 1974: A67), can be regarded as complete. Kant's own interpretation must nevertheless be designated as inadequate. For when Kant, following his unsurpassable formulation of this, tries to explain the example of suicide, he strengthens the dualism when he maintains that I "cannot dispose in any way of the human being in my own person" (Kant 1974: A67). This interpretation, which, as we have already remarked, is definitive for Kant's practical conception of dignity, follows to the letter Kant's own definition, but not the spirit. This interpretation is literal inasmuch as it defends the transcendental concept of the human being as an end in itself against human being's instrumentalization. This interpretation nevertheless stands in opposition to the spirit of the definition of dignity because it, in the dualistic division of human being, does not preserve people's unity. And it is human unity which has to be regarded as a condition of every self-preservation in the sense of a protective self-purposiveness. Another consequence of this division is that one "part" of human being (the "physical being") serves as a means for the preservation of the other "part" of human being (the "moral being"), which is the end or purpose of human being. The moral being alone earns the title "person" as a recognition of its highest rank. This consequence of reductionism is fatal for human being and its dignity, and must be avoided even as one holds firmly to the "authentic subject" of human being (see Merleau-Ponty's critique of Kant in Merleau-Ponty 2002: 150). In this way, we can also put a stop to the division and internal hierarchization of human beings (into the "physical" and "moral" parts), which finds its origin in a concept of autonomy that situates dignity, even as it rests on it, in the explicit suppression of physicality and thereby settles the highest protective value outside of the authentic subject. But autonomy thus does not suffice as a foundation for dignity, as opposed to what Kant maintained in the passage mentioned earlier (Kant 1974: BA69). To the contrary, the foundation of dignity must be conceived in such a way that it finds a foothold in itself and not in an agreement with a transcendental concept, because only in this way is the precondition for a self-determination in contrast to a foreign-determination assured.

A natural orientation should therefore take the place of the transcendental orientation. This orientation is natural, in distinction to the transcendental, because it binds itself to experiences which are radically subjective insofar as they start from their own prevailing bodily nature, which rests on a natural basis. But, as the existence of phantom limbs proves, a bodily nature is also able to constitute itself beyond a natural basis. The leading of the concept of dignity to the self, and the underlying critique – namely, that a ban on instrumentalization sets an unsurpassable criterion, the formulation of autonomy in Kant's terms, while at the same time undermining it – have the effect of replacing the concept of autonomy with that of authenticity. The integrity of the self should be conceived under authenticity, more precisely, as it is reflected in the renowned formulation of the basic law set forth in the inviolability of dignity. Bodily authenticity gives bodily self-relationality, which averts the division discussed above, and also already wards off a first form of instrumentalization. As a result, dignity can be defined as a mode of inviolable being with oneself. This understanding offers two approaches relevant to dignity: first, dignity is described as a perspective from which the perspectives of the possessor of dignity are made valid; second, related to the first, this perspective is recognized as radically subjective, founded in the bodily nature of the respective possessors of dignity. These approaches appear appropriate for this topic: to describe dignity from the perspective which is only accessible to the possessor of dignity, because it is founded in the lived-body, offers a maximum of protection against instrumentalization. It lies now in the nature of the matter that if we are to avoid abridging dignity by taking up an external perspective on it, we cannot give a positive description of it, which is why the *via negationis* alone is feasible. This approach shows when dignity is infringed and consequently injured. In what follows it will become evident that shame is valid as a strong indication of injury (albeit not a sufficient indication, as we will explain below).

The injury of dignity produces shame

The ashamed reactions of people who have suffered far-reaching injuries to their dignity supply evidence that shame provides a signal of injuries of dignity: victims of torture – one thinks for instance of prisoners of concentration camps or rape victims –

react to their experiences with shame (Blume 2003). The feeling of shame, like feelings in general, is situated in the lived-body, which is to say that feelings are only perceived as such, that is, felt, in the body and consequently are radically subjective.[6] The body is consequently the organ which, by feeling, lets feelings reach subjective reality. Following the understanding of the lived-body introduced above, feeling signifies not only the receptive perception of a reality, of a feeling, but also the progressive self-constitution that goes along with the feeling. In this sense it holds that whoever feels shame (just as with any other feeling) becomes someone other than what he had been up to that point: the ashamed person feels humiliated. The feeling of being humiliated covers one with shame, if, as in the case of the injuries of dignity that we have alluded to, the humiliation that is suffered through others is experienced as shame. It is different from the shame that someone feels because of one's own misconduct (cf. Landweer 1999: 45). In the latter case, one feels likewise affected in one's dignity, but one identifies oneself nevertheless as aggressor and experiences the humiliation that is manifest therein as shame. Independently of this difference, shame shows itself as a feeling which concerns us affectively and the feeling of which therefore articulates itself in bodily ways. The singularity of shame does not show itself as such in the affectedness which is experienced through it – this affectedness applies to all feelings. Instead, the singularity of shame lies in the intensity with which this affectedness is experienced. The intensity of shame builds up in its indeceivability, which leaves no escape, overcomes and overwhelms, or crushes, a person. It makes one wish to evaporate or sink into the ground; it consequently functions in a self-annihilating fashion.[7] With reference to the self's containment in a lived-body, as it expressed itself in the above quotation from Merleau-Ponty, and the ways of experiencing shame that are colloquially described and analyzed by Schmitz, the tendency toward the annihilation of the self out of shame becomes recognizable in the self's minimizing movements of contraction, oppression, and depression. Shame acts, therefore, regressively and reverses the course of development and unfolding. This is true, by the way, independently of the supposed "legitimacy" of the shame. One cannot, as a result, count as cases of "illegitimate" shame those in which others insist to the one who is ashamed that this or that presents no reason to be ashamed. This form of judgment from an external perspective, as with all talk in the context of the theme of dignity that is based in an external perspective, is for its part to be rejected as degrading. So let us discuss, as an example of "illegitimate" shame, the following.

It is the case of someone who feels shame for a reason which, upon closer examination, turns out to be mistaken: Mr. Taylor is ashamed not to have greeted his neighbor in the subway, although it later becomes evident that the woman across from whom he sat without acknowledging her was not his neighbor at all. Consequently his shame lacks a real reason, although this does not change the fact that Mr. Taylor, whether it is justified or unjustified, has experienced shame. If one were to ask Mr. Taylor why he was ashamed, he could offer the specific answer, "because I didn't greet my neighbor," or more generally, "because I can't reconcile my failing to greet a person I know with my self-respect." This general explanation makes it clear why Mr. Taylor's shame was justified, whether he actually met his neighbor in the subway or not: he failed to live up to his own self-image, and he experiences this deficiency as humiliating, that is, degrading, and this makes him ashamed. But how is it when the case is reversed?

485

Someone is not ashamed, although he comported himself in a way for which, according to the common view, shame would be an appropriate reaction. One calls people who comport themselves in this way "undignified." Thus, take for an example those who, without apparent consideration or hesitation, openly inflict significant harm on other people. They are "undignified," either because it is considered inconsistent with an office they hold, or because it is regarded as generally unworthy for people to act in this way. What about the dignity of the shameless? Is their shamelessness evidence that, while shame is indeed to a considerable degree a reliable indicator, it does not present a universally sufficient indication of an injury to one's dignity? This obvious assumption does not seem to hold up to a psychoanalytic analysis of shameless comportments and persons, as their comportment is all too often understandable as a consequence of some grave injury to their dignity, with its accompanying deep shame, that lies in their past.[8] With those who are shameless, dignity expresses itself, out of phase; likewise in the shame that accompanies their injury. Accordingly, it thus holds that there is neither unjustified shame, nor shame without injured dignity. However, the reverse does not follow – namely, that where no shame is experienced, human dignity remains untouched. In addition to the cases we have already alluded to of an injury to dignity without immediately being accompanied by shame, we must also note the two following cases: first, someone's dignity may, unbeknown to him, be injured, for example, through defamation, which is why he experiences no shame – for the time being – over this injury. Second, think of the dignity of people who are not in position to experience shame bodily, or only do so in a restricted sense – such may be the case with embryos, premature babies, and the severely ill. It would consequently be deficient to connect the injury to their dignity to the experience of shame alone. Nevertheless it should have become clear that the recourse to the feeling of shame offers both a more reliable and also a more appropriate approach to dignity than the construction of the autonomy of a rational subject. In conclusion, authenticity, which took the place of autonomy, should thus be considered in the light of the preceding discussion.

4 Bodily Authenticity

Proceeding from phenomenological investigations of the second, post-Husserlian generation, the lived-body has proven itself to be self-contained in the sense that it not only forms the natural basis for being a self, but also that to represent a self outside of the body can be maintained only as a fiction. But how can we view a consciousness thinking concretely of itself? The following two ways can be distinguished: first, that one which comes to a concept of self on the path of self-reflection ("reflexive self-knowledge"), which then corresponds to the established concept of self-consciousness; and second, a pre-reflexive knowledge of the self.

Whereas the reflexive self-consciousness ascribes something to itself, which it holds for itself, the pre-reflexive knowledge of the self makes do without any such ascription, and even shows itself to have priority as opposed to the reflexive knowledge of self. The non-intentional knowledge of the self is even indispensable for every form of reflexive knowledge of the self, which becomes explicable through the bodily nature which the possessor of a body affectively fulfills by knowing about himself without having to make a detour through reflection.[9] Even if the experience of shame, in distinction to other feelings, is reflexive, thus it reflects on anyone who experiences this feeling, so that the suffering from shame grounds itself in the inescapable relatedness to one's self, the injury to dignity that indicates it is grasped on the basis of the pregivenness of the pre-reflexive knowledge of itself. This pre-reflexive knowledge establishes itself on the affective affectedness that, for its part, is based in the bodily nature which the primary and likewise pre-reflexive mode of being-with-itself forms. Here is the possessor of a lived-body by itself, one can also say, here he is wholly himself, he is authentic. Just as the pre-reflexive knowledge of the self is a prerequisite and presupposed for the reflexive knowledge, thus also authenticity is a prerequisite for autonomy. Shame announces – reflexively – dignity in the way of negation. In the same way, the pre-reflexively constituted authenticity points further; consequently dignity allows us to suppose through the essences that are not gifted to reflection, which bring themselves to expression in the safeguarded self-possession or "presubjective subjectivity" that defends itself against foreign determination (Blume 2003: 40).

Notes

1   In chronological order, these are the "Charter of the United Nations" (June 26, 1945); "Universal Declaration of Human Rights" (December 10, 1948); "International Agreement for the Elimination of Every Form of Racial Discrimination" (March 7, 1966); "International Pact on Citizens' and Political Rights" (December 19, 1966); and "Agreement against Torture and Other Cruel, Inhuman or Humiliating Treatment or Punishment" (December 10, 1984).

2   By way of example, see Rawls 1971 and Margalit 1996, which show on different levels of complexity that the State should respect human dignity and how this charge can be wasted.

3   See Freedman 2001: ch. 23. The corporeal understanding of body is also to be found in John Locke's theory of self-ownership (see Locke 1963: §27, 353).

4   At the same time, the Husserlian example, as innovative as it has become for the discussion of the lived-body, leads in this respect to a limited knowledge of the body, as it builds on exterior stimulation and conveys a (false) impression of the intentionality of bodily experience, even though bodily sensing reveals that no object is required, and consequently that the body suffices for itself. For a corresponding critique of Husserl, cf. Böhme 2003: 21.

5   On this subject, see Nydahl and Bartoszek 2000: 32.

6   Hermann Schmitz's theory of body and feeling, which I follow, utilizes the concept of "atmosphere" to describe what feelings are. This atmosphere exists objectively, but the important thing for our analytic purpose is that it is lived-bodily experienced. For atmosphere of feelings, see Schmitz 1965: 50f.; for experience of feelings, see Schmitz 1969: 169 and 2002.

7   For proofs and examples, see Landweer 1999: 39ff. and Blume 2003: 84f.

8   For shamelessness, see Blume 2003: 89f.

9   Cf. Schmitz's corresponding analysis in Blume 2003: 17–34.

References and Further Reading

Bienstein, A., and Fröhlich, C. (1991) *Basale Stimulation in der Pflege: Pflegerische Möglichkeiten zur Förderung von wahrnehmungsbeeinträchtigen Menschen* [Basal stimulation in treatment:

treatment possibilities for the improvement of the perceptually impaired]. Düsseldorf: Bundesverband für Körper- und Mehrfachbehinderte e.V.

Blume, A. (2003) *Scham und Selbstbewusstein. Zur Phänomenologie konkreter Subjektivität* [Shame and self-consciousness. Toward the phenomenology of concrete subjectivity]. Freiburg and Munich: Hermann Schmitz.

Böhme, G. (2003) *Leibsein als Aufgabe: Leibsphilosophie in pragmatischer Hinsicht* [The bodily character as task: philosophy of body in pragmatic hindsight]. Kusterdingen: Die Graue Edition.

Freedman, E. M. (2001) *Habeas Corpus: Rethinking the Great Writ of Liberty*. New York: New York University Press.

Fröhlich, A. (1998) *Basale Stimulation: Das Konzept* [Basal stimulation: the concept]. Düsseldorf: Bundesverband für Körper- und Mehrfachbehinderte e.V.

Heidegger, M. (1994) *Zollikoner Seminäre* [Zollikon Seminars]. *Gesamtausgabe* vol. 89. Frankfurt am Main: Klostermann (original correspondence took place 1947–71).

Husserl, E. (1952) *Ideen zu einer reinen Phänomenologie und phänomenologischen Philosophie* [Ideas pertaining to a pure phenomenology and phenomenological philosophy] (ed. M. Biemel). Vol. 4 of *Husserliana*. The Hague: Martinus Nijhoff (original work published 1913).

—— (1973) *Zur Phänomenologie der Intersubjektivität* [On the phenomenology of intersubjectivity] (ed. I. Kern). Vol. 15 of *Husserliana*. The Hague: Martinus Nijhoff (original texts written 1929–35).

Kant, I. (1974) *Grundlegung zur Metaphysik der Sitten* [Groundwork for the metaphysics of morals]. *Werkausgabe* vol. 7. Frankfurt am Main: Suhrkamp (original work published 1785).

—— (1976) *Träume eines Geistersehers* [Dreams of a visionary]. *Werkausgabe* vol. 2. Frankfurt am Main: Suhrkamp (original work published 1766) (*Dreams of a Spirit Seer* (trans. J. Manolesco). New York: Vantage Press, 1966.)

—— (1977) *Die Metaphysik der Sitten* [The metaphysics of morals]. *Werkausgabe* vol. 8. Frankfurt am Main: Suhrkamp (original work published 1797).

Landweer, H. (1999) *Scham und Macht: Phänomenologische Untersuchungen zur Sozialität eines Gefühls* [Shame and power: phenomenological investigations of the sociality of an emotion]. Tübingen: Mohr Siebeck Verlag.

Locke, J. (1963) *Two Treatises of Government. The Works of John Locke* vol. 5. Aalen: Scientia (original work published 1690).

Margalit, A. (1996) *The Decent Society*. Cambridge, MA: Harvard University Press.

Merleau-Ponty, M. (2002) *Phénoménologie de la Perception* [Phenomenology of perception]. Paris: Gallimard (original work published 1945).

Nydahl, P., and Bartoszek, G. (2000) *Basale Stimulation: Neue Wege in der Intensivpflege* [Basal stimulation: new paths in intensive treatment]. Munich: Urban & Fischer.

Rawls, J. (1971) *A Theory of Justice*. Cambridge, MA: Harvard University Press.

Schmitz, H. (1965) *Der Leib* [The body]. Bonn: Bouvier.

—— (1969) *Der Gefühlsraum* [The space of emotion]. Bonn: Bouvier.

—— (2002) The "new phenomenology." In A-T. Tymieniecka (ed.), *Phenomenology World Wide. Foundations, Expanding Dynamics, Life Engagements* (S 491–4). Dordrecht: Kluwer.

33

Sexuality

ANN V. MURPHY

Any examination of what the traditions of existentialism and phenomenology have brought to bear on the discourse on sexuality is complicated first by the fact that – for many of the thinkers in these traditions – sexuality was dealt with in problematic ways, if it was considered at all. At the same time, the traditions of phenomenology and existentialism have been major contributors to philosophical discourse on sexuality, and remain so to this day. While phenomenologists such as Husserl, Heidegger, Sartre, and Merleau-Ponty have been criticized for their elision and/or outright neglect of sexuality, their work has also been enthusiastically – if critically – appropriated by those interested in exploring what it is that phenomenology and existentialism might bring to bear on contemporary discussions of sexuality. Objections to assumptions of sexual neutrality and universality that have tended to pervade many phenomenological accounts of experience are ubiquitous. Notwithstanding these criticisms, it would be impossible to trace the history of sexuality studies, and indeed what has come to be known as queer theory, without making recourse to these traditions. Consequently it is quite possible to trace the evolution of this relationship, particularly with reference to the varying elaborations of sexual embodiment that have emerged from the existential and phenomenological traditions.

The 1990s saw the publication of a number of important books on feminist theories of the body, including Judith Butler's *Gender Trouble* (1990) and *Bodies that Matter* (1993), Susan Bordo's *Unbearable Weight* (1993), Elizabeth Grosz's *Volatile Bodies* (1994), and Moira Gatens' *Imaginary Bodies* (1996). While these texts explore the themes of embodiment and sexuality in different ways and with different aims, they all employ phenomenological and existential resources (albeit in more or less acknowledged ways) in their attempts to give voice to sexually specific experiences of the body. Corporeal feminism is that subset of feminist theory that emphasizes the importance of lived, sexed embodiment, and takes as its starting point the claim that the sexed body is central in the figuring of experience. Drawing in particular on insights from the phenomenological tradition, corporeal feminists have argued that sexual difference cannot be theorized apart from the particular experience of sexed embodiment. Insofar as corporeal feminism is oriented around the claim that it is the body that is central in the figuring of subjectivity, it may be read as a critique of the philosophical tradition's privileging of reason and the mind over and above embodied experience. For this reason, corporeal feminism might be read as a critique of Cartesian dualism, attacking the assumption that the ready dissociation of mind and body, reason and emotion, is even possible. While corporeal feminism draws attention to the sexually specific dimension of embodiment, this return to the body need not provoke the accusation of essentialism. This is because corporeal feminism advocates an understanding of the body as culturally and historically specific and is, in this sense, far removed from the idea of a natural or essential body that prefigures culture. While corporeal feminism brought to the fore the ways in which phenomenology might be employed in the service of feminist aims, existentialism has also emerged recently as a lucrative resource for those seeking to give an account of gender identity that avoids the pitfalls of essentialism.

Cartesian Legacies: The Sexual Body in Existential Phenomenology

In the 1940s, three major texts were published in French existential phenomenology: Jean-Paul Sartre's *Being and Nothingness* (1943; cited as Sartre 1956), Merleau-Ponty's *Phenomenology of Perception* (1945; cited as Merleau-Ponty 1962), and Simone de Beauvoir's *The Second Sex* (1949; cited as Beauvoir 1989). While considerations of embodiment were not evenly treated in these texts, the theme of sexuality was prevalent in them all. As a group, the authors worked to reconcile and move beyond Cartesian dualism, and to grant more attention to the experience of the lived body, or the experience of one's body as it is immersed in a culture and a world that gives it meaning and value. It is for this reason that the work of the French existential phenomenologists in particular has been of interest to theorists working on issues surrounding sexuality and embodiment.

The French Existentialists interrogate the Cartesian rift between body and mind with an eye toward generating new elaborations of experience, freedom, and embodiment. It is nonetheless the case that this dualism proves to be a recalcitrant influence in these works. This much seems clear, given Beauvoir's treatment of women's embodiment in *The Second Sex*. While Beauvoir does situate women's identity in her experience of her body, Beauvoir's descriptions of the nature of this experience are in many ways ambivalent and perplexing. This is due to her loyalty to the existentialist rendering of the body as the site of immanence, which she shares with Sartre. On this reading, subjectivity is thought to be situated in consciousness, and in the self's capacity for rational reflection and deliberation. To be sure, both Sartre and Beauvoir endeavored to bring the situated and embodied nature of subjectivity and freedom to the fore. But it must be acknowledged that these attempts met with varying degrees of success. The body is frequently portrayed as an entity that complicates and hampers the capacity for freedom and deliberation, by making the mind subject to the influences of the concrete world. This understanding of embodiment commits itself to the claim that subjectivity is realized in transcendence, in the transgression of the limitations imposed by the situated body. Hence while Beauvoir and Sartre recognize that there is no disembodied subjectivity, the body is occasionally rendered as the other of consciousness, implying a rift between the two.

While it may be disingenuous to claim that Sartre subscribed to untenable and absolute notions of human agency, it is important to take note of those places in his texts that gave his readers this impression. For all of Sartre's interest in describing human freedom as contingent and situated, his descriptions of the body in *Being and Nothingness* betray his investment in the idea that the body is, in an important sense, the other of consciousness, and in many cases an impediment to the exercise of human freedom. He writes of the body: "either it is a thing among other things, or else it is that by which things are revealed to me. But it cannot be both at the same time" (Sartre 1956: 402). While clearly cognizant of the ways in which the body enabled one's being subject and object at once, the early Sartre is in some ways reluctant to reconcile the two, insisting that they remain incommensurable and irreducible to each other. In a description that anticipates but defies the later Merleau-Ponty's rendering of the flesh, Sartre claims that the phenomenon of "double sensation" – the feeling that one is touching and the feeling that one is touched – is a contingent and inessential phenomenon of human embodiment. The experience of one's body as subject and object, Sartre claims, are "radically distinct," existing on "incommunicable levels" (Sartre 1956: 403). The lived body and the body as object cannot be reduced to each other. Hence the experience of subjectivity and agency is compromised by the recognition that one's body is an object for others: "Thus to the extent that my body indicates my possibilities in the world, seeing my body or touching it is to transform these possibilities into dead-possibilities" (ibid.). Inasmuch as the body facilitates an understanding of one's lived possibilities, it also represents the finitude and limitation of one's freedom and agency. However, in describing the body as a "transcended transcendence," Sartre points to the fact that the body could never be an object in the same sense as an inanimate object; rather it is an object insofar as its possibilities are compromised and restricted by the contingencies of the situation and by others.

Neither brute object, nor free and unencumbered consciousness, what Sartre names the "third ontological dimension of the body" is that lived body wherein I know myself as a body known by others. Caught in the gaze of the Other, one experiences one's transcendence transcended. In this sense, the experience of sexual embodiment is one wherein one utilizes the concepts of the Other to understand one's own self. While the body is necessary for the realization of subjectivity in transcendence, the experience one may have of that body may actually serve to limit and thwart certain projects. Concretely this is best demonstrated through consideration of the ways in which women may internalize certain societal expectations regarding beauty, and judge themselves in accord with these "norms." Hence it does not suffice to say that we are objectified as sexually embodied beings by others; we internalize and take up the norms according to which our bodies are interpreted, and ultimately use them to judge our own selves. This is what Sartre means when he claims that I know myself as a body known by others. The experience of sexed embodiment is intersubjective through and through.

Despite – or perhaps because of – the fact that Sartre's descriptions of concrete relations with others in *Being and Nothingness* render them as inherently conflictual and alienating, his theory has proven to be useful in describing the more oppressive dimensions of objectification, and for this reason has been engaged by thinkers seeking to address the manner in which some groups have had their agency unjustly compromised by the gaze of the oppressor. The Sartrean resonance is clear, for instance, in Frantz Fanon's *Black Skin White Masks* (1952; cited as Fanon 1967), where he describes the experience of the colonized as being "sealed into crushing objecthood," deprived of subjectivity in the eyes of racist colonizers. Similar analyses are employed by Beauvoir in *The Second Sex* when she seeks to give voice to the experience of women's objectification within a misogynist society. What Beauvoir's descriptions betray, however, is an uneasy ambivalence when it comes to the way in which the sexual body should be understood.

Like Fanon and Sartre, there are clearly moments wherein Beauvoir explicitly adopts the existentialist understanding of the body as the site of immanence. Although she claims that biological facts in and of themselves have no significance, and that biology cannot dictate for women some inevitable destiny, there are surely moments where Beauvoir herself describes the sexual body in quite negative terms (Beauvoir 1989: 34). That Beauvoir understood the body as the site of immanence that must be overcome should women attain equality is of little doubt. In *The Second Sex*, her phenomenological descriptions of birth, menstruation, and sexuality demonstrate the recalcitrance of the conflict between consciousness and flesh in her texts. Through her phenomenological investigations of sexed embodiment, Beauvoir renders the woman's body not only as an impediment to her quest for subjectivity and transcendence, but also as a being from which she is, in an important sense, alienated. Menstruation is described in these terms: a woman's body is said to become other than itself, an "obscure and alien" thing, held hostage by "a foreign life." This sense of alienation is iterated in Beauvoir's descriptions of the experience of pregnancy; she goes so far as to argue that morning sickness is the manifest "revolt" of the maternal body against the "invading species" (Beauvoir 1989: 29).

That Beauvoir employs a rhetoric of alienation and violation in her rendering of female embodiment is of some significance. It is not simply the case that women struggle to realize themselves in transcendent projects set over and against the carnal confines of the body, as this seems to be universally the case in existentialist descriptions of an individual's project. For women, Beauvoir claims, this striving for transcendence is doubly complicated by the fact that women as a group are associated with the body, and thought to be tethered to it, in ways that men are not. So it is not simply the case that women understand their bodies as a hindrance to transcendence, but that this understanding is also made more acute by the fact that women, more so than men, are identified with reference to their sexual body. Indeed, the history of philosophy is predicated upon the association of men with rationality and spirit, and women with the body, emotion, and passion. Sartre may indeed claim that all individuals have an experience of objectification as they are embodied in the gaze of others. Beauvoir argues that this objectification is all the more problematic when it masquerades as neutral, which it does in the case of women as they are always already understood as flesh and immanence. This is simply to claim that the objectification of women's bodies becomes all but invisible within the confines of a culture that always already assumes that the feminine is synonymous with the carnal and the sensuous.

Despite her attention to the manner in which the association of women and the body is culturally reproduced, there are moments when Beauvoir seems to adopt the very understanding of the body that she is critiquing. In her discussion of the lesbian in *The Second Sex*, Beauvoir is careful to note that "sexuality is in no way determined by an anatomical 'fate'" and yet she persists in the opinion that homosexuality is something to which one might be "doomed" (Beauvoir 1989: 405). What comments such as these indicate is that while Beauvoir may have been concerned with the social and cultural mores in which the body is interpreted, she persists in reading corporeality as a hindrance to transcendence. In rendering lesbianism as that to which one might be "doomed," and in describing pregnancy and menstruation as experiences of violability and alienation, Beauvoir appears to be subscribing to the Western philosophical tradition's rendering of sexuality and embodiment as hindrances to rationality and autonomy. This much is clear, given her contention that lesbianism is a woman's attempt to "reconcile her autonomy with the passivity of her flesh" (Beauvoir 1989: 407). To be fair, Beauvoir is not trying here to pathologize lesbianism. Indeed, her aim is quite the contrary. In claiming that "homosexuality is no more a perversion deliberately indulged than it is a curse of fate," Beauvoir argues that every type of eroticism "expresses some general outlook on life" (Beauvoir 1989: 417). Knowing this, however, one is certainly shocked to read Beauvoir's somewhat outrageous claim that love between women is "more contemplative" than heterosexual love, and the "carnal affection" between women "more even" (Beauvoir: 1989: 420)! Such claims are worrying, indicating, as they do, that Beauvoir was too comfortable issuing prescriptions concerning lesbianism that now seem at best presumptuous and at worst downright essentialist. Hence in spite of her desire to defend lesbianism against certain discourses that would render it pathological, there are moments in which Beauvoir appears unable to resist this tendency herself.

However, if Beauvoir's phenomenological descriptions testify to her loyalty to a Cartesian framework wherein body and mind are at odds, it is crucial to remember that Beauvoir is not describing what she takes to be some unchanging reality, but rather an experience of immanence or vulnerability that is culturally prescribed. "Woman is determined not by her hormones or by mysterious instincts, but by the manner in which her body and her relation to the world are modified through the action of others than herself" (Beauvoir 1989: 725). There is, in woman's experience of her body, an alienation born of the fact that this body is understood as lesser and abject in a misogynist cultural order. To be sure, *The Second Sex* is a perplexing text to the degree that it is difficult at times to dissociate Beauvoir's descriptions of embodied alienation from her criticisms of the way in which this experience is enabled by certain cultural norms. Nevertheless, it is disingenuous to claim that Beauvoir remained naively committed to a certain Cartesianism that granted priority to the reason over and above the experience of one's own body, as some of her critics have claimed. As Emily Zakin has noted, Beauvoir was interested in proffering phenomenological descriptions of the experience of women in a masculinist and patriarchal society. Doing so involved the exploration of the ways in which the concept of the human has been appropriated by men. This in no way renders Beauvoir complicit in the conflation of masculinity and humanity; indeed, it is precisely this conflation that her work endeavors to undermine (Zakin 2000).

Beauvoir concludes in the chapter "The Independent Woman" by noting of woman that "it will be through attaining the same situation as theirs that she will find emancipation" (Beauvoir 1989: 715). Comments such as these have spawned the accusation that, for Beauvoir, women's liberation was to be achieved in the struggle to be more like men. But as Zakin notes, such an interpretation evades consideration of the manner in which Beauvoir's largely phenomenological methodology would prevent her from coherently making such a claim. Equality feminism is marked by its reluctance to concede the irreducibly different nature of the experience of differently sexed bodies. Insofar as *The Second Sex* reads as a description of women's embodied experience, it can hardly be coherently argued that Beauvoir's humanist tendencies represent equality feminism in any straightforward way. Indeed, it is even possible to read Beauvoir as advocating some romanticized version of difference feminism when she claims that the liberation of women will in no way curtail or compromise the wonder and passion that is the "genuine significance" of the human couple in its "true form" (Beauvoir 1989: 731). She writes that "the reciprocity of their relations will not do away with the miracles – desire, possession, love, dream, adventure – worked by the division of human beings into two separate categories" (Beauvoir 1989: 731). In her mention here of a miraculous love and wonder that will always abide between the sexes, Beauvoir places herself in proximity to Luce Irigaray, who has argued – with and against phenomenology – that the question of sexual difference is the question of our time. It is in this sense that Beauvoir's philosophy seems to rest on certain tenets that would be familiar to both equality and difference feminists; indeed, she has been critiqued along both lines. Not only have feminists worried over her claim that women will find emancipation in becoming more like men; they have also resisted the potentially heterosexist tenor of her claims about sexual difference.

What is clear is that Beauvoir's work cannot be readily categorized, and does not neatly conform to the genres of feminist theory as we have come to know them. This has prompted critics such as Tina Chanter and Penelope Deutscher to argue that her work is best received when its internal contradictions and tensions are left intact and unresolved, allowed to speak for themselves (Deutscher 1997; Chanter 2000). Hence to claim that the inconsistencies in Beauvoir's figuring of the body are demonstrative of some deficiency on her part are disingenuous. As Deutscher notes, the suggestion that Beauvoir was somehow "out of control" of the inconsistencies in her philosophy may work to infantilize Beauvoir as they portray her as an incompetent author (Deutscher 1997: 170). In truth, the tension to which Beauvoir's writing on the body attests is one that still structures much of the work done in feminist theory, and recent work in queer theory as well. Indeed, should one follow the advice of Chanter or Deutscher, a productive reading of Beauvoir's philosophy of the body is one that takes the ambivalence in her descriptions of female embodiment to be indicative of an important tension that has yet to be resolved. As Judith Butler has recently noted, there are certain thinkers in queer theory that have suggested that if one is not born, but rather becomes a woman, then becoming itself becomes the vehicle for the realization of gender (Butler 2004: 65). This lineage can indeed be traced to Beauvoir, who as early as 1949 defined woman as a "becoming."

Sexual Being as Becoming: Merleau-Ponty and Sexual Being

Beauvoir's appeal to the notion of "becoming" in *The Second Sex* is made with reference to Merleau-Ponty, who understood "humanity" as an historically embedded and evolving idea, and not a static essence. It is in reference to this notion of the individual as a culturally located becoming that Beauvoir argues that women should define their possibilities. Indeed, for the Merleau-Ponty of *Phenomenology of Perception*, "neither body nor existence can be regarded as the original of the human being, since they presuppose each other, and because the body is solidified or generalized existence and existence a perpetual incarnation" (Merleau-Ponty 1962: 166). His descriptions of sexual life as "one more form of original intentionality" conceive sexuality as an influence at the very origin of experience, knowledge, and expression. This means that sexuality is irreducible to an object of analysis and is not a finite and isolated dimension of existence. Sexuality imbues one's experience of the world in myriad ways, and to greater and lesser degrees: "Sexuality without being the object of any intended act of consciousness, can underlie and guide specified forms of my experience. Taken in this way, as an ambiguous atmosphere, sexuality is coextensive with life" (ibid.). In this sense, sexuality is not an autonomous entity available for analysis, but influences the form of experience through and through. Sexuality can never be reduced to a content or attribute of experience, for in phenomenology there is no content of experience that does not inherently contribute to its form. Put differently, sexuality cannot be said to be the discrete content of experience, but rather a fundamental influence on the way in which experience is structured.

Merleau-Ponty's discussion of the body in its sexual being is in many ways bound to the notion of the lived-body, a figure that pervades much of his early work. With reference to the Heideggerian notion of being-in-the-world, Merleau-Ponty intends the lived-body to be understood in terms of the body's thrownness into a world in which it always already finds itself situated. For him, the "corporeal schema" or body image is the figure of the lived-body as it is taken up by the subject, neither grasped intellectually, nor understood objectively. In descriptions that foreshadow his later discussion of the chiasm in *The Visible and the Invisible*, Merleau-Ponty claims that human embodiment is defined by a fundamental ambiguity. As the fundamental locus of intentionality, the body is a in a sense responsible for the constitution of a world, yet it is also bound to this world, and subject to its influence. Merleau-Ponty explores the manner in which the body is habituated in the world, indeed, using habit as an example to demonstrate the inadequacy of explanations of embodiment that would appeal solely to claims about the consciousness of one's body (intellectualism) or to mechanistic and material conceptions of the body as a thing. Habits testify to the body's being given over to a world which it constitutes and by which it is in turn constituted: "The world is already constituted, but also never completely constituted; in the first case we are acted upon, in the second we are open to an infinite number of possibilities" (Merleau-Ponty 1962: 453).

Beauvoir and Merleau-Ponty share much of their approach to the sexual being of the body. Both are critical of a Cartesian understanding of an abstract and immaterial *cogito* somehow suspended apart from the flesh. And both recognize the philosophical importance of describing the lived ambiguity of human embodiment, though for Beauvoir this exercise was doubtless informed by more explicitly political concerns. Yet insofar as she understood human subjectivity to be realized in transcendence, and insofar as the body remains the site of the immanent frustration of these projects, the degree to which Beauvoir manages to break with a dualistic way of thinking through the body remains ambiguous. Merleau-Ponty's thought is motivated by the critique of transcendental idealism and its attendant conception of an intentional and volitional consciousness. There are ways in which this is and is not the case for Beauvoir. While there are moments wherein she insists on the inherently embodied and concretely situated nature of consciousness and freedom, there are others in which she seems reluctant to move beyond the rhetoric of choice and intention. However, *pace* suspicions of a recalcitrant Cartesianism, her understanding of woman as an embodied and historically situated becoming resonates deeply with more contemporary elaborations of gender identity.

More specifically, despite (and because of) the ambiguities that Beauvoir's account may manifest, her existential and phenomenological descriptions of embodiment might be read as forerunners to more contemporary theories on the performativity of gender, where "performativity" is meant to connote the fluid and culturally imbued sense of gender as opposed to a binary and biologistic understanding of sex. As accounts of gender performativity tend to accentuate the manner in which gender is accomplished in time as an effect of performance, they are indebted to two main tenets in the existentialist philosophy of identity, first the claim that existence precedes essence, and secondly the claim that the accomplishment of an identity is a project undertaken in the eyes of others. Indeed, there is no making sense of a performative elaboration of gender apart from some understanding of the inherent other-directedness of our actions. Nor is the influence of the existential tenet "existence precedes essence" in many places more lucratively employed than in discourse on sexuality and performativity.

Performativity as Existential Practice

Judith Butler is the most renowned philosopher of gender performativity. In her seminal book *Gender Trouble* (1990), she argued for a certain ambiguity that plagues Beauvoir's account of the construction of gender. Butler applauds Beauvoir's claim that "one is not born a woman, but rather becomes one," as well as the challenge her work posed to essentialist notions of gender that would bind it to an irreducible material sex. Yet while Beauvoir may have been one of the first to introduce a feminist discourse on social construction, some have argued that she failed to sufficiently interrogate the assumption of an agent that somehow prefigures or precedes the appearance of the subject. While Butler may agree with the variability of gender on Beauvoir's account, the rhetoric of volition and intent that pervades her existential descriptions of embodiment is worrisome for Butler. The worry here is that Beauvoir reduces the discourse on construction to a discourse on choice. Ironically, while Butler goes some distance toward dissociating herself from this view, which she attributes to Beauvoir, Butler herself is accused of assuming too wilful a subject in her model of gender performativity. This is a criticism that Butler takes up in *Bodies that Matter* (1993) and more recently in *Undoing Gender* (2004).

In a sense, the fact that Butler is frequently accused of adopting a voluntaristic notion of subjectivity is ironic, given the fact that much of her work is intended as an explicit criticism of such an understanding of the relationship between sexuality and agency. Having claimed in *Gender Trouble* that there are certain regulatory practices that govern not only gender norms, but also the gender identities that these norms admit as intelligible, Butler argues that there is no static "truth" to sex or gender; rather one's gender is accomplished in time as an effect of certain performances. "In this sense, gender is always a doing, though not a doing by a subject that might be said to pre-exist the deed . . . There is no gender identity behind the expressions of gender; that identity is performatively constituted by the very 'expressions' that are said to be its results" (Butler 1990: 25). Clearly Butler does not imply that there was a voluntaristic agent free to adopt, or cast off at will, one gender identity or another. Indeed, for Butler, the stakes of performance are high indeed, as they are legislated and to some extent determined – though not in their entirety – by cultural norms that govern the limits of sexual intelligibility, and more urgently the liveability of one's sexuality. Hence in claiming that gender was constituted performatively, Butler argued against a static and naturalist conception of the sexual subject, and for a subject whose gender is realized in time, through a sequence of acts that are governed by cultural norms. In this sense, performativity must be differentiated from performance. Performance presupposes a subject, while the idea of performativity is meant to combat the very notion of the subject, stressing instead the ways in which subjectivity is constituted in particular historic moments as the effect of certain acts. In this sense, "femininity" must not be conceived as the exteriorization of some innate and inherent essence; rather, femininity is actualized as the effect of certain gendered performances culturally coded as feminine. "Femininity" is a cultural construct, malleable and impermanent; it cannot be conceived as some sort of preexistent essence that is exteriorized as gender. Hence to say that identity is performative is not to say that the performance masks a more foundational subject that assumes or performs certain roles. Indeed, a performative understanding of sexual subjectivity contests the notion that there is a thinking self that precedes and remains unchanged through action.

There is clearly both symmetry and dissymmetry here between Butler's account and an existentialist understanding of identity. The proximity between a performative account of gender and the phenomenological and existential approach is evident should one remember Merleau-Ponty's discussion of the body in the chapter on "The Body as Expression and Speech," from *Phenomenology of Perception*. Merleau-Ponty's aim here is to give an account of embodiment that debunks transcendental idealism and materialism alike. Through his descriptions of the simultaneous constitution of language and thought in expression, Merleau-Ponty belies the intellectualist assumption that thought exists for itself prior to expression (Merleau-Ponty 1962: 183). He subordinates reason and the intellect to the expressive powers of the body. When Merleau-Ponty exposes the myth of disembodied thought, he argues for the simultaneous constitution of thought and language, such that there is no thought apart from its expression in the flesh. So, too, when he writes of a particular "corporeal style" with which one approaches the world, he provides resources for thinking through the relationship between materiality and language that does not reduce each to the other, but forces an examination of their ambiguous relationship. One might read Merleau-Ponty's work not only as a criticism of the cogito, but also as a critique of the idealist tradition more broadly construed. When he claims that speech does not translate thought, but accomplishes it, he aims to undermine intellectualist understandings of language that would take language as a superficial vessel, one that was meant to convey or translate

497

thoughts that were already preformed. For Merleau-Ponty, thought was accomplished in language and expression, meaning that consciousness is realized in an embodied and animate subject and does not exist apart from its embodied instantiation and expression. In this sense, Cartesian dualism is undone. If thought is accomplished as embodied expression, it ceases to live when it is torn free of the body. Moreover, insofar as Merleau-Ponty is also concerned to elaborate the manner in which the body both maintains and disrupts habit, the temporal dimension of his philosophy of existence is not unlike the one that comes to inform the model of gender as performativity. According to the performative account, the accomplishment of gender is a forward-looking temporal unfolding. It is not in the realization of isolated acts that one's gender comes to be, but rather through the repetition or iteration of certain acts that gender is instantiated.

If gender identity is defined as an effect of multiple culturally meaningful practices, it is also the case that performativity, as a model for the accomplishment of gender, is quite far removed from a model wherein there is a strong sense of volition and agency detached from cultural prejudice and influence. When read in light of the trajectory that Butler's work has taken, the accusation that she presupposes too volitional an agent is strange indeed. Stranger still is the fact that when the Butlerian account of gender does not stand accused of voluntaristic humanism, it is subjected to the exact inverse of this criticism, namely, the charge that this model of gender and sexuality forecloses the possibilities for agency that one would like to think should accompany any account of gender formation that is motivated by an emancipatory politics. It is precisely in the incommensurability of these criticisms that one might locate the ties that bind the Butlerian approach to sexuality with those put forward by the existentialists before her. There are important ways in which Beauvoir's project, for instance, might be read as an attempt to reconcile the hope for an increased political agency on the part of women, with the acknowledgment that the possibilities for the liberation of women were radically impinged by misogynist cultural norms that severely compromise a woman's sense of agency. In this sense it resonates quite clearly with Beauvoir's discussion of women in *The Second Sex*, Sartre's discussions of freedom and alienation, and Merleau-Ponty's rendering of human embodiment as an expressive mélange of language and materiality. It is clear that the French existentialists were motivated by the desire to proffer an account of human subjectivity that took seriously the political necessity of articulating some sense of agency, even if this articulation must negotiate and respond to the ways in which this agency is limited in hierarchical and oppressive societies. Sartre was concerned throughout his work with the manner in which political agency was always a work in progress, a contingent endeavor enacted in a climate weighted by history, cultural norms, and the expectations of others. In this respect, Butler would be quite amenable to his approach. It is for this reason that Alan Schrift has suggested that a certain proximity exists between Butler's own work and that of Sartre, Beauvoir, and Merleau-Ponty (Schrift 2001). In this sense, the theory of gender performativity can be said to be an existentialist theory of some ilk, despite the fact that Beauvoir and the other existentialists may have presupposed a more robust and substantive sense of agency and volition than the one that Butler's account would allow.

Queering Phenomenology from Beauvoir to Butler

Recently, existentialist and phenomenological notions of embodiment have been re-surfacing surrounding narratives of transgenderism and transsexuality. Indeed, the consideration of these narratives is in many ways a requisite consequence of the fact that feminist theory has evolved in the way it has, namely as a series of arguments, at times contentious, concerning the degree to which one's body is decisive in identifying one's gender. In this context, these narratives are of interest insofar as they point to what at times is a radical symmetry – and at others an obvious dissymmetry – between one's own gender identification and the material contours of one's own body. While some read the transsexual's desire to inhabit a different body as the valorization of a traditional correspondence between gender identification and embodiment, others read transsexualism as pushing sex, as a discursive entity, quite beyond the body.

Jay Prosser has argued that poststructuralist theories of gender have neglected con-sideration of the manner in which subjects construct their identities as much as they are constructed; they are themselves constituting agents to some degree. It is for this reason that Prosser charges poststructuralist theories with having forsaken "valences of cultural belonging" (Prosser 1998: 11). Transgender and transsexual narratives work against the poststructuralist celebration of the fluidity and contingency of identity; they do so by forcing remembrance of the "ongoing foundational power" that gender categories continue to maintain. Citing the fluid, fictional, and transient dimensions of sexuality that he charges poststructuralists with celebrating, Prosser argues that transsexual narratives demand redress of poststructuralism's evasion of materiality, accomplished in its favoring of discourse. On this account, discourse on the body has not adequately taken up notions of materiality and flesh; in the poststructuralist tradition, the body has been instead been rendered as the locus for the operation of language, power, and science. For these reasons, Prosser takes issue with the claim – which he associates with Butler and Beauvoir – that sex is "really gender all along," a contention that seems at odds with transsexual narratives insofar as they resist departure from the literality of material sex. As these narratives frequently invoke the importance of a correspondence between material sex and gender identity, along with a concomitant desire to "belong" to one's body, they disrupt and complicate several theses of recent queer and feminist theory. For these reasons, it may be fair to argue that Prosser is reviving existentialist concerns about the limits of embodied agency and the importance of narratives on materiality. Perhaps more importantly, Prosser seems to be stressing the phenomenological importance of feeling as though one belongs to, and inhabits, one's body.

Critics have taken issue with Prosser's analysis and those like it. Gayle Salamon (2004) is critical of Prosser's desire to return to the "simplicity of materiality" as this move seems to presuppose the feasibility of an appeal to a body beyond discourse. While Salamon would in no way contest the claim that the experience of embodied subjectivity is essential to subject formation, there is nothing in this claim that pre-scribes or enables a return to a body beyond discourse. Prosser's worry that "the materiality of language in contemporary thought has taken the place of the materiality of the body" is grounded in what is a fundamentally untenable breach between the body designated in theoretical discourse and some "real" materiality that is said to subtend it. Phenomenology can help to make sense of the *experience* of this distinction, however, and therein lies its relevance to the most contemporary debates concerning sexual identity. Even as phenomenology is itself a theoretical discourse, it offers resources for thinking through what it would mean to experience a difference between one's "real" body and the body as it is discursively or culturally represented. Even though the implied schism here is itself a discursive one, phenomenology enables the validation of experiential narratives that testify to its power.

References and Further Reading

Bartky, S. L. (1990) *Femininity and Domination: Studies in the Phenomenology of Oppression*. London and New York: Routledge.

Beauvoir, S. de (1989) *The Second Sex* (trans. H. M. Parshley). New York: Vintage Books (original work published 1949).

—— (1996) *Ethics of Ambiguity* (trans. B. Frechtman). New York: Citadel Press (original work published 1948).

Bordo, S. (1993) *Unbearable Weight: Feminism, Western Culture and the Body*. Berkeley: University of California Press.

Butler, J. (1989) Sexual ideology and phenomenological description. In J. Allen and I. M. Young (eds.), *The Thinking Muse: Feminism and Modern French Philosophy* (pp. 85–100). Bloomington: Indiana University Press.

—— (1990) *Gender Trouble*. London and New York: Routledge.

—— (1993) *Bodies That Matter*. London and New York: Routledge.

—— (2004) *Undoing Gender*. London and New York: Routledge.

Chanter, T. (2000) Abjection and ambiguity: Simone de Beauvoir's legacy. *Journal of Speculative Philosophy*, 14(2), 138–55.

Deutscher, P. (1997) *Yielding Gender*. New York and London: Routledge.

Diprose, R. (1994) *The Bodies of Women*. New York and London: Routledge.

—— (2002) *Corporeal Generosity: On Giving with Nietzsche, Merleau-Ponty and Lévinas*. Albany: State University of New York Press.

Fanon, F. (1967) *Black Skin White Masks* (trans. C. L. Markmann). New York: Grove Press (original work published 1952).

Gatens, M. (1996) *Imaginary Bodies: Ethics, Power, and Corporeality*. London and New York: Routledge.

Grosz, E. (1994) *Volatile Bodies: Toward a Corporeal Feminism*. Sydney: Allen & Unwin; Bloomington: Indiana University Press.

Irigaray, L. (1993) *An Ethics of Sexual Difference* (trans. C. Burke and G. C. Gill). Ithaca, NY: Cornell University Press.

Kruks, S. (2001) *Retrieving Experience: Subjectivity and Recognition in Feminist Politics*. Ithaca, NY: Cornell University Press.

Merleau-Ponty, M. (1962) *Phenomenology of Perception* (trans. C. Smith). New York and London: Routledge (original work published 1945).

—— (1968) *The Visible and the Invisible* (trans. A. Lingis). Evanston, IL: Northwestern University Press.

Prosser, J. (1998) *Second Skins: The Body Narratives of Transsexuality*. New York: Columbia University Press.

Rubin, H. (1998) Phenomenology in trans studies. *GLQ: The Transgender Issue*, 14(2). Durham, NC: Duke University Press.

Salamon, G. (2004) The bodily ego and the contested domain of the material. *Differences: Journal of Feminist Cultural Studies* 15(3), 95–122.

Sartre, J-P. (1956) *Being and Nothingness* (trans. H. Barnes). New York: Simon & Schuster (original work published 1943).

Schrift, A. (2001) Judith Butler: Une nouvelle existentialiste? (Judith Butler: A new existentialist)? *Philosophy Today*, 12, 35–50.

Weiss, G. (1999) *Body Images: Embodiment as Intercorporeality*. New York and London: Routledge.

Zakin, E. (2000) Differences in equality: Beauvoir's unsettling of the universal. *Journal of Speculative Philosophy*, 14(2), 104–120.

34

Feminism

SARA HEINÄMAA

The classical feminist question concerns the relation between man and woman: Is it possible and adequate to evaluate women and men by the same standards and argue for *equality*, or is there a principal *difference* between the sexes which requires that we use two different standards of evaluation? In contemporary feminist theory this dilemma is known as the equality–difference debate. The controversy is old, however, having its roots in the Renaissance and early modern discussions about human nature and human good.

Another central problem concerns the basis of the sexual identity: Is it mainly inborn, or is it learned and established in social interaction? In earlier phases of feminist discussion this was known as the nature–nurture dilemma; in the feminist discussions of the 1970s it was reformulated as the sex–gender controversy.

Phenomenology allows a radical investigation into the transcendental foundations of these dilemmas by offering an account of the constitution of objectivities: sexual identities and differences, goals and values, natural things and artifacts, men and women, sexes and bodies. It explains what it *means to be* a human person, man or woman, and how such persons can relate to each other and to the world. By disclosing the basic structures of embodiment and intersubjectivity, phenomenology makes possible a radical philosophical investigation into central topics of feminism, such as sexual hierarchy, androcentricism, eroticism, expression, generation, and maternity.

Phenomenological accounts of sexual difference are based on Husserl's analysis of *embodiment*. In classical phenomenology, the living body can be studied as it is given and constituted in perception and affection. This primary phenomenon is distinguished from the body as an object of the natural sciences, that is, the physical body or the mere material thing. So the phenomenologist does not posit the sexed body as a thing in itself, but studies the body in its various modes of givenness. He or she also investigates the mutual dependence of various phenomena, and thus is able to argue, for example, that the perceived body is more primary than the extrapolated objects of natural sciences. Neither nature nor culture, neither bodies nor souls are simple givens in this framework; all such realities have foundations and origins in the constitutive process. By inquiring back into these foundations, phenomenology prepares the way for a critique of naturalistic and constructionistic accounts of sexuality and sexual difference.

However, to suggest that phenomenology merely functions as a conceptual and methodic resource for feminism is misleading. Feminist phenomenology is not just an application of phenomenology proper; the relation between the two traditions is more complex. Two facts especially need to be emphasized.

First, some of the most prominent phenomenologists have been women – and some explicit feminists. Simone de Beauvoir is perhaps the best known of the early thinkers who combined phenomenology with feminism, but even before her, in the 1930s, Edith Stein wrote phenomenological treatises on personality, embodiment, and intersubjectivity, and published philosophical reflections on the woman question. Both Stein and Beauvoir challenged prevailing views of men and women with phenomenological tools, but both also questioned philosophical orthodoxy with feminist insight.

Second, feminist phenomenologists have argued that the notion of a sexually neutral self is prejudiced and based on the neglect of women's experiences. It has even been suggested that the question of sexual difference is not restricted to constituted objects but also concerns the transcendental foundation itself – whether it be called the "transcendental self" or "Dasein." Luce Irigaray's thesis is probably the best known of such arguments, but other feminist scholars also have challenged the idea of a sexually neutral foundation. This line of argument becomes possible in phenomenology, because it finds the transcendental foundation, not in subjectivity, but in intersubjectivity.

Kant's transcendental self was nontemporal, universal, and equally shared by all human subjects. Husserl's transcendental person and Heidegger's Dasein are temporal individuals with geneses, histories, and acquired habitualities and possessions. Thus in phenomenology, the problem of sexual difference can also be formulated at the transcendental level: Is it possible to distinguish between two principally different types of personality with two different geneses or internal histories and with two modes of passivity and embodiment? Husserl himself hints at this possibility when he includes "the problem of the sexes" among the genetic transcendental problems in the late work *The Crisis of European Sciences and Transcendental Phenomenology* (*Die Krisis der europäischen Wissenschaften und die transzendentale Phänomenologie*, 1936–7) (Husserl 1988: 187–8).

So the relation between feminist inquiries and phenomenological inquiries is twofold. On the one hand, phenomenology offers methodological and conceptual tools for the development of a philosophical alternative to contemporary feminist naturalism and constructionism. On the other hand, contemporary feminism challenges the idea of a sexually neutral subject, and thus poses the question of whether the transcendental self discovered by the phenomenologists is of one type or of two (or several).

To understand this double questioning, we must familiarize ourselves with phenomenological analyses of embodiment, personality, and sexuality. The concept of the living body provides the foundation for subsequent feminist inquiries into the self–other relation, sexual hierarchy, and difference.

Two Starting Points: The Living Body and the Sexual Person

The phenomenological understanding and framing of "the problem of the sexes" is based on Husserl's account of the ontic meanings that *living bodies* have in our experience.

In the second book of *Ideas* (*Ideen zu einer reinen Phänomenologie und phänomeno-logischen Philosophie*; cited as Husserl 1993), Husserl argues that the primary way in which living bodies are given to us is *expressive*. We do not perceive our own bodies or the bodies of others (animals and humans) primarily as biomechanisms or as cultural artifacts, but as expressive means, motivated by sensations and feelings, directed by intentions and purposes, and responsive to affects and appeals. More fundamentally, my own body is given to me as the field of sensations and as the zero point of orientation and movement. It stands out from all other things in being the only "thing" that I can move immediately and spontaneously. The bodies of others are similar to my own body but, at the same time, they express sensations, feelings, desires, and volitions which are irrecoverably beyond my reach. As such our living bodies are not fully constituted things, but, as Beauvoir puts it, "our grasp upon the world and the outline of our projects" (1972: 66; translation modified).

The expressivity of the body has two aspects. First, a living body appears as an *expression* of a conscious life, a stream of experiences. Second, this expressive relation binds the different parts, movements, and sections of the body into an indivisible unity. Thus, the body cannot be broken up or divided into discrete parts and pieces. It is an expressive whole, and its gestures, postures, movements, and organs contribute to its formation. As such bodies are like works of art: they can be classified as belonging to different *styles* and *types* but they cannot be conceived as replaceable or interchangeable particulars.

Accordingly, sexual identities and sexual differences are not primarily given to us as properties or subsystems of biological organisms (sex) or as cultural artifacts (gender); they belong to expressive living bodies of *persons*.

This was argued by Husserl's early followers in France, by Maurice Merleau-Ponty and Simone de Beauvoir. Both knew Husserl's work on embodiment and based their accounts on his conceptual distinctions. Merleau-Ponty had already studied Husserl's manuscripts in 1937 in the newly established Husserl archive in Louvain, and Beauvoir familiarized herself with the phenomenological understanding of embodiment through Merleau-Ponty's interpretation and through the works of Sartre, Levinas, Heidegger, and Fink.

The common belief and the usual, recurring claim is that in classical phenomenology, the self or the ego is nothing but a performer of acts and a solitary creator of objectivities. As such the self would be pure activity, not affected by anything outside itself. This picture is misguided: Husserl argues in *Cartesian Meditations* (1950; cited as Husserl 1960) that the self is a *person*, a temporal formation with a past and with an origin. It is not a series of punctual acts, but a sediment formed in the continuity of flowing experiences. Its acts are motivated by earlier acts as well as by other forms of lived experience, such as feelings and sensations. Thus defined, the concept of person is a *genetic concept*, and questions concerning its temporal structure, its origin and continuity, are genetic ones.

Further, Husserl argues that the personal self has an individual, unique *style* of experiencing and acting. He writes:

> Every man [human being] has his character, we can say, his style of life in affection and action, with regard to the way he has of being motivated by such and such circumstances.

And it is not that he merely had this up to now: the style is rather something permanent, at least relatively so in the various stages of life, and then, when it is changed, it does so again . . . in a characteristic way, such that, consequently upon these changes, a unitary style manifests itself once more. (Husserl 1993: 283)

The personalistic concepts of style and type offer a possibility of formulating the question of sexual identity and sexual difference in a specific way. We do not need to restrict ourselves to explaining such identities and differences by empirical realities: hormones, genes, stimulus response-systems, social roles, or historical facts. More fundamentally, we can understand sexual difference by intentional and temporal concepts as a difference between two types of personality. As components of personal identities, masculinity and femininity, manhood and womanhood, are not anchored on any particular objects, but are given as two different modes of relating to objects, acting on them and being affected by them. Sexual identities are constituted *together with* our own bodies, those special "things" which connect us to all material things and to the world as a open totality of them.

When sexual identity is understood as a stylistic identity, it runs through the whole life as a way or manner in which lived experiences and acts follow each other, continue, and change. And when this manner of changing itself changes – for example, in childhood, adolescence, sickness, or old age – then "it does so in a characteristic way, such that a unitary style manifests itself once more."

In his *Phenomenology of Perception* (*Phénoménologie de la perception*, 1945; cited as Merleau-Ponty 1995), Merleau-Ponty uses the Husserlian concepts of *person* and *style* to account for the different aspects of human sexuality. He argues that causal explanations of sexual behavior, even if useful for certain purposes, cannot grasp the essence of sexual behavior but instead presupposes a prior understanding of it. This holds for biological and physiological accounts of sexuality but also for psychological, sociological, and anthropological explanations. The task of the philosopher is to investigate their common basis, that is, their shared presuppositions about the meaning of sexuality and its constitution in experience.

For Merleau-Ponty, sexuality and sexual identity belong primarily to persons, to their living bodies, and not to natural objects or cultural artifacts. He explains his phenomenological approach as follows:

In so far as behavior is a form, in which "visual" and "tactile contents", sensibility and motility appear only as inseparable moments, it remains inaccessible to causal thought and is capable of being apprehended only by another kind of thought, that which grasps its object as it comes into being and as it appears to the one experiencing it, with the atmosphere of meaning surrounding it, and which tries to infiltrate into that atmosphere in order to discover, behind scattered facts and symptoms, the subject's whole being. (Merleau-Ponty 1995: 120; translation modified)

The methodological claim is that sexuality must be investigated from the point of view of the experiencing subject. The philosophical question is not how sexually aroused individuals relate to the object of their attraction, when studied from a third-person perspective. Rather, we must ask how the attractive other appears to the person who lives in desire having an individual history of desiring. And to capture the meaning of sexuality, we must study the different ways in which bodies are given to persons in affection and aversion, excitement and arousal, passion and indifference. The task is not to generalize over such cases but to capture their essential features.

In *Phenomenology of Perception*, Merleau-Ponty studies two cases in particular: a man who had lost his ability to see any sexual significance in the world, and a girl who had ceased to speak and eat because her love was forbidden. Merleau-Ponty argues that when studying particular sexual experiences and behaviors, we should not proceed by subsuming them under general laws about human or animal behavior. We must first insert them into the totality of the person's life. Only as moments in a comprehensive unity of an individual life can particular behaviors and experiences be compared with other modes. Sexuality is not a separate level of human life ("animal" or "primitive") but is inseparably intertwined with other modes of experience, including motility, perception, and cognition. "The genital life is geared to the whole life of the subject" (Merleau-Ponty 1995: 158).

Merleau-Ponty argues that the connection between sexuality and other modes of experience is expressive. The styles that manifest in our cognitive and practical lives also run through our erotic lives. We can even say that sexuality "condenses" a person's general manner of relating to others. But this should not be misunderstood: sexuality is not more primary or more basic than the other modes of experience and behavior. It is given in a relation of mutual expression with them all.

According to Merleau-Ponty, this captures the sound core of Freud's writings: sexuality is "interfused" with the whole life. The mistake of reductionistic interpretations of psychoanalysis is that they assume that the interfusion can be understood and described in causal terms. Husserl's concept of the living body allows Merleau-Ponty to argue that instead of causing other forms of behavior, sexual experiences express them, and conversely, are expressed in them. He states: "Thus sexuality is not an autonomous cycle. It has internal links with the whole of active and cognitive being, these three sections of behavior manifesting but a single typical structure, and standing in a relationship to each other of reciprocal expression" (Merleau-Ponty 1995: 157).

Sexual Difference: Phenomenological Analysis and Feminist Questions

Merleau-Ponty also uses the concepts of manner and style to describe the difference between men and women. He writes, for example,

> A woman passing by . . . is a certain manner of being flesh which is given entirely in her walk or even in the simple shock of her heel on the ground – as the tension of the bow is present in each fiber of wood – a very noticeable variation of the norm of walking, looking, touching, and speaking that I possess in my self-awareness because I am body. (Merleau-Ponty 1964: 54)

In Merleau-Ponty's understanding, being-a-man or being-a-woman is not a question of possessing some one fixed property. Sexual identities are not founded on objectivities, biological or social, historical or natural. They are forms of behavior and action,

506

stylistic continua that run through all levels of experience from motility and perception to emotion and cognition, intellect, understanding, and reflection. Even if they develop and change in time, we perceive or conceive permanence, not the constancy of a substance or an attribute but the unity of acting, continuing action and changing it, being affected and responding to affects.

Ultimately, maleness and femaleness are, in Merleau-Ponty's account, two variations of our basic corporeal way of relating to the world; they are two general types that include uncounted individual styles of behavior. Every individual creates an interpretation or a modification of one of these two principal types. Most modifications develop and amplify the duality, but some work to undo or annul it. The development of a sexual identity, in any case, is not accounted for by objectivities, but by imitation and mimicry, repetition and modification of action.

This does not mean that sexual identity is a question of choice. To suggest that we *decide to be* men and women is to commit an intellectualistic fallacy. Sexual identities are not and cannot be determined by will; they are experienced and formed already on the level of perception and motility.

To summarize, Merleau-Ponty applied the Husserlian concepts of person and style to account for sexual experiences and sexual identities. He also outlined an account of sexual difference, but did not go deeper into this problematics.

We have to turn to Simone de Beauvoir's feminist classic, *The Second Sex* (*Le deuxième sexe*, 1949; cited as Beauvoir 1993), in order to find descriptions and analyses of the difference between men and women. Here the phenomenological account of embodiment is combined with a feminist interest in equality and freedom. For Beauvoir, freedom is not just a juridico-political concept but also includes the critical theoretical demand to liberate our thinking from all prejudged and dogmatic views.

Phenomenologically orientated accounts of embodiment, the accounts of Sartre, Merleau-Ponty, and Levinas, encouraged Beauvoir to develop a new way of inquiring into the relationships between men and women. Instead of looking for causal explanations – biological, psychological, or sociological – she suggests that we need to focus on lived experiences and try to find concepts that articulate women's experiences and their identities.

Beauvoir begins her reflections on sexual relations in *The Second Sex* by introducing the phenomenological concept of the living body. She emphasizes: "it is not the body-object described by the biologist that actually exists, but the living body of the subject" (Beauvoir 1972: 69; translation modified). Beauvoir's feminist argument is that male writers, from Antiquity to her own time, have assumed that their bodies function as universal instruments in the exploration of the material world. As such, the body would guarantee a neutral view of the world; but in fact the bodies of philosophers, like all bodies, are finite and limited. Beauvoir states: "He [man] sees his body as a direct and normal connection with the world, which he believes he apprehends in its objectivity, whereas he regards the body of woman as weighed down by everything peculiar to it" (Beauvoir 1972: 15; translation modified). In the case of phenomenology, this comes down to the argument that the descriptions that phenomenologists give of bodily experiences are not based on proper variations but restricted by a male paradigm. Beauvoir argues that the human body, as described by Husserl's followers, lacks concreteness; it is an abstraction based on male experience. At the end of the book she states: "There is a whole region of human experience which the male deliber-ately chooses to ignore because he fails to *think* about it: this experience woman *lives*" (Beauvoir 1972: 622; translation modified).

Beauvoir's main argument is indebted to two discourses that called into question the neutrality of the philosophical canon. First, and most importantly, Beauvoir is a feminist thinker, influenced by the works of Christine de Pisan, François Poulain de la Barre, Mary Wollstonecraft, John Stuart Mill, Virginia Woolf, and Colette. On the other hand, her treatise is indebted to the ideology critique that she found in the works of Kierkegaard and Nietzsche. The works of feminist critics and women writers disclosed a wide area of human experience which was lacking from the stock of philosophy, human sciences, and biosciences. The fathers of existentialism argued that woman – as we know her – is a creation of men; she is the fantasy or projection which relieves man's anxiety of his own carnality and finitude. Nietzsche's *The Gay Science* (*Die fröliche Wissenschaft*, 1882; cited as Nietzsche 2001) suggested that this fear dominates our scientific and philosophical traditions: "The unconscious disguise of physiological needs under the cloaks of objective, ideal, purely spiritual goes frighteningly far – and I have asked myself often enough whether . . . philosophy has been no more than an inter-pretation of the body and a *misunderstanding of the body*" (Nietzsche 2001: 5).

Together these sources assured Beauvoir that most claims about women and men are motivated by prejudices and interests. So it is not by accident that the two mottos of *The Second Sex* are from Pythagoras and François Poulain de la Barre. Whereas Pythagoras argues that "[t]here is a bad principle that has created the chaos, the darkness, and the woman," Poulain de la Barre answers: "All that men have written about women should be suspect, for they are at once the judge and the party" (Beauvoir 1993: 7; my translation). This variance captures the core of Beauvoir's project: she wrote in order to subject to doubt everything that men have written about women, not in the interest of construing an alternative theory of women's being, but in the interest of winning a disillusioned view of the traditions of philosophy, science, and religion.

The Self and Its Other

The Second Sex shows that there are two areas of life that need special attention, if we want to question androcentric preconceptions about embodiment and open existential –phenomenological descriptions to the full concreteness of human experience. These two areas of life are *eroticism* and *pregnancy*. Beauvoir's main argument is that we need to study pairing, pregnancy, and childbirth, not as facts – biological, psycholo-gical, or economical – but as they are experienced and lived by women. Her work sug-gests that if we pay attention to women's erotic experiences and their experiences of pregnancy and childbirth, then we must modify the standard account of the bodily relation between the self and the other.

Beauvoir presents this argument in a non-technical existentialist vocabulary. She states: "The transcendence of the artisan, of the man of action is inhabited by one subjectivity, but in the becoming mother the opposition between subject and object *is* abolished. She forms with this child from which she is swollen an equivocal couple overwhelmed by life" (Beauvoir 1972: 512; translation modified).

In the standard account, the self and the other are presented as visible to one another and as separated by a spatial distance. Beauvoir points out that these conditions are not realized in the case of a woman carrying a child in her womb: The infantile other is not given to the woman in visible perception, but through tactile sensations. There is not spatial distance between these two. On the contrary, the other seems to occupy that special place which constitutes the privileged "here" of the woman and the zero-point of her orientation in space.

Many commentators have criticized Beauvoir for focusing on the negative aspects of women's experiences of their own bodies. There is certainly a strong negative tone in Beauvoir's descriptions of pregnancy and nursing. However, the philosophical core of her discussion of embodiment is not in these undertones but in the argument that we still lack a nonbiased philosophy of the living body of the person. Despite voluminous accounts of embodiment, we still develop our concepts, descriptions, and analyses within the paradigm of the male body. Even the alleged *eidetic* descriptions of living body offered by phenomenologists are in fact restricted by the preconception that women's bodies, as experienced, are fundamentally similar to male bodies, or else deviations from the male norm. This is not the case, as accounts by women testify.

The Beauvoirian argument is repeated and elaborated in later French feminist philosophy, by Julia Kristeva and Luce Irigaray. Both are usually presented as critics of Beauvoir's existentialism, but in their discussions of pregnancy and maternity, both clearly have benefited from *The Second Sex*. Kristeva starts her essay "Motherhood according to Giovanni Bellini" (Kristeva 1980), for example, by writing: "Within the body, growing as a graft, indomitable, there is an other. And no one is present, within that simultaneously dual and alien space, to signify what is going on. 'It happens, but I am not there.' 'I cannot realize it, but it goes on.' Motherhood's impossible syllogism" (Kristeva 1980: 237). Irigaray, on her part, describes the couple of the mother and the unborn child in *An Ethics of Sexual Difference* (*Éthique de la différence sexuelle*, 1984; cited as Irigaray 1993) as follows: "the one who is still in this night does not see and remains without a visible (as far as our knowledge is exact). And the other who sees cannot see him. The other does not see him, he is not visible for the other, who nevertheless sees the world, but without him" (Irigaray 1993: 144/152). Following Beauvoir, both Kristeva and Irigaray argue that the experience in which the woman feels a child moving in her own body constitutes an anomaly in the descriptive framework of classical phenomenology. Thus their critique is not the principled suspicion that Levinas presents against Husserl's analysis; they are not arguing for the general impossibility of replacing any other. More precisely, their reflections point to the difficulty of imagining oneself taking the place of someone who *lives in me*. This difficulty raises new questions about the sense of ownness and one's own body.

The experience of a pregnant woman diverts from the paradigmatic case in three respects (for a detailed explication of this argument, see Heinämaa 2005a).

First, the other's body that the woman experiences is *not* somewhere *there at a distance* but here present with her, in every movement and position of her own body. There is no variable distance between the two but a permanent closeness or proximity. Second, the woman *cannot see* the movements, positions, and gestures of the other inside her, but she *can feel* them. This means that the spatiality of her own moving body proves to be more complex than in the paradigmatic cases studied in the tradition.

509

The body is not a solid closed volume but has an internal space capable of opening to an other. Third, woman's relation to her unborn child lacks that particular form of *reciprocity* that is characteristic of the paradigmatic examples of phenomenology: two visible subjects gazing at each other at distance. The symmetry of such perceptions had already been described by Husserl in the fifth Cartesian Meditation; and later his followers repeated the description in their own terminology, Sartre, for example, by writing: "if the other-as-object is defined in contact with the world, as the object which sees what I see, then my fundamental contact with the other-as-subject must be able to be referred back to my permanent possibility of *being seen* by the other" (Sartre 1966: 345).

Against this Beauvoir and her followers, Kristeva and Irigaray, point out that women relate to their unborn children in a different way. Reciprocity – this particular mode of symmetrical reciprocity – is not (yet) established. For even if we could perhaps say that the child's body is, or lives, in the perceptual field of the woman, we should not assume that the woman's body is given to the child in a similar or analogous way as a perceptual object. Rather the maternal body constitutes for the child the whole field of possible tactile sensations.

At the core of these feminist discussions is the claim that experientially the feminine body has a specific proprioceptic, kinesthetic, and morphological organization, different from that of the male body. For the woman, her body is not constituted as a solid object but rather as a fold which is capable of opening up to form an inner space that can house another sensing being. This opening is experienced in erotic encounters but more vigorously in pregnancy. Thus the others that are crucial for the constitution of intersubjective space and objectivity are not always "there at a distance" but can also be "here within me."

Sexual Hierarchy

Beauvoir's *The Second Sex* also includes a powerful argument against sexual hierarchies. Beauvoir argues that the inequality between men and women has no basis in nature or in any historical telos, but is established by human activity and practice – and reestablished and reaffirmed by our own actions. Thus, we ourselves are responsible for the existence and permanence of the sexual hierarchy. To understand and evaluate this argument, one must go into Beauvoir's account of the origin of values. Beauvoir did not include this account in *The Second Sex* – she took it for granted, because she had already presented it a few years earlier, in the essays *Pyrrhus et Cinéas* (1944) and *The Ethics of Ambiguity* (*Pour une morale de l'ambïguité*, 1947; cited as Beauvoir 1994).

Many commentators have assumed that Beauvoir explains the sexual hierarchy through the biological differences that we can detect between males and females. Some have argued that Beauvoir's account is noncoherent or self-contradictory, as it includes an extensive discussion on bodily differences and the well-known antinaturalistic thesis "One is not born, but rather becomes, a woman" (Beauvoir 1972: 295). So it seems that Beauvoir vacillates between two incompatible opinions, between foundationalistic biologism and extreme constructionism.

510

Such readings disregard Beauvoir's existentialist–phenomenological approach. In the first chapter of the work, entitled "Destiny," Beauvoir indeed introduces three explanatory factors: biological differences (strength), psychological differences (virility), and practical–economical differences (tools). However, she does not present these explanations as her own but takes a critical stand and calls into question their explanatory power and experiential basis. Instead of affirming these grounds she concludes that none of them suffices to account for the sexual hierarchy. Even when combined, they fail to show how the hierarchy was, or could have been, established.

Beauvoir then argues that we can only understand the nature and establishment of the hierarchy if we turn to existentialist ethics. For a long time this was taken as a reference to Sartre's philosophy. Scholarly work has shown, however, that Beauvoir did not base her ethics on Sartre's concepts. She had her own original account, which was motivated and influenced also by the insights of existentialists (Kierkegaard and Nietzsche), phenomenologists (Husserl, Heidegger, Levinas, and Merleau-Ponty), and feminists (Wollstonecraft and Woolf).

In *The Ethics of Ambiguity*, Beauvoir rejects all absolutist – naturalistic as well as historicistic – theories of values by arguing that values are dependent on our own activities. Thus no value or end is absolutely given; everything refers back to human activities and practices. Beauvoir writes: "It is desire which creates the desirable, and the project that sets up the end. It is human existence which makes values spring up in the world on the basis of which it will be able to judge the enterprise in which it will be engaged" (Beauvoir 1994: 15). *The Second Sex* applies this idea in its account of sexuality. Beauvoir states: "It is by exercising sexual activity that men [humans] define the sexes and their relations, just as they create the sense and the value of all the functions that they accomplish" (Beauvoir 1972: 38; translation modified).

Beauvoir's argument about the sexual hierarchy is not based on any system of values but on the realization that we must be ready to call into question all values that we find implied in the descriptions of the sexual relation. In the case of the bioscientific paradigm, this means that the goals of survival and reproduction that form the basis of all biological explanations of sexual relations must be problematized. In the case of psychoanalytic explanations, it is necessary to study how the implicit privileging of the phallus directs the interpretation of women's desires and pleasures (for a detailed explication of this argument, see Heinämaa 2005b). And finally, in the case of historical materialism, one needs to study the origins of the ideas of ownership and technology. Beauvoir ends the introductory chapter of *The Second Sex* by writing:

> In our attempt to discover woman we shall not reject certain contributions of biology, of psychoanalysis, and of historical materialism; but we shall hold that the body, the sexual life, and techniques exist concretely for man only in so far as he grasps them in the total perspective of his existence. The value of the muscular strength, of the phallus, of the tool can be defined only in the world of values: it is determined by the fundamental project in which the existent transcends himself toward being. (Beauvoir 1972: 91; translation modified)

To sum up, Beauvoir argues that a truly philosophical inquiry into the sexual hierarchy cannot be founded on the values of life, procreation, or physical strength. On the contrary, it must also include a critical examination of these values, how they are constituted, in what kinds of activities, and how these activities relate to sexuality and sexual difference.

Later Developments

Later feminist phenomenology develops further Beauvoir's accounts of embodiment, sexuality, difference, and identity, but it also questions many results and starting points of classical phenomenology.

On the constructive side, investigations mainly focus on three areas of experience: motility and spatiality, pregnancy and maternity, and erotic relations and sexual pleasure. Combining phenomenological concepts with pragmatist insight and empirical results from anthropology, psychology, and social sciences, American and British theorists illuminate differences in men's and women's experiences of their own bodies and spatial relations. Iris Marion Young argues, in her well-known essay "Throwing like a girl" (Young 1990), that men and women experience the spatiality and motility of their own bodies differently. In Young's account, this difference is established in early interactive situations and strengthened by social norms. Young's work also includes investigations into the experience of pregnancy and the experience of being "breasted." Carol Bigwood (1991), Jean Grimshaw (1999), and Amy Mullin (2002) further develop such experiential accounts of motility and pregnancy.

Many feminist thinkers influenced by phenomenology have focused their investigations on the phenomena of birth, natality, and maternity. Two simple facts of experience have been emphasized as being overlooked by the philosophical tradition: all humans are born from women, and only women can nurse other human beings in their own bodies. Feminist theorists, from Julia Kristeva to Christina Schües, argue that if we take these facts into consideration, then we must radically change our understanding of the human condition, finitude and mortality, love and desire.

Still other feminist phenomenologists have articulated the difference in men's and women's experiences of desire and erotic love. This was a central topic in the so-called "French feminism" or "écriture féminine" of the 1970s and 1980s but is also a recurrent theme in Beauvoir scholarship. Thus we can find discussions on women's sensual pleasures, enjoyment, and desire in Irigaray's and Hélène Cixous's early essays as well as in contemporary readings of Beauvoir, for example by Debra Bergoffen (1997) and Eleanor Holveck (2002).

In the destructive or deconstructive side, feminist critics have claimed that classical phenomenology suffers from and is restricted by Husserl's foundationalist epistemological interests. Based on the works of Heidegger and Merleau-Ponty, feminist phenomenologists have problematized the focus on science and cognition, and argued that our primary relation to the perceived world is practical and affective. We do not see things from a disinterested position but handle them as instruments, tools, and materials in our practical encounter with the world. Sciences are not simply elements of an objective universal movement of reason, but serve the interest in domination and control.

These critiques emphasize crucial factors of experience and correct severe misunderstandings about the resources of phenomenology, but they often present the classical phenomenological position in a partial light. First, Husserl does not claim that the disinterested view is our primordial or concrete relation to the world as humans; he argues that it is one of our possibilities. Second, his idea of a rigorous science is not intended as a description of the factual state of the sciences or of philosophy. Rather it aims to capture the sense that motivates all scientific enterprises.

More fundamentally, post-phenomenological thinkers have questioned the idea of a universal science and phenomenology as its self-conscious foundation. The most challenging critiques take their starting point in Nietzsche's and Foucault's genealogies and inquiry back to the contingent historical roots of phenomenology itself. In this vein, Judith Butler (1990) questions the Beauvoirian legacy. She rejects the phenomenological account of sexual difference as subjectivistic and voluntaristic. Further, she argues that our understanding of the relations of sex, bodies, and power remains naïve as long as we understand power as merely restrictive. Basing herself on Foucault's works, Butler argues that sexual identities are not founded on anything internal or immanent in the subject, but are contingent effects and products of external forces. This critical Nietzschean insight is shared by other feminist scholars influenced by Foucault and Deleuze, such as Moira Gatens (1996), Elisabeth Grosz (1994), and Rosi Braidotti (1991, 1994). They all argue that the phenomenological approach boils down to a form of internalism or essentialism.

Some leading feminist phenomenologists have indeed suggested that sexual difference is a necessary essential part of human experience. Based on such statements, phenomenology has been classified among essentialistic and even biologist positions. But such characterizations are misleading in suggesting that the main contribution of phenomenology is in an argument for the existence of essences. This is not the case, for even if phenomenology includes descriptions and analyses of the essential aspects of sexuality, sexual identity, and sexual difference, it also necessitates a fundamental inquiry into the constitution of all essences.

References and Further Reading

Arp, K. (2001) *The Bonds of Freedom: Simone de Beauvoir's Existentialist Ethics*. Chicago and La Salle, IL: Open Court.

Bauer, N. (2001) *Simone de Beauvoir, Philosophy, and Feminism*. New York: Columbia University Press.

Beauvoir, S. de (1972) *The Second Sex* (trans. and ed. H. M. Parshley). Harmondsworth: Penguin (original work published 1949).

—— (1993) *Le deuxième sexe I: Les faits et les mythes* [The second sex: the facts and myths]. Paris: Gallimard (original work published 1949).

—— (1994) *The Ethics of Ambiguity* (trans. B. Frechtman). New York: Carol Publishing Group Editions (original work published 1947).

Bergoffen, D. B. (1997) *The Philosophy of Simone de Beauvoir: Gendered Phenomenologies, Erotic Generosities*. Albany: State University of New York Press.

Bigwood, C. (1991) Renaturalizing the body (with a little help from Merleau-Ponty). *Hypatia* 6, 3, 54–73.

Braidotti, R. (1991) *Patterns of Dissonance: A Study of Women and Contemporary Philosophy* (trans. E. Guild). Cambridge: Polity Press.

—— (1994) *Nomadic Subjects: Embodiment and Sexual Difference in Contemporary Theory*. New York: Columbia University Press.

Butler, J. (1990) *Gender Trouble: Feminism and the Subversion of Identity*. New York, London: Routledge.

Chanter, T. (1995) *The Ethics of Eros: Irigaray's Rewriting of the Philosophers*. London and New York: Routledge.

Fisher, L., and L. Embree (eds.) (2000) *Feminist Phenomenology: Contributions to Phenomenology vol. 40*. Dordrecht: Kluwer.

Gatens, M. (1996) *Imaginary Bodies: Ethics, Power and Corporeality*. London and New York: Routledge.

Goto, H. (2004) *Der Begriff der Person in der Phänomenologie Edmund Husserls: Ein Interpretationsversuch der Husserlschen Phänomenologie als Ethik im Hinblick auf den Begriff der Habitualität*. [The concept of the person in the phenomenology of Edmund Husserl: an attempt at an interpretation of Husserlian phenomenology as ethics in view of the concept of habituality]. Würzburg: Königshausen & Neuman.

Grimshaw, J. (1999) Working out with Merleau-Ponty. In J. Arthurs and J. Grimshaw (eds.), *Women's Bodies: Discipline and Transgression* (pp. 91–116). London and New York: Cassell.

Grosz, E. (1994) *Volatile Bodies: Toward a Corporeal Feminism*. Bloomington and Indianapolis: Indiana University Press.

Heinämaa, S. (2003) *Toward a Phenomenology of Sexual Difference: Husserl, Merleau-Ponty, Beauvoir*. Lanham, MD; Boulder, CO; New York, and London: Rowman & Littlefield.

—— (2005a) On Luce Irigaray's inquiries into intersubjectivity: Between the feminine body and its other. In M. Cimitile and E. Miller (eds.), *Returning to Irigaray* (pp. 15–35). Albany: State University of New York Press.

—— (2005b) "Through desire and love": Simone de Beauvoir on the possibilities of sexual desire. In E. Mortensen (ed.), *Sex, Breath and Force*. Lanham: Lexington, forthcoming.

—— (2005c) Verwunderung und sexuelle Differenz: Luce Irigarays phänomenologischer Cartesianismus [Wonder and sexual difference: Luce Irigaray's phenomenological Cartesianism] (trans. S. Stoller). In L. Fisher, S. Stoller, and V. Vasterling (eds.), *Feminist Phenomenology and Hermeneutics*. Würzburg: Köningshausen & Neumann.

Holveck, E. (2002) *Simone De Beauvoir's Philosophy of Lived Experience*. Lanham, MD; Boulder, CO; New York, and London: Rowman & Littlefield.

Husserl, E. (1960) *Cartesian Meditations* (trans. D. Cairns). Dordrecht and Boston: Martinus Nijhoff (original work published 1950).

—— (1988) *The Crisis of European Sciences and Transcendental Phenomenology: An Introduction to Phenomenological Philosophy* (trans. D. Carr). Evanston, IL: Northwestern University Press (original work published 1954).

—— (1993) *Ideas Pertaining to a Pure Phenomenology and to a Phenomenological Philosophy, Second Book: Studies in the Phenomenological Constitution* (trans. R. Rojcewicz and A. Schuwer). Dordrecht, Boston, and London: Kluwer (original work published 1952).

Irigaray, L. (1993) *An Ethics of Sexual Difference* (trans. C. Burke and G. C. Gill). Ithaca, NY: Cornell University Press (original work published 1984).

Kristeva, J. (1980) Motherhood according to Giovanni Bellini. In T. Gora, A. Jardine, and L. S. Roudiez (eds.), *Desire in Language* (pp. 237–70). New York: Columbia University Press (original work published 1975).

Lundgren-Gothlin, E. (1996) *Sex and Existence: Simone de Beauvoir's* The Second Sex (trans. L. Schenck). London: Athlone (original work published 1992).

Marion, J-L. (2002) Flesh or the givenness of the self. In *In Excess: Studies of Saturated Phenomena* (trans. R. Horner and V. Berrand) (pp. 82–103). New York: Fordham University Press (original work published 2001).

514

Merleau-Ponty, M. (1964) *Signs* (trans. R. C. McCleary). Evanston, IL: Northwestern University Press (original work published 1960).

—— (1995) *Phenomenology of Perception* (trans. C. Smith). New York: Routledge & Kegan Paul (original work published 1945).

Mullin, A. (2002) Pregnant bodies, pregnant minds. *Hypatia*, 3(1), 27–44.

Nietzsche, F. (2001) *The Gay Science with a Prelude in German Rhymes and an Appendix of Songs* (trans. J. Nauckhoff and A. Del Caro; ed. B. Williams). Cambridge: Cambridge University Press (original work published 1882).

O'Brien, W., and L. Embree (eds.) (2001) *The Existential Phenomenology of Simone de Beauvoir. Contributions to Phenomenology, vol. 43*. Dordrecht: Kluwer.

Oksala, J. (2004) What is feminist phenomenology? Thinking birth philosophically. *Radical Philosophy*, 126, 16–22.

Sartre, J-P. (1966) *Being and Nothingness: A Phenomenological Essay on Ontology* (trans. H. E. Barnes). New York: Washington Square Press (original work published 1943).

Simons, M. (ed.) (1995) *Feminist Interpretations of Simone de Beauvoir*. University Park: Pennsylvania State University Press.

Stein, E. (1959) *Die Frau: Ihre Aufgabe nach Natur und Gnade* [The woman: her role according to nature and grace]. *Edith Steins Werke 5*. Freiburg: Herder.

—— (2000) *Die Frau: Fragestellungen und Reflexionen* [The woman: questions and reflections]. *Edith Stein Gesamtausgabe 13* (ed. M. Linssen). Freiburg, Basel, and Vienna: Herder.

—— (2004) *Der Aufbau der menschlichen Person. Vorlesung (1932/33) zur philosophischen Anthropologie* [The constitution of the human being: lectures on philosophical anthropology], *Edith Stein Gesamtausgabe 14* (ed. B. Beckmann-Zöller). Freiburg, Basel, and Vienna: Herder (original work published 1994).

Stoller, S., V. Vasterling, and L. Fisher (eds.) (2005) *Feministische Phänomenologie und Hermeneutik* [Feminist phenomenology and hermeneutics]. Würzburg: Köningshausen & Neumann.

Stoller, S., and H. Vetter (eds.) (1997) *Phänomenologie und Geschlechterdifferenz* [Phenomenology and sexual difference]. Vienna: Universitätsverlag.

Welton, D. (1998) Affectivity, eros and the body. In D. Welton (ed.), *Body and Flesh: A Philosophical Reader*. Oxford: Blackwell.

—— (1999) Soft, smooth hands: Husserl's phenomenology of the lived-body. In D. Welton (ed.), *The Body: Classical and Contemporary Readings* (pp. 38–56). Oxford: Blackwell.

Welton, D. (ed.) (1999) *The Body: Classical and Contemporary Readings*. Oxford: Blackwell.

Young, I. M. (1990) *Throwing Like a Girl and Other Essays in Feminist Philosophy and Social Theory*. Bloomington and Indianapolis: Indiana University Press.

Zahavi, D. (1994) Husserl's phenomenology of the body. *Études phénoménologiques*, 19, 63–84.

35

A Life Worth Living

JULIAN YOUNG

Camus opens the *Myth of Sisyphus* with the famous assertion that "There is but one truly serious philosophical problem and that is suicide. Judging whether life is or is not worth living amounts to answering the fundamental question of philosophy" (Camus 2000: 11). And he is, I would say, right. The traditionally most fundamental question, the question of the nature of the good life, makes the presupposition that there *is* such a thing as a good life and is therefore logically posterior to Camus's question.

Of course, a question can be both fundamental and very quickly answered. Camus's view is that for much of the history of the West the answer was indeed both quick and affirmative. For modern humanity, however, this is not the case. For us, there is something of which we are, to one degree or another, aware which makes the question of life's worth a genuine "problem." He calls it "the absurd." This threatens suicide because, from time to time, it produces the "feeling of the absurd" (Camus 2000: 32) or, "as a writer of today [namely, Sartre] calls it," "nausea" (Camus 2000: 21); a great "weariness" (Camus 2000: 21), a saying "no" to life (Camus 2000: 14), a "longing for death" (Camus 2000: 13).

* * *

What, then, is the source of this deadly feeling? What is "the absurd"? Camus says, and reemphasizes several times, that the absurd is not a property the world has by itself. Rather, it is the product of a confrontation between "human need," on the one hand, and "the unreasonable silence of the world" (Camus 2000: 32), on the other. The absurd lies in the failure of reality – a failure of "absurd" proportions – to satisfy a fundamental human need. What is this need?

One thing that is clear is that it is a need that used to be satisfied, for Western humanity, by Christianity. The problem of the absurd, Camus is quite explicit, is created by the death of God (Camus 2000: 7).

Unfortunately for the clarity of *The Myth*, Camus cites no less than three different, supposed human needs as needs which used to be satisfied, but which, in a post-death-of God-universe, no longer are. In fact, therefore, he proposed no such thing as "*the* absurd," but deals, rather, in three types of absurdity which, *prima facie* at least, are quite distinct from each other.

The first of the alleged needs which Camus takes to be fundamental to the human being is the desire for a "meaning of life" (Camus 2000: 12), for "a great idea that will transcend [life] . . . and give it meaning" (Camus 2000: 15). What "life" means, here, is "history." In this sense, Christianity gave meaning to life by postulating a last judgment, an end of history. Camus observes that Hegelian Marxism preserves this idea within a post-supernaturalistic context in that it posits the coming into being of the communist paradise, "a miraculous event at the end of time." For this reason, together with the evident spuriousness of its claim to scientific status and its cruelty (Camus is defending himself, here, against Sartre and the French Marxist intelligentsia), he classifies it as a religion, a new "faith," a "new mystification" (Camus 2000: 188–9).

The sense of life's absurdity as consisting in the absence of an end of history figures quite prominently in *The Myth*: the disillusioned Marxist, for example, who thinks that "the one useful action [is] that of remaking man and earth" – remaking them once and for all – finds all action futile and life nauseating since, in the end, "nothing of himself lasts, not even his doctrines" (Camus 2000: 81–3). And, of course, the figure of Sisyphus himself, condemned by the gods, for all eternity, to push his rock to the top of the mountain only to see it roll to the bottom again, is, *inter alia*, supposed to suggest the futility of an existence in which every human achievement – Goethe's works and even his name – will, in ten thousand years, be nothing but dust (Camus 2000: 74).

The second supposed need that figures prominently in the *Myth* is the desire that reality should be intelligible through and through. It is "an appetite for clarity," for "understanding the world [by] . . . reducing it to the human, stamping it with the human seal" (Camus 2000: 27). Christianity satisfied this desire by postulating a God who created both the human mind and the ultimate structure of reality in the image of his own mind. But with the death of God we are no longer able to believe in such isomorphisms. Reality has become fundamentally opaque, "dense . . . foreign and irreducible to us" (Camus 2000: 20). And hence, Camus suggests, nauseating.

The third fundamental desire, the one most obviously left unsatisfied by the death of God, is the desire for an assurance of the non-finality of death.[1] Now that we can no longer believe Christianity's "pretty little speeches about the soul," Camus observes, nothing protects us from the "horror" of death as absolute extinction. In such horror, he claims, we have an "elementary and definitive" experience of the absurd (Camus 2000: 21).

*   *   *

The first of these alleged types of absurdity I shall not discuss further since it is, I believe, a fiction. Given the general significance of Schopenhauer's observation that, having placed every trial and tribulation in this life there was nothing left for Christian writers to assign to the hereafter save boredom (a point essentially repeated in Margaret Atwood's simple but telling observation that "there is no narrative without conflict"), I do not believe that anyone genuinely desires an "end of time."[2] My topic, rather,

517

is the third type of absurdity, though toward the end of the chapter I shall have something to say about the second.

*   *   *

Camus lived his entire life under the shadow of tuberculosis. Correspondingly, *The Myth of Sisyphus* is, as James Wood observes, "an extraordinarily death-visited work" (Camus 2000: x). Like all really important philosophy, one is tempted to say, it is, above everything else, a meditation on death.

Throughout Camus's works, death is presented as the *summum malum*, as "man's worst enemy" (Camus 2000: 21), "the supreme abuse" (Camus 2000: 84). For modern humanity, death, death as absolute extinction, is, not merely "bitter," but a "hideous" (Camus 2000: 134) and terrifying object of "horror" (Camus 2000: 21, 135). Such horror is not, for Camus, something that hits us only in bad moments or special circumstances. Rather, as Woods remarks, for Camus "the very image of the human is the man condemned to death" (Camus 2000: x). Though it may be acknowledged with greater or lesser degrees of clarity, the menace of death – the fact that it must claim us and may do so at any moment – gives our lives the permanent character of "anxiety" and "anguish" (Camus 2000: 19, 28). It is no wonder, then, Camus implies, that we find life nauseating. Given a choice between never having existed and life on death row, who would ever choose the latter?

Camus says that "great feelings" such as the feeling of the absurd carry with them the picture of an entire universe (Camus 2000: 17–18). Borrowing a term from Heidegger (whom Camus regards as delineating with great accuracy the absurdity of the human condition (Camus 2000: 19, 27–9)), we may say that fundamental to Camus's portrait of the universe is "the nothing" (Camus's own word is actually "the night" (Camus 2000: 110). The bleakness of the post-death-of-God universe is created by the fact that that which lies on the other side of this life and world – that which *is* the other side – is the nothing, the absolute void, the abyss which we must enter one day and may enter at any moment. The primary object of nausea, we may say, is the nothing.

*   *   *

Camus's aim, however, is to show that in spite of the menace of the nothing life is still worth living. Even in the face of a clear and distinct knowledge of the abyss, life remains a magnificent enterprise, suicide absolutely "not legitimate" (Camus 2000: 7). His strategy for convincing himself and us of this is to construct a portrait of "the absurd man," as he calls him: someone who lives in the light of a vivid and unflinching knowledge of the nothing but lives, nevertheless, a life that, in both his own and our eyes, is clearly – indeed splendidly – worthwhile.

*   *   *

The first defining characteristic of the absurd hero is "integrity." He[3] lives "without appeal" (Camus 2000: 53), without the "solace" of comforting "myths" (Camus 2000: 135). This distinguishes him from someone like Kierkegaard who makes what Camus calls "the leap" into absurd belief. The "leaper," that is, is someone who, recognizing that "reason" says that there is no God, but believing, too, that the consequence of this conclusion is "despair," decides to reject reason. If belief in God is irrational, he decides, so much the worse for reason.

Strangely indifferent to the question of whether it is even possible to *choose* to believe in God, Camus views this amputation of the one distinctive and ennobling human attribute as a form of self-mutilation, an insult to human "pride" and "dignity." He views it, indeed, as a form of suicide; "philosophical suicide," he calls it (Camus 2000: 32–51). Though tempted by the leap, the absurd hero, sharing Camus's "scorn" (see Camus 2000: 109) for self-mutilation, rejects it. Indeed, recognizing the threat of backsliding, he turns the preservation of *both* a clear and vivid awareness the nothing *and* his need for a transcendent "something" into an "*ascesis*," a daily discipline. He is careful, that is, to avoid "negating [either] . . . of the terms of the opposition" that constitute the absurdity – the absurdly conflicted character – of the human condition (Camus 2000: 53, 104).

The second defining characteristic of the absurd hero is what Camus calls "revolt." To have vividly in mind both the nothing and the fundamental need for a transcendent "something" is to be aware of the fundamentally nauseating character of human existence. And to be aware of that is to receive an "invitation" to suicide. Life in the valley of the shadow of death is intolerable. Better, therefore, that its end should come sooner rather than later. "Revolt," however, is the *refusal* of this invitation to easeful death. "Revolt is the certainty of a crushing fate, without the resignation that ought to accompany it" (Camus 2000: 54).

It is revolt which, according to Camus, gives value to the absurd hero's life; "the dogged revolt against his condition," "perseverance" with a thoroughly unsatisfactory existence is what constitutes "man's sole dignity" (Camus 2000: 104). Revolt gives the absurd hero's life "majesty." "There is," Camus writes, no finer sight" (Camus 2000: 54).

* * *

This "finest sight" is embodied, above all, in the figure of Sisyphus. Not, of course, Sisyphus the immortal (an odd figure after whom to name a discussion of the pros and cons of suicide), but rather Sisyphus, that "proletarian of the gods" (Camus 2000: 109), who is the modern industrial worker performing his repetitive tasks on the assembly line. Really, however, Sisyphus is all of us as we live out the endlessly repeated patterns – office, work, home, sleep, office, work – which, as Camus points out (Camus 2000: 19), make up our daily round.

The Sisyphean is entirely "lucid" about the nauseating character of his condition. The question "why?" – why carry on with life of toil and anguish in the valley of the shadow of death? – receives no answer (Camus 2000: 19). Fully acquainted with the nothing, he knows the emptiness of those "pretty little speeches about the soul," knows that the tale that through his works he can attain eternal salvation is a complete fiction. Nonetheless he carries on with "dogged" heroism, full of "scorn" for the weakness of those who give in to literal or philosophical suicide. The words that best sum up Sisyphus' self-appreciation are, says Camus, those of Oedipus: "despite so many ordeals . . . the nobility of my soul makes me conclude that all is well" (Camus 2000: 109). "We must," concludes Camus, "imagine Sisyphus happy" (Camus 2000: 111) – happy at his own noble heroism.

Notice that Sisyphus is an essentially "macho," in Camus's own language "virile" (Camus 2000: 11), figure. (Hence my observation in note 2 about the necessity for the masculine pronoun.) The virtues by which he judges himself an admirable figure are intelligence, scorn for the telling of lies (either to others or oneself), courage, and "perseverance" or "doggedness" (Camus 2000: 104). Sisyphus is, above all, *tough*. He is the big boy who never cries. He is an embodiment of "warrior" or, as Nietzsche calls it, "master" morality.

*   *   *

This, however, is not the end of the account of what makes Sisyphus' life worth living. Quite abruptly – abruptly, because up to now his life has been described as one of "torment" and "torture" (Camus 2000: 108–9) – a further reason for his happiness appears. Oedipus' phrase "all is well" sums up Sisyphus' self-appraisal not only on account of his "nobility," but also because "all of Sisyphus' silent joy is contained therein." The "absurd man," that is to say – Sisyphus and he have now become one and the same – by fully acknowledging the nothing, has become the one who "silences all the idols." But this means that "[i]n a universe suddenly restored to its silence, the myriad wondering little voices of the earth rise up" (Camus 2000: 110). Living in the light of the nothing, that is to say, the Sisyphean becomes intensely aware of the fragile wonder of existence. His rock becomes "his thing" (ibid.). He loves its sensuous, stony surface and, one may imagine, the feeling of his own bodily health, as he pushes it up the mountain. (We may, perhaps, picture the happy Sisyphus as a fitness freak working out in a great, outdoor gym, happy to replace the un-music of the indoor gym with the great silence of nature.) "There is," says Camus, "no sun without shadow, and it is essential to know the night" (ibid.). We *need* the nothing, that is to say, to become alive to the wonder and value of the "something."

*   *   *

This idea, the idea of a rapturous, ecstatic existence facilitated by and dependent on an acute sensitivity to the nothing, the idea that "happiness and the absurd are two sons of the same earth" (Camus 2000: 110),[4] is the root notion behind the figures of Don Juan and "the actor" (Camus 2000: 66–79) offered, in *The Myth*, as "examples" or "images" of the absurd hero. Vividly aware of the nothing, vividly aware of the menace of death, vividly aware, as we put it, that "life is not a rehearsal," Don Juan and the actor live lives that are characterized by the urgency, intensity, and heightened awareness that comes from living on the edge of "danger" (Camus 2000: 53). They live by what Camus calls the "ethics of quantity" (Camus 2000: 69), live lives of, by all normal standards, extraordinary "excess" (Camus 2000: 78). The Don seduces more women in an evening than most men manage in a lifetime, the person who lives like an actor lives, "in three hours," an entire life and then flings himself into another. Devoted to "dispersion," his existence represents (here Camus alludes to the Church's traditional disapproval of actors and – especially – actresses) a "heretical multiplication of souls" (ibid.).

*   *   *

This idea of an extraordinary "passion for living" (Camus 2000: 12), of a rapturous, intense, urgent existence tied, essentially, to an aliveness to the nothing, is further pursued in the lyrical essays written a few years either side of *The Myth*, specifically, "Summer in Algiers," "The Minotaur," and "Helen's Exile." Writing amid the grimness of wartime and immediately post-war Paris, Camus recalls the Algeria of his youth, recalls, above all, its summertime. He recalls Algiers as a place where "whoever is young and alive . . . finds occasions for triumph everywhere: in the bay, the sun, the red and white games on the seaward terraces, the flowers and sports stadiums, the cool-legged girls" (Camus 2000: 128). Algeria, he writes, is a place where

> every summer morning seems to be the first in the world. Each twilight seems to be the last, the solemn agony announced at sunset by a final glow that darkens every hue. The sea [Camus's palette, here, seems very close to Van Gogh's] is ultramarine, the road the colour of clotted blood, the beach yellow. Everything disappears with the green sun: an hour later the dunes are bathed in moonlight. There are incomparable nights under a rain of stars. (Camus 2000: 160)

Algiers is a place where one says not "go for" but rather "indulge" in a swim. It is a place where people are not, as in Europe, "nudists" – those tedious "Protestants of the flesh" – but are simply "comfortable in the sunlight." It is a place where people live with Greek "*naiveté*": "living through the body," the young men, as they run along the beaches, "repeat the gestures of the athletes of Delos" (Camus 2000: 129). And it is a place where (like the happy Sisyphus) one cannot fail to "participate in [the] . . . dialogue of stone and flesh in tune with the seasons" (Camus 2000: 130). Camus recalls returning to the inner harbor from a day-long canoeing expedition with the friends of his boyhood: "how," he asks, "can I fail to feel that I am piloting through the smooth waters a savage cargo of gods in whom I recognise my brothers?" (ibid.).

How do these beings – at once friends of Camus's youth and reincarnations of the Greeks – live? Like the absurd hero of *The Myth*, they live "without solace," without appeal to comforting "myths" (Camus 2000: 135), to any "deceptive divinity" (Camus 2000: 136). They live with total "lucidity" with respect to the nothing (Camus 2000: 127), and as a consequence live, like Don Juan and the actor, with "a haste that borders on waste" (Camus 2000: 132). In this land where "a thirty-year old workman has already played all the cards in his hand" (ibid.), life is "not to be built up but to be burned up. Stopping to think and becoming better are out of the question" (Camus 2000: 133) for "this race wholly cast into its present lives" (Camus 2000: 135).

A final remark elevates Camus's memories to the status of philosophy: "I have the mad hope that, without knowing it perhaps, these barbarians lounging on the beaches are actually modelling the image of a culture in which the image of man will at last find its true likeness" (ibid.). Camus is playing, here, for high stakes. The absurd hero is offered as the model for a European renewal which is to take the form of a renaissance of the pre-birth-of-God age of the Greeks.

* * *

I turn now to the task of clarifying and, where necessary, rethinking Camus's account of how to live a worthwhile life in a post-death-of-God universe. As the discussion proceeds, I shall turn to Heidegger for assistance.

For the absurd hero, as we have just seen, life is not to be "built up" but rather "burned up." Unlike "everyday man" who "lives with aims," the absurd man has none (Camus 2000: 56). No long-term aims, at least. Short-term intentions, of course, must surely flit across the minds of the barbarian gods along with all the other flotsam of consciousness. What, however, is entirely excluded from their lives is "building"; that is, as the Germans call it, *Bildung* (self-education in the broadest sense of the word). What is entirely "out of the question" is "becoming better" (Camus 2000: 133), scripting one's life as if writing a *Bildungsroman*, a novel of education, a narrative of progression through "learning experiences" from immaturity toward a fully realized self. What is excluded is the formation of an ideal conception of the self that then provides the basis for a life of disciplined self-development. "Men with a purpose," says Camus scornfully, live in the city. In Algiers (though technically a city, Camus treats this provincial backwater as little more than a backdrop to the beaches) there is nothing for them (Camus 2000: 142). Their state of mind is captured in the remark of Hegel (the arch-*Bildungsroman*cer, of course) that "Only the modern city offers the mind a field in which it can become aware of itself" (Camus 2000: 169).

But what, actually, is so wrong with "everyday man" and his "aims"? What is wrong with "building up" a life? What is wrong, Camus claims, is that the man with aims "weighs up his chances, . . . counts on 'some day,' his retirement, the labour of his sons" (Camus 2000: 56). He lives, in short, a modified form of the Christian life, lives "in the future." The absurd hero, on the other hand, manifests nothing but "indifference" toward the future (Camus 2000: 59). He lives in "the present and the succession of presents" (Camus 2000: 62).

Here, I think, Camus falls into error. To be sure, there is a kind of "living in the future," the kind Camus talks about, which the absurd hero – indeed anyone with any sense – will abhor. This is the life of perpetually "deferred gratification," the life in which the present is seen as nothing but an end in itself, valueless means of arriving at a supposed Shangri-La of the future, the life that is so brilliantly pilloried by Schopenhauer. People, Schopenhauer writes, usually live

> In the expectation of better things . . . On the other hand the present is accepted only for the time being, is set at naught, and looked upon merely as the path to the goal. Thus when at the end of their lives most men look back, they will find that they have lived throughout *ad interim*; they will be surprised to see that the very thing they allowed to slip by unappreciated and unenjoyed was just their life, precisely that in the expectation of which they had lived. (Schopenhauer 1974: 285–6)

The absurd hero, always aware of the menace of death, will avoid this error of *Lebensweisheit* (life-wisdom).

But that this is an error does not at all mean that every life lived in the light of a projected future is an error. Specifically, it does not mean that the life of *Bildung* is one. For it may very well be that a major part of living intensely "in the present" consists, precisely, in knowing oneself to be in the process of "building up" a life.

Nietzsche remarks that the "will to power" is always the will to more power. On one reading this is the plausible claim that a sense of development, growth, ascending movement, continual self-overcoming, is essential to a flourishing human life, to a life, specifically, that flourishes "in the present." It is in the light of this remark that we can see, I think, that there is something wrong with the lives of Don Juan, the actor, and the friends of Camus's youth – given that the latter are offered as models, not merely of youth, but of an entire life. The problem with these lives is that they are entirely *static* and in the end, therefore, boring. The Don learns nothing from his love affairs; no affair is in any way enriched by its predecessors. And the same is true for the actor – for Toad of Toad Hall or the "democratic soul" of Plato's *Republic*. In short, though Camus is right to insist that life must be lived "in the present," and right to warn against the kind of obsession with the future that ruins the present, he is wrong to exclude "building" from the life of the absurd hero. On the contrary, the right kind of building, I would, with Nietzsche, suggest, is actually essential if such a life is to be a flourishing one. Certainly – to indulge in a momentary *ad hominem* – Camus himself abandoned Algeria for the Paris, became himself a "man of purpose."

* * *

Camus's insufficiently nuanced attitude to "aims" is not, however, the major difficulty in his account of the absurd hero. The major problem is as follows.

What we have seen is that the "happiness" of the absurd hero, Sisyphus' happiness, is, in fact, over-determined. On the one hand, we are compelled to "imagine Sisyphus happy" because of his (somewhat self-congratulatory) awareness of his own "nobility" of soul, his refusal to resign from a life ruined by the lucid awareness of death and with nothing to recommend it other than his own refusal to resign. On the other hand, however, Sisyphus is said to be happy because of his rapturous awareness of the "wondering little voices," the sensuous joys, of the earth, a rapture made possible precisely by lucid knowledge of the nothing. But if that is true, then Sisyphus' life has, in fact, a *great deal* to recommend it and there is no possibility of gaining "dignity" through a "dogged revolt" (Camus 2000: 104) against the "resignation" demanded by an intolerable condition.

There is, in short, a fundamental *contradiction* contained in Camus's description of the absurd hero. Sisyphus cannot *both* be happy on account of his own noble "perseverance" in the face of a condition that is nothing but "torment" and "anguish" *and* live a life that is filled with rapture. The absurd hero cannot be *both* "in revolt" and "in rapture."

How should we proceed from here? How should we modify the description of the absurd hero so that his life is an at least *possible* life? It seems to me clear that what we should do is to abandon the idea of "revolt" which, in fact, seems to me to have almost nothing to be said in its favor.

* * *

The idea of persevering with a life that has nothing to recommend it save perseverance itself is exemplified by someone who perseveres with a utterly unsatisfactory marriage

523

simply for the sake of "not being a quitter." Or the life of a cancer patient who, facing ever-more intense regimens of chemotherapy for ever-shorter remissions, refuses ever to give up. In both cases we are disposed to use the "heroic warrior," master morality, rhetoric favored by Camus. We talk of "soldiering on" with the marriage, of the long, and by implication heroic, "battle" against cancer. But of course, if we reflect a little, we do not really believe that the life of the marital soldier or of the cancer battler is really heroic. Such lives are, rather, foolish. As Socrates pointed out long ago (in Plato's *Protagoras*), unconditional courage is not a virtue. Courage, resistance to adversity, is only a virtue when it is exercised in conjunction with the knowledge of what it is proper to resist and what not. So what we should do is to bid farewell to the idea of "revolt." Since unconditional resistance is not a virtue, the idea that a life can be worthwhile simply in virtue of exhibiting it was, from the start, a bad one.

* * *

Abandoning "revolt" leaves us with a slimmed-down account of the absurd hero. What remains now is simply the idea of him (or her, now that we have disposed of this macho idea) as an embodiment of *joie de vivre* made possible by, and only by, a lucid awareness of the nothing. Problems, however, still remain.

In this slimmed-down account, death/the nothing still plays an essential role. It is only through a lucid awareness of the nothing, maintained by an "*ascesis*," a kind of mantric self-discipline, that life acquires and retains its urgent intensity. Yet has Camus not also said that death is the *summum malum*, a "horrendous" "hideous" phenomenon, knowledge of which blights our entire existence? How, then, can a life so blighted be full of rapture? How can the nothing simultaneously blight and delight?

One might be tempted to say: well, that's just how it is. Camus's image of the man on the way to the gallows (Camus 2000: 83) who catches a fleeting sight of, let us say, a beautiful flower, precisely captures the bittersweet character of the human condition.

Life, you might say (swept away by the delight of philosophizing through images), is like one of those seventeenth-century Dutch still lifes: a sensuous delight of hyper-realistically portrayed bread, meat, and fruit, but always containing a tiny hint of corruption – the fly on the mold on the orange or the skull-like appearance of the hollowed-out pomegranate.

Sometimes this seems to be precisely the image of life Camus wishes to present. Rather than speaking of Sisyphus' "secret joy," he speaks of the Greeks' knowledge of life as a "gilded calamity" and of the "stifling quality" of beauty (Camus 2000: 167) – notice that "stifling" air is precisely what facilitates the corruption in the Dutch still life.

In fact, however, the image of the still life ("dead nature" in French) reveals just what is unsatisfactory about Camus's position. For the still lifes about which we have been talking are, in fact, so-called *vanitas* paintings, paintings which, by reminding us of the presence of death even at the summit of sensuous delight, are intended to remind us of the "vanity," the transitory and trivial nature of earthly delights (see Chapter 38).

Camus's aim, let us recall, is not to show that life has its small compensations. It is rather to produce in us an intense "passion for living" (Camus 2000: 12) that will convince us that suicide is absolutely out of the question. But the bittersweet, *vanitas-*painting view of things comes nowhere near to such a ringing endorsement.

* * *

The problem, of course, lies in Camus's conception of the "night," of the nothing. It cannot both be the source of rapture and an object of horror. Given that it is to be the former, what Camus needs to do is to take away its horror. In Dylan Thomas's meditation on his father's death, in the angry lines "Do not go gentle into that good night / Rage, rage against the dying of the light," the use of the word "good" is presumably sardonic. But Camus needs to be able to use the word without spin. For him, the night must *really* be a "good" night, since otherwise it cannot highlight the fragile preciousness of existence without at the same time blighting it.

In other language, what Camus needs, in fact, to do is to abandon the absurd; to "negate," not the non-existence of God and personal immortality, but rather the idea that they represent the object of our most fundamental spiritual need. For the truth is that if life really is, in this sense, absurd there is actually no compelling way of showing that "suicide is not legitimate."

Camus needs to abandon, at least, his official notion of the absurd according to which *both* the nothing *and* human need for personal immortality are its necessary ingredients. Much of the time, however, he slips into using "absurd" simply to refer to the fact of the nothing. Speaking of Sisyphus' "secret joy," for example, he observes, as we saw, that "happiness and the absurd are two sons of the same earth" (Camus 2000: 110). This is a repetition of the point that "there is no sunlight without shadow" and treats "the absurd" simply as a name of the nothing.

If, then, the nothing is to facilitate a life filled with rapture – the possibility of a life that is so *intensely* valuable as to rebut *clearly* the "legitimacy" of suicide – Camus needs to remove its life-blighting character, needs to enable us to face personal extinction with, not horror, but rather equanimity. The resources for this are not, however, to be found in Camus.

* * *

This can be seen if we return, for a moment, to the second of the three types of absurdity identified at the beginning of this chapter; the refusal of reality to satisfy our supposed desire for its intelligibility.

Given that Camus calls questions of science such as the truth or otherwise of Galilean astronomy mere "games" compared with the "real" problem of suicide (Camus 2000: 11), it is initially puzzling that he should postulate the desire for intelligibility as a fundamental human need. It turns out, however, that this desire is not an end in itself but rather a means to "unity" (Camus 2000: 23). Since "understanding" is "reducing to the human," to confront reality's refusal to be understood is to confront the fact that "it has a nature foreign and irreducible to us"(Camus 2000: 20). To confront, for example, the "inhumanness" of the landscape, to discover the inhuman in the human – for example, the stranger in the face of the woman one once loved – is to discover reality's essential otherness than, indeed its "primitive hostility" to, oneself. And this is

525

an anguishing experience because, says Camus, it "leaves one so alone" (ibid.). Alone, of course, in the face of death. The desire for unity with nature is a form of the desire for immortality. Rather than being genuinely autonomous, the second type of absurdity reduces, in the end, it seems to me, to a version of the third.

Camus is a lyrical nature poet of wonderful gifts. But most of the time he feels himself to be fatally excluded, a mere spectator of the magic show of nature.[5] Why should this be? Hegel could only overcome his "alienation" from the world by postulating that the human "spirit" is, in fact, the substance of everything. It is the same with Camus. "If man realised that the universe like him could love and suffer," he writes, "he would be reconciled to it" (Camus 2000: 23), would be able to discover immortality in the form of unity. For Camus, it is only by discovering the "other" to be essentially human that he can overcome his alienation from it. The opposite thought that unity might exist because the self is more than the human, does not arise. Like Hegel he feels utterly disconnected from everything that is other than his own ego. It is this obsessive, clinging to the ego which means that death has to be, for him, the "hideous" object of "horror" he describes it as being. What is missing in Camus is the ability to expand the concept of the self beyond a tiny pinpoint of Cartesian light and out into the darkness of nothing.

The resources for such an expansion, for an appropriation of the nothing, are to be found, perhaps, in Eastern thought. And they are sometimes hinted at by German idealism. To find them clearly articulated within Western philosophy, however, we need to turn to Heidegger.

* * *

The Heidegger regarded in *The Myth* as sharing in a lucid awareness of the absurd is the early(ish) Heidegger of *Being and Time*. The two philosophers share essentially the same conception of death and the nothing. In *Being and Time*, "being-towards-death" is what gives life its intensity and urgency – "authenticity," as Heidegger calls it.[6] Yet facing up to death does not take away the "anxiety" with which every "Dasein" lives. Anxiety in the face of death, anxiety in the face of the "abysmal" (Heidegger 1962: 152) nothingness that "threatens" (Heidegger 1962: 343) to break through into "the clearing" of world at each and every moment, is something with which even – and especially – authentic Dasein must always live.

Early Heidegger concludes from this that security, being safe in the world or, as he calls it, "dwelling," is impossible. In *Being and Time* radical insecurity, "*Un-heimlichkeit*," not being at home, is an essential feature of all Dasein (Heidegger 1962: 188–9).

As Camus tells it – though sometimes he averts his eyes from the fact – it is *Un-heimlichkeit*, Heideggerian anxiety, which underlies the absurd hero's determination to "burn up" his life, to indulge in the greatest possible "excess." But (along with boredom) there is a febrile, feverish quality to such an existence, a kind of desperate consumerism, a quality that is certainly something other than the "silent joy" of Sisyphean rapture. Rather than portraying a flourishing human life that can be accepted as an ideal of existence for post-death-of-God humanity, the portrait is, in reality, it seems to me, a portrait of spiritual sickness, a sickness that consists in radical disharmony with Being. To recover health, the absurd hero must overcome his terror of the night. He must come to see that, while the approach of night makes it important to live the day to the full, the night we will enter is one that is not to be feared. Only with this assurance can the joys of the day remain unsullied by that approach.

* * *

Whereas early Heidegger (articulating Camus's underlying thought) concludes that radical security, "dwelling," is impossible for humanity as such, for later, post-"turning," Heidegger, it is only *modern* humanity that has, by and large, lost the capacity to dwell. This is because modern culture has been overcome by what Heidegger calls "metaphysics." One way of understanding what it is that constitutes "metaphysics," in Heidegger's idiosyncratic use of the term, is to say that it consists in a misunderstanding of the nothing and of death of precisely the kind indulged in by both *Being and Time* and *The Myth of Sisyphus*.

"Mortals dwell," says later Heidegger, "in that they initiate their own nature – their being capable of death as death – into the use and practice of this capacity" (Heidegger 1971: 151). Death, he says, is the "shrine of the nothing." (Note that the shrine of a god is holy because it is a place where the god comes into the world.) It is not, however, the shrine of the "*empty* nothing" (emphasis added). Rather, it is "the mystery of Being itself." To understand this is to be capable of "the good death" (Heidegger 1971: 151).

In the essay "What are poets for?" Heidegger talks of "the abyss." In the face of the abyss, he says, we are incapable of "read[ing] the word "death" without negation" (Heidegger 1971: 125). And it is because of this that our lives are "destitute" (Heidegger 1971: 92), are the constant yearning for a security that always eludes us.

In truth, however, our lives are *not* lived before the abyss. This is so because (here and throughout most of the essay Heidegger thinks with, and through the words of, the poet Rainer Maria Rilke) if we think "Being" (the totality of what is) properly, we see that it resembles the moon, with our world corresponding, merely, to its lighted side. To understand this is to understand, as Rilke puts it, that "death and the realm of the dead," like the dark side of the moon, "belong to the whole of beings as its other side." Thinking Being in Rilke's way we see that "There are regions and places which, being averted from us, seem to be something negative, but are nothing of the kind if we think of all things as being within the widest orbit of beings" (Heidegger 1971: 124–5). In other words, "the nothing" that lies beyond the manifest world is not the abysmal, "empty" nothing of *Being and Time* and *The Myth of Sisyphus*, but is, rather, something "positive (the *positum*)" (Heidegger 1971: 124). To put the point in philosophers' jargon, the nothing that is the other "side" of our world is not an *ontological*, but rather an *epistemological* nothing – nothing intelligible to us.

To read the nothing in this way enables us to face death "without negation," to die "the good death." And this, in turn, enables us to dwell in the world without the shadow of terror under which Camus's absurd hero always lives. Death, to be sure, is the end of the ego. But the end of my ego appears as the end of my *self* only if I fall under the illusion of "metaphysics," the illusion that only the abysmal, empty nothing lies on the other side of the manifest world.

* * *

But why should we believe that "metaphysics" *is* an illusion? Is not the idea of a "positive" nothing, the image of the world as the lighted side of the moon just that – a poetic image? And is it not the case that the decision to read the nothing "positively" rather than "negatively" is a case of wishful (or, as one might say, "New Age") rather than philosophical thinking, in which case, is it not a decision that, in reality, is merely an exotic version of Camus's despised "leap"? Is it not, therefore, a decision that someone as committed to the Cartesian life of tough-minded "reason" as Camus must absolutely oppose?

Heidegger argues against this. Rilke's image of Being is a poet's intuitive insight into fundamental philosophical truth. The evidence for this is to be found in a proper understanding of the concept of truth. I shall now try to describe Heidegger's account of truth on the back of a postage stamp.

Truth, we know, depends on correspondence to the facts. But what the facts are, what possible range of facts can come up for discussion, depends on what kinds of things can be referred to. And this in turn depends on what Heidegger calls "horizons of disclosure." If I say, pointing to the river, "you'll never bathe in that again," you, intending to bathe the very next day, dispute what I say. Unbeknownst to you, however, what I actually intended to refer to was not the river but the body of water that currently makes up its visible stretch.

This example is, of course, far-fetched and, as philosopher's examples usually are, tedious. But it nonetheless serves to highlight the fact that different ranges of facts, and hence different possibilities of truth and falsehood, are disclosed by different horizons.[7] According to Heidegger, our ultimate horizon of disclosure, the limit of what is, to us, intelligible, is constituted by the language we speak. If our world is everything that is intelligibly the case for us, then our world is constituted by our language.

Disclosure is, however, always concealment. Behind every disclosure lies "a reservoir of the not-yet-uncovered," the "concealed" (Heidegger 1971: 60). (In my river example, the ordinary-natural-object horizon "conceals" the stuff-horizon, and conversely.) Every world-disclosure reveals a "facet" or "aspect" of Being (Heidegger 1971: 124). Simultaneously, however, it conceals a "plenitude" (ibid.) of "the not-yet uncovered, the un-uncovered" (Heidegger 1971: 60), a plenitude "beyond number" (Heidegger 1971: 128) of undisclosed aspects of Being.

From which it follows, as Rilke says, that death is but "the side of life that is averted from us." A proper understanding of truth and Being, while it reveals death to be indeed utterly mysterious ("the mystery of Being itself"), takes away the terror of the abyss, the terror of absolute extinction. For a proper understanding reveals the failure to distinguish the self from the ego to be, not just a fundamental error in *Lebensweisheit* (life-wisdom), but a fundamental error, too, in philosophy – the error Heidegger calls "metaphysics." Camus can, therefore, be assured that there is no anti-rational "leap" involved in the positive reading of the nothing. Such a reading, on the contrary, is something reason *demands*.

* * *

But, it may finally be objected, if Rilkean–Heideggerian insight takes away the horror of death, does it not also take away the possibility of joy and intensity? Is it not, in reality, the case that the bittersweet view of the human condition alluded to earlier represents the tragic truth about the human condition? Is it not the case that to take away the bitterness of death is simultaneously to take away the savor of life?

I think not. For what makes present experience uniquely precious is knowledge of, not the abyss, but rather departure. An elegiac sense of ephemerality, not horror before the void, is what endows life with its fragile beauty.

Notes

1   Schopenhauer, indeed, takes the desire for God and the desire for personal immortality to be essentially the *same* desire. Were it to be proved, he observes sardonically, that immortality is independent of or even incompatible with the existence of gods (the immortality of the soul might, for example, be shown to presuppose its "originality"), people "would soon sacrifice th[e] gods to their own immortality, and be eager for atheism" (Schopenhauer 1966: 161–2).
2   Camus appears to suggest that if there is no "end of time" then history is the repetitive futility of the eternal return of Sisyphus' stone to its starting point. But this is a fallacy: that history is endless does not entail "the eternal return of the same," as Georg Simmel proved (against Nietzsche) in 1907 (Simmel 1986: 172–3 n.1).
3   As will emerge, the absurd hero is, for better or worse, an essentially *masculine* figure. The masculine pronoun, here, is *de rigueur*.
4   Notice an implicit change in the meaning of "absurd," here, a point to which I shall return.
5   The great exception here is "Return to Tipasa," which recounts Camus's ecstatic experience of "homeland" (Camus 2000: 178), of "at last com[ing] to harbour" (Camus 2000: 180), amid the Roman ruins above the Algerian bay of Tipasa. One of Camus's many attractive, if frustrating, features is the integrity which compels him to contradict himself.
6   A major difference between *Being and Time* and *The Myth of Sisyphus* is that whereas the latter's response to the nothing is to reject the life of *Bildung*, the former's is to affirm it. Facing up to death, for Heidegger, entails "resolute" commitment to an ideal account of the self which one "projects" into the future. Though Heidegger perhaps exaggerates the point, I have already supported this view by arguing (pp. 520–1 above) against Camus's exclusion of "aims" from the absurd hero's life.
7   Notice that while the possibility of a given range of propositional truths *depends on* a given horizon of disclosure, this does not mean that the truth in question is *relative to* that horizon. What determines whether propositions are true or false is the nature of reality. What makes it possible to *grasp* a given truth is disclosure. This disposes of the familiar objection that if all truth is merely relative to a horizon then Heidegger's theory of truth is itself only "relatively" true. The fact of the matter is that truth is *never* relative to anything save the nature of reality.

References and Further Reading

Camus, A. (2000) *The Myth of Sisyphus* (trans. J. O'Brien). London: Penguin (original work published 1942).

Heidegger, M. (1962) *Being and Time* (trans. J. Macquarrie and T. Robinson). Oxford: Blackwell (original work published 1927). Page numbers given refer to the pagination of the seventh German edition, which are given in the margins of this translation.

—— (1971) *Poetry, Language, Thought* (trans. A. Hofstadter). New York: Harper & Row (original works published 1935–6, 1946, 1947, 1950, and 1951).

Schopenhauer, A. (1966) *The World as Will and Representation*, Vol. II (trans. E. F. J. Payne). New York: Dover (original work published 1818, rev. edn. 1844).

—— (1974) *Parerga and Paralipomena*, Vol. II (trans. E. F. J. Payne). Oxford: Clarendon Press (original work published 1851).

Simmel, G. (1986) *Schopenhauer and Nietzsche* (trans. H. Loiskandl, D. Weinstein, and H. Weinstein). Amherst: University of Massachusetts Press (original work published 1907).

Young, J. (2002) *Heidegger's Later Philosophy*. Cambridge: Cambridge University Press.

36

The Search for Immediacy and the Problem of Political Life in Existentialism and Phenomenology

MICHAEL ALLEN GILLESPIE

"To the things themselves!" While this aphorism encapsulates the project of both phenomenology and existentialism, its meaning for political life is elusive. Both of these schools of thought focus on the individual and generally see political institutions as impediments to immediacy. Both thus only come to a consideration of political life indirectly and secondarily. Moreover, when they do turn to the political realm, they generally reject everyday politics, Weber's "slow boring of hard boards," in favor of radical efforts to bring about totally new forms of communal life.

Both phenomenology and existentialism were responses to the crisis of modernity. Modernity itself was a series of attempts to solve the crisis of late medieval thought engendered by a new view of God as radically omnipotent, and a corresponding end to teleology, theological certainty, and philosophical justification. Two often-antagonistic streams of thought predominate within this project, rationalism or idealism on one hand and materialism or empiricism on the other. The first begins with Descartes, the second with Hobbes. Both thinkers (and the traditions they founded), however, have a great deal in common. They both attempt to develop a new science of motion that will allow human beings to become masters and possessors of nature. They both also believe that the actual world is inaccessible to human beings because we only have veridical knowledge of our own sense impressions. They both seek to overcome this disability by representing the world as a picture. In Descartes's case, concrete things become abstract objects, and the world of experience becomes a system of mathematical relationships. For Hobbes, the experiential world is replaced by a world constructed in words, which are ultimately only useful fictions. The notion of knowledge as representation that these two thinkers share forms the heart of the Enlightenment, and culminates in Kant's transcendental idealism that denies we have access to the things-in-themselves and that confines human understanding to an "island of truth," which is in fact only an island of appearances. Dissatisfaction with life on this island in the late eighteenth and early nineteenth centuries led to a more radical speculative idealism on one hand and to a more ardent materialism on the other. During the course of modernity, the world of experience thus seems to dissolve into either mere concepts or brute material forces.

Phenomenology and existentialism are efforts to tear aside the web of concepts that replaced the actual, pre-theoretical experience of the world, and to regain a sense of the concrete immediacy of life, reestablishing a connection to everything that the conceptual structure of modernity brackets out, including an immediate relationship with God, and an authentic sense of one's own unique being. Both thus begin with the conviction that the modern project, especially in its final Hegelian form, not only misconstrues reality but closes off the possibility of authentic experience. This condition is variously described by these schools of thought as nihilism, the crisis of European humanity, world-midnight, absurdity, atheism, and abandonment; and is thought to evoke dread, anxiety, anguish, forlornness, boredom, despair, nausea, and alienation.

For the most part, phenomenology and existentialism seek to solve these problems through a reorientation of the individual with respect to God and the world. In contrast to the Marxist or liberal traditions, the idea that this crisis has a political or social solution is scarcely considered until the 1930s. In large part this is because the mediating institutions of political and social life seem more to separate than to connect the individual and the absolute. Here the impact of Hegel was profound.

Hegel was a profoundly communitarian thinker but his communitarianism was rooted in the mediation of the individual and the whole. Hegel's system rests upon a notion of general consciousness or spirit out of which both the individual and the absolute arise. While he saw individual consciousness as an abstraction, he did not reject it in favor of pure communitarianism. In fact, he criticized both German Classicism for its attempted revival of the immediacy of the ancient polis and the Romantics for their effort to establish a folk community. Still, he did deny the ultimate reality of the concrete individual as an immediately created being. In his view, the individual, the community, and the absolute have their being ultimately in and through the rational state.

Hegel's existentialist and phenomenological successors were unhappy with this communitarianism for a variety of reasons, but fundamentally because it seemed to deny the ultimate reality of the individual, to make an immediate relationship to God impossible, and thus to undermine human spirituality. Like Kant's island of truth, Hegel's system constrained the individual in decisive and unacceptable ways. The world it defended was banal, bourgeois, philistine, decadent, and dispiriting. While other critics sought to reform these institutions or overthrow them, existentialism and phenomenology turned away from communal life in pursuit of the intense individual experiences, particularly of God and the superhuman.

There are four stages in the development of existentialism and phenomenology: (1) the early existentialism of Dostoyevsky, Kierkegaard, and Nietzsche, (2) the development of phenomenology by Brentano and Husserl, (3) the conjunction of these two and a turn from the theoretical to the practical in the phenomenological existentialism of Heidegger, Jaspers, and their successors, and (4) the rapprochement of phenomenological existentialism with the thought of Hegel and Marx in French existentialism. I will argue that these schools of thought begin with a critique of Hegelianism and everyday life and politics in favor of individual authenticity based upon an immediate encounter with the absolute, but that they then come to believe that such individual authenticity is only possible on the basis of collective authenticity, which itself is only possible as the result of a truly radical transformation of everyday life and politics.

Early Existentialism

Kierkegaard, Nietzsche, and Dostoyevsky were the founders of existentialism. Their work is as much literary as it is philosophical. Their thought is at its core a critique of idealism, and it is in this context that they see the political realm as a barrier to an authentic encounter with the highest things. Within Hegel's system, political philosophy is presented in the sphere of objective spirit as the philosophy of right. He argues that individual freedom and rights, moral goodness, and communal life (the family, economy, and politics) can be reconciled with one another only in the rational bureaucratic state. This state in the person of its officials (including professors and pastors) is also the home and source of spirituality. Dostoyevsky in a number of his works is critical of this bureaucratic state, and while Kierkegaard and Nietzsche pay little attention to it, this is not because they like it. Indeed, they see the goods this state provides – individual property rights, functional families, a thriving bourgeois society, and an efficient bureaucracy – as impediments to a real spiritual life, and particularly to the ecstatic aesthetic or religious experience they believe is essential to give life meaning. The Hegelian state, in their view, produces only an empty and banal existence that culminates in nihilism. Only by means of an act of will – a leap of faith, in Kierkegaard's case, and an act of poetic creation in Nietzsche's – can nihilism be overcome. While this might entail a political transformation, that is a distant possibility that is clearly subsidiary to the creation of an individual of real faith or profound genius.

Their critique of idealism and particularly Hegelianism is comprehensive. In place of idealism's self-conscious, rational individual, Nietzsche and Dostoyevsky emphasize the role of subconscious passions, affects, and drives. Liberal rights are seen as mere camouflage for a deeper will to power. Dostoyevsky, for example, turns to an examination of the deeper and darker side of the soul. For Nietzsche, morality is a means the weak use to dominate the strong. For Kierkegaard, ethical life is superior to aesthetic life, but it is ultimately unable to achieve real goodness, which depends on God alone. The institutions of civil society are also subjected to trenchant critique. The family for Nietzsche is useful only as a means for self-overcoming, and is in general a distraction. The only philosopher to marry, in his view, did so as a joke. For Kierkegaard, as well, the choice of a single over a married life was of central importance, and for Dostoyevsky the corruption of the family is the premise of his greatest work *The Brothers Karamazov* (1879–80). While Dostoyevsky does not abandon the family, he does seek a new more natural or perhaps more mystical ground for it that is quite different than that of Hegel. Economic life, in their view, is also unsatisfying and is not a legitimate outlet for human efforts. Nietzsche argues that it is precisely the emphasis on moneymaking that is turning students away from the classical values and the love of the beautiful that might save them from nihilism.

For these thinkers the bourgeois world that Hegel praises is not a home for human beings but a place of alienation and estrangement. Dostoyevsky's Underground Man is a profound example of such estrangement. Zarathustra also sees the immense distance between himself and the hedonistic "last men" devoid of love, creativity, longing, and wonder (see Nietzsche 1966: "Zarathustra's Prologue," §5). For early existentialism, there is no political solution to this problem. According to Zarathustra in "On the New

Idol," the "state is the name of the coldest of all cold monsters" (Nietzsche 1966: 48) that subverts the people and seduces the creators who might respiritualize the people by giving them a new faith and love. It is perhaps even worse when it is democratic, for democracy subverts the rule of the spiritual creators. Kierkegaard too detests majoritarianism since it undermines individual moral choice. Revolution is no better. Dostoyevsky's *Devils* (1871–2) is a trenchant critique of revolutionary immorality, duplicity, and ineffectiveness. Nietzsche's Zarathustra refers to revolutionaries as scum- and overthrow-devils, and suggests that their success would not weaken but only strengthen the state.

For Nietzsche and Kierkegaard, the chief objection to the bureaucratic state is that it undermines human spirituality. For Nietzsche, *Staat* and *Kultur* are invariably at odds with one another. Since the German state was formed, German culture has declined. The modern state does not produce those who need art, nor does it produce the art that alone can justify existence; it produces only philistines who need to be moved or entertained. For Kierkegaard, the state is antagonistic to spirituality because of its corrosive effect on religion, which has become merely formal and thus inimical to real faith. He particularly dislikes the Hegelianism of the Danish Church, which seems to him to be a step toward paganism, subordinating Christianity and thus God to dialectical rationality.

In constructing an alternative to Hegelianism, these thinkers lay great weight on the extraordinary individual. For Kierkegaard, each individual is a unique, finite being. We are incomplete and can know nothing with certainty or finality. Despite this fact, we have to choose, and because of it, we always choose in dread. Taking responsibility means choosing a way of life despite having insufficient grounds for our choice. In Kierkegaard's early thought this means choosing between the aesthetic path and the ethical-religious path. In his later thought, he argues that the ethical and the religious paths are distinct. Hegel combined these three in his system. Kierkegaard believes they are mutually contradictory and that a fundamental choice between them is unavoidable. In his own case, he feels that the aesthetic life can never be satisfying because it is based on sensory experience, and human beings are not merely sensory beings. Thus, as Kierkegaard suggests in *Either/Or*, the aesthetic life ends in despair. The ethical life is better, but while in some instances one can act morally through one's own efforts, only God makes it possible to do so consistently. To live a truly religious life, one thus must recognize that human will is insufficient to attain the good. In this sense, Kierkegaard aims to reveal the inadequacy of the ethical life that was central to Hegelianism.

Kierkegaard's path is radically opposed to Hegel's. He is concerned not with objective spirit or conceptual truth but with subjective existence in relation to the living God. Moreover, spiritual life is not something that can be inculcated or taught, but something that must be chosen. Free will is thus necessary for authentic Christianity. For Hegel, the individual subject encounters absolute spirit through art, religion, and philosophy, which operate within the framework of the rational state. For Kierkegaard the institutions of the state and society separate man from God. It is not mediation and reconciliation that are needed but immediacy and union with the divine. As a matter of principle, Kierkegaard's thinking thus cannot be anything other than solitary mediation (Luijpen and Koren 1964: 18). It is true that the religious man returns to his fellows and assists them, but this return is itself absurd, and is made possible only by divine omnipotence that overcomes all contradictions. In the end, Kierkegaard thus not only does not develop a political philosophy, he sees the political realm as an obstacle to authentic existence.

Nietzsche follows a different path. Where Kierkegaard turned to religion in search of a God unfettered by the conceptual web of modern rationality, Nietzsche turns to art to find a replacement for a God dead beyond all hope of resurrection. The death of the Christian God has two possible outcomes in Nietzsche's view, the last man and the overman. Humanity will either degenerate into a bovine hedonism or develop a new discipline and a new order of rank that will make possible a higher existence and the development of a superhuman being who will live beyond good and evil.

Nietzsche, like Kierkegaard, thus confronts humanity with a decision, but it is a decision that has nothing to do with choice or free will. Rather it is rooted in the unconscious force of life itself that manifests itself in and through the individual genius. Where Hegel held up the philosopher and Kierkegaard pointed to the saint, Nietzsche presents the artist as the means for the transfiguration of existence. Transfiguration, however, entails the destruction of the existing order, and destruction is generally only reactive, an effort to destroy what constrains us. Nietzsche argues that at the most fundamental level destruction is a manifestation of the spirit of revenge that lashes out against the omnipotent dead hand of the past. Authentic transfiguration thus depends on overcoming the spirit of revenge, and this is only possible if one can accept all that has been as if one had willed it. This is what Nietzsche calls *amor fati*. This absolute affirmation is attained by saying yes to the doctrine of the eternal recurrence of all things, i.e., by affirming everything as it has been, is, or will be.

This is an existential reorientation. Hegel had suggested that all the misery and suffering of "the slaughtering bench of world history" was redeemed by the union of the individual, society, and God in absolute knowledge. Dostoevsky's Ivan Karamazov argues that no final reconciliation can justify the pain and suffering of the innocent, indicting both the Christian and Hegelian visions of a final reconciliation. Nietzsche believes it is necessary to affirm precisely this abysmal vision, not of a world in which suffering is redeemed but one in which it is eternally *not* redeemed, in order to escape from the spirit of revenge. Only in this way can he attain the innocence needed for the transvaluation of all values that will overcome nihilism and create a new order free from the slave morality of Christianity, and guided by a being Nietzsche epigrammatically characterizes as "Caesar with the soul of Christ."

All of this is important for political life, but it is not political philosophy, and it does not involve engagement with actual politics. The superman that Nietzsche longs for will not be a politician or statesman, but what Nietzsche calls an artist-tyrant. His task is the aesthetic transfiguration and justification of life itself. This heroic figure practices what Nietzsche calls great politics, but neither he nor Nietzsche is concerned with every-day politics. It is precisely this petty politics that must be swept away by new wars that will breed a people capable of bearing the new values necessary for great politics. Yet in Nietzsche's mind, this is a distant possibility. In the present, he thus can only long for a radical transformation of humanity and politics that will produce his superhuman artist-tyrant. For Nietzsche, the political realm, even at its highest, is thus merely instrumental to the creation of this being who alone can justify human existence.

535

Phenomenology

Phenomenology is more an academic and less a literary movement than existential-ism. It clearly had an academic origin in the thought of Franz Brentano, who first opened up the possibility of phenomenology. Moreover, it was his student and fellow academic Edmund Husserl who gave it determinate form. In his early career Husserl opposed idealism, and characterized his thought as realism. Later, he came to believe that empiricism (which he calls naturalism, objectivism, and positivism) and psychologism (the notion that the content of ideas is determined by the psychological conditions of their acquisition) posed a greater danger. He therefore came to believe (to the astonishment of many of his students) that phenomenology should be understood not as realism but as a form of transcendental idealism.

Like Kierkegaard, Husserl gives prominence to consciousness and subjectivity, re-jecting the notion of positivists, neo-Kantians, and Nietzsche that the real things and events are outside or beyond or beneath consciousness. In contrast to earlier idealists, however, he denies the existence of an empty *cogito* – consciousness is always con-sciousness of something. The goal of his early thought is to come to terms with these things themselves, a pure seeing without intervening conceptual distortions that lets things show themselves from themselves. One begins by suspending belief in the reality of external objects (the "natural attitude"). Through a phenomenological reduction one then turns one's attention from the object of consciousness to the process of con-sciousness. The objects of perception are in this way replaced by their meaning for consciousness. Through an eidetic reduction one then moves from the process of con-sciousness of the object (i.e., *that* it is) to an understanding of its essence (i.e., *what* it is). Finally, through a transcendental reduction, one turns to the a priori structures of consciousness itself. Thus one comes to absolute consciousness or the transcendental ego, which constitutes all things and thereby gives them meaning and significance.

Just as consciousness is always consciousness of something, things are only in and through consciousness, and this consciousness is always directed by a particular intentionality. The being and meaning of things is thus always a being in or a mean-ing for a consciousness that is directed in a particular way. Intentions thus constitute the meaning and being of the things we encounter. There are no facts "out there" to discover; the facts come to be and have meaning only within a normative framework of values established by a particular intention or attitude. Husserl thus maintains a radical view of the autonomy of consciousness as normative or law-giving and thus as teleological (Velkley 1987: 877).

In his early work, Husserl was preeminently concerned with the individual subject. After 1900, he came to recognize the importance of intersubjectivity and communal life. He had originally believed that the natural attitude was the source of the modern crisis, but realized that this naturalism was predicated on the naïve assumption that the everyday world (including our political and religious communities) is simply "given" (Velkley 1987: 881). Thus, establishing philosophy as a rigorous science depends upon a prior understanding of the intentional structure of communal life.

The communal world for the later Husserl is the accretion of all past attempts to give it meaning and significance. That is to say, the normative or intentional orientation of consciousness establishes and continually modifies the practical/political world that we inhabit. Husserl was influenced here by Dilthey and historicism. Dilthey had argued that each human being exists within a historical horizon that determines his values and actions. There is no objective point of view. Husserl rejected Dilthey's historicism because he believed it led to relativism. Historicism, in his view, did not recognize the crucial fact that human beings have an intrinsic infinite end that distinguishes them from all other beings.

World War I heightened Husserl's sense of the practical significance of phenomenology. Only phenomenology could reveal the true end of human life and save humanity from the death spiral of naturalism, positivism, and historicism. The defense of this argument became even more urgent after Hitler took power. In his last works, Husserl sought to demonstrate the true nature of rationality and freedom as well as to explain the origin of the erroneous views of consciousness that had come to dominate and debilitate the modern world. He sought to achieve this by means of a historical reduction that removed the layers of historical sediment in order to reveal the reality at its core. Husserl suggests that at the heart of things there is a lifeworld that is the foundation for the scientific constitution of meaning. He thus adopts a rationalist position in opposition to historicism and relativism.

Such a rationalism was first articulated by the Greeks, in Husserl's view, but was later displaced by the modern naturalism of Galileo and Descartes. These moderns brought a different intentionality to the experience of the world, a practical and technical concern, abandoning philosophy's previous concern with theory. This led to the loss of a clear sense of the unique telos of European man. Husserl believes that by reopening this original path phenomenology will allow human beings to understand their true goal and their own transcendent character.

All forms of communal life for Husserl arise from attitudes that are transformations of the primitive but socially agreed-upon attitude of those who live immersed in the lifeworld. The lifeworld, however, is not itself originally experienced as a world, because human beings are absorbed in everyday affairs. Their view of the larger shape of things is constituted by mythology and religion, but both of these are rooted in the finite and produce a culture rooted in tradition. This was all changed by the eruption of philosophy in pre-Socratic Greece. Wonder induced a passionate love of theory, which was itself thoroughly unpractical and based on a deliberate suspension of all practical interests. Rooted in theory, the Greek philosophers produced a new idea of an infinite cosmos and a new form or community on the model of the philosophic group. The philosophers thus came to recognize themselves not as citizens of any state but as citizens of the cosmos. Their goals were not finite ends but, beginning with Socrates, infinite ideals. They thus rejected the norms and practices of the traditional communities and as a result came into conflict with them (Husserl 1970: 276–89).

From the perspective of philosophy, "all the beloved expressions about community spirit, the will of the people, the ideal and political goals of nations, etc., are so much romanticism and mythology" (Husserl 1970: 294). The Greek philosophic culture in its super-nationality became the spiritual form of Europe and, through Europe, of all humanity. While the European crisis seems to be the result of the collapse of rationalism, it is thus really the result of the absorption of ancient rationalism by modern naturalism, and it can end in two ways: either the ruin of Europe alienated from rational sense of life, or the phenomenological rebirth of Europe from the spirit of philosophy through the heroism of reason.

Husserl's late thought is thus more concerned with communal life, although it is not itself a political philosophy. In the end he sees everyday politics as an impediment to philosophic activity. Communal life is necessary, but the model for the human community is not the ancient city or the modern state but the Epicurean garden devoted to contemplation. Like Plato, Husserl sees the life of the philosopher as the supremely human life, but in contrast to Plato and in keeping with the Enlightenment, he believes that life is possible for all human beings. The authentic political realm is thus the universal community of autonomous human beings, eschewing practical political life, devoted to theory, and led by a phenomenological science that can answer all questions. His thought thus remains distant from real politics. What is particularly missing is an engagement with praxis in general and human action in particular. The changing tenor of the times, however, brought this question to the forefront for his successors.

Phenomenological Existentialism

Heidegger, Jaspers, and their followers build upon both existentialism and phenomenology but turn in a more practical direction. We see this clearly in the case of Heidegger. Heidegger was trained in neo-Kantianism and Thomism but grew dissatisfied with them because he felt their conceptual framework shut him off from an immediate experience of life. In pursuit of greater immediacy, he turned to the Augustinian tradition (Paul, Augustine, and Luther), historicism, existentialism (first Kierkegaard and then increasingly Nietzsche), and phenomenology. While generally considered a phenomenologist, he differed with Husserl on a number of points. Like Dilthey and Nietzsche, he did not believe in an unchanging reality that could be grasped through a phenomenological or historical reduction, and thus rejected the notion of the lifeworld. Like Kierkegaard, he was impressed by human finitude and did not believe that the end of man lies in infinity and the theoretical life. In fact, he saw theory as an obstacle to an encounter with the things themselves. While he agreed with Husserl that modern rationalism was fundamentally mistaken, he did not believe that ancient rationalism was any better. Like Husserl, he rejected all naturalism, but he was also critical of idealism. Thus he abandoned the language of consciousness and subjectivity and defined human being as *Dasein* (literally, "being-there"). This concept is akin to intentionality but moves beyond it in decisive ways. Dasein is not a *cogito* (the *here* from which we perceive the world out *there*), but is always *there*, i.e., it is being-in-the-world. Husserl believed the world appeared to us as things. Heidegger suggests it is primarily disclosed as equipment, that it appears to us not as a what but as a how. We thus need to know not the natures or essences of things, but how they work or function. Correspondingly, we must understand the self not as a detached observer but as a practical actor. Consequently, the fundamental mode of being-in-the-world for Dasein is not theory but praxis.

Aristotle's account of the intellectual virtues played an important role in the development of Heidegger's thought. For Aristotle the world is divided into things that change and things that do not. The knowledge of the unchanging is theory. It includes intuition of first principles (*nous*) and deduction based on these principles (*epistêmê*). Together these constitute wisdom (*sophia*). Theory, for Aristotle, ends in contemplation, and thus produces no human action. The knowledge of what changes is praxis and includes knowledge of things made (*technê*) and of things done (*phronêsis*). This last guides action, and particularly political action.

This account served as Heidegger's framework, although he modified it in keeping with his belief that there are no unchanging things and consequently no theory independent of praxis. Heidegger saw theory as a moment of praxis, associated particularly with *technê*, and within the realm of praxis, sees *phronêsis* as preeminent. In contrast to many other twentieth-century thinkers, however, Heidegger did not think of *phronêsis* as knowledge learned from experience, but radically reconceived it (drawing on Augustine and Luther) as "historicity," which he understands as a revelatory insight into what is necessary here and now, a "moment of vision" more akin to a divine revelation than to everyday prudence.

This argument is central to *Being and Time*. Heidegger argues that we typically experience the world theoretically as presence-at-hand or technically, as readiness-to-hand or equipment. He suggests that both of these need to be subordinated to Dasein's experience of time as historicity or *phronêsis*. This turn from theory and technical rationality to *phronêsis* is decisive in the development of both existentialism and phenomenology, redirecting them toward praxis in general and political praxis in particular. Moreover, Heidegger's "theological" interpretation of *phronêsis* gives his thinking about politics a radical and indeed a millenarian character.

This "theological" element was at the heart of Heidegger's thought from the beginning in his focus on the question of Being. Dasein for Heidegger stands in a unique relationship to Being (*Sein*). Dasein is not merely being-in-the-world; Being is in the world only in and through Dasein. Being (*Sein*) for Heidegger is ontologically different than beings (*Seienden*), and thus appears to us always as no-thing, i.e., as a profound mystery, therefore always as a question and never as an answer. Dasein can confront this question because it is the only being that has its own Being as a question. Dasein experiences this question not intellectually (there is no word or concept adequate to Being), but "affectively," through a variety of moods. In *Being and Time* anxiety in the face of death is the means by which Dasein grasps its finitude and experiences the question of Being. In his later thought, Heidegger suggests that great joy and existential boredom can also open up the question of Being.

The awesome and terrifying nature of this experience generally induces Dasein to conceal and forget this question by dwelling on and in its everyday concerns, living as everyone else lives, as "they" live. Such a life, in Heidegger's view, is inauthentic because it does not confront the truth of existence, i.e., it is uniquely ours and radically finite. Metaphysics since Plato has been such a forgetting and concealing. With Hegel and Nietzsche, Heidegger believes that metaphysics comes to an end. He thus feels that it may be possible to raise the question of Being, and thereby come to understand our authentic historical task or destiny.

Heidegger's account of anxiety and human finitude draws on Kierkegaard, and his thought was initially read in this light as radically individualistic. For Heidegger, however, the experience of death or nothingness does not isolate the individual, but propels him toward his people and generation, i.e., toward political life. Following Aristotle,

539

Heidegger understood Dasein as *Mitsein*, i.e., as being-with-others. Dasein is not as an individual subject related to others intersubjectively, but the *zôon logon echon* (rational animal or literally, "life that has speech") and thus the *zôon politikon* (political animal). We live in and out of a communal logos and our being at its core is concerned with action. While contemplation may be a solitary activity, praxis is only possible in a community. *Dasein* in its very being is thus political.

For the most part, we are lost in our daily concerns that arise out of the world that is already formed. It is only when this world is broken that we experience the nothingness that is Being and that is also our Being as Dasein. Only a few are able to confront this question, and they are the *phronimoi*, the geniuses of practical wisdom who recognize their historical task or destiny. They live authentically by choosing their ownmost possibilities. While this sounds Kierkegaardian, Heidegger argues that such a choice does not mean abandoning the community, retreating into solipsism, and relating only to God. It means Dasein's choosing its ownmost possibilities within, with, and for the community.

The political meaning of this becomes evident in Heidegger's attachment to National Socialism. The bureaucratic state, in Heidegger's view, was a technical apparatus composed of Hegelian/Weberian bureaucrats who imagined themselves masters of technology but in fact were simply its servants. While this machine might coordinate everyday life, it only had meaning and legitimacy within a (largely Hegelian) metaphysics that the waning faith in absolute truth was undermining. The brokenness of this machine became evident with the political collapse of the early 1930s that catapulted Germany into a confrontation with nothingness and thus with the question of Being.

This crisis was not a theoretical crisis, as Husserl had suggested, but a crisis brought about by the hegemony of theory that blinded human beings to the guiding question of Being. For Heidegger, this crisis thus could only be resolved by a turn to *phronêsis*. The liberal parties were rooted in a theoretical understanding that was no longer tenable. The socialist and communist parties were focused on praxis, but they were guided not by *phronêsis* but by *technê* understood as the dialectical development of the means of production. Only National Socialism rested on *phronêsis*, on the leadership of a *phronimos*, a man who had faced his own mortality and now stood in the service of his people and generation. In Heidegger's opinion, Hitler was a man of such an "unprecedented will," who had "awakened this will in the entire people and welded it into a single resolve," and who consequently "is alone the present and future of German reality and its law" (Wolin 1991: 47, 49, 60). Hitler may have lacked spiritual depth in Heidegger's view, but he had a unique practical insight into what was necessary in the moment. And in the event Heidegger was convinced that he himself could provide the philosophic depth that was missing in Hitler and the National Socialist movement.

Heidegger was not oblivious to the dangers of this path. In *Introduction to Metaphysics*, he portrays the true leader as a wielder of the awesome and uncanny power of Being itself, a power that allows him to lead his people into a new way of being. Heidegger recognizes, however, that the leader himself, like Oedipus, is necessarily entangled in perversity and therefore beyond the city (*apolis*), in Aristotle's sense both a beast and a god. He also knew that the philosopher who participates in such efforts might also become entangled in this perversity. Nonetheless, he aligned himself with the Nazi movement, became the rector of his university, tried to reorganize it on the

Führerprinzip, and sought to become the leader of all higher education in Germany in order to help create a new political existence for the German people.

His failure did not convince him he was wrong, but only that he had underestimated the continuing power of the metaphysical tradition, and particularly the power of technology. He thus turned in his later thought to a deconstruction of metaphysics and an attempt to transform technology by coming to terms with its source in primordial making or *poiêsis*. In his late thought, Heidegger thus seeks to transfigure technology poetically. At the heart of this attack, however, is not an aesthetic but a theological and political motive. This is the result of the fact that he came to believe that it was not the *phronimôs* who is the voice of Being in our times but the poet. If Hitler occupied the place of Oedipus in Heidegger's thought of the 1930s, Hölderlin occupies the place of Tiresias in his later thought. In the end Heidegger's concern with the practical does not lead to political philosophy but to a prophetic and millenarian political theology, typified by his claim that only a god can save us. He thus longs in the end for apocalyptic change and sees all lesser political reform, however important it may be for human well-being, as insignificant.

French Existentialism

After World War II, Heidegger sought to minimize his commitment to Nazism and in doing so deemphasized the political character of his thought. French existentialists, by contrast, remained openly and deeply committed to politics. This was in part the result of their struggle against fascism, but also a consequence of the revival of Hegelianism in France as a result of Alexander Kojève's famous series of public lectures in the 1930s. The French existentialist movement of the 1940s and 1950s largely comprised those who heard or read these lectures.

Kojève's Hegel was not the conservative Hegel of the later system, but the young, dynamic, and revolutionary Hegel of the *Phenomenology*; a Hegel read through Marx and Heidegger who was concerned with the dialectical/historical development of consciousness. The central feature of human beings in his account is the life-and-death struggle essential to self-consciousness and the master–slave dialectic. This Hegel spoke deeply to the generation that had experienced World War I and the Russian Revolution, and continued to resonate with them in their struggle against fascism. For Kojève there are two basic human tasks, the self-assertion of the warrior and the liberating transformation of the world by the worker. History is shaped by these two forces. The remarkable claim that Kojève makes is that these tasks are completed and history is at an end. In contrast to Hegel and in keeping with Marx, however, Kojève asserts that history ends not with the establishment of multiple rational states, but with the institution of one universal state. At the end of history the task of the intellectual is thus not thinking but acting, not reflection on what ought to be, but the institutionalization of what has already been finally and truly determined.

This reading of Hegel and history gave French intellectuals a framework for their struggle against fascism. Fascism was an atavistic rejection of the rationality of history, a denial of universalism. The intellectuals' engagement with politics was thus generally in resistance to the enemies of historical necessity. They thus saw themselves not as political partisans but as agents of the human spirit, engaged in a life and death struggle by which they could attain autonomy and liberate humanity from slavery. In other words, the advent of fascism and the outbreak of World War II opened up again, and perhaps for the last time, the possibility for participating in the world-historical task of human liberation. The political goals of French existentialism were thus radically different than those of liberalism. They aimed not at the reform of existing political institutions and a more decent politics of interest and compromise, but at an authentic and universal communal life. Their political struggle, however, was continually beset by a deep anxiety, for they knew from Kojève and Heidegger that the vitality of their struggle might well die with its success. The fear of such an outcome led many of them to reject all lasting political orders and to promote a doctrine of permanent resistance and revolution.

Sartre is a case in point. Human beings, for Sartre, are characterized in Hegelian and Nietzschean fashion by the fact that they continually transcend or surpass themselves. For Sartre, the principle of identity only holds for being-in-itself which characterizes unconscious, nonhuman things. As being-for-itself (or self-consciousness), human being is self-surpassing or self-overcoming, i.e., it is always outside itself, transcending itself. As bodily beings we are in-ourselves, always in our factical situation (thrown into the world, to use Heidegger's formulation), and yet we are also always more than this situation (Sartre 1956: 310).

For Sartre, at the core of human being is thus an existential freedom. We are free because we are always transcending ourselves. We make and remake ourselves through our choices. Humans are not driven by passion, as Nietzsche and Dostoyevsky suggested, but fashion themselves in Kierkegaardian fashion by spontaneous and thus groundless acts of will. Things have value not in themselves but because they are chosen (Sartre 1956: 294). Choice is a leap of commitment that makes us what we are. In choosing we are guided not by reason or God (who does not exist) but by an aesthetic sensibility: "I am creating a certain image of man as I would have him be. In fashioning myself I fashion man" (Sartre 1956: 292).

Our choices are thus governed only by something like a aesthetic categorical imperative: "one ought always to ask oneself what would happen if everyone did as one is doing; nor can one escape from that disturbing thought except by a kind of self-deception" (Sartre 1956: 292). While humans are free in their choices, they are beset by a grave responsibility, for each of their choices plays a role in shaping humanity. This inescapable responsibility leads to anguish and despair. As Sartre puts it, we are thus "condemned to be free" (Sartre 1956: 295). Sartre agrees with Heidegger that we typically flee from this responsibility into the banality of everyday life and live inauthentically. We can pretend to live as if we were merely something in-itself, but in fact we are not. To live thus is to live in bad faith. It is true that we are determined, that we are something in-itself, but we are also for-ourselves, i.e., self-conscious and thus free. Our choices are not unlimited, and, contrary to Heidegger, we can never know with certainty that our choice is correct, but we can always make something out of what we have been made into.

In Sartre's early thought this notion of authenticity is radically individualistic. Indeed, he considers others a danger because they objectify us and endanger our subjectivity and freedom. *No Exit* is a denial of intersubjectivity, summed up in the famous observation that "hell is other people." In his later thought, however, he concludes that individuals cannot will their own freedom without willing the freedom of others. Being-for-itself is intimately connected to being-for-others. Individual authenticity is only possible on the basis of collective authenticity. Psychological and political freedom are inextricable. The individual thus must be political and must have as his aim collective authenticity.

In order to achieve such collective authenticity, society must be restructured so there is no need for bad faith and so that each individual can freely form himself according to his own will. Following Marx, Sartre argues that scarcity is the source of conflict and inequality. Therefore, liberation is only possible on the basis of a socialism that provides abundantly for all human beings. Similarly, classes must be eliminated because they engender role-playing and bad faith. Among the existing political parties Sartre made common cause with the communists, although he believed that such an alliance was only appropriate in the particular situation of the times, and in fact abandoned the party for the Maoists late in life because he believed the communists were unwilling to act in the revolutionary manner the times demanded.

Given his commitment to the existential freedom of the individual, however, Sartre had little patience for democratic centralism. He rejected Machiavellianism, and was more a libertarian socialist than a Leninist. Still he believed that what counts is total commitment. These countervailing commitments could only be reconciled in a society in which all individuals freely determined and were able to actualize their own ends. The political ambivalence of both existentialism and phenomenology is thus reflected in Sartre's thought, as he is pulled toward both a millennialist transfiguration of the political and a radical and at times solipsistic assertion of individuality.

The Problem of the Political in Existentialism and Phenomenology

Existentialism and phenomenology are extraordinarily ambivalent about politics and thus about political philosophy. On one hand they are apolitical or antipolitical, retreating from a political realm that seems to stand between them and an immediate experience of God or existence, while on the other they seek a radical transformation of the political realm into a community of authenticity in which they can immerse themselves in the immediacy of their fellow beings. Political life for them is thus either all or nothing. For the most part, the concern with interests, with institutions, and questions of right or justice, of constitutions, etc., are not merely matters of indifference, but tainted by their origin in the banality, inauthenticity, and hypocrisy of everyday life. Their goal is to recapture the immediacy of existence, the intensity of living that is lost in the complicated mediating institutions of political life. The fact that this intensity always seems to elude them produces no disinclination to proceed. They believe that "tomorrow we will run faster, stretch out our arms further, until one fine day . . ." Existentialism and phenomenology thus live always in anticipation of a radical change that at its core may be unattainable. In this sense they remain millenarian even when they preach atheism above all things. They are thus not likely to be the source of a lasting or a stable politics, but they are likely to be a continuing voice of dissatisfaction with politics in its everyday incarnations.

References and Further Reading

Detweiller, B. (1990) *Nietzsche and the Politics of Aristocratic Radicalism*. Chicago: University of Chicago Press.

Gillespie, M. A. (1984) *Hegel, Heidegger, and the Ground of History*. Chicago: University of Chicago Press.

—— (1995) *Nihilism Before Nietzsche*. Chicago: University of Chicago Press.

Husserl, E. (1970) *The Crisis of European Sciences and Transcendental Phenomenology* (trans. D. Carr). Evanston, IL: Northwestern University Press (original work published 1936 and 1954).

Luijpen, W. A., and Koren, H. J. (1964) *Existential Phenomenology: A First Introduction*. Pittsburgh, PA: Duquesne University Press.

Nietzsche, F. (1966) *Thus Spoke Zarathustra* (trans. W. Kaufmann). New York: Penguin (original work published 1883–92).

Rosen, S. (2003) *Hermeneutics and Politics*, 2nd edn. New Haven, CT: Yale University Press.

Safranski, R. (1998) *Martin Heidegger: Between Good and Evil* (trans. E. Osers). Cambridge, MA: Harvard University Press (original work published 1994).

Sartre, J-P. (1956) Existentialism is a Humanism (trans. P. Mairet). In W. Kaufmann (ed.), *Existentialism from Dostoyevsky to Sartre* (pp. 345–68). New York: World Publishing (original work published 1946).

Velkley, R. (1987) Edmund Husserl. In L. Strauss and J. Cropsey (eds.), *History of Political Philosophy*, 3rd edn. (pp. 870–87). Chicago: University of Chicago Press.

Wolin, R. (ed.) (1991) *The Heidegger Controversy*. Cambridge, MA: MIT Press.

37

History and Historicity

CHARLES GUIGNON

Phenomenology and the Problem of History

The idea that all human understanding is contextualized in history seems to be at odds with the ideal of phenomenology as originally conceived. In his earliest formulations of phenomenology as a method, Edmund Husserl insisted that this approach should describe how things show up for consciousness, not provide historical explanations of how they came to be. His 1911 essay, "Philosophy as Rigorous Science" (Husserl 1965), rejected all accounts of our beliefs as historical products on the grounds that such genetic approaches promote "historicism," a form of historical relativism that sees all belief and interpretation as relative to the historical worldview in which they appear. Historicism, as a general account of our situation, is deeply problematic, for it not only undermines science's aim of discovering timeless truths, it is also self-defeating, since its truth would entail that it itself is only a transient, historically relative product.

Martin Heidegger, Husserl's protégé, challenged this conception of phenomenology in his 1927 work *Being and Time* (Heidegger 1962). For Heidegger, temporality and historicity are central to any understanding of being whatsoever. Drawing on the explicitly historical approaches of Friedrich Nietzsche and Wilhelm Dilthey, Heidegger shifts the focus of phenomenology from the intuitions in the consciousness of a subject to what emerges into presence in a temporal and historical unfolding. As Heidegger's student, Hans-Georg Gadamer, describes this radicalization of phenomenology, "*the whole idea of grounding itself underwent a total reversal*" from Husserl's early conception. "Heidegger's thesis was that being itself was time. This burst asunder the whole subjectivism of modern philosophy" (Gadamer 1989: 257; emphasis added).

It was in response to Heidegger and others that Husserl in the mid-1930s attempted to incorporate the historical into a new, genetic conception of phenomenology (Husserl 1970). The following account of the concept of history in phenomenology and existentialism will start with Husserl's 1930s view of history, will then turn to Heidegger's characterization of history in 1927, and will conclude with remarks about the conception of history in the work of more recent phenomenologists and existentialists.

Husserl: The "Inner History" of Europe and of Humanity

Husserl's aversion to a historical approach to knowledge is best understood by comparing it to Dilthey's conception of our epistemic situation. Throughout his most productive years, Dilthey's primary aim was to lay a foundation for history in an account of human beings as temporal unfoldings. According to this account, everyday life in the world is made up of "life-experiences" (*Erlebnisse*), where these are understood as meaning-filled interactions with the world. What makes possible the meaningful whole (*Zusammenhang*) of life, for Dilthey, is the agent's reflection (*Besinnung*) on experience, where "reflection" is understood as the process of "making sense" in which we take stock of our lives (Dilthey 2002: 217–22, 259). Historical understanding, in turn, is made possible by this inbuilt structure of reflective life – as Dilthey says, "We are historical beings before we are observers of history, and only because we are the former do we become the latter" (Dilthey 2002: 297). We exist as "bearers" and "carriers" of history, products of historical developments that make up our "facticity" and shape our outlook in ways we can never make totally explicit. This embeddedness in history gives us access to a sense of the meaning of history and provides the basis for grasping the historical.

Husserl, in contrast, holds that a historical point of view such as Dilthey's leads to the sort of "worldview" philosophy that undermines science's claim to discover universally valid truths. Focusing especially on the exact, nondescriptive sciences – especially pure mathematics – Husserl argues that there must be knowledge that is grounded in apodictic evidence presented to consciousness. Historical information is not only irrelevant to the truth of a proposition, it is a major source of the presuppositions that need to be bracketed if we are to inquire into the grounds for science.

Starting with his 1935 Vienna lecture on "Philosophy and the Crisis of European Humanity," however, Husserl's writings underwent an important shift. The subject matter of this lecture is "the philosophical–historical idea (or the teleological sense) of European humanity" (Husserl 1970: 269). According to this lecture, what is distinctive about European humankind is the way it is driven by a defining idea, the idea of achieving rational, theoretical knowledge of the "totality of beings" (*Allheit des Seienden*) (Husserl 1970: 291). The lecture speaks of an ideal of pure, detached *theoria* in which "man becomes a nonparticipating spectator" (Husserl 1970: 285). This ideal originated in ancient Greece in an experience of *wonder* and it has defined the "vocation" of European humanity ever since. The ideal of theoretical knowledge is grounded in a *resolve* not to accept anything handed down from tradition, but rather to inquire into what is true in itself. Through the historical formation of this *telos* of European humanity, norms drawn from truth itself have become absolute values for all humans. The result has been a global "transformation of human existence [*Dasein*] and its whole cultural life" (Husserl 1970: 289). As Husserl puts it in a later essay, the Greek conception of "the whole of Being" (*Seinsall*) creates "a final form [*Endgestalt*] . . . which is at the same time a beginning form [*Anfangsgestalt*] of a new sort of infinity," that is, the task of carrying through the "infinity of exhibitings whose harmonious identity – *idealiter* – [is] the thing itself" (Husserl 1970: 339, 347).

The idea that the West has brought into existence a unique "sending" (*Sendung*) for all humanity is central to Husserl's uncompleted last work, *The Crisis of European*

Sciences and Transcendental Phenomenology (1936; cited as Husserl 1970). In this unfinished book, the crisis of European existence is said to stem from the failure of Western humanity to fully realize its overarching *telos*, the goal of achieving freedom by undertaking the task of rationally grounding all belief and action. What defines Europe's spiritual idea (and distinguishes it from merely "empirical anthropological type[s] like 'China' and 'India'") is its "being toward a *telos*," that is, its being underway in a shared project in which we, as philosophers, are "*functionaries of mankind*" (Husserl 1970: 16–17). In order to disclose this hidden "entelechy" that underlies and makes intelligible all historical events, Husserl says, we must "strike through the crust of externalized 'historical facts' of philosophical history" and exhibit "their inner meaning and hidden teleology" (Husserl 1970: 18).

Revealing the "inner history" of Europe means recovering the founding of the end, which was at the same time the founding of the beginning, of that history. In an appendix to the *Crisis*, Husserl sketches out part of this inner history in terms of the "two epochs" of modern history (Husserl 1970: 339–40). The first crucial epoch begins when Descartes posits intentionality, takes up the demand of apodicticity, and insists on bringing all evidence back to the *cogito*. Descartes's crucial move sets modern Europe on its course. At the same time, however, this Cartesian thrust forward is covered over by a misunderstanding of what the project of rationalism truly entails. Like Galileo before him, Descartes falls into "naturalism" or "objectivism," where this means the "reduction of the infinite task of knowing to the mathematico-physical knowing" of modern science (Ricoeur 1967: 154). With the uncritical conception of reality as *res extensa* and the conception of the "I" as a psychological ego rather than the "absolute ego," Descartes falls prey (*verfällt*) to a distorted understanding of what rationality is. This *falling* into an uncritical acceptance of objectivist and naturalistic presuppositions, with its accompanying loss of any commitment to genuine grounding, represents the "greatest danger" of Western civilization: the loss of freedom and responsibility for meaning-giving that defines not only Western humanity but, through it, all humanity. When the insights achieved through transcendental reflection are covered over, the potential and significance of the first epoch are concealed.

But even though Descartes's own formulation of his project led to a falling away from the ideal of rationality, the moves made by his successors led toward the recovery of the transcendental standpoint. Kant is a pivotal figure in this story, of course, but Husserl surprisingly gives credit to Hume who, despite his "absurd skepticism," achieved a genuine philosophy by "shaking objectivism" (Husserl 1970: §24). These developments in philosophy have opened the way to the second epoch of modernity, the "renewed beginning" achieved in Husserl's own return to the "primal ground [*Urboden*] . . . of all philosophy." The new epoch is achieved through a "reappropriation of the Cartesian discovery, the fundamental demand of apodicticity." It breaks with objectivism by bringing to light the idea of the philosophizing ego as "absolute intersubjectivity," "as the bearer of absolute reason coming to itself," and its correlate, "the 'existing world,' the meaning of being [*Seinssinn*] of which [is] transcendentally constituted" (Husserl 1970: 340). Overcoming the "greatest danger" of European civilization – the danger created by objectivism – requires the courage and resolve to carry through the West's mission for humanity.

Husserl's addendum to the text of the *Crisis*, "The Origin of Geometry," provides a vivid example of what an "inner history" is supposed to be. The aim of this essay is not to expose what Derrida calls the "de facto historical culture" in which geometry as a practice arose. Its aim, rather, is to reveal the "culture of truth, whose ideality is absolutely normative" (Derrida 1978: 59) because it arose, at some distant point in the past, out of creative acts endowed with self-evidence.

The distinction between de facto history and the culture of truth can be clarified by reflecting on the current situation of mathematical practice. In the present world, we find ourselves using a geometry that is "ready-made," already on hand for our use, the offshoot of a sedimented tradition about which we know very little. Much of our practice in geometry involves using propositions and symbols that have trickled down to us through a long process of passing the word along. Our activities in geometry are a sort of game: we make the moves that seem appropriate given the game that is in play, for the most part with no insight into the grounds of this game. Our thinking is, in the terminology of Brentano and Husserl, "inauthentic" (*uneigentlich*), operating with unfulfilled intentions. But even though we have almost no knowledge of what grounds this practice, we have an "implicit knowledge" of primordial grounds, a knowledge "which can thus also be made explicit, a knowledge of unassailable self-evidence" (Husserl 1970: 355). If we can recover this primal evidence through a "regressive inquiry," we will be able to do geometry in a way that is "authentic" (*eigentlich*), or, as Husserl more often says in this context, "genuine" (*echt*).

So the attempt to retrieve the authentic origins of geometry does not involve going back to "some undiscoverable Thales of geometry" (Husserl 1970: 369). Instead, its aim is to *reactivate* the founding intuitions and meaning-giving acts that must have occurred for there to be such a thing as geometry. In Husserl's words,

> our interest shall be the inquiry back into the most original sense in which geometry once arose, was present as the tradition of millennia, [and] is still present . . . we inquire into that sense in which it appeared in history for the first time – *in which it had to appear*, even though we know nothing of the first creators and are not even asking after them. (Husserl 1970: 354)

The assumption is that there was an initial founding or establishing (*Stiftung*) of geometry, an initial spiritual accomplishment fully present in its first execution. This founding of a beginning (*Anfang*) must at the same time be the founding of a goal or end, since any intentional act always intends its fulfillment. For this reason, Husserl can say that geometry just *is* the history of its development from its beginning through its practice today as it develops toward its (perhaps never fully realizable) future fulfillment. Because asking "What is geometry?" is equivalent to asking about this history and tradition, the "ruling dogma" of a separation between epistemological elucidation and historical explanation must be rejected (Husserl 1970: 370): to know what geometry is *just is* to know its inner history.

"Asking backward" to the source seeks to reactivate "the submerged original beginnings of geometry as they must have been in their 'primally establishing' [*urstiftenden*] function" (Husserl 1970: 354). What is recovered in this inner history is not the various things actual people have said and written at various times, but, for example, the *one* Pythagorean Theorem that exists as an "ideal" objectivity and is accessed time after time by different practitioners and students in different languages. Seen from this standpoint, the inquiry into the origins of geometry is concerned with bringing to light the essential structures of the one self-identical geometry that has been passed down to us from its originators, *despite* the crablike, halting movements that make up actual historical development. Such a recovery of origins brackets de facto history and is concerned solely with returning to the primal wellsprings (*Quellen*) from which our current conceptualizations and practices were originally drawn.

In section 9.1 of the *Crisis*, Husserl points out that the regressive method of recovery for any science has an unavoidably circular structure. At the outset, all we have to go on is the ready-made practice of the science in which we are already participants. "The understanding of the beginnings is to be gained fully only by starting with science as given in its present-day form, looking back at its development" (Husserl 1970: 58). But this de facto historical vantage point does not immediately reveal the *sense* that defines the science's development and so makes it the science that it is. As Husserl says, "in the absence of an understanding of the *beginnings*, the development is mute as a *development of meaning*." Moreover, as we have seen, the present-day self-understanding of science is generally distorted by the prevalence of objectivism. The dominance of objectivism is the source of the "'breakdown'-situation" in which we live today, a time in which the fullness of the phenomena is covered over by busy puzzle-solving within the parameters of objectivism's uncriticized assumptions (Husserl 1970: 58).

In order to grasp the essential structures that define the science, therefore, it is necessary to use our initial "implicit knowledge" of the scientific practice as a clue to recovering the originating meanings of that science. In Derrida's words, "only retroactively and on the basis of its results can we illuminate the pure sense of the subjective praxis which has engendered geometry." Based on our understanding of our own goals and purposes as practitioners of the science, we attempt to reactivate the founding meanings that define the teleological project of the science, for "only a teleology can open up a passage, a way back toward the beginnings" (Derrida 1978: 64). As a result, the inquiry involves a shuttlecock movement between present and past: as Husserl says, "we have no other choice than to proceed forward and backward in a zigzag pattern" (Husserl 1970: 58). We use the projection of ends into the future that is definitive of our current practice in order to grasp the beginnings that defined this science as a unified, meaningful possibility. Then we use that interpretation of the origins as a basis for selecting events that count as developments in that science. So the inner history must be understood in the light of the de facto history, while the de facto history is intelligible only in the light of the inner history. In this sort of interpretation (*Auslegung*), "relative clarification on one side brings some elucidation on the other, which in turn casts light back on the former" (Husserl 1970: 58).

In "The Origin of Geometry," Husserl addresses the question of how geometrical ideality proceeds "from its primarily intrapersonal origin, where it is a structure within the conscious space of the first inventor's soul, to its ideal objectivity" as a structure for consciousness as such (Husserl 1970: 358). The answer is that this shift from a subjective, personal intuition to a "we-horizon" is achieved through language. Language is the medium through which the shared life-world "can be an open and endless one,

549

as it is always for humans" (Husserl 1970: 358). Through speaking and, even more important, through writing, the meaning-structure becomes sedimented and is passed down in the form of a tradition that holds for everyone. This sedimentation has both a positive and negative aspect. On the one hand, it preserves and makes accessible the discoveries of the past. On the other hand, it leads people to "fall prey to the *seduction of language*," so that entire regions of life degenerate into mere talking (*Reden*) and reading, where there is only "a passive taking-over of ontic validity [*Seinsgeltung*]" (Husserl 1970: 362, 364). It is because of this fallen state of what is transmitted by the tradition that what is passed along must be cashed in by a reactivation of genuine meanings. Only then can the grounding level of those "elemental concepts" that sprang originally from prescientific life be recovered so that the tradition becomes genuine (Husserl 1970: 366).

The entire process of falling into tradition and retrieval of original wellsprings of meaning displays the fact that all sciences exist as historical. To understand this, Husserl says, is also to see that both history and life's own historicity have essential structures that "can be revealed through methodical inquiry" (Husserl 1970: 369). The continuum of the past has a *unity* of sense that becomes apparent when we see that initial founding creative acts, traditionalization, sedimentation, and reactivation are bound together in a way that preserves an underlying self-evidence. A historical continuity of this sort is necessary *for there to be such a thing as a science*. The process defines "the universal a priori of history": as Husserl says, history "is from the start nothing other than the vital movement of coexistence and interweaving of original formations and sedimentations of meaning" (Husserl 1970: 371). This a priori of history must be teleological: it is a forward thrust toward the realization of the aim of reason. All cases of de facto history are intelligible only insofar as they reflect and embody this underlying historical a priori. The historical a priori therefore makes possible all the "historical facticities" (Husserl 1970: 373) that might be adduced in arguments in favor of a historical relativism. In other words, the very idea of historical relativism presupposes a priori, essential structures that undermine the claims of relativism.

In a section of the *Crisis* on methodology (§15), Husserl echoes Dilthey's claim that we have access to the historical only because we ourselves are participants in and carriers of a historical tradition. As philosophers, we embody the teleological mission that defines all human history, and so we can grasp the historical "from the *inside*" by reflecting on the spiritual heritage (*Erbe*) that is truly our own. Because we are functionaries, heirs and cobearers of the direction of the will that pervades humanity, every recovery of the primal founding act of our historical tradition is at the same time a recognition of the motivation underlying our own assigned task. As for Dilthey, historical inquiry must be rooted in a sensitive reflection on meaning (*Besinnung*) in which we grasp what is most truly our own and thereby come into our own as the beings we are. Or alternatively, using the language of Brentano and Husserl, we could say that, by fulfilling one's intention as a forward-moving thrust toward one's proper telos, the philosopher becomes *authentic*.

Reflection on sense enables us to move from dispersed experiences to a grasp of what binds those experiences into a unity of sense. But it also enables us to see ourselves as belonging to a greater story: the project of Western civilization and, thereby, of human history as a whole. As Husserl puts it,

A historical, backward reflection . . . is thus actually the deepest kind of self-reflection aimed at a self-understanding in terms of what we are authentically [*eigentlich*] seeking as the historical beings we are. Self-reflection serves making a decision: and here this naturally means immediately carrying on with the task which is most truly ours [*eigensten Aufgabe*] . . . the task set for us all in the present. (Husserl 1970: 72, translation modified)

Although Husserl insists that history is an "infinite task," his final picture of "inner history" is in other respect strikingly similar to Hegel's "Philosophy of History" with its conception of "the cunning of reason" working behind the scenes and employing individuals and communities to achieve its ends (Löwith 1970: 52–9).

Heidegger: History as Destruction and Retrieval

Husserl's conceptions of inner history and historicity are always transcendental in the sense that they presuppose a reduction to pure immanence throughout: only the meaning-world is examined, and the reflection remains within the meanings constituted by subjectivity (Patočka 1996: 168). When Heidegger turns to the topic of history, however, he no longer sees it as immanent in subjectivity. Increasingly struck by the way world, community, and history work behind our backs, shaping our sense of things in ways we can never fully objectify and comprehend, he concludes that history is part of the "factical" thrownness that constitutes our being enmeshed in a non-totalizable context. Although *Being and Time* follows Husserl in trying to grasp history and historicity as essential structures (or "existentials") of human existence, what emerges is an awareness of the limits of our ability to achieve total clarity about the nature of our historical embeddedness. Because we are always caught up in a historical context we can never totally master, the Husserlian ideal of all-embracing "theoretical reason" is untenable.

Being and Time begins with an account of the worldhood of the world, where "world" is understood as the all-pervasive background of meaningful relations in which agents are always already thrown. In our average, everyday ways of being involved with things, we are "being-in-the-world" in the sense that our very being as humans (or *Dasein*) is inextricably bound up with a background of significance and relevance relationships. This world is always a shared world: it is from the outset made accessible through the interpretations and practices of a linguistic community, what Heidegger calls the "one" or "anyone" (*das Man*). As participants in a shared social context, we interpret things in terms of the standardized "interpretedness" deposited in our public language (Heidegger 1962: 211). As Heidegger notes, "this discoursing has lost its primary relationship-of-being toward the entities talked about," and so "it does not communicate in such a way as to let entities be appropriated in a primordial manner, but communicates rather by following the route of . . . *passing the word along* . . . What-is-said-in-the-talk . . . takes on an authoritative character. Things are so because 'one' [*Man*] says so." The result is a process in which Dasein's "initial lack of grounds to stand on [*Bodenständigkeit*] becomes aggravated to complete groundlessness [*Bodenlosigkeit*]" (Heidegger 1962: 212; translation modified).

Heidegger asks about the essential structures of Dasein that make up the phenomenon of being-in-the-world and discovers three existentials that determine the being of any human whatsoever: situatedness (being "already-in"), discursiveness (being "among" entities in ways that articulate them), and understanding (being "ahead-of-itself" in projecting possible ways of being). These three existentials define the being of Dasein as *care*, and the meaning of care itself is found to be temporality. Dasein is an entity whose being is defined by the fact that it is projected toward the future in undertaking projects, operating out of a past it "always already is" as "having-been," and involved with what shows up in the mode of "making present." In this temporal structure, the future has priority: it is because we take a stand on our lives by undertaking concrete projects that we can encounter the past as resources for our activities and thereby engage ourselves with what is present. At the same time, it is characterized by an inveterate tendency to "fall" (*Verfallen*) in line with the "anyone" and follow socially accepted norms.

Heidegger's conceptions of history and historicity (*Geschichte, Geschichtlichkeit*) grow out of his account of Dasein as temporality. Temporality, he says, is "the condition for the possibility of historicity as a temporal mode of being of Dasein" (Heidegger 1962: 41). In other words, it is because Dasein is a "movement" or "happening" (*Geschehen*) with a distinctive structure that historical unfolding, and hence "world-history," are possible. To say that Dasein's being is characterized by historicity is to say that it has two related characteristics. First of all, it means that Dasein *is* its past, where this past is given meaning and salience by Dasein's future-directed projects (the past, Heidegger says, "'happens' out of its future on each occasion" 1962: 41). Secondly, it means that whatever way Dasein has of understanding itself at any time stems from the traditional or handed-down (*überkommene*) way of interpreting itself into which it has grown up in the first place. "By this understanding, the possibilities of its being are disclosed and regulated" (Heidegger 1962: 41). The concrete range of possible roles and self-definitions we can take over in realizing our identity are all drawn from the pool of self-interpretations handed down to us by our history. This past "is not something which *follows along after* Dasein, but rather [the past is] something which already goes ahead of it" (Heidegger 1962: 41): the possibilities we receive from the past give us guidance and direction in taking a stand on the future.

On Heidegger's account of history, therefore, we are always embedded in a historical context that defines our possibilities of understanding. For the most part, this history is encountered in the form of a "tradition" (*Tradition*), where this is understood as the calcified set of uprooted and groundless presuppositions that determines in advance how we think and act. Heidegger says that we "fall prey" (*verfällt*) to this tradition in such a way that it becomes master of us: the tradition "takes what has come down to us and delivers it over to self-evidence," with the result that we lose the ability to grasp what it transmits. Tradition "blocks our access to [the] primordial 'well-springs' [*Quellen*]" from which our concepts spring in such a way that we "forget that they have had such an origin." Caught up in the swirl of tradition, oblivious to the primal sources of our concepts, we have no "ground of our own [*Boden*] to stand on" (Heidegger 1962: 43).

To counteract the fallenness and forgetfulness that results from our immersion in the tradition, we need a way of "destroying" or "destructuring" the tradition. To destructure is to peel off the hardened layers of concealment superimposed by tradition in order to recover or "retrieve" the "primordial experiences in which we achieved our first ways of determining the nature of being – the ways that have guided us ever since." The aim of this destructuring and its accompanying retrieval of origins is to demonstrate the sources of our basic concepts – those *"most elemental words* in which Dasein expresses itself" – by "an investigation in which their 'birth certificate' is displayed" (Heidegger 1962: 262, 44).

So far, Heidegger's account of history seems to be quite in tune with Husserl's. It is because we are living in the house of cards constructed by tradition, uprooted from the rough ground of primal experience, that we need a historical investigation that will lead us back to the sources from which all understanding springs. But the conceptions of history and historicity Heidegger develops toward the end of *Being and Time* show important differences from Husserl's account. These differences become apparent in "The Basic Constitution of Historicity" (§74), where Heidegger tries to characterize the forms of "authentic" historicity and historiography (*Geschichtlichkeit, Historie*) that make destructuring and retrieval of the past possible.

At the beginning of this section, Heidegger repeats the claim that Dasein "always understands itself in terms of those possibilities of existence which 'circulate' in the 'average' public ways of interpreting Dasein" in the "anyone" (Heidegger 1962: 435). Our understanding is always shaped and given content by the ways of thinking and acting found in our cultural context. But these passages now refer to a new way of encountering those public possibilities. If Dasein is authentic, Heidegger says, then it encounters the public possibilities not as a tradition, but as a "heritage" (*Erbe*), and this experience of the heritage in turn opens Dasein to the possibility of experiencing its own life as participating in the shared "destiny" (*Geschick*) of a "community, of a people [*Volk*]" (Heidegger 1962: 435–6). What this description of authentic historicity suggests is that being authentic involves, not the identification of one overarching project, as in Husserl's view of history, but rather experiencing oneself as a participant in a range of meaningful undertakings defined by one's heritage. But even though Husserl and Heidegger differ in their view of the eschatology definitive of human existence, they agree in holding that "history has its essential importance . . . in that authentic happening of existence which arises from Dasein's *future*" (Heidegger 1962: 438). The "happening" of human existence, at both the personal level and at the level of world history, is made possible by what Husserl calls a "teleology."

When Heidegger turns to describing the authentic relationship to history, he draws on Nietzsche's "The Use and Abuse of History." At the time Heidegger was writing, Nietzsche was generally seen as holding that there is a deep tension between historical research and life. "The Use and Abuse of History" suggests that, because historical reflection cuts us off from the needs of the present and encourages a detached, antiquarian curiosity about the past, it saps our ability to live fully in the here and now. As an alternative to the prevailing tendency in historical research, Nietzsche considers three possible approaches to history and to historiography that might be more conducive to the needs of life: the antiquarian, the critical, and the monumental. Nietzsche seems to hold that these perspectives toward the historical are fundamentally irreconcilable with one another, and that they are all fictive in the sense that they read events in a light of a prior point of view that determines in advance how events can show up as meaningful.

In *Being and Time*, Heidegger draws on Nietzsche's account of history in formulating his own conception of historiography, but instead of seeing the different modes of history as irreconcilably opposed, he tries to bind them into a single, overarching approach. Authentic historiography is, first of all, futural to the extent that it projects *monumental* possibilities of human existence as enduring models for how life might be lived. Second, it is *antiquarian* in the sense that it reverently preserves what came in the past as a reservoir of assets for understanding what sorts of goals are genuinely worthwhile. And, third, it is *critical* in the way it criticizes traditional interpretations circulating in the public world in order to bring to light alternative possibilities that are grounded in history's underlying projects and commitments.

Through spelling out the concrete form temporality takes as authentic historicity, Heidegger shows how historical destruction and retrieval are possible. This account is similar in many ways to Husserl's conception of "inner history" as a method of "questioning back" and reactivation. But there are also important differences. First, though Heidegger sees the need to project a telos for history if we are to have a basis for selecting what is to count as relevant to the historical story, he does not assume that there is a single project – that of *reason* – underlying all European and, indeed, world history. For Heidegger, there was a "founding" (*Stiftung*) of history in ancient Greek philosophy, a first beginning that needs to be retrieved and rethought in a new beginning for our times. But this primal founding of history is concerned with the question of being, not with the aims of "reason," and it is a beginning that can be radically reinterpreted in various epochs (Heidegger 2002: 47–9). Second, the respect in which history is a shared project, undertaken by "a community, a people," is made explicit and clear in Heidegger's conception of "destiny." There is no need to posit what Husserl calls an "absolute spirit" (Husserl 1970: 298) lying above or beneath the undertakings of real people in the world. And third, history is pictured not so much as something *we make* as something that *makes us*: it is an ongoing happening carrying us along as we try to make something of our situation. The idea of an "inner history," in the sense of a history immanent to consciousness, has no role to play. Instead of history being played out within subjectivity, Heidegger gives us a picture of subjectivity as a sort of side effect of the unfolding of history.

Phenomenological and Existentialist Developments after Husserl and Heidegger

In his monumental phenomenology of the human sciences, *Truth and Method* (1989), Hans-Georg Gadamer develops and transforms Heidegger's account of history in interesting ways. Where Heidegger placed special emphasis on the role of futurity in characterizing history, Gadamer stresses the way the past is always assimilated in ever-new ways though the unfolding of history. Treating the past as the source of all meaningful possibilities of understanding, Gadamer sets out to counteract "the Enlightenment prejudice against prejudices," arguing that constructive prejudices (or "prejudgments") provide us with a frame of reference in which we can question the texts passed down to us and encounter the past as answering our questions in the present. In Gadamer's view, the past lives on in the way it is assimilated into the horizon of the present as this rolls on into the future. We are ourselves products of what Gadamer calls "effective history," where this term refers to the way history is effective in constituting the paths and possibilities of understanding definitive of a community. Because we are always carried along by history, our mode of being is characterized as *belongingness* to something greater than what can be comprehended within subjectivity.

The hermeneutic phenomenologist Paul Ricoeur appropriates Heidegger's account of temporality and extends it by showing the relation between different forms of lived temporality and forms of narrative. In Ricoeur's view, human agency always has a "prenarrative quality" or "inchoate narrativity" that is inherent in life itself. This already preconfigured flow of events is then reconfigured through the emplotting that occurs in the reflective, post facto "telling" of what occurred. Historiography (and hence our understanding of history) grows out of this primal structuring built into the life process itself. In order to display the narrative dimension in all historical emplotment, Ricoeur calls attention to the way that following a story involves (1) anticipating some conclusion to the story, and then (2) making sense of the recounted events in terms of that prior anticipation. The futural anticipation, which provides a basis for knitting the events into a unified storyline, must be constantly reinterpreted in the light of the recounted events. The teleological movement involved in following a story supports the Heideggerian claim that any attempt to understand a course of events must be essentially futural, starting from a sense of what the whole story adds up to and then trying to see the episodes as realizing that overall whole (Ricoeur 1980).

Writing in the 1930s, the existentialist thinker, José Ortega y Gasset developed an especially interesting account of history (Ortega y Gasset 1961). Ortega rejects the conception of humans as static objects with a pregiven nature that arises from "physico-mathematical reasoning," and instead proposes we see humans as self-fashioning beings whose "nature" or "essence' is something they create through their ongoing choices as they act in the world. To be an agent, on this view, is to find oneself standing before an open range of possibilities where one chooses one's identity by choosing one set of possibilities over others. In this sense, "man is the entity that makes itself" (Ortega y Gasset 1961: 201). As we reach maturity, we have mapped out some general program for our lives, and this program provides a basis for making choices among the possibilities open to us. But the possibility of choice does not mean that "anything goes." The choices we make are limited in part by the "repertory of usages" making up the cultural context in which we find ourselves. But they are also limited by what we ourselves have been in the past. In Ortega's view, life has a dialectical structure insofar as moving beyond any particular possibility always involves reacting to and negating what came before. This negation means that our current self-interpretation gains its meaning from what came before (Ortega y Gasset 1961: 208). For Ortega, the dialectical unfolding of life also characterizes history in general: each new development in history gains its meaning from the way it negates what went before. The systematic order in history that results is something that can only be grasped through a "historical reason," "*a substantive reason constituted by what has happened to man,*" which is qualitatively different from physico-mathematical reason (Ortega y Gasset 1961: 231).

Although the quintessential existentialist Jean-Paul Sartre never discusses history in his main work, *Being and Nothingness* (1943; cited as Sartre 1984a), history became a central theme in his later writings. It might be argued, however, that these later,

"Marxist" writings were no longer "existentialist" in the same way his earlier works were. For this reason, in discussing Sartre's views on history, we will focus on Sartre's writings of the 1940s, in particular, the *War Diaries* (Sartre 1984b), composed in 1939–40, and his *Notebooks for an Ethics* (Sartre 1992) of the late 1940s, relying primarily on Thomas R. Flynn's excellent studies of Sartre on history (1992, 1997).

The *War Diaries* are in part a reply to Raymond Aron's 1938 dissertation, *Introduction á la philosophie de l'histoire* (Aron 1948). Aron opposes both Hegel's absolutist philosophy of history, with its faith in a knowable telos of history, and the late nineteenth-century positivist approach to history, with its assumption we can know the past "as it really was." In line with Nietzsche's claim that God is dead, Aron suggests that, if there is no absolute standpoint outside history from which history as a whole can be comprehended, then it must be the case that each historian interprets the historical record in terms of her own prior theoretical perspective. Since there are no uninterpreted historical facts discernible independent of the perspectives historians bring to historical research, historical relativism is inescapable. There can be only a plurality of partial and historically conditioned accounts of history, no "history as such." Moreover, given human freedom, there can no such thing as historical unity in the sense of a definitive culmination of history.

In response to Aron's rejection of the idea of historical facts, Sartre proposes a notion of a historical event (*événement*) as a way to defend historical realism. In addition to the way things have being for an individual subject, Sartre holds, there is also a way something is *for us* together, and this being *pour autrui* gives the historical event a facticity that makes it objective. The event, in relation to our *Mitsein* or "co-being," has the mode of being of the "always already" there: it is "having-been" as described by Heidegger. "[I]t is this event in its absolute existence that the historian intends" (Sartre 1984b: 299, cited in Flynn 1997: 18).

Sartre's thoughts on history are existentialist insofar as they make the individual the ultimate agent of history. We need to start from "the man projecting himself through situations and living them in the unity of human reality" (Sartre 1984b: 301, cited in Flynn 1997: 19). To understand the individual as the agent of history, it is necessary to show how humans act in *situations*, where the word "situation" refers to the seamless whole of individual and significant context of action. For Sartre, there is a circular interdependence between agent and situation: the situation always arises through one's "being-for-others," while one's actions in the situation modify the significance of that context. So action is grounded in an intelligible context one shares with others: "one is oneself only by projecting oneself freely through situations constituted by the Other's project" (Sartre 1984b: 21, cited in Flynn 1997: 21).

With these concepts, Sartre is able to move toward the notion of a social fact that *Being and Nothingness* could not achieve. In the *Notebooks for an Ethics*, written after the war, Sartre expands on this conception of shared situations and events in developing a general characterization of action. Action (or what Sartre later comes to call *praxis*) involves both internalization and externalization. In acting, the agent both *internalizes* or appropriates facticity in the form of the "past" of a situation and *externalizes* or expresses his or her own being as an agent by transcending this facticity. The product of any action is the work (*oeuvre*), and understanding an action involves grasping, in addition to the agent's intention, the work that results.

556

Sartre recognizes that historical events have a deep-seated ambivalence: they involve both facticity and free choice, the in-itself and the for-itself. The givenness of the historical act is crucial, yet Sartre also sees how historical events become other than they were intended to be as they are taken up and given meaning by a community. The event, a bearer of meanings ascribed to it by others, has a life of its own as it unfurls itself over time. It is part of the "inertia" of the historical that it is subject to chance happenings in the physical and social world.

The most pressing question about history for Sartre is how to define the wholeness or unity of history. Because human reality is characterized by transcendence, human phenomena have an open nature: there is no possibility of a final self-coincidence in which the *being* of the human is defined once and for all. For this reason, it seems that there is no way we can make sense of the idea of an endpoint of human history. Yet humans *need* a way of seeing history as adding up to something if their actions are to have a point. Sartre's late, two-volume *Critique of Dialectical Reason*, published in 1960 and 1976, draws on Hegel and Marx in an attempt to conceive such wholeness.

References and Further Reading

Aron, R. (1948) *Introduction á la philosophie de l'histoire: essai sur les limites de l'objectivité historique*. Paris: Gallimard.

Carr, D. (1974) *Phenomenology and the Problem of History: A Study of Husserl's Transcendental Philosophy*. Evanston, IL: Northwestern University Press.

Derrida, J. (1978) *Edmund Husserl's* Origin of Geometry: *An Introduction* (trans. J. P. Leavey, Jr.). Stony Brook, NY: Nicolas Hays (original work published 1962).

Dilthey, W. (2002) *The Formation of the Historical World in the Human Sciences*, vol. 3, *Selected Works* (trans. R. A. Makkreel and F. Rodi). Princeton, NJ: Princeton University Press (original work published 1910).

Flynn, T. R. (1992) Sartre and the poetics of history. In C. Howells (ed.), *The Cambridge Companion to Sartre* (pp. 213–60). Cambridge: Cambridge University Press.

—— (1997) *Sartre, Foucault, and Historical Reason*, vol. I, *Toward an Existentialist Theory of History*. Chicago: University of Chicago Press.

Fynsk, C. (1993) *Heidegger: Thought and Historicity*. Ithaca, NY: Cornell University Press.

Gadamer, H-G. (1989) *Truth and method*, 2nd rev. edn (trans. J. Weinsheimer and D. G. Marshall). New York: Crossroad (original work published 1960).

Heidegger, M. (1962) *Being and Time* (trans. J. Macquarrie and E. Robinson). New York: Harper & Row (original work published 1927).

—— (2002) The origin of the work of art. In J. Young and K. Hayes (ed. and trans.) *Off the Beaten Path* (pp. 1–56). Cambridge: Cambridge University Press (original works published 1935–46).

Husserl, E. (1965) Philosophy as rigorous science. In Q. Lauer (ed.), *Phenomenology and the Crisis of Philosophy*. New York: Harper & Row.

—— (1970) *The Crisis of European Sciences and Transcendental Philosophy* (trans. D. Carr). Evanston, IL: Northwestern University Press (original work published 1936).

Löwith, K. (1970) *The Meaning of History*. Chicago: University of Chicago Press.

Nietzsche, F. (1997) *Untimely Meditations* (ed. D. Breazeale, K. Ameriks, and D. M. Clarke; trans. R. J. Hollingdale). Cambridge: Cambridge University Press (original works published 1873–6).

Ortega y Gasset, J. (1961) *History as a System and Other Essays toward a Philosophy of History* (trans. H. Weyl). New York: W. W. Norton (original work published in 1939).

Patočka, J. (1996) *An Introduction to Husserl's Phenomenology* (trans. E. Kohák). Chicago: Open Court (original work published 1965).

Ricoeur, P. (1967) *Husserl: An Analysis of His Phenomenology* (trans. E. G. Ballard and L. Embree). Evanston, IL: Northwestern University Press (original work published 1943).

—— (1980) Narrative time. *Critical Inquiry*, 7, 169–90.

Ruin, H. (1994) *Enigmatic Origins: Tracing the Theme of Historicity through Heidegger's Works*. Stockholm Studies in Philosophy, 15. Stockholm: Almqvist & Wiksell.

Sartre, J-P. (1984a) *Being and Nothingness* (trans. H. E. Barnes). New York: Washington Square Press (original work published 1943).

—— (1984b) *The War Diaries of Jean-Paul Sartre* (trans. Q. Hoare). New York: Pantheon (original work written 1939–40).

—— (1992) *Notebooks for an Ethics* (trans. D. Pellauer). Chicago: University of Chicago Press (original work published 1980).

38

Bubbles and Skulls: the Phenomenology of Self-Consciousness in Dutch Still-Life Painting

WAYNE M. MARTIN

The proper methodology of phenomenology has been endlessly debated; it is not my intention to enter that debate here. But it is worth noticing an assumption shared by most of the parties to the dispute. Whatever the proper method for phenomenology – be it empirical or pure, transcendental or historicist, straight or hetero – it is generally assumed that the product of phenomenology is words. Lots of them, preferably in German, or French, or academic English. The literary form of the product may vary dramatically (a treatise or a meditation, a manifesto or research article, an ontological poem or an essay), but the medium remains the same. This chapter questions that assumption by examining a set of phenomenological studies undertaken not in words but in oil: Dutch still-life paintings of the first half of the seventeenth century.[1]

My most general thesis here – that still-life painting can be viewed as phenomenology – may be surprising or indeed offensive to some. (I imagine the objection that one diminishes the art by treating it as some kind of cognitive science – a complaint to which I am sensitive but by which I find myself undeterred.) But in one sense the general thesis borders on the trivial: it is hard to deny that the still-life painter undertakes studies (that is indeed what we call them) of the appearance or manifestation of things – phenomena – and expresses the result of this attention in the work he produces. The result is not *logos*, if by *logos* we mean narrowly words; but there is an articulation in Heidegger's sense: a disparting display of phenomenological results.[2] But I also seek here to defend a narrower and no doubt more vulnerable thesis, concerning specifically the phenomenology of *self*-consciousness. It is perhaps unsurprising to find that in a painting of a collection of objects we can find insights into the structure of our experience of such objects. The painter of the *trompe l'oeil* certainly exploits his understanding of our perceptual awareness in order to trick us into seeing what is not there. But it is more surprising to find here important insights into the elusive problems concerning the phenomenological structure of *self*-consciousness – particularly since a still life typically displays only inanimate objects.[3] Nonetheless I shall argue that we find in the still-life tradition the working out of two rival phenomenologies of self-consciousness – one Cartesian and one anti-Cartesian.

Let me take some care with these terms. I here take no stand on any questions of direct influence between the still-life Masters and Cartesian philosophy. As we shall see, the painters of this tradition were conversant with philosophical ideas and figures from the history of philosophy. Moreover, the rise of Dutch still-life painting coincides almost exactly with Descartes's residence in the Netherlands. (Descartes first visited with the army in 1618 and lived there from 1630 to 1649; the oil still-life tradition in the Netherlands began around 1603 and reached its peak during Descartes's residence there.) But aside from one minor detail, I shall here make no claims about direct contact or influence in one way or another. Nonetheless I shall argue that there is a substantive sense in which Cartesian and anti-Cartesian views about the phenomenological structure of self-consciousness are worked out by rival schools in the Dutch still-life tradition.[4]

A Very Brief Primer on Dutch Still-Life Painting

I begin with a short primer on Dutch still-life painting. I apologize to readers for whom this background is familiar; I rehearse it here for several reasons. First, much of the argument and analysis that follows turns on semiotic analysis of some representative and exceptional paintings from the age of the Dutch Masters. Interpreting a Dutch still life requires sensitivity to its symbols, which are themselves rooted in and reflect the distinctive cultural context in which the tradition emerged and developed. So I here briefly sketch in some of that context as a prolog towards the interpretation that follows. I also try to be explicit about the background I presuppose here, in order to expose my assumptions to scrutiny and correction.

So start with basics. What is a still life? The still life is a genre of painting and drawing, standing alongside portraits, landscapes, etc., as a distinct formal subgenre of representational art. It is found across a range of media: in vase paintings, watercolors, drawings, etchings, and photography, for instance – and in oil. A still-life painting presents an array of objects, typically arranged on a table in an interior space. The objects are "still," both in the sense of unmoving but primarily in the sense of not-living.[5] This may include both inanimate objects (a coin or candle) and/or once-living things: a cut flower, a bowl of fruit. As we shall see, however, the principle of stillness was not always observed as the tradition progressively pushed the boundaries of this strictest of painterly disciplines.

It is safe to assume that the drawing and painting of still lifes has long been used as an exercise in the training of painters. But it is chiefly among the Dutch Masters that still life became a high art in its own right. Even in the Dutch context, the repute of the still life is subsidiary. We all know the names of Rubens, Rembrandt, and Vermeer, and perhaps a handful of other Dutch Masters: van Dyck, Frans Hals, de Hooch. . . . But these are chiefly painters of the human form. The names of their contemporaries in the still-life tradition are for the most part quite obscure: de Heem and de Gheyn, Johannes Torrentius, Claesz-Heda and Claesz. But although their names may be unfamiliar, their accomplishment was considerable. To some of these accomplishments a contemporary audience is now almost thoroughly deadened. The technological achievement of hyperrealistic representation is now everywhere in our lives – at every turn and in many media. But in the seventeenth century, the art of producing (in any medium) a representation which could trick the eye was still novel and remarkable.[6] The Dutch appropriated and perfected Italian techniques of perspective drawing and advanced the technologies for the manufacture and application of paints to produce obsessively exact representations of objects.

Three pieces of background concerning the Dutch context of this painterly tradition must be introduced here, since they are indispensable to an understanding of the tradition. The first point is political. During a period of Spanish (and hence Catholic) hegemony in western Europe, the Netherlands were unique in having fought off Spanish control. The Union of Utrecht (1579) is a landmark in the intense, costly, and sometimes violent conflict between the various states of the Netherlands and Spanish/Catholic powers, and it led to the emergence of a Dutch republic in the Northern Lowlands. Its political independence and relative religious tolerance made it a destination for many refugees of the period. Among philosophers the most famous are, of course, Descartes and Spinoza. Spinoza's family fled Spanish intolerance of Jews and became merchants in Holland. Descartes found in the Netherlands greater freedom from the Catholic censor and also (among other things) access to public dissection of human corpses, which was banned in Catholic lands.

The second piece of background is economic. In short, the Dutch of this period were rich – fabulously rich. The title of Schama's study, *The Embarrassment of Riches* (1988), reflects something of the scale and cultural context of an unprecedented accumulation of capital assets among the Dutch burgher class – perhaps the greatest concentration of wealth on the planet until the emergence of Wall Street as a financial center in the latter half of the nineteenth century. The basis for all this wealth was banking and trade, set amid the first stirrings of the global economy. The lucrative but risky traffic in spices, coffee, chocolate, rum, slaves . . . was carried in Dutch vessels and financed by Dutch banking firms and some of the earliest stock exchanges. The Dutch East Indies trading company was formed in 1602, became one of the first corporations with global reach, and exerted considerable autonomy in its operations overseas. The company eventually had its own standing army of ten thousand and was effectively the governing authority in many of the regions whose resources it brought to the European market. At its peak the governors of the company were probably the richest individuals in the world outside of royalty. Many in this new business class lived in a dense urban setting (hence, *burghers*), where dry real estate was perhaps the most elusive commodity – another set of parallels with modern New Amsterdam.

The third piece of background is religious. The Dutch of this period were Calvinists. This statement is, of course, a massive oversimplification of an enormously complex matter. In fact an array of religious traditions were represented in the Netherlands at this time, and the question of the toleration of religious difference was itself one of the central political, religious, and philosophical issues of the day. Nonetheless, the predominant religious institutions of Dutch life followed Calvin's central teachings, notably concerning the preordination of the select, salvation by grace, and the intense distrust of worldly goods and pleasures.

This background is of considerable importance for understanding the art of the period. If nothing else, these developments had a rather dramatic effect on the structure of the art market. The iconoclasm of Calvinist religious practice and the effective banning of Catholic institutions meant the elimination of the Church as the major financer of fine art. But at the same time the emergence of a wealthy burgher class created a new market with a ferocious appetite. The private art collection became a cultural and economic force which created quite a broad market. A visitor from England wrote home in 1641: "pictures are very common here, there being scarce an ordinary tradesman whose house is not decorated with them."[7] Some of those works were painted on commission, following the traditional market structure established by the Church, but there also emerged the novel institutions of the art gallery and auction houses, where uncommissioned works were sold to private buyers, principally for display in private homes and businesses.

It was not just the mode of exchange of art that changed in this new setting; its mode of production also shifted, and both the form and the content of the art itself. The demand for artworks produced a highly competitive marketplace. When we hear the term "Dutch Masters" we should think not only of the mastery of an art form (or cigars!), but also the master of a workshop, where apprentices both trained and contributed to the production of a valuable commodity.[8] A market of this structure itself had noticeable effects on the aesthetic values of the period. With many different workshops producing very similar paintings – endless variations on a theme – a premium came to be placed on virtuosity and technical accomplishment. In the still-life tradition this meant choosing the most difficult objects to paint (delicate crystal or lace, for instance, intricate visual textures, multiply reflective surfaces) and then competing to re-create them as exactly as possible in oil. The vivid realism of Dutch still lifes was thus in part the product of a marketplace where the ability to outperform the competition marked the difference between business success and failure. But for our purposes the most important consequences of these other shifts in the Dutch situation concern the content of the art. In the combination of Dutch business success and Calvinist theology there emerges a kind of spiritual tension in the Dutch situation: unbalanced between unprecedented worldly success and anxiety over that success – a situation perhaps not unlike our own today. I turn to the paintings to explore this tension.

Let us start with a late work from the period, but one that will serve usefully as a point of entry: de Heem's *Vanitas Still-Life with Musical Instruments* (1661).[9] The painting portrays, in vivid detail, a rich assortment of objects. The central panel of the painting is densely filled, with the presented space intricately managed to maximize the visible array. In interpreting a still life, one must be guided in the first instance by the objects chosen for representation. The primary theme in this case is the delights of the senses. The collection is carefully arrayed to suggest a range of sensory pleasures, indeed something for every sense: music to be heard, ripe fruit to be tasted, the sweet smell of flowers and ripe, cut melons, the feel of satiny silk. The whole visual scene presents an array of delights. Hanging on the wall in a private home, such a painting bespeaks wealth: an extravagant sensory feast capped by the decadence of an overturned jug – a symbol of wealth enough to waste, consumption without restraint.[10]

But interwoven with this first theme we find a number of others. The human form is represented here, together with a number of variations on a sexual theme: the shape of the viola suggests the female form, while a cut melon bespeaks female sexuality. The juxtaposition of the orifice of the mandolin and the bagpipes in the background symbolically conveys a sexual act. This symbolic lead itself takes us to the deeper sense of the painting: this is not only a *celebration* of the senses but also a systematic document-ing of the *passing* of such pleasures. The fruit is at the peak of its ripeness; soon it will begin to rot. The instruments are fragile and the pleasure they produce is fleeting. The sexual pleasure is represented here as passing: notice that the bagpipes are deflated, its pipes sagging; the overturned vase now a symbol of pleasures that have slipped away. To punctuate this counter-theme, and in violation of the principle that still lifes must be still, we see a snail (itself a sexual image), sliming in from offstage, ready to transform ripe into rotten. This layering of meaning is characteristic of the still life. The painting pulls in two directions – the two spiritual directions at the heart of the Dutch predicament: between enjoying and celebrating an unprecedented wealth, while also questioning its true worth.

This tension between themes is found in each of the main subgenres of the still life.[11] Within this tradition there were several established and recognized subgenres, each with recognized masters, and workshops largely keeping to their niche. Four in particular deserve mention. Beert's *Dishes with Oysters and Sweetmeats* (1615) is an example of the banquet piece (*Bancketje*). A banquet still life presents us with a table set for a party, a lavish display of foods and tableware. The painting is again an invitation to delight, but the portrayal carries other symbols as well: here the seashells are a refer-ence to the seafaring which brought the wealth; indeed, particular species of shell are often painted to represent particular trading destinations of a patron. The method of composition in a banquet piece is additive: the scene was flooded with bright light and the elements of the banquet were painted one at a time, under the illumination of candle arrays. Accordingly there is only minimal overlap or shadowing of the presented objects (see Bergström 1956). A closely related additive genre is the breakfast piece (*ontbijt*). Again, here a meal is set out (not necessarily a morning meal, but any a meal that breaks a fast, perhaps at an inn after a journey). In this case the meal is set not for a party but for a solitary diner, changing the mood of the piece by a degree from festive to somber. Van Schooten's *Breakfast (Ontbijt)* (1640) presents the tableware of an inn, together with cheeses, fruit, and bread. Once again we find the bivalence or tension of themes; a knife figures prominently (a hint of morbidity), and the broken crust of the mince pie suggests the decay of the body.

A third genre of the tradition brings us closer to recognizably philosophical issues. Van Hoogstraten's *Trompe L'oeil Still Life* (1666–8) carefully sets out to deceive the viewer into seeing represented objects as themselves physically present. It is certainly tempting to imagine Descartes, on arrival in Amsterdam, visiting one of the new Dutch galleries and musing over these reminders that the senses deceive. The senses, it seems, are both cognitively and connatively dialectical, attracting us to false delights and tricking us into false beliefs. The best of the *trompe l'oeil* are astonishing in their illu-sion, and were often hung in ways that heightened the effect: a painting of a wall cabinet full of musical instruments deceives at the end of a hallway; a letter board is real enough to invite the viewer to reach out for one of the objects tucked into its straps. In the possibility of deception we find one principled extreme or ideal which defines a standard of realism in painting. The perfect realism is the complete illusion; this ideal serves to constitute a domain of representational practice.

The fourth distinct genre that deserves mention here is the floral display. Flowers have long been a Dutch obsession, and the rise of the still-life market coincided with what has become known as "tulip-mania" or "the war of the flowers."[12] Flowers exemplify the fragile balance between beauty and pleasure on the one hand and decay on the other: both a symbol and instance of beauty, they are always already dying at the peak of their bloom. The red and white tulip in van der Spelt's *Trompe L'oeil with Flowers and a Curtain* (1658) is a flower we find represented repeatedly in this period – valued for its dramatic color variegation. The variegation was produced, as it happens, by infecting the sprouting bulb with a viral disease, thus reiterating the link between beauty and mortality. Van der Spelt heightens the illusion by including within the painting a realistic curtain, drawn to one side so as to suggest that the represented space of the painting is an interior space of the room in which it is hung – a nook in which the floral display has been set. Much like a mirror, the curtain thus functions to create the illusion of additional space in the cramped internal quarters of a Dutch urban residence. As we shall see presently, the curtain also figures as one in a wave of symbolic images of death and human mortality.

Themes of death and decay find their highest development in the so-called "vanitas still life," which receives it name from the opening passage of the Book of Ecclesiastes, usually quoted in Latin: *vanitas vanitatum et omnia vanitas* ("vanity of vanity: all is vanity"). Vanitas is sometimes counted as a distinct subgenre of the still life, but it is better viewed as a theme that runs through all the genres, sometimes subtly, sometimes at a crescendo. Like the Book of Ecclesiastes, the still-life tradition catalogs and celebrates the very worldly pleasures and accomplishments which it at the same time submits to a critique. In van Oosterwijk's *Vanitas Still Life* (1668) we see the symbol of a merchant's wealth – a globe, a ledger and quill, coins and a money-sack – and the pleasures that go with it: flowers, music, exquisite Asian porcelain. But amid all this comes the theme of death: sand runs through an hourglass, a butterfly lives briefly and passes away, a skull. Formally, the vanitas still life is often very complex. The bright light of the banquet and floral pieces gives way here to a darkened space illuminated by a single light source; the objects overlap and reflect one another, multiplying the compositional complexity.[13] We shall return below to its symbolic complexities.

Let me conclude this brief primer with a few more theoretical remarks. The first concerns the semiotic structure of the paintings. Semiotics is the study of the structure of meaning in signs and symbols. As we have seen, a still-life painting is dense with symbols, and seeing the work comes in part by way of understanding and responding to that symbolic code. The requisite literacy rests in large part on a common stock of cultural symbols derived from the lived world of everyday life, combined with what Grice called natural signs. (No convention or intention is needed to link the skull with death, but to appreciate the significance of a quill or hourglass one must know something of how they are used.[14]) But there is also an underlying formal structure to this symbolic code. Here I resort to some semiotic jargon; call this structure "dialectical polysemy." "Polysemy" here means simply a multitude of meanings, the accumulation of multiple symbolic codes. A polysemic accumulation is dialectical where one set of meanings (pleasure, accomplishment) is balanced by an opposing one (vanity, death). It is in part this dialectical structure that makes the paintings such hermeneutically rich objects – particularly in a cultural setting that is itself caught in a tension between accomplishment and anxiety. In this sense the semiotic structure of the paintings articulates a structure of meaning in the world of Dutch burghers.

Having recognized these tensions, it is natural to ask whether the paintings provide any resolution of them. Do the two themes remain in tension? Does one side "win" in some sense? Is there some resolution the paintings preach? Here it is useful to distinguish between semiotically open and semiotically closed systems of representations. In a closed semiotic system, a particular set of meanings predominates and dictates a particular interpretation; to miss it is simply to be wrong. Street signs are semiotically closed, so are waving flags on the Fourth of July. A semiotic system is open where it leaves unresolved what meanings are to be taken from it; the chaplain's parable in *The Trial* is semiotically open (see Kafka 1937). In many still-life paintings one finds semiotic closure, often effected through the use of a motto, usually taken from biblical or classical sources (particularly the Stoics) or from common proverbs. Torrentius' *Allegory of Temperance* (1614) presents a glass between a jug of wine and a jug of water (themselves rather dramatically gendered) together with a horse's bridle mounted on the wall behind. The message here – that worldly pleasures must be taken in moderation – is rendered explicit as the lyric in a score set beneath the assembled objects. It reads: "That which is without measure is immeasurable evil" – a maxim the painter seems to apply both to wine and to sex. But the lessons of a still life are not always so clear and explicit. What lesson does one take from the insistent reminder of the vanity of worldly pleasure and accomplishment? What ethics is prescribed by a skull? Here we may be tempted to close the semiotic structure by presupposing a Christian moral: Lay up your stores in heaven; live not for pleasure but for final judgment; pursue the good rather than delight. As we shall see, however, the paintings sometimes resist or at least question such hopeful closure.

This brings us to the final point in our primer – the issue of hope. Part of the perennial attraction of the vanitas tradition lies in its visual exploration of nihilistic themes. Indeed, in retrospect we can see in Dutch still life a first exploration of nihilism – the themes of skepticism, somber morbidity, even despair, that reappear with increasing insistency in the modern period. The very term "vanitas" suggests a connection with nihilism. *Nihil* – nothing, *vana* – empty: the two Latin roots are nearly synonymous. But one must tread carefully here. There is considerable danger of anachronism in reading modern nihilistic despair back into these artworks from an intensely Christian context. For the Christian (as indeed for the Platonist), the death of the body marks not so much ending as beginning.[15] The passing goods of the world are balanced by genuine and lasting goods, with the painting then serving as a spiritual exhortation to pursue the lasting goods rather than the fleeting pleasures. I do not wish to deny that this movement toward a hopeful semiotic closure is present in the paintings, but we should not simply presuppose it. As we shall see, there is within the tradition an opposing theme, a movement toward a nihilistic closure.

Bubbles and Skulls: Pieter Claesz and the Transformation of a Visual Theme

I turn now from generalities to something more specific, particularly with an eye for phenomenological leads and clues. Start from bubbles. Soap bubbles and various other bubble-like objects are not uncommon in the still-life tradition, and when they appear

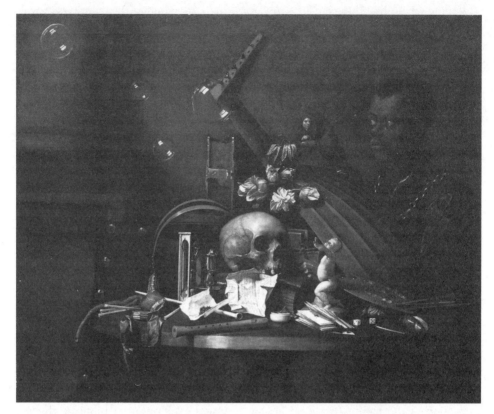

Figure 38.1   David Bailly (1650): *Vanitas Still Life with Portrait*. Oil on canvas
(94.6 × 116.2 cm). Gift of Louis V. Keeler (Class of 1911) and Mrs. Keeler, by exchange.
Courtesy of the Herbert Johnson Museum of Art, Cornell University, Ithaca, NY

they can seem oddly out of place. In David Bailly's *Vanitas Still Life with Portrait* (1650;
see Figure 38.1), a group of bubbles floats through an otherwise somber but familiar
vanitas scene: broken instruments, an hourglass running down, a skull. The painting
is unusual for a number of reasons, most prominently for its inclusion of a living man,
an African bearing a chain. The man in turn holds a second portrait, in this case of the
patron. We shall return to the issues posed by such iteration below, as also to the inclusion here of the artist's own palette and brushes, but consider first what the bubbles
are doing in this somber scene. No small part of the answer must involve the painterly
challenge bubbles present: how does one create, in oil, a convincing representation of
a maximally transparent object? It is worth taking note of the technique that is used: a
light circle conveys a visual edge, while the distortion of a doubly-reflected window
(top left, bottom right) is used to convey the bulbous form. In short, one paints a bubble
by painting what it reflects. Bubbles also capture, reflect, and thereby reproduce light,
yielding a glimmering effect in the darkened spaces of a vanitas composition.

But what do bubbles contribute to the semiotic complexity of the painting? Here it
useful to draw on an older but related representational art: the emblembook, of which
Visscher's *Sinnepoppen* (1615) is perhaps the most famous. An emblembook typically

Figure 38.2   Jacques de Gheyn the Elder (1603): *Vanitas Still Life*. Oil on wood panel
(82.6 × 54 cm). Metropolitan Museum, New York

collects together several woodcuts or etchings, usually combined with moralizing verses
or mottos. In this older (and cheaper!) medium one finds the concatenation of bubbles
and skulls, often combined with the figure of the putto: a cherubic young child. Hendrik
Goltzuis' *Quis Evadet?* (1594) draws on a common emblem: a young child happily
blowing bubbles while leaping over a skull and other symbols of death – a smoking
lamp, wilting flowers. The motto makes the lesson clear – *Quis evadet?* ("Who escapes?")
– while an accompanying text elaborates the moral.[16] Here the symbolic significance
of bubbles seems clear. Bubbles are objects of childlike delight, but also of ephemeral
pleasure and (particularly in conjunction with the skull) symbols of death. In another of
Goltzius' etchings the association is made explicit: *Homo Bulla Est* ("Man is a bubble").[17]

But I believe we must look further to appreciate the concatenation of bubbles and
skulls. Let us start with one of the most important paintings of the tradition, and one of
the oldest. De Gheyn's *Vanitas Still Life* (1603; see Figure 38.2) is probably the oldest

567

surviving Dutch still-life painting, and is still very directly connected to earlier Germanic representations of the macabre: de Gheyn's skull is gruesome, its setting a gravesite. We find here many of the symbolic elements to be found in the later paintings (tulip, coins, and a smoking lamp), albeit in this case dramatically subordinated to the presentation of the skull. The motto, inscribed in the capstone of the arch, reads *Humana Vana* ("human emptiness"). But the painting also tells a more specific story. The tomb, it seems, is a royal tomb, and the painting contains multiple references to Catholic monarchy. The most prominent and specific are the two coins at bottom left and right, showing the obverse and reverse of a Spanish coin, minted to commemorate the Hapsburg Emperor Charles V, and his mother, Joanna of Aragon and Castile. Death, we are shown, befalls even the mighty. But what place does the bubble have in this work? Certainly the association with death predominates over any hint of innocence or pleasure. The bubble might be taken as a hope for immortality (a soul rising from the body), but when we look closer we see that there is more to it than this. Notice first that the bubble is used here to make a political point. Reflected within it we find a further set of objects, a motley assortment, difficult to discern. Several of these reflected objects allude further to royalty (a crown, a scepter); and the most prominent object – the wheel at lower right in the bubble – is the rack of torture, a reference to the methods of Spanish and Catholic power in this period. The bubble is thus used here as a representational medium of its own, and provides a commentary of its own – a painting within a painting.

In de Gheyn's use of the bubble as a representational medium, we find a technique that would be refined, perfected, and exploited in the subsequent tradition. It is in this device, I want to argue, that we find a first exploration of the phenomenological structure of self-consciousness. Before taking up this issue directly, however, we should take note of a much more direct relation to philosophy inscribed with the de Gheyn painting itself. Mottos attributed to philosophers (particularly to Seneca and other Stoics, but also to Lucretius) are not uncommon in vanitas paintings. But de Gheyn is notable for including representations of the philosophers themselves. Standing top left and right, in the positions that might be occupied by angels or saints on a Christian tomb (notice the halo on the figure at left), de Gheyn incorporates statuary figures of Democritus and Heraclitus. They are identified by an implicit reference to a saying attributed to Seneca: "Heraclitus weeps while Democritus laughs." (The reference is to *On Tranquility*, Seneca's answer to Serenus, section 12; see Seneca 1935: 272). The two are indeed presented as weeping and laughing while pointing down at the bubble below. The pre-Socratic figures are included here as symbols of ancient materialism, and in their placement serve as emblems of a counter-Christian metaphysics, a counterweight to Christian hope. If all is atoms (Democritus) and everything changes (Heraclitus), then the hope for immortality expressed by the rising bubble is void. We thus find here an example of the resistance of the paintings to a Christian appropriation, and indeed a gesture toward a fully despairing semiotic closure: worldly accomplishments and pleasures are fleeting vanities and there is no enduring soul; nothing survives death, hence there are no lasting goods.[18]

Rather than pursuing these metaphysical leads further, however, I want now to keep our focus on the use of the bubble as a representational sphere – a use established by de Gheyn and developed in the subsequent tradition. Among the masters of the still

Figure 38.3 Pieter Claesz (*c.*1633): *Still Life with Römer and Tazza*. Oil on wood panel
(42 × 59 cm). Staatliche Museum, Berlin. Photo: Bildarchiv Preussischer
Kulturbesitz/Art Resource, New York

life, the inclusion of bubbles and bubble-like objects becomes increasingly common
and complex. A prominent example is the Römer, the heavy-stemmed, bulbous goblet
that is found in an enormous number of still lifes from the period, typically set in the
background of a banquet setting or breakfast-piece. The bubblelike Römer serves a
number of aesthetic purposes and presents a complex technical challenge, with each
facet of its knobbed stem providing occasion for a further study in reflective projections.
But I would also like to argue here that these representational spheres themselves
reflect and articulate a model of the self-conscious representation of objects – in short:
a phenomenological model. The viewer is invited to see himself in the bubble, and
indeed to see himself as seeing from inside a representational sphere.

I have previously tried to make this case in connection with Claesz's 1633 *Still Life
with Römer and Tazza* (Figure 38.3).[19] In this piece we find Claesz taking up the genre of
the breakfast piece, albeit now with the formal complexity and somber, almost
monochromatic palette of a vanitas composition. The piece presents the aftermath of a
solitary meal: pewter plates scattered with crumbs, empty oyster shells alongside an
overturned platter. Here again we see the use of a bulbous form as a representational
medium: the visually complex tazza is here carefully and systematically distorted
in the projected reflection on the various bubblelike surfaces of the glass. Notice that
the Römer has moved here from its traditionally subordinate place to become the
centerpiece and focal point of the composition. My admittedly adventurous thesis about

this painting is that we find in it a systematic self-consciousness. Indeed, there are at least two forms of self-consciousness suggested in the painting. The first comes by way of the olive. Still-life paintings often include references to the painter's own art; we have seen an example above in the incorporation of a painter's tools in a vanitas assemblage. This might be read as an expression of modesty, a key Calvinist and Stoic virtue. The inclusion of a palette or brushes marks the painter's accounting of his own accomplishments – however hard won – as among the ephemeral goods of the world. In Claesz's breakfast-piece, the olive stands as a kind of ironic self-reference to the painter's art of deception. In a painting portraying dozens of circular forms (ten in the base of the tazza alone), each represented in two dimensions as ellipses, the olive is the one object which is actually elliptical in life. The olive thus reminds us that the work is the contrivance of a painter, and that its representations, however exact they may seem, are themselves deceptions.[20] If this is right, then we can see a number of themes of Cartesian philosophy worked out in the painting: the study of geometry and optics, the concern with perceptual deception and skepticism.

But what is more central to my argument here is a second trace of self-consciousness in the painting, in this case connecting specifically to the Cartesian model of consciousness as a sphere of representation, a mediating sphere on which things are projected for experience. The representational sphere in this case is the Römer, which resembles a bubble both in its physical form and in the compositional strategy Claesz uses to represent it. Claesz's bubble, I suggest, is specifically linked with his own self-consciousness as a painter: in the curved shadow in the lowermost reflected window we can discern the artist's silhouetted head, partially blocking the light as he constructs the represented scene – as if from inside the bubble. This last claim may seem fanciful, and indeed I myself advanced it somewhat fancifully in my earlier discussion of this work. But I can now provide some supporting evidence for this thesis in the form of an obscure painting, hanging in (of all places) the French galleries at the Getty Center, Los Angeles. *Vanitas Still Life* (1634; Figure 38.4) is probably not a work from Claesz's own hand. The Getty attributes it simply as "after Claesz"; likely it is the work of an advanced apprentice from Claesz's studio, with the composition established by the master. The painting is dramatically divided into two fields – a technique that became common in the later development of the still-life tradition. To the right we have a vanitas assembly: shells, a ledger and quill, a skull and bones, a Römer. The gleaming diagonal of the ceremonial cup divides the assembled objects from a reflective orb or spherical mirror presiding over the left of the panel. I believe that this painting, though perhaps not executed at the same level as the others we have been considering, serves to confirm a number of the claims I have been advancing.

Certainly it is tempting to interpret the painting in the framework of Cartesian dualism: divided left and right, the painting can be read as a representation of mind and body, with a toppled urn signifying the union of the two, now severed in death. But what is important for my argument here is specifically the representation of self and self-consciousness in the work. By 1634, the objects represented on the right side of the painting all have clearly established symbolic significance: shells for seafaring and trade; ledger, quill, and sealed contracts for commerce; skull and bones for death. But what should we say of the bubblelike sphere at left? If we look closely we see that it is used here to represent the painter himself, whose figure is hidden but unmistak-

Figure 38.4   Attributed to Pieter Claesz (1634): *Vanitas Still Life*. Oil on wood panel
(54 × 71.4 cm). The J. Paul Getty Museum, Los Angeles

able, sitting at his easel, brush in hand.[21] The sphere is in this way explicitly linked to self-representation; it is a self-portrait, albeit a highly unusual one. And how does this portrait represent the self? The parallels to the Cartesian ego are striking: the self is shown here inside a bubble, engaged in the act of representation. The bubble itself is a representational medium, reflecting and re-presenting the other objects in the painting. As viewers, we can see that those representations are themselves distortions, twisted by the medium of representation itself. But to one who understands the principles of optical reflection (as clearly the representing painter himself does), those distortions betray a systematic and fully intelligible order. The spherical mirror thus reiterates the form of the bubble, now as a maximally *reflective* rather than maximally transparent object. This bubble, however, is neither fragile nor ephemeral, but solid and enduring: a symbolic rendering of the Cartesian hope for the immortality of the representing self.[22]

  This form of self-representation is not unique to Claesz, by any means. The inclusion of self-representations in a spherical mirror can be traced back to van Eyck's *Arnolfini Portrait* (1434). We find it in the still-life tradition as early as 1612 in the paintings of Clara Peeters, where a ceremonial cup is covered with bubblelike protrusions, each of which captures and reflects the figure of the artist, peering out from inside a representational sphere (see Figure 38.5.) My conclusion regarding bubbles is accordingly as follows: From symbols of transient pleasures and fragility in the Emblembooks, bubbles become in Claesz's still lifes a symbolic enactment of the Cartesian mind: site of

Figure 38.5   Clara Peeters (1612): *Ceremonial Cups and Flowers in a Jug* (detail).
Oil on wood panel (59.5 × 49 cm). Staatliche Kunsthalle, Karlsruhe, Germany.
Photo: Erich Lessing/Art Resource, New York

consciousness and self-consciousness, locus of the self as a cognitive representational medium, and crucially, marking a division between what is inside the bubble (the representing subject: the self-conscious painter and his representations) and what is outside it (a represented world, the objects of such consciousness).

Having come this far we must now at least acknowledge the historical elephant in this argument: Although I have been calling all this Cartesian, it seems it cannot be derived from Descartes himself. The *Discourse on Method* was not published until 1637, the *Meditations* not until 1641. Rather than counting this an objection, however, or speculating about some independent knowledge that Claesz may have had of Cartesian philosophy, I suggest that we find here a striking confirmation of a thesis advanced by Hegel, Marx, and Heidegger and emphasized more recently by Charles Taylor and

Figure 38.6   David Bailly (1651): *Vanitas Still Life with Portrait of a Young Painter.*
Oil on wood panel (89.5 × 112 cm). Stedelijk Museum de Lakenhal, Leiden.
Photo: Erich Lessing/Art Resource, New York

Hubert Dreyfus: philosophers do not invent their philosophies out of whole cloth, nor are their works isolated and wholly rational cultural phenomena; rather, philosophers distill and articulate their philosophical views from the cultural practices in which they are embedded. In this case we find that central elements of the Cartesian account of the phenomenological structure of our self-conscious relation to the world are worked out and manifested in seventeenth-century Dutch practices – in particular the representational practices of the still-life tradition – in advance of Descartes's own verbal distillation.

The Temporality of Self-Consciousness in a Late Painting of David Bailly

In this section I turn to a defense of the second part of my thesis; I argue that the broadly Cartesian phenomenology of self-consciousness we find in Claesz's work is challenged within the still-life tradition by a rival, counter-Cartesian articulation of the phenomenology of self-consciousness. I focus my attention here on a single painting: David Bailly's 1651 *Vanitas Still Life with Portrait of a Young Painter* (Figure 38.6). This painting is enormously complex, and there are many issues about it which remain unresolved. The sheer number of objects and symbols is here overwhelming: an

573

assortment of portraits, a Römer and skull, bubbles, an hourglass, a curtain and table-cloth, two books, a pipe, a knife, a string of pearls, a smoking candle, two statues, several flowers in a vase and others scattered on the table, a tall, half-filled flute glass, two musical instruments (the partially hidden recorder on the table and the lute in the uppermost portrait), two pieces of paper, a scroll, coins, a silver orb on a chain, some kind of open silver box, two pieces of painterly equipment (the palette hung on the wall and the long maulstick used to steady the painter's hand), at least one unidentified object (the silverwork standing on the book), and a motto: *vanitas vanitum et omnia vanitas*. The whole assembly comprises more than fifty discrete objects. Once again here we find a sharp division of the visual field. But where Claesz had played very strictly within the rules of the still life, Bailly actively challenges them. The division of the field in this case produces, at right, a vanitas assembly, and at left, a collection of portraits – a crossing of genre boundaries that Bailly had explored on other occasions (see Figure 38.1). Notice that two vertical forms separate these two fields of the paint-ing: the vertical form of the candlestick and the vertical line created by the protruding interior corner of the room. I return below to consider Bailly's use of these dividers.

Although Bailly's painting does indeed include bubbles and skulls, I shall argue here that it does not simply reiterate the treatment of self-consciousness we found in Claesz. In order to see this, however, we need to know more about the painting and the circumstance of its composition. The first thing to know is that Bailly was by profes-sion not a still-life painter but a portraitist, and a very successful one. He had trained with the younger Jacques de Gheyn (himself a portraitist), and had a successful studio near the university in Leiden. In 1650 he was named Dean of the Guild of St. Luke.[23] There are a few earlier still lifes among Bailly's portraits: he seems to have painted in a small still-life arrangement for a portrait his friend de Keyser made of him, and we have already seen the 1650 vanitas (Figure 38.1);[24] but he seems to have taken up the still-life form seriously only late in life, after a very successful career in portraits, and quite probably in response to personal tragedy. It is perhaps worth noting that the professional portrait artist makes a business of putting people in bubbles – the stand-ard oval framing common in commercial portraits then and now. Bailly includes a humorous reference to this practice in the copy of the famous Frans Hals lute player, which here hangs nailed to the wall; Bailly has altered the composition to place the player inside a portraitist's oval bubble.

The next thing to know is that the portrait is here a self-portrait. We can recognize in the eyes that distinctive self-examining stare characteristic of self-portraiture. (It is almost impossible to paint one's own eyes in any other way.) Indeed, the painting is usually taken to be a double self-portrait. Almost everything in the painting is doubled: there are the same number of flowers as figures, and most of the represented objects have clear (or hidden) counterparts within the painting (two glasses, two papers, the curtain and tablecloth, the shape of palette and lute, etc.). The two self-portraits depict the painter as a young man (the largest figure, seated at left) and then grayed and aging (in the oval portrait). Clothing is here used as a clue for the pairings: notice the similarities of dress between the two primary male figures, as also between the oval female portrait and the bust of the Bacchante. All this systematic pairing reflects one of the primary themes of the painting: this is a painting about love, about marriage, and about loss.[25]

To fill this in we need two further biographical details. First, the work was painted in 1651, when Bailly was 67 years old. Hence the closest self-portrait here is not the youthful figure at left but the older figure in the oval portrait.[26] The second detail concerns Bailly's wife, Agneta van Swanenburgh, who had been gravely ill, and according to many accounts had recently died.[27] In a second oval portrait we see Agneta, whose figure is echoed by a ghostly portrait painted into the surface of the wall behind the half-filled glass. The wife's illness may also be remembered here by way of the figure of St. Sebastian – the standing figure in statuary, portrayed in his traditional pose: tied to a tree and pierced with arrows. Sebastian was a figure from the third century (a victim of Roman persecution of Christianity under Diocletian), but he is also closely associated with the Great Plague, which was said to strike down its victims as if by random arrows. The painting, then, presents a study in mourning and remembrance: a self-portrait undertaken as a form of grieving. In this unique representational medium we find once again an exploration of the phenomenology of self-consciousness. Grief and mourning are themselves a form of self-awareness, as a survivor comes progressively to terms with his vulnerability and loss. Here the theme of self-consciousness is intensified by the complex act of self-portraiture: the artist must have spent many hours in the studio, studying and remembering himself while also remembering and mourning his wife. How, then, is self-consciousness understood and articulated in the painting? Here, I submit, self-consciousness is portrayed not as life inside a Cartesian representational bubble, but rather in terms of its distinctive and paradoxical temporality.

Time is a pervasive theme in Bailly's self-portrait. The composition explores a number of temporal complexities and directly challenges some of our common assumptions about the temporal structure of experience. To unravel the temporality of the work, start from the vertical dividing lines identified above. Notice first that the vertical line formed by the corner of the wall also serves to bisect the artist's contemporary (aging) self-portrait and the bubble above it, serving thereby as a marker of the present moment. The folding of the rear wall then serves to divide the painting into a brightly illuminated past (the young artist with his unused palettes), the present (the aging self-portrait), and a darkened future: the many symbols and reminders of death. The vertical established by the smoking candlestick then fittingly serves to divide the living from the dead in this temporal sequence: to its right are the two images of the deceased wife, along with the skull and figure of St. Sebastian; to its left lie the portraits of the living artist and various other references to living contemporaries. (The uppermost portrait is an homage to Frans Hals, Bailly's near-exact contemporary and fellow Antwerper, still living at the time of this composition.) The painting in this way plots the familiar timeline, left to right, of past, present, and future.

But there are other temporal structures at work here as well. Many of the assembled objects are very specific markers of events in Bailly's life. The rendering of the Hals luteplayer reproduces an earlier copy he had undertaken as a novice; the saint is likely a figure he encountered and painted on his Grand Tour;[28] the portrait of his wife is an idealization of the portrait he made at the time of their wedding; and of course the two self-portraits mark his own youth and maturity. What we have here, in short, is a narrative of Bailly's life, knit together by way of reproductive reenactments of his labors as an artist. This marks the first in a series of dramatic contrasts to the Cartesian model of self-consciousness. For Descartes the privileged moment of self-consciousness is always the present instant. "So long as I think, I am and know that I exist," he famously writes in the Second Meditation.[29] In Bailly's painting, by contrast, self-knowledge and self-representation are essentially narrative and hence diachronic: he comes to self-knowledge by knitting together and making present these episodes of his own past and projected future.[30]

Amid these several temporal structures in the painting, however, the most important is the temporal paradox at the heart of the painting. Taken together, the two self-portraits present a temporal anomaly: a young man holds a picture of himself as an aging gentleman. I am aware of two interpretative approaches to the temporality of the portraits, themselves curiously opposed to one another. One approach treats the relation between the two portraits strictly in terms of the passage of time, with the two portraits reiterating the ephemerality of human life, and the artist thereby modestly including himself among the passing vanities of the world. The opposed treatment sees here a celebration of the artist's power over time – the power to stop it with his preserving art (note the paper halted in flight), or to reverse it with the deceit of his brush. On this approach the painting is an arrogant celebration of the power of the painter to overcome death and achieve immortality through his works. But while each of these interpretations makes sense of various elements of the temporal structure, neither offers a direct resolution of the temporal anomaly. Is this deceit simply a lie?

At the risk of rather dramatic anachronism, it may help to approach the problem by way of two other famous paradoxes about experienced time. Let us start with Wordsworth's temporal paradox in his motto to *Intimations of Immortality*: "the Child is father to the Man." Though we ordinarily think of parents producing their children, there is a sense in which children produce the adults they themselves become. Applying this to the present case, we might see the young artist displaying in prospect his own progeny: his older self, and the work of his career as a painter. His endeavors produced not only works of art but also the mature artist himself. The young painter faces his future (note the empty, as-yet unused oval palettes), showing us the ambition of what he himself will become and accomplish (the painted ovals of the portraits). We come closer yet to a solution if we recall the whole of Wordsworth's motto:

> The Child is father to the Man.
> And I could wish my days to be
> Bound each to each by natural piety.

There is, in Bailly's painting, an attempt to bind together the events of a life, to knit together the elements into a whole that makes sense. In this undertaking Bailly's self-conscious subject is not alone inside a reflecting sphere, cut off from the world by a deceptive veil of perception; he is much rather embodied, situated among things, and under the gaze of others. Note the gaze of the unidentified bearded man, looking directly into the young Bailly's eyes. Along with the reference to his contemporary, Hals, and the images of his wife, the portraits display self-consciousness not as solitary (as in Claesz and Descartes), but as intersubjectively situated.

But we come closer yet to a solution in one of Heidegger's temporal paradoxes: the thesis that Dasein is always outside itself in time – what Heidegger dubs the ekstatic character of temporality. To be self-conscious, in Bailly's rendering, is to confront one's own embodied mortal existence as unfolding among things, before others, in time, and toward death. This temporal structure is anything but simple. In part it is a progression from past through present to future – represented here in the folding of the chipped and pocked wall against which the scene is set. But at the same time Bailly's temporal paradox alerts us to a very different temporal structure, captured here in the temporal anomaly. Experienced time runs in two directions: a young man projects himself into a finite future that inexorably approaches him (the remainder of his terrestrial life, available to make himself into a good husband and a great painter); a looming future approaches which inevitably includes one's own death. This future which approaches me is what Heidegger called "the existential concept of the future" – a time "available for this or that," a time whose direction is not trailing off into an infinite distance, but much rather comes inexorably toward the present moment, looming from up ahead (Heidegger 1982: §19bγ. See also Heidegger 1962: §§67–71). The temporal anomaly displays this double direction of time in self-consciousness: from past, to present, to future, but also from a looming future back to a fraught and complex present. As to the question of what happens after death, the painting presents a skeptical balancing of opposed metaphysical possibilities. To the right, the figure of the immortal saint is bathed in light, with the ghostly Agneta gazing upon it. But the other figures here all face away from this Christian hope, and in the figures of the lute player and the bearded man we once again find the rendering of the counter-Christian figures of Democritus and Heraclitus, laughing and mourning, and separated by a bubble.

In her classic and controversial study, Svetlana Alpers (1983) argued for an interpretation of Dutch painting in terms of the Baconian ambition to make things show their nature through being subjected to a disciplined observation – rigorous experiments designed to squeeze the nature of a thing into view. In this sense, Alpers argues, the enterprise of the Dutch Masters should be seen alongside the endeavors of the fledgling Royal Academy as answering to this Baconian call. Applied to the works we have been investigating here, we can say that they too set out to use disciplined observation to articulate and describe the attributes or natures of the things they show. Bailly's painting presents us with many materials and physical media (wood, clay, silk, glass, silver . . .), each painted so as to display its characteristic materiality and distinctive mode of appearance. Among the natures described in the painting we must include human nature, and in particular the distinctive nature of self-conscious human existence. Its nature is made to show itself through Bailly's exacting observation, which reveals its distinctive ekstatic self-relation and temporality.

A Concluding Word about Two Portraits

A famous portrait of Descartes hangs in Gallery 27 of the Louvre. It is a copy of a work by Frans Hals, the same painter whom Bailly honors, both early and late, with his portraitizing copy. There are a number of questions about the provenance of the Hals portrait, and in particular about how many portraits Hals actually painted. An apparently identical painting is listed among the possessions of a Berlin archive;[31] and countless copies have appeared on textbook covers and professorial walls. The original seems to have been lost. In addition to the copies and forgeries there may also have been a number of preliminary studies by Hals himself. What we do know, however, is that there was at least this direct contact between the painterly and philosophical masters: Descartes must have sat for many hours for the painter. In one of the smaller Hals portraits Descartes has a more wild and disheveled appearance, suggestive perhaps of Hals' own lost rendering of "The Boy in the Bubble."[32] In that study of Descartes, Hals gives the philosopher the characteristic eye-locking stare and pose of a self-portrait – a feature which is preserved, albeit less dramatically, in the Louvre portrait. In casting Descartes's portrait as a self-portrait, Hals shows his understanding of the basic doctrine of Descartes's philosophy: the insistence that self-conscious self-knowledge is the foundation of philosophy and the defining characteristic of human nature. There is at least this evidence, then, that the painters of this period were conversant not only with the great philosophers of the classical tradition, but also with the philosophical developments among them. If we find in Hals' portraits an understanding of Descartes's most fundamental doctrine, we find in the contemporary Dutch still-life tradition both a visual articulation of Cartesian self-consciousness and a phenomenological analysis pointing beyond the limits of the Cartesian account.

Notes

1　For the canonical positions in the debate over phenomenological method, see Husserl 1931 and the respective Introductions to Heidegger 1962 and Merleau-Ponty 1962. For recent naturalistic approaches to phenomenology see Dennett 1991 and Petitot et al. 1999. On the contrast between "straight" and "hetero" phenomenology, see Cerbone 2003. There are some important counterexamples to the general assumption that phenomenological articulation must be verbal. Most notably, Merleau-Ponty treats Cézanne's paintings as phenomenological studies (Merleau-Ponty 2004). Foucault's treatment of *Las Meninas* is perhaps less directly phenomenological, but nonetheless serves as an important example of the use of painting to explore structures of representation (Foucault 1970). For a recent discussion of phenomenology in the medium of film see Dreyfus and Dreyfus 2002.

2　On Heidegger's treatment of assertion as disparting display, see Heidegger 1962: §33 and 1982: §17b.

3　The problems of self-consciousness have been among the most persistent and unresolved of the modern philosophical tradition since Descartes, and have resulted in a number of contortions within the specifically phenomenological tradition. The canonical sources are of course Descartes's *Meditations* (1641); Hume's *Treatise* (1739), particularly Book I, Part IV, ch. vi; and Kant's *Critique of Pure Reason* (1781, 1789), particularly the Transcendental Deduction in B. For a survey of more recent treatments see Cassam 1994 and the essays collected in *The Monist* 87(2) (April, 2004). The most famous trace of Husserl's struggle over the problems of self-consciousness comes in a note to the second edition of the *Logical Investigations*, where after having insistently denied in the first edition that there is any self to be found in experience, he happily announces a decade later that he has indeed found one (Husserl 2001: Inv. V, §8n.).

4　This chapter builds on work I started in my review of Mark Sacks' book, *Objectivity and Insight* (2000), and I am grateful to Mark for drawing me in. Many people have since contributed research assistance. Let me thank specifically Leslie Bussis Tait (Metropolitan

Museum, New York), and the many friends, colleagues, and students at UC San Diego who helped me with this material, in particular Philip Gunderson, Nellie Wieland, Doug Ebrahimi, Donald Rutherford, Mason Withers, Dana Nelkin, and Sam Rickless. Over the years a number of undergraduates have written papers on particular paintings discussed here, and many have provided information and leads that I exploit. I apologize for thanking them here only collectively.

5   The French term for still life, *nature mort*, invokes the theme of death more explicitly; the seventeenth-century Dutch term, *vie coye* (literally, calm life), conveys both senses of the English "still." See Bruyn 1951.

6   There are tales from Antiquity of paintings that fooled even birds (the grapes of Zeuxis) and horses (Apelles), but no such works have survived. For reports, see Pliny, *Natural History*, Book 35.

7   *The Diary of John Evelyn* (1641); quoted in Schama 1988: 318.

8   On the seventeenth-century Dutch art market, see Alpers 1988. Dash 1999 recounts a contract involving tulip bulbs (a capital asset in the Dutch horticultural economy), cash, and 11 paintings.

9   De Heem 1661. It has not been possible to reproduce in this volume all the paintings discussed in what follows. A list of paintings cited is included at the end of this chapter, together with details of current provenance. Halftone reproductions of the six works most central to my argument are reproduced within this chapter; I am grateful to the museums for permission to reprint them here. Color reproductions of most of the works discussed here can be found in Chong and Kloek's landmark catalog (1999), which has been an indispensable research tool in this project. All of the works cited here can, at least at the time of writing, be found in digital color reproduction on various internet sites, and can usually be located quickly by searching for the paintings by artist and title. The quality of these reproductions varies dramatically, however, and in some cases even the titles are inconsistent. The titles of Dutch still-life paintings are typically the product of some dubbing in the marketplace, in some cases centuries after their composition; hence one finds considerable variation in the literature. (Not only the painters but the paintings have a degree of anonymity.) In the critical apparatus of this chapter, I have tried to follow the titles used by the current owners of each painting (using English translations, where necessary), but even this is subject to variation and other scholars follow different naming conventions.

10 Naomi Popper Voskuil has suggested that this presentation of commodities in complete detachment from the mode of their production reflects the new form of economic life of the burghers: consuming goods without any contact with their production, a novelty of emerging urban life. As we shall see, however, the form of production of the painting itself is often very elaborately represented within these works. See Voskuil 1973.

11 Like a number of other fine-art traditions of this period (notably the baroque musical tradition), the still life develops within a system of quite rigid rules. The principle of stillness is the first (and often the first to be broken with effect, as we see with de Heem's snail). The principle of realism is the second. The question of what amounts to realism in painting is a vexed problem of aesthetics. As we shall see, the still-life painters themselves explored and struggled with it. Virtuosity, reflected both in the choice of challenging subjects and exacting execution, was an ideal rewarded. The genrification of the form is a less rigid principle, useful mainly to collectors and catalogists, but also notoriously a product of the market setting and commodification of art (witness contemporary music).

12 A note on tulips: tulip-mania reached its height in 1636–7. At its peak a single tulip bulb reached a peak price of 5,200 guilders. By comparison, 40 gallons of brandy sold for 60 guilders; a ton of herring cost 13 guilders. A well-off merchant might earn 3,000 guilders

annually. By comparison, Rembrandt's *The Night Watch* sold for 1,600 guilders in 1642. See Dash 1999.

13   There is much more work to be done on van Oosterwijk's painting. I chose it as exemplary of vanitas, but have since discovered that this designation is disputed, and it may well be more exceptional than exemplary. Its most prominent motto, *SELF-STRYT* ("self-strife," or "self-struggle"), provides occasion for another chapter in itself.

14   On the notion of natural meaning, see Grice 1957.

15   This is complicated considerably by the Calvinist context, which is distinctive among the Christian traditions in its insistence on predestination.

16   "The fresh silvery flower, fragrant with the breath of spring, withers instantly as its beauty wanes. So the life of man, already ebbing in the newborn child, disappears like a bubble or like fleeting smoke." The Latin verse comes from Franco Estius, the humanist poet; this translation is modified from Strauss 1977: 588. I am grateful to Donald Rutherford for his assistance with the Latin.

17   For a classic discussion of this theme see Janson 1937.

18   For discussion of the Democritus/Heraclitus theme, see Blankert 1967. Wind 1937 traces some of the history of what he calls *Democritus Christianus* and *Heraclitus Christianus* and includes a reproduction of Rubens' renderings of the pair. See also Voskuil 1973: 68–9. A related example of this counter-Christian closure can be found in an even older German composition: Barthel Bruyn the Elder's *Vanitas Still Life: Omnia Morte* (undated, mid-sixteenth century). In Bruyn's composition we find a skull and jawbone being scoured by a housefly, alongside an extinguished candle. The motto is a saying attributed to Lucretius: *Omnia morte cadunt, mors ultima linia rerum* ("Everything passes with death; death is the ultimate limit of things"). Here again we find the counter-Christian conclusion: death is not a passing but an ultimate limit. In Bruyn's work, this message is itself hidden on the back of a portrait, a radical device for balancing opposed semiotic structures. Note, however, that in both these cases the ancient reference may also sustain a non-Christian hope. For Seneca the laughter of Democritus is explicitly identified as an expression of hope, and Lucretius' poem had famously argued that death at least is not to be feared.

19   Martin 2001.

20   In reading Claesz's olive as a commentary on the deceptive art of painting, I follow Chong and Kloek 1999: 143. Several formal features of the work serve to draw attention to the olive. It is brightly illuminated by the light reflected from the base of the tazza, and it is a small, visually dense object placed in the position on the canvas where an eye accustomed to reading (left to right, top to bottom) naturally comes to rest. The placement of small, dense objects in this position was often used to provide a clue for unraveling hidden meanings in a painting. Another example can be found in de Heem's snail, discussed above.

21   A zoomable, high-resolution color reproduction of this work is available on the Getty Museum website, www.getty.edu, where it is possible to study the self-portrait in closer detail. In preparing this chapter for publication I have also been made aware of a virtually identical use of the glass orb in a work by Claesz at the Germanisches Nationalmuseum in Nuremberg: *Vanitas Still Life with Violin and Glass Ball* (1628).

22   There is much more to be learned about this spherical object. It figures in a number of contemporary emblems identified as a tool of learning, specifically in connection with geometry and astronomy. It seems likely that it was also a painter's tool, used to study the projections that the painting reproduced. In some paintings it is also used to echo the spherical form of the Earth or as a symbol for the astronomical heavens. For a discussion of the technology of hyperrealism see Hockney 2001. For some examples of the spherical emblems in connection with the sciences, see Goltzius' emblems of the Muses (1592); reproduced in Strauss 1977, vol. 2, figs. 299–307.

23 Biesboer 1989.

24 On de Keyser, see Adams 1985. In addition to those just mentioned, there is a very early pen-and-ink miniature vanitas still life inscribed by Bailly in his student days in the *Album Amicorum* of Cornelis de Glarges. (An *Album Amicorum* is the seventeenth-century Dutch equivalent of an autograph book.) For a reproduction see Bruyn 1951, fig. 1. It is worth noting that the same album also includes an inscription by Descartes himself, providing one indicator of the proximity of the philosophical and painterly communities.

25 There is a long-standing scholarly dispute about the identification of the figures in Bailly's paintings. I here follow Bruyn (1951) and Voskuil (1973) in treating the piece as a double self-portrait. This interpretation has been vigorously challenged by Maarten Wurfbain (1969, 1988), who argues that the young painter is Frans van Mieris and the woman in the oval portrait is Anna Maria van Schuurman, perhaps with the image of Anna Roemers Visscher painted into the wall. Wurfbain's reading, in turn, shapes the treatment offered by Alpers 1983. But recent treatments have largely returned to Bruyn's position. Chong and Kloek go so far as to describe Wurfbain's proposal as "a theory both unconvincing and irrelevant" (Chong and Kloek 1999: 191, n.1). Voskuil's position is that the representations are idealized self-portraits. ("The similarity is obvious from the similarity of features, postures and details of the garments"; Voskuil 1973: 63.) Chong and Kloek call this reading "the most convincing and most poetic" (1999: 191, n.1.)

26 Even this may not be the painter as he saw himself in the mirror in 1651; the oval self-portrait seems to have been executed around ten years earlier. By the time Bailly was 67 the portrait was indeed an object among the others on his studio table. Bailly had used this technique of copying his own self-portrait – a reiteration of self-representation – in some of his portraits. For an example, see *Portrait of an Unknown Professor or Preacher*, reproduced in Bruyn 1951, fig. 13. Recall that the 1650 vanitas (with slave and bubbles) also used the iteration of portraiture.

27 There is scholarly disagreement on this point as well. I follow Bruyn's treatment in assuming she was dead, but again, Wurfbain denies it, and claims that Bailly was outlived by his wife by some thirteen years. There seems little dispute that she was in fact ill (she composed a will in 1644), and the painting incorporates a number of references to her illness: the ball and chain is a bezoir (a seventeenth-century medical device for steeping medicines); the flute is a glass used at funerals. For a systematic assessment of the evidence see Voskuil 1973 and Chong and Kloek 1999.

28 The worship of saints is, of course, not a feature of Calvinist religious practice. Wurfbain suggests that Bailly's model was the Allessandro Vittoria sculpture in the Venetian church of San Francesco della Vigna, but this attribution has been challenged by Voskuil, and there are countless other candidates.

29 "And deceive me as he will, he can never bring it about that I am nothing *so long as* I shall think I am something . . . 'I am, I exist' is necessarily true *every time* it is uttered or conceived" (Descartes 1979, Second Meditation).

30 This is the place to resist Alpers' thesis that Dutch painterly practice contrasts with the Italian tradition in being descriptive rather than narrative (Alpers 1983). I am not qualified to assess this thesis in its generality, but it is hard to see how it can be applied to Bailly's *Vanitas*, which is rich with narrative structure. Even if one follows Wurfbain's questionable lead in repudiating the double self-portrait, the backbone of this autobiographical structure remains: even Wurfbain recognizes that the oval male portrait is Bailly's self-portrait, and that the Hals copy is a work of Bailly's youth, set along the unused palettes. Despite this difference with Alpers, I wholeheartedly endorse her treatment of the painting of this period as "experiential observation" (Alpers 1983: 107); that is in part what I mean by

581

calling it phenomenology. I return briefly to the Baconian aspect of Alpers' treatment below. On narrative knowledge see, inter alia, Danto 1985.

31 *Berlin Archiv for Kunst und Geschichte.*

32 For a reproduction see Schama 1988.

References and Further Reading

Adams, A. J. (1985) The Paintings of Thomas De Keyser (1596/7–1667): A Study of Portraiture in Seventeenth-Century Amsterdam. Doctoral dissertation, Harvard University, Cambridge, MA.

Alpers, S. (1983) *The Art of Describing: Dutch Art in the Seventeenth Century.* Chicago: University of Chicago Press.

—— (1988) *Rembrandt's Enterprise: the Studio and the Market.* Chicago: University of Chicago Press.

Bergström, I. (1956) *Dutch Still-Life Painting in the Seventeenth Century* (trans. C. Hedström and G. Taylor). London: Faber & Faber (original work published 1947).

—— (1970) De Gheyn as a vanitas painter. *Oud Holland*, 85, 143–57.

Biesboer, P. (1989) The Burghers of Haarlem and their portrait painters. In S. Slive et al., *Frans Hals* (exhibition catalog) (pp. 23–44). National Gallery of Art, Washington, DC; Royal Academy of Arts, London; and Frans Hals Museum, Haarlem. London and Munich: Royal Academy of Arts.

Blankert, A. (1967) Heraclitus en Democritus in het bijzonder in de Nederlanse kunst van de 17de eeuw. *Netherlands Kunsthistorische Jaarboek*, 31–124.

Boström, K. (1949) David Bailly's stilleben. *Konsthistorik Tidskrift*, 18, 99–110.

Bruyn, J. (1951) David Bailly: Fort bon peintre en vie coye. *Oud Holland*, 66, 148–64, 212–67.

—— (1953) Twee late portretten van David Bailly. *Oud Holland*, 68, 113–14.

Cassam, Q. (ed.) (1994) *Self-Knowledge.* Oxford: Oxford University Press.

Cerbone, D. R. (2003) Phenomenology: Straight and hetero. In C. G. Prado (ed.), *A House Divided: Comparing Analytic and Continental Philosophy* (pp. 105–38). Amherst, NY: Humanity Books.

Cheney, L. de Girolami (1989) Dutch vanitas paintings: The skull. In *The Symbolism of Vanitas in the Arts, Literature, and Music.* London: Edwin Mellen Press, 113–76.

Chong, A., and Kloek, W. (1999) *Still-Life Paintings from the Netherlands 1550–1720.* Zwolle: Waanders.

Danto, A. (1985) *Narration and Knowledge.* New York: Columbia University Press.

Dash, M. (1999) *Tulipomania: The Story of the World's Most Coveted Flower and the Extraordinary Passions it Aroused.* New York: Three Rivers Press.

Dennett, D. (1991) *Consciousness Explained.* Boston: Little, Brown.

Descartes, R. (1979) *Meditations on First Philosophy* (trans. D. Cress). Indianapolis: Hackett (original work published 1641).

Dreyfus, H., and Dreyfus, S. (2002) Existential phenomenology and the brave new world of *The Matrix.* In *Philosophy and The Matrix.* http://www.whatisthematrix.warnerbros.com

Foucault, M. (1970) *The Order of Things: An Archaeology of the Human Sciences.* New York: Random House (original work published 1966).

Grice, P. (1957) Meaning. *Philosophical Review*, 66, 377–88.

Heezen-Stoll, B. A. (1979) Een vanitasstilleven van Jacques de Gheyn II uit 1621: Afspiegeling van neostoïsche denkbeelden. *Oud Holland*, 93, 217–45 (English summary at 246–50).

Heidegger, M. (1962) *Being and Time* (trans. J. Macquarrie and E. Robinson). New York: Harper & Row (original work published 1927).

—— (1982) *The Basic Problems of Phenomenology* (trans. Albert Hofstadter). Indianapolis: Indiana University Press (text of lecture course delivered in 1927).

Hockney, D. (2001) *Secret Knowledge: Rediscovering the Lost Techniques of the Old Masters*. New York: Viking Studio.

Husserl, E. (1931) *Ideas: General Introduction to Pure Phenomenology* (trans. R. Boyce-Gibson). London: George Allen & Unwin (original work published 1913).

—— (2001) *Logical Investigations* (trans. J. N. Findlay). London: Routledge & Kegan Paul (original work published 1900–1).

Janson, H. W. (1937) The putto with the death's head. *Art Bulletin*, 446–8.

Kafka, F. (1937) *The Trial* (trans. W. Muir and E. Muir). New York: Alfred A. Knopf (original work published 1925).

Martin, W. (2001) Claesz in the window. *Inquiry*, 44, 481–500.

Merleau-Ponty, M. (1962) *Phenomenology of Perception* (trans. C. Smith). London: Routledge (original work published 1945).

—— (2004) Cézanne's doubt. In *Merleau-Ponty: Basic Writings* (trans. T. Baldwin). New York: Routledge (original work published 1945).

Petitot, J. et al. (eds.) (1999) *Naturalizing Phenomenology: Issues in Contemporary Phenomenology and Cognitive Science*. Stanford, CA: Stanford University Press.

Rorty, R. (1979) *Philosophy and the Mirror of Nature*. Princeton, NJ: Princeton University Press.

Sacks, M. (2000) *Objectivity and Insight*. Oxford: Oxford University Press.

Schama, S. (1988) *The Embarrassment of Riches: An Interpretation of Dutch Culture in the Golden Age*. New York: Knopf.

—— (1993) Perishable commodities: Dutch still-life painting and the empire of things. In J. Brewer and R. Porter (eds.), *Consumption and the World of Goods* (pp. 478–88). London, Routledge.

Seneca (1935) *De Tranquillitate Animi*. In *Seneca: Moral Essays*, vol. 2 (trans. J. W. Basore). Cambridge, MA: Harvard University Press (original work published *c*.60).

Slive, S. et al. (1989) *Frans Hals* (exhibition catalog). National Gallery of Art, Washington, DC; Royal Academy of Arts, London; and Frans Hals Museum, Haarlem. London and Munich: Royal Academy of Arts and Prestel Verlag.

Straus, W. (ed.) (1977) *Hendrick Goltzius: The Complete Engravings and Woodcuts*. New York, Abaris Books.

Voskuil, N. P. (1973) Self-portrait and vanitas still-life painting in 17th-century Holland in reference to David Bailly's vanitas oeuvre. *Pantheon*, 31, 58–74.

Wind, E. (1937–8) The Christian Democritus. *Journal of the Warburg Institute*, I, 180–2.

Wurfbain, M. (1969) Vanitas-stilleven David Bailly. *Openbaar Kunstbezit*, 13.

—— (1988) David Bailly's vanitas of 1651. In R. Fleischer and S. Munshower (eds.), *The Age of Rembrandt: Studies in Seventeenth-century Dutch Paintings* (pp. 49–69). University Park, PA: Penn State University Press.

Paintings Cited

Bailly, David. 1650: *Vanitas Still Life with Portrait*. Oil on canvas, 95 × 116 cm; Cornell University Art Museum; Ithaca, NY.

Bailly, David. 1651: *Vanitas Still Life with Portrait of a Young Painter*. Oil on wood panel, 65 × 97 cm; Stedelijk Museum de Lakenhal, Leiden.

Beert, Osias. 1615: *Dishes with Oysters and Sweetmeats*. Oil on wood panel, 52.9 × 73.4 cm; National Gallery of Art, Washington, DC.

Bruyn the Elder, Barthel. (undated): *Vanitas Still Life (Omnia Morte)*. Oil on wood panel (reverse of *Portrait of Jane-Loyse Tissier*), 61 × 51 cm; Rijksmuseum Kroller-Mulle, Otterlo.

Claesz, Pieter. 1628: *Vanitas Still Life with Violin and Glass Ball*. Oil on wood panel, 36 × 59 cm; Germanisches Nationalmuseum, Nuremberg.

Claesz, Pieter. 1633: *Still Life with Römer and Tazza*. Oil on wood panel, 42 × 59 cm; Staatliche Museen, Berlin.

Claesz, Pieter (attributed). 1634: *Vanitas Still Life*. Oil on panel, 20 × 28 cm; J. Paul Getty Museum, Los Angeles.

de Gheyn the Elder, Jacques. 1603: *Vanitas Still Life*. Oil on wood panel, 83 × 54 cm; Metropolitan Museum of Art, New York.

de Heem, Cornelis. 1661: *Vanitas Still-Life with Musical Instruments*. Oil on canvas, 153 × 166 cm; Rijksmuseum, Amsterdam.

Goltzius, Hendrik. 1594: *Quis Evadet?* Engraving, 21.2 × 15.3 cm; Rijksmuseum, Amsterdam.

Hals, Frans (copied from). 1649a: *Portrait of Descartes*. Oil on canvas, 78.5 × 68.5 cm; Louvre, Paris.

Hals, Frans. 1649b: *Portrait of Descartes*. Oil on wood panel, 19 × 14 cm; Statens Museum for Kunst, Copenhagen.

Torrentius, Johannes. 1614: *Allegory of Temperance*. Oil on wood panel; 52 × 50.5 cm; Rijksmuseum, Amsterdam.

van der Spelt, Adriaen. 1658: *Trompe L'oeil with Flowers and a Curtain*. Oil on wood panel, 46.5 × 63.9 cm; Art Institute, Chicago.

van Eyck, Jan. 1434. *The Arnolfini Portrait*. Oil on wood panel, 81.8 × 59.7 cm; National Gallery, London.

van Hoogstraten, Samuel. 1666–8: *Trompe L'oeil Still Life*. Oil on canvas, 63 × 79 cm; Staatliche Kunsthalle, Karlsruhe.

van Oosterwijk, Maria. 1668: *Vanitas Still Life*. 73 × 88.5 cm; Kunsthistorisches Museum, Vienna.

van Schooten, Floris Gerritsz. 1640: *Breakfast (Ontbijt)*. Oil on panel, 50 × 82 cm; Koninklijk Museum voor Schone Kunsten, Antwerp.

39

Mathematics

MARK VAN ATTEN

to philosophise in regard to their mathematics (a hard task!)
Kant, *Critique of Pure Reason* (Kant 1965: B753)

Connecting Phenomenology and Mathematics

Three different ways of connecting Husserlian phenomenology and mathematics come to mind at once: (1) One can study the role of mathematics in the historical development of phenomenology; (2) One can study differences between phenomenology and mathematics as sciences; and (3) One can apply phenomenology to mathematics considered as a performance of consciousness.

(1) Mathematics as part of Husserl's motivation to develop phenomenology

Husserl obtained his Ph.D. in mathematics in 1883 (under the supervision of Leo Königsberger), and became interested in the philosophy of mathematics. The more he thought problems in the philosophy of mathematics through, the more he realized that he would need to address more general problems of mind and language first. It is quite probable that certain mathematical developments and conceptions of mathematics made it easier (heuristically) for Husserl to arrive at some of the fundamental tenets of his phenomenology, such as the primacy of intuition, and, arguably, his method of eidetic variation. In the period before the *Logical Investigations*, Husserl read widely in the literature on the foundations of mathematics of the time. In particular, he was well acquainted with the work and thought of Cantor, Frege, Hilbert, Kronecker, Schröder, and Weierstrass. In 1906, Husserl described the question that had been central to his philosophical development so far as follows:

> I was tormented by those incredibly strange realms: the world of the purely logical and the world of actual consciousness – or, as I would say now, that of the phenomenological and also the psychological. I had no idea how to unite them; and yet they had to interrelate and form an intrinsic unity. (Husserl 1994: 490–1)

Gradually, Husserl came to lose contact with mathematics and the contemporary discussion of its foundations, although, especially in the early 1920s, he would hear of certain developments from students and friends such as Hermann Weyl and Oskar Becker. In 1927, he wrote on the eve of his visit to Amsterdam, where he would meet L. E. J. Brouwer, that he would certainly disappoint Brouwer as he no longer could speak about the foundations of mathematics (letter to H. J. Pos, December 26, 1927). In spite of that confidence, Husserl shortly after published his *Formal and Transcendental Logic*; conceivably, an effort to catch up with recent developments in the foundations of mathematics might have resulted in a somewhat less programmatic work.

(2) Mathematics and phenomenology can be described as two (different) types of science, with correspondingly different types of knowledge and of reasoning

Husserl offers such descriptions in, for example, sections 71 and 75 of *Ideas I* (Kant also discusses the topic, e.g., Kant 1965: B740–66). One function of such a description is to show that it is harmful to try to model philosophy too closely after mathematics (see also "The pernicious influence of mathematics on philosophy" (Rota 1997: ch. VII)). But seeing the difference may also serve to open up a possibility:

> In terms used by Kant (Kant 1965: A713) – philosophy analyses and mathematics builds up concepts – Gödel looked for a combination (where Kant saw only a distinction): for a given problem one may have the choice between a solution by means of philosophical analysis and easy mathematics and one by elaborate or otherwise subtle constructions. The simplest example is a solution by new axioms, discovered and justified by means of philosophical analysis. (Kreisel 1980: 150)

This brings us to a third way of connecting mathematics and philosophy.

(3) Phenomenology of mathematics

From a phenomenological perspective, mathematics is a performance of consciousness; we constitute our awareness of the objects and their relations. Thus, one can study types and degrees of evidence in mathematics, phenomena of presence and absence of mathematical objects, mathematical intuition, idealization, the arithmetical versus the geometrical, the noetic–noematic correlation in mathematics (as Tragesser 1973: 293 put it: "Something is recognizable as being a mathematical object if it can be recognized that it can be completely thought through mathematically"). The first contributions to the phenomenology of mathematics were made by Husserl himself (e.g., in his *Philosophy of Arithmetic*, 1891; cited as Husserl 2003); but, as mentioned above, Husserl gradually lost contact with developments in (the foundations of) mathematics.

As the phenomenologically fundamental concepts of intentionality and constitution both have to do with the notion of object, it lies close to hand that phenomenological investigations of mathematics will also be (not exclusively, but primarily) concerned with mathematical objects. In this respect, phenomenology's concerns are very similar to the traditional ("foundationalist") concerns in the philosophy of mathematics – say, as practiced in the first decades of the twentieth century: What is the nature of mathematical objects, and how can we have knowledge of them? But after a few decades of focusing on these questions, more recent work in the philosophy of mathematics has seen a shift of emphasis to a number of other aspects of (successful) mathematical experience; for example, applicability (What explains what has been called the unreasonable success of pure mathematics in physics?), explanation (What distinguishes an explanatory proof from an uninformative one?), probabilistic reasoning (What role does or can it have in a deductive science?), visualization (What is the role and epistemological status of diagrams and pictures?), beauty (What is its relation to mathematical truth and to insight?), and reasoning by analogy. (For a number of eloquent and insightful essays based on a phenomenological view of mathematics that pays attention to those aspects and is not overly concerned with the more traditional questions, see Rota 1997.)

According to a view congenial to me, shifts of emphasis (here, away from foundationalist concerns) are tantamount to shifting one's grounds. This may be readily (and probably enthusiastically) admitted by those thus shifting, but a further point to be made is that the different grounds are not always related symmetrically. Two ways to make this clear are the following. First, an unenlightening proof is still a proof; a theorem that is not beautiful is still a theorem; a mathematical theory without applications is still a mathematical theory. This means that for a complete account of mathematics, at some point one will have to address some of the more traditional questions. Second, as a matter of conceptual priority one needs to have an (at least tentative) idea of what mathematics consists in before one can begin to investigate the role of, say, beauty in mathematics. Otherwise, how would one confidently select the data for such an investigation? For example, someone who does not accept certain infinite sets that are talked about in Cantor's set theory will not include such sets (and their relations) among the data in an investigation of mathematical beauty (although for such a person they still may exemplify other types of beauty, in the way fictional objects can).

The rest of this chapter will be limited to (3), the phenomenology of mathematics, with an emphasis on its foundations.

Transcendental Phenomenology as a Foundation of Mathematics

The phenomenology of mathematics can be viewed from at least two perspectives, according as to whether one refers to phenomenology as an ongoing tradition or, more abstractly, as a particular approach to philosophical problems. Obviously, the two perspectives are largely overlapping; but distinguishing them points to the possibility of investigations that, although neither their author nor the text explicitly identifies with phenomenology and therefore cannot be said to be part of the historical movement, can profitably be read as exercises in phenomenology all the same. The second perspective also serves as a reminder that study of writings on mathematics in the phenomenological tradition may give rise to second thoughts about (aspects of) that tradition. We will be concerned with this second perspective.

587

Phenomenology gives an analysis of (certain aspects of) mathematical thought, but does not bring in (alleged) aspects of consciousness that are essentially different from those that mathematicians (with or without being aware) use already. A common objection to phenomenological analyses of mathematics, in particular with its elements of (categorial) intuition and eidetic variation, is that this simply does not seem an accurate description of one's experience when doing mathematics. A response one finds already in early Husserl is to invoke the difference between having an ability and being able to describe that ability (see, e.g., p. 57 of his review of Ernst Schröder's "Vorlesungen über die Algebra der Logik" in Husserl 1994). One may be a good mathematician and at the same time have no or mistaken ideas about philosophical accounts of mathematics. In other words, what, philosophically speaking, we do when we do mathematics need not be immediately transparent to our awareness. By (systematized, developed) introspection, phenomenology analyzes the way in which we form our conscious ideas on the basis of what is truly given to us. (Gödel once remarked: "Both Husserl and Freud considered – in different ways – subconscious thinking" (Wang 1996: 167).) Thus, phenomenological analysis is not an alternative or competitor to mathematical analysis, but rather a deepening of it (at the level of the fundamental concepts).

How does transcendental phenomenology position itself relative to traditional philosophies of mathematics? One idea is that the latter, who are all in conflict with each other, may be (over)emphasizing different aspects of mathematical thinking at the cost of others:

> In his publications Gödel used traditional terminology, for example, about conflicting views of "realist" or "idealist" philosophies. In conversation, at least with me, he was ready to treat them more like different branches of the subject, the former concentrating on the things considered, the latter on the processes of acquiring knowledge about these objects or processes . . . Naturally, for a given question, a "conflict" remains: Which branch studies the aspects relevant to solving that question? (Kreisel 1980: 209)

The question posed by Kreisel here presupposes an answer to another question: What aspects of our experiences when we are doing mathematics are actually relevant to mathematics, be it from an "idealist" or from a "realist" perspective? This question can, of course, only be answered if one has a prior conception what mathematics is. Gödel indicated a characteristic feature of mathematical objects when he pointed out that: "they can be known (in principle) without using the senses (that is, by reason alone) for this very reason, that they don't concern actualities about which the senses (the inner sense included) inform us, but possibilities and impossibilities" (Gödel 1986–2003: 3.312n.3). Phenomenologically, this characterization can be rendered and amplified by saying that the objects of mathematics are purely categorial objects (pure forms or structures); these are studied not to the extent that they are (or have been) factually given but with respect to their possibility or impossibility. Paul Bernays has described mathematics as "the science of possible idealized structures" (Wang 1996: 336ff). To these possibilities and impossibilities of categorial objects correspond possibilities and impossibilities of categorial intuition: "The ideal conditions of the possibility of categorial intuition as such are correlated to the conditions of possibility of the objects of categorial intuition and of categorial objects as such" (Husserl 1970: 6.62). By the fundamental principle of transcendental idealism, as formulated by Husserl in section 142 of his *Ideas I*, the existence of an object (of any kind) is equivalent to the existence of a possible consciousness to which this object is given originally and adequately. So as a special case, a mathematical object can be said to exist if it can be given adequately and originally with purely categorial evidence to a possible mind. Because of this straightforward relation between existence in mathematics and the conditions of possibility of categorial intuition, mathematics is particularly close, and therefore particularly interesting, to phenomenology; and there is a sense in which mathematics is part of phenomenology. A pertinent question, also for transcendental idealism in general, is what exactly the notion of possibility amounts to here.

Note that Husserl's transcendental idealism combines (selected aspects of) traditional "realist" and "idealist" philosophies, and thereby allows one, as Gödel did, to think of them as branches of the same subject. (In fact, Gödel told Kreisel that he had formed this view while reading Husserl. Two places in Husserl that Gödel may have been referring to are sections 18–23 of *Ideas I*, and section 16 of his article for the *Encyclopaedia Britannica*. See van Atten and Kennedy 2003: 464–5 for further discussion.)

The question of what aspects of our experiences when doing mathematics are actually relevant to mathematics as such can now be answered by saying that the relevant aspects are exactly those that, ultimately, pertain to the constitution of purely categorial object (for an elaboration of this view on mathematics, see Tragesser 1973; van Atten 2002). From the point of view of transcendental phenomenology, all reality, including its abstract aspects or components, is constituted reality; the position of transcendental phenomenology relative to traditional or non-phenomenological foundations of mathematics then is one of a standard to which the latter may be tested. In particular to the extent that the latter may be in conflict with each other, phenomenology will view each of them as an exaggeration of one or more particular aspects of mathematical experience at the cost of others. Any genuine insight on the nature of mathematics obtained on the basis of one of those non-phenomenological philosophies of mathematics should, precisely to the extent that it is genuine, admit of a phenomenological reconstruction or, perhaps more aptly, rediscovery. Conversely, one may try to be efficient and look at questions in the foundations of mathematics directly from a phenomenological perspective (see Gödel 1986–2003: 3.374–87; Rota 1973). A particularly attractive topic is what has been called, by Palle Yourgrau (2005: 182), "the Gödel Program." While Hilbert focused on formal aspects of mathematics, and Brouwer on intuitive aspects, Gödel focused on the interplay between these two aspects: his "Program" (or what in any case can, with hindsight, be presented as such) consisted in the investigation of the limits of formal methods in capturing intuitive concepts (besides logic and mathematics, also in relativity theory).

To hold that a phenomenological investigation cannot contribute to the foundations of mathematics for the reason that formal rigor is the only type of rigor possible is question-begging (Gödel 1986–2003: 3.383; Rota 1997: ch. VII). When formalizing a certain subject and its intuitive notions, surely some other kind of rigor must have been at work in devising the axioms and in verifying that they hold for the intended meaning. Kreisel has called this other kind "informal rigour," and has emphasized that this is often sufficient to settle mathematical questions (Kreisel 1967). It is not to be thought of as a new kind of rigor, or as a new method coming in from outside mathematics (competing with mathematicians' methods); rather it is simply the kind of rigor that mathematicians have always been applying when not working formally (and unlike rigor, formal systems are a late arrival in the history of mathematics). This includes the correction of earlier mistakes by the application of more informal rigor (see also section 24 of Husserl's *Ideas I*). Of course, both kinds of rigor may be combined by first analyzing a mathematical problem informally but rigorously, and then formalizing the solution; and formal problems may often be due to insufficient prior informal analysis. Husserl's *Wesensschau* is an instance of informal rigor; and *Wesensschau* as such is not a radically new technique but rather a common and age-old method made fully conscious and then developed further. Husserl has described the great care that has to be taken in performing eidetic variations (e.g., Husserl 1981: §§86–93); similarly, Gödel has observed that intuition requires more, not less, caution and experience than (formal) proofs (Wang 1996: 301). On the other hand, the rewards are proportionally higher. None of this is to belittle or deny the virtues and uses of formalization, which is a practical necessity; but it is to set straight the relation between the formal and the intuitive. In formalization, generally a particular kind of rigor is gained, but (part of the) evidence is lost. In the specific case of arithmetic, this can even be demonstrated by formal means, by Gödel's incompleteness theorem (see Example 5 below). That theorem also shows that occasionally a formal result suffices to refute a philosophical position, in this case Hilbert's formalism in its original sense. Another example is the completeness of the formal theory of elementary geometry (Tarski), which proves that Kant was wrong when he said that in doing geometrical proofs one will always need geometrical intuitions (Kant 1965: B743–5). Such intuitions will, of course, have been used in setting up the axioms of the appropriate formal system, but Tarski showed that no more of it is needed to arrive at the propositions that follow from these axioms.

There are three different ways to see the relation between philosophy and the (actual practice of) mathematics: philosophy describes, but has no right to impose limits or other changes on mathematical practice; philosophy tests, according to some philosophical standard, what is acceptable in mathematical practice; philosophy has the right to impose, according to some philosophical standard, limits but also extensions of mathematical practice. These three conceptions may be called non-revisionism, weak revisionism, and strong revisionism, respectively. Husserl repeatedly has claimed that (a) mathematics without a philosophical foundation is not a science but a mere technique; (b) philosophical considerations may lead to the rejection of parts of mathematical practice; but (c) they cannot lead to mathematical innovations. So he certainly saw a phenomenological foundation of mathematics as a form of weak revisionism. In *Ideas III* (e.g., §14), Husserl introduced the idea that transcendental phenomenology provides the universal ontology (see also versions 3 and 4 of the *Encyclopaedia Britannica* article), that is, the idea that transcendental phenomenology is the science of all possible being. As such, it plays a founding role in any eidetic science (see also Rota 1973). Moreover, it can be argued that from the point of view of transcendental phenomenology Husserl's claim (3) is not correct. Clearly, Husserl had no aim of revising classical logic or mathematics; it can, however, be argued that this has more to do with Husserl's own background and psychology than with what his philosophical principles imply, and that these principles warrant a strong revisionism (van Atten 2002). If that is correct, this means that mathematics is exceptional in science in that it is possible to argue from (structures of) consciousness to objects in mathematics (phenomenology would have this in common with the traditional philosophy of mathematics of intuitionism). Such arguments from philosophy to mathematics are likely to find their motivation, however, in a certain mathematical problem. Whether Husserl's claim (c) is correct or not, in either case transcendental phenomenology treats the mathematical tradition, including traditional foundations of mathematics, with a certain reserve. It asserts a certain autonomy.

Directly opposed to such a (weak or strong) revisionism is the currently popular form of non-revisionism known as naturalism, according to which no point of view external to the practice of mathematics, in particular no philosophical one, can demand changes in mathematical practice. A naturalist may well acknowledge that it is possible to exaggerate the agreement between practicing mathematicians; for example, within the one field of contemporary set theory there is much disagreement over the acceptability of various principles and of certain (very large) objects, and the small but significant minority of constructive mathematicians persists in rejecting various principles from classical mathematics. But a naturalist might go on to say that the disagreement is considered not to be amenable, or not in need of, philosophical adjudication; rather, mathematics with its methodologies that have been developed through the ages could take care of itself. A problem with that line is that those disagreements are frequently motivated (and kept alive) by philosophical considerations of the mathematicians themselves.

Note that Husserl once radically changed his ontological account of mathematics for a reason that had nothing to do with the content of mathematics: when instead of saying that mathematical objects are outside of time (*unzeitlich*, e.g., Husserl 1970: 2.8) he came to hold that they are in all time (*allzeitlich*, e.g., in texts from around 1917 that became part of Husserl 1981: ¶64c), this was not at all motivated by anything in mathematics specifically, but by Husserl's new insight that constitution of objects of any kind presupposes the constitution of time. This also serves to illustrate a point that is not always appreciated by mathematicians: mathematical objects may have properties that, though not of mathematical interest, are of philosophical (in particular, metaphysical) interest.

The two (overlapping) perspectives mentioned above – phenomenology as an ongoing tradition and as an abstract system of thought – suggest various (overlapping) tasks. One task is to arrive at a historically responsible and coherent reading of texts on mathematics in the phenomenological tradition; another, to take as point of reference the debate in the foundations of mathematics (as it raged in the first decades of the twentieth century – note that the reasons why the debate came to an end are mostly of a sociological and psychological nature, rather than philosophical: from the latter point of view, many of the issues are still open) and try to determine Husserl's position (or what would or should have been his position) with respect to the schools participating in that debate (in the widest sense): logicism, Platonism, formalism, intuitionism. (For a phenomenological reflection on problems and issues in the various traditional schools, see Tieszen 1995.) At present, different positions in the philosophy of mathematics have gained clarification from phenomenological investigations; but it is likely that instead of eventually coming to favor one of them over the others, further

591

phenomenological investigations will clarify and corroborate the picture sketched above of one subject with different branches, where the branches differ according to aspects taken into account and according to degrees of evidence and idealization accepted. Below, attention will be drawn to examples of cases where explicit considerations on the notion(s) of evidence in mathematics have led to concrete mathematical developments. In other words, some cases are touched on in which what was (either explicitly or in effect) adopting a phenomenological perspective led to a deeper understanding of a mathematical issue.

Examples

Six examples of (explicitly or implicitly) phenomenological thought in contemporary foundations of mathematics now follow. They are mostly concerned with (varieties of) constructive mathematics; this is not a necessity but is easily explained by the fact that classical mathematics involves idealizations that go much farther than those in constructive mathematics; to that extent, these idealizations are harder to evaluate, and less work has been done on specifically classical topics. That is not to say, of course, that such work cannot be done, and such work would constitute considerable progress in the phenomenology of mathematics.

1 Intuitionistic logic (Mancosu 1998; van Atten 2004b)

Brouwer's "intuitionism" views mathematics as an activity of making constructions in the mind, the fundamental construction material being the intuition of the passage of time. Intuitionistic logic is just the logic of those constructions. A proposition P is true if we have (or have a method to obtain) a mental construction that is correctly described by P. On this view, that the proposition P: $2 + 2 = 4$ is true is accounted for as follows: Construct the number 2 (by abstracting all the content from the experience of the passage of time from one "now" to another, leaving the pure form); construct it again; put the two results together. Now construct the number 4; comparison with the result of $2 + 2$ shows they are the same, and therefore P is true. In the case of the proposition Q: $2 + 2 = 5$, a similar procedure would have led us to see that 4 and 5 cannot be made to coincide; hence Q is false, or, put differently, $\neg$Q is true. The proposition P$\lor$Q is true, because I have a construction that makes one of the two disjuncts true. Similarly, the proposition P$\land$Q is false.

One's actual, essentially languageless activity of making constructions can be described, and logic is taken to be a description of observed regularities in these descriptions. Logic, according to Brouwer, is thus first of all an empirical science. However, it is possible to establish essential laws on the basis of eidetic insight into the nature of constructions. In this way (but without explicitly invoking phenomenology), Brouwer's (former) student Heyting formalized intuitionistic logic (see Heyting 1998); after that, he gave an explicit interpretation, and this time he did invoke phenomenology (see Heyting 1983). He knew the work of Husserl's student Oskar Becker (Becker 1927) and corresponded with him (see Peckhaus 2005); he adopted Becker's idea that intuitionistic logic can be thought of as a logic of intentions:

We here distinguish between propositions and assertions. An assertion is the affirmation of a proposition. A mathematical proposition expresses a certain expectation. For example, the proposition, "Euler's constant C is rational", expresses the expectation that we could find two integers a and b such that C=a/b. Perhaps the word "intention", coined by the phenomenologists, expresses even better what is meant here . . . The affirmation of a proposition means the fulfillment of an intention. (Heyting 1983: 58–9)

Thus, the intention expressed by a proposition is fulfilled exactly if we know a mathematical construction that shows that things are the way the proposition at which the intention is directed says they are. From this general principle of interpretation, the following explanations of the meaning of the logical constants are derived (for brevity, only the clauses for propositional logic are given):

Conjunction: (the intention expressed by) P∧Q is fulfilled exactly when P is fulfilled and Q is fulfilled.

Disjunction: P∨Q is fulfilled exactly when at least one of P, Q is fulfilled.

Implication: P→Q is fulfilled exactly when the subject has a construction that transforms any construction (proof) of P into one of Q.

Negation: ¬P is fulfilled exactly when the subject has a construction that transforms any proof of P into a proof of a contradiction.

Intuitionistic logic is different from classical logic. Classically, P∨¬P is always true (the principle of the excluded middle, abbreviated PEM); intuitionistically, the intention P∨¬P is fulfilled exactly when one of P, ¬P is fulfilled. But while it is true that not both can be fulfilled, it is not the case that for every P, we have, at any given moment, either a construction fulfilling P or a construction fulfilling ¬P. For example, P may be a still open problem. Therefore, intuitionistically, PEM is not valid. (Which is not to say that it is false; it just is not always true.)

Because to have a construction that fulfills an intention directed at a proposition is to have a proof of that proposition, Heyting's interpretation can also be stated in terms of having proofs; and in that more widespread form, it has become known as "the proof interpretation."

2 Choice sequences

It has been known since Aristotle that treating a line (a continuum) as a set of discrete points cannot do justice to its continuous nature, as on that conception the points are isolated from one another. Brouwer showed how the continuum can be dealt with in a more satisfactory way if one introduces so-called choice sequences into mathematics (Troelstra 1985; van Atten et al. 2002). A choice sequence is a potentially infinite sequence of (say) numbers, chosen at will, one after the other, by the individual mathematician. At any particular moment, only finitely many choices will have been made, and therefore a choice sequence is always becoming and never finished. Without going into the technical details of how choice sequences are used to arrive at an alternative theory of the continuum, it can be indicated how Brouwer's work in two ways depends on (what is, in effect) phenomenological analysis. First, the recognition that a continuum is a whole in a different sense than a set is. A line is continuous through and through: each of its parts exhibits this property just as the whole does. (In section 19 of his third *Logical Investigation*, Husserl calls wholes of this type "extensive" (Husserl 1970: 3.19)). Second, an analysis of the notion of mathematical construction is needed to show that choice sequences are a genuine type of object (that can be constituted with evidence, and have identity conditions) and, moreover, are genuinely mathematical objects, in spite of the fact that classical mathematicians do not accept them as such.

Another aspect of choice sequences that is of phenomenological interest is that they force intuitionistic logic for theories about them. For example, if one begins a choice sequence by choosing 0 three times in a row, then there is (assuming one has not imposed certain conditions or restrictions on one's own choices) no fact of the matter whether all numbers in the sequence will be 0 or not. So, by intuitionistic logic (see above), we have no sufficient evidence to assert that either all numbers are 0 or they are not. Thus, PEM does not generally hold for choice sequences. This illustrates a theme from Husserl's genetic analysis of judgment (in *Formal and Transcendental Logic* (Husserl 1969), and in *Experience and Judgment* (Husserl 1981)) that has been developed further in ch. IV of Tragesser 1977: with different domains of objects, different logics are associated. Minimal experience with choice sequences shows that, whatever a universally valid logic may look like, it will not be classical logic.

3 The "bar theorem"

A full explanation of Brouwer's "bar theorem" from 1927 cannot be given here, but for the purpose of getting an idea of its philosophical interest it suffices to know that it is an implication that roughly states: if in a tree structure a particular kind of subset of nodes (a "bar") exists, then this subset contains a small tree that can be constructed in an ordered way. (Brouwer applied this theorem to trees in which the branches are choice sequences.)

In Brouwer's intuitionism, as described above, to say that something exists is to say that we have a construction method for it. Correspondingly, to say that a proposition is true is to say that we know a proof of it. The truth of a proposition is evidenced by, and only by, a proof. Brouwer's argument for the bar theorem starts by assuming that the antecent is true. He then proceeds by asking what a proof of the antecedent of the theorem can possibly be like. He then argues that any such proof can be analyzed into a particular canonical form; finally, he shows how that canonical form of the proof can be transformed into a construction of the small tree, which proves the consequent. The phenomenologically interesting step here is Brouwer's analysis of what proofs of the antecedent can be like. For here he reasons that mathematical proofs are (in general) infinite, mental objects of a certain structure. (At the time, Brouwer saw this as his main argument against Hilbert's formalism.) It is the structure of proofs considered as mental objects that will be the basis for the construction of the tree mentioned in the consequent. Brouwer's analysis of the nature of mental proofs can be accounted for in terms of introspection, the notions of horizon and intentional implication, and the temporal structure of (mathematical) acts; such an account is given, together with a full explanation of the theorem, in van Atten 2004b: ch. 4.

4 Hilbert's Program (Mancosu 1998)

How much evidence is needed to be convinced of (not the truth, but) the consistency of classical analysis? David Hilbert hoped to show that the answer was "as much evidence as is needed to be convinced of the truth of finitary mathematics." This was one of the most important parts of what is known as "Hilbert's Program," one of the efforts to provide a foundation for classical mathematics. Generally, Hilbert's Program consisted in the effort to show that all of classical mathematics could be captured in one formal system, and that that system could be shown to be consistent by finitary means.

The "finitary mathematics" that Hilbert wanted to use deals with only finitely many, concrete objects, that is, objects that one can survey. One never makes actual use of an infinity of objects, or of objects that are infinitely complex, or of objects that are abstract and cannot be made concrete or visualized. Finitary mathematics is therefore constructive. (A good example of finitary mathematics is the arithmetic one learns in primary school.)

Because it stays away from the infinite and from abstract objects, finitary mathematics was (and in some corners still is) taken to be especially clear and secure. The idea, then, was to show by finitary means that formal systems for classical analysis are consistent, that is, that in these systems it is not possible to derive both P and ¬P. The rationale was that these formal systems can themselves be reasoned about finitarily.

There are a number of aspects to Hilbert's Program that are of phenomenological interest: there is the question of the exact nature and range of Hilbert's notions of intuition and evidence, which go back to Kant; the question which of the known principles of mathematics can be (re)interpreted so as to be acceptable in finitary mathematics; the question as to the relation between language and objects in mathematics. From a historical point of view, there is a close relation between Hilbert's method of ideal elements and Husserl's "Double Lecture" in Göttingen in 1901.

The final two examples are both, in different ways, reactions to Hilbert's Program.

5 Incompleteness and intuition

One formulation of the results Gödel published in 1931 (Gödel 1986–2003: 1.144–95) is:

> First incompleteness theorem: Any formal system (satisfying some mild conditions) that contains arithmetic is either incomplete (i.e., leaves certain of its propositions undecided) or inconsistent. Moreover, for any consistent formal system of the appropriate type, undecidable propositions (are not merely known to exist but) can actually be specified.
>
> Second incompleteness theorem: Among the undecidable propositions is one that (formally) expresses the consistency of the system.

But these propositions that are undecidable in the system are decidable by evident (informal) inferences which, first, cannot (on pain of inconsistency) be reflected formally in the original system and, secondly, are exactly as evident as the inferences possible in the original system. The second incompleteness theorem shows that one example is a proposition that (formally) expresses the consistency of the original system: any ground for doubting that proposition is a ground for doubting the original system, and to the extent that one believes that the original system is sound, one believes that it is consistent.

Both incompleteness theorems serve to refute Hilbert's Program in its original sense. The first, because it shows that it is not possible to capture all of mathematics in one system – as soon as it contains arithmetic, there are propositions it cannot decide – the second, because it shows that a formal demonstration of the consistency of a given system needs means at least as strong as those supplied by the system itself.

Another philosophical doctrine refuted by Gödel, again using his incompleteness theorems, is Carnap's position that mathematics is merely the (conventional) syntax of a certain language and has no content of its own (Gödel 1986–2003: 3.334–62). On that conception, only empirical propositions have content. (This, of course, would be contested also by Husserl, on phenomenological grounds.) One of Gödel's arguments against this position is that, even though rules of syntax may be chosen arbitrarily, they stand in need of justification to the extent that one has to ensure that they are consistent. For if they are not, then they will allow one to deduce, from any given (empirical) proposition accepted as true, every other possible proposition (the mathematical as well as the non-mathematical ones), including the incorrect ones. But the second incompleteness theorem shows that a proof of the consistency of the syntactical rules will require a mathematical intuition of the same power as those rules; therefore, non-empirical content cannot be eliminated.

6 The Dialectica Interpretation

How much evidence is needed to be convinced of (not the truth, but) the consistency of classical arithmetic? By Gödel's incompleteness theorems, more evidence would be needed than can be provided by the finitary mathematics from Hilbert's Program (see above). In particular, this means that abstract evidence is needed. But how much? The Dialectica Interpretation, which was published in 1958 (in the journal *Dialectica*, hence the name) under the significant title "On a hitherto unutilized extension of the finitary standpoint," is an attempt to answer that question (Gödel 1986–2003: 2.240–51).

The first step is to invoke Gödel's translation of 1933 (Gödel 1986–2003: 1.286–95) of classical arithmetic into intuitionistic arithmetic, also known as Heyting Arithmetic: it consists of Peano's axioms for arithmetic joined not to classical logic but to Heyting's system of intuitionistic logic. In the translation the interpretation of the statements is changed, and from an intuitionistic point of view the translations obtained are weaker than the original statements (classically they are equivalent). However, the translation of a statement like $1 = 0$ is $1 = 0$. Hence, if a contradiction can be derived in classical arithmetic, then a contradiction can be derived in intuitionistic arithmetic (the converse is immediate). In other words, classical arithmetic is consistent if and only if intuitionistic arithmetic is consistent.

In the second step, the Dialectica Interpretation proper provides an interpretation of Heyting Arithmetic. As we saw above, intuitionists interpret intuitionistic logic in terms of proofs; what Gödel wanted to show was that, in the context of arithmetic, it can also be interpreted in terms of objects that are, like proofs, abstract, but (in a sense that can be made more precise), less so. The objects that Gödel suggests are computable functionals of finite type; roughly, functionals of type 0 are the natural numbers, and functionals of higher type are defined by constructive operations that assign to finite tuples of functionals of already defined types another functional of already defined type.

The Dialectica Interpretation may by itself constitute a significant advantage from an epistemological point of view, but what Gödel had in mind is the following application. The interpretation shows that intuitionistic arithmetic indeed is consistent. Combined with the translation, one obtains a consistency proof for classical arithmetic. So the answer the Dialectica paper provides to the question of how much evidence is needed to establish the consistency of classical arithmetic is: more than for Hilbert's finitary reasoning, but less than for the intuitionistic notion of proof.

However, for technical reasons, a necessary condition for this epistemological advantage is that the notion of a computable functional of finite type is taken as immediately intelligible, or primitive. A comparative phenomenological investigation of these functionals and the intuitionistic notion of proof may be required to determine to what extent the advantage is real. An interesting remark by Gödel in this respect is that "One may doubt whether we have a sufficiently clear idea of the content of this notion [of computable functional of finite type], but not that the axioms [given in this paper] hold for it. The same apparently paradoxical situation also obtains for the notion, basic to intuitionistic logic, of a proof that is informally understood to be correct" (Gödel 1986–2003: 2.245n.5).

It may be considered odd that a proof of the consistency of arithmetic, that is, of a theory of the natural numbers, should be attempted in terms of a notion that is more complicated, that of computable functional of finite type, which even includes the natural numbers as type 0. But both classical and intuitionistic arithmetic appeal to non-constructive or abstract notions via their logic, which is, after all, also part of these systems. This appeal has so to speak to be made up for, and this is exactly what the functionals are used for: to reduce logical complexity.

A revised version from 1972 (published posthumously in Gödel 1986–2003: 2.271–80), adds, among other things, more details on the notion(s) of evidence in play; it is not impossible that Gödel had further developed his sensitivity to such aspects during his wide reading in phenomenology that he begun shortly after completing the original version from 1958.

Acknowledgment

I am grateful to Professor Georg Kreisel for correspondence and conversation on some of the issues discussed in this chapter.

References and Further Reading

Becker, O. (1927) Mathematische Existenz. Untersuchungen zur Logik und Ontologie mathematischer Phänomene [Mathematical existence: investigations on the logic and ontology of mathematical phenomena]. *Jahrbuch für Philosophie und phänomenologische Forschung*, 8, 439–809.

Benacerraf, P., and H. Putnam (eds.) (1983) *Philosophy of Mathematics: Selected Readings*, 2nd edn. Cambridge: Cambridge University Press.

Bernays, P. (1976) *Abhandlungen zur Philosophie der Mathematik* [Essays on the philosophy of mathematics]. Darmstadt: Wissenschaftliche Buchgesellschaft.

Gödel, K. (1986–2003) In S. Feferman et al. (eds.), *Collected Works*, 5 vols. Oxford: Oxford University Press.

Heyting, A. (1983) The intuitionist foundations of mathematics (trans. P. Benacerraf and H. Putnam). In P. Benacerraf and H. Putnam (eds.), *Philosophy of Mathematics: Selected Readings*, 2nd edn. (pp. 52–61). Cambridge: Cambridge University Press (original work published 1931).

—— (1998) The formal rules of intuitionistic logic (trans. P. Mancosu). In P. Mancosu (ed.), *From Brouwer to Hilbert: The Debate on the Foundations of Mathematics in the 1920s* (pp. 311–27). Oxford: Oxford University Press (original work published 1930).

Husserl, E. (1969) *Formal and Transcendental Logic* (trans. D. Cairns). The Hague: Martinus Nijhoff (original work published 1929).

—— (1970) *Logical Investigations* (trans. J. N. Findlay). New York: Humanities Press (original work published 1900–1).

—— (1981) *Experience and Judgment* (trans. J. S. Churchill and K. Ameriks). In P. McCormick and F. A. Elliston (eds.), *Husserl: Shorter Works*. Notre Dame, IN: University of Notre Dame Press (original work published 1939).

—— (1994) *Early Writings in the Philosophy of Logic and Mathematics* (trans. D. Willard). Dordrecht: Kluwer (original works published 1890–1910).

—— (2003) *Philosophy of Arithmetic: Psychological and Logical Investigations – with Supplementary Texts from 1887–1901* (trans. D. Willard). Dordrecht: Kluwer.

Kant, I. (1965) *Critique of Pure Reason* (trans. N. Kemp-Smith). New York: St. Martin's Press (original work published 1781; rev. edn. 1787).

Kreisel, G. (1967) Informal rigour and completeness proofs. In I. Lakatos (ed.), *Problems in the Philosophy of Mathematics* (pp. 138–86). Amsterdam: North-Holland.

—— (1980) Kurt Gödel. 28 April 1906–14 January 1978. *Biographical Memoirs of Fellows of the Royal Society*, 28, 149–224.

Lohmar, D. (1989) *Phänomenologie der Mathematik. Elemente einer phänomenologischen Aufklärung der mathematischen Erkenntnis nach Husserl* [Phenomenology of mathematics: elements of a phenomenological clarification of mathematical knowledge after Husserl]. Dordrecht: Kluwer.

Mancosu, P. (ed.) (1998) *From Brouwer to Hilbert. The Debate on the Foundations of Mathematics in the 1920s*. Oxford: Oxford University Press.

Peckhaus, V. (ed.) (2005) *Die Philosophie und die Mathematik: Oskar Becker in der mathematischen Grundlagendiskussion* [Philosophy and mathematics: Oskar Becker in the discussion of the foundations of mathematics]. Munich: Wilhelm Fink.

Rota, G. C. (1973) Husserl and the reform of logic. In D. Carr and E. Casey (eds.), *Explorations in Phenomenology* (pp. 299–305). The Hague: Martinus Nijhoff.

—— (1997) *Indiscrete Thoughts*. Boston: Birkhäuser.

Tieszen, R. (1989) *Mathematical Intuition: Phenomenology and Mathematical Knowledge*. Dordrecht: Kluwer.

—— (1995) Mathematics. In B. Smith and D. Woodruff Smith (eds.), *The Cambridge Companion to Husserl*. Cambridge: Cambridge University Press.

—— (2005) *Phenomenology, Logic, and the Philosophy of Mathematics*. Cambridge: Cambridge University Press.

Tragesser, R. (1973) On the phenomenological foundations of mathematics. In D. Carr and E. Casey (eds.), *Explorations in Phenomenology* (pp. 285–98). The Hague: Martinus Nijhoff.

—— (1977) *Phenomenology and Logic*. Ithaca, NY: Cornell University Press.

Troelstra, A. S. (1985) Choice sequences and informal rigour. *Synthese*, 62, 217–27.

van Atten, M. (2002) Why Husserl should have been a strong revisionist in mathematics. *Husserl Studies*, 18, 1–18.

—— (2004a) Intuitionistic remarks on Husserl's analysis of finite number in the *Philosophy of Arithmetic. Graduate Faculty Philosophy Journal*, 25(2), 205–25.

—— (2004b) *On Brouwer*. Belmont, CA: Wadsworth.

van Atten, M., and Kennedy, J. (2003) On the philosophical development of Kurt Gödel. *Bulletin of Symbolic Logic*, 9, 425–76.

van Atten, M., van Dalen, D., and Tieszen, R. (2002) Brouwer and Weyl: The phenomenology and mathematics of the intuitive continuum. *Philosophia Mathematica*, 10(3), 203–26.

Wang, H. (1996) *A Logical Journey: From Gödel to Philosophy*. Cambridge, MA: MIT Press.

Yourgrau, P. (2005) *A World Without Time: The Forgotten Legacy of Gödel and Einstein*. New York: Basic Books.

Index

600